# FROMMER'S
# NEW YORK
# ON $60 A DAY

## JOAN HAMBURG
## and NORMA KETAY

D0110760

**PRENTICE HALL**

New York □ London □ Toronto □ Sydney □ Tokyo □ Singapore

Published by Prentice Hall Trade Division
A Division of Simon & Schuster Inc.
15 Columbus Circle
New York, NY 10023

ISBN 0-13-332669-1
ISSN 8755-5433

Manufactured in the United States of America

## A Disclaimer

Readers are advised that prices fluctuate in the course of time and travel information changes under the impact of the varied and volatile factors that affect the travel industry. The authors and publisher cannot be held responsible for the experiences of the reader while traveling. Readers are invited to write the publisher with ideas, comments and suggestions for future editions.

# CONTENTS

**Introduction** NEW YORK ON $60 A DAY     1
     1. Frommer's Dollarwise® Travel Club—How to Save Money
       on All Your Travels   20

**I.** FINDING A BUDGET HOTEL     26
     1. New York on a Shoestring—Hostels, Ys, and
       Nontraditional Hotels   28
     2. Low-Cost Permanent Residences   34
     3. Rooms for Service Personnel   36
     4. Hotels for General Occupancy   37
     5. Rooms for Families   50
     6. Bed-and-Breakfasts   52
     7. Weekend and Other Packages   53

**II.** EATING CHEAPLY AND WELL     55
     1. Midtown West/Times Square   55
     2. Midtown East   67
     3. Upper East Side and Yorkville   75
     4. Upper West Side   89
     5. Lincoln Center   98
     6. Pennsylvania Station/Chelsea   101
     7. Greenwich Village   106
     8. SoHo   119
     9. Lower Manhattan/TriBeCa   124
     10. Chinatown   132
     11. Little Italy   138
     12. Lower East Side/East Village   141
     13. Murray Hill/Gramercy Park   150
     14. Brighton Beach, Brooklyn   162
     15. Especially for Brunch   163
     16. Around the Clock   165
     17. Early-Bird Dinner Specials   167
     18. Big-Splurge Restaurants   167

**III.** THE TOP SIGHTS AND CULTURAL
    ATTRACTIONS     169
     1. Sights Not To Be Missed   170
     2. Museums   180
     3. Galleries, Theater, Concerts, Opera, and Dance   192
     4. Entertainment   208
     5. Zoos and Botanical Gardens   210
     6. Sports and Recreational Facilities   213

7. More Sights 220
8. Churches and Synagogues 223
9. Historic Houses 227

**IV.** A STROLL OR TWO 230

1. Greenwich Village 230
2. The Lower East Side 232
3. The Garment Center 234
4. Yorkville 234
5. SoHo 236
6. The Upper West Side: Columbus Avenue 236
7. Chinatown and Little Italy 237
8. Chelsea 237
9. TriBeCa 240
10. Central Park 240
11. Times Square 241

**V.** ONE-DAY EXCURSIONS FROM NEW YORK 242

1. Up the Hudson Valley 242
2. Long Island 249
3. New Jersey 250

**VI.** BARGAIN NIGHTSPOTS 251

1. Bar Hopping 251
2. The Music Spots 260
3. Dance, Dance, Dance 267
4. Theatrical and Nightclub Entertainment 271

**VII.** THE BEST SHOPPING BUYS IN TOWN 275

1. Men's and Women's Clothing 275
2. An Alphabetical Miscellany 288
3. Food 315

**VIII.** NEW YORK WITH CHILDREN: BUDGET TIPS     322
    **1. Cultural and Educational Attractions  323**
    **2. Recreation  333**
    **3. Entertainment  335**
    **4. Shops for Children  338**
    **5. Services for Children  340**
    **6. Eating Out With Children  341**
    **7. Mapping Out Your Days  342**

**IX.** FAST FACTS FOR NEW YORK     345

**Index**  355

# MAPS

**The Five Boroughs of New York City  5**
**Manhattan Areas  7**
**New York City Subways:**
   **IRT Broadway–7th Avenue Subway  10–11**
   **IRT Lexington Avenue Subway  12–13**
   **Independent (IND) Subway (8th Avenue)  14–15**
   **Independent (IND) Subway (6th Avenue)  16–17**
   **BMT Subway  18**
**Midtown Manhattan  57**
**Upper East Side  77**
**Upper West Side  91**
**Rockefeller Center  174**
**Upper Manhattan  187**
**Central Park  218–219**
**Greenwich Village  233**
**Downtown Manhattan  235**
**SoHo, Little Italy, and Chinatown  238–239**
**Getting Out of New York City  243**
**The Hudson River Valley  247**

## Amtrak and the Big Apple

New York City is Amtrak's most popular destination with more than six million passengers arriving and departing its two stations each year. Penn Station, located in downtown Manhattan at 33rd Street and Eighth Avenue, is by far the busiest of Amtrak's 500 stations nationwide. More than 90 trains arrive and depart daily with frequent service to and from Washington, Philadelphia, Boston, and points in between, as well as daily service to and from Florida, New Orleans, Montreal, and Chicago.

Visitors to New York who want to spend a day in Atlantic City can use Amtrak's daily direct Atlantic City Express or any of Amtrak's New York–Philadelphia trains that connect with service to Atlantic City.

Grand Central Terminal, on the East Side, is an architectural landmark. It is the terminus and departure point for service to and from Albany, Niagara Falls, Toronto, Cleveland, and Chicago, with 20 trains arriving and departing daily, as well as to hundreds of suburban and other northern and southern points.

Amtrak service from Washington to New York includes North America's only high-speed rail service—the 125-mph Metroliner. Reserved seating, Railfone service, wide, reclining seats, and dinette service are just a few of the amenities included in the $74 fare. For an added $41.50 you can reserve a Club Service seat with meals included. The downtown to downtown trip takes only 2 hours, 39 minutes to 2 hours, 55 minutes, depending on the number of intermediate stops. Metroliner to Boston is only on Fridays.

Readers might find Amtrak's unreserved trains from Washington to Boston more appealing. For just $59, (and about 30 extra minutes) you can use any of Amtrak's hourly departures from Washington. Since no reservations are needed, you have the flexibility of changing your mind at the last minute and taking an earlier or later train. From Boston, the fare is just $44.50 with a choice of 12 daily trains. If you're traveling any time but Friday or Sunday from 11 a.m. to 8 p.m. ask about off-peak, round-trip excursion fares for extra savings.

Amtrak offers several hotel and tour packages in the Big Apple with prices from $55.50 per person, double occupancy, for two days, one night at the Penta Hotel, to $421 per person, double occupancy, for a "Big Apple" Deluxe 3-day package at the Plaza that includes Broadway shows and sightseeing options. Rail fare is extra, but all can be arranged by calling Amtrak toll-free at 800/USA-RAIL.

## Mass Transit and Taxi Fares

The Metropolitan Transit Authority and the Taxi and Limousine Commission increased all fares and rates as we went to press. The basic changes are: Subways and buses now cost $1.15; 55¢ for senior citizens and the handicapped. Initial charge for taxis is $1.50; 25¢ for each additional one-fifth of a mile; 20¢ per minute for waiting charge; 50¢ night surcharge.

# NEW YORK ON
# $60 A DAY

## 1. FROMMER'S DOLLARWISE TRAVEL CLUB—
## HOW TO SAVE MONEY ON ALL YOUR TRAVELS

**W**ith this printing, *New York on $60 a Day* is 30 years old. When it first came out in 1960, its two authors were younger than the book is today, but their love affair with the city has lasted through three decades.

New York has weathered many changes in the intervening years: steel skyscrapers have given way to glassy postmodern corporate palaces; the Spanish barrios of the West 60s gave way to the opulence of Lincoln Center; nouvelle cuisine and health food have, for many, edged out the heavier cuisine of old.

But in this city of constant change, one thing remains the same. Whether you are a seasoned New Yorker or a first-time visitor, New York never exhausts its ability to surprise. Most New Yorkers are not born or brought up here. They become New Yorkers when the city's magic spell of excitement, intrigue, and glamour makes them realize that it's the most exciting place in the world.

For 30 years this book has been a trusted guide. If you want to sample the city's magic brew on a limited budget, this small classic will help you do it.

### THE TWO NEW YORKS

It's not true that New York is a city only for the rich. There is no other city in the world that offers the diversity in price range for a variety of goods and services. New York has been called the world's number one performing arts city, and many of the best cultural events in the city are free or available at low cost. The city devotes itself to providing both residents and visitors with a dazzling array of unusual and exciting events. Shakespeare in the Park (Central Park) is presented by the New York Shakespeare Festival. Stars such as Linda Ronstadt, Cleo Laine, Meryl Streep, Kevin Kline, and Dustin Hoffman have played on the open-air stage in Central Park's Delacorte Theatre. Tickets are available on a first-come, first-served basis—absolutely free.

Restaurants to fit any budget can be found with no trouble at all. This book will provide you with enough choices to keep you busy eating out for years. Hotels, on the other hand, are another thing altogether. We have more than our share of good ones with correspondingly high prices—the Helmsley Palace, the Regency, the Waldorf, the Plaza, among others—but finding the smaller, off-beat hotels with satisfactory rooms at lower cost takes a lot of looking. We have nonetheless uncovered several of these hotels with adequate accommodations at budget prices.

If it's nightlife you've come for, there are offerings galore—the widest range of nighttime entertainment possibilities in the world! You can spend evenings on end without exhausting the supply of discos, country-music haunts, belly-dancer palaces, showcase theaters, concert halls, etc.

For food, the selections are even better: hundreds upon hundreds of restaurants where good meals are still in the budget to moderate range. These are in the not-so-easy-to-find category for the inexperienced visitor, but every New Yorker knows that these low-cost finds exist. What we've done is to collect scores of those "little places around the corner" into one volume.

To do that, and to find the rest of the information contained in this book, we devote five to six months yearly to walking, searching, questioning, tasting, and trying. Each edition includes new selections, as well as revisions of acceptable old ones. We've been irritating pests (especially to our friends whom we "shake down" for every restaurant tip they possess), but we've come up with information that we sincerely believe can save you hundreds of dollars over the course of time.

## NOTE ON PRICES

The information in this anniversary edition is correct as of the early 1990 publication date. Because prices are changing weekly everywhere, we cannot assume New York will be immune to price revisions. Therefore we cannot be responsible for price changes that occur after publication.

## $60 A DAY—WHAT IT MEANS

Our main goal is, of course, to show you how to enjoy New York without spending a fortune. To do that you have to begin with a moderate per-day cost of living. By living costs we refer to basic necessities: your hotel room and three meals. Obviously your transportation, sightseeing, and entertainment costs will all be in addition to this, but we will show you how to enjoy these and other activities with a reasonable expenditure of money.

Inflation, as we all know, has become a way of life across the nation, and New York City is no exception. Prices continue to skyrocket. In updating this book we were truly surprised at some of the gigantic price leaps. Good values in hotels are, alas, becoming almost impossible to find. You can just about squeak by on food for $20 a day and, by traveling with a companion and sharing a double-occupancy room, spend $40 to $50 a day for your lodgings. For those of you with a little more to spend, we have included more expensive choices; your flexibility will make it a bit easier.

The $60-a-day standard won't bring you a Hilton or a Plaza, but it will usually produce an adequate room, plus very good meals—and this we say without reservation—for our many small foreign restaurants especially offer what we consider gourmet-quality food.

By cataloguing all the choices, *New York on $60 a Day* hopes to service the entire range of budget visitors who come to or live in New York: from the extremely cost-conscious visitor or resident to those who have more to spend but want to get the best value for every penny he or she puts out.

## SOME PRIOR ORIENTATION

New York vies with Mexico City and Tokyo for the distinction of being the world's most populous city. Some 7½ million people live within our city limits, and 5½ million more are located in the surrounding suburbs.

New York prides itself on its polyglot mix. It is an ethnic, racial, and religious smörgåsbord. Italians, Irish, Jews, Hungarians, Scandinavians, Chinese, Japanese, Hispanics—you name it, New York's got it. The rich blend of cultures is the solid underpinning on which the city is built. Every few decades a new generation of immigrants emerges as the latest entrepreneurial hotshots. Everyone gets a turn and the city respects, even salutes, the hard workers who make it to the top. New York is not the town of the vested interest. It is instead the personification of the American Dream. Just looking at any list of who's who in the city clearly confirms that the strength of New York lies in the sons and daughters of its recent immigrants.

New Yorkers have also always prided themselves on being in the vanguard of social and political movements. It is here that you can find headquarters for various civil rights organizations; political organizations from far right to far left; sexual rights organizations, both gay and heterosexual; and women's organizations.

New York offers groups for whatever your interest, problem, or cause may be. And the "live and let live" attitude of most residents guarantees you the freedom to pursue your chosen path.

No other American city, with the possible exception of Washington, D.C., has the importance of New York. The city is the center of America's communications industry and the advertising and public relations world. The offices of the major fashion houses and magazines are located here, as is virtually the entire book-publishing industry. New York is the home base of America's commercial theater, the nation's major opera company, and key art galleries. Many of the country's major industrial concerns maintain their headquarters in the skyscrapers of Manhattan. The city is so full of celebrated public figures and important cultural, political, and economic events that most New Yorkers remain blasé and unconcerned about things that would dazzle and excite the residents of almost any other town. We admit, of course, the many flaws and inconveniences of New York, but as you can see, we love our exciting city and grow more aware of its endless opportunities and gifts with every passing day.

Tourists may not be tempted to savor all the unusual neighborhood areas of New York, but to us there is nothing more interesting than the people who live here. Everyone knows us for our culture, but the huge ethnic population is what makes this city great. We will give you a rundown on these neighborhoods elsewhere in this book. Visit them and meet real New Yorkers. You'll like them. New Yorkers are friendly, open people, and they are proud of their city.

## A City of Boroughs

New York is made up of five distinct sections, called "boroughs": **Manhattan, Brooklyn, the Bronx, Queens,** and **Staten Island.**

The island of Manhattan—in the very center of New York—is where the key public buildings are located, and where the most important commercial, industrial, and cultural activities take place. It's here that you'll find virtually all the sights and entertainments you've come to see, all the hotels and restaurants that we'll recommend, and all the other famous places and landmarks that are customarily identified with New York. That's not to say that the other boroughs don't possess some of these attractions, but you'll have more than enough to do if you try to canvass merely the sights of Manhattan. We have, however, included several sights to be seen in other boroughs.

Manhattan is only a small residential section of New York—a fact that ought to clear up the bewilderment you may experience over the predominantly commercial appearance of the island. Most New Yorkers live in the other boroughs of New York and travel back and forth each day to their jobs in Manhattan. If you take a trip into Brooklyn, or the Bronx, Queens, or Staten Island, you'll see the areas in which most New Yorkers live; you'll find streets with trees, private homes, little community centers, schools, fields, and parks similar to those you'd find in the residential districts of any other town. And if you travel into the suburbs of New York—to the villages on Long Island or the county of Westchester, north of Manhattan—then you'll encounter the greener areas in which many New Yorkers live, and from which they commute to Manhattan to work.

## The Geography of Manhattan

Actually, it's lucky that you'll be staying and sightseeing in Manhattan, because it's the easiest of the boroughs in which to find your way around. Except for the bottom third of Manhattan—that is, the portion below 4th Street on the West Side, 1st Street on the East Side—virtually the entire island is laid out exactly like a grid: the streets and avenues of the town crisscross each other almost at precise right angles.

The **avenues** of New York run directly north and south (uptown and downtown).

The **streets** of New York run directly east and west (crosstown).

With a few exceptions, all these avenues and streets bear consecutive numbers, enabling you to know at all times where you are.

Thus, starting at 14th Street on the West Side or 1st Street on the East Side, and going north, the streets of New York are numbered 5th, 6th, 7th, 8th, etc., all the way up to around 212th Street at the northern tip of Manhattan. If you're at 42nd Street and want to go to 82nd Street you simply go directly north for 40 blocks.

Similarly, the avenues begin with First Avenue on the East Side of Manhattan, and then proceed across town. Second Avenue, Third Avenue, Fourth Avenue, Fifth Avenue, and so forth until you arrive at Twelfth Avenue on the west side of Manhattan. Thus if you're on Seventh Avenue and want to go to Ninth Avenue, you simply go west for two blocks.

## How to Find the Nearest Cross Street on an Avenue Address

New Yorkers have the following system for finding the cross street on an avenue address: Drop the last digit of the number of the address and divide the remaining number by two. Then add or subtract the following appropriate number:

| | |
|---|---|
| Avenue A, B, C, or D | add 3 |
| First Avenue | add 3 |
| Second Avenue | add 3 |
| Third Avenue | add 10 |
| Fourth Avenue (Park Avenue South) | add 8 |
| Fifth Avenue | |
| 1 to 200 | add 13 |
| 201 to 400 | add 16 |
| 401 to 600 | add 18 |
| 601 to 775 | add 20 |
| From 776 to 1286 | cancel last figure and subtract 18 |
| Sixth Avenue | subtract 12 |
| Seventh Avenue below Central Park | add 12 |
| Eighth Avenue below Central Park | add 10 |
| Ninth Avenue | add 13 |
| Tenth Avenue | add 14 |
| Eleventh Avenue | add 15 |
| Amsterdam Avenue | add 60 |
| Broadway | |
| 1 to 754 | below 8th Street |
| 754 to 858 | subtract 29 |
| 858 to 958 | subtract 25 |

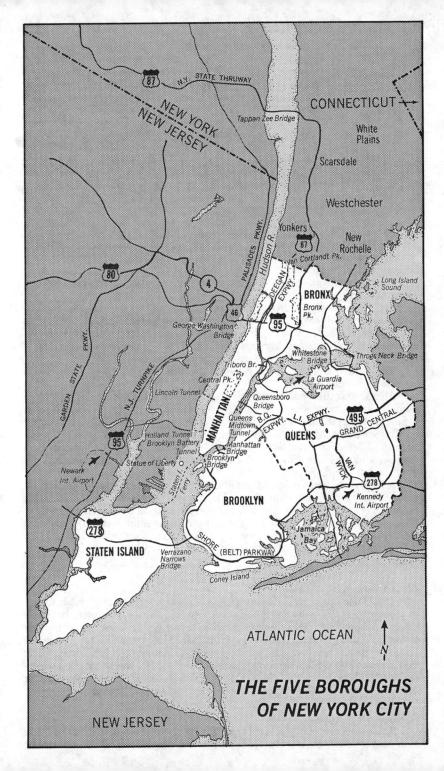

THE FIVE BOROUGHS
OF NEW YORK CITY

| Above 1000 | subtract 31 |
| Columbus Avenue | add 60 |
| Lexington Avenue | add 22 |
| Madison Avenue | add 26 |
| Park Avenue | add 35 |
| Riverside Drive | divide number by 10 and add 72 |
| West End Avenue | add 60 |

For example, if you were trying to locate 645 Fifth Avenue, you would drop the 5, leaving 64. Then you would divide 64 by 2, leaving 32. According to the chart, you would then add 20. Thus 645 Fifth Avenue is at about 52nd Street.

As we've said, there are some exceptions to this general layout, and these revolve around the fact that several avenues bearing names have been interspersed among the avenues bearing numbers. Thus Broadway (an avenue) appears between Seventh and Eighth Avenues on the Upper West Side (and proceeds *diagonally* downtown); Madison, Park, and Lexington Avenues are placed between Fifth and Third Avenues.

And, incidentally, Fourth Avenue is the same as Park Avenue and is called Fourth Avenue only from 8th Street (where it begins) to 14th Street. From 14th to 34th Streets, it's Park Avenue South, and then Park Avenue proper begins. And Sixth Avenue is officially named "Avenue of the Americas"—but everyone calls it Sixth Avenue, and you'll see both names used in these pages.

The most central avenue in New York, cutting directly through the island lengthwise, is Fifth Avenue.

All east-west street addresses in New York begin at Fifth Avenue and increase in number as they move away from Fifth Avenue. Thus the address 2 West 9th Street would denote a building on 9th Street just a few steps to the west of Fifth Avenue; 56 West 9th Street would indicate a building that is even farther west, and so on. The address 12 East 45th Street would denote a building just a little to the east of Fifth Avenue, while 324 East 45th Street would indicate a building on 45th Street that is way, way east of Fifth Avenue.

A look at the maps printed throughout this book should make it all clear instantly. But as for the bottom portion of Manhattan—that is, the portion below 4th or 1st Streets—there simply is no way that you can easily find your way around. For this is the oldest section of New York (the city grew from south to north), and streets there follow the outlines of old cowpaths and the like. They twist and turn in no defined fashion and bear names instead of numbers: Wall Street, Canal Street, Whitehall Street, etc.

## About Times Square

The Times Square area is having a renaissance, although it's only visible to date in a few tall new structures and hotels. Visit Times Square for its theaters, but don't forget our neighborhoods: offbeat Greenwich Village, SoHo, TriBeCa, and the East Village; dignified Gramercy Square; elegant Park, Madison, and Fifth Avenues (a Fifth Avenue bus ride is an absolute must); and Chinatown and Little Italy, where the flavor is entirely different from the rest of the city. After you've traversed the entire city, you'll realize that life in New York isn't well characterized by the souvenir shops, hot-dog stands, and porno shops of the midtown Broadway area.

## A Note on Safety

Perhaps because of exaggerated reports in the media, some first-time visitors to New York approach the city with fears that border on paranoia. While it would be

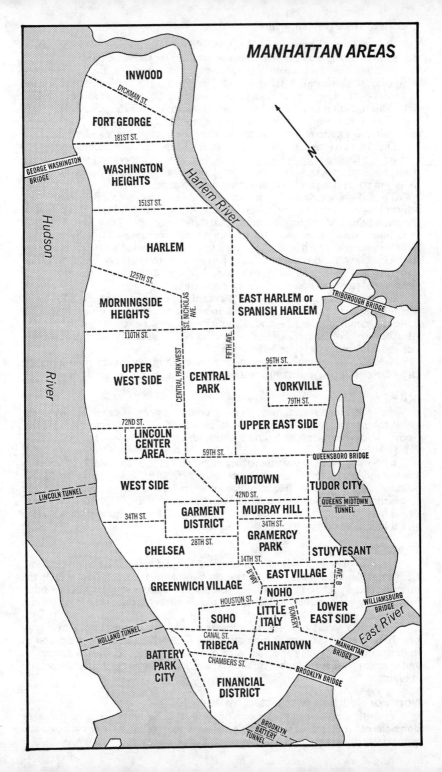

foolish to discount the crime problem, it should not be magnified. New York *can* be dangerous—like any metropolitan area—but there are ways to keep safe.

Strolling New York streets alone at night isn't usually safe, and in some areas should be avoided entirely. These include Harlem, Spanish Harlem, Times Square, and parts of the Upper West Side, Upper East Side, East Village, and Lower East Side. This doesn't mean that you must stay away from the city's nightlife. Take cabs to the bars, restaurants, and clubs. Travel in a group, stay on the brightly lit avenues, and avoid the numbered and side streets, which are usually darker and quieter.

During the day or night, walk purposefully. Keep your purse tucked under your arm (or if a shoulderbag, worn *diagonally* over your shoulder) and your wallet in front, not back, pockets. Don't wear expensive jewelry or keep passports and all money in your purse, wallet, or any other single place.

The subways are cheap and fast but also require extra caution. The system is not self-explanatory, so make sure about directions before using it. Don't stand close to the tracks; choose crowded, not empty, cars, and once riding, stay alert. We don't recommend using the subways for late-night travel; the buses are usually safer. But keep in mind that at rush hour, the heavy jostling crowd provides a good camouflage for pickpockets. Neither are hotels and department stores always safe. Don't leave passports and money in hotel rooms, and be aware that some criminals view department-store customers as lucrative and easy targets.

In some parts of the city, people play cards and dice in the streets. Don't join them. First, these games are illegal. But more important, you'll probably lose because the games are rigged—and if you win, you may be relieved of the money. Also, be careful of the traffic. The cars and trucks and especially the cabs move very fast and don't always stop for pedestrians.

*A Final Note:* New York is fascinating and exciting, but on the flip side are the city's dangers. If you're alert and cautious, you can enjoy the city safely.

## MAPS

We've included several maps to make orienting yourself easier. For more detailed color maps, we recommend the *"I Love NYC" Travel Guide,* available free from the New York Convention and Visitors Bureau, 2 Columbus Circle, New York, NY 10019; and (our favorite) the Flashmaps *Instant Guide to New York* ($5.95), which has maps showing restaurant, theater, hotel, and museum locations, as well as subway and bus routes. Another popular map is *Hagstrom's Quick and Easy Metropolitan Area* ($4.95). For a free full-color subway or bus map of any borough (be sure to specify), send a self-addressed stamped envelope to "Maps," New York City Transit Authority, Room 875, 370 Jay St., Brooklyn, NY 11202. Subway maps are also available at most subway station token booths.

## TRANSPORTATION

New York has few rivals when it comes to fast and inexpensive transportation. Cabs are available 24 hours a day, and except during the rush hours (8 to 9:30 in the morning and 4:30 to 6 in the evening) the subway and bus systems work wonderfully, getting you anywhere in Manhattan and the other boroughs as fast as a private car and with considerably less anxiety.

The charge for all the buses and subways is $1.15, which must be paid in change or tokens. The bus is the most interesting way to travel and its routes are easiest to understand. The subway system is faster, but crimes in the subway have increased, and in recent years even some New Yorkers have been reluctant to use the system late at night.

### North or South in Manhattan by Bus

Virtually every one of the avenues of Manhattan has buses that go either up or down the entire length of that avenue; and since most of the avenues have one-way traffic restrictions, most of the buses go in only one direction.

Along the following avenues, the buses go *north* (uptown) only: First Avenue, Third Avenue, Park Avenue (to 40th Street only), Madison Avenue, Sixth Avenue (Avenue of the Americas), Eighth Avenue, Tenth Avenue.

Along the following avenues, the buses go *south* (downtown) only: Second Avenue, Lexington Avenue, Fifth Avenue, Broadway (below 59th Street), Seventh Avenue (below 59th Street), Ninth Avenue.

Along York Avenue, Riverside Drive, and Broadway above 59th Street, the buses go in *both* directions (uptown and downtown).

## East or West in Manhattan by Bus

There are also a number of so-called crosstown buses that go east or west across the entire island, along certain of the important streets of Manhattan.

Along the following streets, the buses go *east* only: 8th Street, 50th Street, and 65th Street. (*Important note:* This last bus travels along 65th Street on the West Side of Manhattan; after it crosses Central Park to the East Side, it continues on 65th Street to Madison Avenue, turns north for 3 blocks and continues east.

Along the following streets, the buses go *west* only: 9th Street, 49th Street, Central Park South (that's 59th Street between Fifth and Eighth avenues), and 67th Street. (*Another important note:* This last bus travels along 67th Street on the East Side of Manhattan only; after it crosses Central Park to the West Side, it continues its westbound route on 66th Street.)

And along the following streets, the buses go in *both* directions (east and west): 14th Street, 23rd Street, 34th Street, 42nd Street, 57th Street, 59th Street, 79th Street, 86th Street, 96th Street, 116th Street, 125th Street, 145th Street, and 155th Street.

If transferring from one bus route to another is necessary, a free "transfer" ticket is available to passengers who have already paid the full fare. The ticket allows you to change from one bus to another, but only where routes intersect (ask for your transfer when you pay your fare). Senior citizens, those 65 and over, who are New York City residents pay half fare (55¢), except during rush hours. For information about the transit system, call 718/330-1234.

## Traveling by Subway

Despite the noise and occasional discomfort, especially during the hottest days of summer, the quickest, cheapest, and most efficient way to move around the city is by subway. And from the point of view of pure experience, we recommend that every visitor ride the subway at least once: if you haven't ridden the subway you haven't seen New York.

Tokens currently cost $1.15 apiece and are obtained at token booths inside the stations. Purchase tokens with small bills; anything larger than a $20 bill will not be accepted. Buy ten-packs for $11.50 to avoid complicated transactions.

To the stranger, the system might appear to operate in an extremely mysterious way, and to unravel its complexities would require a separate tome. Our first and most important piece of advice, therefore, is to obtain a good map. You can pick up a free map at most token booths. Because it is complex, you may want to supplement it with a copy of the aforementioned Flashmaps *Instant Guide to New York,* which contains excellent maps not only of the subway system, but of everything in town. Almost every bookstore carries it, as do large newsstands.

Having said all this, here are a few pointers to smooth your subway riding:

There are three subway lines running through Manhattan: Interborough Rapid Transit (IRT), Brooklyn–Manhattan Transit (BMT), and the Independent Line (IND). Keep in mind that there are *three* IRT lines: the East Side IRT–Lexington Avenue line, the West Side IRT–Seventh Avenue line, and the no. 7 Flushing line. The East and West branches of the IRT are connected by the Grand Central–Times Square Shuttle and the 14th Street Canarsie (BMT) line. The BMT runs mostly from Brooklyn through lower and midtown Manhattan out to Queens and back.

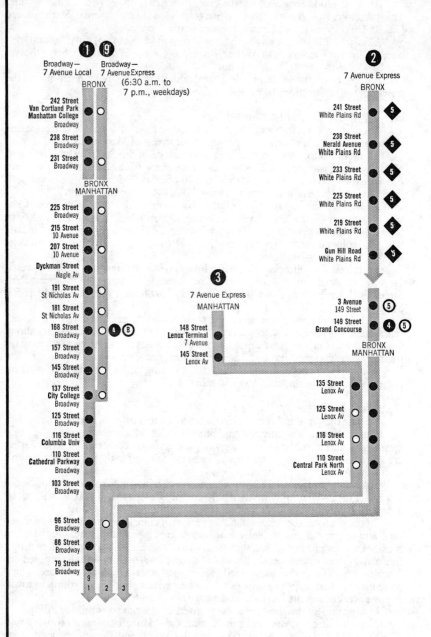

# IRT BROADWAY—7TH AVENUE SUBWAY

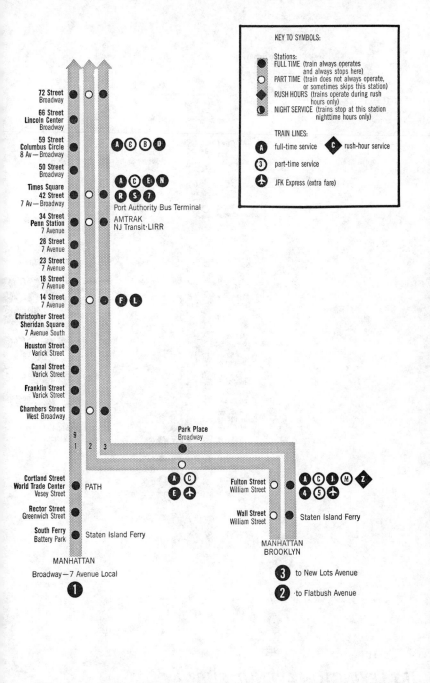

KEY TO SYMBOLS:

Stations:
FULL TIME (train always operates and always stops here)
PART TIME (train does not always operate, or sometimes skips this station)
RUSH HOURS (trains operate during rush hours only)
NIGHT SERVICE (trains stop at this station nighttime hours only)

TRAIN LINES:
Ⓐ full-time service
Ⓒ rush-hour service
③ part-time service
✈ JFK Express (extra fare)

72 Street
Broadway

66 Street
Lincoln Center
Broadway

59 Street
Columbus Circle
8 Av — Broadway
Ⓐ Ⓒ Ⓑ Ⓓ

50 Street
Broadway

Times Square
42 Street
7 Av — Broadway
Ⓐ Ⓒ Ⓔ Ⓝ
Ⓡ Ⓢ ⑦
Port Authority Bus Terminal

34 Street
Penn Station
7 Avenue
AMTRAK
NJ Transit·LIRR

28 Street
7 Avenue

23 Street
7 Avenue

18 Street
7 Avenue

14 Street
7 Avenue
Ⓕ Ⓛ

Christopher Street
Sheridan Square
7 Avenue South

Houston Street
Varick Street

Canal Street
Varick Street

Franklin Street
Varick Street

Chambers Street
West Broadway

Park Place
Broadway

Cortland Street
World Trade Center
Vesey Street
PATH
Ⓐ Ⓒ
Ⓔ ✈

Fulton Street
William Street
Ⓐ Ⓒ Ⓙ Ⓜ Ⓩ
④ ⑤ ✈

Rector Street
Greenwich Street

Wall Street
William Street
Staten Island Ferry

South Ferry
Battery Park
Staten Island Ferry

MANHATTAN
BROOKLYN

MANHATTAN

Broadway — 7 Avenue Local

① 

③ to New Lots Avenue

② to Flatbush Avenue

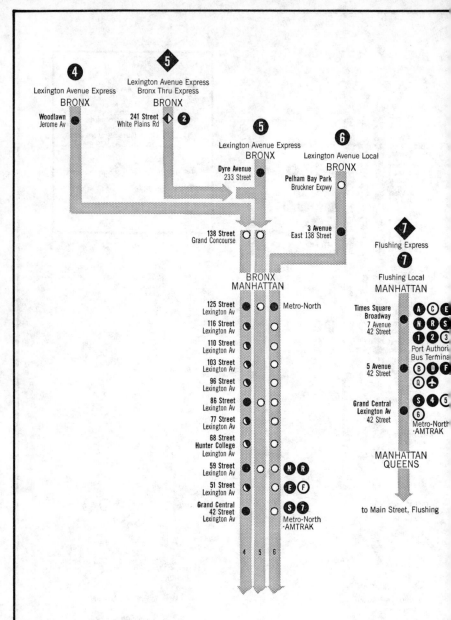

**IRT LEXINGTON AVENUE SUBWAY**

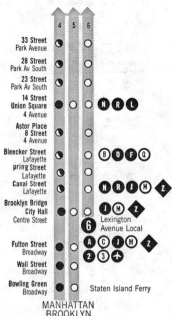

| | 4 | 5 | 6 |
|---|---|---|---|

**33 Street**
Park Avenue

**28 Street**
Park Av South

**23 Street**
Park Av South

**14 Street**
Union Square
4 Avenue  Ⓝ Ⓡ Ⓛ

**Astor Place**
8 Street
4 Avenue

**Bleecker Street**
Lafayette  Ⓑ Ⓓ Ⓕ Ⓠ

**pring Street**
Lafayette

**Canal Street**
Lafayette  Ⓝ Ⓡ Ⓙ Ⓜ ◆Z

**Brooklyn Bridge**
**City Hall**
Centre Street  Ⓙ Ⓜ ◆Z

❻ Lexington
Avenue Local

**Fulton Street**
Broadway  Ⓐ Ⓒ Ⓙ Ⓜ ◆Z
❷ ❸ ✈

**Wall Street**
Broadway

**Bowling Green**
Broadway  Staten Island Ferry

MANHATTAN
BROOKLYN

❹ to New Lots Avenue

❺ to Flatbush Avenue

KEY TO SYMBOLS:

Stations:
● FULL TIME (train always operates
  and always stops here)
○ PART TIME (train does not always operate,
  or sometimes skips this station)
◆ RUSH HOURS (trains operate during rush
  hours only)
◐ NIGHT SERVICE (trains stop at this station
  nighttime hours only)

TRAIN LINES:
Ⓐ full-time service    Ⓒ rush-hour service

❸ part-time service

✈ JFK Express (extra fare)

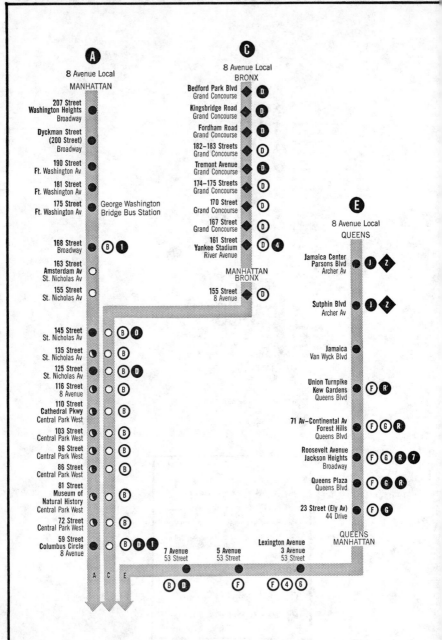

# INDEPENDENT (IND) SUBWAY (8TH AVENUE)

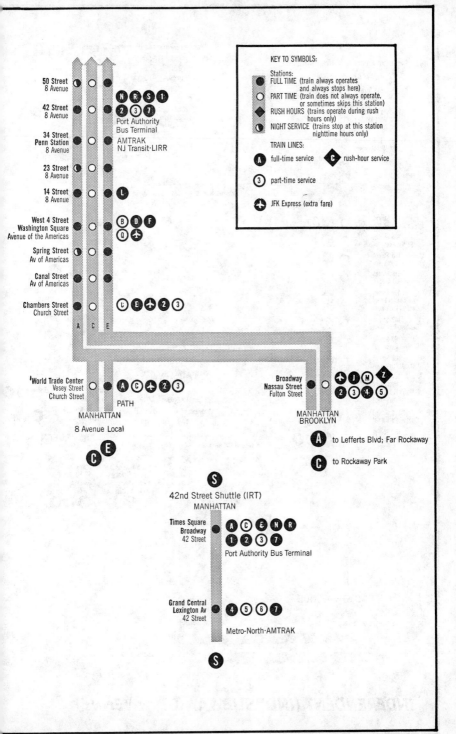

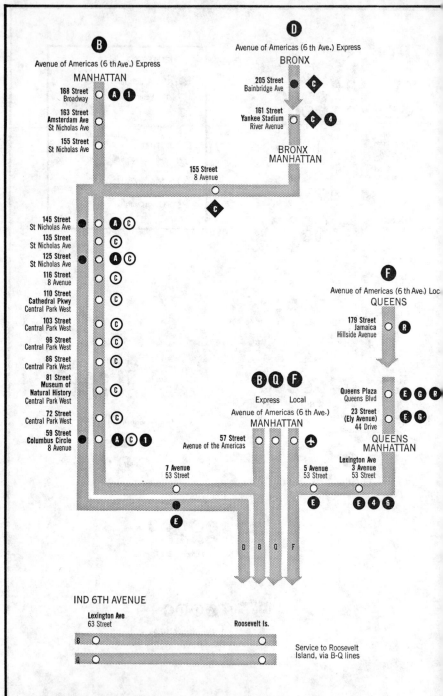

# INDEPENDENT (IND) SUBWAY (6TH AVENUE)

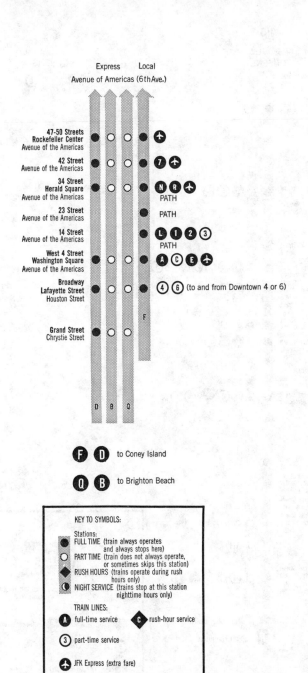

Express　Local
Avenue of Americas (6th Ave.)

**47-50 Streets**
**Rockefeller Center**
Avenue of the Americas

**42 Street**
Avenue of the Americas

**34 Street**
**Herald Square**
Avenue of the Americas
PATH

**23 Street**
Avenue of the Americas
PATH

**14 Street**
Avenue of the Americas
PATH

**West 4 Street**
**Washington Square**
Avenue of the Americas

**Broadway**
**Lafayette Street**
Houston Street
(to and from Downtown 4 or 6)

**Grand Street**
Chrystie Street

D　B　Q

**F** **D** to Coney Island

**Q** **B** to Brighton Beach

KEY TO SYMBOLS:

Stations:
**FULL TIME** (train always operates
and always stops here)
**PART TIME** (train does not always operate,
or sometimes skips this station)
**RUSH HOURS** (trains operate during rush
hours only)
**NIGHT SERVICE** (trains stop at this station
nighttime hours only)

TRAIN LINES:
**A** full-time service　　**C** rush-hour service

**3** part-time service

**✈** JFK Express (extra fare)

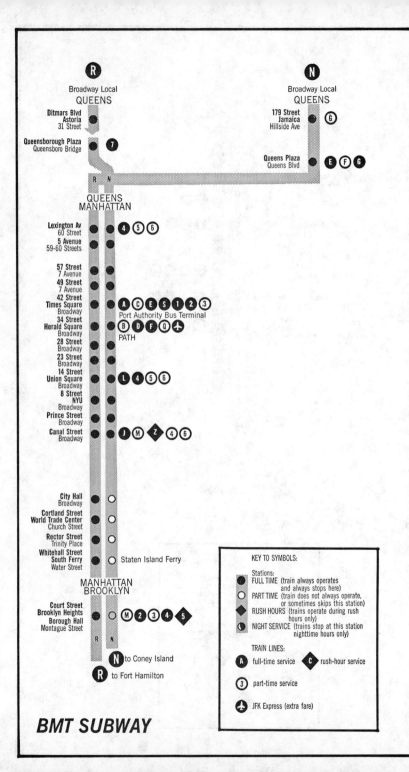

# BMT SUBWAY

IND trains run along Sixth and Eighth avenues, with major stops in Greenwich Village at West 4th Street and Sixth Avenue (both lines), at the Port Authority Bus Terminal at 41st Street (Eighth Avenue line), at Rockefeller Center (Sixth Avenue line), and at Columbus Circle (59th Street; Eighth Avenue line). You can switch from line to line—look for the transfer points on your subway map.

Each subway train is clearly numbered or lettered, indicating its specific route. (IND and BMT trains are lettered; IRT trains are numbered). Since differently routed trains will pull into the same station, it is best to know which letter or number you should take. Consult your subway map.

Both express and local trains run on each line. Locals stop at all stations on the route. Express trains do not. For example, if you ride an express (A) train uptown from 42nd Street on the IND Eighth Avenue line, you'll stop first at 59th Street and then zoom right through seven stations to the next stop, 125th Street! So you might be advised to stick to local trains until you know the system. Riding only in Manhattan, you won't lose much time doing this, and it could lessen the strains and frustrations of getting lost, or being whisked 60 blocks north of your destination.

Avoid the rush hours—8 to 9:30 in the morning, 4:30 to 6 in the afternoon. Pushing and shoving is the rule then—as it is most other times—but at rush hour there are at least 100 people per car pushing and shoving (feels more like a thousand).

To avoid waiting in line to buy tokens, carry extras with you—they can also be used on the bus.

It is not a particularly good idea to ride at night. If you do, avoid empty cars. Transit policemen patrol the trains at night, and the conductor rides in either one of the center cars in a tiny compartment at all times.

Do not hesitate to ask questions. Subway personnel (token sellers, conductors, transit police officers) are the best sources of information on exactly which train goes where—and how to negotiate the maze of underground passageways to the entrance to the train you're looking for, or to the exit to the street.

## Traveling by Taxi

Obviously the most convenient way to travel around town is by cab, but it's not cheap. At press time, fares start at $1.50 the minute you step into a cab, and thereafter the charge is $1.25 for each additional mile and an additional 20¢ for every minute of waiting time in traffic. The rider pays bridge, tunnel, and/or highway tolls. Also, as of this writing there is a 50¢ surcharge tacked on each fare after 8 p.m. every day, and all day on Sunday. Of course you are also expected to tip, but don't let any driver intimidate you—give 15% on all fares.

On short rides, if a group of people hop a cab together it can often cost less, or at least the same, as taking a subway. You can often find willing cab sharers at bus stops.

Check the *Yellow Pages* under the heading "Taxicab Service" for radio-dispatched cabs, which operate on regular meter rates, though sometimes there's an extra charge if you reserve in advance. Although it's usually easy enough to walk out and hail a passing cab, there may be occasions when you'd prefer door-to-door service. We usually call **MinuteMen** (tel. 718/899-5600, or toll free 800/345-6636), **Communicar** (tel. 718/457-7777), or **Bell Radio Taxi** (tel. 691-9191).

Cabs are hard to come by during morning and evening rush hours, and furthermore any trip at these times will cost you a fortune in waiting time.

Avoid gypsy cabs. These cabs do not have a medallion on top, many have a somewhat battered appearance, and they offer somewhat questionable service—we ourselves have been taken for more than a ride. There are, however, some fine private-car services with radio-dispatched late-model sedans. If you find yourself in an area not serviced by regular yellow cabs, ask a local person for a recommendation or check the *Yellow Pages* under "Car Service" or "Taxis." Ask for the rate when booking service.

## Parking Your Car

People in New York have been known to have fistfights over street-side parking places. Usually the only way to get one is to catch someone leaving a spot, which can take as long as a half hour. Don't wait to see a car pulling out. Watch for telltale signs. A person reaching into a pocket for keys, opening a car door, or even just walking purposefully toward a vehicle often means a space may be free in a few minutes.

Finding inexpensive garage parking is no easy task either. The average price for a space can be $5 or more an hour and more than $20 a day. One way to beat prices is to find a lot with a low maximum and a set charge for minimum parking time. **Square Industries** has several low-cost parking locations in Manhattan—including ones at 40 E. 89th St. (tel. 534-9421), and at 303 W. 46th St. (tel. 664-8224). The first charge is $18 (plus tax) for ten hours; the second $9.50 for ten hours.

The **municipal garages** managed by the city are the cheapest in Manhattan. In the **midtown** area, for instance there's one on Eighth Avenue between 53rd and 54th Streets (tel. 997-8901). Parking costs $2.40 an hour; it's open daily 24 hours. Another municipal garage is on the **Lower East Side,** at 105-113 Essex St., near Delancey (tel. 475-9814). Parking is 50¢ per half hour with a $4 minimum between 7 a.m. and 7 p.m. and $6 for 24 hours.

## Low-Cost Car Rentals

**Not Nu Car Rental,** 415 W. 54th St., between Ninth and Tenth avenues (tel. 265-3120), rents cars for $25 day, with a charge of 12¢ per mile. Cars are seven to eight years old and in good condition. Open Monday through Friday from 8 a.m. to 6 p.m. and on Saturday until 2 a.m.

**Tried and True,** 241 W. 28th St., between Seventh and Eighth avenues (tel. 268-9444), rents at a daily rate of $35 with 100 free miles (20¢ for each additional mile). A three-day weekend rental costs $120 with 300 free miles. Tried and True is open Monday through Friday from 7 a.m. to 7 p.m.

**ABC Rental Car,** 739 Broadway, at Astor Place (tel. 228-6690), rents daily at $49 with 150 free miles (30¢ for each additional mile). Weekend rates are $54 per day with 150 free miles; however, you must rent the car for three days over the weekend. ABC is open Monday through Saturday from 7:30 a.m. to 7 p.m.

**Rent-a-Wreck,** 280 Culver St. (N.J. 44), in Jersey City, N.J. (tel. 201/451-9500), does what its name promises. It rents older cars (but not more than three years old) at $24 a day, and new cars at $28. The price includes 50 free miles on the older cars, 100 miles on the new cars, plus 18¢ for each additional mile. Rent-a-Wrecks are individually owned franchises; this is the low-cost member—expect to pay more if you rent from the Manhattan branches. You can get to Jersey City via the PATH trains and a bus. Open Monday through Friday from 8 a.m. to 7 p.m. and on Saturday until noon. Try to reserve in advance.

**U-Drive,** 301 Bowery, between Houston and 1st streets (tel. 982-9680), rents cars for $39.95 a day on weekdays. There are also weekend specials, which include 500 free miles (15¢ for each additional mile) and insurance as well. Open Monday through Friday from 7:30 a.m. to 5 p.m. and on weekends until noon. They usually have same-day availability.

# 1. Frommer's Dollarwise® Travel Club—How To Save Money On All Your Travels

In this book we'll be looking at how to get your money's worth in New York, but there is a "device" for saving money and determining value on *all* your trips. It's the popular, international Frommer's Dollarwise Travel Club, now in its 30th successful year of operation. The club was formed at the urging of numerous readers of the $-A-Day and Frommer Guides, who felt that such an organization could provide continuing travel information and a sense of community to value-minded travelers in all parts of the world. And so it does!

In keeping with the budget concept, the annual membership fee is low and is immediately exceeded by the value of your benefits. Upon receipt of $18 (U.S. residents), or $20 U.S. by check drawn on a U.S. bank or via international postal money order in U.S. funds (Canadian, Mexican, and other foreign residents) to cover one year's membership, we will send all new members the following items.

## (1) Any *two* of the following books

Please designate in your letter which two you wish to receive:

### Frommer $-A-Day® Guides

Europe on $40 a Day
Australia on $30 a Day
Eastern Europe on $25 a Day
England on $50 a Day
Greece on $35 a Day
Hawaii on $60 a Day
India on $25 a Day
Ireland on $35 a Day
Israel on $40 a Day
Mexico (plus Belize and Guatemala) on $35 a Day
New York on $60 a Day
New Zealand on $45 a Day
Scandinavia on $60 a Day
Scotland and Wales on $40 a Day
South America on $35 a Day
Spain and Morocco (plus the Canary Is.) on $40 a Day
Turkey on $30 a Day
Washington, D.C. & Historic Virginia on $40 a Day

($-A-Day Guides document hundreds of budget accommodations and facilities, helping you get the most for your travel dollars.)

### Frommer Guides

Alaska
Australia
Austria and Hungary
Belgium, Holland, & Luxembourg
Bermuda and The Bahamas
Brazil
California and Las Vegas
Canada
Caribbean
Egypt
England and Scotland
Florida
France
Germany
Italy
Japan and Hong Kong
Mid-Atlantic States
New England
New York State

Northwest
Portugal, Madeira, & the Azores
South Pacific
Southeast Asia
Southern Atlantic States
Southwest
Switzerland and Liechtenstein
USA

(Frommer Guides discuss accommodations and facilities in all price ranges, with emphasis on the medium-priced.)

## Frommer Touring Guides
Australia
Egypt
Florence
London
Paris
Scotland
Thailand
Venice

(These new, color illustrated guides include walking tours, cultural and historic sites, and other vital travel information.)

## Gault Millau
Chicago
France
Hong Kong
Italy
London
Los Angeles
New England
New York
Paris
San Francisco
Washington, D.C.

(Irreverent, savvy, and comprehensive, each of these renowned guides candidly reviews over 1,000 restaurants, hotels, shops, nightspots, museums, and sights.)

## Serious Shopper's Guides
Italy
London
Los Angeles
Paris

(Practical and comprehensive, each of these handsomely illustrated guides lists hundreds of stores, selling everything from antiques to wine, conveniently organized alphabetically by category.)

## A Shopper's Guide to the Caribbean
Two experienced Caribbean hands guide you through this shopper's paradise, offering witty insights and helpful tips on the wares and emporia of more than 25 islands.

## Beat the High Cost of Travel
This practical guide details how to save money on absolutely all travel items—accommodations, transportation, dining, sightseeing, shopping, taxes, and more. Includes special budget information for seniors, students, singles, and families.

## Bed & Breakfast—North America
This guide contains a directory of over 150 organizations that offer bed & breakfast referrals and reservations throughout North America. The scenic attractions and major schools and universities near the homes of each are also listed.

## California with Kids
A must for parents traveling in California, providing key information on selecting the best accommodations, restaurants, and sightseeing attractions for the particular needs of the family, whether the kids are toddlers, school-age, preteens, or teens.

## Caribbean Hideaways
Well-known travel author Ian Keown describes the most romantic, alluring places to stay in the Caribbean, rating each establishment on romantic ambience, food, sports opportunities, and price.

## Frommer's Belgium
Arthur Frommer unlocks the treasures of a country overlooked by most travelers to Europe. Discover the medieval charm, modern sophistication, and natural beauty of this quintessentially European country.

## Frommer's Cruises
This complete guide covers all the basics of cruising—ports of call, costs, fly-cruise package bargains, cabin selection booking, embarkation and debarkation—and describes in detail over 60 or so ships cruising the waters of Alaska, the Caribbean, Mexico, Hawaii, Panama, Canada, and the United States.

## Frommer's Skiing Europe
Describes top ski resorts in Austria, France, Italy, and Switzerland. Illustrated with maps of each resort area. Includes supplement of Argentinian resorts.

## Guide to Honeymoon Destinations
A special guide for that most romantic trip of your life, with full details on planning and choosing the destination that will be just right in the U.S. [California, New England, Hawaii, Florida, New York, South Carolina, etc.], Canada, Mexico, and the Caribbean.

## Marilyn Wood's Wonderful Weekends
This very selective guide covers the best mini-vacation destinations within a 200-mile radius of New York City. It describes special country inns and other accommodations, restaurants, picnic spots, sights, and activities—all the information needed for a two- or three-day stay.

## Manhattan's Outdoor Sculpture
A total guide, fully illustrated with black-and-white photos, to more than 300 sculptures and monuments that grace Manhattan's plazas, parks, and other public spaces.

## Motorist's Phrase Book
A practical phrase book in French, German, and Spanish designed specifically for the English-speaking motorist touring abroad.

## Paris Rendez-Vous
An amusing and *au courant* guide to the best meeting places in Paris, organized for hour-to-hour use: from power breakfasts and fun brunches, through tea at four or cocktails at five, to romantic dinners and dancing 'til dawn.

## Swap and Go—Home Exchanging Made Easy
Two veteran home exchangers explain in detail all the money-saving benefits of a home exchange, and then describe precisely how to do it. Also includes information on home rentals and many tips on low-cost travel.

## The Candy Apple: New York with Kids
A spirited guide to the wonders of the Big Apple by a savvy New York grandmother with a kid's-eye view to fun. Indispensable for visitors and residents alike.

## The New World of Travel
From America's #1 travel expert, Arthur Frommer, an annual sourcebook with the hottest news and latest trends that's guaranteed to change the way you travel—and save you hundreds of dollars. Jam-packed with alternative new modes of travel that will lead you to vacations that cater to the mind, the spirit, and a sense of thrift.

## Travel Diary and Record Book
A 96-page diary for personal travel notes plus a section for such vital data as passport and traveler's check numbers, itinerary, postcard list, special people and places to visit, and a reference section with temperature and conversion charts, and world maps with distance zones.

## Where to Stay USA
By the Council on International Educational Exchange, this extraordinary guide is the first to list accommodations in all 50 states that cost anywhere from $3 to $30 per night.

## (2) Any *one* of the Frommer City Guides
Amsterdam and Holland
Athens
Atlantic City and Cape May
Barcelona and the Balaerics
Boston
Cancún, Cozumel, and the Yucatán
Chicago
Denver, Boulder, and Colorado Springs
Dublin and Ireland
Hawaii
Hong Kong
Las Vegas
Lisbon, Madrid, and Costa del Sol
London
Los Angeles
Mexico City and Acapulco
Minneapolis and St. Paul
Montréal and Québec City
New Orleans
New York
Orlando, Disney World, and EPCOT
Paris
Philadelphia
Rio
Rome
San Francisco
Santa Fe, Taos, and Albuquerque
Seattle and Portland
Sydney
Tokyo

Vancouver and Victoria
Washington, D.C.

(Pocket-size guides to hotels, restaurants, nightspots, and sightseeing attractions covering all price ranges.)

## (3) A one-year subscription to *The Dollarwise Traveler*

This quarterly eight-page tabloid newspaper keeps you up to date on fast-breaking developments in low-cost travel in all parts of the world bringing you the latest money-saving information—the kind of information you'd have to pay $35 a year to obtain elsewhere. This consumer-conscious publication also features columns of special interest to readers: **Hospitality Exchange** (members all over the world who are willing to provide hospitality to other members as they pass through their home cities); **Share-a-Trip** (offers and requests from members for travel companions who can share costs and help avoid the burdensome single supplement); and **Readers Ask . . . Readers Reply** (travel questions from members to which other members reply with authentic firsthand information).

## (4) Your personal membership card

Membership entitles you to purchase through the club all Frommer publications for a third to a half off their regular retail prices during the term of your membership.

So why not join this hardy band of international budgeteers and participate in its exchange of travel information and hospitality? Simply send your name and address, together with your annual membership fee of $18 (U.S. residents) or $20 U.S. (Canadian, Mexican, and other foreign residents), by check drawn on a U.S. bank or via international postal money order in U.S. funds to: Frommer's Dollarwise Travel Club, Inc., 15 Columbus Circle, New York, NY 10023. And please remember to specify which *two* of the books in section (1) and which *one* in section (2) you wish to receive in your initial package of members' benefits. Or, if you prefer, use the order form at the end of the book and enclose $18 or $20 in U.S. currency.

---

Once you are a member, there is no obligation to buy additional books. No books will be mailed to you without your specific order.

---

### Share a Ride

The Gray Line Air Shuttle is the only share-ride service operating between all metro New York airports and midtown hotels. Fares are $13 for Kennedy, $10 for LaGuardia, and $15 for Newark International. Arrangements for pick-ups can be made in the airline's baggage claim area at the ground transportation desk or by using the Gray Line Air Shuttle courtesy telephones located in the same area. Pick-ups from hotels to the airport can be arranged by the hotel transportation desk or by calling toll free 800/451-0455. The shuttle operates seven days a week from 8 a.m. to midnight.

---

### New York in Your Wallet

John Tauranac, who designed the official MTA map 11 years ago, has produced a three-paneled fold-out map *The Manhattan Traveler* ($2.95) with bus, subway, and places of interest panels. Available at map stores throughout the city.

# I

# FINDING A BUDGET HOTEL

1. **NEW YORK ON A SHOESTRING—HOSTELS, Ys, AND NONTRADITIONAL HOTELS**

2. **LOW-COST PERMANENT RESIDENCES**

3. **ROOMS FOR SERVICE PERSONNEL**

4. **HOTELS FOR GENERAL OCCUPANCY**

5. **ROOMS FOR FAMILIES**

6. **BED-AND-BREAKFASTS**

7. **WEEKEND AND OTHER PACKAGES**

**Y**ou're planning your first trip to New York, or maybe the first one in some years. When it comes to choosing a hotel, confusion reigns. You've heard rumors that Manhattan hotel rooms are vastly overpriced and that some neighborhoods are not safe. Should you choose to stay in midtown near Times Square, in the Lincoln Center area, or over on the East Side? What about that big new hostel uptown? And how much *will* you have to pay for a decent room? Finding a suitable budget hotel is the most difficult task, and the hardest, trickiest, most important job of all. Read and reread this chapter carefully; we have spent months researching the hotel scene, and if you read on, you'll find your choice of clean, comfortable accommodations within your budget.

Like many other major cities of the world, New York has an area or district noted for the cluster of good, inexpensive hotels: Times Square and the midtown theater district. Other budget hotels are widely scattered, and it's necessary to search them out. Nevertheless, they exist. Some, of course, have no fancy doormen or brocaded lobbies, but they do have adequate accommodations whose prices can still be considered reasonable in today's highly inflated hotel market.

And what does a reasonable, budget-minded hotel cost in New York these days? More than it does in most other cities, alas. Plan on spending between $80 and $100 for a double if you wish to stay in one of the regular tourist hotels (see "Hotels for General Occupancy," ahead). High as these rates may seem, they are actually budget by New York standards—in many hotels, rates of $150 and more per night are commonplace, and luxury hotels *start* at $200 and go up. If you stay in a hostel, a Y, or a women's hotel, or are a student or young working person and can qualify at certain places, you will, of course, pay much less. Weekly or longer stays bring down the rates. A bed-and-breakfast arrangement in a private home can save you money. And the best deal of all is to plan your trip for a weekend when first-class and luxury hotels often have special packages—meals, theater tickets, and such—for not much more than the cost of a budget hotel. We outline all of these options in the pages ahead.

Finding the best bargain rooms is an art, so here are a few tips that all tourists on a budget should know. First of all, the rates that hotels quote, known as "rack rates," are not necessarily what you will have to pay. When you make reservations, always ask if there are special discounts that might apply: corporate rates, family rates, package deals, senior-citizen rates (almost all hotels have these), rates for students or government employees or clergy or airline employees, or whatever is appropriate. If you call a hotel directly, rather than a toll-free "800" number in the case of a chain, you have a better bargaining advantage. We do suggest advance reservations, of course, but sometimes you can walk into a hotel late in the afternoon and if it is not completely booked, you may luck into a room at a considerably reduced rate. (*Warning:* Don't try this unless you have relatives or dear friends with an extra bed to fall back on.)

It is advisable, however, to write or call well in advance for reservations. New York hotels are busier than ever with many foreign tours and convention groups coming into Manhattan. But to take advantage of the special discount rate that some hotels offer to readers of this book, you *must write* well in advance stating specifically what price room you require. If you don't write ahead you may find that the cheaper, bargain rooms have been snapped up, and that only the higher-priced variety remains available. You may not get the same discount if you arrive without advance reservations, even if you flash a copy of this book upon registering.

If you haven't written for reservations, then make good use of a phone booth (25¢ per call) before you rush to a particular hotel. In some of the lower-priced establishments, you may want to see your room before paying or registering; quality varies from floor to floor in some budget hotels. It is also possible for hotels to change their rates at will, depending on what the traffic will bear.

Although there are many hotels in Europe offering rooms without baths, the number of those that do so in New York are dwindling. However, a few New York hotels still have some rooms available without private baths. Request them when you can: savings are great. This doesn't mean that you have to give up bathing to enjoy these low costs—it means you share a connecting bath with the adjoining room or trek down the hall a few doors to a bath.

Here's another tip: Travel in threes. By forming your own threesome, you will cut costs considerably. A triple is usually a large double-occupancy room with one double bed and one twin. It's three for little more than the price of two.

Or as an alternative, if you're a couple you can travel with another couple and share a suite, which usually consists of two well-furnished bedrooms and one bathroom. Some even have kitchen units. By sharing a bathroom here, you'll discover that the cost of a luxury suite doesn't equal the cost of two private rooms with bath.

## TELEPHONE TRAPS

Before you pick up the phone in your hotel room to call home or chat with local friends or business associates, beware. Phone calls can take an enormous toll on your bill. Back in the days before the Bell system broke up in 1984, charges for long-distance calls from hotel rooms were regulated by law. Not anymore! Now, with a variety of phone systems available, you may find yourself linked up with an alternative company you've never heard of that charges exorbitant rates. Hotels, seeing phone service as an easy source of extra revenue, often add extra charges onto regular long-distance calls, credit-cards calls, and local calls as well—and they may even charge you for calls that have not been completed. The safest—and cheapest—way to make phone calls is to use the public phones in the lobby. If you do make calls from your room, be sure to look for the card outlining the costs: by law it must be posted by the main phone in your room. If it isn't, check with the front desk. And keep a record of all calls you make, just in case things get out of hand when you get your bill.

## OTHER PRELIMINARY POINTS

Remember that inflation being what it is, hotel rates may well be higher as time goes on. The rates quoted in this guidebook were correct at press time.

Also note that the prices we quote for rooms do not include the dismaying amount of hotel taxes: 8¼% for New York State, plus another 5% for New York City, plus a flat fee of $2 per day imposed by the city on every hotel room in New York.

Got the general picture? Then let's begin. . . .

---

# 1. New York on a Shoestring—Hostels, Ys, and Nontraditional Hotels

---

## NOT FOR HOSTELERS ONLY

The **New York International Youth Hostel,** 891 Amsterdam Ave. (at the corner of 103rd Street), New York, NY 10025 (tel. 212/932-2300), may well be New York's best budget lodging choice. For little more than the cost of parking a car in the midtown area, you can park yourself in a clean, comfortable, and secure hostelry, at a tab that could be as low as $19 per night! And the new hostel, which opened in the fall of 1989, is not just for international students and others traveling with a pack on their back and a bicycle on the rack (although they make up the largest percentage of guests): couples, families, people of all ages are welcome. And all are guaranteed an experience unlike that in the average, impersonal New York hotel.

The fee of $19 a night (no hotel taxes are added on) is for members of American Youth Hostels; nonmembers may purchase a membership on the premises (around $25), or pay a guest membership of $3 a night. Linen rental for those not carrying their own is $1 a night.

The new hostel is unique on many counts. It is the first American Youth Hostel in New York, the largest in the country, and the most ambitious hostel project in the world. It is housed in a century-old city landmark listed on the National Register of Historic Places, which was designed by the famed 19th-century architect Richard Morris Hunt (who was also responsible for the base of the Statue of Liberty and the Metropolitan Museum of Art). The four-story, Victorian Gothic building, which had been abandoned and allowed to fall into a sad state of disrepair, has been given a $15-million total renovation, and superbly restored following the most minute (and costly) city, state, and federal landmark requirements. The building meets all the latest health, fire, and handicap-accessible codes. In addition to providing accommodations for 477 guests, it also offers handsome common rooms (one for quiet pursuits, another for television), spacious gardens for dining and sunning (still under construction at the time of this writing), a kitchen where hostelers may prepare their own meals if they wish, a self-service cafeteria with an outside dining area, an off-off-Broadway theater, and a commercial restaurant. Also on the premises are conference rooms and facilities for nonprofit groups (organizations from all over the world hold meetings and house participants here). The building also houses the regional office of the Metropolitan New York Council, an American Youth Hostel reservations center, and a full-service travel agency. And, yes, there are bike racks, and vans to meet groups at the airports. The hostel is located one block away from the IRT subway station at 103rd Street and Broadway, in a multiethnic neighborhood that is undergoing gentrification. Seven blocks north is the Cathedral of St. John the Divine, and four blocks farther north begins the campus of Columbia University. Midtown is about a 15-minute subway ride or a 30-minute bus ride away.

As for the sleeping rooms, they are quite spacious and sunny, with high (eight- or ten-foot) ceilings and either two, three, or four bunk beds with drawer space underneath. Rooms are carpeted and have individual heat/air-conditioning controls. Baths are down the hall (a ratio of eight people to one bathroom), and have individual showers and dressing rooms. There are four hotel-quality family rooms that have queen-size beds and two bunk beds, as well as private baths. Rates for these are also $19 per person per night (children under 17 are charged half price). Security is excellent, since rooms have electronic key locks, and only those with keys are allowed access to the bedroom floors.

Unlike other hostels, NYIYH has no curfews or closing times, making it fully accessible to guests 24 hours a day. Guests are not required to do chores. All the facilities have been designed to bring people together, to promote a lively cross-cultural exchange in a relaxing atmosphere, and to give people "an alternative to the sterile environment of the New York hotel scene," according to director Eliot Winick. And all for $19 a night! Advance reservations are suggested.

Practically an unofficial "annex" to the New York International Youth Hostel, located as it is just around the corner at Broadway and 103rd Street, the **Malibu Studios Hotel,** 2688 Broadway, New York, NY 10025 (tel. 212/222-2954), is another excellent choice for offbeat budget lodgings. Decorated in California palm-tree motif, the place is always packed with new–in–New York singles—many would-be actors and actresses, performers and entertainers, students from nearby Columbia University—as well as businesspeople on a budget, European and American tourists, all in search of clean, comfortable, and safe no-frills lodging at excellent prices. The very best bargains are for those who stay at least a week. A small studio room with a single or double bed, freshly painted and nicely decorated with quilted spreads and drapes, a desk/dresser and chair, and a small refrigerator topped by a two-burner electric hotplate, plus a sink, rents for $150 a week for one, $175 for two. The bathrooms, shared with three or four other people, have both tub and shower and are kept immaculately clean. On a daily basis, such a room goes for $50 single, $60 double. Then there are larger rooms, which have private baths and TVs as well as the cooking facilities; on a daily basis these rent from $60 single, $70 double.

At the time of our visit the management was expanding the original 100-room building and creating 50 more rooms in an adjoining building. Some of these rooms are quite large and will have double beds and a sofa bed, so a family of four could be accommodated. Families and large groups can also be put together in adjoining rooms. The best thing to do is to call the reservations manager, tell him your exact needs, and he will most likely be able to work something out for you.

The Malibu is about 15 minutes by subway or 30 minutes by bus from midtown Manhattan, in a lively, multiethnic neighborhood. Unlike more expensive midtown hotels, the Malibu does not have daily maid service, private phones, air conditioning, and TVs as standard features (there are, however, TVs in the larger rooms; in the studios, TVs can be rented for $15 a week, and fans are available on request). There is 24-hour switchboard and message service, and pay phones in the lobby. Bathrooms are cleaned by the housekeeping staff, but guests are expected to care for their own rooms (they'll loan you a vacuum cleaner at the desk). And there's a laundromat next door. Security is no problem, since they use a closed-circuit-TV security system, have someone on duty at the front desk 24 hours a day, and keep the front door locked (guests must be buzzed in). There is no elevator. Although every room has its own cooking facilities, most people eat out—there are dozens of ethnic restaurants in the neighborhood—or have food delivered from the Chinese restaurant on the corner, or, in a pinch, go to the nearby fast-food chains. A travel agency next door can assist guests with airline tickets.

Malibu Studios is not fancy, but it's clean (rooms are painted every few months), it's convenient, and the price is right. It attracts a congenial clientele who often become friends. (Recent guests have included an 80-member French contingent who had arrived to take part in the New York Marathon!) The management goes out of its way to be helpful, and even provides free passes to local clubs and discos. The formula has worked so well that there are hopes of opening another branch of Malibu Studios at another Upper West Side location in the near future. Write or call for advance reservations.

## THE CAMPUS AS HOTEL

Some of New York's best budget accommodations are not in New York at all. They're ten minutes away, across the Hudson River, at the campus of **Stevens Institute of Technology** in Hoboken, New Jersey. From the scenic, 55-acre campus sitting on a high bank of the Hudson known as Castle Point, guests can view New York's fabled skyline from a myriad of viewpoints; enjoy safe, secure, and clean accommodations at very low prices; and pop into Manhattan in all of ten minutes via convenient PATH trains that travel beneath the Hudson River. In addition, they have access to a low-cost cafeteria for meals, and can partake of all the sports and leisure activities on campus, including tennis courts, an indoor track, indoor swimming pool, sauna, weight machines, and squash, basketball, and racquetball courts —free. And all this at rates that can be as low as $20 per night!

Here's how it works. Stevens Institute is one of the very few colleges in the area that has dormitory accommodations to spare: usually about 400 rooms are available to visitors in summer, and around 50 in winter. Visitors live right in the dorms alongside regular students; the dorms are very quiet, we're told (these are serious students of technology and they usually spend their time glued to their computers), except for a few days after exams. Rooms are scrupulously clean (which is often not the case in college dorms in New York). Visitors may choose a standard dorm room, which consists of a bunk bed (beds may be placed side by side on the floor), a desk, and a chair; baths are down the hall, and the rooms are not air-conditioned. If you want the room to yourself, it's $30; if there are two of you, it's $22 per person. Deluxe rooms, in Technology Hall, are more comfortable, with regular twin beds, air conditioning, carpeted floors, and private bath. For one person, the rate is $50; for two, it's $30 per person. All rates include taxes. If you stay three or more nights there is no charge for linens; for one or two nights, the linen package is $4. Families should know about the beautiful suites in Technology Hall, complete with two twin beds (two rollaways can be added), a full bath with tub and shower, TV, air conditioning, and a fully equipped kitchen with utensils provided—a terrific family bargain at $90 per night.

There are two ways to save money on even these low rates. First, Campus Holidays, the rental agent of Stevens Institute residence halls, has agreed to offer readers of this book a 10% discount, which also applies to their three-day "Big Apple on a Budget" tour; inquire when you make reservations. An option for those traveling alone is to indicate that you would be willing to be matched with a roommate, and you will pay only the per-person double-occupancy rates—$22 in standard rooms, $30 in deluxe, instead of $30 or $50—whether or not you are actually given a roommate. (Chances are good that you won't.)

Stevens Institute is located in Hoboken, New Jersey, a working-class waterfront town currently being gentrified by New Yorkers. Its major claims to fame are that it was the birthplace of the game of baseball and the hometown of Frank Sinatra. The campus is a seven-block walk, a 40¢ bus ride, or a $2 taxi ride to the PATH trains, which run to the World Trade Center, Greenwich Village, or midtown Manhattan (near Madison Square Garden) for $1, 24 hours a day. Public buses also make frequent runs into New York. The campus is convenient for motorists, since it's halfway between the Lincoln and Holland tunnels. And parking on campus is free.

To make reservations or to get further information, contact Campus Holidays,

USA, Inc., 242 Bellevue Ave., Upper Montclair, NJ 07043 (tel. 201/744-8724, or toll free 800/526-2915 outside New Jersey).

## LIFE AT THE Y

For the young and young at heart (men, women, even families), the **Vanderbilt YMCA,** 224 E. 47th St. (between Second and Third avenues), New York, NY 10017 (tel. 212/755-2410), is the safest and best of the city's Ys. A 435-room, ten-story structure, it offers some of the finest athletic facilities (including a large pool, gym, and sauna) in town, plus an excellent cafeteria and a self-service laundry. The atmosphere of the place reminds us of a European youth hostel—relaxed, young, and friendly—but visitors of any age can stay. It's not a bad idea for families willing to rough it. The cafeteria is a terrific money-saver; it's quite pleasant, and offers big, filling meals in the $4 to $5 range. Guests are given automatic Y membership for the length of their stay and can use all the Vanderbilt Y facilities. The hospitality desk is helpful with sightseeing and other information.

Rooms are small and spartan, but very clean, located off attractive hallways with carpeted walls. All accommodations are air-conditioned and have single or bunk beds, dresser, and desk. Some have sinks in the room, but baths are down the hall. Phones are also in the hall; the desk will take messages for you.

Rates for single rooms with single beds are $34 to $44 per night; doubles (with bunk beds) are $44 to $50. Triples (with bunk beds) are $60 to $65; quads (with bunk beds) are $76 to $80. Credit cards are accepted. Considering the superb East Side location and facilities, this Y is quite a bargain. It's also the kind of place parents can feel at ease sending their young sons and daughters. Write or call for reservations.

The **WestSide YMCA,** 5 W. 63rd St. (between Central Park West and Broadway), New York, NY 10023 (tel. 212/787-4400), has an excellent location—just seconds away from Lincoln Center and Central Park. Subways and bus lines can have you in midtown in about ten minutes. Students and tourists can all feel comfortable here. Both single and double rooms for men and women are offered, with special rates for students and groups. Services include daily maid service, mail and message service, and 24-hour uniformed security guards. Television is available in some of the rooms, and air conditioners can be rented for $3.25 per day.

You must be 18 years of age or older to stay in any of the rooms at the Y. Rates start at $32 a night for a single room without bath. Twin-bedded rooms without bath start at $46, and twins with bath start at $52 per night. For more details, call the reservations office at extension 120 or 121.

All guests of the WestSide YMCA are members for as long as they stay. That means free use of the excellent Health and Fitness Center, which features two gyms, two pools, a banked and cushioned indoor running track, Nautilus and Universal weight systems, and handball, racquetball, and squash courts, plus a steamroom and sauna, and much more. A good choice if you need to stay in shape while visiting New York!

## FOR WOMEN ONLY

For many years New York had three major hotels solely for women. Now one of them has been converted into a first-class hotel for general occupancy; another is still operating as a women's hotel, but, unfortunately, is located in a part of town where vast numbers of the city's homeless have been dumped into welfare hotels, with concurrent neighborhood problems. So for women traveling alone who would like the comforts of a respectable women's hotel, there is really only one viable choice, and that's **Allerton House,** 130 E. 57th St. (at the corner of Lexington Avenue), New York, NY 10022 (tel. 212/753-8841), which has been holding forth for many years, a dowdy but doughty dowager among its kind. Its lobby looks more like that of an office building than a hotel, with only a plaque to mark its entrance. The location is excellent, in a busy midtown business and shopping neighborhood, with

Bloomingdale's just two blocks away. The atmosphere is rather sedate (about three-quarters of the rooms are occupied by permanent residents, mostly older women), but there are also enough 20- to 30-year-old guests for younger women to feel at home. Pluses include a terrific wrap-around rooftop terrace ideal for sunbathing, and a laundromat. Tommy Makem's atmospheric Irish Pavilion restaurant, with candlelight, beamed ceilings, and a popular bar, adjoins the hotel. And there's usually a smart crowd lined up at the elevators waiting to gain access to the Living Well Lady Figure Salon on the mezzanine floor (hotel guests are usually entitled to one free visit) or to the Beverly Bridge Club, one of the city's busiest and best (lunch and an afternoon's worth of bridge for $8), on the third.

Almost half the Allerton's 369 rooms have recently been redecorated with new furniture and accessories; they are small but pleasant, with high ceilings, direct-dial phones, sinks, and dressers; TV sets can be rented. The remaining rooms could be described as clean and respectable, but without much charm. The units on the 17th floor, however, are another story; attractive hotel rooms, they have twin beds, private bath, black-and-white TV, air conditioning, nice furnishings, and are an excellent value at $75 double.

A bathless room (facilities down the hall) is $45 per night for one person; a room with connecting bath (you share with an adjoining room), $50; a room with a private bath or shower, $60. The 17th-floor twins are $75. Weekly rates are available for stays of two weeks or longer: $175 for a bathless room, $195 for a room with connecting bath, $210 for rooms with private bath or shower.

## STUDENTS—MEN AND WOMEN

New York may be expensive for the average visitor, but flash your student ID card and it get's a bit easier. Several establishments put out a big welcome for students and young international travelers. (See, also, "Not for Hostelers Only," above.)

University students aged 21 or above (with student IDs) and those with academic affiliations should consider the vacation-time (May 15 to August 15 and December 15 to January 15) accommodations at the famous **International House of New York,** 500 Riverside Dr. (at 122nd Street, overlooking the Hudson River), New York, NY 10027 (tel. 212/316-8400). Bus and subways are close by. During the school year, International House accommodates, on a permanent basis, over 500 students from all over the world. About 65% of the students are foreigners, and though many of the American residents attend Columbia University, over 45 educational and training institutes are represented each year. But when the permanent residents leave on vacation (during the periods stated above), the house rents its rooms to students visiting New York.

Accommodations are just part of the offerings. There's a low-priced cafeteria, a small dining room and kitchen for informal parties, a laundry, music practice rooms, a general store, and several public lounges including a TV room and study rooms. There's also a gym with volleyball, basketball, and table tennis facilities, and there are dance and aerobics classes. Special activities of interest to students and newcomers to New York occur almost daily.

Rooms are simple but neat and clean, with light walls, linoleum-tile floors, and the necessary furnishings—bed, linens, blanket, pillow, dresser, desk, chair, bookcase, lamp, and private telephone. They are all singles, two-thirds with sinks; bath and toilet facilities are shared in the hall. There is no maid service, but linens can be exchanged for fresh ones for a small fee. Vacuum cleaners and irons are available at no extra cost.

The rates are $25 a night; monthly rates average $18 a day. (Applications are required for stays of longer than a month.) A limited number of cots are available for guests to stay in your room for $10 a night for a maximum period of two weeks. Expanded facilities can now accommodate academic-year residents; there are apartments for couples and groups of four to six students. Rooms are occasionally available to transient students during the academic year, but advance reservations cannot be confirmed more than a week in advance. Write or call for reservations.

Despite its name, the **International Student Hospice,** 154 E. 33rd St. (between Lexington and Third avenues), New York, NY 10016 (tel. 212/228-7470 or 228-4689), is not for internationals only: this reconverted Murray Hill townhouse is the place where Oxford scholars swap stories with Ohio collegians, where students from St. Louis bunk in the opposite room from those from the Sorbonne. Sponsored by a nonprofit foundation, and in business since 1958, ISH can house 20 guests (students are preferred, but others are sometimes accepted), and charges them $20 per night in rooms for four; there are just a few tiny private rooms. Bathrooms and showers are down the hall. Rooms are small but clean, and there's a library for studying, and even a tiny lounge with color TV. Guests must observe a midnight curfew. The hospice is within walking distance of Grand Central Terminal, Penn Station, Madison Square Garden, and the United Nations, in a mixed residential-business neighborhood, right in the shadow of the Empire State Building. Write or call in advance, or call at any hour: the phone is on 24 hours a day.

Is it an avant-garde art gallery pretending to be a hotel, or is it a hotel pretending to be an avant-garde art gallery? The answer is a little bit of both. Surely, there is no other hostelry in New York quite like the **Carlton Arms Hotel,** 160 E. 25th St. (at the corner of Third Avenue), New York, NY 10010 (tel. 212/684-8337). The artistic inventions of a friendly staff and their friends in the art community have turned this once rather decrepit hotel on a shabby street into a congenial place for young travelers. Especially popular with counterculture types and students from Europe and Asia, this four-story hotel has ancient furniture, but the beds are all new and good, and the place is kept clean, safe, and comfortable. The amazing thing about it is the décor: vivid color schemes (some halls and doors are painted in black accented by vivid fluorescent colors); hallway and wall murals climbing up the staircase, filling every inch of wall space and reaching up to the ceiling; and theme rooms (like the Roses and Car Crashes room, for example), create an atmosphere unlike anything to be found at your neighborhood Holiday Inn. The management has hit upon a brilliant decorating scheme: every three months they turn over four rooms to aspiring artists and give them a free hand; their wall murals then become a permanent part of the décor. When all four rooms are completed, an art opening is held. As of this writing, 42 of the hotel's 54 rooms had been done. These rooms have attracted so much attention—some are lovely; some verge on the grotesque; some, like Brian Damage's vision of the interior of a submarine looking onto the lost underwater world of Atlantis (Room 40) are artistic *tours de force*—that they have appeared as backdrops for fashion shots in one of Europe's most prestigious fashion magazines. Advice to those who want peaceful dreams: Before you choose your room here, have a look to see if the art agrees with you. There is no air conditioning here, but the rooms do have fans. Some 40% of them have private baths; other rooms share communal facilities. Those with bath are $39 single, $50 double; those without bath are $33 single, $44 double. Students and international travelers are offered discounts of 20%. Not for middle-class comfort, but acceptable for casual types. Two telephone calls are requested to secure a reservation.

The Carlton Arms shows what can be done with little money but lots of imagination—it's one-of-a-kind.

## FOR INTERNATIONAL STUDENTS AND TRAVELERS

The office of the **International Student Center,** 38 W. 88th St. (between Central Park West and Columbus Avenue), New York, NY 10024 (tel. 212/787-7706), is jammed with backpacks; you know you're in a student hostel the moment you set foot in the door. Sponsored by the Association for World Travel Exchange, which has a similar house in Holland, ISC has been hosting foreign students and travelers (young people between the ages of 18 and 30) since 1956. They've converted an old brownstone in a pleasant residential neighborhood into seven single-sex dormitory rooms, each with from four to ten beds. Downstairs is an old kitchen that students are free to use, and a ramshackle lounge with TV, the scene for lots of lively socializing. This is a good place to meet someone to travel with. Most summer guests are from Western Europe; in winter the largest number are from New Zealand, Australia, and Japan. Rates are $10 per night, with a five-day limit from May 1 to the end of October. Robert Tesdell, the cordial manager, advises that advance reservations are not accepted; the best thing is to call them as soon as you arrive in town. Passports are required. The residence is open daily from 8 a.m. to 11 p.m.

The **Chelsea Center,** 511 W. 20th St. (between Tenth and Eleventh avenues), New York, NY 10011 (tel. 212/243-4922), circa 1981, is perhaps the homiest hostel in town. The teakettle is always on and a warm welcome is always available from hostess Heidi Dubose of Germany and her staff, who have remodeled the first floor of an old loft building and turned it into a real home-away-from-home for wandering students and travelers from abroad. They have a large, sunny, L-shaped room, very clean, with white-washed walls and six double-decker beds, plus another room with eight bunk beds; facilities are completely coed. Rates are $16 per night, and that includes sheets, blankets, showers, and breakfast—three slices of bread and butter and jam, tea, coffee, and milk. The center welcomes backpackers, hikers, and other travelers as well as students, but always gives first preference to foreigners. Stays are limited to one week during the summer. The location, although it seems a bit out of the way in a mixed residential/light-industrial area, is actually excellent: it's a two-minute walk to the 23rd Street crosstown bus that takes you to the heart of Manhattan, and a short walk to Greenwich Village. Several nearby discos are open until the wee hours (free or low-cost admission passes are usually available). Guests have the use of the cozy kitchen, and you can usually find them there, having a snack, chatting with Heidi or the staff about goings-on in New York, or perhaps celebrating a birthday. One student from Australia wrote in the guestbook: "Definitely the most friendly place in the U.S.A. and a 'secure' place to feel welcome in New York." The house is closed between 11 a.m. and 4 p.m. Advance reservations are welcome; without them, be sure to call in advance before your arrival. An excellent choice for a personal welcome in New York.

*Note:* If they can't put you up, the people at the Chelsea Center will do their best to find you another good, low-cost accommodation.

## 2. Low-Cost Permanent Residences

For those of our readers who are planning a fairly lengthy stay in New York—say, two months or more—we've scoured the city for good, low-cost, permanent residences. These we'll break down into two categories: permanent residences for students and young working people, and permanent residences for women.

### RESIDENCES FOR STUDENTS AND YOUNG WORKING PEOPLE

The **YM-YWHA,** 1395 Lexington Ave. (at 92nd Street), New York, NY 10128 (tel. 212/427-6000), is a cultural paradise for those young men and women who plan to stay at least three months. Rates include light housekeeping privileges, and this is one of the city's most exciting institutions. It was here that Dylan Thomas gave his celebrated poetry readings in the 1950s; and the Y continues to present excellent cultural programs ranging from the Juilliard String Quartet (one of countless musical events) to lectures and appearances by writers such as John Updike, I. B. Singer, and Bharati Mukherjee. There are also Jewish operas, Israeli and Jewish-themed films (such as *Hester Street*), Yiddish theater and theater on Jewish themes (like Paddy Chayefsky's *The Tenth Man*) productions. Residents often get reduced-price or free tickets to these events. Other facilities include, of course, the adjoining gymnasium and pool, with steam and sauna rooms; exercise rooms and equipment;

basketball, volleyball, racquetball, handball, and paddleball courts; etc. Other on-premises amenities include social, TV, and study lounges for residents; laundry facilities; a library; an art gallery with changing exhibits; and kitchens on every floor. The Y is located in a good residential neighborhood, and is convenient to public transportation.

As for the rooms, they're immaculate and cheerful, with coordinated drapes and curtains and linoleum-tile floors. Furnishings include a single bed or beds, dresser, desk, bookshelves, and lamps. Some are air-conditioned; baths are communal; phones are in the hall (they take messages). If you so desire, you can install a phone in your room at regular New York City rates.

The Y accepts young men and women between the ages of 18 and 26, regardless of race or religious belief, but only if you are a full-time student or employee, or a combination of the two. Every applicant is required to have a personal interview with a member of the Y staff (by appointment) prior to admission. (Special arrangements can be made with those coming from another part of the country or from overseas.) Shared rooms start at about $400 per month per person for a minimum stay of three months; singles begin at about $560. For short-term stays (sometimes available in summer) rates are on a weekly basis, starting at $168 per week per person. In addition, residents are required to purchase a Y membership ($75 annually), and a $35 fee is payable upon submission of your completed application.

When writing for an application form, specify that you are between the ages of 18 and 26, and employed or in school; otherwise you will first get a letter explaining eligibility requirements. Write as far in advance as possible, and follow up your application with repeated phone calls or further letters. Highly recommended.

## RESIDENCES FOR WORKING WOMEN AND STUDENTS

Some of the nicest of the city's permanent residences for women are maintained by the Salvation Army. On the East Side they have the **Parkside Evangeline,** 18 Gramercy Park South (at Irving Place), New York, NY 10003 (tel. 212/677-6200). Located right off lovely Gramercy Park in one of New York's most exclusive neighborhoods (some of the rooms overlook the park, and residents can use this otherwise-locked private facility), the Evangeline has 300 rooms for students and working women aged 18 to 35 of any race or religion. It's the kind of place in which you'd feel good about having your young daughter stay. Facilities include a fireplace lounge off the lobby, two outdoor rooftop terraces with chaises longues for sunbathing, a sewing room, music practice rooms, washing machines (irons and ironing boards available), exercise machines, hairdryers, a library, and a very attractive second-floor lounge where women can entertain visitors. There's also a lovely carpeted dining room with old-fashioned wallpaper and tables covered in white linen cloths.

Rooms (singles and doubles) are small, but clean and rather charming, with curtained windows and maple Ethan Allen furnishings (chairs, dresser, desk, and hutch), switchboard phones, and sinks. Most have a bath in the room; some share a connecting bath. No men are allowed in the rooms.

A personal interview or two letters of recommendation are required, and you must show that you work or go to school full time. Rates at this amazing facility are just $135 and up per week, including breakfast and dinner daily! A visiting friend or sister can get a cot in your room for $12 a night, and occasionally rooms for family members only are available on a daily basis for $30 per night, meals extra. A few double rooms are also available. The minimum stay is 90 days (during the summer, six weeks). Contact Miss Pierce or Maj. James Miller.

In Greenwich Village, there's the lovely **John and Mary Markle Evangeline Residence,** 123 W. 13th St. (between Sixth and Seventh avenues), New York, NY 10011 (tel. 212/242-2400). Here, on one of the prettiest tree-lined streets in the Village, the Salvation Army runs another superb facility. Its 200 rooms are divided equally among college students, businesswomen, and senior citizens, which makes for a stimulating mix; you might find students from Parsons School of Design and NYU, nurses from St. Vincent's Hospital, and even an octogenarian retired professor from Columbia! A $7-million renovation has made the 58-year-old building better than ever; now all its rooms have a private bath and shower, and a telephone, and are attractively furnished with Ethan Allen colonial furnishings. Weekly maid service is provided. Everyone has use of a typing room, a TV room, a piano studio, a lounge, study halls, and a beautiful roof garden. There's also a snackbar and counter on the first floor—and the rates also include two meals a day! Single, double, triple, and quad rooms are available, at rates that begin at $88 per person a week. Of course there is a waiting list, but rooms are also assigned on the basis of need. Several guest rooms are available on a nightly basis at $52.50 per night, including two meals. Inquiries should be directed to Maj. Daniel Moore.

During the summer months, when the college students have gone home, rooms are often taken by young ballet students (accompanied by chaperones) who have come to New York on scholarships from some of the leading ballet companies.

Another Salvation Army facility for women is the superbly located **Ten Eyck-Troughton Memorial Residence,** 145 E. 39th St. (between Third and Lexington Avenues), New York, NY 10016 (tel. 212/490-5990), which is for women aged 35 to 60 who are employed full time. Rates average over $120 per week, including two meals.

## Working Women Only

The **Webster Apartments,** 419 W. 34th St. (between Ninth and Tenth avenues), New York, NY 10001 (tel. 212/967-9000), is an outstanding hostelry with permanent-residence accommodations for 400 women. Heavily endowed by Charles and Josiah Webster, who founded the residence in 1923 and left means to fund the enterprise, it provides the comforts of home (a very stately and elegant home) to young working women at low cost. Facilities of the 13-story brick structure include a gracious lobby, a handsome library with deep leather chairs, an elegant drawing room, television rooms, a charming wicker-furnished garden room, a card-playing room, and even a series of small intimate rooms with no doors that serve as "beau parlors" for entertaining "gentleman callers" (the latter are not permitted upstairs). Other amenities are a lovely garden (quite a luxury in Manhattan), sewing machines, typewriters, laundry, and daily maid service.

The rooms themselves, all singles, are pretty and quaint, with freshly painted walls, carpeting, and all necessary furnishings, including a sink. All rooms have direct-dial phones. Baths are in the hall. Rooms have electric fans; air conditioning is available at extra cost.

Weekly rates (subject to change) are between $95 and $136, depending on your salary, and including breakfast and dinner seven days a week. Although most of the residents are young, women of any age who are employed full time may apply. You can write to the above address, but if you're in the city, come in for an interview any Wednesday evening between 5 and 7:30 p.m. (no appointment necessary).

## 3. Rooms for Service Personnel

For active-duty military personnel, male and female, the **Soldiers', Sailors' and Airmen's Club, Inc.,** 283 Lexington Ave. (between 36th and 37th streets), New York, NY 10016 (tel. 212/683-4353), rents out semiprivate rooms (most rooms have only two beds) for just $20 per night, and there are adequate bath facilities on each floor. Separated personnel (six months or less) pay the same rate. The rooms are homey, neat, and cheerful, with nice furnishings, cream-colored walls adorned with framed prints, and very high ceilings; many have shuttered windows. Phones are in the hall; they take messages. The building itself is like a gracious old home with elegantly furnished lounges (one houses a jukebox and piano), a library/writing room, a pool room, and a TV room. A budget-priced cafeteria on the premises, open Saturday and Sunday only, offers continental breakfast. The club also provides free tickets (when available) to movies, plays, and such, and can arrange hotel accommodations for married personnel or at reduced military rates at other hotels.

While the USO does not have hotel rooms, it can help service personnel on active duty, and their families, get New York hotel rooms at rates of 20% to 40% off regular prices. Temporary headquarters of the **Gen. Douglas MacArthur Memorial Center** are at 587 Seventh Ave. (between 41st and 42nd streets), New York, NY 10036 (tel. 212/719-5433). The USO provides many other services as well. They often have free tickets to movies, Broadway shows, and sports events on a day-to-day basis, and provide information on New York sightseeing and nightlife. Free refreshments are often available, too, with volunteers doing the cooking.

---

# 4. Hotels for General Occupancy

Now we come to the regular nonspecialized hotels, which accommodate everyone. We list them according to the area of New York in which they are found. The average price of these rooms will be around $100, some a bit lower, and a few a bit higher for those visitors who don't mind a relative "Big Splurge." By New York standards, even these are very well priced. Whatever hotel you choose, be sure to write well in advance for a reservation. Advance reservations are your best guarantee for getting the lowest rates possible.

## MIDTOWN WEST/TIMES SQUARE AND ENVIRONS

This is by far the most convenient neighborhood to stay in if you wish to take advantage of the Broadway theater. Some of the other aspects of this area—shoddy cinema houses, sleazy bars, and cheap penny arcades—are not so attractive and best avoided. However, the area is being improved constantly (though some enormous construction projects create lots of noise and dirt), and the streets get better as you go north of 42nd Street and east of Seventh Avenue. And the hotels here are working harder than ever to maintain strict security standards and to make visitors feel comfortable. We were impressed with several hotels and the genuine value they offer.

The 600-room **Century Paramount Hotel,** 235 W. 46th St. (between Broadway and Eighth Avenue), New York, NY 10036 (tel. 212/764-5500, or toll free 800/225-7474), has long been one of our favorite hotels in this area. Now that a dynamic new management has taken over (it was close to completion of a $30-million renovation at press time) it's going to be better than ever. There will be a new lobby and new elevators, and every guest room will be redecorated. All the amenities that always made it seem like a far-higher-priced hotel—doormen, a bustling marble-walled lobby, a newsstand, and so on—will still be there, but in addition there'll be some state-of-the-art facilities not seen in most New York hotels: a day-care center where parents may leave their kids while they're out seeing the town, a business center, and a fitness center, free for the use of guests. Not to mention four restaurants: a gourmet deli, a breakfast room, a brasserie, and a supper club. And the new management will still pride itself on offering three things: convenience, comfort (they have better mattresses than many more expensive hotels), and cleanliness. Rooms are of good size, with individually controlled air conditioning, direct-dial phones, cable TV, and nice décor; at least 45% of the rooms have two double beds.

Of course rates have gone up, but the hotel is still in the "tourist" category, and since the management has agreed to continue the policies of its predecessors and provide a 10% discount to those readers who contact them directly, the hotel is still affordable. Here are the regular rates: singles run $95 to $115 and doubles go for

$105 to $125; an extra person in the room pays $15; up to two children in the same room with their parents, using existing bedding, stay free. If you've brought your car, you can garage it across the street for a reasonable fee.

When a hotel has been in business for over 50 years and is still going strong, you know they must be doing something right. Such a one is the **Hotel Edison,** 228 W. 47th St. (just west of Broadway), New York, NY 10036 (tel. 212/840-5000, or toll free 800/367-7070), where the owner-management works hard at pleasing guests. What we like best here is the feeling of spaciousness that the newer hotels, even the more expensive ones, cannot afford to have. You'll sense it in the large lobby (plain but comfortable), the wide halls, and the 1,000 nicely decorated rooms. The lobby bustles with guests (many of them theater groups from Europe, South America, and Japan), and has a transportation desk and gift and tobacco shop. Right on the premises is the Café Edison, open from 7 a.m. to 11 p.m. daily, which serves homemade cheese blintzes, bread pudding, and cabbage soup, among other offerings; the owner makes fresh corn muffins every morning. A bit of a legend in the area, it's been dubbed the "Polish Tea Room" by its regular crowd of Broadway moguls, television actors, successful and aspiring thesbians, and a group of retired magicians who have their regular table in the back; it's reputed that as many deals are made here over the gefilte fish and chopped liver as are made at the more glittering Russian Tea Room on 57th Street. The owners are a Polish immigrant couple; most of their East European Jewish dishes are not listed on the regular menu, so ask. Sofia's, on the other side of the lobby (once the Green Room, home to the big bands and names like Blue Baron), serves hearty meals, and the Rum House Bar and Lounge is a popular theater-district watering hole.

The rooms themselves are large and comfortable, many with two double beds and two large closets; all are air-conditioned with combination tub and shower, direct-dial telephone, and cable color TV. Many rooms have fashionable laminated "shipboard" furniture. Double-paned windows help control noise. The one-bedroom suites offer particular value: warm and homey, beautifully furnished, and renting for $125 to $140 per night for two persons, they are a far better buy than bedrooms alone in many fancier hotels.

Rates for singles range from $90 to $100 per night; doubles or twin-bedded rooms for two are $98 to $108; family rooms with two double beds and bath, for three or four family members, are $120 to $130. Rollaway beds are available for $10 per night. Parking is available, at an additional charge, directly across the street.

The name "Chatwall" may well become a generic term in midtown Manhattan meaning "a comfortable inn at an affordable price." At least that's what international hotelier and restaurateur Sant S. Chatwall seems to have in mind. In the last two years, Chatwall's company acquired seven architecturally significant or landmark properties in midtown Manhattan (among them the former President and Tudor hotels), revamped them totally, and created some very attractive lodgings that keep the budget traveler well in mind. And to make them even more attractive, the management has agreed to provide special reduced rates at four of its properties to those readers who call them directly, mentioning this book. The rates, for our readers alone, will be $90, $105, and $120, single or double—a savings of at least $20 off regular rates. In addition, depending on availability, rooms will be upgraded whenever possible. Now here's a look at the four hotels that will honor these rates in 1990. (Rates may be slightly higher in 1991.)

**Chatwall Inn on 48th Street,** 234 W. 48th St. (between Broadway and Eighth Avenue), New York, NY 10036 (tel. 212/246-8800, or toll free 800/826-4667, 800/621-4667 in Canada). The old President Hotel was never like this! Total remodeling has created a handsome 16-story, 367-room hotel with a spectacular postmodern lobby, complete with its skylit Atrium Court and waterfall and floors of Italian marble. Guests can have complimentary continental breakfasts here. Caffè Primavera is a stunning room for Italian and continental cuisine, and the Lobby Bar is a popular spot for drinks and conversation. Newly redone guest rooms are most attractive, with mauve spreads and drapes, nice furnishings, attractive prints on the walls, handsome tile or marble bathrooms with luxury personal-care items, cable color TVs, direct-dial phones, and individual heating/air-conditioning controls. Room sizes vary, but all are respectable, and some of the smaller rooms even have little balconies. Beds are twins or doubles, with some queen-size beds. There's concierge service and a multilingual staff. This location is corporate headquarters for the Chatwall company.

At the **Chatwall Inn on 47th Street** (also known as **The Ashley**), 156 W. 47th St. (between Broadway and Eighth Avenue), New York, NY 10036 (tel. 212/245-6090, or toll free 800/826-4667, 800/621-4667 in Canada), a residential atmosphere pervades this "olde New York"–style hotel, with 200 rooms, including 4 executive suites and 28 deluxe suites. On one side of the attractive lobby is La Veranda, a tasteful restaurant for northern Italian cuisine. The guest rooms, of decent size, are furnished in a maroon-and-white color scheme, and have handsome beige tile or marble bathrooms, cable color TVs, direct-dial telephones, and individually controlled heating/air conditioning. Ice machines are available, and so is valet parking. Guests are served complimentary continental breakfast in a pretty little room on the lobby floor.

The **Chatwall Inn on 45th Street,** 132 W. 45th St. (between Broadway and Avenue of the Americas), New York, NY 10036 (tel. 212/921-7600, or toll free 800/826-4667, 800/621-4667 in Canada), has only 75 rooms on 8 floors, each done in American Federal or Queen Anne–style furnishings, in soft pastel-green tones. Cable color TVs, direct-dial telephones, and individually controlled heating/air-conditioning units are available in all rooms. Again, bathrooms are all new in tile or marble, with luxury personal-care items. Complimentary breakfast is served in the building's original wood-paneled dining room, complete with fireplace. The Greenhouse Wine Lounge, in a plush Riviera-like setting, and the Croissanterie for pastries and light snacks were on the drawing board at the time of our last visit.

*Note:* All three of the above Chatwall Inns are located in the very heart of the theater district and are within walking distances of all major Broadway theaters.

On the East Side of town, special rates for our readers will be available at some of the rooms at the **Chatwall Inn on Park Avenue,** 429 Park Ave. South (at 30th Street), New York, NY 10016 (tel. 212/532-4860, or toll free 800/826-4667, 800/621-4667 in Canada), a small hotel with a homey atmosphere. The restored Park Avenue mansion will have newly redone guest rooms and baths, again with cable color TVs, direct-dial telephones, and individual heating/air-conditioning controls. There's a multilingual staff and valet parking. Guests enjoy complimentary continental breakfast. The use of a complete health and exercise center, offering aerobics, free weights, Nautilus equipment, and a health bar is also available to guests at an adjacent facility for a modest fee.

To repeat: Readers of this book can save at least $20 on rooms at these hotels by calling central reservations for Chatwall Inns (tel. toll free 800/826-4667, 800/621-4667 in Canada).

The **Hotel Iroquois,** just off Fifth Avenue at 49 W. 44th St., New York, NY 10036 (tel. 212/840-3080 or toll free 800/332-7220), is a real surprise. Once a dreary-looking spot that had been allowed to decline, it's undergoing a metamorphosis, and the changes are so lovely that it may well be on its way to becoming "the poor man's Algonquin" (the famed theater hotel is just a few doors away). The location is excellent, out of range of the noisy, congested theater district yet just a short walk away, and security is excellent. The lobby is small and inviting, with shell chandeliers, a large sunburst on one wall, pastel leather chairs, and Jan Wallman's restaurant, bar, and cabaret off to one side. Of the 86 rooms, some 60 are suites; and 45 of these have recessed kitchenettes, very hard to find in New York hotels. These are all-in-one units complete with a small refrigerator topped by two burners, a sink, and an oven. The suites are very large (one has a closet the size of a small room!), beautifully furnished with Queen Anne–style mahogany furniture, mauve drapes with floral motif, and thick carpeting. In the living room are usually a secretary desk, an armoire containing the TV set, a fireplace (for decoration only), a sofabed, and Impressionist prints on the walls; in the bedroom are either twins, a double, a king, or a Hollywood king (slightly larger than regular). At rates of $95 to $125 for two (children free, but $10 for each extra adult guest), these suites are among the best deals in town. All rooms and suites have acoustic windows, cable color TV, direct-dial phones, and air-conditioning. For regular rooms, the rates are $75 to $85, single or double. Constance Sawyer, the General Manager, will work with guests on rates. You're liable to find members of rock bands sleeping here (they're very quiet guests, says Ms. Sawyer), or casts of Broadway plays. A pleasant choice.

Just a few steps from Fifth Avenue, the 200-room **Mansfield Hotel,** 12 W. 44th St., New York, NY 10036 (tel. 212/944-6050), is a modest but acceptable budget choice, popular with European, South American, and Japanese guests. What it has going for it is a good location, on the same block as the Harvard Club and the New York Bar Association, and a friendly staff; and a small lobby that adjoins O'Lunney's, a delightful Irish pub that offers country music and folk singing four nights a week. Limited room service is available via the Sandwich Shop. What it lacks—aside from the splendid staircase intact in this Sanford White 1907 building—is charm. Rooms are clean, and all have either a tub or shower, air conditioning, direct-dial phones, and cable color TV, but they are small and rather minimally decorated. The cozy suites are perhaps the best buy here, and refrigerators can be furnished on request.

Single rooms go from $60 to $65; doubles or twins, from $70 to $75; junior suites for three from $85 to $95; suites for four to six, $100 to $140. A discount is offered on parking at a nearby garage.

It's hard to find a more convenient location to the Broadway theater than the **Hotel Consulate,** 224 W. 49th St., New York, NY 10019, west of Broadway (tel. 212/246-5252); the Eugene O'Neill Theater is next door, the Ambassador is across the street, and so is the Actor's Church. This remodeled oldtimer (once the Forrester Hotel, home to the likes of Walter Winchell and Jose Greco), has about 225 rooms, and they have been tastefully—if rather sedately—decorated and furnished with brown-and-white spreads and drapes, and brown carpeting. All have color TV with AM/FM radio, direct-dial phone, air conditioning, and private bath. There are reproductions of old prints on the walls and safety locks on every door. The hotel is very careful about security; the staff keeps an eye on everyone who comes in, and the owner surmises that the Consulate "probably has less theft than any other hotel in New York." A restaurant is on the premises, and a moderately priced coffeeshop, open from 7 a.m. to 7 p.m., will provide room service. The Consulate is popular with both businessmen and tourists, and with many Europeans and Canadians; they take Canadian money at par, which means very respectable savings of about 15% (other discounts do not apply in this case).

The management has agreed to offer those readers who contact them directly and mention this book a discount of 10% on their rates; this means singles from $65 to $85; doubles from $85 to $105; and suites that will sleep up to four, from $105 to $140. There is no charge for up to two children under 16 in the same room as their parents.

The **Portland Square Hotel,** 132 W. 47th St. (between Avenue of the Americas and Seventh Avenue), New York, NY 10036 (tel. 212/382-0600, or toll free 800/388-8928), has been, under another name, a theater hotel since 1904 (James Cagney was one of the famous names who stayed here). At this writing the hotel was undergoing a complete renovation (it will definitely be in full swing by the time you read this) by the same management in charge at the Herald Square Hotel in Herald Square and the Washington Square Hotel in Greenwich Village. If the loving restorations of these two properties are any indication, the Portland Square should be a delightful budget oasis in the midst of the busy Times Square area. It's ideally situated for theater-goers, as it's just half a block from TKTS, the popular half-price, same-day box office service; half a block in the other direction is New York's famed "Diamond District." The newly modernized hotel, with all-new plumbing, electricity, etc., is decorated with Broadway photographs and other memorabilia of the '20s and '30s. It boasts a small and stylish lobby, and 120 rooms, all of them comfortably furnished with individual heat/air-conditioning controls and direct-dial phones. Rates begin at just $35 for one person sharing a bathroom with several others. A standard room for one person, with private bath, is $55; a standard room for two people (with one bed) is $60. A large double room for two with one bed is $65; a standard room for two with two beds is $70. A large double room with two beds is $75 for two, $80 for three, and $85 for four.

The newly redecorated **Ramada Inn** at 48th Street and Eighth Avenue, New York, NY 10019 (tel. 212/581-7000, or toll free 800/2-RAMADA), looks very handsome these days, with its chrome-and-glass, hi-tech modern lobby, softened by comfortable furniture and a marble terrazzo floor. Its 336 guest rooms are very attractive too, and so is the rooftop pool on the 15th floor, which affords skyscraper views while swimming or basking on a chaise longue in the sun. The open-air poolside cocktail lounge is quite pleasant, and even more pleasant is the New Yorker Restaurant on the lobby floor—sunny, plant-filled, with posters on the walls, flowers on every table, and three moderately priced American/continental-style meals a day. As for the rooms, they have been newly redecorated in soft tones of mauve and teal, are of good size, and have individually controlled heat and air conditioning, oversize closets with safekeepers at nominal charge, direct-dial telephones, AM/FM radios, and color TVs with in-room, first-run movies—among other amenities. Beds are either double, or two doubles, queen-size, or king-size. The hotel boasts a tight security system: security guards in and out of uniform patrol the hotel constantly. Although rates can go a bit high for our budget—singles at $98, $108, $118, $128, and $138; and doubles or family rooms at $110, $120, $130, $140, and $150—the hotel is large, and you can usually get something at the lower rates.

Most of the guests at the **Hotel Remington,** 129 W. 46th St. (between Sixth and Seventh avenues), New York, NY 10036 (tel. 212/221-2600, or toll free 800/223-1900), seem to be from Brazil, Venezuela, or other South American countries. They—and the large numbers of Europeans who frequent the hotel in summer—know the very good value that can be had at this small, 80-room hotel that was totally renovated a few years ago and is continually improving itself. The lobby looks larger than it really is, thanks to its mirrored walls and crystal chandelier; there is one small elevator to navigate the nine floors of the hotel. Rooms are very nicely furnished with white furniture with a swirl motif, floral wallpaper and bedspreads, and all have air conditioning, cable color TVs, radios, direct-dial telephones, and insulated windows, which makes for quiet. All the bathrooms are new, and some are quite special, with colored tubs and marble vanities. Rooms with private bath are $65 single, $70 double, $75 triple, and $80 quad. Some rooms do not have private bathrooms, but they do have a sink, and a very clean bathroom is shared by three rooms. These are an excellent buy at $55 for a single, $55 for a double, $65 for a triple. With its central location, cheerful and clean accommodations, plus a very friendly staff, the Remington is by far one of the best budget values in New York.

If you can't get into the Remington, consider a larger establishment run by the same management, where the rates are a bit higher but also reasonable by New York standards. This is the **Hotel Wentworth,** 59 W. 46th St. (between Fifth and Sixth avenues), New York, NY 10036 (tel. 212/719-2300). The Wentworth offers some 250 pleasant rooms, cheerfully decorated with flowered wallpaper and spreads; all rooms have air conditioning, cable color TVs, private bathrooms, and direct-dial phones. Singles are $70; deluxe singles, $80; twins, $80; deluxe twins, $85; doubles, $80; and deluxe doubles, $85. A room with two double beds runs $85 to $105; and suites run $100 to $150. An additional person is charged $10. The Wentworth is well located, close to Fifth Avenue and the charming People Plaza, a mini-park between 45th and 46th streets, laced with interlocking gardens, outdoor sculpture, and cascading waters. In spring and fall, midtown workers pause here for lunch under umbrellaed tables and free noontime entertainment. The hotel's winding, crystal-chandeliered lobby boasts its own 60-booth Jewelry Exchange, to give guests a head start on New York shopping. The staff is multilingual, the better to serve a preponderance of South American and European guests.

One of the stars of New York theater hotels is Best Western's **Milford Plaza,** 270 W. 45th St. (at Eighth Avenue), New York, NY 10036 (tel. 212/869-3600, or toll free 800/221-2690, 800/522-6449 in New York state). There's an air of excitement about this place, which begins in the graceful marble lobby with its three-story-high ceiling, so pretty with its red carpets and black chairs, and extends right up the 28 floors to the 1,300 rooms, all of which have a star on the door and views from their windows of Broadway's theater marquees. Guest rooms have new carpeting and attractive spreads and wallpaper, and the bathrooms have been handsomely retiled. Rooms are compact, rather than large, but they have everything you need, including color TV, AM/FM radio, direct-dial phone, and self-controlled air conditioning and heat; there is free ice on every floor. Security is excellent, since everyone coming up to the rooms must show a key.

Milford guests can take all their meals right at home if they wish. A lavish breakfast buffet, featuring something like 27 items (with eggs cooked to order), costs under $10 and is on from 7 to 11 a.m. The Stage Door Canteen specializes in barbecued food and nostalgia: its walls are decorated with photos of the original Stage Door Canteen. Mama Leone's, one of the city's most famous Italian restaurants, is now on two levels of the Milford Plaza—and the food is still great, after all those years! The Celebrity Deli is popular with just about everybody, especially with traveling Texans, who fall in love with the corned-beef sandwiches. The lobby also offers a travel and theater-ticket desk, a sundry shop, and a unisex hair salon.

Although regular rates are $95 to $135 for a single and $110 to $150 for a double, they've kept us budget folks in mind with their "Lullabuy of Broadway" deal, functional any day of the week (unlike most packages). Subject to availability, they offer a room plus continental breakfast, a meal, and a welcoming cocktail for the rate of $49.50 per person in a double. And on regular rates, the management will extend a 10% discount if you reserve directly and identify yourself as a reader of this book.

## Two Motor Hotels in the Heart of Town

The **Travel Inn Motor Hotel,** 515 W. 42nd St. (between Tenth and Eleventh avenues), New York, NY 10036 (tel. 212/695-7171), has always been popular with visitors who want the convenience of a central location, free parking, and a refreshing swim when they come home from a hard day's sightseeing or business. A total renovation of the 250-room property—all-new rooms, hallways, and public areas —was completed a few years ago, making the Travel Inn better than ever, and still an excellent value for New York, despite the fact that its rates have now gone up to $85 for a single and $105 for a twin. Even standard rooms are enormous, most furnished with two double beds, imported white furniture from France, matching draperies and spreads done in seashell motifs on blue-and-pink or wine backgrounds. A few rooms have chintz spreads and Japanese lamps; all have a desk and chair, air conditioning, direct-dial phone, and color TV. The halls are handsome, with marble and glass panels on the walls. The lobby is small, but the gathering places here are an Olympic-size outdoor swimming pool (reserved strictly for guests of the hotel), several pretty courtyards, and sunbathing areas decked out with garden furniture. All of this makes the hotel an excellent choice for families with children.

The Travel Inn offers several package deals that can cut the cost of a New York vacation considerably. The most popular, which is called "Big Apple by Air, Land & Sea," includes, in addition to accommodations for three days, a helicopter ride, a Circle Line boat cruise, tickets to the Empire State Building or the USS *Intrepid* Sea-

Air-Space Museum, a full American breakfast every day and a complete dinner at Curtains Up Restaurant—all for $330 single, or $220 per person in a double. And the nice thing about this—and the hotel's one- and two-day packages—is that they are available any day of the week, and not limited to weekends as is often the case.

The location is excellent, one block from the off-off-Broadway 42nd Street Theater Row, and just a few blocks from Times Square (easily accessible by crosstown bus). There is free self-parking in an indoor garage with no in-and-out charges. With all this going for it, the Travel Inn is very popular, so try to reserve at least two weeks in advance if possible, especially in the summer.

Right on the premises is the Bistro 42nd Restaurant, serving three meals a day. Walk one block to the corner of Ninth Avenue and 42nd Street and you're at Ninth and Natural, a natural-foods restaurant for gourmets with very low prices and a wonderfully congenial atmosphere. A delicious find.

Things are looking very good indeed over at Best Western's **Skyline Motor Inn,** 49th to 50th streets on Tenth Avenue, New York, NY 10019 (tel. 212/586-3400, or toll free 800/433-1982, 800/327-6542 in Canada), which was completely redone several years back, from its skylit glass-and-marble lobby with its comfortable seating areas to the new coffeeshop-restaurant-cocktail-lounge and piano bar called Café 50, to each of its 230 rooms. This is a large hotel, with the rooms spread out over two buildings, a free garage (although there is a $2 in-and-out charge), and best of all, a beautiful glass-enclosed rooftop swimming pool, complete with sundeck and sauna, heated and open all year. There's exercise equipment—a rowing machine, bikes, a treadmill, and so on—in the pool area too, so guests need never miss their daily workouts.

The rooms are very large, done in attractive color schemes; each has color TV with radio and wakeup alarm clock, direct-dial telephone, individually controlled air conditioning and heat, and a modern tile bath with tub-shower combinations. These run $92 to $105 for a single and $98 to $115 for a double. Comfortable suites, with a sofabed in the living room, run $150 and up. Up to two children, aged 14 and under, can stay free in the same room with their parents. Each additional person is charged $10.

## THE WEST FIFTIES

One of the best areas for New York sightseeing, the West Fifties provide easy access to Broadway theaters, Rockefeller Center, Carnegie Hall, Lincoln Center, Central Park, the art galleries of 57th Street, and the shops of Fifth Avenue. There are at least five good choices here for the dollar-conscious traveler.

The **Gorham Hotel,** 136 W. 55th St. (between Sixth and Seventh avenues), New York, NY 10019 (tel. 212/245-1800), is especially nice for families who appreciate its spacious bedroom suites and cooking facilities. But it's also very popular with theater people, buyers, independent business people, and many Europeans. Close to the theater district, but away from the hustle-bustle of Times Square, it couldn't be more conveniently located. The mirrored, all-oak lobby with its crystal chandelier is small and charming, indicative of the friendly service offered at the Gorham. A concierge is always on hand to provide help with sightseeing or theater tickets. Adjoining the lobby, but out of our price range, alas, is one of New York's most rarified restaurants, Castellano, a northern Italian establishment, which has the food crowd agog.

Rooms at the Gorham are immaculate and attractive, all equipped with air conditioning, modern bath, cable color TV, pushbutton phones, in-room safes, many closets, comfortable furnishings, and wall-to-wall carpeting. But the most important offerings are the kitchenettes in each room, which consist of a coffee-maker, toaster oven, sink, refrigerator, and necessary light housekeeping utensils. Many of the larger suites at the Gorham have been redone to consist of one large bedroom with two double beds, table, and chair, plus a smaller bedroom with one double bed; there are 40 such rooms, and they're a big hit with families.

At this writing, a new management had taken over the Gorham, and a huge renovation was in process. The result will be an almost deluxe facility—even with Jacuzzi whirlpools in every room! Of course rates will go up then, but for the present, and for quite a while to come, we can expect singles to run $85 to $105; doubles, $95 to $115; and suites, $120 to $140. Additional persons pay $10 to $20. Since the Gorham does most of its business from repeat customers, it's advisable to write or call collect well in advance for reservations, especially if you want the lower-priced rooms.

Days Inn, the national lodging chain, moved into the Big Apple just a few years ago, took over and totally renovated (to the tune of $8 million) the old Holiday Inn, and emerged with **Days Inn,** W. 440 57th St. (between Ninth and Tenth avenues), New York, NY 10019 (tel. 212/581-8100, or toll free 800/325-2525). It's a big hotel with a lot going for it: an excellent location, 596 comfortable rooms, an attractive plant-filled lobby, The Greenery Restaurant for all three meals plus room service, an on-site garage, and especially welcome in the hot and humid New York summer, a handsome swimming pool and rooftop café. Rooms are quite large by New York standards, are attractively decorated in pastel and earth colors, and all have cable color TV, direct-dial phones, air conditioning, and a mini-bar/refrigerator. Bedding can be either two double beds or a king-size bed; more expensive king leisure and deluxe rooms also have sofas. Regular rates run $109 to $129 for a single and $129 to $144 for a double, which makes them a bit high for us. Definitely worth trying for is their "Bonanza Days" package: for $99 a day, two people can get a room, a continental breakfast, free parking, and even a free newspaper; up to two children under 17 can stay in their parents' room free. For an extra night, the price is $90. This offer is good for any-day arrival, subject to availability. Seniors can get rooms for $103 single, $115 double.

Just opposite Central Park, around the corner from Carnegie Hall and a short walk from Lincoln Center, is a little hotel worth knowing about: the **Westpark Hotel,** 308 W. 58th St., New York, NY 10019 (tel. 212/246-6440). This 100-room, nine-story hotel has plenty going for it: it's an old, well-insulated building, which makes it very quiet; and it's been totally remodeled and decorator-designed with a graceful touch, which makes it charming. Yet all this comes with a moderate price tag: $70 to $90 for a single, $80 to $105 for a double, $90 to $120 for a twin-bedded room, and $130 to $170 for a one-bedroom suite. Those readers of this book who write to the hotel directly will be given a discount of 10% off these rates.

Just a few years old, the Westpark has become a hit with businesspeople, tourists, and small groups. The modernistic lobby, with glass doors, mirrored columns, a fireplace, and soft-green velvet chairs to sink into, adjoins the Café Comedy next door. The rooms are lovely, many decorated with deep-maroon quilted bedspreads, ginger-jar lamps, and other nice touches; of course, all have direct-dial phone, air conditioning, color TV with AM/FM radio, and private bath. The higher-priced rooms have views of Central Park. Especially handsome are the one-bedroom suites: one of our favorites has pink drapes, a four-poster bed, two television sets, velvet sofas, a desk, and lovely lamps and prints. Discount parking is available at a nearby garage. Many languages are spoken at the Westpark, and service is helpful and friendly.

Your fellow guests at the **Hotel Wellington,** Seventh Avenue at 55th Street, New York, NY 10019 (tel. 212/247-3900, or toll free 800/652-1212), are apt to be a motley crowd: perhaps dancers from a ballet company appearing at City Center just down the street, flocks of visitors from Scandinavia and Western Europe, businesspeople and tourists—all attracted by a good location and a good price. The Wellington is one of New York's older hotels, which consists, all told, of three buildings with about 700 rooms; there are 400 transient rooms in the main building, and other buildings house both long-term visitors and transients. Standard rooms, which have either twin or double beds, are small but pleasant, with bamboo headsteads, perhaps rose-colored spreads (color schemes vary from floor to floor), air conditioning, color TVs, and direct-dial phones; most rooms have both tub and shower, though some have shower only. A number of rooms have been completely redone, with laminated headboards and furniture and a more modern décor. Very nice indeed are the Tower Rooms, quite large, with space for a table and chairs. And nicest of all are the suites, very large and lovely, with double beds in the bedroom, and a double convertible sofa in the living room; some of these have a stove and refrigerator. Single rooms go for $89 and $94; Tower singles are $99 and $104. Double/twin rooms go for $99 and $104; Tower doubles are $109 and $114. Family rooms, which consist of two double beds and two bathrooms, are $120 and $125. One-bedroom suites cost $120 to $175. An increase of about 10% over these rates may be forthcoming soon. The Wellington's lobby, recently renovated, is quite attractive. The Park Café adjoins it, and also provides room service from 6 to 11 p.m. daily. The popular Alpine Tavern, on the other side of the lobby, is open daily from 11 a.m. to 4 a.m.

## HERALD SQUARE

New York's original *Life* magazine building has been given a new lease on life. The landmark Beaux Arts building, built in 1893 by Carrère and Hastings, served as the magazine's offices until 1936; upstairs lived such renowned New Yorkers as illustrator Charles Dana Gibson. Decades later the building was a run-down hotel. But all that has changed now, thanks to a hotel family with a passion for history and nostalgia. The Puchall family has transformed the building into the charming **Herald Square Hotel,** 19 W. 31st St., New York, NY 10010 (tel. 212/279-4017, or toll free 800/727-1888), and it's been an instant success with European tourists and South American buyers. This is a small, limited-service establishment that's just perfect for the budget traveler: single rooms without bath are available for as little as $35! And while the location is not as fashionable as it was back in the 19th century, it is certainly convenient—around the corner from Macy's Herald Square, three blocks south of the Empire State Building, and close to the Fifth Avenue department stores. The 130-room, nine-story building has been renovated from top to bottom, inside and out, and the restoration is lovely, beginning with the gilded sculpture, Philip Martiny's *Winged Life,* over the entrance. A small, sparkling lobby is decorated with reproductions of old *Life* magazine covers, as are the halls and guest rooms. All rooms are nicely decorated in pastel tones, and have cable color TVs, AM/FM radios, direct-dial phones, and individually controlled air conditioning; the bathrooms are brand new. Rooms vary only in size and beds, and are priced accordingly.

Rates are excellent, starting with those singles at $35, which are small and share a bathroom with only one other guest; there are two of these on each floor. A very small single or double with one bed, toilet, and shower, is $50; a standard room for one person with one bed and a bathroom with shower and tub is $60; a standard room for two people with one bed is $65. A large double room for two with one or two beds is $75; a large double room for three is $85, and for four, $95.

The same management runs the Portland Square Hotel (see "Midtown West/Times Square and Environs") and the Washington Square Hotel in Greenwich Village, all of them clean, comfortable, nicely restored, and budget-priced.

## LOWER WEST SIDE—CHELSEA

In a city where the old is often torn down to make way for the new and modern, the **Chelsea Hotel,** 222 W. 23rd St. (between Seventh and Eighth avenues), New York, NY 10011 (tel. 212/243-3700), has stood since 1882, catering to the bohemian, the creative, the offbeat, and those who thrive among them. It was the first hotel in the U.S. to be proclaimed a national landmark. This is the place where Andy Warhol made the movie *Chelsea Girls;* where Dylan Thomas, Brendan Behan, Lenny Bruce, Jane Fonda, and Elliot Gould all came to rest, retreat, and get inspiration. Among the works that have been written at the Chelsea are Arthur Clarke's

*2001,* Thomas Wolfe's *You Can't Go Home Again,* Arthur Miller's *After the Fall,* and William Burroughs's *Naked Lunch.* Manager Stanley Bard reigns over the scene, and his art collection (including many works from grateful tenants) turns the lobby here into a veritable art gallery. Note especially the sculpture called *Chelsea People*— you'll recognize many of the celebrities who have called the Chelsea home. A half-million-dollar renovation a few years back has spruced up the French Louisiana façade of the building with its wrought-iron balconies and made it more attractive than ever. A good Spanish restaurant, El Quijote, adjoins.

Many of the guests stay here for a long time—or forever—attracted by the soundproof walls (three feet thick!), the friendly family feeling, and the enormous rooms, each with unique features (perhaps working fireplaces or kitchens). Short-term visitors come from all over the world, attracted by the legend of the hotel. Even the smallest of the transient rooms is large by New York hotel standards. The furnishings are not luxurious (there are, for example, no pictures on the walls, since most tenants want to hang their own; bedspreads and drapes can be a bit somber, and the furniture is not brand new), but the rooms are adequate, and usually kept up. About half the rooms have air conditioning, all have direct-dial phones, and color TVs can be rented for $15 per week.

Room rates offer good value. Singles run $65 to $85, doubles go for $75 to $125, and rooms with kitchenettes begin at $85 and go way up. However, a better deal, if you require a kitchenette, is to take one of the suites for four people, which rent for $150 to $165. The management advises that readers of this book will be given the seventh night of a week's stay free if the week is prepaid.

Wouldn't it be nice for the budget traveler if there were places like the Chelsea Inn on every block in town! The **Chelsea Inn,** 46 W. 17th St. (just west of Fifth Avenue), New York, NY 10011 (tel. 212/645-8989), is an "urban inn," designed especially for businesspeople and family vacationers who prefer an intimate, small establishment in a quiet part of town, complete with that big money-saver—a kitchenette. Close to the Javits Convention Center, the "Photography District," the "Flower Market," the Toy Center, the Gift Building, and the Garment Center, the Chelsea Inn is very popular with those who need to stay in New York for a bit—the average guest stays about five days. Owners Linda Mandel, Mindy Goodfriend Chernoff, and Harry Chernoff bought this old building a few years ago, totally renovated it, and created just 13 rooms that offer homey comforts and more than a touch of charm. All rooms have kitchenettes (usually a sink and a small refrigerator with a stovetop above it), color TVs with AM/FM radios, direct-dial phones, and individually controlled air conditioning. Rooms are also nicely decorated—bathrooms have murals on the walls, and some rooms have a view of the garden. Those rooms on the first three floors are all walk-ups. Single rooms that share a bath with just one other room are $68 per night; studios with a queen-size bed are $95, single or double. Families do best in the two-room suites, with a double bed in one room and a high-rise that opens into two separate beds in the other; these go for $120 to $130 per night for up to four. One-bedroom suites with a double bed and a convertible sofa are $125 for two. Rollaways can be added to any room for $10 a night. The front desk closes every night at 9 p.m., so guests are given their own front-door keys.

## GREENWICH VILLAGE

There's only one tourist hotel in the Village, and luckily for us, it's a budget hotel. The **Washington Square Hotel,** 103 Waverly Pl. (between Sixth Avenue and Washington Square Park), New York, NY 10011 (tel. 212/777-9515 or toll free 800/222-0418), couldn't have a better location. It's steps away from Washington Square Park and in the very heart of the Village "scene," with its restaurants, jazz clubs, shops, and lively street life. At the time of our visit, the hotel, which was once known as the Earle, in a 1902 building, was in the throes of a massive restoration: all its 200 rooms and bathrooms were being redone; there were plans for blue/green/peach color schemes for bedspreads and drapes, gray carpets, olive wood furniture, headboards, and mirrored closets. All rooms will have color TVs, air conditioning, and direct-dial phones. The new lobby is already functioning, and it's a beauty, with tile floors, a wrought-iron gate, greenery, and a winding staircase. Guests, who may be European or Japanese tourists, or jazz musicians who play the local clubs, get lots of friendly service and sightseeing tips here. They have the use of Fax and Telex machines in the office; there's a room with lockers where they can store their belongings if they must check out early. Rates are reasonable: $55 single, $80 double, $85 twin, $100 for quad. A rollaway bed is $7.

## LINCOLN CENTER AND THE UPPER WEST SIDE

Just north of Lincoln Center are some of New York's best-kept hotel secrets. They are all on the Upper West Side, which in recent years has burgeoned into one of New York's most lively and desirable neighborhoods, with its new luxury condominiums, wonderful shops and restaurants on practically every block, and convenient bus and subway connections to midtown. For the tourist, going above 72nd Street is one of the wisest moves to make: it means spacious rooms, often apartments with kitchenettes, at far less than what you'd pay for comparable accommodations in midtown. Plus a chance to be part of one of Manhattan's most enjoyable environments. Cabs and buses are plentiful, and the subway can have you in the Broadway theater district in 15 minutes, tops.

Many of the guests who stay at the **Hotel Olcott,** 27 W. 72nd St. (between Columbus Avenue and Central Park West), New York, NY 10023 (tel. 212/877-4200), are performers at nearby Lincoln Center, diplomats, and U.N. personnel. The Royal Ballet of London calls it their New York home, and so do half a dozen singers from the Metropolitan Opera Company and a few movie and sports celebrities, as well as lots of businesspeople and visitors from overseas. Happily for us, this largely residential hotel still has plenty of space for transients. It offers a terrific location, close not only to Lincoln Center, but also across the street from Central Park and in the very heart of the exciting Columbus Avenue scene; a subway station is on the corner. Its Dallas Jones Bar-B-Q Restaurant is one of New York's best inexpensive restaurants, serving meals averaging $5 or $6 in the plushest of settings (more details in Chapter II).

As for the studios and suites, they're spacious, clean, and comfortable, with attractive furnishings, big closets, nice prints adorning the white walls, and carpeted floors. Homey—very comfortably homey—would be the best way to describe them. All have direct-dial phones, cable color TVs with AM/FM radios, air conditioning, tub and shower baths, and fully equipped kitchenettes with hotplates and refrigerators. The suites, which are very spacious, also have living rooms, and two-bedroom suites have two baths.

Here's how the rates go: studios are $70 single, $80 double; $425 weekly for a single, $475 for a double. One-bedroom suites are $100 for one or two persons, $600 per week; an extra person is charged $15 daily or $70 weekly (up to four can be accommodated). Long-term rates are lower. The management advises that you reserve four weeks in advance for an extended stay of a week or more; for three or four days, a week in advance; and for one night only, call during that week.

Up until a few years ago, there was nothing to distinguish **The Milburn,** 242 W. 76th St., New York, NY 10023 (tel. 212/362-1006), from any of the other gracious old West Side apartment buildings that line this street just west of Broadway. But now it's one of the nicest places to stay in the area, thanks to a decision by its management to convert 70 of its 120 apartments into hotel rooms. Some $3 million was spent on the renovation of the lobby and the rooms, and the results are a delight. The lobby is small but handsome with its Oriental carpet, chandeliers, and original paintings on the walls. Concierge service is available 24 hours a day. Studios are spacious, done in a cheerful modern mode, with either a king-size or queen-size bed or two twin beds. All have glass tables with four chairs, cable color TV, air conditioning, direct-dial phones, attractive modern furniture, and new baths, and all are fully carpeted. Best of all, they each have modern, fully equipped kitchenettes with microwave ovens and utensils, so it's easy to save money by cooking in—and some of New York's most popular gourmet markets, like Zabar's and Fairway, are within walking distance. And the rooms are quiet—there's no midtown construction noise here. There's a laundromat right on the premises. Studio rooms run $90 to $99, single or double, depending on their location in the hotel (rooms with views are on the higher side). Suites are impressive, a bedroom plus a parlor, with the living room sofa opening into a queen-size bed. These are priced at $130 to $140 for two. Children under 12 stay free in their parents' room; $20 for each additional person.

Word about the Milburn has gotten around quickly. It has many international and corporate clients—architects who were redesigning the French consulate were staying there at the time of our visit—as well as vacationers attracted by the warmth and hospitality of the staff, who are attentive to personal needs and requirements. Readers of this book who contact the hotel directly will be given a 10% discount on weekends and at other times, subject to availability.

Some of the largest hotel rooms in New York can be found behind the doors of the **Hotel Esplanade,** 305 West End Ave. (at 74th Street), New York, NY 10023 (tel. 212/874-5000, or toll free 800/367-1763, 800/553-0567 in New York state). Move into one of their suites—even bedrooms—and you'll be inclined to throw a party! More than 60 years old, this has long been one of the fine residential hotels of the West Side; now its rooms are available to short-term visitors. A new management recently took over the hotel and has redecorated the lobby in an elegant design. You'll be in heaven if you can get one of the 30 rooms with a view of the Hudson River. River view or not, the rooms are lovely, very large, nicely furnished, with cable color TVs, direct-dial phones, air conditioning, bathrooms with both tub and shower, and huge closets, many of them walk-in. There's a small kitchenette too, and again note that you're within short walking distance of Upper West Side gourmet markets like Zabar's and Fairway. Rooms are well priced for quality of this kind, at $99 for one or two people. Suites are enormous; the bedroom consists of two double beds, plus a huge living room and kitchenette; at $109 for two, and $10 for each extra person up to four, these have to be considered one of the best bargains in town. Two-bedroom suites rent at $199, and these can sleep up to six. Prices are subject to an increase. Readers of this book who write directly to the hotel will be granted a 10% discount between November 1 and March 1.

Your fellow guests at the Esplanade are liable to be from London or Paris or next door—people who are having their apartments painted or redecorated often move in for a few days. And members of musical groups sing its praises.

Across the street from the American Museum of Natural History, in a residential block, is the 300-room **Excelsior Hotel,** 45 W. 81st St. (just off Central Park West), New York, NY 10024 (tel. 212/362-9200), a charmer in the European manner. In fact, many European visitors—including consular people and titled types—are frequent guests. Curators and couriers from the Metropolitan Museum of Art and the Museum of Modern Art stay here (and so do neighbors from nearby apartment buildings, like Liv Ullmann, who might move in when their own apartments are being redecorated or painted). Three marble steps lead down to a graceful, high-ceilinged lobby, with an accommodating coffeeshop off to one side to provide room service at breakfast. Rooms, constantly being updated and renovated, are done in pale tones, nicely if not lavishly decorated with furnishings of light woods, blue quilted bedspreads and matching draperies, plus color TVs, individual air conditioning, direct-dial telephones, and large closets. Upper-floor rooms at the front of the house offer views of the museum's park and the midtown skyline; those in the rear, of the gardens of houses on 82nd Street. The management prides itself on running "a respectable hotel, one where you can bring your children and not have to worry." They will not book conventions, carefully screen wedding parties, and quickly dispense with noisy or obstreperous guests. It's easy for families to save money and cook in here, as the suites have fully equipped kitchens, and there's a supermarket just around the corner on Columbus Avenue. You could comfortably stay here for quite a while.

Single rooms go for $65 to $75; doubles, $75 to $85. Very comfortable kitchenette suites that can sleep four (sofabed in the living room, twin beds in the bedroom) are $94 to $108 for four people. Two-bedroom suites run $130 to $150. The Excelsior is at the top of the Columbus Avenue shopping-and-restaurant neighborhood, 16 blocks from Lincoln Center and a short bus ride to midtown shops and theaters. The management is helpful, and security here is excellent. A find.

## MIDTOWN EAST/UPPER EAST SIDE

You simply can't beat the location of the **Pickwick Arms Hotel,** at 230 E. 51st St. (between Second and Third avenues), New York, NY 10022 (tel. 212/355-0300), in a lovely East Side residential neighborhood, a few blocks from all major shopping, cinemas, and restaurants. It's a surprise to find a budget hotel here. This half-century-old hotel, which is being spruced up all the time, is quite pleasant, offering an attractive lobby with a Tudor-style fireplace, a rooftop sun deck, airport limousine service, and some 370 economy-minded rooms. It's one of the busiest hotels on the East Side, and definitely the most reasonable.

The Pickwick Arms is one of the few hotels left in New York where you can realize major economy by sharing the bath down the hall. Some of the older singles, small but quite cozy, have washbasins only, and share a bath/shower with five or six other rooms; these rent for $36. Two such rooms sharing one shower are $42 each. Many of the smaller, older rooms, however, have been converted into large guest rooms (most with twin beds; only 40 have doubles), which are color coordinated, have direct-dial phones, air conditioning, attractive furniture, cable color TVs, and AM/FM radios, and in-room safes large enough to handle bulky objects like cameras. These rent for $75 and $85. The management prides itself on excellent mattresses, careful housekeeping, and good security; guests must be buzzed in late at night.

Families who don't mind all living in one room can take advantage of the eight family rooms. They're furnished with one or two double beds or twin beds and a sofabed, and their own bathrooms. These rent for $75 for two, $85 for three, $100 for four or five. We especially liked the ones in the rear, overlooking the garden.

Although the neighborhood abounds in restaurants, the Pickwick Arms has a few of its own. On one side of the building is the Beekman Deli, open from 7 a.m. to midnight daily, with all kinds of take-out food that can be delivered to the rooms. On the other is the world-famous (and expensive) Spanish restaurant, Torremolinos.

Many of your fellow guests at the Pickwick Arms will be South Americans or Europeans here on tours. The multilingual staff can handle Spanish, French, German, and Hebrew. Reserve several weeks in advance during the summer months.

Carnegie Hill, which begins at 86th Street and Madison Avenue, is one of New York's most agreeable residential areas, dotted with art galleries, lovely shops, and a plethora of sophisticated restaurants. And it's close to major subway and bus lines. The **Hotel Wales,** 1295 Madison Ave. (between 92nd and 93rd streets), New York, NY 10028 (tel. 212/876-6000), has long been a standby in this Upper East Side neighborhood, offering gracious rooms at reasonable rates. A new management took over the hotel recently and undertook a major renovation and redecoration of the venerable building, redoing all the rooms with handsome traditional furniture, installing new windows that enhance the views of Central Park available from many rooms, and stripping the painted wood surfaces down to their original beauty. New lighting, carpeting, bedspreads, TVs, phones, and air conditioning have all been installed, and the petite lobby, with its vaulted ceiling and colonnaded winding marble staircase, is prettier than ever. Prices have risen, but value is good for a hotel with this kind of European charm. Singles or doubles rent for $95 to $125 per day; suites are $145 to $175. The suites have either queen- or king-size beds, plus a sofabed in the living room, so they can sleep four. Third and fourth guests in a suite pay $5 per day, with a limit of four people. Some of the rooms and suites have refrigerators, but there are no longer any kitchenettes.

Two restaurants adjoin the lobby of the Hotel Wales. Sarabeth's Kitchen has been around for several years and is a New York gourmet favorite for quiches, omelets, and other light food; they serve three meals a day, beginning with a luscious breakfast. Scheduled to open as we go to press is the new Busby's, a bistro-type restaurant for fine continental cuisine.

## 5. Rooms for Families

Many of our hotels possess unusually large rooms in which additional cots can be placed, or cater specifically to families traveling with children. Here is a recap of those previously mentioned hotels and a few others that have family rooms or large suites.

**IN THE TIMES SQUARE AND ROCKEFELLER CENTER AREAS** The **Hotel Consulate,** 224 W. 49th St. (west of Broadway), New York, NY 10019 (tel. 212/246-5252), has suites that can sleep up to four people for $105 to $140.

Very large rooms with two double beds can easily house you and the kids, and there's a swimming pool too, at the **Travel Inn Motor Hotel,** 515 W. 42nd St. (between Tenth and Eleventh avenues), New York, NY 10036 (tel. 212/695-7171). Doubles are $105; $10 for each extra person.

The kids will enjoy the pool and all of you can bunk in rooms with two double beds for $98 to $115 (or in a suite starting at $150) at the **Best Western Skyline Motor Inn,** 49th to 50th streets on Tenth Avenue, New York, NY 10019 (tel. 212/586-3400, or toll free 800/433-1982, 800/327-6542 in Canada).

Family rooms with two double beds, sleeping three or four, run $120 to $130 at the **Hotel Edison,** 228 W. 47th St. (just west of Broadway), New York, NY 10036 (tel. 212/840-5000, or toll free 800/367-7070).

Large, spacious suites, beautifully furnished, run $95 to $125 for two (children stay free in their parents' room) at the **Hotel Iroquois,** 49 W. 44th St. (between Fifth and Sixth avenues), New York, NY 10036 (tel. 212/840-3080).

Doubles and family rooms are $110 to $150 at the **Ramada Inn,** 48th Street and Eighth Avenue, New York, NY 10019 (tel. 212/581-7000, or toll free 800/2-RAMADA). The kids will love the rooftop pool.

Utilizing the "Bonanza Package" at the **Days Inn,** 440 W. 57th St. (between Ninth and Tenth avenues), New York, NY 10019 (tel. 212/581-8100, or toll free 800/325-2525), a couple can get a room, continental breakfast, and free parking for $100; and up to two children under 17 can stay in their parents' room free.

Cozy suites sleep four to six at the **Hotel Mansfield,** 12 W. 44th St. (just west of Fifth Avenue), New York, NY 10036 (tel. 212/944-6050), and cost $100 for four, $120 for five, or $140 for six.

Up to six family members can share a spacious two-room unit (two double beds in one room, one double in the other) at the very fine **Hotel Gorham,** 136 W. 55th St. (between Sixth and Seventh avenues), New York, NY 10019 (tel. 212/245-1800). Suites run $120 to $140 for two people, plus $10 to $20 for each extra person.

Family rooms are a good buy at the **Hotel Wellington,** Seventh Avenue at 55th Street, New York, NY 10019 (tel. 212/247-3900, or toll free 800/652-1212). Rooms with two double beds and two bathrooms are $120 and $125; elegant one-bedroom suites go for $150 to $175.

A pretty room with two double beds is just $75 to $80 at the **Hotel Remington,** 129 W. 46th St. (between Sixth and Seventh avenues), New York, NY 10036 (tel. 212/221-2600, or toll free 800/223-1900). And similar rooms are $85 to $105, while suites rent for $100 to $150, at a sister establishment, the **Hotel Wentworth,** 59 W. 56th St. (between Fifth and Sixth avenues), New York, NY 10036 (tel. 212/719-2300).

**IN CHELSEA**  The renowned but offbeat **Chelsea Hotel,** 222 W. 23rd St. (between Seventh and Eighth avenues), New York, NY 10011 (tel. 212/243-3700), has family apartments for four—two rooms with kitchen—from $85 a night, less for weekly stays and longer.

There are kitchenettes in all the units at the cozy little **Chelsea Inn,** 46 W. 17th St. (just west of Fifth Avenue), New York, NY 10011 (tel. 212/645-8989). Families can enjoy one-bedroom suites at $95 per night for two ($10 for each additional person, up to four) or two-room suites with a convertible sofa for $120 to $130 per night for up to four people.

**IN THE HERALD SQUARE AREA**  Families who enjoy togetherness can share a large room with two double beds at the newly renovated **Herald Square Hotel,** 19 W. 31st St. (just west of Fifth Avenue), New York, NY 10010 (tel. 212/279-4017, or toll free 800/727-1888).

**AT COLUMBUS CIRCLE**  Not far from Lincoln Center, decorator-designed, luxuriously appointed one-bedroom suites that can sleep four can be found for $130 to $170 at the **Westpark Hotel,** 308 W. 58th St. (between Eighth and Ninth avenues), New York, NY 10019 (tel. 212/246-6440). Even more reasonable are the lovely rooms with two double beds for two to four people at $90 to $120. (A 10% discount is offered to our readers.)

**ON THE UPPER WEST SIDE**  A very good bet is the **Hotel Olcott,** 27 W. 72nd St. (between Columbus Avenue and Central Park West), New York, NY 10023 (tel. 212/ 877-4200). Two to four people in a spacious one-bedroom suite with fully equipped kitchenette and living room pay $100 to $130 a night. Larger suites are sometimes available in summer, and weekly rates are especially good here. Inquire of the management.

Another Upper West Side favorite is the sedate **Excelsior Hotel,** 45 W. 81st St. (off Central Park West), New York, NY 10024 (tel. 212/362-9200), across from the American Museum of Natural History, which offers beautiful suites with full kitchens, housing two to five people, for $94, $101, and $108.

You and the kids can all stretch out in the very large suites at the **Hotel Esplanade,** 305 West End Ave. (at 74th Street), New York, NY 10023 (tel. 212/874-5000, or toll free 800/367-1763, 800/553-0567 in New York state). One-bedroom suites are $109 for two, plus $10 for each extra person up to four; two-bedroom suites run $199 for up to six people.

At the attractive **Hotel Milburn,** 242 W. 76th St., New York, NY 10023 (tel. 212/362-1006), families can relax in bedroom and parlour suites, at $130 to $140 for two people; children under 12 stay free with their parents.

**ON THE EAST SIDE**  Families who don't mind sharing the bath can stay at the **Vanderbilt YMCA,** 224 E. 47th St. (between Second and Third avenues), New York, NY 10017 (tel. 212/755-2410). Triples and quads (with bunk beds) rent for $60 to $65 and $76 to $80 respectively, and full use of all health-club facilities—including a terrific pool—is included. (Summer rates are slightly higher.)

The **Pickwick Arms Hotel,** 230 E. 51st St. (between Second and Third avenues), New York, NY 10022 (tel. 212/355-0300), is a budget hotel in a fashionable location. Family rooms with one or two double beds, or twin beds plus a sofabed, go for $75 for two people, $85 for three, and $100 for four or five. A few rooms in the rear overlook a garden.

Farther uptown, the **Hotel Wales,** 1295 Madison Ave. (between 92nd and 93rd streets), New York, NY 10028 (tel. 212/876-6000), has newly redone suites that can sleep up to four people for $125 to $145 for two, plus $5 each for the third or fourth guests. There's a sofabed in the living room, and queen- or king-size beds in the sleeping room.

On weekends only, several luxurious residential hotels of **Manhattan East Suite Hotels** offer studio apartments and suites at reduced rates: $93 for a studio, $100 for a junior suite, and $120 for a one-bedroom suite accommodating up to four people. For full details, see "Weekend and Other Packages," below.

**JUST ACROSS THE HUDSON RIVER** On the campus of the **Stevens Institute of Technology** in Hoboken, N.J. (tel. toll free 800/526-2915), families can enjoy a suite with two twin beds, two rollaways, and a fully equipped kitchen, for all of $90 per night.

---

# 6. Bed-and-Breakfasts

---

What with the unusually high cost of New York hotel rooms, the bed-and-breakfast concept of staying in a private residence and receiving breakfast as part of your rent is growing more popular than ever. New York has at least three major B&B organizations at this writing. The oldest and largest is **Urban Ventures,** which offers comfortable, carefully chosen rooms in private apartments—mostly on Manhattan's Upper West Side, Upper East Side, and Greenwich Village, and also in close-to-Manhattan areas of Brooklyn—at rates that are often less than those at budget hotels. Singles go for $38 to $60, doubles run $50 to $75, and entire apartments can also be rented: a studio apartment for about $65 to $90, a one-bedroom apartment for $90 to $160. Stays usually average several nights to two weeks (there is a two-night minimum). This is a good bet if you'd like not only to save money, but to establish some personal contact with New Yorkers, since Urban Ventures' hosts are usually outgoing types who genuinely like people. Contact Mary McCauley at Urban Ventures, P.O. Box 426, New York, NY 10024 (tel. 212/594-5650).

Another popular outfit is **City Lights Bed and Breakfast Ltd.,** P.O. Box 20355, Cherokee Station, New York, NY 10028 (tel. 212/737-7049), which makes placements in Manhattan, Brooklyn, Queens, and even Long Island. Owner Dee Staff Neilsen usually has singles for $40 to $70, doubles for $60 to $95, and apartments for $95 to $200, although in many cases prices can be lower, especially on doubles.

Many people in the arts and related professions are hosts at Judy Goldberg's **Bed, Breakfast (& Books),** 35 W. 92nd St., New York, NY 10025 (tel. 212/865-8740), which got its name from her husband, who is in the book business; city guides and B&B directories are also available. Mrs. Goldberg works with each client and host personally; she has units available all over Manhattan, from SoHo to the Upper West Side and the Upper East Side. Most rooms in hosted apartments go for $65 to $70 single and $75 to $80 double. Unhosted apartments start at $90 and $95 for studios and go up to about $120 and $125 for a one-bedroom apartment. Two-bedroom apartments for four people could be $160 a night.

All three of these agencies do not require a membership fee. They do, however, request that you make reservations in advance (the farther in advance the better), and there will be a charge should you cancel out. All accommodations and hosts are inspected and screened, and an attempt is made to bring together people of similar interests. And the letters of appreciation all these groups have received from satisfied guests are truly impressive.

---

# 7. Weekend and Other Packages

---

Many New York hotels and travel companies offer weekend package deals that prove to be relatively inexpensive. Here's how it works. During the week, most of the city's top hotels are occupied by out-of-town business executives. When the weekend comes, off they go, back home. This leaves many rooms empty. To fill the gap, the hotels can offer couples excellent rates for a two- or three-day period, throw a few breakfasts and dinners in the package, and sometimes a few theater tickets as well. Some packages are also available during the week.

For a complete rundown on hotel packages, pick up or write for a free pamphlet called *New York City Tour Package Directory.* It's available from the New York Convention and Visitors Bureau, 2 Columbus Circle, New York, NY 10019. Your travel agent will also know of many packages.

Keeping in mind that all rates are subject to change, and that bookings are based on availability, here are some examples. The hotels, of course, can be approached directly.

If you'd much rather stay in a suite with your own kitchen than in a hotel bedroom, you can't do better than to reserve one of the extraordinary weekend packages offered by the **Manhattan East Suite Hotels.** This company manages (among many others) nine of the city's most prestigious luxury suite hotels, including the **Shelburne Murray Hill,** 303 Lexington Ave., at 37th Street; the **Beekman Tower,** 49th Street and First Avenue, opposite the United Nations Plaza; the **Eastgate Tower,** 222 E. 39th St.; the **Dumont Plaza,** 150 E. 34th St.; **Lyden Gardens,** 215 E. 64th St.; **Lyden House,** 320 E. 53rd St.; **Plaza Fifty,** 155 E. 50th St.; and the **Southgate Tower,** 371 Seventh Ave., at 31st Street, opposite Madison Square Garden and Pennsylvania Station. When corporate guests go home for the weekends, their exquisite apartments become available at much lower prices; a studio for one or two people, normally renting for $150 to $195, is $93; a junior suite (a very large, L-shaped room with a dining area) that usually rents for $160 to $220 for up to three people, is $100; a one-bedroom suite for up to four people, normally renting for $175 to $240, is $120. A rate increase is expected, so prices may be higher than the rates quoted here. Still, this has to be one of the best deals in town; a large family or two couples traveling together can realize enormous savings. And the suites are simply beautiful: large, gracious, decorator-designed, exquisitely furnished, all with large and fully equipped kitchens, down to the dishwasher, silverware, and glassware. Of course all the usual hotel services and amenities are available.

Which of these hotels to choose is your only problem. Since all are lovely, base your decision on what part of town you wish to be closest to. The Eastgate Tower and Southgate Tower have on-premises garages. Lyden House and Southgate Tower have no two-bedroom suites. Rooms will be assigned on the basis of availability (you may get your second choice, but that will be no hardship). Reservations can be made up to two months in advance. Some fall weekends may not be available. Reservations are easy: phone 212/744-5660, or toll free 800/ME-SUITE.

*Note:* Rates are good on Friday, Saturday, or Sunday night, but you must arrive on Friday or Saturday to qualify for the Sunday rate.

"No Frills" weekends are offered at the five Helmsley hotels in New York, and the value is very good at these other times rather pricey places. Best deals of all are at the **Helmsley Windsor,** 100 W. 58th St., New York, NY 10019 (tel. 212/265-2100), and the **Helmsley Middletowne,** 148 E. 48th St., New York, NY 10017 (tel. 212/755-3000), where the price of a double room is $109 per night, Friday and/or Saturday arrival. The Middletowne has kitchenettes. The **New York Helmsley,** 212

E. 42nd St., New York, NY 10017 (tel. 212/490-8900), has deluxe accommodations for $130 per room per night, Friday and/or Saturday arrival. All these can be
booked by calling their toll-free number: 800/221-4982.

If you're the kind of person who hates to break your exercise routine when
you're on vacation, take advantage of the "No Frills" package offered by **Loew's
Summit,** Lexington Avenue at 51st Street, New York, NY 10022 (tel. 212/752-
7000). For $99 per room per night (Friday or Saturday), you have unlimited use of
the Summit Health Club in addition to deluxe accommodations, with children under 14 free in their parents' room, a 10% discount on food and beverage in Maude's
Restaurant and Lobby Bar, and storage of your car.

The luxurious **New York Hilton and Towers,** 1335 Ave. of the Americas (between 53rd and 54th streets), New York, NY 10019 (tel. 212/586-7000), has a fabulous two-night package called "Midtown Magic." Included in the $269 price tag is
the sumptuous Sunday Buffet Bruncheon in Hurlingham's, plus use of the hotel's
new fitness center, which includes aerobic equipment, Universal weight equipment,
and a sauna. Also inquire about other single-night and two-night packages; there is
always some sort of very good deal here. Children stay free when they share a room
with their parents.

"Le Weekend Français" offers luxury with a French touch at the lovely **Le Parker Meridien,** 118 W. 57th St., New York, NY 10019 (tel. 212/245-5000, or toll
free 800/543-4300). Two nights' (Friday arrival) accommodations, breakfast in Le
Patio, chilled champagne waiting in the room, and membership in the hotel's health
club (year-round pool, Nautilus equipment, sauna, and so on) are included for the
price of $170 per night for two people, with a two-night minimum.

The **Sheraton Centre Hotel and Towers,** 811 Seventh Ave. (between 52nd
and 53rd streets), New York, NY 10019 (tel. 212/581-1000) offers a "Best Value
Weekend" on Friday and Saturday, subject to availability, at $114 per night. Chil-
dren under 17 occupying the same room as their parents stay free. For availability
and reservations, call Sheraton toll free at 800/325-3535 or Sheraton Centre toll
free at 800/223-6550.

The attractive **Doral Inn,** 541 Lexington Ave. (at 49th Street), New York, NY
10022 (tel. 212/755-1200, or toll free 800/847-4135), has a "No Frills" package
for a neat price: $99 per room per night, for single, double, or triple occupancy.

The **Doral Park Avenue,** 70 Park Ave. (at 38th Street), New York, NY 10016
(tel. 212/687-7050, or toll free 800/847-4135), is a European-style hotel with the
only sidewalk café on Park Avenue. All rooms have refrigerators, premier movie
channels, and marble baths with dryers. Their "Weekend in the Big Apple" package
for one or two nights (Friday, Saturday, or Sunday arrival) offers accommodations in
deluxe rooms plus continental breakfast, parking, and a copy of Sunday's *New York
Times,* for $129.50 per room per night, single or double.

The **Shoreham,** 333 W. 55th St., New York, NY 10019 (tel. 212/247-6700),
is a charming small hotel. Its "Weekend Special," for two to three nights, with a
Thursday or Friday arrival, includes accommodations with serving pantry (refrigerator and coffee maker) and cable color TV. Doubles are $84 per night.

# II

# EATING CHEAPLY AND WELL

**1–14. RESTAURANTS BY NEIGHBORHOODS**

**15. ESPECIALLY FOR BRUNCH**

**16. AROUND THE CLOCK**

**17. EARLY-BIRD DINNER SPECIALS**

**18. BIG-SPLURGE RESTAURANTS**

New York's melting pot is home to the world's largest array of cuisine. Here you can sample everything from hearty peasant fare to refined French cooking, take in the friendly atmosphere of a family-run trattoria, or sip wine in chic art deco surroundings. The biggest problem you'll have is deciding where you want to go—there are more than 17,000 eating spots in the city.

As an aside, we'd be remiss in not pointing you in the direction of *The New York Restaurant Guide,* a new 50-page guide to eating spots in all five boroughs compiled by the New York Convention & Visitors Bureau. For a free copy, write to: Restaurant Guide, NYC Visitors Bureau, 2 Columbus Circle, New York, NY 10019.

This chapter will introduce you to nearly 400 restaurants. We've arranged them by geographic location. At the end we have included a list of good brunch spots and restaurants with early-bird specials. We've also listed the restaurants open 24 hours a day and those worth a once-in-a-blue-moon splurge.

## 1. Midtown West/Times Square

Here, in an area encompassing the Broadway theater district and the "Diamond District," there is an abundance of restaurant discoveries for the budget traveler. Midtown West is bounded roughly by 40th Street on the south, 57th Street on the north, Fifth Avenue on the east, and Ninth Avenue on the west.

### AMERICAN/CONTINENTAL

If you want to eat at reasonable prices in unpretentious surroundings and still find yourself in the company of stars, try **Joe Allen's,** 326 W. 46th St., between Eighth and Ninth avenues (tel. 581-6464). We've seen Al Pacino, Roy Scheider, and Angela Lansbury here on separate occasions. The atmosphere is warm, if too noisy to be intimate. Exposed brick walls bear framed theatrical posters that are an inside joke—the shows are either flops or little known. Tables are covered with red-checkered tablecloths and plants hang in brick archways that separate the busy bar from the larger dining area. Out in back there's dining beneath a skylight.

Prices on the blackboard are usually low. There are generally three or four dinners in the $9 to $12 range. Recommended are the sautéed calves' liver ($15) or grilled chicken ($14). Huge salads, priced from $4 to $13, are meals in themselves. Try the Belgian endive salad ($4). Brunch—served seven days a week until 2:45 p.m. (to 3:35 p.m. on Saturday and Sunday)—has omelets, and other egg variations for about $6.50 each. For dessert, there is the caramel apple cake or coconut custard pie for $3.75.

Open daily from noon to 1 a.m. (from 11:30 a.m. on Wednesday and Saturday for matinee-goers). Reservations advised.

A similar restaurant is **Sam's,** 263 W. 45th St., between Broadway and Eighth Avenue (tel. 719-5416). It has exposed brick walls, a bar and dining room separated by brick archways, and baby-blue tablecloths. While the ambience here is just as warm, Sam's blackboard menu has a wider selection of lower-priced items: hamburgers and chili are $4.50 to $5.50, quiche with salad is $9, and daily specials run $7 to $9.50. Try half a broiled chicken for $12 or barbecued ribs for $11. Desserts made on the premises include cheesecake and lime pie at $4.

Open daily from 11:30 a.m. to 4 a.m.; the kitchen closes at 1:30 a.m. Reservations suggested.

For a taste of "Anywhere U.S.A.," head a little out of the way to the **Market Diner,** 572 Eleventh Ave., at 43rd Street (tel. 244-6033). There's nothing special about the diner, but that's what makes it so familiar: a sweeping coffee counter, large orange booths, a foyer filled with video games, and a parking lot where customers can park one hour for free.

The menu is virtually endless. There are some 40 kinds of sandwiches, priced from $1.50 for a fried egg to $6.25 for a toasted bagel with cream cheese, lox, sliced onion, and tomato. Full dinners—including a meat dish, potato or rice, and vegetable or salad—run from $5.25 for baked breast of lamb or chicken chow mein to $10 for veal parmigiana. There are more than a dozen seafood dinners priced from $7 to $10.50, including fried sole or clams at the lower end, up to the garlicky shrimp scampi. And with any entree of $7 or more, you get a "bonus" cup of soup or glass of juice. For dessert, there are baked-on-the-premises fruit pies, muffins, and cakes—most for under $1.50—and ice-cream treats made with Breyer's ice cream. A super-sundae is $2.50.

Open 24 hours a day, as is its other location downtown on the corner of West and Laight streets.

Rise above it all—18 stories—and encounter the classiest university cafeteria you'll probably ever see. It's **City University's Graduate Center Dining Commons,** 33 W. 42nd St. (18th floor), between Fifth and Sixth avenues (tel. 642-2013). It's not just a university cafeteria, either. There's a lounge and bar, where hot hors d'oeuvres are served gratis from 5:30 p.m. "until they're gone," which is usually by 6:30 p.m.

The lounge has a large oak bar with caned chrome barstools. Along one of the exposed brick walls is a row of chrome-and-canvas lounge chairs, where studious customers can sit back with a book and a drink. The more gregarious gather around the low, round tables. The dining area has cream-colored walls and plants hanging in shutter-framed windows.

The service is cafeteria style, but the food is first rate. It consists of soup ($1.25), sandwiches (about $2 to $4.50), and a salad bar. For about $5.50 you can order hot entrees like braised beefsteak with scallions or the fish of the day, served with a gourmet vegetable and potato.

Breakfast is available from 8 to 11:15 a.m.; lunch, from 11:30 a.m. to 4:30 p.m.; and dinner from 4:30 to 8 p.m. The Commons is a good place to stop by for a cheap cup of coffee (55¢), and dessert (pies and cakes run $1.25 to $2), or for an afternoon drink (house drinks are $3; call drinks, $3.25; draft beer, $1.75).

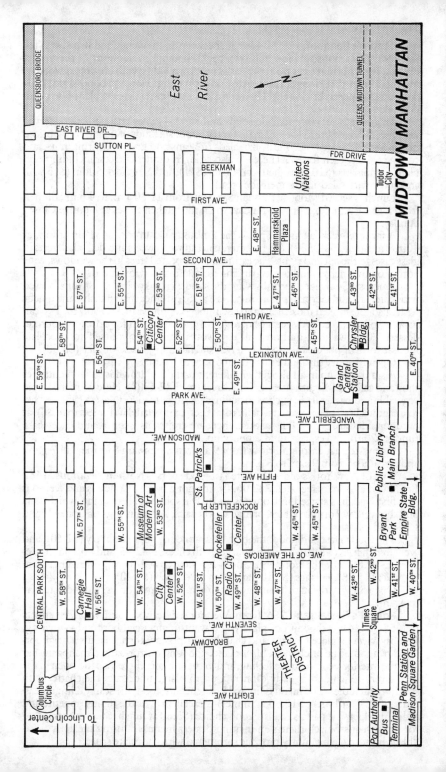

**Beggar's Banquet,** 125 W. 43rd St., between Sixth Avenue and Broadway (tel. 997-0959), is a not-so-typical midtown bar/restaurant in the heart of the theater district. It's a warm retreat from the flashy midtown lights, with an almost woodsy, mountain feel that derives from rich wood paneling, wooden booths, brick-tile floors, and exposed brick walls. Up front there are a few tables in a plant-filled window area.

There are hearty homemade soups and stews—types change daily—served with freshly baked bread for under $5. Or try one of six kinds of quiche, most priced under $8. There are large, meal-size salads of beans and greens, or fruit, nuts, and cottage cheese, each for $7. There are also a dozen dinner entrees, including eggplant parmigiana ($10), spaghetti carbonara ($11), and New York sirloin ($15). All are served with salad and homemade bread.

Lunch is served Monday through Saturday from 11:30 a.m. to 4 p.m.; dinner, from 5 to 11 p.m. (except on Monday, when the kitchen closes at 8 p.m.). Closed Sunday.

A favorite weekday lunch spot is the **Embassy Gourmet,** 1431 Broadway, at 40th Street (tel. 354-0550). As you enter, you can view sweets and deli salad treats in glass cases to the left and right. The eating area has potted trees in the windows, wine bottles on the shelves, and plants hanging from latticework overhead.

Embassy Gourmet's specialties are the salads: chunky chicken or tuna, served with cole slaw and German potato salad, is $8.25. Another special dish is the quiche with salad, or smoked mozzarella and cucumber on pumpernickel ($6.75). Two can happily split a cheese-and-sausage board ($10) and save room for a dreamy gourmet dessert. After walking midtown all day, you might treat yourself to chocolate mousse torte or praline cake ($4), or a rich and fattening Blackout cake ($3.50).

Open Monday through Friday from 6 a.m. to 7 p.m.

A similar set-up in an altogether different part of midtown is **Juliana** gourmet shop and café, 891 Eighth Ave., at 53rd Street (tel. 582-4503). Here you can sample vegetable and pasta salads, such as tortellini al pesto or fusili primavera ($5), or "heroic sandwiches" of soppressata, ham, roast beef, or mortadella (for less than $6), at outdoor sidewalk tables. For snackers there are croissants, scones, and cheesecake (under $2.50), and espresso and cappuccino.

Open Monday through Friday from 9 a.m. to 8 p.m., on Saturday till 7 p.m., and on Sunday from 9 a.m. to 5 p.m.

One of New York's oldest favorite fast-food spots is **Nathan's Famous,** 1482 Broadway, at 43rd Street (tel. 382-0620). It's got a happy, Coney Island feel to it (the first Nathan's started in Coney Island). The split-level restaurant, which seats 500, has yellow Formica tables, orange vinyl chairs, and paintings of Coney Island scenes on its walls.

The food is fast and good: the best New York hot dogs you'll try ($1.60), and great french fries ($1.40). The superburger with cheese is $2.75, and a bacon cheeseburger, $2.80. For the nonburger, non–hot dog crowd there's other fare: clam chowder ($1.75), knishes ($1.10), and corn on the cob ($1.20).

Open Sunday through Thursday from 7 a.m. to 2 a.m., on Friday and Saturday to 4 a.m.

**Robert's Restaurant,** 736 Tenth Ave., tucked between 50th and 51st streets (tel. 581-4244), is the kind of place you'd want in any neighborhood—inviting, friendly, clean, a place to drink and chat. Not surprising, then, that it's a neighborhood hangout. The brick walls, black piano, and long mirror-backed mahogany bar give the interior a comfortable feeling, and in the summer there's a patio open in the rear. Every lunch and at early dinners a piano player undercuts the chatter with soothing melodies. The menu is limited but generally good; the seafood linguine in red sauce ($9 at lunch, $10.50 at dinner) is excellent. For the lighter appetite and tighter budget, the pasta salad is a good choice ($5.50 at lunch, $6 at dinner). And for the rich-at-stomach there's an inviting dessert menu, featuring the aptly titled "black bottom," a big, nutty brownie smothered with chocolate sauce.

Open seven days a week from noon till whenever the bar closes, which can go into the wee hours of the morning if the mood is festive.

Everything is up-to-date at the **20th Century Café**, 795 Ninth Ave., between 52nd and 53rd streets (tel. 691-4587). This open and airy eatery is designed in a black-on-white motif. High ceilings, checked tile floors and walls, and black tables are nicely offset with soft track lighting alongside trendy hints of neon.

Lunch includes a mouthwatering variety of fresh (not frozen), seven-ounce burgers from $2.10 to $4.50. Sandwiches span about the same range with the Monte Cristo topping the bill. Quiche (Lorraine, broccoli and cheese, or spinach and cheese) with salad are $5.75. A cheddar-cheese-smothered baked potato is $3.75, and a do-it-yourself chef's salad is $5.50. For those whose culinary needs demand something more substantial, homemade fettuccine Alfredo and salad ($5.75) should do the trick.

Dinners here are just as reasonable and just as good. Appetizers include zucchini sticks ($4.25) and fried mozzarella sticks with a dip of marinara for $4.25. Entrees come with vegetable, rice or potato and cost between $6 and $10. They include beer-batter chicken with honey-mustard sauce ($7) and broiled scallops in garlic butter ($8.25). Desserts include chocolate layer cake ($1.25), cheesecake ($1.50), and ice-cream sundaes ($2). A full complement of hot and cold beverages is available, including espresso ($1.50) and egg creams for $1.

The 20th Century Café is open from 6 a.m. to midnight seven days a week.

There are chain restaurants, and there are great chain restaurants. **Tony Roma's—A Place for Ribs,** 1600 Broadway, on the corner of 48th Street (tel. 956-3130), originated in Florida. But good food, like good news, travels fast. While there are six locations in Manhattan, here in the midst of midtown's heaviest hustle and bustle a mecca for meat lovers is especially welcome. The interior is cool and welcoming. Swirling ceiling fans, touches of brass and etched glass, bentwood chairs, and old-fashioned lamps give the restaurant an oasis-like feel.

Ribs are the name of the game here. At lunch a small order of tenderloin baby back pork ribs, St. Louis–style pork ribs, or truly bountiful beef ribs will cost you $9. Those with a more than hearty appetite can order the dinner-size portion for $13. The pork ribs have tender, ready-to-fall-off-the-bone meat. The beef ribs are more sturdy, and are enormous. All come with cole slaw and a choice of barbecued beans, baked potato, or french fries.

For those not in the mood for ribs there is other ample fare to be had. Half-pound burgers with fries range from $6 to $7. There are soups, salads, seafood platters, and chicken. If you haven't eaten in several days, try the Roma feast for two. A groaning home-style platter will bring half a slab of baby back ribs, half a slab of pork ribs, three huge beef ribs, half a barbecued chicken, two ears of corn, two potatoes, and cole slaw for $27.

Open Monday through Thursday from 11:30 a.m. to midnight, on Friday and Saturday from noon to 1 a.m., and on Sunday from noon to 11 p.m.

## ARGENTINIAN

To see where the New York Argentinian community socializes, go to **La Milonga,** 742 Ninth Ave., at the corner of 50th Street (tel. 541-8382). It has a Latin club atmosphere that is festive and convivial. A busy bar greets the visitor, and the dining areas bear travel posters of Argentina and memorabilia of Argentinian tango singer Carlos Cardel.

At dinner there's an $8 minimum, and for that you can get Italian spaghetti with meat sauce. Or try a dinner platter that reflects the Argentinian predilection for meat; it has sweetbreads, kidney, steak, sausage, short ribs, and salad, for $12. Seafood specials such as lobster gumbo, paella Valenciana, or marinara are more, but not overpriced at $15.

Open from 3 p.m. to 2 a.m. daily, with a limited late-supper menu available until 3 or 4 a.m. On Friday, Saturday, and Sunday nights there's live Argentinian folkloric or tango music from 9 p.m. with a moderate cover charge, and dinner prices are a couple of dollars higher. Reservations are suggested for weekend nights.

## BRAZILIAN

Climbing the stairwell up to **Cabana Carioca,** 123 W. 45th St., between Sixth Avenue and Broadway (tel. 581-8088), is like coming upon the gay and gaudy minstrel caravan in the movie *'Bye 'Bye Brazil*. Cabana Carioca is one of the least expensive, and certainly the most colorful of midtown's Brazilian restaurants. The restaurant on the second and third floors is almost as colorful as the folkloric scenes painted on the stairway walls. A large window overlooking 45th Street is filled with plants, the walls are hung with oil paintings by a South American artist, and the tables are gaily covered with yellow linen cloths and brown napkins.

Three specials are offered daily, priced from $9.25 to $13. Portions are generous enough to share between two. Try the broiled chicken gaucho style ($10) or fish stew Brazilian style ($13). These come with rice, more black beans than you can eat, and a basket of fresh bread. The Brazilian national dish, feijoada completa, is a stew of black beans and three kinds of meat—pork, beef, and sausage ($10). At the lower-priced end of the menu there's a Portuguese omelet, made with sausage ($5). Consider sampling the desserts ($2.50); select from guava with cheese, coconut custard with cheese, or Portuguese pastry. Highest recommendation.

Open daily from noon to 11 p.m. Reservations suggested.

More in the style of modern Rio is a lovely, sophisticated little bar and restaurant called **Via Brazil,** 34 W. 46th St., between Fifth and Sixth avenues (tel. 997-1158). The décor is very '80s, with mahogany-stained wainscoting trimmed in jungle green and watercolors of Brazilian scenes hung above on white walls. There is seating to the side in semiprivate cubicles, or at the front in a glassed-in patio. Samba music plays in the background.

The menu offers an extensive selection of entrees with a Brazilian accent for under $15. There's fried fish served with fried bananas, a shrimp omelet, broiled lamb, veal, and pork, all served with rice and salad, and priced from $10.25 to $16. Via Brazil serves several versions of muquecas—a herby fish stew made with tomatoes and coconut milk—priced from $14 for cod stew to $16 for a stew with fish, shrimp, and lobster tail. All come with rice, beans, and salad. If you decide to share an entree, expect to be charged $2.50 for an extra plate.

Open Sunday through Tuesday from noon to 10 p.m. and Wednesday through Saturday until midnight.

## CHINESE

Another culinary find is the **Westside Cottage Chinese Restaurant,** 788 Ninth Ave., between 52nd and 53rd streets (tel. 957-8008). At this attractive midsized eatery, the light-plum-colored walls are adorned with contemporary Oriental prints. The unadorned butcher-block tables are set with darker-plum napkins. The lunch specials here are inexpensive and varied. For $4.50 or under you can get any one of no fewer than 20 entrees, accompanied with soup or eggroll and egg-fried or white rice. Brown rice is also available.

For dinner you might start with barbecued pineapple chicken or some Szechuan dumplings in a spicy sauce for $3.50. A full compliment of soups includes the house special for two, which is a tangy meat-and-seafood combination ($4). Some of the more popular entrees include eggplant with garlic sauce ($5.50) and crispy prawns with walnuts ($9.25). On the spicier side of things there's sliced beef or lamb Hunan style ($7), or diced chicken with eggplant ($6.50). Ten-ingredients pan-fried noodles is a hearty fare, and has indeed ten ingredients, including chicken, shrimp, and beef.

We've saved the best for last. The days of the free lunch may be over, but the days of free drinks are not. With any dinner, Westside Cottage will quaff your thirst with a bottomless glass of house wine. And for dessert, complimentary pineapple, orange chunks, and a fortune cookie will accompany your modest check.

Open daily, 11:30 a.m. to 11 p.m.

There is also a Westside Cottage II at 689 Ninth Ave., at 48th Street (tel. 245-0800). Reservations are recommended at both places.

## CUBAN/CHINESE

Thanks to a sizable Chinese immigrant population in Latin America, Chinese food is as popular south of the border as it is in the U.S. With the post-revolutionary exodus from Cuba, many Chinese restaurateurs settled in New York and established a number of binational eateries that are a budget-minded, ethnic-food-lover's paradise. One of Manhattan's best and friendliest is **Asia Number 7,** 854 Eighth Ave., between 51st and 52nd streets (tel. 247-5696). Its interior is uncharacteristically—for Chinese/Latino restaurants—attractive, with butcher-block tables and caned chairs.

The food is cheap and served in ample portions. You can go either Latin or Chinese—the cuisines are kept distinct—or combine the two. Though China and Cuba are several oceans apart, their cuisines are remarkably compatible. Where else might you eat egg foo yung alongside fried plantains? Our favorite Cuban entree is ropa vieja (Spanish for old clothes), shredded beef with a spicy Cuban sauce, served with black beans, rice, and fried plantains ($8). Daily Cuban specials include beef stew Cuban style, codfish, and oxtails, all served with rice and beans or plantains ($8). On the Asian side of the menu are such traditional Cantonese favorites as tomato or pepper beef ($5.25), and shrimp with lobster sauce or sweet-and-sour pork ($7.25). For dessert, try coconut, guava, or papaya served with cream cheese ($2.50). Tropical shakes are $2.

Open daily from 11:30 a.m. to 10 p.m.

## ENGLISH/IRISH

A little out of the way, but one of New York's most charming dining places is the **Landmark Tavern,** 626 Eleventh Ave., at 46th Street (tel. 757-8595). An inn-like, Irish tavern that dates back to 1868, the Landmark has an antique feel to it that few New York restaurants can match. There is dining on the second floor, in what served for a century as home to the Carly family, the Landmark's first owners. It is still the restaurant's homiest part; eating there is much like having Thanksgiving dinner at grandmother's. There are old floor rugs, antique furniture, brick fireplaces, and even a functioning grandfather clock.

Downstairs in the main dining area is a gorgeous old Victorian bar with huge, beveled mirrors. Tables are covered with white linen and adorned with candles and fresh flowers.

The old mahogany bar at the Landmark offers 6 beers on tap, 25 single-malt scotches, and 17 varieties of brandy and cognac. For lunch there is shepherd's pie ($10) or fish and chips ($10.50). There are also sandwiches ($5.25 to $7) and Irish potato soup with bacon ($3.50). Dinner entrees run about $2 higher than their lunch counterparts, and come with potato, vegetable, and a relish dish. They include lamb steak marinated in rosemary and red wine ($15), grilled Mako shark with shallot butter ($15), and a prime rib with Yorkshire pudding ($23). After dinner there is a rotating selection of desserts in the $5 range.

Sunday brunch at the Landmark offers four types of omelets ($10), Irish oatmeal pancakes with Irish bacon ($10.50), or mashed-potato pancakes with bangers for the same price. Have a Bloody Mary, screwdriver, brandy-milk punch, fruit juice, or glass of champagne on the house with your brunch.

Open daily for lunch from 11:30 a.m. to 4:15 p.m. and for dinner from 5 p.m. to midnight (on Friday and Saturday to 1 a.m.). Sunday brunch is served from noon to 4:15 p.m.

There's always a boisterous Irish-pub crowd gathered around the bar at the

**Shandon Star,** 938 Eighth Ave., near 55th Street (tel. 664-8181). At lunchtime the locals are joined by broadcast and business types who come from nearby for the restaurant's famous meat sandwiches, filled with generous portions of corned beef, pastrami, ham, or roast beef ($3.75), and for sandwich platters, which come with two vegetables ($5.75). Drinks at the bar are priced very reasonably.

Open daily from 8 a.m. to 4 a.m.

## FRENCH

In fair weather, dine on a terrace overlooking 55th Street on the second floor of **La Bonne Soupe,** 48 W. 55th St., between Fifth and Sixth avenues (tel. 586-7650). In winter there's warmth and intimacy inside on the street level. Low ceilings, subdued lighting, walls covered with red-and-white checked gingham, and tables covered with red-and-white checked tablecloths give La Bonne Soupe a close, cozy ambience. So does the small bar in back, which you'll pass if you go upstairs to sit on the outdoor terrace, or to view the restaurant's collection of Haitian primitive paintings which adorn the upstairs walls.

Lunch and dinner at La Bonne Soupe are from the same menu, at the same low prices. Omelets, filled with ratatouille or Gruyère cheese, are $7, and a meal of soup, bread, salad, dessert, and coffee or wine is only $7. Soups are mushroom-barley with lamb, sweet-and-sour cabbage, and French onion. There are also salads—Niçoise, chef's, or "Popeye" (spinach)—for $8.25, and fondues of cheese ($6.75) or chocolate ($4.75).

Open daily from 11:30 a.m. to midnight (on Sunday to 11 p.m.).

There is a distinct French accent at the **Film Center Café,** 635 Ninth Ave., between 45th and 46th streets (tel. 262-2525). This clean and simple bar, booth-and-table–style restaurant has been pepped up with a multicolored tile ceiling, touches of art deco glass, and mirrors. The overall effect is down home, upscale. The softly played tunes from the '50s and '60s make the atmosphere even more homey. From the small wood bar up front, $2.50 will get you a large glass of any of the eight beers available on draft.

The food here is fresh, imaginative, and homemade. At lunch, soups such as cold gazpacho, cream of cucumber, hot lobster bisque, or split pea can be had for $2.25. Entrees range from $6 to $11.50. One of the favorites here is a very French steak tartare of prime beef, filled with capers, onions, radishes, parsley, and a delicate mix of spices, served with fries, for $9.50. For the same price you can get a superlative meatloaf with real mashed Idaho potatoes and fresh vegetable. But don't miss the creative sandwiches du jour ($8.50) like the duck or soft-shell crab, both served with those very french fries.

At dinner, appetizers such as crab cakes ($5.50) or boudin blanc (a white veal-and-chicken sausage) with apple purée and sautéed onions ($4.50) may lure you. Entrees ranging from $7.50 to $13 include Cajun or lemon chicken, both served with rice and vegetables for $11.25. For those of you who missed lunch, the steak tartare and meatloaf are still available. Desserts at lunch or dinner are only $3.25, and include frozen chocolate mousse and a fantastic fruit salad that boasts kiwi, banana, papaya, orange, grapes, and pineapple.

Lunch is served weekdays from noon to 4 p.m. Dinner is daily from 4:30 p.m. until 1 a.m. You can brunch on Saturday and Sunday from 11 a.m. to 4 p.m. No credit cards or checks accepted.

The entrees are expensive at **Café Un, Deux, Trois,** 123 W. 44th St., between Sixth and Seventh avenues (tel. 354-4148). But this restaurant's distinctive ambience may be worth the price. Boisterous, bustling, brightly lit, and airy like a loft, it's the kind of restaurant to go to when you don't want intimacy. In the heart of the theater district, the café is packed both before and after shows.

Butcher paper instead of linen serves as tablecloths, and with crayons supplied by the café, your table becomes an adult playground. Waiters will demonstrate their remarkable memories by reproducing the evening's menu on your tablecloth—that is, if your own graffiti doesn't take up all the space before your waiter arrives. If it's your birthday, by all means request a serenade. The waiters' chorus sounds professional.

Though entrees run upward from $15 to $20, including roast duck for $16, there are omelets for $7.50 and appetizers for under $6.25. Try pâté de campagne ($3.75) as a before- or after-theater snack. Or for a big-splurge sweet, consider ordering profiteroles—three cream-puff pastries filled with vanilla ice cream and topped with bittersweet fudge sauce ($5.50).

Open daily from noon to 12:30 a.m. Prices are somewhat lower before 5 p.m.

## GREEK

The dining is elegant at the **New Acropolis,** 767 Eighth Ave., at 47th Street (tel. 581-2733). Lamb entrees here start at $8.25, except for a recommended combination plate of baked lamb, eggplant moussaka, baked macaroni, stuffed grape leaves, spinach, and cheese ($11.75). There are dozens of other entrees and daily specials, from fried or broiled shrimp ($15.25) to roast baby veal ($11.75) or chicken ($7.25). Acropolis serves its own version of Greek antipasto, with caviar and eggplant salads, stuffed grape leaves, feta cheese, and tzatziki (yogurt seasoned with garlic, oil, salt, and cucumber) at $6.25. This dish includes a huge hunk of fresh bread and butter.

Open daily from 11 a.m. to 11 p.m.

## INTERNATIONAL

Want a chance to meet New Yorkers, have a good dinner or brunch, and get to practice a foreign language too? An evening at **The Language Club** has to be one of the best values in New York. Started in April 1984 by the popular broadcast talk-show host Barry Farber, the club has caught on so quickly that any given week should see at least five or six meetings in the metropolitan area. Farber, a student of 14 languages, thought he was the only language freak around; when he mentioned the fact on a radio show, hundreds of others came forward, and now the meetings are extremely popular, especially with older singles who would like to meet people in a congenial and cultural environment. For between $10 and $14, the visitor receives a drink, a buffet meal that runs from "generous to limitless," depending on the restaurant, and a chance to converse in small groups in any number of tongues, everything from Albanian to Zulu, though the most popular languages are French, Spanish, Italian, and German. There's no guarantee that you'll find somebody with whom to discuss world affairs in the language of your choice, but the chances are good. A joint program on teachings and tactics (that is, learning to memorize words once and for all) is presented to the entire group. And students are also offered discounts on classes at language schools, cassette courses, books, dictionaries, and more. The purpose of the club is to bring together those who wish to begin, refresh, improve, or practice a language, so you are welcome at whatever your level of skill. Internationals are especially welcome: they quickly become "superstars, celebrities," says Farber, and get a chance to make American friends and practice their English in a pleasant, non-threatening environment."

As for the restaurants, they are always of excellent quality, from dinners at La Maganette or J.J. Starr, to Sunday brunches at Victor's Café. Says Farber: "The bargain is so good it pays to come to the Language Club even if you keep your mouth shut!"

For information on all Language Club activities, phone their 24-hour hotline at 877-1413.

## ITALIAN

That New York institution, **Mama Leone's,** has a spacious and bright new home at 261 W. 44th St., near Eighth Avenue (tel. 586-5151). Every evening, strolling musicians serenade you while you dine.

Dinner prices are high, but the lunches are reasonable and filling. Pasta entrees ($11) are your best bet. Try the spaghettini or the tortellini primavera. For large groups, an all-you-can-eat buffet lunch is available Monday through Saturday.

Mama Leone's is open Monday through Friday from 11:30 a.m. to 2:30 p.m. for lunch, and 4 to 11:30 p.m. for dinner. Saturday hours are 11:30 a.m. to 11:30 p.m., and on Sunday, 1:30 to 9 p.m. Reservations are necessary for large groups.

It's on the pricey side, but the budget-minded traveler might make an exception for **Patsy's,** 236 W. 56th St., between Broadway and Eighth Avenue (tel. 247-3491)—especially if the traveler is in the mood for star-gazing. This famous, family-run restaurant has been serving up hearty Italian specialties for more than 45 years. Frank Sinatra, Barbra Streisand, Michael J. Fox, and their friends appreciate the tradition and are frequent patrons of Patsy's.

A visit to this decidedly New York scene need not break your budget if you watch what you order. Enjoy one of the ten pasta selections or mussels marinara for $12.25. Broiled chicken à la Patsy's and whiting in cassuola are under $15. Lunch can be done for less.

Patsy's is open Tuesday through Friday for lunch from noon to 3 p.m. Dinner is served Tuesday through Thursday and on Sunday from 3 to 10:30 p.m., and on Friday and Saturday from 3 to 11:30 p.m. Reservations suggested.

## JAPANESE

For excellent Japanese food at reasonable prices, try **East,** 251 W. 55th St., between Broadway and Eighth Avenue (tel. 581-2240). Lunch entrees (priced between $7 and $10) come with soup, a small salad, and rice. Sushi and sashimi platters range from $6.25 to $12. For dessert, try the green-tea or red-bean ice cream ($2). At dinner there is a greater selection of entrees at slightly higher prices.

East is open for lunch every day except Sunday from noon to 2:30 p.m., and every evening for dinner from 5 p.m. to midnight. Reservations are recommended for dinner.

Tucked away up a dingy apartment-house stairway is an excellent little restaurant called **Hide** (pronounced "hee-day"), 304 W. 56th St., between Eighth and Ninth avenues (tel. 582-0030). Almost totally lacking in ambience. Hide nevertheless draws a loyal crowd for its hospitality and delicious, moderately priced Japanese dishes. Favorites are chicken teriyaki ($12) and beef teriyaki ($14), and shrimp and vegetable tempura ($12). Complete dinners, including entree, soup, pickled vegetable, rice, and dessert, run up to $14 for negimaki. There are assorted sushi platters for $9.25 and $11.25.

Lunch is served weekdays from noon to 2:30 p.m.; dinner, Monday through Saturday from 5:30 to 11 p.m.

For a more expansive sushi setting, there is **Café Iroha,** 1634 Broadway, on the corner of 50th Street (tel. 315-3808). The sushi bar twists around a whole side of the room, manned by traditionally garbed Japanese sushi chefs, who yell orders in their native tongue to waiters dashing to and fro. As with most places in New York, the sushi is not cheap—prices can run up to $14 ($16.50 at dinner) for the deluxe sushi platter—but the presentation of the food is sheer beauty, a masterful demonstration of raw-fish-as-art-form. Individual pieces, ordered one by one at the sushi bar between sips of hot sake rice wine, range from $2 to $3.50. There is good food other than sushi as well. In particular, the chicken curry, served with soy-bean soup, steamed rice, and a Japanese salad, is exquisite at $9.50 ($11 at dinner).

Open for lunch Monday through Friday from noon to 2:45 p.m., and for dinner Monday through Saturday from 5 to 11:15 p.m.

## JEWISH DAIRY

**Diamond Dairy,** 4 W. 47th St., just west of Fifth Avenue (tel. 719-2694), is a tiny, coffee-counter luncheonette that serves kosher cuisine to Orthodox Jews working in Manhattan's diamond district. Sit near the mezzanine window and watch the trade in precious gems below.

The food here is tasty, healthful, and inexpensive. Traditional dishes like potato pirogie and cheese kreplach are $5.25, as are the salads of vegetables and chopped egg. Pickled herring is $5.50. Gefilte fish, salmon cutlet, and fish balls with spaghetti cost $6 or less. Sandwiches are generally around $3.50, and desserts—freshly baked —are $2 or less.

Open Monday through Thursday from 7:30 a.m. to 5:30 p.m., on Friday to 3 p.m.

## JEWISH DELI

The sandwiches are colossal at the **Stage Delicatessen and Restaurant,** 834 Seventh Ave., at 54th Street (tel. 245-7850). Even if you can get your mouth around the first half of any sandwich you order, you may need a doggy bag for the second. In short, the corned beef and hot pastrami are piled high. Bagels and lox, potato pancakes, and other deli favorites are served up in equally generous portions. Prices range from $5 to $12.

This theater district hangout has been serving showbiz schmoozers and other colorful characters for more than 50 years. And here's a reflection of the times: The menu is conveniently printed in English and Japanese.

The Stage Deli is open daily from 6 a.m. to 1:30 a.m.

## MEXICAN

Texans and others "in the know" will complain that there is no real Mexican food in New York (Mexicans will agree). But among the best the city has to offer is the Mexican cooking at **Caramba!,** 918 Eighth Ave., at 55th Street (tel. 245-7910). Relax, enjoy the festive, colorful décor of woven wall hangings and Indian masks. Tables are covered with pink linen tablecloths and glass. The floors are rustic cement, and there's a patio-garden in the back beneath a sunny skylight.

Forget about authenticity and fill up on truly tasty food. Start with nachos, covered with melted cheese and jalapeño peppers ($3); then go for one of the combination plates ($9.50). The pork burrito, with green chiles and salsa verde, approaches the authentic. And you should consider a chile relleno, stuffed with chicken or cheese, dipped in egg batter, and fried. If you have trouble choosing only two dishes, pay another $2.75 and get a third choice. But arrive hungry; with beans and rice on the side, you'll be leaving stuffed. If you're restrained, save room for the delicious Mexican doughnuts, buñuelos, served with New York's favorite Häagen-Dazs ice cream ($3.50).

Open daily. Lunch is served from noon to 4 p.m. (prices are slightly lower), and dinner is from 4 p.m. to midnight. There's a brunch served on Saturday and Sunday from noon to 4 p.m. featuring various Mexican versions of eggs and a cocktail or wine ($7).

If the wait at Caramba! is too long, which it often is, try the Mexican restaurant just across the street, **Cancún,** 937 Eighth Ave., near 55th Street (tel. 307-7307). Its owners are also its chefs, and though not Mexican, they come with experience from other New York Mexican restaurants. The food here—if not authentically Tex-Mex, much less Mex-Mex—is tasty and priced right.

Cancún has combo plates, with a choice of either enchiladas or tacos priced at $8 (for three items, $10). Cancún also serves Mexican-flavored casseroles of eggplant and beef for $9, and seafood entrees for $10 to $13. For "gringos" who don't like chili and cumin, there are hamburgers and cheeseburgers (around $5) and California chicken, sautéed in wine ($9).

Cancún is open Sunday through Thursday from 11:30 a.m. to midnight, on Friday and Saturday to 1 a.m., with weekend brunch ($6) served until 4 p.m.

In competition with Caramba! for the well-heeled crowd is **Arriba Arriba,** 762

Ninth Ave., between 51st and 52nd streets (tel. 489-0810). The restaurant feeds a steady clientele of young professionals and theater types—both goers and doers—who enjoy the socializing as much as the margaritas (from the $2.25 "bebe-size" to $9.50 "mama-size") and the nachos, layered with beans, cheddar cheese, and jalapeño (single portion at $3.75).

While dining at pink-linen-covered tables surrounded by colorful Mexican murals on the stucco walls, enjoy a combination platter, choosing from tacos, tostadas, burritos, enchiladas, or tamales, all with refried beans and rice on the side. (Prices range from $6 to $8.75, depending on the number of dishes in your combination.) If after that you still have room, finish with homemade flan, an authentic Mexican recipe of rich custard covered with brandy-caramel sauce ($3.50) or a deep-fried flour tortilla dusted in cinnamon and sugar, topped with chocolate or vanilla ice cream ($3.25).

Open daily from noon to midnight (on Friday and Saturday to 1 a.m.). Brunch, featuring five different selections with a cocktail and coffee, is served on Saturday and Sunday from noon to 4 p.m. for $7.25.

## MIDDLE EASTERN

If you want to eat good, natural Middle Eastern food at reasonable prices, try the **Lemon Tree Café,** 769 Ninth Ave., between 51st and 52nd streets (tel. 245-0818). This friendly little café with wood-latticed walls serves up such Middle Eastern favorites as baba ghanouj, hummus, falafel, and tabouli salad. The vegetarian combination platter gives you a portion of each of these with pita bread for $5.25. Combination meat platters are around $7.50 and are served with a choice of rice and hummus, or french fries and salad. Try the thinly sliced, marinated flank of turkey (schwarma), for $7. Pita sandwiches range in price from $2.50 to $3.50. The Lemon Tree offers an excellent, homemade baklava for dessert at $1.

Open daily from 11 a.m. to 11:30 p.m.

## SEAFOOD

**King Crab,** 871 Eighth Ave., at the corner of 52nd Street (tel. 765-4393), is a thoroughly classy restaurant with superb seafood at reasonable prices. The interior is exceptionally pretty, with a black marble bar, gilt-framed mirrors, oak floors, ample greenery, and Tiffany-style lamps.

Fish of the day costs between $8 and $15; shrimp scampi, less than $11.50; and a seafood combination or seafood brochette, $12. At dinner the menu is more varied, and entrees like sea bass, cod, brook trout, flounder, and bluefish are all under $12. Among the shellfish entrees, shrimp scampi and scallops are within budget, just under $14. Lunch and dinner come with vegetable, potato or rice, bread, and butter; dinner adds a salad. Favorite desserts at King Crab are the carrot cake and pecan pie ($2.50).

Open Monday through Saturday from noon to midnight (lunch specials served until 3:30 p.m.) and on Sunday from 4 to 11 p.m. No reservations.

If waiting at King Crab doesn't suit you, there's a newer, very similar operation called **K.C. Place,** 807 Ninth Ave., between 53rd and 54th Streets (tel. 246-4258). The décor and menu are equally appealing. Lunch is served daily from noon to 4 p.m. and dinner from 4 to 11:30 p.m. (to 10 p.m. on Sunday), and brunch from noon to 4 p.m. on Sunday—and here you *can* get reservations.

## THAI

Slightly more exotic than either Szechuan Chinese or Korean, but similar to both, is the cuisine of Thailand. **Bangkok Cuisine,** 885 Eighth Ave., between 52nd and 53rd streets (tel. 664-8488), is one of New York's most popular Thai restaurants. Metallic Thai paintings are hung on black walls; Thai figurines keep vigil from strategic vantage points; huge fish tanks soothe the eye. Cozy or crowded, depending on your mood, the restaurant's center tables are close enough for eavesdropping.

If you go in for spicy, by all means go for it here: try any of the dishes so designated by a little star. For a dish like few you've tried before, have minced pork with lime juice and peanuts, served on a bed of iceberg lettuce—$9, a generous serving. Less spicy dishes are still perfectly tasty. There's double delight—with chicken and shrimp in sauce—for $14, and egg noodle topped with chicken curry and Chinese vegetables for $12. Slightly higher, but a real treat, is roast duck with the chef's special sauce for $16.

For vegetarians or just stricter budgetarians, meatless dishes include sautéed mixed vegetables with hot curry and sautéed bean curd with oyster sauce, each $9.

Open Monday through Saturday from 11:30 a.m. to 11:30 p.m., on Sunday from 5 to 11:30 p.m.

**Siam Grill,** 586 Ninth Ave., between 42nd and 43rd streets (tel. 307-1363), is one of the few Thai places in the city that offers take-out and delivery service. Fortunately, the take-out area does not intrude on the colorful dining area. House specialties include sautéed chicken and shrimp with mixed vegetables and chile ($9), and pla mug pad bai gra prou, a sautéed squid with basil leaves and chili ($9.25). In addition, there are fine soups and appetizers ranging from $2 to $5.25.

Open Monday through Friday from 11:30 a.m. to 11:30 p.m., and on Saturday and Sunday from 5 to 11:30 p.m. Delivery is free with a $10 minimum order.

Perhaps the best Thai cuisine in all of Manhattan is at **Siam Inn,** 916 Eighth Ave., between 54th and 55th streets (tel. 489-5237). The cozy restaurant space is not too cramped, not too spacious—perfect for parties of three or four—and the food is exquisite. There is a five-stool bar near the entrance at which to wait for a table, but rarely is a wait necessary. Up and down the menu one can't go wrong, be it the cold spring rolls with tamarind sauce ($4 for one, $7.25 for two), the sautéed chicken with mushrooms and baby corn ($8), or the sautéed squid with onion and chile ($8). Save room for dessert: The house-made ice cream—in banana, mango, and green-tea flavors—is a treat at $2.50.

Open Monday through Friday from noon to 3 p.m. for lunch and 5 to 11:30 p.m. for dinner, on Saturday from 4 to 11:30 p.m., and on Sunday from 5 to 11 p.m.

## 2. Midtown East

With the chic lunchtime hustle of suited-up business crowds, U.N. diplomats, and elegant shoppers, the Midtown East section of town, located between 42nd and 60th streets east of Fifth Avenue, seems like a formidable challenge to budget-conscious diners. But there are a surprising number of restaurants in this area that are reasonably priced.

### AMERICAN/CONTINENTAL

With a dark-wood interior and regular patrons from the neighborhood, the **Mayfair Restaurant,** 964 First Ave., at 53rd Street (tel. 421-6216), has a familiar old-fashioned feel. There's a large bar at the front, decorated with a huge set of antlers. Leather-covered wooden booths are in the back of the restaurant for diners. Green checkered tablecloths, green curtains hung on thick brass rods, and softly lit green lamps add the proper accent to the mahogany-colored wood paneling.

Special entrees change on a rotating basis throughout the week, but all are hearty and filling. Prices for entrees range from $10.50 to $16.50, but there is usually at least one item on the low end of the scale for each day. Chopped steak ($10.50) and broiled chicken ($11.25) are items that are offered at all times. Try the beef stew ($10.50), offered Monday, or the beef goulash with noodles ($10.50) on Wednesday. We suggest pie at $3.25 or the peach Melba for $4 for dessert.

Open daily from noon to midnight. No reservations, except for parties of four or more.

A beautiful varnished blond-wood exterior is the first clue that the **Electra Restaurant,** 949 Second Ave., at 53rd Street (tel. 421-8425), is no ordinary Greek coffeeshop. While the interior reverts to familiar Formica tables and brown booths, the wide variety of dishes is anything but "run of the mill."

Everything from breakfast dishes to hamburgers is served throughout the day. Try the special feta cheese with tomato omelet for $5.25. For a full meal, order the breaded veal cutlet ($9). The roast beef plate costs $8.25, and is served with potato, vegetable, and a salad. There are also Greek specialties like lamb shish kebab ($9). Hamburger specials cost between $2.75 and $6.25. Try the homemade baklava or galaktoboureko for dessert ($2).

The Electra is open from 6 a.m. to 1 a.m. weekdays, until 2 a.m. on weekends.

The placement of **Extra Extra!** in the Daily News Building, 767 Second Ave., at 41st Street (tel. 490-2900), inspired big-time restaurant designer Sam Lopata to do it up in newsprint. The walls are covered with snips of oversize newsprint. The floors are splattered with ink spots. But it's also more than a cute "theme" restaurant. The food is astonishingly varied and good, and the menu is fun. For lunch, try dilled chicken in pita bread, ($9) or your own pizza with everything from tomato and mozzarella ($10) to pickled jalapeño slices ($12).

Open from 11:30 a.m. to 10:30 p.m. Monday through Friday, with a piano bar nightly. On the weekends the restaurant is open from 5 p.m. to 1 a.m.; Sunday brunch is from noon to 4 p.m. and includes free babysitting for the kids.

For a quick sandwich in art deco surroundings, try the **Horn and Hardart Automat,** 200 E. 42nd St., at Third Avenue (tel. 599-1665). Food at the Automat is dispensed from glass boxes decorated with art deco mirrors. Coffee pours with a turn of a crank and comes out of ornate dolphin-shaped spouts.

To "order," you must go to a central booth and buy silver and brass tokens to use in the machines, although some dispensers accept quarters. Hot sandwiches cost $3.75 and up; cold sandwiches, between $2 and $3.25; roll and butter, 60¢; and pie, $1.10. Baked chicken, broiled fish, meatloaf, and other hot entrees are available in a cafeteria-style line for $4 to $5.25. On the way out, grab a few fresh-baked David's Cookies for $7.25 per pound.

Open daily from 6 a.m. to 10 p.m.

**The Café at Grand Central,** West 42nd Street in Grand Central Terminal, West Balcony (tel. 883-0441), is located in one of New York's biggest attractions, Grand Central Terminal, and if you can eat while you sightsee, so much the better. Make sure you look up—the constellations on the huge domed ceiling shouldn't be missed—and from the vantage point of the café you can take in the whole main terminal. Lunch is the only meal served here, but the handsome bar attracts a good crowd of waiting commuters at 5 p.m. every day. A sandwich of sopressata, salami, and imported swiss on a baguette is $5.50. The special changes daily and is always a good bargain. Salads are large: Niçoise is $6 and chicken is $5.50. Steak tartare, when available, is custom-made to taste ($7.25). For dessert, try the extra-chocolatey chocolate cake ($2.75).

Open daily from noon to 4 p.m.

"Come hungry," advises Joey Horn, the owner of **Goodfellow's,** 1009 Second Ave., between 53rd and 54th streets (tel. 759-8775). His restaurant offers "a taste of old New York," which means excellent prime rib and filet mignon for $11. Other house specialties include the veal scaloppine piccata ($11) and the cold Irish smoked salmon platter with capers, onions, and tomato ($14). All dinners are served with salad or vegetable and choice of baked potato, french fries, or rice. Top off a hearty meal with the irresistible rum chocolate fudge cake ($2.50). Like the television show "Cheers," there is a downstairs bar—with piano music on Thursday and Friday evenings—and an upstairs dining room.

Open daily from 11:30 a.m. to 4 p.m. for lunch, 5 p.m. to midnight for dinner, and until 2:30 a.m. for late supper.

**J.R.'s 8 Oz. Burgers,** 250 E. 58th St., between Second and Third avenues (tel.

980-1421), is a great burger house, which also serves hearty breakfast and dinner basics. The restaurant is nicely attired (for a burger house) in oak tables, an oak counter, tin ceilings, and tiled floors. The burger patties, which weigh no less than eight ounces, are made from huge mounds of lean red meat, slowly grilled with whatever extras you can think of ordering. The house specialty is the East Side burger, with bacon, cheese, ham, mushrooms, and fried onions for $5.50. Burger items come as a platter with french fries, lettuce, and tomatoes for about $1 extra. For breakfast, french toast with ham and two eggs is $6.75.

Breakfast hours are 6 to 11:30 a.m. The restaurant closes at 10 p.m. daily.

On the rise in New York are charcoal grill houses like **Checkers Char-Grilled Chicken & Ribs,** 1047 Second Ave., between 55th and 56th streets (tel. 355-0994). The black-and-white-tiled restaurant holds a number of small tables, from which you can watch the grill man work in his tall white chef's hat. Special combination plates (served with salad, bread, and sauce) include a barbecued-beef-and-onion sandwich ($4.50) and a half portion of baby back ribs ($6.75).

Open weekdays from 11:30 a.m. to 11 p.m., on Saturday from 4 to 10 p.m., and on Sunday from 4 to 11 p.m.

When the urge for steak and potatoes strikes, try **Kenny's Steak Pub,** 565 Lexington Ave., between 50th and 51st streets (tel. 355-0666). The old wooden bar in the front of the restaurant is a good place to watch sporting events; when the bar opened in the 1950s, it was a favorite watering hole for pro baseball players. Red-and-white checkered tablecloths and brass fixtures add to the sense that this is a classic steakhouse. Prime rib at lunch is $13.50, with dinner prices higher. In addition, you can also get a delicious shrimp cocktail for $8.50.

Kenny's is open from 7 a.m. to 11 p.m. daily.

If midnight munchies are a problem, try **Jumbo Bagels & Bialys,** 1070 Second Ave., between 56th and 57th streets (tel. 355-6185). Along with some of the best bagels in the city, the shop in front of the bakery serves bialys, muffins, and croissants, and offers accompanying salads and juices. Any of the dozen types of bagels are 50¢ each, and fruit muffins are $1. Whitefish or baked salmon salads are $4. For only $5 you can get a lox, bagel, and cream-cheese sandwich—the bagel combination New Yorkers adore. No tables, but late-night munchers often sit in the large bay window facing the street.

Open 24 hours daily.

## CHINESE

Just around the corner from the U.N. is the **Wan Fu** restaurant, 801 Second Ave., between 42nd and 43rd Streets (tel. 599-1231). It offers reasonable prices and a pleasant, relaxing décor. There are two dining rooms, one at ground level and one up on an interior balcony. The wall-to-wall carpeting is red, but Chinese paintings and murals are of subdued tones. Every table is set with silk flowers.

Lunch platters, served from noon to 3 p.m. on weekdays, range in price from $4.25 to $8.50. The wide variety of dishes includes cold sunsee noodles with sesame sauce ($4.25). Try the assorted-flavor soup ($3.50) or the combination platters ($5.50 to $7). The house specialties are more expensive—$7.25 to $12—but worth it. The chef will make dishes only as spicy as you want, and will skip the salt or MSG upon request. A small, full bar at the front of the restaurant gives the place a clubby feeling.

Open from noon to 10:30 p.m. Monday through Saturday. Reservations are suggested for lunch.

**Lai Lai,** 690 Third Ave., between 43rd and 44th streets (tel. 867-4620), has a California décor and Hunan cuisine. Some choice dishes include filet mignon with sesame seeds ($8.50), Hunan-style lamb ($8), and crispy prawns with walnuts ($9). The lunch specials, served from 11:30 a.m. to 3 p.m., are a standard $5.50. The restaurant uses no MSG, and the staff is happy to alter the spices to suit your tastebuds. Another plus: There's brown rice upon request.

Open Monday through Wednesday from 11:30 a.m. to 10 p.m., on Thursday and Friday from 11:30 a.m. to 11 p.m., and on weekends from 1 to 10:30 p.m.

True to its name, the **Beijing Duck House,** 144 E. 52nd St., between Lexington and Third avenues (tel. 759-8260), serves Peking duck throughout the day. There is no need for advance notice, but the limited supply goes on a first-come, first-served basis. The cost is $34 for two people. The restaurant is small, with white tablecloths and fresh red carnations on every table.

The specialty here is the crisp-skinned duck, prepared through a sophisticated process that includes pumping air into the skin before roasting; it's served with thin pancakes. But there are other, less expensive dishes for those who don't want to splurge. Entrees range in price from $10 for vegetable dishes to $18 for seafood. Poultry dishes average about $12. Try the sliced duck meat with green scallions and hoisin sauce ($13), a kind of Peking duck without the skin.

Open from noon to 10 p.m. Monday through Thursday, to 10:30 p.m. on Friday, Saturday, and Sunday.

## FRENCH

It's hard to find a reasonably priced good French restaurant in New York, so **Les Sans-Culottes,** 1085 Second Ave., at 57th Street (tel. 838-6660), is a gem. The ceiling and walls are a patriotic shade of blue, the latter hung with eclectic prints. The tables are as likely to be filled with French people as Americans.

The lunch entrees average $10 and include Cornish game hen, omelets, and lamb kidneys. For lighter fare, try the special: the standard appetizer—vegetable basket, various sausages that you cut yourself and chef's pâté—and an hors d'oeuvre or dessert ($10). The hors d'oeuvres include onion soup gratiné, escargots, and green salad; the desserts are masterpieces, such as delicate ice-cream crêpes or candied chestnuts in fresh whipped cream. Dinner is prix fixe at $20, and includes the appetizer, entree, and dessert. You can also order these courses à la carte: appetizer ($10), entree ($15), or dessert ($3). The service is friendly and unpretentious. The wine list is superb, as is the house wine at $6 a carafe. As the menu says (in French), "A day without wine is like a day without sun!"

Open daily for lunch from noon to 3 p.m., and for dinner from 5 to 11 p.m.

The best fast food to be had in midtown is from **Le Croissant Shop,** 459 Lexington Ave., at 45th Street (tel. 697-5580), one of several dotting midtown. The service in this small bakery-deli is speedy and cheerful, and the ingredients fresh and satisfying. The croissants and other specialties are baked daily on the premises, and some stores offer a closeup view of the baking. For a people-watching lunch on the marble steps of the New York Public Library (Fifth Avenue, between 40th and 42nd streets), try the Dijon chicken salad on a fresh-baked croissant or ham and brie on a French roll (prices average $3.50). The quiche is a fine pick for $2.50, as are the hearty soups for about the same price. For dessert, try one of their many French pastries ($1 to $2.25).

Open Monday through Friday from 6:30 a.m. to 7 p.m., on Saturday from 8 a.m. to 6 p.m., and on Sunday from 8:30 a.m. to 4:30 p.m.

## IRISH

For a taste of Ireland, stroll into **Tommy Makem's Irish Pavilion,** 130 E. 57th St., between Park and Lexington avenues (tel. 759-9040). The long dark wooden bar up front leads into a dining area with wooden beams and dark-green décor, which give the area a cozy and earthy feel. The Irish smoked salmon is prepared in the old Gaelic manner with capers and lemon for $8.25. Mixed-grill specialties, including pork or lamb chops, sausage, bacon, black pudding, and kidney and tomatoes, cost $16, but they're enough for two people. Although most of the kitchen help is Chinese, most of the waitresses and barmen speak Irish with a brogue. And folk musicians of international renown, including owner Tommy Makem, play here on a regular basis.

Open from noon to 2 a.m. Monday through Saturday; closed Sunday.

## ITALIAN

Jazz up a pasta meal by going to **Mimi's,** 984 Second Ave., at 52nd Street (tel. 688-4692). This Italian piano bar has a glassed-in terrace that looks out onto Second Avenue. Three stained-glass windows from an old temple serve as dividers between the terrace and main dining room. Tables are set with flowers in Perrier bottles. Mimi's has many loyal local patrons, who can often be found singing around the piano. Thursday and Friday are particularly crowded evenings.

Though many of the entrees may strain your budget, pasta dishes for dinner range from only $8 for spaghetti to $9 for fettuccine Alfredo. Chicken parmigiana is $10, and cacciatore is $9.50. For dessert, try spumoni or tortoni, both $1.50.

Open from noon to 4 a.m. Monday through Saturday and from 5 p.m. to midnight on Sunday.

**Ray's Original Pizza,** 961 Second Ave., at 51st Street (tel. 752-2143), serves thick Sicilian and thin Neapolitan pizzas. Ray's is frequented by customers wearing everything from Gucci's to rollerskates as the night wears on; rock music plays at a reasonable decibel, and the tables are simple. Slices start at $1.35 and whole pies begin at $7.50; sausage, ricotta and mozzarella cheese, green peppers, eggplant, and spinach are among the toppings and fillings you can order. You can also get calzones—a small "pizza-hero" sandwich—for $3 and up.

Ray's is open daily from 10 a.m. to about 2 a.m.

**Café Fonduta,** 120 E. 57th St., near Lexington Avenue (tel. 935-5699), offers light northern Italian fare and a pleasant atmosphere for conversation before or after the theater. Owner Luis Levero will usher you into the restaurant past a glass cabinet stocked with an excellent selection of Californian, French, and Italian wines. Be sure to taste the pasta dishes, among them: rigatti a quattro formaggio, with cheddar, swiss, fontina da osta, and parmesan cheeses, mushrooms, and zucchini; tagliarini and chopped spinach in a light cream sauce; fettucine Alfredo with vegetables and a cream sauce; and angel-hair fonduta, a mixture of pasta, tomatoes, and basil. All are $10 to $14.

Open weekdays from 11:30 a.m. to 10 p.m., on Saturday to 4 p.m. Closed Sunday.

With its wide windows and eclectic décor, **Pastamore,** 820 Second Ave., at 44th Street (tel. 983-4666), is a clean and cheerful spot to down a soul-enriching bowl of pasta. From angel hair primavera to fettuccine carbonara to linguine in clam sauce, all dishes are a reasonable $8. Another good bet is an individual pizzamore ($5) or a nine-inch traditional pizza for $8. The tartufo ($2.75) is worth saving room for. There is a minimum of $6 per person.

Open weekdays from 11 a.m. to 11 p.m. and weekends from 4 to 11 p.m.

Located in the Pan Am Building, **Trattoria,** 45th Street, between Vanderbilt and Lexington avenues (tel. 661-3090), is a lively spot for a fulfilling Italian repast. "The Trat," as it's known by the regular business-lunch crowd, offers an interesting range of pasta and fish, as well as some house specialties like risotto with parmesan cheese and asparagus ($12). The Caesar salad ($10) is a meal in itself, but you'll want to sample the carpaccio ($7) or an individual pizza with chicken and wild mushrooms ($11). And save room for the tiramisu, ladyfingers soaked in espresso with a layer of mascarpone mousse ($4). A friendly bar is available inside and on the outdoor patio, which is open from May to October, weather permitting.

Open Monday through Friday for breakfast from 7 to 11 a.m., for lunch from 11:30 a.m. to 5 p.m., for complimentary buffet from 5 to 7 p.m., and for dinner from 5 to 10 p.m.

## JAPANESE

The **Larmen Dosanko Noodle Shop,** 423 Madison Ave., between 48th and 49th streets (tel. 688-8575), features huge steaming bowls of noodles mixed with a variety of meats and vegetables. The décor is informal, with seats at the counter up front or in orange booths toward the back. While the Dosanko chain may strike you as the Japanese equivalent of "fast food," the noodles are good, inexpensive, and filling.

There are six larmen noodle dishes to choose from, and you can order any of them with beef or pork for $4.50. The chef's special, which changes daily, is $6. You can also order combination platters for between $5.75 and $6.25. Ice cream is served for dessert for $1.60. Alcoholic beverages are also served ($1.50 to $2.25).

Open from 11 a.m. to 10 p.m. Monday through Friday, and from noon to 8 p.m. on weekends. There are several Larmen Dosankos located elsewhere in the city.

Modern and stylish, **Hatsuhana**, 17 E. 48th St., between Fifth and Madison avenues (tel. 355-3345), offers exciting Japanese cuisine that is beautifully served. If you eat at the sushi bar, your orders will be served on ti leaves from Hawaii. The décor includes individual booths with blond-wood dividers and round portholes.

Prices are a little high, but the food is worth the splurge. A tempura luncheon with fried shrimp, seafood, and vegetables is $13.75. Salmon teriyaki is the same price. Dinners are more expensive, with specials ranging from $18 to $25. There are sushi items on the dinner menu for $15; sushi à la carte is $2.25 per piece.

Open Monday through Friday from 11:45 a.m. to 2:30 p.m. for lunch, and from 5:30 to 10 p.m. for dinner, and Saturday from 5 to 10 p.m. Closed Sunday. Reservations suggested.

## MEXICAN

Named for the Mayan Empire's sacred city of warriors, **Bonampak,** 235 E. 53rd St., between Second and Third avenues (tel. 838-1433), is authentically decorated with velvet paintings, desert plants in the window, and Mexican pottery and other curios displayed in nooks and crannies along the stucco walls. Pretty, multicolored blown-glass lamps give off a warm glow to the relaxed atmosphere.

Bonampak offers a mix of Tex-Mex and interior Mexican dishes. Try the chicken in unsweetened chocolate sauce for $8.75, or the beef with lime and garlic juice for $11. Combination platters with tacos, tostados, burritos, and tamales are reasonably priced from $5 at lunchtime. For dessert, we suggest the mangos flambés for $4. The menu is in both Spanish and English, and the staff is quite friendly.

Open from 11:30 a.m. to 10 p.m. Monday through Friday, and 5 to 10 p.m. on Saturday. Closed Sunday.

## MIXED BAG

For relief from the hustle of midtown, the **Citicorp Center,** which covers the block from 53rd to 54th streets, bordered by Lexington and Third avenues, is a greenery-filled escape. The three-story skylit atrium below the shimmering steel office tower with a dramatically angled roofline, is a bustling, but not hectic, arcade of shops and restaurants. Citicorp sponsors frequent concerts and exhibits in the central public space, and tables and chairs are scattered about, suited to brown-bagging and people-watching.

If you bring your own lunch, you can top it off with a freshly baked chocolate-chip cookie from the **Famous Chocolate Chip Cookie** on the second level. Variations on the chip theme are 60¢ to 70¢ apiece and about $6.50 a pound. Muffins are $1.20 each. Cookies and pastries are also sold at **Café Buon Giorno** on the main level. Soups, sandwiches, and quiche are also served for take-out only. The scents of freshly baked bread wafting across the main floor from **Au Bon Pain** (tel. 838-6996) are enough to send you heading for their take-out croissant sandwiches made with ham, turkey, salami, tuna, and French cheese ($3.25 and up). Breads, from rye to challah, are made fresh daily. No seating, only take-out.

If the weather is cooperative, take a stroll to the Citicorp plaza below Lexington Avenue, and stop at the **Bear Café**, famous in midtown for its cinnamon coffee at 65¢ a cup ($5.50 by the pound). The Bear also features stuffed potatoes, filled with your choice of nacho cheese, chili jalapeños, or sour cream ($2.75). Homemade soups include chicken vegetable and gazpacho. And to go with the fragrant coffee, homemade muffins ($1.25) in every conceivable flavor, from banana to cranberry, are made fresh daily.

Open daily from 6:30 a.m. until 7 p.m. (closes earlier on rainy days, and from December until April). Chairs and tables fill the plaza in warm weather, so you can have your lunch al fresco.

For less casual fare, there are seven other restaurants to choose from inside the Citicorp Center. Some can be expensive, but most offer weekly specials well worth the visit.

**Auberge Suisse** (tel. 421-1420) is an elegant restaurant, specializing in Swiss and French dishes. Prices are high for entrees, but they include a salad. A unique specialty here is fondue for two, for $19, which includes a salad and fresh, crusty bread for dipping into the bubbling cheese concoction. Other specialties include sautéed breast of chicken in tomato basil butter ($11), and veal sausage, St. Gallen style, with potatoes and onions ($10). Dessert here is truly a treat, thanks to the variety, from chocolate mousse to apple crêpes in Swiss pear brandy ($4 each). Appetizers are also unusual and reasonably priced, and two are ample for a meal.

Open Monday through Saturday from noon to 2:30 p.m. and 5 to 10 p.m.

**Avergino's** (tel. 688-8828), with white stucco walls and colorful hangings, and a kitchen open to full view, serves authentic Greek food like taramosalata, fish roe dip, at $5 for an appetizer (but ample) portion, stuffed grape leaves at $5 as an appetizer, and moussaka at $12. Lunch and dinner menus vary by a few dollars, with most entrees in the $10 to $15 range. Lunchtime here is sometimes frenetic, but always fun, with Greek music and waiters at your service. There is an $8 minimum per person from 11:30 a.m. until 2 p.m.

Open daily from 11:30 a.m. until 10:30 p.m.

**Charley O's Bar and Grill** (tel. 752-2102) has the feeling of an old pub: dark-green walls, copper lamps, brass-framed mirrors, and a large round clock. Tables in the dining room sport crisp white tablecloths and individual booths are separated by etched-glass dividers. Checkered-glass skylights in the back take in lots of natural light in the daytime.

Main courses at lunchtime are priced between $7.25 and $10. Meat sandwiches and hamburgers run between $6 and $9.50. You can also get large salads for $9 to $11.75, and omelets for $9. Desserts run between $2.75 and $3.50. There's a free hot-and-cold buffet (appetizers and hors d'oeuvres) during happy hour after 5 p.m. in the bar.

Open from 11:30 a.m. to 4 p.m. for lunch, from 4 to 9 p.m. for dinner on weekdays, from noon to 5 p.m. for brunch on the weekends.

**The Market** (tel. 935-1744) has a stand-up counter with tables, where you can get coffee and pastry as well as a limited number of sandwiches. Sandwiches run between $3.25 and $5.50. Pita specials (tuna melt, etc.) run between $5.25 and $5.75. Salad platters range from $2.75 to $6.75. Pastries range from $1 to $2.

Hours are 7:30 a.m. to 7:30 p.m. on weekdays, and 9 a.m. to 7 p.m. on weekends.

**Healthworks** (tel. 838-6221) is a busy health-food restaurant, brightly decorated with red chairs and green trim. There are daily specials like vegetarian lasagne ($6), as well as numerous salads and quiches for about $6. Fresh baked goods can be purchased for dessert, along with frozen yogurt. You can order items for take-out, but some take-out prices are more expensive.

Open from 7 a.m. to 9 p.m. weekdays, from 11 a.m. to 9 p.m. on Saturday, and from 11 a.m. to 6 p.m. on Sunday.

**Alfredo's** (tel. 371-3367), whose founder in Rome lays claim to the original recipe for fettuccine Alfredo, specializes—naturally—in pasta. Best bets here are the special Sunday brunch offerings, served from noon until 4 p.m. Brunch ($7.50) is a choice of soup, tomato juice or melon, along with your choice of an Italian omelet, eggs Benedict, any pasta, veal bocconcini, eggplant, or sautéed chicken. Dessert and coffee are also included. On the regular menu, veal and chicken dishes start around $13. Daily specials are $8.50 for dinner and $5.50 for lunch. Lunch is always a good buy, with fettuccine Alfredo at $8.50. Salads are included with specials.

Open from 11:30 a.m. until 11:30 p.m. weekdays and Saturday, and on Sunday from noon until 11:30 p.m.

**Les Tournebroches** (tel. 935-6029) is a quiet French enclave in the midst of the hustle of the Citicorp Center. Prices here can be high, but an evening special dinner for $11 is a bargain. It includes soup du jour, choice of roast half chicken, fish of the day, or mixed-grille brochette, salad, and coffee. Hors d'oeuvres here are also delicious, with pâté and truite fumée for $5.50. Clam chowder is $4; French onion soup, $3.50. Grilled swordfish is $17. The prices are all in the $11.50 to $20 range. Wine is $10 a carafe and is also sold by the glass. Lunch has a minimum of $11.50 per person.

Open Monday through Saturday from 11:30 a.m. to 3:30 p.m. and 5 to 10 p.m.

## MOROCCAN

Taking up hardly more than a parking space, **Teva,** 122 E. 42nd St., between Park and Lexington avenues (tel. 599-1265), is a Moroccan take-out gem in the basement of the Chanin Building. If you can find it, the rewards are numerous. The food is kosher, vegetarian, and great. Sandwiches in pita are very filling, falafel is $2.75, and the excellent hummus is $3.25 for a sandwich. One special to look for is the couscous platter for $2.50. If you like things spicy, ask for the harissa pepper sauce, and to cool fired-up taste buds, try the yogurt sesame sauce.

Open Monday through Friday from 7 a.m. to 4 p.m. Closed weekends.

## NATURAL FOODS

Naturally beautiful people flock to **Au Natural,** 1043 Second Ave., at 55th Street (tel. 832-2922), where butcher-block tables, tiles, mirrors, and fresh flowers give the place the feel of a designer's kitchen nook. Among the many entrees are soybean steak and vegetables for $10.50 and vegetable fettuccine for $12.50. Salads, omelets, yogurt, and juices round out the menu. Sunday brunch features cottage-cheese blintzes for $6.50, and eggs Benedict au naturel with a country chicken sausage patty for $8.

Hours are 8 a.m. to midnight daily, with brunch served on Sunday from 10 a.m. to 3 p.m.

## SEAFOOD

Boasting fresh fish that's caught right off Montauk Point, **Hobeau's,** 882 First Ave., between 49th and 50th streets (tel. 421-2888), is a midtown seafood find, if you don't mind a packed house. With a typically nautical interior, Hobeau's is best for lunch, as dinner prices generally run $1 or $1.50 more for most dishes, and the service is fast and no-nonsense. (You're even entitled to a free cocktail if your waiter doesn't tell you his name or he forgets to take your drink order—it doesn't happen often.) Fish is it at Hobeau's, and from fried shrimp stuffed with crabmeat ($6.25) to a mixed seafood platter ($10), the fish is the main attraction. There are also poultry and beef entrees—from $5.25 for a hamburger platter to steak teriyaki for $7, and steak and crab legs for $14. Appetizers include oysters Rockefeller ($1.25 each) and baked mushrooms stuffed with shrimp and crabmeat ($4). Lobsters range from $11 for a 1¼-pound crustacean to twin pound-and-a-quarters for $19 ($5 charge for sharing twin lobsters). Brunch, which comes with a half carafe of Bloody Marys, screwdrivers, wine, or beer, is $6 on Saturday, Sunday, and holidays.

Hobeau's is open for lunch from 11:30 a.m. until 4 p.m. daily, for brunch from 11:30 a.m. until 4 p.m. on Saturday, Sunday, and holidays, and for dinner from 4 p.m. until 3 a.m. daily.

The graceful arches of Grand Central Terminal are echoed in the **Oyster Bar and Restaurant** in the station's lower concourse, East 42nd Street, between Vanderbilt and Lexington avenues (tel. 490-6650). Here the tiled arches are festooned with white lights, giving them an added elegance. The large restaurant has a main dining room, counter service for quick meals, a cocktail lounge, and a redwood-paneled saloon. Opened in the 1930s when trains were widely used, the restaurant serves up seafood with style. There is a take-out booth modeled after a ship's deck for commuters on the go.

The seafood is all fresh, and the menu changes daily to accommodate the current catch. Prices are high, but you can get oyster stew for $9 and pan-roasted oysters for $9.50. Broiled fish runs between $17 and $26, and main dishes like bouillabaisse and coquilles St-Jacques are $21.50 and $22 respectively. Lobster is $21 a pound.

Open Monday through Friday from 11:30 a.m. to 10:30 p.m. The last seating is at 9:30 p.m., and reservations should be made for both lunch and dinner.

---

# 3. Upper East Side and Yorkville

East of Central Park at Fifth Avenue, between 61st and 96th Streets, is what New Yorkers call the Upper East Side. Once pooh-poohed by Village and SoHo types who found it too plastic, and scorned by Upper West Siders proud to be "roughing it," the Upper East Side has a chic all its own. It is home to young professionals and established executives. On Madison Avenue in the 60s you'll find some of the world's most exclusive shops, and on Park Avenue you'll see the brass shingles of Park Avenue doctors, renowned for their skill—and fees! And you'll also find traces of old German New York, in the 80s along First and Second avenues in the area still known as Yorkville. Along the East River there is everything from modest apartments of five-story walkups to the beautiful homes of Sutton Place—some of the most expensive real estate in the country. The East Side is also home to the mayor. Gracie Mansion, his manor house at 89th Street and East End Avenue, is the last remaining 19th-century country seat on the East River. It's no longer country up here, but there's lots of good walking—and eating—to be done!

## AMERICAN/CONTINENTAL
Exclusive Park Avenue has a neighborhood secret in the Armory at 643 Park Ave. at 66th Street—a restaurant with good food at reasonable prices. It's the **Seventh Regiment Mess** (tel. 744-4107), run by the U.S. Army! In spite of all the combat fatigues you'll see in the Armory, the public is welcome and the mood at ease. We think you'll agree that the Mess is a unique find!

You can't miss the Armory—this 19th-century red-brick building occupies the whole block. You enter through massive wooden doors studded with iron. Tell one of the soldiers inside the door that you'd like to go to the Mess—he'll show you to the elevator to the left side of the Great Hall. Take time to look around. The Grand Staircase is grand indeed, and the Great Hall is full of antique cannons, military portraits, and flags that are black with age and so thin you can see through them. The Mess is on the fourth floor.

You can take a drink first in the long lounge, where there are comfortable green tweed sofas, red leather chairs, and small metal plaques on the walls honoring members of the Seventh. The dining room, like the lounge, has a beamed ceiling, half-timbered walls, and mounted heads of long-dead moose and rams. The dining room also has a beautiful wood floor, tables covered with blue and white linen, and pleasant waitresses. Entrees come with tomato juice, consommé, or the day's soup, as well as vegetable, potato, and coffee. Most prices are under $14. Choices include scrod or fried butterfly shrimp ($10), baked manicotti ($7), chicken à la Seventh au gratin ($8.50), and chef's salad ($6). Desserts are $2.50.

The Mess is open weekdays only, from 5 to 9 p.m. (*Note:* The restaurant closes for the summer, late June until Labor Day.)

**Mumbles,** 1622 Third Ave., at 91st Street (tel. 427-4355), has been home-away-from-home for legions of East Side singles, many of whom live just down the block in the massive Ruppert Towers. Mumbles even looks homey, with wooden shingles inside and out, multipaned windows with lots of plants in them, a timbered ceiling, a well-trod wood floor, and small tables covered with green-and-white checkered cloths. Most of Mumbles' menu and all the specials are written on blackboards—the fare runs from hamburgers to veal marsala. Most items cost less than $10. (See the Murray Hill/Gramercy Park section for more details on the extensive menu.)

Mumbles keeps longer hours than most of us did at home, however. It's open daily from noon to 4 a.m. Food is available until 2 or 3 a.m., but for the day's specials, come before 11 p.m. After that you can still have sandwiches, salads, and steaks. No reservations.

The newest **Mumbles,** 1491 Second Ave., at 78th Street (tel. 772-8817), is all white and airy. You can dine inside near the bar or in a glass-enclosed terrace decorated with lush green plants. When the weather's warm, the sidewalk surrounding the restaurant becomes a lively outdoor café—an excellent spot to relax and people-watch. Open daily from 11:30 a.m. to 4 a.m.

**The Green Kitchen,** 1477 First Ave., at 77th Street (tel. 988-4163), is a fancy coffeeshop with something for everyone. There's an oval-shaped area with your basic booth set-up; but there's also a small bar, and an attractive restaurant-style porch with tablecloths, fresh flowers, and glass walls.

The extensive menu also has a little of everything. There are "Famous Salads," for $6.25 and up, and sandwiches for $2.75 and up. Most popular here are the daily chef's specials. For $7.25 you can have your choice of entree—veal, beef, pasta, chicken, or fish—served with soup, salad, and homemade dessert. The dessert choices are vast, with prices starting at $1.35. All desserts are baked on the premises. Chocolate cheesecake, assorted pastries, fruit pies, layer cakes, and cookies are under glass and temptingly on display.

The Green Kitchen is open 24 hours daily. And there's brunch too, from noon to 4 p.m. on weekends.

In this age of diversity it's nice to find a place that does one thing and does it cheaply and extremely well. **Chicken Kitchen,** 301 E. 80th St., at Second Avenue (tel. 517-8350), does exactly that. Succulent char-broiled chicken is the name of the game here, and we think it's at the top of the chicken-restaurant pecking order. The interior is tasteful and simple. High-backed carved wooden chairs, butcher-block tables, and marble counter tops adorn this small split-level, black-and-white tile-floored establishment. The chicken is cooked on an open grill and the walls are covered with what can only be called "chicken arcana," obscure facts and drawings of the mighty bird.

The menu is even simpler than the décor: broiled, juicy, flavorful chicken, $4.25 for a half and $8 for a whole. Each order comes with pita bread and a choice of quite delectable homemade sauces, including cranberry, barbecue, hot Mexican salsa, or a mustard curry. Side orders of gourmet rice, spinach and rice, tabouli, green salad, slaw, or potato salad can be had for less than $2.

Chicken Kitchen also has free delivery in 30 minutes to anywhere in the city. They have several other branches, located at 1177 Second Ave., at the corner of 62nd Street (tel. 308-9400); 982 Second Ave., at the corner of 52nd Street (tel. 980-5252); and 461 Sixth Ave., at the corner of 11th Street (tel. 929-1100).

It may have something to do with the way New Yorkers look at the rest of the world. There's only one real Jackson Hole, but there are **Jackson Hole Hamburger Restaurants** all over the Upper East Side. They're everything from the very small original restaurant to the glass-walled spaciousness of the one at 91st Street and Madison Avenue. They all have attractive if simple décor, ski posters of a Wyoming

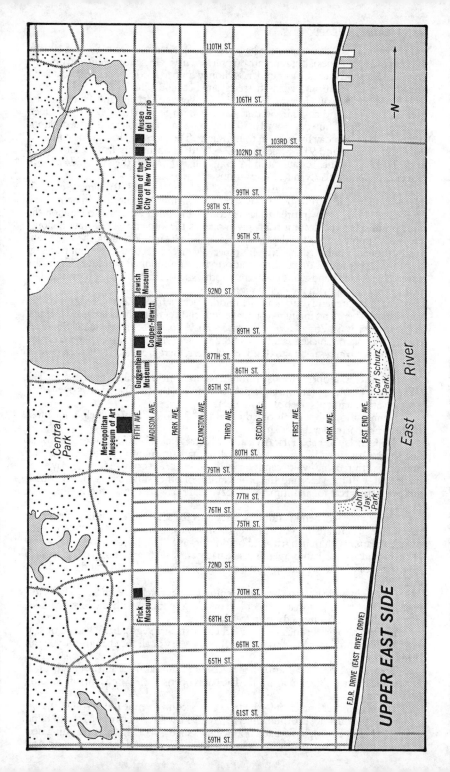

ski resort, and good, inexpensive hamburgers. Prices range from $4 to $10 (the highest the menu goes), but most are $6 or less. There's lots more: eggs and omelets for $3 to $6; sandwiches, most under $4; honey-dipped fried chicken with salad and french fries for $6.50; and salads, desserts, and beer and wine.

There are Jackson Holes at 232 E. 64th St., between Second and Third avenues (tel. 371-7187), and at 1633 Second Ave., at 85th Street (tel. 737-8788). Open Monday through Thursday from 10:30 a.m. to 1 a.m., on Friday and Saturday until 4 a.m., and on Sunday from noon to midnight. The Jackson Hole at the corner of Madison Avenue and 91st Street (tel. 427-2820) is open daily from 7 a.m. to 11 p.m. There is another restaurant in Murray Hill and one on the West Side at 85th Street and Columbus Avenue. Reservations not needed.

**J. G. Melon,** 1291 Third Ave., at 74th Street (tel. 650-1310), is made irresistibly charming by its profusion of—what else?—melons: in painting, in neon, even in the real thing. A few retired squash racquets and other objects also hang on the brown walls, but the décor is really given over to the kith and kin of watermelons, etc. J. G. simply stands for the owners, Jack and George. We think the restaurant (really more of a pub) is delightful. It's especially nice to get one of the four tables up front in the bar room, tucked on a platform under mullioned windows. Tables are covered with green-and-white checkered cloths, and the high ceiling is reddish tin—perhaps in keeping with the melon motif.

The tiny kitchen is smack in the middle, across from the bar. From it comes simple fare. There's no menu—you make your choices from the blackboard listings. A hamburger is $4.75; a bacon burger, $5.50. A roast beef sandwich is $5.75. A chef's, Niçoise, or chicken salad costs $8.25. There are also entrees like a Cornish hen with potato and salad for $10.25. For dessert, there are pies ($3.50) and cheesecake ($4).

J. G. Melon is open Monday through Saturday from 11:30 a.m. to 4 a.m. The West Side J. G. Melon (at Amsterdam Avenue and 76th Street) kitchen is open until 1 a.m. Both restaurants open at noon on Sunday.

We are curious about only one thing at J. G. Melon—why no melon liqueur at the bar? The bartender didn't know.

**T.G.I. Friday's,** 1152 First Ave., at 63rd Street (tel. 832-8512), was New York's first singles bar. It's still a show-stopping landmark, in an outrageously blue corner building with red-and-white candy-striped awnings at every window. Friday's has mellowed with the years and the proliferation of other singles bars, but the small tables are still great for an intimate rendezvous. Friday's décor is a fun hodgepodge of Victoriana.

The eight-page menu is full of suggestions for solid American fare. Prices are reasonable. There are 11 ways to order a hamburger, including the "name your own"; a platter with french fries and onion rings is $7.75. Burgers come on an English muffin or on hamburger buns. Salads are $7.25 and up. The soup-and-sandwich combo is $7. Four-egg omelets with fries, rolls and butter, and a salad start at $7.25.

Entrees include London broil and lemon-pepper chicken, each $11. The "Outrageous Dessert" is just that—chocolate pudding spooned with chocolate chunks, marshmallows, and whipped cream ($4.50).

You can also get brunch—juice; french toast; three eggs; ham, bacon, or sausage; English muffin; coffee or tea; and a Bloody Mary or all the champagne you can drink—for $10.

Open daily from 11:30 a.m. till the wee hours. On Saturday and Sunday brunch is available from 11:30 a.m. to 4 p.m. The bar is open till 1:30 or 3 a.m., depending on the crowd.

There's another branch at 94th Street and Second Avenue (tel. 410-3420).

From the outside, **Brother Jimmy's,** 1572 First Ave., between 81st and 82nd streets (tel. 288-0933), looks like a bootlegger's shed. A corrugated tin awning decorated with melon-size plastic lights shades the entrance to this barbecue joint. And although the interior looks more like a garage than a restaurant, the food is excellent and the prices unbeatable. The unfinished studded walls and whitewashed brick are lined with baseball caps, cowboy hats, and road signs from North Carolina and Texas. Up front in the bar, Skee Ball and a wide selection of beer keeps the crowd happy. In the back, Duke University, North Carolina State, and University of North Carolina bumper stickers cover an old Nordge refrigerator. And in the corner, a 26-inch color console television is silently on.

Back in the dining room, pull your silverware out from the wax-paper folders and dig into the complimentary cole slaw, a fattening but delicious treat. Start with the bucket of chicken wings ($9)—if you're with a crowd, it will feed six. For dinner, there's trout, catfish, a few Mexican entrees, or a whole slew of barbecued sandwiches ($4.25 to $10). The specialty of the house is barbecued pork or chicken. Smoked over hickory wood for 12 to 20 hours, it's tender and satisfying. Try the half chicken ($7.50), or the southern-style ribs ($9) slathered in a spicy vinegar sauce. All dinner entrees are less than $10 and include a vegetable, cornbread, and a generous portion of thick, chunky mashed potatoes with gravy. Brother Jimmy's also offers something that hungry Upper East Side kids and parents have been eagerly awaiting—a Li'l Tykes menu. It's a scaled-down version of the main offerings. The prices, likewise, are scaled down, running from $1.75 to $2.25 for an entree served with potatoes (mashed or fried) and a green vegetable. Clean your plate and Brother Jimmy will give the li'l tyke a free bowl of sherbet.

Brother Jimmy's serves dinner from 5 p.m. to midnight Sunday through Thursday, and until 1 a.m. on Friday and Saturday. The bar stays open as long as there's a crowd, which is usually 2 or 3 a.m.

If you're downtown, check out Jimmy's cousin, **Brother's Bar-B-Q,** 228 W. Houston St., between Sixth Avenue and Varick Street (tel. 727-2775).

**Ruppert's,** 1662 Third Ave., at 93rd Street (tel. 831-1900), takes its name from the former Jacob Ruppert Brewery, once across the street. Its fame comes from its elegant décor, good food, and refreshing prices. Ruppert's is serenely modern, with grays, maroons, and touches of brass at the bar rail and at the stairs to the split-level dining room in back. The two-story ceiling is black and has overhead fans turning lazily. Ruppert's' 54-foot bar is stunning—a gleaming mahogany structure that spent its first 50 years in a newspaperman's bar downtown.

Lunch prices are under $9. Poached eggs over chicken strips on a toasted croissant is $6.75, an omelet with a wide choice of stuffings runs $5.75, and a chicken breast sandwich with peppers and onions goes for $7. There are reasonably priced entrees, such as curried chicken salad with apples and chutney for $7 and penne with eggplant, tomatoes, and fresh mozzarella for $6.25. The waiter will tell you the day's desserts. At dinner there are entrees like chicken breast and brandy mustard ($10.50), grilled leg of lamb with mint mustard ($14), and chicken pot pie ($10). Dinner entrees range from $4.25 to $16; appetizers, from $4 for strips of chicken breast with honey-mustard sauce to $6 for Little Neck clams on the half shell.

We think Ruppert's is at its most lovely at brunch. There's usually a musician playing—a classical pianist, or a guitarist playing mellow '60s music. There are a variety of omelets ($7); other choices include eggs Benedict ($8) or smoked salmon, tomato, onion, and cream cheese on a bagel ($10). Or you might go light and choose an appetizer of fresh melon ($4) and a croissant with fruit preserves ($2.25). Brunch entrees come with a complimentary drink, glass of wine or juice, and coffee or tea.

Ruppert's is open daily from 11:30 a.m. to 4 a.m. Lunch is served until 4:30 p.m.; dinner, from 5 p.m. to 12:30 a.m. Brunch is Saturday and Sunday from 11 a.m. to 4 p.m. There's also live music every night of the week. Reservations recommended.

**Rascal's,** 1286 First Ave., at the corner of 69th Street (tel. 734-2862), is a large, friendly bar-restaurant that attracts an upscale crowd. It offers a standard continental menu, including pasta, seafood, and chops. Dinner specials, served every night between 5 p.m. and midnight, range from $9.50 to $15. On weekends brunch is served from 11:30 a.m. to 4:45 p.m., offering an entree, rolls and fruit, coffee or tea, and all the Bloody Marys or mimosas you can drink, for $13. Sunday brunch is a local tradition at Rascal's.

Rascal's is open from 11:30 a.m. to 4 a.m. seven days a week and no reservations are necessary.

**Mr. Babbington's Restaurant,** 1568 Third Ave., at the corner of 88th Street (tel. 860-1980), remains one of New York's true bargains. Most of its business comes from delivery, take-out, and catering, but the lucky few who visit the restaurant are in for a treat. The plant-filled windows, open kitchen, tile floors, and still-life murals of flowers, fish, and produce combine to give the restaurant a rustic, homey feel.

But the real beauty here is the high quality and low prices of the food. After starting with spicy chicken wings ($2), you might try the pit-grilled half chicken with plum sauce ($7.75) or the poached scrod in white wine and herb sauce ($7.25). All dinner entrees include a help-yourself salad bar and bread basket brimming with fresh-baked pumpernickle and corn muffins. If you still have room for dessert, order the deep-dish apple pie with ice cream, chocolate-fudge cake with chocolate whipped cream, or the hot peach pancake and ice cream, each under $2. You can easily enjoy a complete dinner with appetizer, entree, dessert, and coffee for under $14. Bring your own beer or wine, as the restaurant does not serve alcohol.

Mr. Babbington's serves lunch Monday through Saturday from 11:30 a.m. to 4 p.m. (The lunch prices are unbeatable.) Dinner is served daily from 5 to 10:30 p.m. There's also Sunday brunch served from 11:30 a.m. to 4 p.m. for $11.

**Jim McMullen's,** 1341 Third Ave., near 76th Street (tel. 861-4700), is where many of New York's "beautiful people" go to unwind. This successful restaurant is always crowded with well-dressed people, a sprinkling of celebrities among them. It's an attractive place, with huge vases of flowers, random-width plank floorboards, and exposed brick walls with decorated wood panels. The dining room is more spacious than the elbow-to-elbow bar. Tables are covered with maroon cloths, with white linen set over that. A lavish flower arrangement dresses up each table. Waiters are dressed preppy in white oxford shirts, blue pants or skirts, and black bow ties. There is also an atrium where you can dine overlooking a garden.

The menu is not inexpensive, so stick to the low side. You might start with mozzarella salad ($3.50 at lunch, $4.75 at dinner). Lunch prices start at $6.50 for a club sandwich and go upward of $14. On the low side of the menu are omelets, salads (chicken salad with walnuts, oranges, red onion, and Roquefort gets our attention any day), pastas, and chicken pot pie. Dinner choices range from broiled chicken ($11.50) to a veal loin chop ($19.50). Most prices are in the $14 range. Served with your meal is a bread basket filled with hot buttermilk biscuits and cornbread. Specials change daily, including the wine specials.

This is not the place to skip dessert, thanks to the resident pastry chef. Try the chocolate-brownie pie or cheesecake.

Open daily from 11:30 a.m. till 3 a.m. (food served until 1:30 a.m.). No reservations.

**Camelback & Central,** 1403 Second Ave., at the corner of 73rd Street (tel. 249-8380), has a minimalist décor that is somehow perfect for fine dining. The floor is bare wood, but the center banquette is carpeted. Windows are great expanses of glass, and the brick walls are painted a creamy white. Exquisite floral arrangements, Chagall-like pastel paintings, and more flowers at the tables are the only decoration, and the art deco bar is the oldest thing to be found. The staff is friendly and the food excellent.

There's no need here to go to the high end of the menu to find a superlative dinner (although entrees do go as high as $19 for a grilled veal chop). Pasta Camelback is an exotic combination with plum tomatoes, cilantro, browned anchovy, garlic, and oil, or try the vegetable tempura, each under $12. Roast duck with a port wine–currant sauce is superb ($16). Fresh swordfish with herb or anchovy butter ($17) is an equal delight; you may also find swordfish as a special with the likes of a caper-and-mushroom sauce—making choices difficult. All entrees come with potato, rice, or barley and a vegetable. Desserts here are rich and chocolate-laced—fruit and ice-cream parfait with chocolate sauce, apple fritters with chocolate-brandy sauce, chocolate sin, and chocolate silk pie (priced $2.75 to $5). Certainly one of the city's best culinary buys is the pre-theater dinner offered from 5 to 6:30 p.m. For $15 you have your choice of soups, a salad, a choice of five tempting entrees with rice, barley, or potato, vegetable, dessert, and coffee or tea.

Expect the same inspiration in the weekend brunch. For $12 you can savor a drink, an appetizer (mostly fruits or fruit-based), and an entree such as sautéed whitefish in strawberry sauce, vegetable tempura, or eggs Benedict. The maître d' will tell you with unabashed pride that it's the best brunch on the East Side. Lunch is simpler than dinner and brunch, and comparably lower in price. The soup of the day is a good opener ($3), and there's a seafood antipasto with squid, shrimp, and scallops ($6). Lunch entrees are as American as a hamburger with cottage fries ($6.25), and as European as a pâté salad plate ($8), the highest-priced entree on the luncheon menu.

In the summer, on clear days and mellow Manhattan evenings, the outdoor café is open for lunch, brunch, and drinks.

Lunch is served weekdays from 11:30 a.m. to 3 p.m., and dinner is served weekdays from 5 to 11:30 p.m., weekends till midnight. Camelback & Central is open for brunch on Saturday from 11:30 a.m. to 3:30 p.m. and on Sunday until 4 p.m.

Reservations are usually required. The name, by the way, comes from a crossroads in Phoenix, Arizona—we're glad it migrated this way.

The slogan at the **Polo Grounds,** 1472 Third Ave., between 84th and 85th streets (tel. 570-5590), is "big drinks, good food, great sports." They get a nod from us on all three. Named after the one-time home of baseball's New York Giants, the Polo Grounds offers a selection of over 100 beers from 25 countries; excellent burgers, steak, chicken, and fresh fish; and 11 video screens and an electronic board that continuously updates every conceivable sports score.

The theme here is sports, but don't look for any hot, sweaty jocks. The Polo Grounds draws families, connoisseurs of imported beer, and of course, sports enthusiasts. The walls are covered with sports memorabilia. Even the waiters and waitresses get into the act. They're decked out in the old-style New York Giants baseball jerseys.

The menu pays tribute to many of the great players and coaches who played at the Polo Grounds as well as some of the great players of today. The appetizers, or "starting line-up" as they're called, are under $5. The roster includes Tom Terrific (shrimp cocktail), Pee Wee Reese (a small portion of buffalo chicken wings), and Current Yankee Manager (a different soup every day). For a light meal, order from the "munchies" section. Choose from pizza, chicken nachos, hamburgers, or turkey club and roast beef sandwiches ($5.50 to $9). For a more substantial meal, try the Tony Lazzeri, a grilled sirloin steak with shoestring potatoes ($13); or the John McGraw, sautéed breast of chicken with fresh tarragon and artichoke hearts ($9).

Dinner is served daily from 5 p.m. to midnight. Brunch is served on Saturday and Sunday from noon to 5 p.m. The bar is open until 2 a.m.

If you're hungry for some authentic New Orleans fare, look no further than **Ruby's River Road Café and Bar,** 1754 Second Ave., near 91st Street (tel. 348-2328). The theme is Mississippi Delta. Up front in the bar, the casual, post-college crowd taps their feet to the music of James Brown and Professor Longhair as they slug Delta Beer and gator shots beneath a ceiling covered with three-foot-long plastic alligators. Beyond the bar and the open jaws of two mammoth alligator skulls lies the dining room, where ceiling fans turn lazily above the mauve, gray, turquoise, and black faux-snakeskin tables and chairs.

For an appetizer, try the fiery okra-and-chicken gumbo ($4.50), or our favorite, spicy crab and corn hushpuppies ($5.50). For the main course, jambalaya with grilled sausage and chicken ($10) is one Louisiana specialty that's guaranteed to light your mouth on fire. On the cooler side, try the Sunset Salad, with grilled chicken, fresh spinach, water chestnuts, and mandarin oranges ($11.50).

Ruby's is open daily from 5 p.m. to 3 a.m. The full menu is served from 6 to 11 p.m., and a smaller bar menu is offered until 1 a.m.

## LIGHT AND GRACIOUS

**The Summerhouse,** 50 E. 86th St., at Madison Avenue (tel. 249-6300), is an airy café with a pleasing simplicity. Statuesque floral arrangements and a stunning carousel horse from bygone days are in the windows. Tables are set with white linens, fresh flowers, and candles; chairs are turn-of-the-century oak with high backs. A simulated screen-porch setting keeps things informal.

The menu is appropriately light and summery. A crab cake on an English muffin and a curried chicken salad are each priced at $10.50. An omelet filled with spinach and sour cream is $8.50. A large bowl of Texas chili and a house salad runs $9.25. Lunch prices are about $10, and up to $17 for dinner. For Saturday and Sunday brunch, in addition to the luncheon entrees, there are fluffy pancakes with a seasonal fruit topping at $9.50, and eggs Benedict at $11. A particularly nice touch with every meal is the strawberry butter served with a basket of warm biscuits.

The Summerhouse is open from 11:30 a.m. to 11 p.m., except on Saturday and Sunday when it's open from noon to 11 p.m. Reservations taken only for dinner.

**Sarabeth's,** 1295 Madison Ave., near 92nd Street (tel. 410-7335), is a pastry-lover's dream. It's also a lovely place for a drink, tea, or a meal—morning, noon, or night. The restaurant is early American, with parquet floors, gray marble tables, magnificent sprays of fresh flowers, crown moldings, and rosettes at the ceiling. If you're lucky the gracious Sarabeth (yes, there *really* is a Sarabeth) will be on hand to advise you about the daily specials.

At Sarabeth's you can have omelets any time of the day, apple butter, and cheddar cheese among them, for $6.50 to $8.25. Brunch—including porridge with honey, wheatberries, brown sugar and raisins, and/or bananas—is served until 4:30 p.m. daily. There are always daily specials at dinner. Regular entrees include tortellini with zucchini, wild-mushroom ravioli with fresh basil, chives, and walnuts ($14.50), and chicken breast braised in a white wine and mustard sauce ($15).

The pastries can't be missed—even if you have to take your sticky buns, elephant ears, and fabulous double-chocolate-chip cookies home with you! You may also be tempted to buy one of the delicious homemade preserves (even at $8 a jar).

Sarabeth's is open daily from 9 a.m. to 10:30 p.m. Brunch is served until 3 p.m.; dinner begins at 6 p.m. Reservations accepted for dinner only.

Across the park, the **West Side Sarabeth's,** 423 Amsterdam Ave., at 80th Street (tel. 496-6280), is a spacious, dressier restaurant with a slightly more extensive menu. The delectable pastries and breads are the same though, and there's a bakery in which to indulge the whims of every sweet-tooth.

**Hanratty's,** 1410 Madison Ave., near 97th Street (tel. 369-3420), is a congenial neighborhood spot, decorated with tasteful simplicity. The attractive, long wooden bar runs almost the length of the restaurant, and a large blackboard announces the daily specials. You can sit at a table by the window or in the more private dining area beyond the bar. There are candles on the table at dinner, and flowers in glass vases.

Most of the dinner entrees are available for under $15 and are served with a choice of two side orders—salads, vegetable, potato or rice. The daily pasta and beef specials are about $11; seafood specials are priced at $12 to $15. Always on the menu are sandwiches and salads, from a hamburger on English muffin ($5.50) to a grilled chicken salad ($9). You can find out about desserts from the blackboard. Lunch is reasonable with a large selection of hot and cold sandwiches from $3.50 for a hamburger, to $5.75 for the elaborate Hanratty's sandwich (turkey, avocado, bacon, and lettuce). For a lighter lunch, there's a bowl of chili ($3.50) or homemade soup ($2.50). For weekend brunch, entrees and salads ($8 and under) are served with your choice of two drinks.

Open 11:30 a.m. to 4 p.m. Monday through Friday for lunch, and on Saturday and Sunday for brunch. Dinner is served from 5 to 11:30 p.m. daily. The bar closes somewhere between 2:30 and 4 a.m., according to the whims and energy levels of the customers.

## CHINESE

**Szechuan Kitchen,** 1460 First Ave., at 76th Street (tel. 249-4615), is one of those small, favorite eating places that New Yorkers try to keep to themselves. This simple, cozy restaurant is always packed, but everyone's friendly and the wait is worthwhile. If it's a very busy night you'll be issued a number, but there's a bench to sit on which gives you time to decide what to choose as you watch the waiters bustle by with tempting platters of food. The glass-topped tables are close together so it's not unusual here to get to know your neighbors. When we were there, enthusiastic devoted customers were describing entrees to newcomers at adjoining tables.

For starters, try the cold sesame noodles ($3.50) or the spring roll ($1.50). All the main dishes are reasonably priced; most expensive is the widely praised hot spiced lobster meat at $13. Try the chef's special chicken (diced chicken with vegetables and pine nuts) at $7.75, beef with broccoli at $7, string beans with garlic sauce at $6, or the hot spiced ginger shrimp at $8.25. Fried-rice dishes are $6 and under.

Open daily for dinner only, from 5 to 10:30 p.m. No reservations.

## CZECHOSLOVAKIAN

For more than 35 years **Vasata,** 339 E. 75th St., between First and Second avenues (tel. 988-7166), has been a jewel of a restaurant with true European charm and simplicity. The interior is as warm as the friendly people who run it like a Czech country inn. Soft light from coach lamps illuminates the wood-beamed ceilings and stucco walls of this long, cozy dining room. There is a highly polished wood bar tucked away near the entrance across from old photographs of Prague. Tables, set simply with white linen and fresh flowers, are nestled farther back. Lovely old pieces of Czech pottery decorate the surrounding walls. Appetizers are all around the $5 mark, and include such Czech favorites as eggs à la Prague for $4.50, or head cheese with onions and homemade duck liver pâté with pistachios, each $5.50. There is also a constantly changing menu of homemade soups for $3.25 a bowl, the best of which is the famous cream of mushroom. Entrees come with a choice of two fresh vegetables, and range from $10 to $18. Roast duck Vasata ($13.25), and roast loin of pork ($12.25) are the most popular. But schnitzel Cordon Bleu ($14.50), and Prague filet of beef in red wine sauce and crisp onions ($15) follow close behind. But don't let the regular menu distract you from the daily specials, which include boiled beef in dill sauce ($12.25) and of course, Szekely goulash ($12).

If you still have room for dessert, you're in luck, for delicious desserts abound. The traditional palacinty, thin crêpes filled with apricot preserves or chocolate, are $3. And for $1.50 more you can have them flamed in brandy or Cointreau. The brandied chocolate mousse is $3.50. There is a wide assortment of after-dinner liqueurs, or you can mix your tea with a little 160-proof Austrian rum for $4.50.

If you should visit Vasata between October and March on a Thursday night, you can order their game of the week. Leg of venison, wild hare, roast goose and pheasant, or wild duck are all possible treats.

Open from 5 to 11 p.m. Tuesday through Saturday and from noon to 10 p.m. on Sunday. Reservations are suggested.

## ENGLISH

We love **Drake's Drum,** an English pub at 1629 Second Ave., between 84th and 85th streets (tel. 988-2826). It's favored by rugby players (which one owner used to be and one still is), homesick Brits and other Europeans, and neighborhood fans. Drake's Drum is appropriately dim, with lanterns, dark wood, red-and-white checkered tablecloths, sawdust on the floor, and huge, wonderful oil paintings, including one of the restaurant's interior. Regulars crowd the copper-topped bar to watch the latest world sports competition. The pillars, wound with thick rope from floor to ceiling, are good to lean against if you can't get a bar seat. In warm weather you can dine outdoors under the sidewalk awning. Prices for food are very, very low.

There's an unbeatable lunch special—with a $2 beer or drink, you get a free quarter-pound hamburger on a roll, weekdays from 11:30 a.m. to 4 p.m. Other lunch prices are (almost) as good. You can try a chef's salad for $4.75, a ham-and-cheese omelet with french fries for $5, or a steak sandwich with salad and potato for $6. Dinner prices are slightly higher. The dinner menu also features entrees like chicken parmigiana, pub-style fish and chips, southern fried chicken, broiled scrod, and yes, even quiche—all with varying combinations of salad, french fries or baked potato, rice, and vegetable. The "Draught and Steak" is a good deal with a 12-ounce sirloin, salad, and baked potato, and choice of 32-ounce pitcher of beer or 16-ounce carafe of wine for $13.50. Also, check the menu for nightly low-priced specials; and on British holidays like St. George's Day (April 23), look for extra-specials like "toad in the hole," "bangers and mash," and roast beef with Yorkshire pudding.

Drake's Drum has two weekend brunch selections—the "Rugby," with a charcoal-broiled steak, two eggs, bacon, french fries, English muffin, and a 16-ounce pitcher of sangría or a Bloody Mary for $8; or the "Bicycle," with french toast, bacon, and sangría or a Bloody Mary for $5.50.

Lunch is served daily from noon to 4 p.m., and dinner is from 5 p.m. to 1 a.m. (on Friday and Saturday till 2 a.m.). Brunch is from noon to 4:30 p.m. on Saturday and Sunday. Drake's Drum is open for drinks nightly until the early hour of 4 a.m. No reservations needed.

## GERMAN

Years ago thousands of German families called the Upper East 80s home. Today, even though many have moved away, you'll see that their German influence still makes this an interesting neighborhood. Stroll down East 86th Street between Second and Third avenues, where even the newsstands carry German papers. You might want to stop at the **Bremen House,** 220 E. 86th St. (tel. 288-5500; open between 9:30 a.m. and 7:15 p.m. Monday through Saturday), for a look at everything from imported Belgian pâté to German crystal lamps. And there are plenty of restaurants here, from plain to fancy, many of them German.

**Ideal,** 238 E. 86th St., between Second and Third avenues (tel. 535-0950), is a straightforward luncheonette that's been serving hearty food since 1932. There are a few tables, a long lunch counter stacked with reserves of beer, and fluorescent lighting overhead. Ideal has a character all its own, and it's a good place to eat for $7 or less. A meal of Yankee pot roast with potatoes and red cabbage is $7, as is schweinebraten (fresh ham with sauerkraut and potatoes). Lamb stew is $7.25; potato pancakes with applesauce costs $5. For the more adventurous, there are pigs' knuckles with sauerkraut and potatoes, or liver dumplings, both priced at $6.25. In addition, most meat sandwiches are about $4. Desserts are $1.50; a draft German beer, only $1.10.

Open daily from 7 a.m. to 11 p.m.

**Kleine Konditorei,** 234 E. 86th St., between Second and Third avenues (tel. 737-7130), is another of the block's oldtime German restaurants. It has been around since 1923. In the front windows are exquisite pastries and whipped-cream cakes, and a counter at the front offers pastries and European chocolate. It's all much more elegant than it sounds: The dining rooms up the stairs have flowers, white linen, and burnished brass. The carpet and wallpaper are red, and there's cherry paneling. The shaded sconces and chandeliers are reminiscent of old Vienna.

Complete meals are featured at lunch and dinner. At lunch you might start with a homemade herring salad or chopped chicken liver, with an entree of wiener würstchen (German frankfurter) with potato, salad or vegetable, and a dessert of vanilla pudding ($13.75). Lunch prices range from $9.75 to $14.75; à la carte, the wiener würstchen is $9. Choices for the full dinner are similar, with an appetizer or soup, salad and vegetable, potatoes, dessert, and coffee, tea, or milk. A complete dinner with an entree of rainbow trout amandine is $14.75, and $15.25 with Hungarian goulash. À la carte, an assorted cold-cut platter or herring salad is $11.75.

Kleine Konditorei is open daily from 10 a.m. to midnight Sunday through Thursday, until 1 a.m. on Friday and Saturday. Reservations recommended.

**Café Geiger,** 206 E. 86th St., between Second and Third avenues (tel. 734-4428), will catch your eye with its two front windows: one full of pastries as fanciful as edible elephants, the other with an exquisite tableau of a Bavarian village, complete with cog trains, waterfalls, and a castle atop. Inside there's a spacious, cheerful dining room with elegant touches like wood paneling and oil paintings. The staff is polite, and the Café Geiger has a loyal following.

There are many reasonably priced items on the menu, although entree prices can go as high as $17.50. Potato pancakes with applesauce is $9, as is wiener würstchen (the Vienna-style frankfurter) with sauerkraut and potato. Hard-boiled eggs Russian style come with caviar, vegetable salad, mayonnaise, and fresh greens for $8.50. Daily specials are priced similarly. The menu lists 43 mouthwatering desserts, including fresh-baked tortes, strudels, waffles, cakes, and pies, most under $3.50 each. All bar drinks are available.

Open Sunday through Thursday from 9 a.m. to midnight, and on Friday and Saturday to 1 a.m. Reservations suggested.

## HUNGARIAN

The **Mocca Hungarian Restaurant,** 1588 Second Ave., between 82nd and 83rd streets (tel. 734-6470), is clean and inviting. It's cozy too, even with its turn-of-the-century mosaic floor and marble. Brass wall lamps, mirrored panels, original pressed-tin ceilings, and lace curtains add to the charm.

The Mocca's portions are usually generous, and the food generally good. A three-course lunch special here will cost you $6. Dinner entrees come with potato, vegetable, and salad. You might start with a warming bowl of home-made noodle soup—good broth, fine noodles, and sliced carrots ($2.50). Calves' liver with green peppers and paprika or a crisp breaded wienerschnitzel is $9 each. An entree of stuffed cabbage is $9.25, and there's also a good duck entree on the menu ($9.75). For dessert, definitely give the apple, cheese, or cherry strudel ($2.75) or rich somloi galuska ($4.25) a try. That is, if a cake soaked in rum, with nuts and chocolate sauce, and a smothering of whipped cream doesn't intimidate you!

The Mocca is open daily, for lunch from 11:30 a.m. to 3:45 p.m., and for dinner from 3:45 to 11 p.m. Reservations suggested.

## INDIAN

The **Agra,** 807 Lexington Ave., between 62nd and 63rd streets (tel. 308-8281), is a charming retreat tucked away on the second floor of an otherwise nondescript building (go up the stairs and turn right). The Agra has Indian-print cloth on the walls and ceiling, and tables set in white linen and flowers. Ask for a seat by the windows, which are cut to look like Indian arches. The Agra is sunny and bright by day, dark and mysterious by night. Many regular patrons are Indian or have traveled in India—a good indication of its authenticity.

Come between noon and 3 p.m. Monday through Saturday for a bargain lunch —$5.25 buys a good beef, lamb, chicken, keema (chopped lamb), or vegetable curry, served with fiery red onion relish, mild dhal (a soup-like blend of lentils and onions), a vegetable dish such as cooked cabbage, white or saffron rice, and coffee or a pot of bracing Indian tea.

Dinner prices are also reasonable. For openers, try the coconut soup ($1.50).

The duck curry is a good choice ($8.75). Most prices range from $6.50 for vegetarian dishes to combination dinners like the tandoori dinner with shami kebab (chopped meat), bread, choice of soup and dessert, mango chutney, tandoori chicken, rice pilaf, dhal, and tea or coffee ($13 for one person, $25 for two). And don't pass any meal without one of the excellent Indian breads, such as the poori—puffy, slightly sweet, and large enough for two ($1.50).

The Agra serves wine for $1.50 a glass, $3.75 to $7.50 a carafe. King Fisher, an Indian beer, and other brands are $2.

Open from noon to midnight Monday through Saturday, and from 4 p.m. to midnight on Sunday. Reservations are suggested for one of the window tables, otherwise not necessary.

**Tanjore,** 1229 First Ave., between 66th and 67th streets (tel. 517-7578), is a pleasant Indian restaurant that looks much bigger than it is because of its mirrored walls. There's also lots of brick and many plants, with ceiling fans overhead. Napkins are tucked into stemmed glasses on the linen-covered tables. Tanjore first caught our eye with its lunch special, served Monday through Friday from noon to 3 p.m. The lunch includes rice and soup, and prices vary with the entree. At lunch, chicken curry or mango chicken is $6, and tandoori chicken is $8. Most entrees on the regular dinner menu are priced under $12, and there are complete dinners for $13 to $17. A la carte, you might ask for an appetizer of chicken chat ($4), crisp-fried pieces of chicken in a spicy lemon marinade. For dessert, there's mango sliced over ice cream, or fresh strawberries.

Tanjore is open daily for lunch from 11:30 a.m. to 3 p.m., and for dinner between 5:30 and 11 p.m. Reservations recommended for weekend dinners.

## ITALIAN

No need to go all the way downtown to Little Italy since the reasonably priced **Café and Restaurant Divino** is at 1544 and 1556 Second Ave., between 80th and 81st streets (tel. 517-9269 and 861-1096). Café Divino is *molto buono,* with intimate charm. The small restaurant is decorated in bright greens and crisp white: green-and-white tablecloths, a green awning over the bar, green curtains, with posters of Italy on the white walls. The menu is the same at lunch and dinner. There are 12 different types of pasta, such as tortellini alla Panna and conchiglie ortolana, priced between $8.75 and $9.25. The six or so specials of the day include chicken sorrentina ($11.25) and filet of sole in wine sauce ($12.75). For dessert there are delights like zuppa inglese and torta Divino ($3.50 each), cannoli ($2.50), and Italian ice creams ($3), and of course espresso ($2) and cappuccino ($2.50).

Open Monday through Thursday for lunch from noon to 4 p.m. and for dinner from 5 p.m. to midnight; on Friday and Saturday from noon to 1 a.m. (kitchen open until 12:45 a.m.). On Sunday it's open from noon until 11 p.m.

A huge yellow awning, white stucco walls, and—during the warm summer months—doors that swing out onto a sidewalk café signal rustic Italian food at **Maruzzella,** 1479 First Ave., at the corner of 77th Street (tel. 988-8877). Once inside, the olfactory pleasures of a wood-burning pizza oven, fresh garlic, and olive oil will whet your appetite. The blond-wood tables and chairs fit right in with the red tile floor and sunny personality of this charming place. The waiters, in their blue workshirts and yellow aprons, chat in Italian as the pizza maestro tosses another thin-crusted pie in the open oven.

The food, like the atmosphere, is light and fresh. Split an antipasto for starters. Or try the thinly sliced sun-dried beef with rucola also, known to New Yorkers as arugula ($8.75), the homemade mozzarella with tomato lightly flavored with olive oil ($8.50), or the fresh soups ($5.75) or salads ($5.50 to $5.75). The real specialties, though, are the pasta and pizza. The pasta dishes (under $10) are small but flavorful. And the pizza should not be missed. These thin, crisp, ten-inch delicacies are topped with a mellow tomato sauce and a carefully chosen selection of Italian specialties, including mozzarella, hot salami, anchovies, capers, olives, hot peppers, and/or artichoke hearts. Most cost about $9.50 and can serve as a meal, although you might choose to top it all off with a cappuccino and a slice of the incredibly rich mocha-mousse cake ($5.75).

Maruzzella is open daily for lunch from noon to 3:30 p.m. and for dinner from 5:30 to 11:30 p.m.

## MEXICAN

**Mañana,** 1136 First Ave., between 62nd and 63rd streets (tel. 223-9623), is elegant, with soft lights, white stucco walls, dark heavy woods, tapestry chairs, touches of red in escutcheons, and candles. In spite of its subdued, graceful atmosphere, though, meals are substantial and attractively priced. Lunch appetizers cost under $5; an appetizer of chalupas (chili- and pork-filled mini-tortillas) or nachos are $5 each at dinner. Hearty combination platters of Mexican favorites with rice and beans are $5.75 at lunch, $10 at dinner. Chili con carne is $4.75 at lunch, $6.50 at dinner. For dessert there's crème caramel for $2 at lunch, $3.25 at dinner; or ice cream for $1.75 at lunch, $2.75 at dinner. Or you might want to try something different in the ice cream with fruit and sweet Malago wine sauce ($2.50 and $4, depending on the meal). Sangrita, a hot and spicy Bloody Mary, is also served ($3.75).

Mañana is open weekdays for lunch from noon to 3 p.m. and for dinner until 11:30 p.m., on Saturday and Sunday from 1 to 11:30 p.m. No reservations accepted.

**Blue Moon Mexican Café,** 1444 First Ave., at the corner of 75th Street (tel. 288-9811), is the place for hi-tech tostadas and festive fajitas. Although it's not the most authentic south-of-the-border fare, the atmosphere is fun and the prices are reasonable. Upper East Siders craving a nibble of Mexican food and an exotic frozen drink begin to trickle in around 6:30 p.m., dressed in everything from dark suits to T-shirts and shorts. The décor at the Blue Moon is black, brass, and neon—for example, green neon cacti are mounted on the brick wall behind the bar.

At your table you'll be greeted by a dwarf cactus and a brimming bowl of chips with salsa. If the chips aren't appetizer enough, try the chicken taquitos ($5) or the cheese-smothered nachos ($4). One of the specialties here is prime sirloin chili. The quarter-moon chili is mild, while the full moon is a hotter variety of the same ($3.50 to $7). Dinner entrees, which are all around $11, include chimichangas, enchiladas, fajitas, tostadas, and other Mexican specialties. All include refried beans and rice.

The Blue Moon also serves a $10 Sunday brunch and a $7 lunch special Monday through Friday. The bar is open until 2 or 3 a.m. depending on the crowd. Dinner is served from 5 p.m. to midnight Sunday through Thursday, until 1 a.m. on Friday and Saturday.

## MIDDLE EASTERN

**Falafel 'n' Stuff,** 1586 First Ave., between 82nd and 83rd streets (tel. 879-7023), has lots more imagination than its name. This Egyptian restaurant has the narrowest of dining rooms, with salmon brick walls and white wall lamps. There is also some Egyptian art. On the tables are fresh carnations with babies' breath.

On the menu are 14 vegetarian platters, priced from $7 to $8.50. Each comes with salad, rice, vegetables, and pita bread, making a filling and inexpensive meal. We think these maza dishes—falafel (crisp-fried chickpea balls), tabouli (crushed wheat salad), hummus (chickpeas and tahine)—are the best on the menu. The barbecued Pharaoh chicken is also a good deal at $10.50. Other meat dishes are similarly priced, and go as high as $14.50 for baby lamb rib chops.

Jumbo sandwiches with maza fillings are another low-priced consideration. They start at $3 and none is higher than $4.50. An appetizer of stuffed grape leaves or stuffed zucchini (each $4) is recommended. For dessert, try the magnificent bird's nest, a homemade concoction of phyllo and nuts, baklava, or a not-too-sweet custard (each $2).

Open daily from noon to midnight (till 1 a.m. on Friday and Saturday). Reservations suggested for parties of more than two.

## THAI

For fans of Indian and Chinese food, Thai cuisine can be a refreshing, exciting, and surprising change. It is designed to stimulate the five taste sensations: sweet, sour, hot, salty, and neutral. One of the most charming and affordable of New York's Thai restaurants is the tiny **Thai Express,** 1750 First Ave., between 90th and 91st streets (tel. 831-3813). Fresh orchids sit on each of the ten tables, and the atmosphere is pleasant, relaxed, and comfortable, thanks in part to the unfailingly courteous hostess and waiter.

Satay, curry-marinated chicken or beef on bamboo skewers served with a warm peanut sauce, is a delicious start to any meal ($4.75). For $8 to $11 you can order one of the half-dozen dinner boxes—for example, chicken or beef in a green-curry paste (gang keow wan). All boxes include bean-curd soup, Thai garden (a fresh green salad with peanut dressing), a couple of thick potato chips, white rice, and crunchy, sweet mee krob noodles. You can also get curries (around $8), vegetarian dishes ($5 to $7), and fresh seafood ($10 to $16). Thai dishes are notoriously hot, so be careful when ordering. Most dishes can be spiced to your taste, one star for mild, two for medium, three for hot, and four for smoldering.

Thai Express is open for lunch Monday and Wednesday through Saturday from 11:30 a.m. to 2:30 p.m. Dinner is served Sunday through Tuesday from 6 to 10 p.m. and Wednesday through Saturday from 6 to 10:30 p.m.

## JUST DESSERTS

While you're on 86th Street window-shopping or walking off a hearty German meal, consider the **Treat Boutique,** 200 E. 86th St., near Third Avenue (tel. 737-6619), for an ice-cream cone. The scoop is AlpenZauber ice cream; like many fancy-sounding confections, it's local, not imported (it's from Brooklyn), but still highly recommended. A large cone is $1.25; a double dip, $2.25. There are 15 toppings (crushed M&Ms, trail mix, walnuts, etc.) for 35¢ each, if your sweet tooth is truly insatiable.

Open Tuesday through Saturday from 11 a.m. to 10:30 p.m., and on Sunday and Monday from noon to 10 p.m.

**Peppermint Park,** 1225 First Ave., at the corner of 66th Street (tel. 288-5054), is a favorite for young and old. Everything is fresh (no preservatives), and there's a long list of 40 delicious flavors of ice creams, sherbets, and frozen yogurts. Take-out cones here are $1.50 for a single scoop, and there are also sodas, egg creams, sundaes, and floats. In another case there are mouthwatering Italian pastries. There's also a small dining area behind a green glass partition, where you can order fountain specialties (a banana boat for $4.75, the white crêpe Gatsby for $3.50, or a Belgian waffle with ice cream and fudge sauce for $4.50). You can also have a full meal here —quiches for $4.25, salads for $5.25 to $6.50, entree crêpes in creamy sauces for $4.75, and a cream-cheese-and-salmon sandwich for $6.25.

Peppermint Park is open from 10 a.m. to midnight Monday through Thursday, till 1 a.m. on Friday, till 2 a.m. on Saturday, and from 11 a.m. to midnight on Sunday.

Don't miss **Gran Gelato,** 1614 Third Ave., between 91st and 92nd streets (tel. 289-1200). For those of you not fluent in Italian, gelato is a delectable, super-rich ice cream, which comes in an astounding variety of wonderful flavors. And while it's been several years since the gelato craze first swept New York, we think it's one of the best desserts around, and Gran Gelato is one of the best places to get it. Inside this friendly café, the light is soft and the walls are striking pink and black. Your stomach will applaud such gelato delights as gianduia (chocolate hazelnut), amaretto chip, cappuccino, stracciatella (chocolate chip), and pistachio, among many others. For the calorie-minded, there is an equally impressive array of fresh-fruit sorbettos whose flavors include lampone (raspberry), pink grapefruit, lemon, and orange. All can be had at $2, or $2.50, or $3.50 a cup, depending on the size. But gelato is so rich and thick that a little really does go a long way. If you should thirst during your Italian taste experience, there is cappuccino ($2) and espresso ($1.50) which have received many bravos on their own.

Gran Gelato is open weekdays from noon until 11 p.m., until midnight on weekends.

# 4. Upper West Side

This neighborhood offers a wide variety of international foods and has a lively spirit due to its large student population. Columbia University, at 116th Street between Broadway and Amsterdam Avenue, is the city's only Ivy League institution and wields considerable influence despite its distance from downtown Manhattan. Barnard College is just a block north from Columbia on Broadway; and there are many other schools and seminaries in the area. The Upper West Side is also permanent home to many different groups, and you can see how ethnic flavors change almost block by block. It also is a neighborhood in transition, not from the students who come and go with each academic year, but from the influx of trendy, artsy stores and restaurants moving in next to the older mom-and-pop shops. Some welcome the change; others deplore it. Whatever the outcome, you'll find an exciting and energized neighborhood, where something's always going on.

## AMERICAN/CONTINENTAL

According to its management, "every dog-gone thing" gets ordered at the **West Side Restaurant,** 2020 Broadway, at 69th Street (tel. 724-4000). This family-style diner—with comfortable booths, wooden arches, and red swivel stools at the lunch counter—offers plenty of cheap, tasty food. A grilled cheese sandwich costs $2.50. A beefburger on a toasted bun with cole slaw and a pickle is $2.50. A hot roast beef sandwich with potato and vegetable is $6.75. The West Side also offers a variety of diet delights if you're watching calories. A chicken-salad platter on a bed of lettuce with tomato, scallions, cucumber, cole slaw, and sliced egg is $6.

Open 24 hours.

To enter the **All State Café,** 250 W. 72nd St., between Broadway and West End Avenue (tel. 874-1883), just walk down the few steps and you'll come upon the bar and a crowd of congenial locals, pulling on long-necked beers, feeding the jukebox, and chatting with strangers. Tables are in back, where you can order pasta, around $10.25 and always a good bet, or big, juicy burgers ($3.50) or hot, rich chili ($2.75). The lunch special includes your choice of entree, vegetable, coffee, and soup or salad for $5.75.

The kitchen is open daily from 11:30 a.m. to 1 a.m.

**Amsterdam's Bar & Rotisserie,** 428 Amsterdam Ave., between 80th and 81st streets (tel. 874-1377), is standing-room-only until it closes. Gay red homespun tablecloths, shiny black wood chairs, and freshly painted white brick walls create a cheery atmosphere. The chef guards no secrets from diners, as the kitchen is visible in the center of the restaurant. Whole chickens and cuts of beef roast dramatically on a spit while french fries sizzle in a fryer underneath.

Some prices are high, but the roast half chicken, with a fresh green herb sauce and a pile of crispy thin fries with their skins, is a good and savory buy at $10. By all means try the spicy homemade catsup that sits on every table. Fresh Norwegian salmon ($16) is refreshing and delicious when served with a shot of frosty aquavit, "the water of life," a caraway-flavored Danish liqueur.

Small salads (which come with the entrees) are made with arugula, radicchio, and other flavorful greens, flavored with a balsamic vinegar dressing that would send Peter Rabbit into raptures.

The restaurant is open from noon until 1 a.m. daily. The bar stays open until 2:30 a.m. on weekdays and until 3:30 a.m. on weekends.

**West Side Storey,** 700A Columbus Ave., at 95th Street (tel. 749-1900), is about ten blocks north of the chic Columbus Avenue strip. But if you're willing to take a stroll, a delightful meal is in store for you. This restaurant is a little hidden at the corner, but customers seek it out, and often are found waiting for the doors to open in the morning.

Breakfast dishes feature a special french toast—challah bread dipped in cream and served with real Vermont maple syrup ($5). Three-egg omelets are also a treat, with fillings such as caviar, sour cream, and chives ($7) or mozzarella cheese and sausage ($6).

Lunch brings in another big crowd. The sandwich selection includes bacon, arugula, and tomato ($3.50), served on your choice of bread, or fresh roast turkey for $5. A dish of Moroccan chili with sour cream and a small salad is $6, and a grilled hamburger on a seeded roll with fries is $5. Dinners are quiet, but there is still a good selection that includes chicken gai yang with Thai hot sauce for $10, and chicken livers sautéed in sherry with mushrooms for $9. All entrees are served with two choices of salad, potato, rice, french fries, or the daily vegetable. Meals may also be prepared for low-salt or low-calorie diets.

Hours are 7 a.m. to 11 p.m. daily, with deli take-outs too.

**The Burger Joint,** 2175 Broadway (tel. 362-9238), and **The Pizza Joint,** 2175 Broadway (tel. 724-2010), have been Upper West Side institutions for over 20 years. Located right next door to each other between 76th and 77th streets, they are unpretentious eateries that offer a staggering array of wholesome, reasonably priced food. Since they are run under the same ownership, you can order from both menus at either "Joint."

The house specialties are, logically enough, burgers and pizzas—topped with everything from the conventional cheese to hearty chili con carne. A 100% beef char-broiled burger served with french fries, lettuce, and tomato costs $4; the Big Nick hamburger, named for the Joints' owner, has a half pound of beef and should satisfy even the most ravenous traveler ($5.25 with the above accoutrements). The pizzas range in price from $4.25 for an individual cheese pizza to $8.25 for one with everything on it. Other fare includes heros and submarine sandwiches ($3 to $5.50), spinach, meat, or cheese pie ($4.25), minestrone soup ($2.25), and spaghetti and meat sauce served with fresh bread ($5). The Joints also serve breakfast, with a cheese omelet, fries, and toast ($3.25), and pancakes (about $2).

The Burger Joint and the Pizza Joint are open daily from 6 a.m. to 5 a.m.

**Marvin Gardens,** 2274 Broadway, between 81st and 82nd streets (tel. 799-0578), is instantly appealing, with lots of plants and brick, natural wood, and intimate booths. Dinners, which are in the $8 to $15 range, include the fish of the day, chicken stuffed with bacon and cheese, spareribs, and a fancy shell steak with peppercorns. You could also order from the pasta section. There are also sandwiches and salads to choose from at lunch and dinner, as well as a vegetable plate, and you could have a side order of ratatouille or beansprouts with sesame dressing.

Marvin Gardens opens Monday through Friday at 7:30 a.m. and on Saturday and Sunday at 9 a.m. Sunday through Wednesday it closes at 2 a.m., Thursday through Saturday at 3 a.m. Weekend brunch is served with a full array of omelets, waffles, and daily specials. Reservations are recommended for this popular spot.

**Diane's Uptown,** 249–251 Columbus Ave., between 71st and 72nd streets (tel. 799-6750), is a great find. A stained-glass entry sets the mood. Inside, high-backed wooden booths, mahogany tables, lush green plants, and dark-green walls with judiciously placed mirrors complete a feeling of luxury and relaxation. The menu is an even greater find, with bargains galore. A plain seven-ounce hamburger is $4. But you can create your own combinations with toppings ranging from mush-

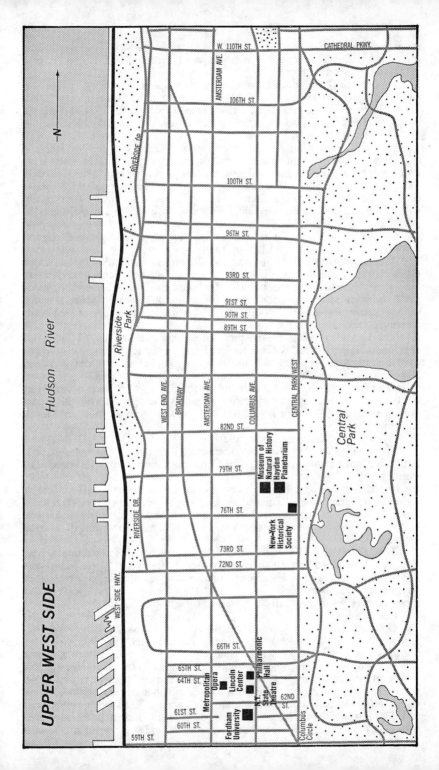

room and bacon to bleu cheese and onions. Each topping is 85¢. If you'd rather try something different, select a Virginia ham and cheese sandwich for $3.75, or a bacon-and-egg sandwich for $2.75.

Devotees of Diane's heartily recommend rounding your meal off with an old-fashioned egg cream, a steal at $1.35. Many customers make the trip to Diane's simply for the delicious desserts. These include French apple pie for $3 or key lime pie for $3.25. There is also a large selection of milkshakes, malts, and double dips.

Open from 11 a.m. to 2 a.m. daily.

**Lucy's,** 503 Columbus Ave., between 84th and 85th streets (tel. 787-3009), is a Cal-Mex surf joint that thrives on carefully orchestrated nonchalance. There is *always* a wait to eat, so arrive prepared to have a margarita or pick out a Lucy's T-shirt (one of which will cost you about the price of an entree). Speaking of which, dinner is cheap and good. Best bets include the blue-plate special—a flauta, burrito, and tostada for $9.50—and chicken fajitas with tomato sauce for $11. Also good is Lucy's grilled swordfish ($14).

Open Sunday through Thursday from 5 to 11 p.m., to midnight on Friday and Saturday; the bar stays open until about 3 a.m.

**The Four Brothers,** 2381 Broadway, at 87th Street (tel. 874-7532), run by four Greek brothers named Lolos, is half coffeeshop, half fancier dining room. There is a homey bar where locals sit and watch TV for hours. Behind the bar is a lamp made from a whiskey bottle with a sombrero perched on top, twinkly Christmas lights, numerous bar mugs and accessories, and a balalaika next to a rope of seed beads hanging on the wall.

The diner offers one of the most reasonable breakfasts in town: $2.25 for two eggs, home-fries, toast, and coffee or tea; or a breakfast of juice, wheat cakes or french toast, and beverage. Lunches and dinners at this local hangout are very good and also quite reasonable. The Greek salad is $5.25, omelets cost around $5, and several roasts and fish and chicken dishes are between $6.75 and $8.25. There is a daily special list every weekday and a wide variety of sandwiches. Drinks from the bar are quite inexpensive ($1.50 for a wine spritzer). Not surprisingly, there are a lot of regulars!

Open from 6 a.m. to midnight daily.

The **College Inn,** 2896 Broadway, between 112th and 113th streets (tel. 663-0257), is a longstanding tradition in the Columbia University neighborhood. The menu, which is almost too extensive to absorb, features American and Greek food. Each wooden table is set with a large, bright-colored plastic water jug, or you can sit at the lunch counter on one of the red swivel stools. There are mirrors on three walls; above, Mediterranean street scenes are depicted on the wallpaper. You are likely to find this diner as crowded with students studying at 3 a.m. as it is during the evening dinner rush.

The daily specials, all between $4 and $8, have plenty of family-dinner appeal. You might be tempted by the Irish lamb stew, with a cup of soup, a green salad, bread and butter; or the baked meatloaf, with potato and vegetable. The shish kebab is always a favorite. Soup here is 85¢ for a cup, and 95¢ for a bowl. And if you have any room left over, splurge with an old-fashioned banana split ($2.50).

Open 24 hours daily.

Columbia University's gracious **Faculty House,** tucked away behind a dormitory at 400 W. 117th St., close to Amsterdam Avenue (tel. 854-1200), is a little-known secret even among neighborhood residents. Delicious buffet lunches and dinners are open to nonmembers. Visitors can eat lunch in the cafeteria or lunch or dinner on the fourth floor, in a lovely large room with a great view of the city. Buffet lunches are $12 for nonmembers, and include two hot entrees, cold selections, vegetables, a full salad bar, and a sumptuous dessert table. The soups are homemade and delicious, including delicate bisques, cream soups, and fresh vegetable creations. Waiters will bring coffee and tea to your table, and you may eat all you want from the buffet tables. The dinner buffet has a set price of $13.50, plus a $1.50 service charge. Dinner often features delectable fish dishes with smooth sauces, coq au vin, and veal and lamb.

Hours are noon to 2 p.m. for lunch and 6 to 8 p.m. for dinner, Monday through Friday. Closed for the summer.

Across Columbus Avenue from the Museum of Natural History, the **Museum Café,** 366 Columbus Ave., at 77th Street (tel. 799-0150), is a longtime neighborhood favorite for lunch, dinner, or late drinks. Its high ceilings and Mediterranean archways lend an elegant but casual feel to the place.

The menu features a wide range of dishes, with interesting twists on the fish-chicken-pasta triumvirate so popular currently. The omelets here are legendary; try one made with tasso, a Cajun spiced pork ($6.50). The café serves individual pizzas with a variety of fillings, priced from $6 to $8.50, and a good selection of sandwiches and burgers.

Open weekdays from 11:30 a.m. to midnight, and on Saturday and Sunday from 10:30 a.m. to 1 a.m.

For a truly daunting burger experience, nothing tops **Jackson Hole,** 517 Columbus Ave., at 85th Street (tel. 362-5177). Priced from $3.75, for a plain burger, to $7.50 for a mountain of chopped beef smothered in bacon, cheese, ham, mushrooms, tomatoes, and fried onions, any of their seven-ounce behemoths is available with fries, lettuce, and tomato for $2.25 extra, but you will almost definitely not have room. For the timid, a good variety of reasonably priced omelets and hot and cold sandwiches are also available. A tile floor, pressed-tin ceiling, and glass doors onto a sidewalk-café area give the place an airy, bright, and bustling feeling.

Jackson Hole opens at 11 a.m. Monday through Friday, and at 9 a.m. on Saturday and Sunday. It closes at midnight Sunday through Wednesday, at 1 a.m. on Thursday, and at 2 a.m. on Friday and Saturday.

**Happy Burgers,** 2489 Broadway, between 92nd and 93rd streets (tel. 799-7719), is a coffeehouse with unbeatable burgers, under all kinds of toppings, priced from $3.25 up. The menu is varied, including such Greek specialties as moussaka and spinach pie, as well as more prosaic sandwiches, salads, and the like. The service is friendly and efficient, another feature that makes this a neighborhood favorite.

Open from 7 a.m. to 11 p.m. seven days a week.

## CHINESE

If you're looking for a nice restaurant for a group, or just a fancier-than-average Chinese place, the **Hunan Balcony,** 2596 Broadway, at 98th Street (tel. 865-0400), is a perfect choice. The comfortable two-story restaurant has a window view and some nice touches: for instance, fruit drinks served with colorful parasols. Service is fast, and the food is delicious and reasonable.

Try the fried dumplings ($3.25) and cold noodles with sesame sauce ($3) for appetizers, and favorite entrees such as beef with four flavors ($8.50), sliced beef and red pepper, garlic, green scallions, ginger, and watercress, or moo shu pork ($7) served with pancakes to make what has been called a "Chinese burrito." Shredded pork with garlic sauce ($7) is also delicious.

Open from noon to midnight on Monday, Tuesday, and Sunday; Wednesday through Saturday until 1:30 a.m. Reservations are suggested for parties of more than five people.

The **Moon Palace Restaurant,** 2879 Broadway, between 111th and 112th streets (tel. 666-7517), isn't one of the area's cozier spots, but its generous portions of good food at low prices have made it a favorite with local students, Columbia faculty, shopkeepers, and secretaries. The weekday lunch special is an especially good deal: an entree with soup, rice, dessert, and a pot of tea costs from $3.75 for vegetable chow mein to $10.50 for lobster Cantonese. The sweet-and-pungent (also called sweet-and-sour) shrimp for $7 is quite tasty and loaded with shrimp.

In addition to the specials, there are six pages of Peking- and Shanghai-style dishes to choose from. The velvet chicken ($7.25) practically melts in your mouth, and if you're feeling adventuresome, you can try sautéed shrimp with pork kidney ($7). Of course, there are customary family dinners, with a five-course meal for two starting at $15. Service is efficient, and low-priced cocktails, wine, and beer are available.

Open daily from 11:30 a.m. to 11 p.m.

The **Empire Szechuans** decorate the corners at Broadway and 97th Street, one at no. 2574 (tel. 663-6004) and at no. 2581 (tel. 666-0555), and have virtually taken over the neighborhood. Oldtimers prefer the original on the east side of Broadway to its glitzy progeny on the west side. But whichever you choose, you'll be well served by the time you crunch into your fortune cookie.

Their weekday luncheon special offers soup, an eggroll, and fried rice with an entree for about $5. The regular menu offers a variety of hot and spicy dishes, which can be toned down—or up!—to suit your taste, plus such exotic dishes as General Tseng's Historic chicken (with red-pepper and hot bean sauce) for $9 and honey crispy duck for $11.

Open from 11:30 a.m. to 1:30 a.m. Wednesday through Sunday, to 11:30 p.m. on Monday and Tuesday. Reservations suggested for dinner.

## CUBAN

The **Ideal Restaurant,** 2825 Broadway, at 109th Street (tel. 866-3224), has the warm, friendly atmosphere of a Spanish *tasca*. The walls have exposed brick and wood paneling, and green plants hang in the windows. Much of the Ideal's clientele comes from the local Latin community, and the restaurant is also popular with the student crowd. During dinner the tables are reserved for those ordering full-course meals, and smaller orders can be eaten at the luncheon counter.

The Ideal offers a variety of meat, seafood, and rice dishes, all prepared in the hearty Cuban style. Pot roast in gravy or beef stew with potatoes—both served with rice and beans or fried plantains and french fries or fried yucca—costs $10; sliced fish is $9.75; and a thick soup of chicken and rice is $9.50. Dessert selections include such tropical treats as guava shells, papaya chunks, or grated coconut with cream cheese ($2.75). Be sure to try their thick, frosty fruit drinks—a dessert in themselves. You can top it all off with one of the Upper West Side's most reasonably priced cups of espresso (85¢). A modest but well-chosen wine list is available.

Open weekdays from 11:30 a.m. to 11 p.m., weekends from 4 to 11:30 p.m.

## CUBAN/CHINESE

Cuba and China merge at **La Victoria-China,** 2536 Broadway, at 95th Street (tel. 865-1810). This restaurant offers an adventure in mix-and-match eating. It's a neighborhood eatery full of New York craziness. It's noisy, bustling, and full of people. It is full of Formica and vinyl booths, with wall hangings and bustling Chinese waiters making it bright and busy. For a Cuban experience, try one of the generous combination plates such as chopped beef, with moros y cristianos (rice and beans) and salad ($5.50). The savory sauce on the beef and the rice studded with black beans is delicious and hearty. Green or ripe plantains make an interesting and tasty dish ($1.50). When you mix a meal with Chinese favorites like moo goo gai pan (chicken with mushrooms, bamboo shoots, and vegetables, at $7.50), a crazy but satisfying blend can be yours.

Open from 11 a.m. to 10:30 p.m. daily. No reservations.

## GREEK

As you go downstairs on a quiet side street near Columbia University, **The Symposium** Greek restaurant, 544 W. 113th St., between Broadway and Amsterdam Avenue (tel. 865-1011), is a pleasant surprise. There are folk-art paintings on the ceiling, painted lightbulbs, Greek art on the walls, and drawings on the tables. The friendly, festive atmosphere will add to a very good meal.

Moussaka (eggplant and meat pie) and pastitsio (stuffed macaroni) are $6.25. "Feta" ccini (Greek spinach noodles with feta cheese) is $5.75. A carafe of wine is

$5.25. For dessert, a full array of Greek delights is offered, including a fabulous baklava. If the weather permits, dine in the lovely rear garden decorated with strings of lights, hanging plants, and more paintings.

Open daily from noon until 11 p.m.

## HUNGARIAN

A lot of restaurants say that they have home-style cooking, but **Charles Green Tree,** 1034 Amsterdam Ave., at 111th Street (tel. 864-9106), really does. Even if your mother never cooked a Hungarian meal in her life, the food will make you think you're eating in somebody's home. The décor is well worn and homey: the wood-paneled walls are decorated with bright plates, and plants are scattered throughout the dining room.

The food is hearty and plentiful. Daily specials include stuffed chicken ($7.50), roast lamb shank ($8.50), and chicken liver à la Budapest ($7.50)—all served with rice, potatoes, and string beans. On Thursday, Friday, and Saturday, roast loin of pork ($8.50) and stuffed veal ($8) are added to the specials; on Friday, roast duck ($12) is also featured, and on Saturday all these specials, plus sauerbraten ($9), are offered.

Try a cup of cold borscht ($2) for an appetizer, and perhaps an entree of plum dumplings ($7), potato pancakes ($5), Hungarian goulash ($7.50), or chicken paprikash ($7). Add $4 to the price of any entree and you'll get an appetizer, coffee or tea, and a dessert. The fresh apple strudel ($1.65) and palacsinta ($1.65), a Hungarian crêpes suzette, are the most popular sweets.

The Green Tree is open from noon to 10 p.m. Monday through Thursday, on Friday and Saturday to 11 p.m.; on Sunday only dinner is served, from 5 to 10 p.m. Reservations accepted only for groups of seven or more.

The best way to top off your meal is to stop in at the **Hungarian Pastry Shop,** one door to the south at 1030 Amsterdam Ave. (tel. 866-4230). Enjoy some of the richest, lightest delicacies in New York with a cup of their special coffee or herbal tea.

Open weekdays from 8 a.m. to 11:30 p.m., on Saturday from 9 a.m. to 11:30 p.m., and on Sunday from 9 a.m. to 10:30 p.m. During the busiest hours, service can be slow—don't come here if you'll be in a rush.

## INDIAN

"Though curry is Indian food, not all Indian food is curry," reads the slogan at the **Indian Kitchen,** 2200 Broadway, at 78th Street (tel. 362-8760). This interesting restaurant has a lot more than its storefront looks suggest. Luciano Pavarotti and Zubin Mehta are reputed to be regulars here, where creative Indian dinners as well as vegetarian Indian specialties are served. Chicken tikka tandoori, chunks of white meat barbecued and served with vegetables and a sauce ($11), and shrimp tikka, jumbo shrimp sautéed in a green masala and steamed with vegetables ($13), are perennial favorites. Four kinds of homemade chutney (tomato, tamarind, mango, and ginger) are available as well.

There are 12 different curry dinners on the menu—egg, shrimp, chicken, and more—and also special pulav dinners made with choice fish or vegetables cooked in rice with vegetables, herbs, and spices. All are in the $9 to $11 range.

Don't leave without trying tofutti, a nondairy ice cream made from tofu, soy milk, fresh fruits, and honey. It's kosher and has only 26 calories per ounce ($1.75).

Open daily from 11 a.m. to 11:30 p.m. You may bring wine or beer.

## ITALIAN

**Genoa,** 271 Amsterdam Ave., between 72nd and 73rd streets (tel. 787-1094), is a little restaurant with a beamed ceiling and amber lights overhead. Owned by Robert Arena, who traces his lineage back to Sicily, Genoa consistently serves great Italian food at great prices. You'll feel the pride he takes in his restaurant as soon as

**96 □ EATING CHEAPLY & WELL**

you walk in. Start with a heaping antipasto, cold or hot ($5), and work your way into one of the wonderful homemade pastas ($8). Veal and chicken entrees run about $10. Check out the daily specials, often the biggest bargains on the menu.

Genoa is open Tuesday through Saturday from 5:45 to 10:30 p.m., and on Sunday from 5:30 to 9:30 p.m.

## JAPANESE

At **Suki's,** 433 Amsterdam Ave., between 80th and 81st streets (tel. 496-8940), the atmosphere is chic and intimate. Rock and roll plays softly in the background. There is a small, sleek black-lacquered wood bar and a vase of elegant fresh flowers at the entrance. Potted plants sitting by the big front window and a wall covered with brightly colored paintings add to Suki's charm.

The food here is excellent and affordable. For the intrepid, sitting at the sushi bar and watching the masterful sushi chefs slice and sculpt colorful mouthfuls of raw fish and seaweed is as much fun as going to the theater. The mackerel handroll, raw mackerel with minced scallops and ginger and rice, wrapped in a cone of toasted seaweed ($4), is fresh and delicious. Grilled eel sushi ($2) is an unusually sweet treat. And if you're really brave, try the creamy raw sea urchin ($2.50)—you'll feel positively affectionate for the spiny species.

The Japanese chef's salad (baby shrimp, crab, and marinated beansprouts with tofu and the chef's dressing at $9) is also good. Kikka yaki, broiled sea scallops with the house sauce ($10.50), and tatsutaage, Japanese fried chicken ($8.50), are more conventional fare but with a unique flair.

Open from 5 p.m. to 1 a.m. Monday through Saturday, and from 5 to 11 p.m. on Sunday.

A bit on the pricey side but still well worth a visit, **Sakura of Japan,** 2298 Broadway, at 83rd Street (tel. 769-1003), serves some of the best sushi in town. Entering this dark, atmospheric spot, you pass two large tanks full of tropical fish. Head for the sushi bar, where you can order a full range of freshly prepared items, either in combination on a platter with miso soup ($13), or individually, starting at $1.25 per piece. There are also delicious entrees like chicken teriyaki priced under $10. Next door is the Loews's 84th Street movie theater, making this an excellent choice for a pre-movie bite.

Lunch is served daily from noon to 2:45 p.m.; dinner, from 5 to 11:45 p.m.

## MACROBIOTIC

With a basis in Eastern philosophy, the macrobiotic diet is intended to balance the two universal principles, yin and yang, within the individual and thus lead to a more harmonious, healthy life. Macrobiotic food is made from whole grains, beans, fresh fruits and vegetables, seafood, and seaweed. Forbidden "fruits" include meat and eggs (too yang), sugar, honey, alcohol, and even seemingly innocuous foods such as dairy products (too yin).

But even if you can't tell your yin from your yang, you'll find enjoyable macrobiotic fare at **Souen,** 2444 Broadway, between 90th and 91st streets (tel. 787-1110). Most of the dishes are based on Japanese cuisine, and as long as you don't have your heart set on meat and potatoes, you'll appreciate the freshness of the food.

Souen is small and spotless, with 16 little tables in two neat rows and a few counter seats as well. The décor is simple without being stark: oak parquet floors and exposed brick lend warmth. You can try some agetofu ($3.50), deep-fried tofu in ginger burdock sauce, along with some brown rice ($1.50 for a small bowl, $2.75 for a large), which comes with a sesame-oat sauce. A bowl of tabouli salad costs $3; vegetable soba (noodles and vegetables in broth) is $5.50.

House specials include karaage (a trout filet deep-fried with ginger burdock sauce) at $12, and seitan (whole-wheat protein cutlets deep-fried, with the same sauce), at $8. If you're not feeling adventurous, you can get broiled sole, shrimp, sea trout, or brook trout for $9. Try some bancha tea (25¢) or mu tea (75¢) with your meal. Sugar-free desserts, such as the tofu pie ($3) or apple crunch ($2.25), are a boon for the less-than-iron-willed dieter, though perhaps not as satisfying as a gooey hot-fudge sundae.

Souen is open Sunday through Thursday from noon to 10 p.m., on Friday and Saturday to 11 p.m.

## MIDDLE EASTERN

**At Our Place,** 2527 Broadway, between 94th and 95th streets (tel. 864-1410), is a great place to come with friends or to relax alone with a good book. The restaurant is a sharp-angled warren of booths and mirrors, but the service is very efficient and the food is good and not very expensive. Try the moussaka, with lamb ($8) or eggplant ($7). Couscous also comes with lamb ($10) or vegetarian ($9). Start off with a falafel ($6.50), and in the summertime, try the iced mint tea. The ingredients are always very fresh and the preparation not to be faulted.

Open from 4 to 11 p.m. on Monday, 4 p.m. to midnight Tuesday through Thursday, and 1 p.m. to midnight Friday through Sunday.

## NATURAL FOODS

**Peter's Pumpkin Eater,** 2452 Broadway, near 91st Street (tel. 877-0132), features "natural cuisine," an eclectic menu of macrobiotic, Middle Eastern, and Mexican fare. This is a quiet, peaceful restaurant, even at its busiest. Classical music plays in the background. The small wooden tables are set with fresh flowers and candles. Abundant green plants hang near the front windows. Diners here all look healthy, which is the best advertisement for this cuisine.

While there's no red meat on the menu, there's a varied selection of broiled fresh fish ($10.50 to $14). Guacamole ($4.25) and hummus ($3.50) are popular appetizers. A hearty helping of coarsely cut vegetables—carrots, zucchini, broccoli, cabbage, and chickpeas on a bed of brown rice, smothered in an unusually sweet-and-spicy cashew sauce—is delicious. A diner at a nearby table was overheard saying, upon tasting this dish, that "it's like coming home." Mango lemonade ($1.50 for a small glass, $2.25 for a large) is a refreshing beverage, or try a cool papaya smoothie ($2.50) that is both thirst-quenching and a reputed digestive aid.

Peter's Pumpkin Eater is open for breakfast. You can start your day here with such fare as homemade scones, carrot-raisin muffins, and fresh-squeezed orange juice.

Open from 9 a.m. to 11 p.m. Monday through Friday, from 11 a.m. to 11 p.m. on Saturday and Sunday.

## SEAFOOD

**Broadway Bay,** 2180 Broadway, at 77th Street (tel. 362-4360), offers a long, art deco bar, a small dining room with leather banquettes and ceiling fans, a glassed-in porch area with a bright, southwestern feeling, and most important, some of the best and most reasonably priced seafood to be found on the West Side.

Lunch is the best deal here: typical specials include baked bluefish with linguine and soup for $4.75, and a Genoa salami and provolone hero with french fries and soup for the same price. During the summer months Broadway Bay serves a refreshing and spicy chilled gazpacho that is a perfect accompaniment to any of the specials.

Dinner entrees are a mixture of straight-ahead seafood dishes and Italian specialties, and include a spectacular linguine Fra Diavolo, covered with clams, mussels, shrimp, and scallops in a spicy tomato sauce, for $11. There are also daily fish specials, such as rainbow trout, tuna steak, and softshell crabs—whatever's fresh.

Open from 11:30 a.m. to 1 a.m. Monday through Saturday. On Sunday, brunch is served from 11 a.m. to 3:30 p.m., and dinner, until midnight.

---

## 5. Lincoln Center

---

The Lincoln Center neighborhood has changed radically since it inspired the Broadway musical *West Side Story*. Although you can still find some oldtime *bodegas* (Spanish neighborhood markets), the area has filled up with slick, expensive restaurants that can gobble up your budget in no time. When you've got tickets to a Lincoln Center concert and want to go someplace nearby for dinner or dessert, we suggest one of the reasonably priced restaurants and cafés listed here. All are within walking distance of Lincoln Center, which is bounded by Broadway and Amsterdam Avenue, between 62nd and 66th streets.

### AMERICAN/CONTINENTAL

The **Opera Espresso,** 1928 Broadway, at 65th Street (tel. 799-3050), is sort of an elegant coffeeshop—a perfect place to have something simple before or after the show without having it cost more than the Lincoln Center tickets. The walls are adorned with framed copies of old Metropolitan Opera programs, a Gregorian chant on parchment, and pictures of performers from Pavlova to Nureyev. Graceful brass chandeliers cast a soft glow. You can sit either at the counter or in one of the comfortable booths.

Entrees run $7.50 to $9.25, including baked eggplant stuffed with ricotta and mozzarella, served with a salad, and chicken with biscuits, gravy, and salad. You can also get sandwiches ($4.25 to $7), burgers ($7 to $8.75), omelets with potato or salad ($7 to $8.50), and a fresh cup of espresso ($1.65) with dessert ($3.50 or $4.50).

Open from 7:30 a.m. to midnight Monday through Saturday, and from 8 a.m. to midnight on Sunday. Reservations accepted for large groups only.

The **Lincoln Square Coffee Shop,** 2 Lincoln Square, between 65th and 66th streets, "where Broadway meets Columbus" (tel. 799-4000), is a world-class coffeeshop. It has all the requisites, like Viennese coffee with lots of whipped cream ($2.75) and hamburgers (from $4.25), soups ($2), sandwiches (from $4 to $6.50), homemade pies and ice-cream sundaes or "brownies all-the-way" ($2 to $4). French onion soup in a crock is $2.25. There are other special entrees like eggplant milanese ($6.75) or Indian curried chicken ($7.25).

Open Monday through Thursday from 6:30 a.m. to midnight, on Friday and Saturday to 1 a.m., and on Sunday from 8 a.m. to midnight.

**The Saloon,** Broadway at 64th Street, across from Lincoln Center (tel. 874-1500), is an outdoor café with roller-skating waiters and a high-ceilinged, exposed-brick gathering spot for West Siders. The menu is huge, in size and assortment, but appetizers and salads are exotic and affordable, as are sandwiches and other specialties. Blue-corn nachos chivera, with goat cheese, jalapeños, and guacamole ($6.50) or Cajun popcorn (deep-fried crayfish tails, $7.50) are almost enough for a full meal. Hot and cold salads are featured, including duckling and macadamia nuts ($12.75), hot gulf shrimp salad ($12.75), and a chef's salad for $9.50. Sandwiches (from $7.50 to $9.50) are inventive—as are the omelet and egg dishes ($6.50 to $9.50). Pizzellas, wafer-thin pizzas, are $6.50 to $8.50 for a lighter meal.

Open daily from 11:30 a.m. to 2 a.m. for food, until 4 a.m. for drinks.

### CHINESE

**Empire Szechuan,** 193 Columbus Ave., between 68th and 69th streets (tel. 496-8778), serves some of the finest dishes from the southwestern Chinese province of Szechuan. There are two dining rooms separated by a short staircase. The first one has a mirrored wall which makes it appear larger, and the one in back is cozy and cheerful.

There are many chef's specials every day, including Paradise Chicken for $8.75, Empire Special Duck for $9.75, and Hunan Flower Steak for $9.75. The regular menu has over 50 entrees listed from $6.25 to $13.50.

Open Sunday through Tuesday from 11 a.m. to 1 a.m., and Wednesday through Saturday until 2 a.m.

## ITALIAN PASTRIES

**Café La Fortuna,** 69 W. 71st St., between Columbus Avenue and Central Park West (tel. 724-5846), is one of those delightful places where you should forget that calories exist. It's the perfect place to linger over a cappuccino ($1.85) or espresso ($1.45) and pastry ($2.25 to $2.50) after the show. The walls are laden with old opera records and pictures of singing stars from Caruso to Pavarotti. One of the owner's favorite photos is the one of John Lennon, Yoko Ono, and their son, Sean— former regulars at the café—mugging it up in oldtime costumes. During the summer you can enjoy the evening on the café's fenced-in patio.

Most of the pastries, including the sinfully rich canoli, are Italian, although there are also some German delights. A variety of cookies, cakes, homemade Italian ices, and gelati ($2.25 to $3) are also available.

Open Tuesday through Thursday from 1 p.m. to 1 a.m., on Friday to 2 a.m., on Saturday from noon to 2 a.m., and on Sunday from noon to 1 a.m. Closed Monday.

## JEWISH DELI

New York's Jewish delis are legendary, and **Fine and Schapiro,** 138 W. 72nd St., between Broadway and Columbus Avenue (tel. 877-2721), is one of the nicest around. Started in 1927, this place has a charmingly simple, old-fashioned décor with cedar walls and brown-painted wainscotting. Dinner is a fancy production, complete with double linen tablecloths on the blond wood-grained Formica tables. Many regular customers have been coming here for decades.

Lunch is the best deal here. For about $7.50 to $9 you can get one of a variety of sandwiches, such as pastrami, chicken salad, or chopped liver, with soup, cookies, and tea or black coffee (no butter or milk is served). You can also choose from a changing list of luncheon specials, such as stuffed cabbage, gefilte fish, or potted meatballs (each $7.50), served with potatoes or vegetables, soup, tea, and dessert. Of course you can also order items à la carte. Potato pancakes cost $1.90; potato salad or cole slaw costs $1.50. A club sandwich is $8.75, a bottle of beer costs $1.90 to $3, and $1.25 buys a glass of Dr. Brown's Celery Tonic or a traditional cream soda. Homemade soups such as pea, lentil, and cabbage are $1.80 for a cup and $2.50 for a bowl. Omelets range from $5.75 for onion to $11 for chicken liver, all served with relish and french fries.

Dinners are huge—served with appetizer, soup, vegetable, potato, dessert, and beverage—and offering everything from corned beef and eggs ($12.50) to stuffed homemade kishke ($14.50) and broiled baby lamb chops ($20.50). If you'd like to turn any of these generous meals into a dinner for two, add a $3 charge for the extra plate. For those on low-sodium diets, Fine and Schapiro offers several salt-free dishes.

Open from 11 a.m. (at 8:30 a.m. for the take-out counter) to 11:30 p.m. daily except Friday, when the deli closes at 9 p.m.

## MEXICAN

If you're in the mood for some south-of-the-border cuisine, try **Los Panchos,** 71 W. 71st St., between Columbus Avenue and Central Park West (tel. 874-7336).

From the street, you step down into a pleasant bar/lounge (known for its Cuervo margaritas at $3.75) into a dining room with white cloths and candles on the tables. The stucco walls are brightened, though not to garish excess, with sombreros, serapes, and Mexican paintings. When the weather is nice, you can also eat in the quiet back patio.

Lunch here is the best deal; most entree prices rise by $3 to $4 for dinner. The menu includes typical taco, tostada, enchilada, and burrito combination plates ranging from $6 to $8.50 with rice and beans. Other dishes include flautas—corn and flour tortillas stuffed with muenster cheese, deep-fried and covered with guacamole—served with tomato sauce, rice, and beans for $9—and a bowl of hot and spicy chili, served with rice on the side for $6.25 ($8.50 at dinner). Guacamole dip ($3.25 at lunch, $4 at dinner) is a popular appetizer, and flan ($2.25) is the perfect dessert after a hot, spicy meal. And you can wash it all down with a complimentary glass of wine.

Open daily from 11:30 a.m. to midnight. Brunch is served on Saturday and Sunday from 11:30 a.m. to 4 p.m. Reservations accepted.

## SEAFOOD

Dining at **Capt. Nemo's,** 137 W. 72nd St., between Columbus and Amsterdam avenues (tel. 595-5600), is fun. You enter through the pleasant front bar area and walk past a tank full of brilliantly colored tropical fish into a dining room fitted out to resemble an art deco submarine. For dinner, white linen cloths cover the tables, and candles add a touch of romance.

At lunch you can start with a cup of New England or Manhattan clam chowder for $1.45, then have a filet of sole, scrod, or bluefish, prepared just about every way possible for $6.75 to $8.25. Scampi broiled in garlic butter is $8, as are fried scallops. Dinner entrees are served with salad and potatoes or rice. If you don't want fish, you can have chicken ($12.25) or choose from a variety of quiches. You'll have to order carefully to avoid breaking your budget: most entrees cost $13 to $14. If you really feel like going all-out, there's a lobster dinner with appetizer, potato or saffron rice, salad, and wine for $22.

Open Sunday through Thursday from noon to midnight, on Friday and Saturday from noon to 1 a.m. Reservations accepted.

## VIENNESE

**Eclair,** 141 W. 72nd St., between Columbus and Amsterdam avenues (tel. 873-7700), is a charming old neighborhood institution with a suitably old-fashioned décor. The dining room is nicely lit and airy; the terrazzo floors and white linen tablecloths speak of the proud Viennese heritage of owner Alexander M. Selinger.

As you might guess from the name, Eclair's specialty for 50 years has been pastries and cakes. You'll have a hard time choosing from over 200 varieties of scrumptious strudels, tortes, eclairs, fruit tarts, danish, croissants—you name it. Prices range from $2 to $3.50. For an extra 50¢ you can have your delicacy à la mode or with a mound of whipped cream. The perfect complement for one of these pastries is a cup of rich, smooth Viennese coffee with whipped cream ($1.50).

But don't write Eclair off as just a coffee and pastry shop. It's a pleasant place for dinner before or after a concert, with such continental treats as Hungarian goulash ($10.50) and Viennese fried chicken ($10)—all served with creamed spinach or the vegetable du jour, potato, and your choice of cucumber, tossed salad, or applesauce. Add $4 to any of these dinners and you can get a soup (perhaps chilled borscht) or appetizer, dessert, and coffee or tea. Check the daily specials, which include paprika chicken with nockerl and tossed salad ($9) or a breaded liver steak with potato salad ($9). A glass of wine with a dinner is only $2.

If you're looking for lighter fare, try the quiche, served with a tossed salad for $6, or one of a variety of sandwiches and burgers, most priced from $4.50 to $6.50.

With a full soda fountain, wine, beer, and apéritifs, Eclair offers such a variety of choices that it's ideal for groups of people with different tastes or appetites.

An excellent breakfast is also served. Open from 8 a.m. to midnight daily. Reservations accepted.

---

## 6. Pennsylvania Station/Chelsea

The area that includes Pennsylvania Station and Chelsea, from 15th Street to 40th Street west of Fifth Avenue, is characterized by two distinct neighborhoods. Located in the heart of the garment district, Penn Station is surrounded by a nine-to-five stream of commuters and delivery trucks. The emphasis here is on fast food—but don't be led astray by the familiar chains. There are plenty of unique eateries here, offering low-priced meals. Farther down, the residential area known as Chelsea is a neighborhood in transition. Developers are moving in quickly, and trendy restaurants, theaters, and stores are popping up on every block. There are still, however, a lot of small, unpretentious restaurants here.

### AMERICAN/CONTINENTAL

There's an "olde" English feel to the **Old Garden,** 15 W. 29th St., between Fifth Avenue and Broadway (tel. 532-8323). It has a Tudor exterior of red brick and black-wood framing. The front arched wooden doorway leads to a cozy dining room and a large bar called the Winery, which is lit by electric gas lamps. Tables are set with patchwork cotton tablecloths, and archways toward the back are hung with curtains of the same material. The exposed-brick walls have still-life pictures of fruits and flowers.

Lunch is your best bet here, with entrees ranging from $6 to $14, and luncheon salads ranging from $5.50 to $9. To begin, you might try the chopped liver or split-pea soup (each $2.50). Entrees are served with potatoes and vegetables. Fried Louisiana shrimp with sauce for dipping costs $9.50, and veal marsala with wild mushrooms runs $10. For dessert, try the strawberry shortcake for $2.50.

Open from 11:30 a.m. to 9 p.m. Monday through Friday, from 4:30 to 9 p.m. on Saturday. Reservations suggested.

The menu changes every two weeks at **Miss Ruby's Café,** 135 Eighth Ave., between 16th and 17th streets (tel. 620-4055), a self-styled haven of "American Eclectic" cooking that features different regional cuisines monthly. Inside, beyond the long bar in front, there's a light and airy room, whose bare-brick walls are done in pastels. Hanging plants, track lighting, and three skylights add to the effect, and the open kitchen at the rear affords a view of your own meal being prepared.

Cooking styles you might encounter here range from New England to Deep South to California; we recently sampled Tex-Mex, feasting on lady's curried shrimp served with rice and beans. In addition to the changing menu selections are the "American Classics," which include such mouthwatering delicacies as chicken-fried steak and cornmeal-fried catfish. Entrees run between $10 and $20. Beer and wine are available, as are specialty drinks and wines that change with each menu.

Desserts are sinfully rich, with the likes of fudge pie ($5) and fried biscotto dough drizzled with honey. Coffee, espresso, and cappuccino are always available.

Much the same fare is offered at lunch, and there is an "interim" menu—soup and salad—in effect between 4 and 6 p.m. Sunday brunch ($10) features blackboards of changing specials.

Open from noon to midnight Monday through Saturday, to 10 p.m. on Sunday. Sunday brunch is from noon to 4 p.m.

You can dine 24 hours a day at the **Empire Diner,** 210 Tenth Ave., between 21st and 22nd streets (tel. 243-2736). This sleek, authentic diner captures the style of the 1930s and '40s. The interior of the restaurant is done in black and chrome, and at night the space is lit with candles. Customers can sit either at the counter that runs the length of the diner or at one of the comfortable booths by the window. In the summer there is seating outside. Piano player John Jarvis is at the ivory keys in the evenings starting at 8 p.m. and during weekend brunches.

The burgers here are large and very good, and range in price from $8 for the steakburger, to $9.75 for the chiliburger. Hot entrees run from $9 for the stir-fried vegetable platter, to $15 for the shell steak. If you're in the mood for something light, try the sesame snow-pea salad ($6), served with the special dressing of the day. Eggs are available all the time for $4 ($5.75 with bacon, ham, or sausage). Omelets start at $8.

The Empire Diner is open 24 hours a day (but closed Monday from midnight to 4 a.m.).

A favorite of some of our musician friends, **Buckwheat & Alfalfa,** 182 Eighth Ave., between 19th and 20th streets (tel. 463-9511), is a rather utilitarian-looking restaurant that surprisingly turns out some of the best vegetarian gourmet dishes we've had in New York. The menu is full of healthy, delicious, and unusual dishes.

For an appetizer, you might want to try the low-salt cold buckwheat soba noodles with a spicy peanut-sesame sauce ($4), or marinated cabbage and aduke beans ($3.50). Vegetarian entrees (served with vegetables and either brown rice or the grain of the day) include barbecued tempeh with kale ($9) and tofu sukiyaki with collard greens ($10). Lunch features oversize sandwiches, priced between $2 and $4.25; a variety of salads for under $6; and a "You won't believe it's vegetarian" chili ($3).

Don't miss Buckwheat & Alfalfa's fresh juices and shakes. One of our favorites is the Royal Rush shake, which includes papaya or mango juice, banana, bee pollen royal jelly, green barley juice, propolis, ginseng, vitamins A, B, C, and D, foti, wu chi, and kelp—a veritable health feast for only $2.75. There's also a noteworthy selection of wine and beers.

Buckwheat & Alfalfa is open for lunch from 11:30 a.m. to 4 p.m. Monday through Friday, and for dinner from 6 to 10:30 p.m. Tuesday through Saturday. Brunch is served on Saturday from 11:30 a.m. to 3 p.m., and on Sunday from 11:30 a.m. to 3 p.m. The restaurant is open for dinner on Sunday from 4 to 9 p.m.

The **Zig Zag,** 206 W. 23rd St., just west of Seventh Avenue (tel. 645-5060), is a relative newcomer to burgeoning West 23rd Street. After its blue neon sign and framed-glass entrance, the first thing you notice about this upscale restaurant is that it's very long and thin. But once inside, the true size of the room is distorted by mirrors covering the side walls and the area behind the bar. Reflected in these mirrors is the jagged "zig zag" dropped ceiling of the bar.

The food here is simple American bistro fare. Grilled baby chicken is served with vegetable and seasoned home-fries ($10), and the fish of the day (grilled rainbow trout with Créole sauce the day of our visit), is $12. A chef's salad made with chicken, shredded red cabbage, and other vegetables is $8. A hamburger is $5, and a delicious smoked-turkey and swiss sandwich on challah bread, dipped in batter and grilled, is served with a spicy horseradish sauce for $8. Desserts include a sinful bittersweet chocolate cake, and apple pie, each $3.50.

Zig Zag is open daily from 11:30 a.m. to 1:30 a.m. The menu stays the same for lunch and dinner.

## CHINESE

**Chinatown Express,** 425 Seventh Ave., between 33rd and 34th streets (tel. 563-3559), is attractively designed with green-and-white tiles at the front counter and behind the stove. Entrees are temptingly displayed in a curved alcove covered by glass slats. Downstairs there are two dining rooms, decorated with plastic shields painted with Chinese characters. An upstairs dining room, with a view of the avenue below, is furnished with orange chairs and live plants. The restaurant is kept bright and clean by a hardworking staff.

The menu features combination platters served in large portions. Wonton soup is $1.60 and eggrolls cost $1. The four platter combinations are all about $4, with a peppersteak, eggroll, and fried-rice platter for $5; a platter of spareribs, fried wonton, chicken wings, fried rice, and shrimp toast is $4. Roast pork lo mein costs $3.75, and a large order of chicken wings is $4.50.

Open from 11 a.m. to 9 p.m. daily, and from 9:30 a.m. to 10 p.m. on nights when there's a big show at Madison Square Garden across the street.

The food at **Sung Ho Lo,** 211 Seventh Ave., between 22nd and 23rd streets (tel. 924-8580), is undeniably fresh; we once watched as the staff sat stemming mountains of green beans at a back table. The informal, quiet restaurant is decorated with framed black calligraphy letters painted on rice paper, and Chinese watercolor prints. Plants adorn the front window and a tall bamboo tree stands by the counter.

Luncheon specials, ranging in price from $4 to $5, are the best deals of the day. Try the chicken with broccoli, the sweet-and-sour pork, or the peppersteak, each $4. Shrimp with cashew nuts is $5. The à la carte menu, for lunch and dinner, includes hot-and-spicy orange beef ($6.75) and lemon chicken that's batter-fried and dipped in lemon and honey sauce ($6.25). For dessert, try the chilled lichee nuts (75¢). Main dishes can be served with brown rice, if you prefer it to the white rice.

Open Monday through Thursday from 11:30 a.m. to 10:30 p.m., on Friday to 11 p.m., on Saturday from 5 to 11 p.m., and on Sunday from 5 to 10:30 p.m.

## CUBAN/CHINESE

Housed in an old shiny aluminum diner, **Mi Chinita** is at 176 Eighth Ave., at the corner of 19th Street (tel. 529-3609). Here the character is set by the diner décor—a long Formica counter and blue Formica tables matched with aqua-colored linen curtains. Two Chinese hanging lamps and a few other Chinese decorator items reflect the Asian half of the menu.

The menu offers a wide selection of both Chinese and Cuban food. Egg-drop soup is $1.35 and two eggrolls cost $2.50. The Chinese menu includes roast pork and mushrooms ($5.75), vegetable egg foo yung ($5), and chicken with broccoli ($5.75). From the Cuban menu you can choose peppersteak with rice and beans ($5.25), tongue with rice and beans ($5), or paella ($14). This is only a small view of the wide number of dishes offered. For dessert, try the flan or bread pudding (85¢).

Open from 11:45 a.m. to 9:30 p.m. Monday through Saturday.

## GREEK

Hidden away behind a freight entrance on 39th Street is **Nick's Place,** 550 Seventh Ave., between 39th and 40th streets (tel. 221-3294). This restaurant is a real find, with delicious homemade Greek specialties. There are only seven tables in the dining area, but the small room is cozily decorated, with dappled wallpaper and old-fashioned French posters.

Traditional Greek offerings include moussaka with vegetable or salad ($5), spinach pie with salad ($5), and stuffed grape leaves ($1.65). There is also a wide variety of salads, including avocado salad vinaigrette ($5), and a spinach salad ($5). For dessert, try the fresh carrot cake or the homemade chocolate cake (each $1.65).

Hours here are limited to 11 a.m. to 3 p.m., weekdays only.

For more elegant dining, there's the **Atlas Greek Restaurant,** 171 W. 29th St., around the corner from Seventh Avenue (tel. 695-6998). Don't be discouraged by the gray stairway leading up to the restaurant. You'll find that the Atlas has a spacious, airy dining room with a good view of Seventh Avenue from the window tables up front. The décor here is simple, with mirrors and warm wood paneling that takes on a golden glow when the sun streams in. Tables are covered in white linen. Many patrons are Greek businessmen, who stop in at lunchtime to sample the authentic food and drink retsina or ouzo.

The menu here changes daily, with most entrees around $6. On Wednesday and Friday there are special fish dishes. Lamb pilaf or shish kebab is $6.75. A Greek salad is $3.50 and wine or beer is $1.50. For dessert, try the fruit custard ($1.50).

Open from 11:30 a.m. to 3 p.m. Monday through Friday.

## ITALIAN

A colorful deli, **Manganaro's Grosseria,** at 488 Ninth Ave., between 37th and 38th streets (tel. 563-5331), consists of a large store that sells imported specialty items, with a small luncheonette in the back. The store is decorated with hanging baskets and a red, green, and white canopy at one counter. It's now run by five of the seven Manganaro sisters, who see to it that the biscotti and the delicious cheeses are all beautifully displayed. The sit-down deli is simply decorated, with a green floor and brown-wood Formica tables.

Sandwiches here are a real treat, served in long, fresh hero rolls. A meatball hero is only $3.75, and an eggplant parmigiana sandwich is $4.75. Baked ziti and eggplant, served only on Friday, costs $6. A cappicola sandwich is only $4, and the Manganaro special, with mixed meats, cheese, and peppers, is $4.75. For dessert, try the extraordinary ricotta cheesecake made with rosewater ($7 per pound).

Open from 8 a.m. to 7 p.m. Monday through Saturday.

## JEWISH DAIRY

Kosher businessmen can be found eating at **Gefen's Kosher Dairy,** 297 Seventh Ave., between 26th and 27th streets (tel. 929-6476). The restaurant is clean and unpretentious, with white Formica tables. The walls are covered with wood paneling and mirrors. There's a sit-down counter along one side, as well as a take-out stand. Waiters, dressed in black outfits with white shirts and black bow ties, add a touch of old-world elegance. The atmosphere here is boisterous, with plenty of lively chatter.

Your waiter will immediately set a metal dish filled with pumpernickel bread and fresh rolls at your table, but save some room for other items. To start, try the borscht with cream ($3.25) or the homemade soup of the day ($2.50). Entrees include baked gefilte fish ($9.50) and broiled salmon ($12), served with a choice of two vegetables and mashed or boiled potatoes. The dairy dishes include potato pirogen and cheese blintzes for $7.50 and potato pancakes for $6.25. There are daily specials, including Hungarian vegetarian goulash on Tuesday and stuffed cabbage on Wednesday (each $7.75). For dessert, try the homemade danish ($1.50) or the homemade cheesecake ($2.50).

Open from 7 a.m. to 7 p.m. Monday through Thursday, on Friday to 3 p.m., and on Sunday from 11 a.m. to 7 p.m. Closed Saturday.

## JEWISH DELI

Smart and sassy, **J. J. Applebaum's Deli Co.** points out on its three-foot menu that it is "sandwiched" between 33rd and 34th streets at 431 Seventh Ave. (tel. 563-6200). Puns like this abound on their long list of offerings, including the "son of a botch" and the "U.R.A. turkey" sandwiches. The décor here is modern and airy, with exposed-brick walls and black-and-white checkered tile floors. Maroon booths are separated by wood siding, lit by large white half-glove lights suspended from lattices on the ceiling.

To start, try the borscht served with sour cream and a boiled potato ($4.75). Sandwiches served with homemade cold slaw, potato salad, and a pickle are huge. The grilled Reuben, a mountain of hot pastrami covered with cole slaw, Russian dressing, and gobs of melting cheese, is $7.75. You can also get zucchini latkes, with sour cream or applesauce ($5.50), and a steak sandwich with charcoal-broiled steak is only $6.50. For dessert, try the fresh pound cake ($1.75) or the carrot cake ($2.75).

Open from 8 a.m. to 9 p.m. weekdays, and until 8 p.m. on weekends.

**Lox Around the Clock,** 676 Sixth Ave., at 21st Street (tel. 691-3535), is located two blocks below the Flatiron Building on Fifth Avenue and its clientele comes from the various nightclubs in the area. The owners call Lox "an international Jewish cuisine restaurant" and it is that and more. Inside, comfortable wicker chairs with padded cushions and wooden tables fill the room and funky neon clocks are hung over the bar. The tables are close, the music is turned up, and the crowd at Lox Around the Clock can get spirited; so it's probably not the spot for an intimate dinner. If you're hungry, though, you've come to the right spot. The portions are huge, and for late risers, breakfast is served throughout the day. Cheese blintzes ($8), lox and cream cheese on a bagel with garnish ($8.50), and kasha varniskes with brisket gravy ($7.50) are some classic Jewish offerings. There are several big sandwiches, including a delicious curried chicken salad in pita bread ($7) and a tasty mozzarella, basil, and tomato sandwich served on garlic challah. Hot entrees include stuffed cabbage ($10) and Romanian steak, grilled and served with steak fries and a vegetable ($11.75). There are also five kinds of burgers, served with fries ($6.50 to $7.50), omelets and salads. If for some reason you still have room, Lox also offers fresh baked desserts like cheesecake ($3.75) and homemade brownies à la mode ($5.50), and a caloric treat called the "Here's the Guilt" banana split ($5).

There is a happy hour at Lox Around the Clock from 5 to 7 p.m.; drinks are $1.50. Lox Around the Clock is, true to its name, open 24 hours a day.

## MEXICAN

One of the most popular spots in Chelsea's burgeoning "Restaurant Row" on Eighth Avenue, **Mary Ann's,** 116 Eighth Ave., at 16th Street (tel. 242-9455), offers a nice variety of well-executed Mexican and Tex-Mex dishes at very affordable prices. Stucco and brick walls, ceiling fans, south-of-the-border decorative crafts, and a tiny candle on each table are the simple but effective design touches that, along with the menu, attract a young neighborhood crowd.

After working your way through a bowl of tortilla chips and pungent dipping salsa, try an entree like the chile relleno plate ($6), two Monterey peppers stuffed with cheese and covered in a delightful sauce, served with rice and beans. Mole poblano ($8), breast of chicken with a red-chile-and-chocolate sauce, comes with hot flour tortillas and is quite good. Such daily specials as roast duck in a mole of green tomatoes and pumpkin seeds, served with rice and zucchini, generally run $8 to $9. From a limited but respectable wine list you can choose a bottle of a good French table white for only $6 (beer is also available). A cup of flan ($2) tops off the meal.

Open from noon to 10 p.m. Monday through Thursday, to 11 p.m. Friday through Sunday.

## MEXICAN/SPANISH

There's a quaint, homey, feeling at **La Cascada Café,** 132 Ninth Ave., at 18th Street (tel. 255-6529). After eight years, René Rubenstein still greets guests at the door and seats them herself. A little off the beaten track, La Cascada caters to a local crowd of regulars, many of whom come back for the Mexican fiesta all-you-can-eat platter. While much of the menu is decidedly Mexican, there is a good variety of Spanish food as well.

The Mexican fiesta special is an excellent value. It consists of a heaping plate of tacos, enchiladas, tamales, burritos, or tostadas. For $8 you get a choice of three. If you're not so hungry you can get a choice of two for $7, or one for $6. The fiesta plate comes with rice and beans. La Cascada has a handsome choice of appetizers (both Spanish and Mexican), ranging in price from $4 to $8. The specialty of the house is mussels à la Cascada, served in a lightly seasoned tomato sauce for $7. Among the Spanish selections is chicken Zapata ($10.25), done in a white wine sauce with tomatillo, mushrooms, bacon, and garlic. For dessert, there's the chocolate decadence cake ($4), baked by the owner's mother. Wine, beer, and liquor are served. Brunch at La Cascada is also an excellent value at $8 à la carte, including two free drinks.

Open Monday through Friday from 5 to 11:30 p.m., on weekends from 11 a.m. to 11:30 p.m.

## SPANISH

From its blue-tiled exterior to its stucco walls, the **Centro Vasco,** 208 W. 23rd St., between Seventh and Eighth avenues (tel. 741-1408), has an authentic Spanish feel. Inside, the restaurant is decorated with original abstract art pieces painted by a Peruvian artist, in addition to more standard paintings of flamenco dancers. The setting here is elegant, with candle-shaped wall sconces and chocolate-colored table-cloths draped over beige linen. Arched doorways and wooden beams complete the Mediterranean setting.

This restaurant is expensive, with entrees between $7 and $24. But dinners, served in large portions, can be split by two people, with a $3 charge for an extra plate. To start, we suggest the black-bean soup or gazpacho ($4). The seafood paella, big enough for two, is $14. The lower-priced entrees—veal parmigiana ($11) and shrimp in wine sauce ($12.25)—are also good. If you really want to go all-out, try the stuffed lobster dinner ($22). For dessert, try the flan ($2) or cheesecake ($2.50).

Open for dinner only, from 3 p.m. to midnight during the week, to 1 a.m. on Saturday.

## THAI

If you're in the mood for something exotic, you might want to check out **Singha Thai Cuisine Restaurant,** at 240 Eighth Ave., between 22nd and 23rd streets (tel. 741-1732). This popular neighborhood restaurant is casual and simply decorated. Thai silk paintings adorn the walls, and dominating the center of the restaurant is a large bronze sculpture of a singha ("lion" in Thai). Tasty multicolored shrimp chips are brought to the table for you to munch on as you peruse the extensive, though simply priced, menu.

The menu offers a wide selection of Thai food from appetizers to desserts. The tom kha gai, chicken-coconut soup spiced with chile, lime juice, and galaga (a ginger-like spice), is excellent and costs only $2.50. Thai spring rolls are $4 and make a nice light appetizer when shared. Most of the entrees are sautéed with fresh vegetables, herbs, and spices. Chicken dishes are $9, shrimp dishes run $11, and noodle dishes are priced between $7 and $8. Pork and beef dishes run $8 to $9. A specialty of the house is fried Rama chicken ($9) served with baby corn, carrots, and green beans, and topped with peanut sauce and fresh coriander. Of course, Singha beer is available to accompany the meal.

Singha Restaurant is open Sunday through Thursday from 4 to 11:30 p.m. and on Friday and Saturday from 4 p.m. to midnight.

# 7. Greenwich Village

Greenwich Village, perhaps like no other place in all the city, encompasses the special diversity that is New York. Centered around Washington Square Park and including New York University, it is both frenetic and serene, commercial and residential. It offers the intimacy of quiet, crooked streets, and is one of the few places where one can wander quite accidentally onto an absolutely still street filled with rows of trees and townhouses that evoke the feel of a European city. Yet within another few blocks one returns to Sheridan Square, the honky-tonk of 8th Street, and the whirl of Washington Square Park.

That park, once a potter's field, then a parade ground, is the hub of the Village —especially on a sunny weekend or a warm summer night, when it's peopled by magicians, musicians, street artists, mothers and their toddlers, men bent intently over chess boards, young people on skateboards and roller skates, hustlers hawking the latest fad to anyone who will buy, and hundreds of spectators soaking up the scene. The entire area is filled with antique stores, unusual boutiques, and small restaurants and bars in all price brackets. The area covered in this section is bounded north and south by 14th and Houston streets, and on the east and west respectively by Lafayette Street and the West Side Highway.

## AMERICAN/CONTINENTAL

The thoroughly quaint little **Ye Waverly Inn** tavern and restaurant, 16 Bank St., at Waverly Place (tel. 929-4377), has been making customers happy since the 1920s, and the building that houses them dates to over a century ago. You can almost smell the age in the yellowing, cracking wallpaper, dark-wood wainscotting, oaken booths, and pendulum clocks. There's even an 1868 engraving of Manhattan to really take you back in time.

In spring and summer there's patio dining in the back (though the patio isn't nearly as charming as the inn-side). In winter, two of the four dining rooms are heated by working fireplaces.

Dinner prices at Ye Waverly Inn have begun to climb over budget, but an early-dinner special, served Monday through Thursday from 5:15 to 6:30 p.m., is worth scheduling your evening around. For $8.75 you get soup, an entree of southern fried chicken, meatloaf, calves' liver, or quiche and Waldorf salad, plus a vegetable, dessert, and coffee. Lunch is also a good deal. You can order soup, fresh muffins, salad, and a variety of sandwiches, like a hearty grilled cheddar or swiss with ham or bacon. And the inn makes its own desserts—pecan pie, Wellesley fudge cake, and carrot cake cost around $3.50.

Perhaps the best time to head for Ye Waverly Inn is on Sunday, when a classical guitarist serenades partakers of a champagne/cocktail brunch. Choose from eggs Benedict, fluffy omelets, quiche, french toast, or apple fritters with bacon and maple syrup. Complete with drink or juice, homemade rolls or muffins, and coffee or tea, the brunch is $9.50.

Ye Waverly Inn serves lunch Monday through Friday from 11:45 a.m. to 2 p.m. and Sunday brunch from 11:45 a.m. to 3:30 p.m. Dinner is served Monday through Thursday from 5:15 to 10 p.m., on Friday and Saturday to 11 p.m., and on Sunday from 4:30 to 9 p.m. Reservations are advised at all meals.

**The Lion's Head,** 59 Christopher St., just off Seventh Avenue South (tel. 929-0670), is known as a popular writers' hangout, the sort of place where at the bar you might meet the body behind a famous byline or the author of one of the books whose jacket covers line one wall. A hand-carved lion's head of oak, dating from the turn of the century, looms above the bar, which adjoins the dining room. With its low ceilings, dark-wood paneling, exposed-brick walls, and amber lighting, the place is dark, den-like, and cozy. Dinners like grilled rib-eye steak in Irish whiskey ($17.50) can easily break a budget, but for a low-priced alternative, order the spinach and fettuccine with pesto sauce, pan-fried brook trout, or the chicken pot pie— all priced under $14.

The Lion's Head serves a reasonably priced brunch from noon to 4 p.m. on Saturday and Sunday, including eggs Benedict with fries; walnut pancakes with bacon, ham, or sausage; or a chef's salad.

Open daily for drinks from noon to 2 a.m. and often till 4 a.m. Dinner is served from 5:30 p.m. to 1 a.m. weeknights, until 2 a.m. on weekends. Reservations are recommended for dinner parties of more than three.

The **Dallas B-B-Q** at 21 University Pl., off 8th Street (tel. 674-4450), is popular with college and high-school students. From the glass-enclosed dining room you can look out on a colorful Village street scene. Inside, the dining room is wildly decorated in black and white—the walls and chairs are zebra-striped, and the tables are black lacquered.

The menu won't disappoint you. At B-B-Q you'll get some of the best barbecue and cornbread in the Village. Try the baby back spareribs, served with a choice of potato and a generous slab of cornbread. You can get a smaller portion of the same meal at lunchtime. If you prefer chicken to beef barbecue, order the finger-licking quarter chicken, which also comes with a potato and cornbread. B-B-Q offers other tidbits—such as corn on the cob or crunchy onion rings—à la carte. The prices range from a low of $2.95 to a high of $8.95. All items on the menu are also available for take-out. B-B-Q has a house wine served by the glass or in a carafe, and a small selection of beer.

Open daily from noon to midnight (until 2 a.m. on Friday).

**The Blue Mill Tavern,** 50 Commerce St., west of Seventh Avenue (tel. 243-7114), is on one of the quietest and quaintest streets in the Village. Just around the corner from the famous Edna St. Vincent Millay House, it's a little difficult to find but definitely worth the search.

Alcino Neves, whose family has run the place for more than 40 years, was raised (and still lives) in an apartment above the restaurant, and is full of memories about the Village as it used to be. The tavern is part of that earlier history; the restaurant was established in the 1920s and was a speakeasy during Prohibition. It once did a thriving tourist business, but now caters mainly to local residents who know the place.

Inside, one can sit at intimate booths, upholstered in leather and across from a mahogany bar, or in the main dining room, where three huge murals, painted to look like Delft tile, establish the Dutch theme.

The food is traditional—the kind that mothers used to make. Chopped sirloin, caldeirada (a Portuguese fish stew), liver and bacon, or a small steak all come on a platter with a potato and either two vegetables or a salad, and are priced under $15.

The Blue Mill is open for dinner from 5 to 10 p.m. Monday through Thursday, until 11 p.m. on Friday and Saturday. Closed Sunday. No reservations.

Bring a good book and a thin wallet to the **Peacock Caffè,** 24 Greenwich Ave., off West 10th Street (tel. 242-9395). It's a quiet, romantic place, with classical music playing in the background, baroque columns, busts, a life-size statue of Pan playing his flute, and a carved-wood peacock perched over what was once a fireplace.

During the day the Peacock serves a variety of sandwiches ($5 to $6) on Italian bread, such as prosciutto and provolone, and salami and provolone. Plates of fruit and cheese, an array of salads, and soups all cost under $8.

At night you can order any of the above, or choose a pasta dish like gnocchi with butter sauce, or tortellini or fettuccine with meat sauce. Prices range from $7 to $9. For dessert, try the homemade Florentine apple torte served with whipped cream, or the Milanese coffeecake served with butter. And of course there's cappuccino, espresso, and special concoctions of coffee, chocolate, cinnamon, and whipped cream.

Open Tuesday through Thursday and on Sunday from 1 p.m. to 1 a.m., on Friday and Saturday until 2 a.m. Closed Monday.

Weary of the New York scene? The **Cottonwood Café,** 415 Bleecker St., between West 11th and Bank streets (tel. 924-6271), may offer the perfect respite from urban overload. A bank of windows facing Bleecker Street lends a bright and breezy air to the front dining room, where the walls are decorated with huge framed photographs of Texas ranching scenes and a state map. The back dining room, just as large but darker, is where the music begins at about 10:30 p.m. on weekdays and 11:30 p.m. on Saturday. Most of the performers are original songwriters, often playing folk or country-and-western music on acoustic guitar. Performances continue until the bar closes, between 12:30 and 2 a.m., depending on the size of the crowd.

The menu is limited and excellent, offering such Tex-Mex culinary delights as chicken and cheese enchiladas with refried beans and rice, and chicken fajitas—

marinated chicken pieces wrapped in a tortilla. Other main entrees, all under $10, include chicken fried steak, pork chops, or smoked barbecued ribs, and come with a choice of two vegetables (also available à la carte). We recommend the mashed potatoes—cooked with their skins and slathered with creamy gravy—and fried okra or blackeyed peas. Come hungry; the portions are Texas size.

When ordering brunch at Cottonwood's, from 10 a.m. to 3 p.m. on Saturday, until 4 p.m. on Sunday, try the huevos rancheros (hot Mexican eggs) or fresh fruit pancakes, and perhaps a bowl of grits.

Dinner is served from 5 to 11:45 p.m. Monday through Saturday, until 11 p.m. on Sunday.

A loud and fun Village hangout, the **White Horse Tavern,** is at the corner of West 11th and Hudson streets (tel. 243-9260). This legendary spot has long been a haven for writers and artists, including Dylan Thomas, who died several days after downing 18 shots of whiskey here in less than 20 minutes.

The place is roomy and the food is simple and cheap: burgers for $3.50, fish and chips for $5.50. The weekend brunch is a bargain. French toast, omelets, corned-beef hash, and basic eggs and bacon are all under $6.

Open daily from 11 a.m. until 2 a.m. Weekend brunch is served from 11 a.m. to 4 p.m.

For another great view of the Village spectacle, try **Woody's,** 140 Seventh Ave. South, between West 10th and Charles streets (tel. 242-1200). Seated in either the glass-enclosed front porch or the sidewalk café, you can watch the parade of pedestrians passing by. Inside there's an elaborate 150-year-old hand-carved mahogany bar from Bavaria and a pleasant lounge area with a view of the street. The bar is always casual and on weekends it's rowdy and noisy. The main dining area is decorated with hunting prints and furnished with oak booths and pedestal tables; in the winter two fireplaces burn brightly, lending a cozy atmosphere.

Woody's international menu includes numerous specials priced under $12. You can order fruit and baked brie, sautéed bluefish, and any number of pasta and Tex-Mex dishes. If you like salad, try the Greek chicken salad—grilled marinated breast of chicken in a bed of feta cheese, tomatoes, black olives, and roast peppers. Or check the blackboard for specials at both lunch and dinner.

Saturday and Sunday brunch, served from 11 a.m. to 5 p.m., includes a drink, muffin or bagel, and coffee or tea ($9). The bar boasts an impressive selection of beers, including Belgian raspberry brew and Samuel Smith's famous porter.

Woody's is open daily from noon to 2 a.m.; dinner starts at 6 p.m., and the bar stays open until 4 a.m. Reservations required for parties of eight or more.

Housed in an old 20th-century bank (there's an old vault downstairs), **Blue Willow,** 644 Broadway, at the corner of Bleecker Street (tel. 673-6480), offers American cuisine with a twist. Its main dining room is decked with marble walls, an antique wooden bar, lofty tin ceilings, and huge glass windows facing a buzz of pedestrians. If you can wade through the sea of Persian rugs and antique furniture in the back room, you can listen to local jazz musicians like talented saxophonist Rob Middleton perform Wednesday and Thursday evenings (9 p.m. to midnight; $5 cover).

A little pricey in the seafood and meat department, Blue Willow offers a variety of other dishes at reasonable prices (under $12). Begin with steamed mussels in Spanish garlic sauce and garlic bread, and then move on to the roast leg of lamb with mint, spinach, and pecan stuffing. Or try any of the pasta dishes, like shrimp, mussels, crabmeat, and scallops on fettuccine or the handmade wild-mushroom ravioli.

Open daily from 11:30 a.m. to 3 a.m. Reservations suggested.

Heapin' helpings are the rule at **Eddie's,** 14 Waverly Pl., near Broadway (tel. 420-0919), where the burger platters and the tostada salads weigh more than most people do when they're born. The crowd at Eddie's is likely to be mostly college kids from New York University, which perhaps explains the sturdy, no-nonsense décor —heavy wooden tables, exposed-brick walls, and pop and rock music on the sound system. There's nothing pretentious or trendy about Eddie's. It's good solid food at a low price in a simple place. It's a fine spot for a weary traveler who has spent the day exploring New York's oddities and is not in the mood for any more surprises.

Besides the basic burgers and Tex-Mex fare, Eddie's offers omelets and bountiful vegetarian selections, including tofu salads, stir-fried vegetables with brown rice, and an avocado-and-mozzarella pita sandwich. The prices are more than reasonable, especially given the portion size. A hamburger alone is $3; burger platters run $5 to $6 and include a pile of fries and a healthy salad. Nothing on the menu is more than $7. Eddie's serves soft drinks, coffee, tea, beer, and wine—no hard liquor.

Eddie's is open Monday through Saturday from 11 a.m. to 11 p.m. Cash or American Express only.

A Village fixture, **Elephant and Castle,** 68 Greenwich Ave., between West 10th Street and Seventh Avenue (tel. 243-1400), is a charming, if crowded, nook well known for its staggering variety of delicious sandwiches, omelets, soups, and burgers. The pesto omelet is $6.50 and the Elephant burger, with sour cream, bacon, tomato, scallions, and cheese ($7.25), are among the house favorites.

Open Monday through Thursday from 8:30 a.m. to midnight, on Friday to 1 a.m., on Saturday from 10 a.m. to 1 a.m., and on Sunday from 11 a.m. to midnight.

**The Corner Bistro,** 331 W. 4th St., at the corner of Jane Street and Eighth Avenue (tel. 242-9502), is a true neighborhood bar, with big wooden booths, sporting events on TV, and a quiet, friendly mood. The menu is short and to-the-point: burgers, chili, sandwiches, and french fries. The burgers are enormous, hand-molded slabs of beef ($3.75 to $5), the chili is straightforward two-alarm, the sandwiches are basic grilled cheese and BLT's, and the shoestring fries are crisp and plentiful. It goes without saying that the bar has the full line of liquors and a sizable selection of draft and bottled beers.

The Corner Bistro is open from 11:30 a.m. to 4 a.m. every day, and its kitchen keeps the same hours. Reservations are unknown.

**David's Pot Belly,** 98 Christopher St., between Bleecker and Bedford streets (tel. 243-9614), is another tiny eatery (45 people is a squeeze) that's popular with the Village crowd and tourists. It has wood-paneled walls, small wooden tables and booths, mirrored walls, and hand-blown amber-colored hanging lamps.

The menu consists primarily of omelets, egg casseroles, burgers, and salads—all priced well below $10. Omelets come with every imaginable filling; corn, jelly, peanut butter, sardines, chutney, olives and pimiento cheese, walnuts, peach, pineapple, eggplant, artichokes, and more. Those and a variety of egg casserole dishes ($9 to $10) are served with potato pancakes, applesauce, and an English muffin. Half-pound burgers ($6) come with an array of toppings—from chili to cream cheese, anchovies to egg. Crêpes, topped with mornay sauce ($8), may be filled with anything from asparagus and mushrooms, tuna and corn, to chopped beef and onions or hot mixed fruit. The menu also offers a variety of salads ($5.25 to $8.50). Desserts consume an entire page of the menu, and include floats ($4) and sundaes ($6) made with Häagen-Dazs ice cream.

Open daily from 11 a.m. to 6 a.m. No reservations.

The **Cedar Tavern,** 82 University Pl., between 11th and 12th streets (tel. 929-9089), is a comfortable joint, as the manager likes to say. Downstairs it's dark and woody. In the back there are cozy booths lit by lantern-like lamps; up front there's an elaborate maple bar, over 100 years old, with panes of stained glass; and on the second floor there's a garden under a peaked glass roof. In the late 1950s and early '60s the tavern, then located around the corner on 10th Street, was a hangout of abstract expressionist artists like Mark Rothko, Franz Kline, and Jackson Pollock. Now the clientele is more likely to be the neighborhood crowd—antique dealers, professionals, and students.

Meals here are tasty, simple, and cheap: sandwiches start at $4; entrees, at $9. You can order a cheese, mushroom, or ham omelet, served with a vegetable, potato, and salad, or pork chops and broiled scallops—two of the more popular items, served with a salad and potato. At the weekend brunch, served from noon to 4:30 p.m., you can get a cocktail, coffee, home-fries, and a choice of eggs Benedict, french toast, or eggs with ham, bacon, or sausage, for $7.25.

Open from 8 a.m. to 4 a.m. daily; the kitchen is on duty from 11 a.m. to 1 a.m. Sunday through Wednesday and until 3:30 a.m. on Thursday, Friday, and Saturday. Reservations accepted.

**Covent Garden,** 133 W. 13th St., between Sixth and Seventh avenues (tel. 675-0020), is lovely to look at. The room is graced by a grand piano that sits near the rear of the main dining room and is reflected in a huge mirror. There is music nightly, with a pianist whose repertoire runs from show tunes to classical to jazz. Out back is an appealing garden terrace under a skylight roof, with abundant hanging plants and an ivy-covered wall.

Lunch is affordable and the menu is large and varied. You can order a French-dip roast beef sandwich or a hamburger, or try the selection of pastas and salads. Most dinner entrees are well above budget, but you can order a Caesar salad for two or filet of sole alla rugulla for under $13.

Sunday brunch is a fair bet. For $12 you can have cocktails or unlimited champagne with an entree of cold chicken breast, quiche, and spinach salad, or a small prime sirloin with eggs.

The real bargain, though, is the late-night supper, served from 9 p.m. to midnight, when burgers, salads, mini-pizzas, and the pasta du jour all cost under $10.

Covent Garden is open for lunch Monday through Friday from noon to 3 p.m. Dinner is served from 5 to 11 p.m. Sunday through Thursday, until 11:30 p.m. on Friday and Saturday. Sunday brunch is served from noon to 3:30 p.m. Reservations advised.

In the twilight zone between East and West Villages, an appropriately amorphous restaurant has made a niche for itself—**The NoHo Star,** 330 Lafayette St., at the corner of Bleecker Street (tel. 925-0070). The menu wanders between China and America, the window panes are slanted, and every column and wall sports a different design. Despite the initial feeling of vertigo, however, few eating places could be more comfortable or more satisfying.

Starting off the day with breakfast, (under $7), one might have eggs Nepal, scrambled with cream and a touch of curry, and served with flaky papadum bread, or yogurt frou-frou, with fresh fruit, hazelnuts, and Vermont maple syrup. The regular dinner menu features particularly good Chinese dishes—among them, crispy jumbo shrimp with pan-blackened stringbeans, and the vegetarian delight. Most dinners, including grilled breast of chicken with lime and coriander, are priced below $12.

Open from 8 a.m. to 12:30 a.m. Monday through Friday, 10:30 a.m. to 12:30 a.m. on Saturday, and 10 a.m. to 11:30 p.m. on Sunday. Reservations are suggested.

**Gray's Papaya,** 402 Sixth Ave., on the corner of 8th Street (tel. 260-3532), is one of New York's favorite fast-food stops. It's strictly stand and gobble—no seats. It's known for its 60¢ hot dogs, fast-moving lines, and wide variety of fruit juices—papaya, coconut, pineapple, and fresh-squeezed orange juice.

Open 24 hours a day.

## CAJUN

Cajun cooking appeared on the New York scene as a wild craze a few years back, with trendy restaurants mushrooming all over town. Now that the fad has died down, the serious business of Cajun food can proceed with less fanfare and more truly good eating. The **Acme Bar & Grill,** 9 Great Jones St., at the corner of Lafayette Street (tel. 420-1934), certainly makes no great claim for itself; its motto is "An Okay Place to Eat." That it certainly is. It is a big, unpretentious space hung with old gas-station signs and kept dark enough to generate intimacy.

Its menus, identical for lunch and dinner but with a $1 to $2 price difference, are made up of a modest number of dishes that focus on fish and cost under $12 on the average. Catfish and trout loom large, whether pan-fried, blackened, or spicy. Oyster lovers can feast on a robust plate of fried or steamed oysters, and non-fish-eaters can console themselves with crisp chicken-fried steak.

Acme serves a weekend brunch between 11:30 a.m. and 3:45 p.m. that features such hearty fare as catfish and eggs. It's open for lunch on weekdays from 11:30 a.m. to 4 p.m., and for dinner between 4 p.m. and midnight. On weekends dinnertime stretches to 1 a.m. Reservations are suggested.

A glassed-in sidewalk café hides the fact that **Sazerac House,** 533 Hudson St., at the corner of Charles Street (tel. 989-0313), is the oldest structure on Charles Street. The 1826 landmark building was once part of a farm.

Sazerac's interior is old-style Village, with an old mahogany bar, rough hard-wood floors, oak booths and tables, and a working fireplace. Menus from New Orleans restaurants and pictures of Dixieland and jazz musicians grace the walls. The atmosphere is cozy and attracts primarily a neighborhood crowd, plus a few celebrities now and then.

The menu offers moderately priced ($8 to $13) New Orleans favorites like jambalaya—a Créole stew—served with garlic bread, and deep-fried oysters. Lower-priced items include more traditional New York fare: hamburgers and cheeseburgers and meatloaf with mashed potatoes. Sazerac is a favorite Village spot for brunch, serving à la carte pain perdu (Louisiana-style french toast), a variety of gourmet egg dishes, hash and eggs, and quiche—all under $7. There are also burgers for the hungrier.

Sazerac serves lunch daily from 11:30 a.m. to 4:45 p.m., and dinner from 5 p.m. to midnight. Brunch is served on Saturday and Sunday from 11 a.m. to 4:45 p.m. Reservations recommended.

## CAJUN/CARIBBEAN

Southern cooking goes all the way to the Caribbean at **Day-O,** 103 Greenwich Ave., near West 12th Street (tel. 924-3160). The resulting dishes are distinctively spicy. Many of the recipes come from Small's Paradise, a reknowned Harlem eatery. Eventually, the owners hope to work a little Italian into the menu to stay true to the restaurant's geographic roots—it is in the same space that for 30 years was home to the restaurant La Marionetta.

From floor to ceiling, Day-O is a rewarding, surprising sensation—and not just because of the food. Four different artists were hired to paint tropical murals on the walls and design the light fixtures. The palm trees really sway and motorized mobiles bob and swing overhead to a reggae soundtrack. The décor and the young, trendy, West Village crowd work together to give their own meaning to the term "urban jungle."

Entrees (priced from $6 to $9) include Dolores's chicken Dixie, Beryl's best (a house secret—Jamaican-seasoned minced sirloin), codfish fritters, West Indian peppersteak, and gumbo Day-O (a hearty portion of seafood stew with Cajun seasonings). The "side stuffers" continue the Cajun/Caribbean theme. Healthy portions of collard greens, black-eyed peas with rice, fried plantains, sweet-potato chips, and cornbread can be had for less than $2 each.

Drinks are an important part of the Day-O menu. Their fluorescent and tropical pastel colors are as pleasing as their taste. The flavored margaritas, daiquiris, Day-O rum punch, and flying baboons, at $4.75 a pop, are a treat.

Day-O is open for dinner seven days a week from 5 p.m. to midnight, serves drinks only from 1 to 4 a.m., and serves brunch on Saturday and Sunday (call for times). Day-O accepts cash only.

## CHINESE

**Sung Tieng,** 334 Bleecker St., between Christopher and West 10th streets (tel. 929-7800 or 924-8314), is a large, cool, airy place with white walls and picnic tables in a little terrace out front. It serves unusual Cantonese, Szechuan, and Hunan dishes with flair, minimal MSG, and prices under $12. The Fisherman's Nest consists of scallops, prawns, fish cakes, and crab prettily served in a wonton basket. The Dragon and Phoenix is a succulent combination of lobster and chicken. This year's house favorites include ginger chicken and orange beef or chicken—served with orange rinds, dried chile peppers, and garlic.

Sung Tieng is open from 11:30 a.m. to midnight Monday through Thursday, to 1 a.m. on Friday, from 1 p.m. to 1 a.m. on Saturday, and 1 p.m. to midnight on Sunday. Reservations are suggested.

## CUBAN

**Bayamo,** at 704 Broadway, between East 4th Street and Astor Place (tel. 475-5151), is one of the more festive Village restaurants. The owners call it a Cuban restaurant with Chinese overtones, but the décor is pure New Wave. If you can, sit at a table in the balcony. From there you can get a great view of the comings and goings of a whole variety of chic-looking Village folk.

When you cast your eyes over the extensive menu, you'll see that you can get almost anything at Bayamo. In the mood for a salad? Try ensalada de pollo escabechado, which is spiced chicken mixed with cold vegetables. Maybe you want eggs. Order the huevos revueltos con camarones—scrambled eggs with shrimp, tomato, and chili. For a taste of the East, sample any of this restaurant's Oriental spring rolls, made to order with your choice of filling, and filling enough to be a whole meal. Most dinners cost between $7 and $12.

There's also a large dessert menu. The homemade flan with pecans and macadamia nuts gets rave reviews. If you want something lighter, try the mandarin orange sorbet.

Open Sunday through Tuesday from 11:30 a.m. to midnight, on Wednesday and Thursday until 1 a.m., and on Friday and Saturday until 2 a.m.

## FRENCH

**Chez Brigitte,** 77 Greenwich Ave., between Bank and 11th streets (tel. 929-6736), is an easy place to overlook: six paces and you've passed it. It has two counters, 12 seats, minimal décor, and a sense of humor: a sign in the window declares, "Chez Brigitte will seat 250 persons at one time." If you don't mind the luncheonette ambience, you'll be pleased with the Provence-style fare at reasonable prices (under $10).

You can begin with pea, onion, or soup du jour, and then choose either a daily special (served with a vegetable and potato, rice, or macaroni) or entrees like beef bourguignon, filet of sole meunière, veal cutlet, or chicken fricassee. Omelets, sandwiches, and fresh homemade dessert—such as chocolate chiffon or banana pie—are also available.

Open from 11 a.m. to 9 p.m. Monday through Saturday.

Unlike most eating spots in the Village, **14 Christopher Street,** right off Gay Street (tel. 620-9594), begins to fill by 6 p.m. That's because of its popular "early-bird special"—a complete dinner, with salad or soup, entree, dessert, and beverage, all for $9. The cuisine is "French country," the chef/owner British, and the décor American 1980s sophisticate.

Early-bird specials change from time to time, but are generally simple, sauceless entrees. The regular menu is more adventurous but also more expensive. Filet of flounder with scallop stuffing, chicken Cordon Bleu, or beer-batter chicken in honey-mustard sauce all cost under $15. Daily specials always include entrees for under $15. Wine dresses it all up, at $6.50 for a half carafe of "house."

An early-bird dinner is served Tuesday through Sunday from 5 to 7:30 p.m. Regular dinner goes until 9 p.m. Lunch on weekdays is from noon to 5 p.m., on Sunday to 4 p.m. Weekend brunch is served from noon to 4 p.m. Closed Monday.

**Restaurant Florent** is a clattering, glittering little diamond in the rough—the meat market district, in the far western reaches of the Village. It's located at 69 Gansevoort St., between Washington and Greenwich streets (tel. 989-5779).

Clearly the owner dreams of Montmartre: his kitchen serves excellent bistro food at reasonable prices (between $6.50 and $9). Coquilles St-Jacques, a wonderful goat cheese salad, and a charcuterie plate, offering three different meat pâtés, are among the more popular dishes. Florent does not serve mixed drinks, but does offer a good selection of wines, beers, and cognacs.

Though the prices are low and the décor diner-hip, take care to dress sharp; behind a deceptively humble storefront, the bright and fancy have come to Florent to talk, flirt, and scheme. Reservations are a must every day at lunch and dinner.

Open 24 hours a day.

## INDIAN

Indian food was scarcely known in New York 15 years ago. Now there are restaurants everywhere, but few as satisfying as **Mitali West,** 296 Bleecker St., at the corner of Seventh Avenue South (tel. 989-1367). This two-story red palace is done up in classic Indian style—or the local version thereof—with red-jacketed waiters, low lights, and printed fabrics on the walls. The food is abundant at fairly low prices, and the savvy diner can feast for under $11.

An entree such as Dopiaz curry will do the trick, filled out with side orders of paratha, a savory flat bread, and perhaps mango chutney. For a splurge, a meal might begin with chicken tandoori or lobster curry. The budget-minded might also look into the combination platters, which juggle various line-ups of appetizer, entree, and condiments, and cost an average of $12. In addition there is an $8 lunch special served Monday through Friday from noon to 3 p.m.

Mitali West is open every day from noon to midnight. Reservations are suggested.

## ITALIAN

You don't necessarily have to head for Little Italy to find a good Italian restaurant in the city, or even to find a cluster of them. Along Thompson Street in the Village, between West 3rd and Bleecker streets, there are two moderately priced Italian eateries.

You may recognize the **Grand Ticino,** 228 Thompson St. (tel. 777-5922), as the gracious restaurant with a restful air and friendly service that was featured in the hit movie *Moonstruck.* Established in 1919, it's the oldest Italian restaurant in the Village. It is a few steps below street level, and entered via a small alcove of plant-filled windows. The deep-green walls are background for black-and-white framed photographs. The tables are covered with white linen, softly lit with individual lamps, and surrounded by simple black chairs. A few pieces of pottery line a shelf that runs across the room and a huge vase of flowers sits beside the bar. The effect is one of understated elegance.

The dinner and lunch menus are essentially the same, with prices running about $1 less at lunch. Most of the soups are priced at about $3 for dinner; pasta dishes run an average of $10. Main entrees come with a vegetable of the day or spaghetti, and desserts like tira misu, a sweet pudding with whipped cream, espresso, and ladyfingers.

Open Monday through Friday from noon to 3 p.m. for lunch, from 5 to 11 p.m. for dinner. On Saturday, open continuously from noon to 11 p.m. Closed Sunday. Reservations recommended.

A few doors away is **Livorno,** 216 Thompson St. (tel. 260-1972), which has a charming, festive air. In the front room there's a bar under a shingled eave, and the walls are decorated with prints, paintings, and maps of Italy. Pass through a lattice-work plastic grape arbor to enter the main dining room in the back, where trompe-l'oeil windows are framed by wood shutters and boxes of plastic geraniums. Tables are covered with white linen over deep-green cloths.

Appetizers such as spinach or escarola in broth, or a hot antipasto, are less than $5. Homemade pasta dishes and entrees like veal scaloppine, veal cutlet, or chicken cacciatore cost between $8 and $14. All include a side order of vegetables or pasta.

Livorno is open daily from noon to 11:30 p.m. Reservations recommended.

Located in the heart of Greenwich Village, **Minetta's Tavern,** 113 MacDougal St., at Minetta Lane (tel. 475-3850), offers Italian dishes in a cozy and casual atmosphere. There are small paned windows, a dark wooden bar, a dessert case filled with pastries, and small tables covered in white linen.

Minetta's is affordable (most entrees cost less than $12) and serves an array of vegetable, poultry, veal, and pasta dishes. We enjoyed the petto di pollo alla fiorentina—breast of chicken sautéed with spinach—and the tortellacci, pasta filled with basil, fontina, and ricotta. Delicious desserts ($5) and coffees are also available.

Minetta's is open from noon to 3 a.m. daily. Reservations suggested.

## JAPANESE
**Shima,** 12 Waverly Pl., between Greene and Mercer streets (tel. 674-1553), serves excellent food at reasonable prices. The décor here is also simple, with wood-paneled walls tastefully decorated with Japanese block prints. A small separate room has knee-level tables and cushions for seating on the floor. Overhead in the main dining area, paper lanterns hang from an Oriental-style peaked ceiling.

For lunch you can order à la carte: vegetable tempura, chicken teriyaki, or suki-yaki. At night, full dinners (for under $11) come with soup, salad, rice, and an appetizer. A bottle of sake, served warm as the Japanese drink it, adds Asian charm to any meal.

Shima is open weekdays for lunch from noon to 2:30 p.m. and for dinner daily from 5 to 11 p.m. Reservations accepted.

**Minami,** 27 Waverly Pl., between University Place and Greene Street (tel. 529-2198), serves the standard New York–Japanese fare in attractive, clean surroundings. The waiters are more than just polite, they are warm without being intrusive; perhaps that's why so many parents like to bring their children here.

The fresh sushi and sashimi, chicken teriyaki, and the more unusual yellowtail teriyaki are all priced under $12.

Minami is open Monday through Friday from noon to 11 p.m., and on Saturday and Sunday from 4 p.m. to midnight.

## MEXICAN
People who hail from places where Mexican fare is usually the best buy in town often greet the prices for New York City's south-of-the-border food with some dismay, but the restaurants are individual enough in personality to make them worth a visit.

You get the real thing at **Gonzalez y Gonzalez,** 625 Broadway, between Bleecker and Houston streets (tel. 473-8787). The restaurant's motto is "Comida típica de México"—that is, "typical Mexican food." The south-of-the-border décor finishes the theme. With its murals, piñatas, and sombreros, Gonzalez y Gonzalez is ready for a Mexican festival, and you will be too, after a few moments inside.

Nothing on the menu is more than $10, and the brilliantly spiced dishes set a new standard for Mexican food. The menu is in both Spanish and English. To start, you might try roast cheese with tomatillo sauce ($3.50) or roast mushrooms with chiles and salsas ($4). Marinated chicken in banana leaves ($10), rice with seafood ($10), and whitefish with garlic ($9) are excellent main-course selections. If you have a light appetite, the seafood soup ($4), thick and spicy with plenty of squid and fish, and a side order of plantain fritters ($3.25) or fried plantains ($2) is more than a meal. There's a tantalizing array of Mexican desserts. Since you won't have room for all of them, try banana and mango flambé with ice cream ($4).

If the authentic food doesn't make this young restaurant famous, maybe its 100-foot-long bar will. A waiter told us that it's the longest bar in New York and the second longest in the country. It's a good place to sip margaritas to the Latin rhythms of live mariachi music every Wednesday through Saturday after 8 p.m. (call for details).

Gonzalez y Gonzalez is open Sunday through Thursday from 11:30 a.m. to midnight, until 1 a.m. on Friday and Saturday.

**Panchitos,** 105 MacDougal St., between Bleecker and West 3rd streets (tel. 473-8963), is a casual, crowded, noisy place, and so popular at peak hours that the lines of hungry customers snake back through the long grotto-like hallway. The wait can be as much as 30 minutes.

The newly renovated restaurant is bright and lofty, with room for 150. It runs the width of a block; in the back, plant-filled windows look out onto a quiet street. The floors are concrete set with marble, and the main dining room is lined with black-walnut booths and Mexican folk art. Overhead, large ceiling fans whir gently. Many evenings a local musician plays Spanish classical guitar.

Panchito's may be as popular for its drinks as for the food it serves. The bar boasts 101 different double-rum piña coladas and frozen daiquiris, 25 types of rum, and 30 cognacs; the drink list consumes almost 3 pages of the menu. But the food is good and affordable, and the portions are generous. In fact unless you're simply ravenous, an order of Panchito's popular combination platters—enchilada, burritto, or tortilla served with rice and beans ($5 to $10)—should be plenty.

Open daily from 11 a.m. to 4 a.m. No reservations; be prepared to wait.

The hi-tech dining room at **Caramba!,** 684 Broadway, at the corner of Great Jones (East 3rd) Street (tel. 420-9817), may not seem particularly south-of-the-border, but after you've tasted the food you'll know why this is considered one of the best Mexican restaurants in the Village.

Caramba! is a favorite hangout for the young, professional crowd, who come on weekend nights to enjoy the giant slush margaritas ($5 for a medium, $11 for a large). If you don't want to wait for a table, come to this restaurant at lunchtime; it'll be far less crowded.

There's a wide selection of appetizers, and many of them are filling enough to be a whole meal if you aren't very hungry. Most of Caramba!'s hearty entrees cost between $7 and $13. Try the chicken or shrimp quesadilla, a soft flour tortilla filled with cheese, shredded chicken or shrimp, and salsa verde, and served with guacamole and jalapeños. For an entree, have a Caramba! combination plate, a choice of two items from a long list of Mexican specialties, or the beef chimichangas, crisp-fried burritos topped with enchilada sauce and served with rice and beans.

Caramba! is open from noon to midnight during the week, until 1:30 a.m. weekends.

**Manhattan Chili Company,** 302 Bleecker St., right off Seventh Avenue (tel. 206-7163), offers a mouthwatering selection of different kinds of chili. What they call the "Real McCoy" is the standard mixture of chili beans, beef, onion, and hot pepper. For variety, you may want to try the seafood chili, or if you like hot food, choose the "Texas Chain Gang" chili. All the chilis cost between $7 and $10, depending on the size of the bowl you order.

Besides chili, the menu includes a few other Tex-Mex favorites like chunky gazpacho or chicken and steak fajitas served on a sizzling platter with onions and red peppers. For dessert, sample the Mississippi mud pie. The restaurant also has a wine list and offers a large selection of beers.

The Manhattan Chili Company is open Sunday through Thursday from noon to midnight, and on Friday and Saturday until 1 a.m.

Those who like to take their meals in a party atmosphere will enjoy the **Caliente Cab Co.,** 21 Waverly Pl., at the corner of Greene Street (tel. 529-1500). The crowd-pleasing menu and the decorating scheme somehow convey a futuristic interpretation of a Tijuana taxi garage.

Popular items include a choice of quesadillas and Mexican pizzas, or a bountiful combination platter of taco, enchilada, tostada, and burrito—all less than $10.

The restaurant opens at noon every day and closes its kitchens at 12:45 a.m. Monday through Thursday, at 2:45 a.m. on Friday and Saturday, and at midnight on Sunday.

The cozy, rustic atmosphere at **Violeta's,** 220 W. 13th St., between Seventh Avenue and Greenwich Street (tel. 255-1710)—candlelit wooden tables, recorded guitar music, and large posters of movie-star Mexicans on the walls—reflects the tastes and enthusiasms of its proprietress, Violeta herself, who is nearly always on hand to oversee the kitchen.

In addition to the regular Mexican offerings—burritos, enchiladas, and tamales (all about $9.50)—there are house specialties that include lamb tacos and mole poblano (chicken in a nonsweet chocolate sauce). Mexican beer and pitchers of fruity sangría are available to quench your thirst. The lunch menu offers lighter versions of the regular dinner menu, with correspondingly lighter prices.

Open seven days a week from noon to 4 p.m. for lunch and 4:30 p.m. to midnight for dinner.

## MIDDLE EASTERN

As travelers often do, you may tire of rich sauces, vegetable-less entrees, and spicy ethnic foods. If so, take a trip to **Boostan,** 85 MacDougal St., between Bleecker and Houston streets (tel. 533-9561). It's a popular, totally unpretentious restaurant that prides itself on large helpings of extremely healthy foods based on Middle Eastern and Mediterranean recipes. You can dine at lacquered tree-trunk tables adorned with flower-filled vases, amid guitars and wooden flutes and weavings hung on the walls. Or if weather permits, you can sit outside at small Formica tables.

Boostan's under-$8 vegetarian dinners are widely appreciated for their freshness and ample servings. A favorite among regulars is couscous (a Middle Eastern grain dish) topped with stewed vegetables, but other dishes are more imaginative and tastier. An expanded menu now offers fresh salmon, halibut, and filet of sole, as well as pasta dinners like fettuccine primavera—all priced under $10.

Desserts at Boostan should not be ignored. Baloza, made of fresh orange or apricot, low-fat milk, and whipped cream, is particularly popular, as is Boostan's carrot cake. Try a Turkish coffee to top it all off.

Open daily from noon to 1 a.m.

## PIZZA

Located in the middle of an Italian neighborhood that has stubbornly maintained its identity through decades of bohemia, commercialization, and gentrification, **John's Pizzeria,** 278 Bleecker St., between Cornelia Street and Seventh Avenue South (tel. 243-1680), represents an older, more traditional style of pizzeria that is rapidly becoming hard to find in New York. John's does not, for example, bow to pressure by selling individual slices, but only serves whole pies, for take-out or on-the-spot consumption.

The décor is resolutely featureless, but the pies are among the best in town. A list of some 40 variations ranges from the small cheese-and-tomato pizza ($8.25) to the giant six-ingredient extravaganza ($12.50).

Open Monday through Thursday from 4:30 to 11 p.m., and on Friday, Saturday, and Sunday from noon to 12:30 a.m. It is a popular place, and it's first-come, first-served—so expect to wait.

There must be at least a dozen pizzerias in the city which all claim to be the "original" **Ray's** pizza house. But most in-the-know New Yorkers seem to agree that this one, on the corner of 11th Street and Avenue of the Americas (tel. 243-2253), is the authentic one and worthy of its fame. The pizza here has a nearly perfect crust and gobs of mozzarella. On any given day—and seemingly at any hour—the line of people waiting for a slice snakes out the door and more are jammed around the stand-up counters and the restaurant's few tables.

Slices of regular pizza sell for $1.50, $1.60 for Sicilian, $3.50 for a "famous" combo slice. Optional extras are 50¢ each. An entire large pie is $11.50; with one topping, $13.

Ray's is open Sunday through Thursday from 11 a.m. to 2 a.m., until 3 a.m. on Friday and Saturday.

**Pizza Piazza,** 785 Broadway at the corner of East 10th Street (tel. 505-0977), is the place to go if you like deep-dish Sicilian-style pizza. The pizzas come in three sizes: small is recommended for one person, medium for two, and large for three or four. The menu features a list of 12 types of pizza ranging from the "Basic," with tomato sauce and three kinds of cheeses ($5.50, $10.50, $19), to the "Californian," with tomato sauce and seasonal vegetables ($6, $11.75, $20). The menu also offers pastas, burgers, chili, and salads.

Cooking the pizzas takes 20 minutes, so you may want to while away the waiting time by trying an appetizer. Guacamole, and broccoli and shrimp vinaigrette, are both tasty.

Open from noon to 10:30 p.m. Sunday through Thursday, until 12:30 a.m. on Friday and Saturday.

## PUERTO RICAN

**La Taza de Oro,** right outside the Village at 96 Eighth Ave., between 14th and 15th streets (tel. 243-9946), is a great place for anyone interested in eating some of the best Latin food around at bargain-basement prices. La Taza de Oro, or "cup of gold," is a simple luncheonette with Formica counters and Formica tables, where the music from the jukebox is Latin and almost everyone speaks Spanish. It's a neighborhood joint, and the menu, posted on two blackboards, is in English as well as Spanish.

Most of the dishes cost under $9 and many people come for the pork chops or the roast chicken, both served with rice and salad. But the specialties are more exotic: tripe soup, pickled fish, and octopus salad are a few among many. Recommended, too, are the drinks—mavi (an apple-cider drink) and tamarindo (a tropical fruit juice).

Open daily from 7 a.m. to midnight; breakfast is served until 11 a.m. daily. Sometimes the owners close on Sunday, so you might call first if you're planning on dropping by that day.

## SOUL FOOD

The **Pink Teacup,** 42 Grove St., near Bleecker Street (tel. 807-6755), is one of the few eateries in the Village where a yearning for true southern cooking can be satisfied. Nearly everything in this luncheonette is pink, including the walls, curtains, menu, and shirts worn by the waitresses and waiters. The entrees include pigs' feet, giblet stew, grits, and freshly baked southern biscuits.

The place is small, with ten counter stools and seven oilcloth-covered tables. The walls are adorned with an assortment of photographs of Stevie Wonder, Martin Luther King, John F. Kennedy, and the Supremes. The menu is remarkable for bounteous fare at budget prices (between $7 and $13). Begin your morning with a breakfast of eggs, grits, and bacon; or dine in true southern style on pecan or blueberry pancakes and a grilled pork chop or fried chicken with a biscuit. Dinner offerings are equally generous: all come with hot bread, soup, salad, two vegetables—such as black-eyed peas, yellow turnips, or okra—and dessert. All homemade, all hearty, all deliciously authentic.

Open from 8 a.m. to midnight Monday through Thursday and around the clock from Friday morning to Sunday midnight. No reservations.

## SPANISH

There's something appealingly unpretentious about **Spain,** 113 W. 13th St., west of Sixth Avenue (tel. 929-9580). This casual and friendly restaurant has been run by the same family for two generations.

The fare is northern Spanish, and seafood is its specialty. Here, too, the portions are large, and you might want to split one portion between two people. The menu at lunch and dinner is the same, with prices running about 50¢ to $1.50 more at dinner. The most popular dish is mariscada with green sauce—a medley of shellfish (clams, lobster, shrimp, mussels) served in a huge metal pot. Entrees range between $7 and $16, and all are served with Spanish rice, a tossed salad, and bread. A half carafe of sangría is $5.50; desserts like caramel custard cost $3.

Spain is open Monday through Saturday from noon to 3 p.m. for lunch, and daily from 3 p.m. to 1 a.m. for dinner. Reservations recommended, especially on weekends.

**Tío Pepe,** 168 W. 4th St., between Sixth and Seventh avenues (tel. 242-9338), is a family-style restaurant serving traditional Spanish cuisine. Overlooking West 4th Street out back is a lovely glass-enclosed garden and Spanish-style patio. A flamenco guitarist adds to the atmosphere.

The best buy at Tío Pepe is the Mexican "all-you-can-eat" combo platters—tacos, enchiladas, tamales, burritos—served with soup, salad, rice, and beans ($6 at lunch, $9 at dinner). Most dinner entrees are in the $10 to $15 range. At lunch, however, most of the same entrees—chicken paella, shrimp in green sauce, rainbow trout with almonds, and others—are recommended. They are all delightful departures from regular Mexican restaurant fare.

Open Sunday through Thursday from noon to midnight, on Friday and Saturday until 2 a.m. Lunch is served from noon to 4 p.m.

## THAI

If you've never eaten Thai food, **A Poy Laung,** 210 Thompson St., between Bleecker and West 3rd streets (tel. 533-7290), is a great place to make the introduction; some swear it's the best in town. The restaurant is a small (only nine tables), unassuming place, and simply decorated. Travel posters of Thailand cover the walls, fish mobiles swing gently from the ceiling, silk flowers top the cloth-covered tables, and Thai music sets the mood. The location couldn't be better (Thompson Street is a delightful Village stretch and the restaurant's big front window provides a fine view of the street), nor could the food. We recommend it highly.

Many of the dishes are hot and spicy, but you may order mild. If you can't distinguish from the menu descriptions, don't hesitate to ask. Those that come with Thai sauce are especially hot, but milder dishes include pork, shrimp, beef, or chicken with eight kinds of vegetables. We tried one of each—beef with eight vegetables and chicken with spicy Thai sauce—and both were excellent. Most pork, chicken, and beef dishes are between $6.50 and $7; most seafood dishes are $8. A bowl of all the rice you can eat is $1. It's a bargain of a meal. A glass of house wine or a refreshing glass of Thai iced tea complements the meal nicely.

Open Monday through Saturday from noon to 11 p.m., and on Sunday from 5 to 11 p.m. Reservations accepted.

# 8. SoHo

This former industrial area, whose buildings date from the last century, derives its name from its location south of Houston Street (thus SoHo). It encompasses the area from Houston to Canal streets, between Lafayette Street and Avenue of the Americas. When New York's industrial center began to shift from Manhattan, many of SoHo's cast-iron warehouses were left empty. They didn't stay that way for long; over the past two decades hundreds of artists and other loft dwellers have moved in, and today SoHo is a lively, colorful, and urbane neighborhood. On the weekend, hundreds of New Yorkers crowd the narrow streets taking in an incredible variety of art galleries, boutiques, gourmet food shops, nightclubs, and theaters. Like the art in its galleries, food in SoHo can be an expensive commodity. There are no rock-bottom bargains in this neighborhood. But below are some of the more reasonably priced places.

## AMERICAN/CONTINENTAL

From noon until early in the morning, the pub-like **Broome Street Bar,** at the corner of Broome Street and West Broadway (tel. 925-2086), is filled with a typically eclectic SoHo crowd of artists, writers, and musicians, all of whom are noisily—and sometimes vehemently—discussing the latest trends in art or literature or exchanging the news and gossip of the neighborhood. Broome Street is especially attractive in the late afternoon when jazz plays on the sound system, and you can sit over a beer or coffee and study the passing SoHo scene through the plant-filled front windows. There's a venerable old mahogany bar, small tables with comfortable bentwood chairs, and old-fashioned "Sydney Greenstreet" fans overhead.

The menu is posted: salads, quiches, burgers, sandwiches, and omelets are $7 or less. There's a wide assortment of desserts at around $3, and the ice cream is a New Yorker's favorite: Häagen-Dazs. Be sure to try the pineapple fizz.

Open Sunday through Thursday from 11 a.m. to 1:30 a.m., on Friday and Saturday until 2:30 a.m. The kitchen is open until closing.

Our favorite place for lunch in SoHo is **Food,** 127 Prince St., at the corner of Wooster Street (tel. 473-8790). It's big, bright, airy, and tastefully adorned with modern art and photographs, many by local artists. People sit at simple butcher-block tables, under high ceilings and surrounded by a forest of greenery.

Meals are served cafeteria style, and the ample portions are absolutely delicious. The homemade soups served with big slabs of whole-wheat bread and butter are meals in themselves, and at $3.25, a bargain. Huge sandwiches are priced $4 to $7, and large, fresh salads run $3.75 to $8.50. But for a real treat, try one of the daily specials. We recently enjoyed Cajun chicken with a mushroom garnish, baked pumpkin, corn on the cob, bread and butter ($7.50). Desserts are homemade and include poppyseed cake and rhubarb-strawberry pie ($3.25).

Food is open Monday through Wednesday from noon to 10 p.m., Thursday through Saturday until 11 p.m., and on Sunday from 11:30 a.m. to 4:30 p.m. for brunch. No reservations, but sometimes there's a short wait for tables during the crowded lunch hour.

The **Cupping Room Café,** 359 West Broadway, between Broome and Grand streets (tel. 925-2898), is simply one of the most comfortable places in town for a leisurely breakfast or brunch. With exposed-brick walls, captain's chairs, blackboard menus, and a working pot-bellied stove, it's suggestive of a charming rural restaurant. A huge vase of colorful flowers sits on an oak counter and more flowers adorn marble-topped tables. The skylight-lit back room is a perfect place to enjoy excellent croissants and delicious freshly brewed coffee, while jazz or classical music plays in the background.

A homemade muffin is $1.75, and a cup of coffee is $1.25. Chicken tarragon salad costs $7.25, as does a hot waffle topped with raisins, nuts, fresh fruit, and homemade whipped cream. For dessert, try the delicious Austrian plum cake or perhaps the fruit torte, each $4. Specials are offered daily.

The Cupping Room Café is open from 8 a.m. to 1 a.m. Sunday through Thursday, on Friday and Saturday to 2 a.m.

Early risers who want to breakfast in SoHo before taking on the galleries should head to **Elephant and Castle,** 183 Prince St., between Sullivan and Thompson streets (tel. 260-3600). Here you'll find 22 different kinds of omelets to choose from, including a delicate fines-herbes omelet ($3.75) and smoked salmon with dill ($7.50). The fresh-squeezed orange juice runs $1.75. Cheerful jam jars decorate the shelves mounted on mirrored walls and give the place a cozy, early-morning feel.

Hamburger lovers may want to lunch at Elephant and Castle. There are 12 different toppings for the juicy thick burgers, including guacamole with cheddar and tomato and sour cream with horseradish ($5 to $7.25). For the famished, there's even the Elephant burger—a colossal creation of chopped beef served with curried sour cream, bacon, scallions, cheddar, and tomato ($7.25). Indulge, but bring a toothbrush for afterward. There's also a variety of sandwiches for $4.75 to $6.25.

Open Monday through Thursday from 8 a.m. to midnight, on Friday and Saturday until 12:30 a.m., and on Sunday from 10 a.m. to midnight.

The **Prince Street Bar and Restaurant,** 125 Prince St., at the corner of Wooster Street (tel. 228-8130), is a comfortable bar-restaurant and hangout, offering reasonably priced food and drink. The crowd here is constantly changing, with an interesting cross section of the SoHo populace. The back of the dining room is dimly lit by pink overhead bulbs and houses a bar covered with framed mirrors; up front, natural light streams in through high, plant-filled windows. The menu offers almost everything under the sun: we counted over 80 separate dishes, including many Indonesian specialties. A small sampling includes guacamole dip ($5.50); tofu parmigiana with french fries or rice, and bread ($6.50); mixed vegetables with lemon butter ($6.50); and a roast beef and creamed horseradish sandwich in toasted pita ($6.50).

Then there are the hot toddies for the winter months ($3.75), refreshing piña coladas for the summer ($4.50), and a slew of fresh-baked desserts—try the "tunnel of fudge" cake ($3).

The kitchen is open Sunday through Thursday from 11:30 a.m. to 1 a.m., on Friday and Saturday until 2 a.m. The restaurant closes an hour later.

Lovers of wine and good, imaginatively prepared food should head for **The SoHo Kitchen,** 103 Greene St., between Prince and Spring streets (tel. 925-1866). In this large loft space, you'll find SoHo-ites and young urban professionals alike clustered at the raised tables along both walls or relaxing at the enormous horseshoe bar. Adding to the atmosphere are the huge contemporary artworks hanging on exposed-brick walls.

The menu offers anything from a light snack to a full meal. Try the gourmet pizzas, like the mozzarella with sun-dried tomatoes, priced around $9. Grilled trout is $9.50, and fettuccine with peas, smoked salmon, and caviar in a cream sauce runs $11.50.

After ordering food, sample wine from their incredible wine list. With 110 selections, it is said to be the most extensive in the world. You can have a five-ounce glass, starting at $4, or a full bottle. For those who want to sample wine of a particular variety or region, have a flight tasting, a serving of four to eight 1.5-ounce tastings, beginning at $7.75.

Open Monday through Friday from 11:30 a.m. to around 1 a.m., on Saturday from 12:30 p.m. to 2 a.m., and on Sunday from 12:30 p.m. to midnight. The kitchen closes at midnight Monday through Saturday, at 8 p.m. on Sunday.

Traditional deco diners were easy on the eyes and difficult on the digestion. At SoHo's **Moondance** diner, 80 Ave. of the Americas (Sixth Avenue), at Grand Street (tel. 226-1191), you can have the best of both worlds. Under a revolving electric moon, you can eat tasty well-prepared food served by exceptionally friendly waiters. Burgers with a variety of toppings cost $5.25 to $7.50, and sandwiches run $5.50 to $7.50. Try the grilled mozzarella with basil and tomato on garlic challah, or the popular chicken-salad sandwich. The patrons are an interesting blend of blue-collar and art-world chic. During warmer months, streetside tables are set out. Breakfast is served all day.

Open from 8:30 a.m. to midnight Sunday through Thursday, 24 hours on Friday and Saturday.

# ETHIOPIAN

**Abyssinia,** 35 Grand St., on the corner of Thompson Street (tel. 226-5959), offers excellent Ethiopian cuisine in an intriguing ethnic setting. Diners are seated on tiny three-legged stools around a short round table decorated with a dome of straw. When the meal is served, the dome is removed and hung on the wall.

The exotic variety of vegetarian, beef, and fish dishes cost an average of $10, and are all accompanied by an ample serving of "injera," the porous Ethiopian pancake that takes the place of knife and fork and can be used to soak up every last bit of the spicy red-pepper sauce known as "berbere." Doro wot, a popular Ethiopian dish of chicken marinated in berbere, is served exceedingly tender and spicy. Also excellent is kitfo, a national dish of steak tartare seasoned with spiced butter and hot chile powder.

Desserts are equally unusual, from a simple plate of papaya with lime ($3.50) to a rich dark African chocolate-chip cake ($4). For those who can never get enough chocolate there's even a trio of handmade chocolate truffles ($4). Cocoa beans never tasted so good.

Open for dinner only, from 6 to 11 p.m. nightly.

## FRENCH

If you become infected with the worldly glamour of SoHo and feel like throwing your money around, **Provence,** at 38 MacDougal St., near Ave. of Americas (Sixth Avenue) (tel. 475-7500), located on a quiet side street, is one of Manhattan's most charming restaurants. Provence's deep-blue exterior, punctuated by wooden windowboxes full of flowers, instantly evokes rural France. The restaurant is well out of our price range for dinner, but lunch is a bit less of a splurge, with most entrees ranging from $10 to $13. Besides, that's when the art world's movers and shakers drop by for their power-lunching.

The menu changes seasonally, but always includes steak frites, omelets, salads, and unusual seafood. (When we visited last they were serving skate wings with capers and olive oil.) But Provence's raison d'être is its informal Provençal entrees, heavy on the garlic and tomatoes, that are more filling and less fussy than formal French cuisine.

Open Tuesday through Sunday from noon to 3 p.m. and 6 to 11 p.m. Closed Monday.

## INTERNATIONAL FARE

Although slightly west of SoHo proper, the **Ear Inn,** 326 Spring St., between Washington and Greenwich streets (tel. 226-9060), is well worth the few extra blocks of walking. This small, casual restaurant is a deservedly beloved neighborhood hangout whose outstanding feature is its clientele of writers, musicians, and artists. The Ear Inn offers its discerning patrons poetry readings and tables covered with butcher paper and crayons, should the creative urge strike while dining. The restaurant is housed in an ancient landmark structure dating from 1817 and the décor is minimal—a collection of old glass bottles on the bar, a few fish on the walls, a wood floor. There are tables with blue-and-white checkered tablecloths in the front and in a small back room. The jukebox, which plays the latest in New Wave, reggae, and jazz, is very, very good.

The Ear Inn's specialty is "homemade international cuisine" and the food is inexpensive and imaginatively prepared. You might sample the cowboy chili ($3.50 a bowl), an excellent hot-and-spicy offering, along with a mixed green salad or salade niçoise ($5.75). Or there are sirloin burgers, pasta of the day, and daily specials ($4.75 to $8). The desserts are all homemade and very large. There's a full bar too.

The kitchen is open from noon to 1 a.m., and there are poetry readings every Saturday at 3 p.m. (except during the summer months). Sunday brunch is served from noon to 5 p.m.

Standing in marked contrast to the rest of the SoHo scene is **Fanelli's,** 94 Prince St., at the corner of Mercer Street (tel. 226-9412). The last of the neighborhood taverns, it's been around for over a century. It's a small place with a handful of tables and an eclectic clientele of SoHo-ites, truckers, and students. The original owner,

Mike Fanelli, was a boxer in his youth, and the walls are lined with photographs of old fights and famous boxers. The food is simple, but filling. For $5 to $7 you can have linguine with marinara sauce, lasagne, or shepherd's pie with salad. New England clam chowder is $3.25. Thick sandwiches run $4.25 to $5.25.

The bar is open from 10 a.m. to 2 a.m. Monday through Saturday, and from noon to 2 a.m. on Sunday; food is served until 1 a.m.

## ITALIAN

A young, sophisticated crowd is already flocking to **I Tre Merli,** 463 West Broadway, between West Houston and Prince streets (tel. 254-8699), the SoHo sister of a wine bar and restaurant in Genoa, Italy. Indeed, the Genovese owners have taken pains to give their New York hangout a sleek Italian look. The trendy interior, including floors and furniture, is a highly glossed black, and the clever modular bar with movable sections encourages an Italian attitude toward meeting strangers.

Wine and champagne come by the glass ($3.50 to $7) or bottle and are imported exclusively from the I Tre Merli vineyards in northern Italy.

The cuisine, like the wine, is Genovese, and the fragrant and spicy dishes served at brunch may bring back memories of lazy afternoons in Italy. An artichoke salad with parmesan cheese is $7.50; gnocchi, potato pasta with a basil-and-garlic sauce, is $9.75; and breast of chicken with herbs is $11.50. Dinner is more expensive, but the view from the mezzanine of the late-night action at the crowded ground-floor bar may make the splurge worthwhile.

Open daily from noon to 2 a.m. (in the summer, until 4 a.m. on Saturday and Sunday).

**La Dolce Vita,** 195 Spring St., between Sullivan and Thompson streets (tel. 431-1315), is truly a sampling of "the good life." Owner/chef John Mazzocchi's special touch is evident everywhere, from the exposed-brick walls lined with stars' photographs from the '30s, '40s, and '50s, to the blue-and-white checkered tablecloths, ceiling fans, and carved-oak bar, to the delicious and innovative food. In warmer weather the restaurant expands for al fresco dining at tables on the sidewalk.

Here you'll find an exciting assortment of northern Italian specialties. For an appetizer, try the mussels marinière served in a white wine and cream sauce in a small or large portion ($4.50 or $8.50) or the fresh roasted peppers and mozzarella ($6). Entrees include spinach fettuccine with four cheeses and walnuts ($8.50), shrimp, clams, and mussels Fra Diavalo in a spicy red sauce ($12), and chicken breast scarparella in a light garlic sauce ($9). If you're lucky, papardelli will be a special. Wide fettuccine with Italian bacon and mushrooms in a tomato cream sauce make it a treat for $10.25. Make sure you leave room for the mouthwatering homemade desserts, which are all $4. We recently enjoyed the amaretto cheesecake and the tartuffo, an Italian chocolate truffle. Since the desserts change frequently, ask your waitress for the daily offerings.

Open Monday through Friday from noon to midnight, and on Saturday and Sunday from 11 a.m. to midnight.

## PASTRY AND COFFEE

All over Manhattan, grocery shopping can be a dramatic undertaking, but only at **Dean and DeLuca,** 560 Broadway, at Prince Street (tel. 431-1691), does it become a spectator sport. For the price of a delicious cup of cappuccino ($1.50) or a looks-too-perfect-to-desecrate pastry ($1 to $5), you can have a ringside seat. Housed in a block-long building that looks more like a gallery than a grocery, Dean and DeLuca is New York's premier gourmet food store. As you enter, work your way to the cappuccino/pastry bar on your left. There are no seats, but prop your elbows up on the elegant marble counters and enjoy the show. Is that Madonna outhustling Richard Gere for the last head of Belgian endive?

Open Monday through Saturday from 8 a.m. to 8 p.m. and on Sunday from 9 a.m. to 7 p.m.

# 9. Lower Manhattan/TriBeCa

Financiers and tourists alike who find themselves in lower Manhattan at lunch or dinnertime would do well to resist the urge to grab a bite around the corner. A much better idea is to stroll a little to the east, toward the waterfront, or to the west and a bit uptown, to TriBeCa (Triangle below Canal Street). Both these areas—the former steeped in history, the latter the site of an old produce market that's redefining itself into a loft-and-office district—offer a number of restaurants with good food at reasonable prices, served in interesting environs.

## AMERICAN/CONTINENTAL

The **Bridge Café,** 279 Water St., at Dover Street (tel. 227-3344), two blocks from the South Street Seaport, has a 19th-century Cape Cod charm other landmark restaurants in the area have lost. From the outside, the red wood-frame building looks as if it's bowing before the towering Brooklyn Bridge above it. Inside, there are photos of the bridge on the café's cream-colored slat-board walls. There are potted flowers in the entry and front windows and red-checked cloths on the tables.

The lunch menu changes daily, but generally offers sandwiches, soup ($5 for a bowl of clam chowder, $9 for a soup-and-sandwich combination), a hot and a cold pasta dish, and fish, chicken, and meat entrees, usually braised with a subtle sauce. Most are priced under $10. Dinner entrees run higher, but there's usually an under-$12 choice, such as tortellini with sausage and tomatoes ($11.50).

Lunch is served daily from 11:45 a.m. to 3 p.m., and dinner from 6 p.m. to midnight (until 11 p.m. on Sunday). Brunches featuring omelets (try the one with sour cream and chili, $8), buckwheat pancakes ($7.25), and pastas such as fettuccine primavera ($9) are served from noon to 3:30 p.m. on weekends.

It's a friendly TriBeCa crowd that frequents the bar and restaurant at **Smoke Stacks Lightnin',** 380 Canal St., at West Broadway (tel. 226-0485). If you can get yourself past the video games at the entry, you can make yourself at home at the large, roomy wooden tables. The green-and-brown motif and lofty, green pressed-tin ceiling give Smoke Stacks a woodsy atmosphere, and lighting from theatrical fixtures lends added drama to the décor.

Smoke Stacks is particularly nice at sundown for a drink and an appetizer, perhaps country pâté ($4.25) or crab-stuffed mushrooms ($5). Bistro fare is served at lunch and dinner, with most entrees under $10. At the lower-priced end of the menu are hearty sandwiches, most under $6, served at lunchtime, and a meal-size Caesar ($4.50) or seafood salad ($7). On Sunday, Smoke Stacks serves a champagne brunch for $10.75—not a bad deal, even for brunch-crazy Manhattan.

Smoke Stacks is open from 11:30 a.m. to 2:30 a.m. Sunday through Thursday, until 4 a.m. on Friday and Saturday. The kitchen closes at midnight on Sunday, at 1 a.m. Monday through Thursday, and at 2 a.m. on Friday and Saturday. Brunch on Sunday is served from 11:30 a.m. to 4:30 p.m.

Less out-of-the-way than most of TriBeCa's warehouse restaurants is **211 West Broadway,** at Franklin Street (tel. 925-7202). This one is cool gray and typically lofty, with a gray pressed-tin ceiling held high by Grecian-style columns and floor-to-ceiling windows screened with venetian blinds. Tables are marble tops on wrought-iron pedestals, graced by bud vases filled with fresh flowers.

The lunch menu offers a number of items for the budget-conscious. Try the breast of chicken with lime-herb marinade ($11.50), tagliarini primavera ($8.50), or the "Two-Eleven burger" ($6.50) with shoestring potatoes. The price goes up at dinnertime, but the juicy house burger is still affordable at $8.50. Penne in spicy tomato sauce is $9.50, and poached chicken salad is less than $13.

The restaurant serves cocktail brunches on Saturday and Sunday. Once again, the house burger with shoestring potatoes costs least ($8.25). Among the other choices: eggs with smoked salmon and salmon caviar ($10.50), and a Spanish peasant omelet ($8.50). All brunch entrees are served with a mimosa, a Bloody Mary, or a screwdriver.

Lunch is served daily from 11:30 a.m. to 4 p.m.; dinner is 6 p.m. to midnight weekdays, to 1 a.m. on weekends; and weekend brunch, from 11:30 a.m. to 4:30 p.m. Live music on an occasional Sunday.

**The Square Diner,** 33 Leonard St., at the corner of West Broadway (tel. 925-7188), has a friendly, unpretentious atmosphere and good-quality Greek and American food at very low prices. On a street full of chic new restaurants, this handsome aluminum diner seems somewhat an anomaly. The interior is decorated in classic Greek diner motif, with pictures of the Acropolis and the Greek islands adorning the walls.

This is one of the few places left in Manhattan where you can still get a deluxe hamburger for under $4. A quarter-pound deluxe bacon cheeseburger is only $4.75. The chopped sirloin steak platter is $5.75, served with soup or salad. Fried filet of sole is $6. The Greek salad platter ($4.75) is a good buy, as is the lamb shish kebab for $6.75. Omelets and sandwiches are all priced under $4.50. Desserts range in price from $1 to $2, and a malted with double ice cream is only $2.

Open from 6 a.m. to 9 p.m. seven days a week.

**Walker's Restaurant,** 16 N. Moore St., at Varick Street (tel. 941-0142), was formerly Vic's Bar, a rough-and-tumble tavern notorious in the neighborhood for its seedy clientele. While Walker's patrons may now be somewhat more upscale, the space still retains a cozy tavern-like atmosphere. In the front half of the restaurant is a beautiful old oak bar behind which hang 19th-century beveled mirrors. In the back of Walker's it's quiet, with wooden tables lit by candles. The place is frequented mostly by local TriBeCa loft dwellers and is usually quite busy for dinner, so making reservations might be a good idea.

The food at Walker's, though basic, is filling and good. Daily specials are written on a blackboard and brought to the table. The night we dined there the specials included grilled lamb with rosemary, Louisiana fried chicken, spinach linguine with seafood, and broiled grouper. Specials usually range in price from $9 to $14. On the menu are salads priced from $3 to $7. Entrees are excellent and reasonably priced. The lunch menu includes a variety of sandwiches priced between $4 and $6, as well as an eight-ounce sirloin steak sandwich for $8. On weekends Walker's has an à la carte brunch for $8, including a free drink.

Open from 11 a.m. to 2 a.m. daily.

A favorite of TriBeCa's "locals"—the loft dwellers who call the district home—is **riverrun,** 176 Franklin St., between Greenwich and Hudson streets (tel. 966-3894). Healthful food, manageable prices, and rotating displays of the work of neighborhood artists are three good reasons for this cozy restaurant's popularity. At lunch, if you're in the mood for a meal-size salad, you can choose among several, including a mixed seafood salad ($7.50), a hearty niçoise ($7.50), and a bracing mixture of lettuce, chicken, apples, walnuts, swiss cheese, and onion ($7.25). Perhaps you'd prefer the full smoked trout with bean salad ($8.25), chicken and vegetables in spicy garlic sauce with rice ($7.50), or a mound of steamed mussels floating in a zesty sauce of garlic, white wine, and tomatoes ($8.50). Omelets with french fries are cheaper still ($6 for one stuffed with smoked trout, sour cream, and scallions), as are sandwiches such as the avocado on whole wheat ($6) and the cheeseburger with french fries ($5.75).

Many of the items on the luncheon menu reappear on the dinner menu at slightly higher prices. Among the additional entrees are shrimp with snowpeas in a spicy garlic sauce ($10); fried chicken with cornbread and homemade potato salad ($8); and angel-hair pasta Fra Diavolo with mixed seafood ($8.25). If you've a yen for something sweet, try the riverrun's three-berry pie ($3.75). The friendly waitresses will bring you extra forks if you want to share.

Their unlimited-champagne brunch, on weekends, features eggs florentine or

Benedict ($7.25), french toast with bacon or ham ($6.50), and a selection of omelets from $5. Also available are items from the regular lunch menu: salads (from $6.50), burgers (from $5.25), and quiche with french fries ($6.50).

The restaurant is open for lunch from 11:30 a.m. to 5 p.m. weekdays and from 11:30 a.m. to 2 p.m. on Saturday. Dinner runs from 5 p.m. to 1 a.m. Sunday through Thursday, to 2 a.m. on Friday and Saturday. Brunch is served on Saturday and Sunday from 11:30 a.m. to 5 p.m.

One block west and one block south from riverrun is another neighborhood hangout, a festive Cajun place, **how's bayou,** 355 Greenwich St., at Harrison Street (tel. 925-5405). By design, there's nothing fancy here. The restaurant is housed in a former meat market whose many doors stay open on summer nights to give diners the feeling they're eating al fresco. Fans hang from the pressed-tin ceiling, as does a large neon sign that spells out the restaurant's name. Paper bags of tortilla chips adorn every butcher-block table—a clue that the kitchen produces Mexican as well as Cajun specialties. The staff makes you feel like an instant regular by snapping Mardi Gras beads around your neck.

How's bayou's food won't win accolades from restaurant critics, who don't hand out stars for good home-cooking. But the food here is hearty and served in generous portions. For lunch you can have chunky chili ($4) or a "Bayou raft" of oysters on fresh hero bread ($6). Specialties from the dinner menu are also served at lunch, including a chicken, sausage, shrimp, and crayfish jambalaya ($6), enchiladas ($6), and southern fried chicken ($7). (These items are about $2 or $3 more at dinnertime.) Evenings, you can choose from Créole meatloaf ($9) and mesquite chicken ($10.50) among the Cajun offerings, fajitas ($10.75) from the Mexican list, and chicken fried steak ($8.50) and barbecued pork ribs ($10.50) from the section of the menu labeled "Southern Hospitality." Round out the meal, if you're still hungry, with homemade apple pie or Créole bread pudding with whiskey sauce ($3). Ya hear? Weekend brunch ($8 and up) offers items from lunch and dinner plus corned-beef hash and eggs, omelets, and side orders of grits, biscuits, and gravy.

Food is served from 11:30 a.m. to midnight Sunday through Thursday, to 1 a.m. on Friday and Saturday. The bar stays open until 2 or 3 a.m.

For some of the city's most acclaimed hamburgers, drop into **Hamburger Harry's,** 157 Chambers St., near Greenwich Street (tel. 267-4446). "Ha-Ha's" décor is a functional mix of butcher block and art deco—just the right setting for charcoaled burgers with a gourmet touch. If you want to watch the red-capped chefs in action, ask to be seated at the counter. Plush seats there are spaced for the maximum in comfort and elbow room. Ha-Ha's hefty but lean hamburgers are broiled over live charcoal and mesquite—the wood that gives these burgers their distinctive taste. You'll have 17 varieties of hamburgers to choose from, ranging from a "number 10" (plain without the roll, $5.50) to burgers topped with béarnaise sauce ($5.50), gorgonzola cheese ($4.50), guacamole and pico de gallo (spicy, $6), or the works (chili, cheddar cheese, chopped onion, guacamole, and pico de gallo, $6). Don't pass up Ha-Ha's fresh curlicue french fries ($2), which, like the burgers, have received top marks from New York's discriminating restaurant reviewers.

Instead of hamburgers, you might try the fajitas—a house specialty that combines char-broiled beefsteak or chicken with pico de gallo, refried beans, guacamole, and steaming flour tortillas ($10 for the chicken, $10.25 for the beef). Other items on this surprisingly eclectic menu: chili ($4.50), and specials such as the shrimp plate ($10.50), corn chowder ($2.50), and desserts such as Mississippi mud cake with whipped cream ($4). Ha-Ha's serves wine and beer.

Open seven days a week from 11:30 a.m. to 11:30 p.m.

What Ha-Ha's is to the hamburger, **Ham Heaven,** 49 Warren St., between West Broadway and Greenwich Street (tel. 513-7224), is to ham. Come here if you want to taste succulent, sweet Virginia ham at its best. Owned by Paul and Kathy Domitrovich and named after Kathy's family's place in Detroit, Ham Heaven is, well, "hamazing," as the proud Domitroviches will be the first to tell you. On the street level, where sun slants in from a skylight, green tablecloths and counter service give this former hardware warehouse a homey warmth. Downstairs, theater seats salvaged from an uptown disco and walls decorated with porcine art put you in the mood for . . . well, ham and dinner theater. They "import" their hams from Michigan—meat from other sources proved too salty—and bake about 20 a day in brown sugar and ginger ale. You can savor the finished product in an overstuffed sandwich ($3.75); in homemade navy-bean or split-pea soup loaded with ham ($2); as healthy slices served with macaroni salad, potato salad, or baked beans ($5.75); in quiche ($5.75) and omelets ($3.50 to $4.75); or chopped and sautéed with fresh vegetables and stuffed into pita bread ($4.75). A popular favorite is the Dixie sweet ham special served with sweet potato and collard greens ($6.75). Breakfast features "Detroit Heavenly Hash" ($4.50) for a hearty mix of hash browns, chopped ham, green peppers, and onions, fried together with an egg added on top. The menu provides options for diners who don't feel like ham—but ham's the thing, and it draws ham lovers from all over town.

The restaurant serves breakfast and lunch all day, opening at 6:30 a.m. weekdays and 8 a.m. weekends. Closing hours in this business district one block below TriBeCa are 4 p.m. weekends and 10 p.m. weekdays, except for blues and theater nights, when the restaurant stays open until 2 a.m.

Sports fans lonely for the home team might find it in action at a unique TriBeCa restaurant, **The Sporting Club,** 99 Hudson St., between Harrison and Franklin streets (tel. 219-0900). The main draw is a ten-foot video screen and its companion, a computerized scoreboard, which tower above the oval bar and can be seen from every table in this mahogany-paneled, multilevel restaurant. TV monitors spotted around the restaurant enable Bill Rose, the owner, to show anywhere from three to six events simultaneously. (Call ahead and he'll tell you if he'll be able to pull your favorite team off a satellite or cable link. The scoreboard keeps almost instantaneous track of every game being played in the nation.) Sports lovers flock to this restaurant as much for the camaraderie as for the food and drink. The clientele, about two-thirds male, often includes well-known sports figures, sometimes working behind the bar. The menu is eclectic and moderately priced, running from "O.J.'s Buffalo Wings" ($6) and "Sporting Club salad" ($5) to the "Larry Bird roast chicken" ($12), and a "George Steinburger" ($8.50). On Saturday and Sunday from noon to 5 p.m., brunch ($7 and up) is popular—only partly because every home run will earn you a free drink during baseball season.

The restaurant opens every day at 11:30 a.m. and closes anywhere from midnight to 2 a.m. The kitchen stays open until midnight on weekdays, until 1 a.m. on weekends.

For a taste of "Nouveau American Grill," head to **Pipeline,** 2 World Financial Center, at 225 Liberty St. (tel. 945-2755). The décor here is very hi-tech, with steel-pipe sheeting covering many of the surfaces and walls painted in neon colors. Multiple television screens above the bar play music videos that diners can select from the video jukebox. Outside, in the shadow of the World Financial Center Towers, is a tree-lined dining terrace with a great view of the Hudson River and Jersey City.

The menu is a little overpriced for bar-and-grill fare, but the food is good and the portions are large. Salads range in price between $8 for the house salad and $10 for the niçoise. Hot entrees run between $10 and $17.50. The linguine with shrimp, peanut oil, ginger, garlic, and lemon grass ($13.50) is excellent. There is a good selection of sandwiches, all served on fresh baguettes with cottage fries and tomato salad, for $10 each. You can also get fresh corn on the cob here for $3. Desserts are $4 to $5.

Open daily from 10 a.m. to midnight.

## FRENCH

By far the prettiest of TriBeCa's warehouse restaurants is **Capsouto Frères,** 451 Washington St., at Watts Street (tel. 966-4900). The neo-Romanesque warehouse is housed in a landmark building dating to 1891, and the restaurant's owners have done wonders with its interior. From the high, exposed-beam ceiling hang gently turning antique ceiling fans and chandeliers of brass with fogged-glass tulip shades. Stately cast-iron columns appear to support the lofty ceiling. The floors are brightly polished hardwood; the walls, exposed brick with large, floor-to-ceiling windows framed by maroon velvet drapes. White linen cloths cover the tables, with fresh flowers on each.

Main entrees run upward of $14, but there's a varied selection of seven "petits plats" with delicious portions of coquilles St-Jacques, soufflés, and a vegetarian plate with wild rice—all for $8 to $13. The dishes are à la carte, but servings are generous. Desserts include pastries and fruits and are irresistibly pretty. They cost about $5.

Capsouto Frères is open daily from noon to 2 a.m., except Monday when it opens at 5 p.m. Lunch is served before 4 p.m., with prices somewhat lower.

## GREEK/MEDITERRANEAN

TriBeCa has a bustling Greek restaurant, **Delphi,** 109 West Broadway, at Reade Street (tel. 227-6322), that is well worth a visit. Delphi has an enclosed terrace and a small room on the ground floor with a room full of hanging plants above. Travel posters advertise Greece from nearly every wall—as if the food weren't advertisement enough. As an appetizer, try the stuffed grape leaves ($3) or the Delphi specialty, spinach cheese pie ($4.25); then move on to a hearty Greek salad ($4) or tomatoes stuffed with pignola nuts, raisins, and rice, and cooked with herbs and spices ($7). For filling meat dishes, you might turn to the souvlaki platter (roasted marinated beef and lamb), the mixed grill of souvlaki, shish kebab, sausage, and eggplant salad, or the golden-baked pastitsio (macaroni layered with ground beef, cheese, and tomato sauce). The meat dishes all cost $7 and include a small Greek salad, rice or baked potato, and fresh broccoli. Definitely a good deal.

Open seven days a week from 11 a.m. to midnight.

Across town, a few blocks from the South Street Seaport, you'll find **Chrisa II,** 76 Fulton St., near Gold Street (tel. 964-4136). Greek specialties here are served in a coffeeshop atmosphere, brightened by Greek island scenes painted on the walls and Greek music playing in the background. The prices are definitely right for the budget traveler. You might lunch on pita-bread sandwiches filled with souvlaki, shish kebab, or sausage ($3.50), or Greek antipasto ($7). There's also cheese or spinach pie ($3.50) and a Greek salad ($4.50).

Open every day except Sunday at 10:30 a.m., Chrisa II closes Monday through Friday at 9:45 p.m. and on Saturday at 8:30 p.m.

## IRISH

The atmosphere is undeniably Irish at **Katie O'Toole's Pub and Restaurant,** 134 Reade St., between Hudson and Greenwich streets (tel. 226-8928). The chatty Irish staff will make you feel at home in this quaint, oak-paneled pub-style restaurant. There's a tree-shaded outdoor terrace where customers can sit and have a drink or meal.

The fare at Katie O'Toole's is simple "pub food." The specialty, bangers and mash (sausages and mashed potatoes), is $6. Burgers range in price from $3.50 to $7. A club sandwich is $6. Hot entrees run $6 to $9. There's authentic English beer on tap.

Open daily from 11 a.m. to 3 a.m.

## MEXICAN

For a true south-of-the-border taste, TriBeCans go to the **Beach House,** 399 Greenwich St., at Beach Street (tel. 226-7800). The interior of this Civil War–era building is dark and warm. Large fans spin lazily from the high ceiling, painted mirrors adorn the walls, and you're as likely to sit at a large booth as at a candlelit table near the bar. You can buy burritos, enchiladas, tacos, and tostadas, served with refried beans and rice, either separately or in combinations of two ($9) or three ($11). For something unusual, try the flautas (deep-fried corn tortillas filled with chicken and topped with guacamole and sour cream, $9.50), or the pollo mole poblano (half a chicken sautéed in mole sauce, $10.50). Prices are as much as $3.50 per item cheaper at lunch.

Open for lunch weekdays only, from noon to 4 p.m. Dinner is served Sunday through Friday from 4 p.m. to midnight, on Saturday from 5 p.m. to midnight. Closed Monday.

For chili that's sure to knock your socks off, join the other downtown regulars at **Exterminator Chili,** 305 Church St., two blocks south of Canal Street (tel. 219-3070). The tiny restaurant is strung with Christmas tree lights year around, and jam-packed with kitschy trinkets ranging from miniature covered wagons resting on the window sill to plastic skulls hanging from the ceiling. The chili is just as eclectic as the décor, subject to daily changes in ingredients, which may include turkey, hominy, beets, or peanuts. Predictably, chili is the favorite item on a menu that doesn't have a thing priced over $12. Chili is available in four varieties: residential (mild), commercial (medium-hot), industrial (painful), and agricultural (vegetarian). Served over rice and beans and topped with sour cream, onions, and aged cheddar cheese, chili costs $6 at lunchtime, and $9 at dinner for a platter that includes cole slaw, chips, and a big hunk of cornbread. Also available at lunch are a variety of sandwiches (all $4 and under), salads (under $5), and burgers (all under $7).

For dinner, if you're not a chili-lover, try the jungle chicken served with rice and beans ($11). The cama camitas (marinated beef or chicken with flour tortillas, avocado, and sour cream, $11) are also tasty, as are the chili burgers ($9) and the Texas spaghetti ($10).

Exterminator Chili serves breakfast from 7:30 to 11 a.m. on weekdays, brunch from 11:30 a.m. to 4:30 p.m. on weekends, and lunch from 11 a.m. to 4 p.m. daily. Dinner is served from 6 to 11 p.m. on weekdays, and to midnight on weekends.

## MIXED BAG

Take a ride into the sky, climb 107 stories in less than a minute, walk through a simulated crystal cave, and arrive at the **Hors D'Oeuvrerie,** One World Trade Center (tel. 938-1111). After 3 p.m. the cocktail lounge is open to the public, and after 4 p.m. you can enjoy spicy ethnic hors d'oeuvres with afternoon or evening drinks.

The corridor leading from the super-smooth, super-fast elevator to the lounge looks like the inside of a precious gem, with glass, mirrors, and enlarged travel photos arranged into a three-dimensional collage. Mounted on pedestals fixed to the floor are giant semiprecious stones: African rose quartz, Eurasian pegmatite, and amethyst geode.

Inside, seating is on multiple terraces, with a 180° view. Pick your table to afford a view of the Statue of Liberty, Staten Island, or the Brooklyn Bridge and Queens.

Though the view is clearly the real treat, the hot and cold hors d'oeuvres run a close second. For under $12 you can choose from sushi and sashimi (raw fish), shrimp tempura, Japanese yakitori, steak tartare, and much more. There are even "main course" entrees: char-broiled beef medallions with guacamole ($15), for example, and sautéed shrimp, chicken, and bok choy ($12). Espresso is $1.75; drinks, upward of $3.50.

The Hors d'Oeuvrerie is open to the public daily from 3 p.m. to midnight for food, until 1 a.m. for drinks. A scrumptious Sunday brunch ($9 and up) runs from noon to 3 p.m. Piano music begins at 4 p.m. daily (a trio at 7:30 p.m.). Men must wear jackets (a very few house jackets can be borrowed); blue jeans of any sort are not allowed.

## SEAFOOD

The **Front Street Restaurant,** 228 Front St., between Beekman Street and Peck Slip (tel. 406-1560), is a madhouse on weekdays from noon to 3 p.m., when it serves some 400 to 500 self-service lunches, all priced between $2.75 and $6. Housed in an 1831 landmark seaport building, the restaurant has a New World, marine ambience. The main dining area has a jukebox, Formica tables, exposed-brick walls, and concrete floors; out back there's outdoor dining at tables on a slat-board patio where empty beer kegs have been tossed out. Fried shrimp, clams, and scallops are the favorites, along with juicy bratwurst, bauernwurst, and knockwurst. There are also quiches, cheesemelts, and seafood salads—none priced above $7 at lunch. A dinner menu offers similar fare, plus barbecued chicken ($5.50) or lamb ribs ($7.25), and broiled fish specials ($7 to $8.50), served with salad, garlic bread, and a choice of rice pilaf or french fries. Beer on tap is $1.25; a glass of house wine, $1.60.

Open weekdays from 10 a.m. to 10 p.m., on Saturday from 11 a.m. to 9 p.m., and on Sunday from noon to 9 p.m. The dinner menu begins at 5 p.m. every day. A musical brunch ($8.50) runs from noon to 4 p.m. weekends and features folk music and a choice of fresh broiled or fried fish, quiche, a burger platter, or three-egg omelets, all served with french fries, salad, garlic bread, and a half liter of beer, wine, or sangría.

A classier, but higher-priced seafood place, also in a landmark building, is **Fulton's Steamer,** 144 Beekman St., at the corner of Front Street (tel. 267-9490). The tavern/restaurant has wood floors and walnut-stained wainscotting beneath mauve-colored walls adorned with chrome-framed photos. The split-level room is cooled in spring and summer by large ceiling fans. There's a lovely mahogany bar that came from the old fish market.

All entrees served at lunch and dinner are fresh seafood, priced between $7.50 and $16. Choose from smoked filet of sole with potato and salad ($9.75), fried clams ($8) or oysters ($9), served with potato, vegetable, and salad, or sautéed shrimps and bay scallops ($11). For dessert there's a sumptuous chocolate cake ($2.50).

Open for lunch Monday through Friday from noon to 3 p.m., and for dinner Tuesday through Friday from 5 to 9 p.m. On weekends the restaurant is open on Saturday and Sunday from 2 to 9 p.m.

## THAI

If you're fond of spicy Eastern dishes, go to **Tommy Tang's,** 323 Greenwich St., near Duane Street (tel. 334-9190), where traditional Thai cuisine is prepared with a creative flourish. Despite the spotless white linen and the exotic flower arrangements, a friendly, intimate atmosphere permeates the restaurant. The dining room, painted in pastels and tastefully lighted, has a sort of "new-wave deco" feel to it.

Entrees include such exotic offerings as shrimp panang (sautéed shrimp and red-pepper points in a strongly spiced curry sauce, $14.50), and rad na noodles (sautéed with chicken, pork, or beef with broccoli in an oyster sauce, $8.50). The ginger chicken with scallions and shiitake and straw mushrooms, served in a mild black-bean sauce ($7.50), is a nice counterpoint to many of the spicier items on the menu.

Tommy Tang's hours are 11:30 a.m. to 3 p.m. for lunch Monday through Friday, 6 to 11 p.m. for dinner Monday through Thursday, and 6 p.m. to midnight on Friday and Saturday. Tommy Tang's is closed on Sunday.

## SEAPORT CHOICES

Dining options at **the South Street Seaport** inviting four-block complex that so remarkably evokes the atmosphere of 19th-century New York include a fantastic variety of fine restaurants (most regrettably too pricey for more than a brief mention here), cafés, and foodstalls. For gourmets and gourmands on a budget, the **second floor of the Fulton Market building** offers the next best thing to an around-the-world food cruise. You can munch on dim sum (Chinese dumplings), empanadas (Argentine meat turnovers), cheese steak sandwiches, burgers, chili, raw-fish bar goodies, Indian tandoori cooking, Greek barbecue, Japanese soup and noodle dishes, chicken and ribs, pizza, sushi, frozen-yogurt sundaes, fresh fruit, salads, sausages, New York delicatessen, and enough cake, candy, and ice-cream specialties to satisfy the most demanding sweet tooth.

**Gianni's,** 15 Fulton St. (tel. 608-7300), an art deco study in black and white, is one of the Seaport's most attractive restaurants, and the one that offers diners the best view of the bustling world outside. Weather permitting, sit at the outdoor café, where Caesar salads are $9, arugula and endive salads are $6.50, and grilled-turkey sandwiches are $14.50. Open daily from noon to 11:30 p.m.

The newly renovated and popular **North Star Pub,** 93 South St., at Fulton Street (tel. 509-6757), is decorated like a British ale house, so it's no wonder the menu has a British flavor. Among the choices are bangers and mash (English sausages and mashed potatoes, $7.50), ploughman's plate (Stilton cheese, claret-red cheddar, pickles, chutney, and crusty bread, $6.75), and a fishmonger's basket (shrimp and fish filet, coated in beer batter and deep-fried, $9.25). The pub offers an excellent selection of English beers (John Courage, Whitbread, Bass) on tap, at $4.25 a pint. Open daily from 11:30 a.m. to around midnight. Sundays they open at 12:30 p.m. The kitchen is closed after 4:30 p.m. on Fridays.

The turn-of-the-century atmosphere in **Roeblings Bar and Grill** (tel. 608-3980), on the mezzanine of the Market building, provides the perfect setting for the hearty (and rather expensive) American fare: steaks, chops, blackened bluefish, grilled half chicken (at $11, the cheapest dinner entree), oysters (raw or fried in beer), and smoked trout. No dinner served on Friday evenings, when the place is crammed with Wall Streeters celebrating the week's end and taking advantage of a *free buffet.* You might want to join them. Open daily from 11:30 a.m. to 11:30 p.m. Saturday and Sunday closing time is at midnight.

For a treat, go to **The Grille,** across from the Trans-Lux Seaport Theatre on Beekman and Front streets (tel. 227-9328). During warm months the Grille moves outdoors and serves lunch and dinner on pink tablecloths. Dinner entrees begin at $10 for hot meatloaf with gravy and mashed potatoes and run to $15.50 for grilled salmon with vegetable and potato. Weekend brunch offers a variety of choices, from a ham-and-mozzarella omelet ($7.25) to filet of sole ($11.50). Open daily Monday to Thursday from 11:30 a.m. to 10 p.m., Fridays to midnight; Sundays to 9:30 p.m.

We would be remiss not to mention two of New York's landmark restaurants still very much in business in the busy Seaport. **Sloppy Louie's** (tel. 952-9657) and **Sweet's** (tel. 344-9189) are both in Schermerhorn Row on Fulton Street. At either place you'll find fresh seafood at moderate prices, with a full dinner ranging from about $10 to $20. Sloppy Louie's is open daily from 11 a.m. to 9 p.m.; Sweet's is open Monday through Friday from 11:30 a.m. with a last seating at 8:30 p.m.

Probably the most inviting of the outdoor cafés on Pier 17 is **Caroline's at the Seaport,** 89 South St., Pier 17 (tel. 233-4900). Be sure to avoid the upstairs portion of Caroline's, which is quite expensive and not nearly as fun as the café, which allows a clear view of the river, as well as a perch from which to distance yourself from the teeming masses. All items on Caroline's café menu are under $11, and there are some very interesting items there indeed. Try the Cajun chicken fingers with honey ($8.50), fried calamari with marinara sauce ($8), or a refreshingly cool seafood salad. There's a shrimp salad ($9) and grilled lobster roll ($11). Whatever you order, make sure you accompany it with Caroline's tortilla chips with guacamole and salsa ($4.50).

Caroline's is open daily from 11 a.m. to 11 p.m.

Right next to Caroline's is the **Café Café,** 89 South St., Pier 17 (tel. 406-2870). Though its menu is not quite as interesting as Caroline's, you still get the same view of the harbor, and you can order a draft beer for $2.50 and a variety of sandwiches ($6.50 to $7.50), salads (ranging from $6.50 for the Caesar to $11 for the seafood salad), and desserts (try the chocolate mousse cake, $3).

Café Café's kitchen is open from 11:30 a.m. to 6 p.m. daily. The bar is open to 2 or 3 a.m. On Saturday and Sunday you can order brunch from 10 a.m. to 1 p.m.

Probably the most pervasive presence on the third floor of Pier 17 is the **Liberty Café**, 89 South St. (tel. 406-1111). Liberty Café is sprawled across one end of the third floor, and offers diners the opportunity to get a view of the harbor from the cool indoors. Surrounded by windows, Liberty Café is a blessed retreat from the hustle and bustle of the pier. Enjoy Liberty's Fulton market chowder ($4.75) and a half-dozen littleneck clams from the raw bar ($8.25). Jumbo shrimp cocktail will cost you about $10.75, and smoked Caesar salad with crumbled bleu-cheese dressing is $9. You can get some interesting but rather expensive entrees (bay scallops and shrimp pot pie for $16, Cornish hen topped with herb butter for $13).

Liberty Café is open from 11:30 a.m. to 11 p.m. Sunday through Thursday, until midnight on Friday and Saturday.

## 10. Chinatown

For street shopping and divine dining, there's no place like Chinatown. This rapidly expanding neighborhood is loosely bounded by Canal Street to the north and by Park Row to the south. Chinatown is a bustling hodgepodge of fascinating shops and restaurants, and its streets are crammed with crowds buying low-priced fish, fruit, and vegetables from a lively market of sidewalk vendors. The biggest crowds come to Chinatown during January or February to celebrate the Chinese New Year with a steady stream of firecrackers.

During the rest of the year Chinatown's main attraction is its restaurants, where you'll probably find the greatest concentration of Chinese cuisine in America. Cantonese, Szechuan, Hunan, Mandarin, and Shanghai—all varieties of Chinese fare from the country's different provinces are represented in force.

Many of these restaurants offer a unique treat called dim sum, the traditional Chinese tea lunch, which is an economical way to sample some of Chinatown's most interesting dishes.

What you'll find lacking in most Chinese restaurants is elegant ambience. The Chinatown standard of interior design is hard Formica furnishings placed under harder fluorescent lighting. Plastic tablecloths and simple spindleback chairs complete the spartan style of décor. But don't be put off by conventionally banal settings, for it's also a Chinatown truism that some of the plainest places serve some of the most memorable meals.

There are a few other rules of thumb to remember while scouting out an authentic Chinese meal. Once seated, you can point to tasty-looking dishes on route to other tables—most restaurants have many dishes not listed on the menu—and experiment as much as you care to (from slightly new, like squid, to very new, like duck toes). And don't go to Chinatown expecting intimate or quiet dining. In fact, you'll often share a large round table with other diners. Relax, enjoy, and concentrate on your main goal: serious eating at a very reasonable price.

### CANTONESE

This is the food served by a majority of Chinese restaurants and characterized by specialties that include fried wontons or wonton soup, roast pork, and shrimp with lobster sauce. Unfortunately, Cantonese fare has been given a bad name by restaurants that serve cliché dishes full of cornstarch and sauces laden with fruit out of a can. In Chinatown, less Westernized versions of Cantonese favorites prove that at its best, Cantonese food can meet the standards of the most sophisticated and demanding gourmet. A word of caution: Some restaurants will doctor dishes served to Westerners, so if you want to sample something Chinese style, make that clear to your waiter.

A Chinatown institution with superior Cantonese fare is the **Yun Luck Rice Shoppe,** 17 Doyers St., near Pell Street (tel. 571-1375). Located on a charming curved side street, Yun Luck was for years an out-of-the-way favorite among Chinatown residents and in-the-know tourists. Then the food critic for the *New York Times* gave the 150-seat restaurant her seal of approval with a rare three-star (excellent) rating. Now it's hard to find a seat for lunch. If you're lucky or patient enough to get a table, stay away from the tried-and-true chow mein and wonton dishes and try some truly inventive Cantonese cooking. Among the house specialties are crabs Cantonese style, stir-fried with a sauce of pork, ginger, black beans, and scallions; and treasurer duck, garnished with jumbo shrimp, roast pork, chicken, mushrooms, and snowpeas. The much-raved-about steamed flounder and steamed bass are not on the menu, so ask your waiter.

Our favorite nonseafood dishes are steak with jade tree, meat that melts in your mouth served on a bed of broccoli; beef with mixed vegetables; and watercress soup ($4.50 for a large tureen serving two to four). The thick, chewy noodle dishes are quite good, with roast duck lo mein near nirvana for noodle nuts.

The price on the à la carte dinners ranges from $4.50 to $10, and $16 for a few seafood and lobster dishes. Most dishes cost between $7 and $9. No dessert is on the menu. Bring your own wine or beer, since the house serves no liquor. Reservations, especially for large crowds, are a must.

Open from 11 a.m. to 10:30 p.m. daily.

Also top-notch is **Wong Kee Restaurant,** 113 Mott St. (tel. 966-1160), a small establishment which provides very good inexpensive noodle and soup dishes without the frenetic fast-food atmosphere found in other Chinatown noodle houses. The place is cheerily decorated in shades of steely gray, lemon yellow, and dark turquoise, and the overall effect is soothing and attractive.

Wong Kee's hearty dishes over rice, such as beef with green peas, cost as little as $2.50, and entrees like sizzling chicken—beans, chunks of chickens, garlic, and scallions—can feed two people for as little as $7. There are other more expensive house specialties, like shrimp with hot pepper and salt, Wong Kee spiced pork, and any of Wong Kee's fresh vegetable dishes. A Chinese friend told us about this place and we can understand why it's his favorite.

Open daily from 11 a.m. to 10 p.m. No bar, but you can bring your own drinks. Reservations accepted for large groups.

The menu of **Hong Ying,** 11 Mott St., near Chatham Square (tel. 962-9821), boasts that "all our Chinese food is delicious, the price reasonable." Critics and customers agree. Here you can find offbeat Cantonese seafood delicacies like mussel casserole with black beans and garlic, and eggplant with garlic.

Our favorite meal is wor shu opp—fried duck with a thin coating of finely chopped almonds under skin as crisp as parchment and topped with a delicate sauce. Also on our interesting yet inexpensive meal list is lor hon jai, mixed vegetables in bean-curd sauce topped with sesame seeds; Canton-style crabs or snails; steamed fish; and a unique dish called fun gone har kew, fried chicken livers and jumbo shrimps with water chestnuts, bamboo shoots, snowpea pods, and other vegetables. Most à la carte dishes cost between $4 and $9. Hong Ying also offers many low-priced basic Chinese noodle dishes.

Open Sunday through Thursday from 11 a.m. to 2 a.m., on Friday and Saturday to 4 a.m. No reservations. No bar.

For the freshest Cantonese-style seafood in Chinatown, try **Sun Lok Kee,** 13 Mott St., near Chatham Square (tel. 285-9856 or 732-7295). This small restaurant with nondescript décor is always packed, but service is fast and so is the line. Its menu offers hefty entree portions that cost between $5 and $9. Some of our favorite dishes are mussels in black-bean sauce, steamed fish, steamed shrimp, and crabs Cantonese style. The fresh vegetable and pork dishes make delicious accompaniments.

Open from 11 a.m. to midnight seven days a week.

Another Cantonese restaurant adept at handling crowds is **Phoenix Garden,** 46 Bowery Arcade, between Bowery and Elizabeth streets (tel. 962-8934 or 233-6017). This clean, loud, and very friendly restaurant was given a two-star rating by the *New York Times* several years ago and so is frequented by many uptowners. As is common with many restaurants in Chinatown, the real challenge here is picking only a few dishes from the extensive menu. Phoenix Garden offers more than 26 soups to start with (about $5.50). Other specialties, priced between $6.50 and $9, include roast squab, pepper-and-salty shrimp, sizzling chicken with ginger and scallions in casserole, and pan-fried noodles.

Open daily from 11:30 a.m. to 10:30 p.m.

Another place to go for quality Cantonese food is the **Kam Bo Rice Shoppe,** 51 Bayard St. (tel. 233-5440). In addition to inexpensive yet filling noodle dishes ($3.25 to $5.25), you can get stir-fried vegetable and beef dishes with rice, and for seafood lovers there's mussels in a black-bean sauce served in a hot clay pot ($8), or the "Three Stars Sea Food Pot," with lobster, crabmeat, jumbo shrimp, and mixed Chinese vegetables.

Open daily from 11 a.m. to 3 a.m.

## SZECHUAN

The hot-pepper province in southwestern China is a center for savory, spicy cooking where dishes are seasoned with generous portions of garlic and scallions. Some of the better-known Szechuan dishes are twice-cooked pork, shredded beef with garlic sauce, chicken with hot peppers, and hot-and-sour soup.

A hard-to-find little restaurant, but well worth the search, is the **Little Szechuan,** 31 Oliver St., off Chatham Square, between Henry and Madison streets (tel. 349-2360). The name is appropriate: the tiny place has only eight tables. A golden dragon covers most of the one wall, tables are clothed in red and covered with glass, and newly installed track lighting adds a touch of modernity.

The service is extremely hospitable, the food is superlative, and the prices are unbeatable. Most dishes cost under $7.50. We've feasted on ginger shrimp, sautéed hot pork shreds, orange beef, ta-chien chicken, hot-and-spicy vegetables, and the cold noodle appetizer with sesame sauce. You'll be hard-pressed to find either better or cheaper fare.

Open daily from 11:30 a.m. to 10 p.m.

The **Szechuan State,** 22 Chatham Square (tel. 619-1435), serves excellent yet inexpensive food in a comfortable environment. Golden Tiffany-style lamps cast a warm glow on the wood- and mirror-paneled room and its rust-colored vinyl booths.

In the past we've taken the waiter's advice and tried the delicious sliced scallops and prawns in garlic sauce. Also highly praised are the imperial shrimp with peanuts, sesame chicken, double-sautéed pork, and shredded beef with hot sauce and peanuts. Most dishes are reasonably priced, with lamb, poultry, and beef à la carte dinners costing an average of $6. Fish dishes are the most expensive meals on the menu, priced at an average of $9. Pork, vegetable, bean, and noodle dishes are the least expensive.

Open from 11 a.m. to 11:30 p.m. Sunday through Thursday, to 1 a.m. on Friday and Saturday. Reservations accepted.

## SHANGHAI

Chefs from every part of China were drawn to this sophisticated city in days of yore and combined their regional culinary skills to create what we know as Shanghai cuisine.

One of the best places in Chinatown to sample Shanghai delicacies is **Say Eng Look,** 5 East Broadway, off Chatham Square (tel. 732-0796). *Say eng look* means "four, five, six" in Shanghai dialect—an unbeatable combination in Chinese games of chance. Indeed, owner/chef A. K. Chang leaves nothing to fate as he fixes such sure-fire winners as finely sliced deep-fried pork cutlets, special mixed vegetable, shrimp with sizzling rice, sweet-and-sour sliced fish, and shrimp with kidney. You might also try the casseroles—another Shanghai specialty—particularly the fish-head casserole or the chicken with cashew nuts. Most à la carte dinner dishes cost between $6 and $13.

Say Eng Look's interior is spotless and attractive. Subdued lighting tones down the flamboyant red walls and the beamed ceiling gives the restaurant a homey charm.

Open from 11:30 a.m. to 10:30 p.m. Sunday through Thursday, to 11 p.m. on Friday and Saturday. Reservations are necessary for large groups.

Under the same ownership and bearing the same name in English, **Four Five Six,** 2 Bowery, at the corner of Doyers Street (tel. 964-5853), offers a similar menu in slightly less appealing surroundings. It's also more touristy, offering Westernized versions of Shanghai specialties; so if you want the real thing, talk to your waiter or go to Say Eng Look.

Open from 11:30 a.m. to 10 p.m. Sunday through Thursday, to 11 p.m. on Friday and Saturday. Reservations suggested for large groups.

## MIXED BAGS

There are some restaurants in Chinatown offering the culinary specialties of several provinces, the variety of which allows you to put together an interesting meal and to sample a few types of cooking at one sitting.

One of the best of the genre is the **Mandarin Inn Pell,** 34 Pell St., at the corner of Mott Street (tel. 267-2092). It's one of the largest restaurants in Chinatown, with seating on two floors for 300 people. The main floor is dominated by two huge electrically lit photomurals of wild horses, and another of a coastal setting. Upstairs the décor is even wilder, with walls bizarrely paneled in aqua and red tiles depicting leaves and berries. There is wine-red carpeting, scarlet drapes, and crystal chandeliers.

Among the chef's prize recipes are those for lobster and black-bean sauce, and Mandarin spareribs. The house offers a complete family dinner for $12, or a gourmet dinner for $18 which includes soup, appetizer, entree, and dessert. Most à la carte dishes range between $7 and $14.

When ordering an à la carte dinner, we like to begin by sharing an order of sizzling rice soup, almost a meal in itself, containing shrimp, chicken, pork, and snowpeas, or perhaps an order of scallion pancakes. Exciting entrees include lemon chicken, Mongolian lamb, spicy Kung Pao shrimp, and spicy sautéed string beans or eggplant. For dessert there's no other choice but the Peking honey crisp banana, deep-fried in batter and then dipped in honey, sugar, and sesame seeds ($3.50 for two).

Open Sunday through Thursday from 11 a.m. to 11 p.m., on Friday and Saturday from 11 a.m. to midnight.

The **Peking Duck House,** 22 Mott St. (tel. 962-8208 or 227-1810), is on Ed Koch's list of his ten favorite restaurants. It's easy to see why. The restaurant is famous for its way of cooking Peking duck. When the chef carves the roast duck ($26 for a whole duck) with surgeon-like skill at your table, the skin has been browned to a golden lacquer. The meat is moistly tender and folds neatly into the paper-thin crêpes served with the meal. A velvety hoisin sauce and cool cucumbers and scallions make the roasted duck sandwich a succulent taste sensation.

The Peking Duck House offers an extensive variety of Mandarin, Szechuan, and Hunan dishes, but the most popular order, as you would guess, is the duck. If duck isn't for you, other house favorites include the sliced pork double sautéed with chile sauce, the spiced cold beef appetizer, or the sliced beef with watercress in hot garlic sauce. Although the duck is expensive, a host of vegetable, beef, chicken, and seafood dishes are available for $5 to $10. Noodle and vegetable dishes are less expensive, costing an average of $4.50.

Open Sunday through Thursday from 11:30 a.m. to 10:30 p.m. and on Friday and Saturday from 11:30 a.m. to 11:30 p.m. No bar, but Chinese beer is served.

**Chi Mer,** 11 Chatham Square, near Doyers Street (tel. 267-4565), offers a tasteful ambience and gourmet Chinese food at affordable prices. Tables are covered with simple white linen over a green cloth; the lighting is recessed and the atmosphere is elegant. With walls of exposed brick, mirrors, and pale paisley wallpaper, the restaurant is a pleasing change from the fire-engine red that covers the walls of many other Chinatown restaurants.

The rave-winning menu of Hunan, Mandarin, and Cantonese fare offers patrons over 150 choices of critically acclaimed Chinese food. Diners recommend the Szechuan orange-flavored beef, the eggplant with garlic sauce, and the beef with watercress. Also recommended are Chi Mer's fried dumplings and Oriental fondue of shrimp balls, pork balls, and lobster liver dipped into a simmering broth.

The beef, chicken, and pork à la carte dinner dishes range from $5 to $14. Seafood and fish dishes are a little more expensive. Dinners of vegetables and noodles generally run about $6.

Open Sunday through Thursday from 11:30 a.m. to 11:30 p.m., on Friday and Saturday until 1:30 a.m. Reservations advised on weekend nights. There is a small bar.

## DIM SUM

Many Cantonese and larger mixed-bag restaurants offer a dim sum brunch, usually served from 10 a.m. to 3 p.m. Waiters bring trays of Chinese delicacies and other food in bite-size portions; you choose what you like and are charged by the number of plates on your table at the brunch's end. A satisfying dim sum brunch generally costs between $4 and $6 per person.

All the popular places for dim sum are very crowded on weekends, but this real Chinese eating experience is worth the wait. You can go during the week for a saner meal, but the weekend crowds are part of the fun.

**The Nice Restaurant,** 35 East Broadway (tel. 406-9510), has become a favorite for dim sum in recent years. Its two floors seat more than 400 people, and the restaurant is often full. This is Hong Kong–style dining at its best: the bigger the better.

Don't be intimidated by the hustle and bustle of dim sum here. You can take cues from other diners, and don't be shy about asking what's in a dish. Many dim sum dishes are some kind of dumpling with shrimp, pork, vegetable, or fish fillings. Some favorites are steamed buns filled with pork, shrimp dumplings, pork wontons, and beef balls. There are also sweet confections to end the meal—typical are small cakes filled with custard, coconut, almond, or red-bean paste. All dishes are priced from $1.60 to $3.

Dim sum are served from 8 a.m. to 4 p.m. daily. Dinner is served from 4:30 to 11 p.m.

**Hee Seung Fung,** 46 Bowery, between Canal Street and Chatham Square (tel. 374-1319), prides itself on offering the largest choice of dim sum in the city. Plates of dim sum are continuously wheeled around the restaurant from 7:30 a.m. to 5 p.m., with each plate costing $1.60 to $3.

The à la carte menu of Cantonese fare offered by the restaurant after noon presents some interesting possibilities for the demanding palate. To snap your taste buds to attention, try the snail with black-bean sauce or the shark fin with shredded chicken soup.

Hee Seung Fung is decorated in gold and chrome, and, because of many favorable write-ups, enjoys a large tourist and uptown crowd along with Chinatown locals. Especially helpful at H.S.F. (as it's commonly known) are the pictorial brochures at each table that describe various dishes. H.S.F. has become so popular in recent years that it now has a branch uptown at 578 Second Ave., at 32nd Street (tel. 689-6969), and another in the exclusive Hamptons.

Open for dim sum from 7:30 a.m. to 5 p.m. daily. Dinner is served to midnight. Reservations accepted.

Dim sum at the **Silver Palace,** 50 Bowery, near Canal Street (tel. 964-1204), has become a Chinatown tradition. An escalator brings you to the second-floor dining room which looks roughly the size of a football field, and is decorated in bright red with many large tables—necessary for its hordes of devoted customers. In fact, the management claims there's seating for 800. Reservations aren't accepted, they say, because they'll *always* find room for you. The food at Silver Palace is fast, fresh, and delicious. Prices for more than 58 kinds of dim sum range from $1.65 to $4.25 per plate.

Open for dim sum from 8 a.m. to 4 p.m. daily.

## NOODLE HOUSES

Throughout Chinatown are many small places specializing in Chinese noodle dishes served in bowls with pork, shrimp, chicken, duck, fish, vegetables, and beef. These noodle meals are filling, delicious, and very low in price.

**Hong Fat,** 63 Mott St., between Bayard and Canal streets (tel. 962-9588), is the premier noodle emporium, but it resonates with the noisy atmosphere of a fast-food burger chain. It's a good eatery for a quick lunch, not a restaurant for a relaxing dinner.

China's four basic noodles are served: lo mein (soft noodles), show fon (broad noodles), chow mai fon (fine rice noodles), and special noodles with gravy—each for between $3 and $4.25. You can also order your noodle dish fixed "your way," with any combination of roast pork, beef, shrimp, fish, chicken, or duck.

The restaurant also serves several non-noodle Szechuan specialties, including beef with Szechuan preserved vegetables, dried sautéed string beans with minced pork, and lemon chicken, all priced under $7.

Open 10 a.m. to 5 a.m. daily.

Chinatown's most popular lo mein eatery has found its formula for success in inexpensively priced food served in heaping helpings so huge that a meal can often feed two people. **Lin's Garden Restaurant,** 53 Bayard St., at the corner of Elizabeth Street (tel. 962-9085), is decorated in the same no-frills style as other Chinatown restaurants, yet Lin's is the place to go for over 40 varieties of noodle dishes priced between $2.75 and $5.25.

In addition to four basic types of noodle dishes, Lin's serves over 100 Cantonese specialties (priced between $5 and $9), including clams Chinese style, served hot in the shell in an oyster sauce; iron steak with broccoli; roast duck; and sweet-and-sour pork.

Open from 9 a.m. to 6 a.m. seven days a week.

**Wo Hop** is actually two restaurants, at 15 and 17 Mott St. (tel. 766-9160 and 406-3973 respectively). The two establishments are different in décor but similar in menu. Devotees of both restaurants recommend the chunky, meat- and seafood-filled soups and noodle dishes. The Wo Hops offer over 50 noodle dishes priced under $5.25. Many of the steamy plates of silky noodles, such as roast pork chow fon and beef chow fon, cost $3 or less. Other low-priced Cantonese fare: roast pork with green peppers and onions, beef with beansprouts, and kam loo wanton—fried wonton, breaded with seafood, roast duck, chicken, pork, pineapple, and sweet-and-sour sauce.

Number 15 is the more attractive place to eat. Decorated with bright-red tiles and electrically lit photomurals of the Chinese countryside, the 50-seat restaurant is cheerful and pleasant. Number 17, located at the bottom of a flight of stairs, has been in that location for over 40 years.

The restaurant at 15 Mott St. is open daily from 11 a.m. to 5 a.m.; the one at 17 Mott is open 24 hours a day. Only 15 Mott will accept reservations.

For some of the best soup in Chinatown, try the **Shanghai Snack Bar,** 14 Elizabeth St. (tel. 964-5640), at the end of the covered Elizabeth Street mall walkway. Offering more than 25 varieties of soup and noodle dishes, this is the perfect place for a quick yet filling meal. Try the Shanghai noodles in a bowl of hearty broth, with diced chicken and pork, shrimp, bamboo shoots, green peas, and Chinese mushrooms, or the several appetizing dumpling dishes that range in price from $2.75 to $3.

Open daily from 10:30 a.m. to 10 p.m. (approximately).

For refined dining, try **Siu Lam Kung,** 18 Elizabeth St. (tel. 732-0974). Here, crisply uniformed waiters serve seafood that's undeniably fresh; in fact, the tank in the window of the restaurant is home to such future dinner fare as frogs, served with black-bean sauce, and eels, served sliced and sautéed in a mild sauce (prices vary seasonally). You can also get a delicious sizzling dish of sang kang scallops in a spicy brown sauce ($12), or lobster prepared in either black-bean sauce or with ginger and scallions (around $13, depending on the season). Another highly recommended house specialty is shrimp with cashew and steamed crab.

Open daily from 11 a.m. to midnight.

## ICE CREAM

Don't fill up on fortune cookies when you dine in Chinatown; some of the most flavorful Chinese desserts can be tasted at the **Chinatown Ice Cream Factory,** 65 Bayard St., between Mott and Elizabeth streets (tel. 608-4170).

This is Chinatown's answer to Baskin-Robbins. Here you can try 36 homemade flavors as Chinese as chow mein or as exotic as the Orient, including almond cookie (our favorite), lichee, ginger, red bean, green tea, papaya, and mango. For the less adventurous, Occidental favorites from vanilla to Rocky Road are on the menu. A cone is 50¢, a pint is $3, and a quart is $6. Open daily from 11 a.m. to midnight.

The five Seid Brothers—William, Henry, Eugene, Philip, and Otis—make all the flavors from all-natural ingredients in a huge freezer on the premises. Try the milkshakes, ice-cream sundaes, banana splits, and ice-cream cakes for a tasty alternative to the double-dip cone.

---

# 11. Little Italy

---

Little Italy is the ultimate ethnic neighborhood for the New Yorker and tourist alike. Its lively street life serves as a magnet to people from all over the city. The area's Italian character is reflected in its plethora of bakeries, coffeehouses, restaurants, and food shops. In the summer and fall, street festivals spring up almost every week. Best known is the feast of San Gennaro, held in September. Cars are exiled from Mulberry Street, fried pastries and sausages steam the air, and you can become part of the gregarious scene. Later, the tired street reveler can rest in a café and indulge in fresh pastries. Some of the best are listed in this section.

No one should miss the experience of eating at **Puglia,** 189 Hester St., near Mulberry Street (tel. 966-6066 or 226-8912). Although the food is excellent, the main attraction is the atmosphere: Puglia is crowded, casual, rowdy (in a friendly way); on weekends the house singer and organist often leads the customers in a sing-along, and the entertainment is all free. Puglia is a venerable New York institution in which patrons have been partying since 1915. The restaurant has marbled floors and walls decorated with friezes of Little Italy scenes and mounted deer heads. The festive diners sit at long tables out front, and there's an adjoining garden-like backroom with a bar. In the summer a few tables grace a small garden outside.

The portions of food are inexpensive (pastas under $8, veal and poultry under $9.50, and seafood dishes under $11) and hefty. There are some unusual dishes—

try the grilled sheep's head, a house special ($3). On the more traditional side is spaghetti with meatballs, mussels, or sausage; a wide selection of veal dishes ($8.50 to $9.50); and lasagne, ziti, or manicotti. An order of garlic bread is $1; a glass of wine with your meal, $1.75. Good food, great fun.

Open Tuesday through Sunday from noon to 1 a.m.

The only Little Italy restaurant that has been around longer than Puglia is **Vincent's Clam Bar,** 119 Mott St., at the corner of Hester Street (tel. 226-8133). Giuseppe and Carmelo Siano established the place in 1904 and the Siano family has been running it ever since. The front room houses a bar and a long counter, behind which Vincent's chefs cook up steaming pots of their famous hot sauce. The main dining room in the back is informal but pleasant, with beamed walls, two big arched windows, and a vase of fresh flowers on every table. On the wall, watching over it all, is a large oil painting of the Siano brothers.

Fresh fish, seafood, and pasta are the specialties here: for less than $11 you can get an order of linguine and clams, calamari, or shrimp with medium or hot sauce, baked mussels, little neck clams, or an Italian seafood combination platter, such as calamari, scungilli (conch), and oysters that costs between $13 and $15.

Open Sunday through Thursday from 11:30 a.m. to 2 a.m., on Friday and Saturday until 5 a.m. No reservations.

One of Little Italy's more reasonably priced restaurants is **Luna,** 112 Mulberry St., between Canal and Hester streets (tel. 226-8657). Like many of the area's kitchens, it's family owned and family run. Luna has a justifiably loyal clientele and at dinnertime the booths (there are only 12) fill quickly, so be prepared to wait.

The antipasto is very good, and comes with stuffed pepper, mushrooms, scallops, and clams. Pasta dishes—spaghetti, lasagne, ravioli, and linguine—are all under $7.50, and seafood and veal dishes like veal cacciatore with mushrooms and peppers cost $9. In general the seafood dishes are outstanding; we favor calamari oreganato, a tender, sliced squid baked with a topping of breadcrumbs, garlic, oregano, and olive oil. There are also healthy platters of steamed mussels and clams, wine by the glass, and a full complement of bar drinks.

Open daily from noon to midnight.

For first-rate, southern-style Sicilian cuisine, **Benito's II,** 163 Mulberry St., between Broome and Grand streets (tel. 226-9012), is the place. It's a rustic restaurant, with a dark wood-paneled ceiling and exposed-brick walls punctuated by floor-to-ceiling wood beams. Neat tables are covered with white linen tablecloths and waiters are sharply dressed in white and black.

The veal, seafood, and pasta are excellent, as are the antipasti. The entrees are all between $9.25 and $13, but you can get a much better deal if you order in courses, Italian style, and share. Two people might begin with the pepper stuffed with vegetables in marinara sauce or the popular mozzarella in carrozza (fried cheese sandwiches); or go on to share one of the pastas, such as spaghetti carbonara style or homemade manicotti; then perhaps a main dish, octopus Sicilian style (with tomatoes, capers, garlic, and black olives), veal scaloppine, or the delicious striped bass, broiled and served in a light tomato sauce with capers and anchovies. You might also order a small carafe of wine with your meal, and if you decide to splurge on dessert, try the zabaglione with strawberries, a popular Benito II custard dessert.

Benito's II is open daily from noon to midnight.

Just down the street is **Benito's I,** 174 Mulberry St. (tel. 226-9171). No longer affiliated with Benito's II, this small restaurant features delicious Sicilian cuisine in a charming, intimate atmosphere.

The entrees are between $10 and $13; we found the scaloppine alla Benito excellent (veal with prosciutto and mushrooms sautéed in marsala wine). An unusual and tasty dish is broccoli di rapé, bitter broccoli cooked with garlic and herbs. Also recommended is the fettuccine Giulio Cesare, veal-based red cream sauce, with mushrooms, prosciutto, and freshly ground parmesan. Pasta dishes are between $6 and $10.

Open Tuesday through Sunday for lunch from noon to 3 p.m., and for dinner from 5 to 11 p.m. (to midnight on the weekend). No reservations are needed.

**Umberto's Clam House,** 129 Mulberry St., at the corner of Hester Street (tel. 431-7545), is perhaps the best known of Little Italy's restaurants. During the wee hours (the real crowds don't start arriving until 3 a.m.) the place is filled with actors, actresses, and other restaurateurs. One whole wall is devoted to autographed pictures of the celebrity clientele—among them Frank Sinatra, Johnny Carson, Cher, Jackie Gleason, and Fellini. Nevertheless, Umberto's is an attractive and unpretentious place with butcher-block tables, large windows, blue-tiled floors, and fishnet and ship models on the walls. In good weather a row of umbrella tables is placed outdoors on a small patio.

Umberto's is most renowned for its clams ($9 for a dozen cherrystone or littlenecks) and its linguine in hot sauce. Seafood, such as calamari (squid), scungilli (conch), and mussels are served with a choice of hot, medium, or sweet sauces and biscuits. House favorites include the fish salad combination—shrimp, calamari, mussels, and scungilli with lemon, oil, garlic, and parsley—and fish and chips or a plate of smelt with french fries, lemon, and tartar sauce. Most of the traditional Italian pastries are $2.

Open from 11:30 a.m. to 6 a.m. daily.

Right down the street is **Teresa's of Mulberry Street,** 117 Mulberry St. (tel. 226-6950), a pretty and intimate little place with barely enough room for its 11 indoor tables and 4 patio tables. It has plant-filled windows, beautiful latticework over room-length mirrors, and tables covered with brown oilcloth. The entire effect is rather charming and very Italian. The menu is the same at lunch and dinner, and the prices are extremely reasonable: most of the pastas are under $8; fettuccine Alfredo, and linguine and spaghetti, are delicious favorites, as is the filette de pomadoro—red sauce, onion, fresh tomatoes, Italian ham, and a dash of red wine.

Open daily from noon to 11:30 p.m. Reservations are recommended at dinner and on weekends.

Housed in a Federal two-story domed brick house that dates from the early 1800s, **Paolucci's,** 149 Mulberry St., between Grand and Hester streets (tel. 925-2288 or 226-9653), is one of Little Italy's top-rated southern Italian (Neapolitan) restaurants, family owned and family run. The décor is classy, with black-and-gold chairs, a pressed-tin roof from which hang huge chandeliers, and white-linen-covered tables. Next to the bar is a large, working brick fireplace.

All the food is homemade and first-rate. Most entrees cost between $6 and $11. Lunch and dinner specials (noon to 5 p.m.) offer manicotti and lasagne, veal parmigiana, and hot or cold antipasti—all under $9. We like to finish up a meal with a dessert of homemade Italian cheesecake and a cup of espresso with anisette. Wine and liquor are also available.

Paolucci's is open on Monday, Tuesday, and Thursday from noon to 11 p.m., Friday through Sunday until 11:30 p.m. Reservations are suggested on weekends.

What would a visit to Little Italy be without a thick slice of pizza or a hefty cheese calzone? For both, go to **Florio's,** 192 Grand St., between Mott and Mulberry streets (tel. 226-7610). Entered via an alcove with large plant-filled windows, the interior has exposed-brick and stucco walls decorated with oil paintings, a beamed ceiling, and tables covered with red tablecloths under glass. There's a very comfortable backroom with a skylight and thriving potted trees and plants.

A thick-crusted regular pizza here is $11 for a large pie. A piece of cheese calzone (sort of like a fried, rolled slice of pizza with filling) is $4.50; you can also get cheese and sausage or cheese and prosciutto varieties. Florio's offers huge hero sandwiches—meatball, sausage and peppers, veal cutlet, and more—for between $4 and $5. There are also homemade pasta dishes, and fish, chicken, and veal entrees (most between $10 and $12). Italian ice creams and pastries cost between $2 and $3.

Open daily from 11 a.m. to midnight. No reservations.

## PASTRY SHOPS AND CAFES

Since 1892, **Ferrara's,** 195 Grand St., between Mott and Mulberry streets (tel. 226-6150), has been tempting New Yorkers with an outrageous variety of cake and pastry. Just a peek at the long marble pastry counter laden with every imaginable confection and cake will have your mouth watering. The demand for Ferrara's goodies has made the café a nationally known business; Ferrara's ships its own brand of coffees, candies, and hundreds of other Italian delicacies all over the world.

The traditional Italian pastries—cannoli, eclairs, babas au rum, babas au ricotta, napoleons, cream puffs, and many others—are $2. Specialties of the house include Gianduja mousse cake, chocolate layer cake with praline paste; chocolate hazelnut mousse encased in a hazelnut chocolate; almond and cheese cakes; and a rustic peasant pie, filled with salami, fresh eggs, and smoked cheese. An espresso, cappuccino, and other Italian coffees cost between $1.50 and $3.

Once you've made your choice, and if the weather is good, walk outside and sit under the white-and-red awning, while the rest of Little Italy strolls by.

Ferrara's is open from 9 a.m. to midnight during the week, until 3 a.m. on weekends.

**Caffè Roma,** 385 Broome St., at Mulberry Street (tel. 226-8413), is a traditionally charming Italian café. The décor is lovely and authentic: high ceilings, white tiled floors, marble tables and counters, with numerous paintings on the wall by Frank Mason, an internationally renowned artist. The long gold pastry case is filled with some of the most delicious pastries in all of New York.

Caffè Roma is known for its milk Sicilian cassatina, a special cake filled with ricotta and frosted with vanilla, and pieces of chocolate. Assorted pastries and ice creams cost between $1.50 and $3; coffees are $1.25 to $3.

Open daily from 8 a.m. to midnight.

**In Bocca Al Lupo** (In the Mouth of the Wolf), 113 Mulberry St., at Canal Street (tel. 431-9755), is a relatively new addition to Little Italy. Its sparkling-clean interior has an exposed-brick wall and floor-to-ceiling mirrors on the opposite wall, which give a feeling of depth to the tiny café. Sit by the working fireplace in fall or winter and enjoy an espresso with Sambuca or a mochaccino, a chocolate-flavored cappuccino. In the summer, sit outside in the fountain garden which is enclosed by brick walls. Large potted plants and twinkling lights on the tree branches add to the festive atmosphere.

Some of the delectable desserts to choose from are the Italian rum cake, chocolate cheesecake, and fruit-flavored Italian ices, all priced between $2 and $4. For the truly decadent, there is coppa cha cha: hazelnut and cappuccino ice cream with tiny rum-soaked balls of cake, nuts, black cherries, and whipped cream ($4.75).

New to the menu are small pizzas ($5 to $8) and "paninis"—small Italian sandwiches made with provolone, salami, or prosciutto ($4 to $5).

Open Monday through Friday from 11 a.m. to 2 a.m., on Saturday and Sunday until 4 a.m. Major credit cards accepted.

---

# 12. Lower East Side/East Village

A stroll through the Lower East Side and the East Village is like entering a time machine that spans six decades of American history. Here you'll find restaurants and coffeeshops that grew up in the '20s, '30s, and '40s, as waves of immigrants, making their way past Ellis Island, landed in Manhattan and made their first homes in places called Hester and Grand streets in the Lower East Side. Today the Orthodox Jewish population still thrives below Houston Street, but it shares this area with new immigrant groups from Latin America and Southeast Asia.

Just to the north is the East Village, traditionally the home of Ukrainian immigrants, and the Ukrainian community is still very much in evidence. Every year a

Ukrainian festival livens up East 7th Street between Second and Third avenues. But in the 1960s St. Marks Place (8th Street) became the center for New York's counter-culture movement—the East Coast's Haight Ashbury. Since then, each new out-of-the-mainstream, "in" crowd has paraded its style through the East Village's streets. The area is also home to artists and actors, and most recently to the New York Public Theater and other off-Broadway companies.

Restaurants here are a bargain hunter's dream. The food here is some of the best and cheapest you'll find in the city.

*A word to the wise:* While the East Village is filled with streets that bustle with activity into the wee hours of the morning, there are some side streets that are deserted and unsafe. Don't miss the excitement here, but exercise a little extra caution, especially at night.

## AMERICAN/CONTINENTAL

**Around the Clock Café,** 8 Stuyvesant Pl., just east of Third Avenue (tel. 598-0402), draws a loyal following, especially for breakfast and lunch. Passersby who stop to admire the café's large, centerpiece clock stay for the delicious food. The menu includes a wide range of salads, burgers, and omelets. Sample the chicken or beef fajitas ($6.50), or try the pasta with fresh seafood of the day ($7.25). Entrees range from $5 to $9.

The café's riverboat-era antique bar, imported from Missouri, adds to the timeless atmosphere.

Open 24 hours every day. Breakfast served anytime.

If you think that **Eat,** 11 St. Marks Pl., between Second and Third avenues (tel. 477-5155), sounds like the name of a rough, no-frills hash house, you're in for a pleasant surprise. This long, low-ceilinged restaurant offers a touch of class with its eye-catching art, wood trim, and fresh flowers on the tables. The menu is a mix of vegetarian dishes and pita (Middle Eastern pocket bread) sandwiches. A few fish and chicken dishes are offered too. Try the cheese and chili-melt pita stuffer or the stir-fried vegetable pita stuffer, each $5.25. Pasta dishes are excellent. We suggest the broccoli fettuccine topped with mushroom sauce for $7.50. Or ask about the fish selection of the day ($8.50).

Eat has an extensive imported beer and wine list. Open from 10 a.m. to midnight Sunday through Thursday, on Friday and Saturday to 1 a.m.

For a break from the whirl of sightseeing, try the peaceful atmosphere of the **Cloister Café,** 238 E. 9th St., between Second and Third avenues (tel. 777-9128). An outdoor garden patio offers its own small fountain and goldfish pond. Ivy-covered brick walls and festive night lighting also add to the patio's charm. If it's raining or cold outside, move indoors to admire the Cloister Café's antique religious stained-glass windows. The Strauss salad, with chicken, crabmeat, spinach, garnishes, and fruit ($8), is a meal in itself. Tortellini al pesto is another favorite here ($9). You are invited to bring your own wine or beer. You can also linger over a café-au-lait, served French style in large bowls ($2.25), or sip on the other delicious teas and coffees.

Don't come here if you're in a hurry, though. The help is as relaxed as the atmosphere. They don't like to rush. Open from noon to 12:30 a.m. Sunday through Thursday, to 1:30 a.m. on Friday and Saturday.

**7A,** 109 Ave. A, at East 7th Street (tel. 475-9001), is a bright, airy café with pink-and-white walls, lots of wood and plants, and outdoor sidewalk seating. For entrees, try the bay scallops sautéed with herbs and wine over linguine, served with a vegetable and your choice of rice or potato ($8.50). Or stay with simpler fare, such as the hearty half-pound burger on pita bread or an English muffin, served with a garden salad or home-fries ($4.25).

If you're getting a late start in the morning, try 7A's weekday breakfast special, served until 1 p.m. For $2.75, order your choice of three eggs any style, with home-fries, toast or an English muffin, and coffee. For the same price you can also get blue-berry pancakes with coffee.

Desserts here are a local treasure. Treat yourself to the pecan pie ($3) or the irresistible chocolate cheesecake ($3.50).

Open from 10 a.m. to 2 a.m. Sunday through Thursday, to 6 a.m. on Friday and Saturday.

**Sidewalks,** 94 Ave. A, at Sixth Street (tel. 473-7373), doesn't have spectacular food. The menu features an ordinary and inexpensive roundup of burgers, salads, and sandwiches priced between $3 and $7. But the endless parade of East Village oddballs strolling past its outdoor tables turns most meals into an unbeatable brand of offbeat dinner-theater. It's definitely one of the best people-watching perches in the city. Don't come for lunch—most of the local color will still be asleep.

Open from 10 a.m. to 4 a.m. every day.

## BRAZILIAN

The walls of **Anaconda,** 29 St. Marks Pl., between Second and Third avenues (tel. 260-6183), are overgrown with large floral murals dense enough to mask a few specimens of the restaurant's reptilian namesake. But the only thing that will wrap itself around you during your meal is a heady dose of hedonistic Brazilian culture. Anaconda is one of New York's new breed of sensuous South American eateries. The waiters are beautiful. The food, like traditional Portuguese paella or pan-fried red snapper marinated in citrus juice and herbs, is beautifully served. And the loud Latin American music will have you shimmying around on your seat. Most entrees are between $7 and $11; sandwiches are also available for $5 or $6. Go ahead. Give in. End your meal with the exquisite strawberries Amazon (marinated in rum and dipped in white and dark chocolate).

Open from noon to 2 a.m. Monday through Friday, until 4 a.m. on Saturday and Sunday.

## CARIBBEAN

If you like a real party atmosphere, try **Sugar Reef,** 93 Second Ave., between 5th and 6th streets (tel. 477-8427). It's gaily decorated with lots of greenery and plastic tropical fruit and you'll feel as though you were suddenly transported from downtown Manhattan to the sunny tropics. The food is spicy, the portions gener-ous, and the atmosphere fun.

Start off with a Jamaican meat pattie, fiery beef wrapped in pastry ($3.75); then try the curried shrimp and coconut ($12), served with pumpkin rice and smothered cabbage. Another favorite is the vegetable roti ($8.75)—sautéed carrots, kale, cab-bage, and potatoes, wrapped in fresh roti pastry. Order beer or wine from the bar to complete your meal, or splurge on an island specialty drink, such as a Blue Curaçao ($4.75), frozen and served in a large souvenir surfer glass.

Keep in mind, however, that this festive restaurant is not recommended for a quiet evening. The reggae music is loud and the tables are small. Friendly table-to-table chatter is the norm.

Open Sunday through Thursday from 5 p.m. to 12:30 a.m., and on Friday and Saturday from 3 p.m. to 1:30 a.m.

## CHINESE

Some local Chinese-food lovers won't eat anywhere besides the **Bamboo House,** 104 Second Ave., at East 6th Street (tel. 254-3502). This small, unassuming restaurant is well known for its heaping portions and tasty dishes. The vegetables here are crisp and the meats are carefully prepared. Try a mixed dish of chicken, shrimp, and scallops in garlic sauce for $7. Or we recommend the sautéed tender chicken with broccoli for $6. Another chicken favorite is the moo goo gai pan, also $6. If you want spicy seafood, try the prawns sautéed with hot spicy paste for $6.75. Most of the cooking is traditional Szechuan, but brown rice is also available.

The medium-sized square dining room features a modest décor, with Chinese prints and calendars and festive red Chinese trim. The candles on each table add a nice touch, but the food here is the main attraction.

Open from 1 to 11:15 p.m. daily.

## CRÉOLE/SOUTHERN

When the **Great Jones Café,** 54 Great Jones St., just off the Bowery (tel. 674-9304), opened several years ago, the owners planned a little neighborhood bar with food as a side attraction. But the word got out about some of New York's finest Cajun cooking. Now the crowds that usually fill up the bar are waiting for a table. Begin your meal with an order of honey-sweetened, fresh-baked jalapeño cornbread ($2.50). Then for a real treat, try the blackened redfish, charred and crunchy outside, succulent and juicy inside, served with a salad and vegetable ($9.50). Another big favorite here is the rich, thick, Louisiana gumbo, cooked old style, and served with a salad and vegetable ($7.25). Don't forget to check the daily specials, posted on the blackboard. If you're caught waiting for a table, join the bar drinkers for a Cajun martini, a shot of straight vodka or gin flavored with jalapeño pepper ($2). You might need a beer chaser. If so, order a Rolling Rock, the café's unofficial beer.

The kitchen is open from 5 p.m. to 1 a.m. Monday through Friday, and until 2 a.m. on Saturday and Sunday. Note: Tables are placed side by side, so privacy is at a minimum.

## ITALIAN

**La Spaghetteria,** 178 Second Ave., at East 12th Street (tel. 995-0900), is an unusually posh East Village restaurant. But don't be intimidated by the plush furnishings and subdued jazz music; jeans are still welcome here. For starters, have the mozzarella e pomodori (mozzarella cheese and tomatoes with olive oil), plenty for two at $4.25. One of the house specialties is the fettuccine con salsice (fettuccine with sausage, mushrooms, and roasted red peppers) for $9.50. Or try the rigatoni al ragu d'agnello (tubular pasta with a light lamb tomato sauce) for $7. Finish your meal with a slice of double chocolate cake ($4).

Open weekdays from 5 p.m. to midnight, weekends until 2 a.m.

If you're prepared to put up with a long wait (often up to an hour) and crowded quarters, **Cucina di Pesce,** 87 E. 4th St., just west of Second Avenue (tel. 260-6800), offers one of the East Village's most interesting scenes. Descend the stairs from the street and mingle with the crowds enjoying complimentary mussels marinara in the bar/waiting room. Once you're seated in the restaurant proper, choose from 13 different kinds of pasta and nearly as many varieties of fresh seafood. A complimentary cold salad is served, and other appetizers are available from $2 to $6. Try the asparagus and stringbeans with broiled mozzarella. Entrees range from $6 to $11, with seafood specials priced a bit higher. A devoted following swears by the seafood fettuccine.

The dining room is a pretty shade of pale blue, and is lined with statues, maps, and mirrors (in which the predominantly young and sleek diners appraise each other).

Open from 6 p.m. to midnight seven days a week.

## INDIAN/BANGLADESHI

The Ahmed brothers were the first to open their small basement restaurant on East 6th Street between First and Second avenues, and soon others followed suit, turning the block into an Indian-food lover's haven.

Boasting that it was "the first on the block," **Shah Bagh,** 320 E. 6th St., between First and Second avenues (tel. 677-8876), is a most unpretentious restaurant in décor, with interior wood paneling and barely a hint of Indian decorator items. There are two dining rooms, filled with small wood tables that are set with flowers and white cloth napkins. Tea is on the house.

To start your meal, you might want to try the coconut soup or the banana fritter. The à la carte menu features vegetable, chicken, beef, lamb, and crabmeat curries for under $5. There are also several kinds of biryani, dishes cooked with saffron rice, coconut, and spices, for between $3.50 and $5.25. All entree dishes are made mild, so ask for hot orders if it suits you. For dessert, try the honey cake or the gulab jaman, a sweet fried cheese ball. Hours are noon to midnight daily.

The Ahmed brothers' second enterprise, **Anar Bagh,** down the street at 338 E. 6th St. (tel. 529-1937), features a similar menu with fancier décor. A bright green, yellow, and red canopy hangs from the ceiling in the interior dining room, and there is an open garden for dining in back.

The menu here is translated into English, with explanations of traditional dishes. Try the poori (puffed Indian bread) as an appetizer, or the mulligatawny tomato soup. Korma dishes, cooked in a creamy sauce with mild spices, cost between $4.25 and $6.25. Curries here run $3.25 to $6. There's a wide selection of seafood dishes, including lobster, for under $8. For dessert, try a roshgolla cheese ball or firni custard sprinkled with rose water. Open daily from noon to midnight.

Each of the restaurants along "Little India" row has its own devoted following. While most of them serve comparable food at comparable prices, **Mitali,** 334 E. 6th St. (tel. 533-2508), is a bit more expensive, and in our opinion, serves the best food on the block. From your comfortable wooden table, you can watch the chef prepare your food behind a wall of plate glass. In addition to the usual curries, Mitali serves a complex and delicious assortment of tandoori dishes. Entrees ($6 to $13) cost a few dollars more than at the neighboring restaurants, but are still reasonably priced. Mitali has a full-service bar and a good selection of wine and Indian beer.

Open from noon to midnight every day.

## JAPANESE

Only in New York would you find a restaurant like the heady, trendy, New Wave sushi restaurant called **Avenue A,** 103 Ave. A, between East 7th Street and St. Marks Place (tel. 982-8109). Immerse yourself in A's black-and-purple interior (the owner's favorite colors) with highlights of blue lighting, irreverent art displays, and two black-lacquered bars, one for sushi and one for drinks. In the back is more intimate seating with fresh flowers on the tables.

You might make a meal by sampling the appetizers and the sushi à la carte. If so, try the Masa specialties, prepared by Masa, a veteran sushi chef. These include the yado-kari—mushrooms, carrots, and bamboo shoots sautéed with crabmeat and baked in a clam shell with a white sauce ($5.50). Or try the "Dynamite"—scallops, mushrooms, and smelt roe baked in white sauce with sesame seeds ($5.50). Another favorite is the "Tiger's Eye"—salmon, spinach, and seaweed surrounded with squid to look like a tiger's eye ($5.50). For bargain entrees, try the katsu tama, a deep-fried pork cutlet and vegetables cooked with egg in a sukiyaki sauce ($7), or the rolled beef, stuffed with scallions, with teriyaki sauce ($8.75).

Open from 6 p.m. to 1 a.m. Monday through Saturday.

Sushi fans will love **Sharaku,** 8 Stuyvesant Pl., between Second and Third avenues (tel. 598-0403). This is a popular Japanese hangout that serves a wide variety of sushi ranging from $1.40 to $3 à la carte. Try the yellowtail ($1.75) or the giant clam ($2). For those of you who prefer your fish cooked, we suggest the shrimp tempura ($5.25). The medium-sized dining room is festively decorated with Japanese prints and bamboo shades. The music is low-key and soothing.

Open for dinner Sunday through Thursday from 6 p.m. to 1 a.m., on Friday and Saturday to 4 a.m.

**Dojo,** 24 St. Marks Pl., between Second and Third avenues (tel. 674-9821), offers a great mix of Japanese dishes, natural foods, and good old-fashioned American meals. Here you will find one of the widest selections and some of the best prices in the East Village. The highest-priced meal on the menu is the steamed seafood plate, with mussels, scallops, shrimp, and fish, served with salad and rice, for only

$6.75. Other bargains include the hamburger dinner, served with salad and home-fries for $3.75, and any of the salad plates ($3.50 to $5), each a meal in itself. For dessert we suggest the chocolate mud cake ($3).

Situated in the heart of the East Village, Dojo's offers a great view of the East Village scene from its canopied sidewalk seating. Otherwise, enjoy yourself in any of the three inside rooms.

Open Sunday through Thursday from 11 a.m. to midnight, on Friday and Saturday to 2 a.m. Breakfast is served until 5 p.m. and after 11 p.m.

With its wooden walls, paper screens, and claustrophobic tables, **Sapporo,** 245 E. 10th St., at 4th Avenue (tel. 260-1330), feels very Japanese indeed. Sapporo is a place where people huddle over their tables and take their sushi very seriously. A 15-minute wait is the norm, but it's worth it. Regulars insist that Sapporo serves the best sushi in the East Village. If you know what you like, à la carte sushi and sashimi range from $1.30 to $3.25. If you don't, try the sushi dinner ($8.50). It includes miso soup, a small salad, and ten varieties of sushi. Don't be startled if, as you leave, the entire staff bows and shouts "Thank you."

Open from 5 p.m. to 12:45 a.m. every day.

## JEWISH DAIRY

The huge, open dining room at **Ratner's,** 138 Delancey St., between Norfolk and Suffolk streets (tel. 677-5588), is reminiscent of a ballroom from the 1940s, with a pink scalloped ceiling and mirrored walls. There are a lot of oldtimers on the staff, dressed in mustard-colored uniforms, who can tell you about the early days when the Harmatz and Zankel families first opened the restaurant. The bakery counter up front offers tempting treats, and the restaurant menu is world famous for its wide selection of Jewish specialties, like matzoh brei and kreplach.

To start, we suggest the cold borscht, with a generous helping of sour cream ($3.50). Try the potato pancakes with applesauce ($7.25), or the cheese, potato, or sour-cream blintzes for the same price. Splurge on the baked gelfilte fish with Créole sauce, vegetable, and potato ($10.25). The matzoh brei with applesauce is $7.25. For dessert, if you have room, try the strawberry cheesecake for $3.

Hours are 6 a.m. to 11 p.m. Sunday through Thursday, until 2 a.m. on Friday and Saturday.

On a smaller scale there's **Yonah Schimmel,** at 137 Houston St., between Eldridge and Forsyth streets (tel. 477-2858). The knishes here are famous city-wide, and on Sunday morning it's not unusual to see limousines lined up outside this un-pretentious eatery, buying knishes for fancy East Side brunches. Inside, a dumb-waiter on rope pulleys still delivers hot knishes and strudels from the kitchen. Lillian Berger, the present owner, is a descendant of Yonah Schimmel, who opened the restaurant in 1910.

While potato and kasha knishes are the star attractions at $1.75, you can also get a homemade borscht with sour cream for $1.25. Cheese bagels and apple strudel are $1.50.

Open daily from 8 a.m. to 6 p.m.

These days, students from the local Seward Park High School are as likely to be found at the **Grand Dairy Restaurant,** 341 Grand St., at the corner of Ludlow Street (tel. 673-1904), as are Jewish matrons stopping for coffee and blintzes after shopping. The dining area is separated from the counter by a long divider, with a battered metal coatrack above it. White Formica tables and orange chairs make for simple décor, with orange curtains in the window and granite-speckled floors. The strictly kosher restaurant has a menu filled with hundreds of dairy items.

Try the cabbage soup (Sunday) for $2.50 or the borscht with sour cream for $2.75. Dairy items include matzoh brei and kasha blintzes, $4.75 each. Omelets here ($3 to $7) are delicious. Fish dishes cost between $4.50 and $8. For dessert there's a wide variety of pastries, including homemade coffeecake ($1) and hamantaschen cakes ($1.25).

Hours are 6 a.m. to 4 p.m. Sunday through Friday. Closed Saturday and Jewish holidays.

You'd never know it by looking at its simple, greasy-spoon set-up, but the tiny counter at **B+H Dairy,** 127 Second Ave., near St. Marks Place (8th Street) (tel. 477-6874), serves up what many consider the city's best soups. A rich and unusual hot tomato/beet borscht and a filling mushroom-barley are two neighborhood favorites among the selection of five or six soups served every day. Soup with challah bread costs $2. Jewish dairy specialties are also reasonably priced. If you ask for water, you'll be setting up the cheeky countermen for their favorite joke. "There's water in your soup," they'll reply, more often than not.

Open from 6 a.m. to 10 p.m. every day.

## JEWISH DELI

Although Abe Lebewohl established his delicatessen late by Lower East Side standards (1954), meals at the **Second Avenue Deli,** 156 Second Ave., at the corner of East 10th Street (tel. 677-0606), have become a thriving tradition. With its flashy green stained-glass windows, the restaurant is easily spotted from a distance. The late Sam Levenson, a great Second Avenue Deli fan, wrote that the "vital ingredient" found here is "common sense based on years of scenting." In addition to common sense, Lebewohl has a good deal of promotional skill, and he has managed to turn Second Avenue Deli events into major New York happenings.

The interior décor is bright, with glass lamps hanging from the ceiling and a large take-home counter. Pickles are set at every table. There's a small café in back as well, decorated with posters and plants.

The mushroom-barley soup ($2.50) is a good bet to start your meal. Matzohball soup is another specialty here (same price). The deli is famous for its pastrami, and a heaping hot pastrami sandwich is $6.50. There are traditional knishes for $1.50 and kugels for $3.75. Hungarian goulash with noodles is $10.50. For dessert, try the warm apple strudel for $2.50.

Open weekdays from 7 a.m. to midnight, weekends until 2 a.m. No reservations.

**Katz's,** at 205 E. Houston St., between First Avenue and Avenue A (tel. 254-2246), is a haven for carnivores who believe that red meat is still king. Take a ticket at the door—you'll need it to pay your bill on the way out. The cavernous main dining room is decorated with a wall of salamis and jars of pickled products. Tables along the left-hand wall are reserved for waiter service. But it's more fun to approach the counter on the right, where meat-slicing men prepare your food right under your nose, then write the price on your ticket. Katz's is famous for its deli sandwiches, most priced around $6, especially its pastrami and corned beef. Your sandwich maker will offer you a plate with a sample of meat. Eat the offering and leave a tip in its place. (Otherwise the quality of your sandwich may suffer.) While you're attacking your mound of meat, see if you can spot the World War II–era sign that still reads "Send a salami to your boy in the army."

Open Sunday through Thursday from 8 a.m. to 10:45 p.m., on Friday and Saturday until 12:45 a.m.

## MEXICAN

The **Life Café,** 343 E. 10th St., at Avenue B (tel. 477-8791), in the East Village, attracts a fringe crowd of punk types, yet-to-be-discovered artists, and 1960s holdovers. The café gets its name from the montage of pictures from old *Life* magazines pasted on its walls.

The food here is mostly Mexican, with assorted burgers and vegetarian dishes. If you've got an appetite, order the "mega burrito," two flour tortillas stuffed with rice, beans, lettuce, tomato, onions, and salsa, topped with more salsa and sour cream ($7.25). Or order the deep-fried chimichangas, topped with salsa, guacamole, and sour cream, and served with rice, beans, and salad ($8). Burgers range from a "regular deluxe," served with Life fries (sweet baby red potatoes with the skins left on) for $5 to the "Ultra Burger" for $6.50.

Open weekdays from 11 a.m. to 1 a.m., until 2 a.m. weekends.

A popular spot for indoor/outdoor drinking and dining is **Bandito!,** 153 Second Ave., between 9th and 10th streets (tel. 777-4505). The dining area is comfortable, with complimentary hot tortilla chips and sauce on every table. For starters, an order of quesadilla (a soft tortilla with cheese, cilantro, and jalapeños) at $5 is plenty for two. But don't fill up on appetizers, because Bandito! believes in heaping platters. We recommend the enchiladas suizas (two chicken enchiladas topped with cheese, salsa verde, and sour cream) for $10, or the avocado stuffed with chicken salad, made with a special cream-cheese and sour-cream dressing ($6). Spicy-food lovers will enjoy the chimichangas, topped with cheese and the secret salsa Bandito ($8.25).

Open weekdays from noon to 1 a.m., until 3 a.m. on weekends.

Behind the steamed-up windows of its little storefront, **Harry's,** 91 E. 7th St., near First Avenue (tel. 477-0773), serves up big servings of California-style Mexican food to the appreciative clusters of young trendy types that crowd its five or six tables. The burritos and enchiladas are served with chicken, beef, or vegetables, and all are priced around $5. If you like no-frills Mexican food in no-frills surroundings, a stop in Harry's will leave you full and happy.

Open Sunday through Thursday from noon to midnight, on Friday and Saturday until 1 a.m.

## MIDDLE EASTERN

On the north side of St. Marks Place, just east of First Avenue, are two Middle Eastern oases in the midst of the East Village's bohemian bustle. **Café Yaffa,** 97 St. Marks Pl. (tel. 674-9302), and **Mogador,** 101 St. Marks Pl. (tel. 677-2226), are both tranquil spots with sidewalk tables, airy dining rooms, and artsy clientele. Yaffa also has a large shaded garden open in the summer.

Yaffa bills itself as an "international" restaurant. It nods to Middle Eastern cuisine with hummus, tahine, and baba ghanouj sandwiches on pita (about $2.50), but has a large menu of salads ($3.75 to $5.50), pastas ($6 to $7.25), and vegetarian specialties ($3.25 to $5.75).

Mogador is more authentic Middle Eastern. Your waiter will tempt you with a tray of a dozen different appetizers. Pick the ones you want for $1.50 each. The menu includes five varieties of couscous, ten different kinds of tahines (exotically seasoned lamb or chicken stew), and an enormous list of daily specials.

Yaffa offers live music weeknights from 8:30 to 11 p.m. Mogador patrons dodge the oscillating hips of belly dancers every Wednesday night.

Yaffa is open from 10:30 a.m. to 2 a.m. weekdays, until 3 a.m. on weekends. Mogador is open every day from 10 a.m. to 1 a.m.

## POLISH

**Christine's,** 208 First Ave., between 12th and 13th streets (tel. 505-0376), is an ordinary-looking diner with extraordinary food. Try the home-made mushroom-barley soup with fresh challah bread ($2.50), or the assorted pirogi platter, with your choice of eight stuffings for these Polish dumplings ($4.25). Delicious breakfasts such as three-egg omelets, french toast, or blueberry pancakes are all under $3. And no matter how crowded the restaurant is (and it usually is crowded, as nearly everyone in the East Village knows about Christine's), the waitresses will always give you prompt service and a bright smile.

Open daily from 6 a.m. to 10 p.m.

Some customers eat three meals a day at **Teresa's,** 103 First Ave., between 6th and 7th streets (tel. 228-0604). This family-run coffeeshop and restaurant offers some of the lowest-priced food in the city, and Teresa and her family are quite rightly proud of their delicious home-cooking and special recipes. Breakfasts here range from blueberry pancakes to western omelets, all under $3. Sandwiches such as grilled cheese with bacon, sausage, or ham are a treat at $2.50. A wide variety of soups are offered too. A bowl of the potato soup is $1.50. So is a bowl of the red Ukrainian borscht. Lunch and dinner entrees are a steal. And here is where Teresa's family recipes really shine. Try one of Poland's national dishes, such as the boiled beef cooked with horseradish sauce, served with a vegetable and potato ($6); or the breaded pork chops, served with vegetable and potato ($5.25). The inside of Teresa's is simple and appealing, with wooden tables, fresh flowers, and an orange lunch counter in the back.

Open daily from 6 a.m. to midnight.

## UKRAINIAN

When a fire destroyed its original home, the many regulars of the **Ukrainian Restaurant** could hardly wait until their favorite restaurant reopened at 132 Second Ave., between St. Marks Place and East 9th Street (tel. 529-5024). Entering the recently redecorated restaurant is like stepping into a Ukrainian chalet. Ukrainian prints, traditional plates, and musical instruments called banduras decorate the stone walls. Ukrainian music is played, and the waiters and waitresses even wear traditional dress.

One thing that hasn't changed is the delicious food. Try the steak tartare, prepared to order with a basket of homemade challah bread, black or rye ($6.50). If you can't decide among all the tempting dishes, then choose the combination plate. It includes one stuffed cabbage, four varieties of pirogies, bigos, slices of kielbasa, tossed salad, and a basket of bread for $6.75.

Open daily from 11 a.m. to 11 p.m.

Owner Michael Hrynenko's success with the Ukrainian Restaurant inspired him to set up **Kiev International Coffee House and Restaurant,** 117 Second Ave., at East 7th Street (tel. 674-4040). Open 24 hours a day, seven days a week, this coffeeshop is the late-night hangout for local residents. The décor is diner style, with a take-out counter in front and Formica tables in the glassed-in dining room toward the back. The challah here is just as delicious as it is at the Ukrainian Restaurant, and the menu includes breakfast items as well as Ukrainian specialties.

Kielbasa and eggs served with bread and home-fries is $3.25, and potato pancakes are $5.75. Meat entrees range in price from $5.75 to $8.50. Pirogen and blintzes are $5.75. Pita sandwiches are also served, filled with falafel or liver for $3.50. A homemade babka with blueberries and ice cream costs $2.50, and apple cake costs $1.50.

The informal décor at the **Odessa,** 117 Ave. A, between East 7th Street and St. Marks Place (tel. 473-8916), includes cheery red booths and bright white Formica tables. There's a sit-down counter in the center of this restaurant, and the menu boasts of fine home-cooking. The Odessa has become a regular hangout for punk crowds, who seem to feel quite at home in the traditional old-fashioned diner with its old-fashioned prices.

The large menu offers everything from Ukrainian specialties to American hamburgers. Potato pancakes are $2.50 and a variety of pirogen cost between $2.25 and $3.75. Homemade blintzes are $3.75. Italian specialties, like veal parmigiana, cost between $3.25 and $6. A broiled salmon steak is $6, and there are daily seafood specials. For dessert, try the homemade cheesecake, a bargain at $1.85.

Hours are 7 a.m. to midnight every day.

## LUNCH ONLY

Every inch of **McSorley's Old Ale House,** 15 E. 7th St., between Second and Third avenues (tel. 473-9148), is covered with historical memorabilia. This bar dates from 1854, when members of General Custer's 69th Army Regiment convinced old McSorley, a blacksmith, to turn his blacksmith forge into an alehouse. The rest is history.

Only McSorley's special recipe ale is served here. Order the light or dark ale, two steins for $2.50. Many regulars swear by McSorley's corned-beef sandwiches ($4.25). Others champion the daily special. Once you're settled with your beer and food, look around at the treasures covering the walls, including a pair of old shoes that the owner, Irishman Matt Maher, swears were worn by Joe Kennedy, father of President John F. Kennedy. Also hanging from the bar is the chair that President Abraham Lincoln reputedly sat in while he made his famous Emancipation Proclamation speech, freeing U.S. slaves. Both students and oldtimers fill McSorley's to the packing point, often smoking up a storm with McSorley's special-order cigars (50¢ each). But bear with the crowds, because you'll never forget your visit here.

Open from 11 a.m. to 1 a.m. daily.

## OPEN 24 HOURS

At **103 Second Restaurant,** 103 Second Ave., at East 6th Street (tel. 533-0769), you'll find the atmosphere of a comfortable diner, but with a twist, such as tables that angle out from the wall. The front window and ceiling with wooden rafters also emphasize slanted angles.

For a hearty meal, try the slow-stewed beef with onions, carrots, and potatoes, with a dinner salad and rolls and butter ($7.25). For a lighter meal, try the delicious salade niçoise ($6.25). Omelets range from $4.25 for an omelet with swiss cheese to $6.25 for an omelet with Nova Scotia salmon and fresh dill. Order beer or wine from the bar to complete your meal, or splurge on a French coffee, with Grand Marnier and whipped cream, for $4.25.

---

# 13. Murray Hill/Gramercy Park

---

These two East Side neighborhoods stretch from 15th Street up to 42nd Street, from the quaint Village to bustling Grand Central Terminal. You'll find towering apartment complexes near the East River, and bucolic surprises like the Third Avenue Organic Garden, a community effort between 31st and 32nd streets complete with summertime scarecrows and zinnias. There are traces of very old New York— the Federal house at 122 E. 17th St. and Irving Place, where Washington Irving used to meet with a literary salon; a white clapboard house at 203½ E. 29th St., still with a wooden fence and carriage house (now a home). The Players Club, founded by Edwin Booth, stands in all its Gothic splendor at 16 Gramercy Park South; the National Arts Club is right next door at 15 Gramercy Park South. A statue of Booth portraying Hamlet is located in the center of the park. There is an order of Carmelite Fathers in a Romanesque church at 26th Street and First Avenue, just behind Phipps Plaza, and the famed Little Church Around the Corner at 1 E. 29th St., scene of many a wedding. There are contrasts—exclusive Gramercy Park, and grimy commercial areas in the 20s between Madison and Third avenues, also home to many Indian and Pakistani restaurants. Which brings us back to the business of eating, of course!

## AMERICAN/CONTINENTAL

**Mumbles,** downtown at 603 Second Ave., at 33rd Street (tel. 889-0750), is a lot like its uptown sisters. The exterior is shingled, and there's a white door and window boxes with real flowers. A low wooden bar takes up half the restaurant, but there are more tables in the window porches. The menu is printed on paper placemats set over the green-and-white checkered tablecloths, and is also written on chalkboards. The blackboard specials change daily, with the likes of asparagus-mushroom quiche with salad, or London broil and sautéed rainbow trout. Entrees, which range from $8 to $15, come with the vegetable of the day. Other recommended dishes are the fettuccine Alfredo, the spinach salad, a Mumbleburger platter, and the tuna-melt sandwich, a meal in itself. End your meal with a rich slice of chocolate chocolate-chip cake.

Mumbles's weekend brunch includes a Bloody Mary or mimosa, and coffee or tea. For $9 you get three eggs with steak, bacon, ham, or sausage; fries; and an English muffin or bagel. Also served are french toast with bacon or sausage, and eggs Benedict or florentine.

Mumbles is open from 11:30 a.m. to 4 a.m. daily, and for brunch on Saturday and Sunday from 11 a.m. to 3:30 p.m. Reservations not necessary.

**Tuesday's,** 190 Third Ave., at 17th Street (tel. 533-7900), was a meeting place for showbiz people, weight lifters, and acrobats during the days of Prohibition; the restaurant still contains secret panels everywhere. In the 1940s and '50s it became a favorite spot for college kids. Today the atmosphere is one of nostalgia for the racy days of yesteryear, as black-and-white photographs of celebrities, inscribed to Joe "the Judge" King (who ran the speakeasy) line the walls.

The menu (encased in a black marble "tablet") is large and varied, and includes a special selection of vegetarian platters, ranging in price from $3 for a tossed salad to $8 for vegetable primavera. Entrees start at $7 and go as high as $14 for filet mignon. Try the Oriental-style chicken, roasted in soy sauce, ginger, garlic, and sesame oil, or if you're in the mood for something lighter, the shrimp-and-avocado salad. Most entrees come with a large tossed salad, a delicious loaf of sesame bread, and potato or vegetable. For dessert we especially recommend the southern-style pecan pie, served warm and with a dollop of whipped cream. Desserts range from $3 to $4.50.

Brunch is served on Saturday and Sunday starting at 11:30 a.m. For $9 you get a choice of omelet, eggs Benedict, or quiche, with french toast or fresh nut bread, potatoes, juice, and all the champagne you can drink. Guest jazz artists perform while you eat, though we're told the music can get a little loud.

Fat Tuesday's, located in the basement, serves up great jazz music every night, but there's a cover charge ($10 to $15) and a $7.50 food-and-drink minimum.

Tuesday's opens every day at 11:30 a.m. and closes at 12:30 a.m. Sunday through Friday; on Saturday they're open until 2 a.m. Reservations are not necessary.

**Pete's Tavern,** 129 E. 18th St., on the corner of Irving Place (tel. 473-7676), opened in 1864 and is the oldest-established bar in New York City. Originally known as Healy's Bar, Pete's (bought in 1935 by Pete De Bella) was a Tammany Hall meeting place. During Prohibition it was one of New York's most notorious speakeasies, operating from behind a storefront florist's shop. Pete's also has a notable literary history—O. Henry penned "Gift of the Magi" while sitting in the very first booth after you enter the main doorway. Butch Cassidy and the Sundance Kid reputedly ate at Pete's, and President Kennedy dined here when he was staying in the Gramercy Park Hotel.

Although the original eating area has been expanded (the two backrooms used to be stables), Pete's has retained the feel of a real neighborhood tavern. Its authentic pub appearance—the original tin ceiling, tile floor, antique mirrors, rosewood bar, and walls cluttered with photographs taken over the past 60 years—has made it a prime set location for TV commercials and films: the Miller Lite ads are filmed here; a scene from *Ragtime* (with James Cagney) was shot here. "Pete's has always played down its image," according to its personable night manager, and today it's a melting pot for everyone—politicians, policemen, tourists, actors, sports figures . . . the list goes on and on.

Menu prices can go as high as $21.50 for a 16-ounce sirloin steak, so you will do best to stick with the more reasonably priced burgers and pasta dishes. Pete's is famous for its eight-ounce burgers, served with fries, cole slaw, lettuce, and tomato. Main entrees, served with baked potato, a mixed green salad (ask for the house dressing, a creamy herb blend) or a side of spaghetti, include eggplant parmigiana, filet of

sole broiled or fried, and London broil with mushroom sauce. Entrees range between $8.50 and $21.50.

The most popular dessert is the hot pecan pie. There is also chocolate cheesecake, rum cake, and zabaglione, a mixture of eggs, sugar, and wine served chilled.

A weekend brunch menu includes a Bloody Mary or mimosa, main entree (an
omelet with fries and french toast with bacon are among the choices), and coffee or
tea for $8.50.

Pete's is open seven days a week. The bar is open daily at 8 a.m. Lunch is served
from 11:30 a.m. to 3 p.m. Dinner is served from 3 to 11:45 p.m. (until 12:45 a.m.
on Friday and Saturday). Brunch is Saturday and Sunday from noon to 4 p.m.

**Caffè Bonnelle,** 208 E. 34th St., between Second and Third avenues (tel. 679-
8688), is a European-style café cheerfully presided over by its owner, Arthur
Bonnelle. The walls are host to revolving art shows, and classical music is played in
the background—but never too loudly to drown out intimate conversations. No
alcohol is served, and patrons are sophisticated yet low-key. There are butcher-block
tables with tablecloths and comfortable chairs. In short, this is the sort of haven
where you want to hang out—quite possibly alone—with the "Arts and Leisure"
section of the *Times*.

A variety of sandwiches, quiches, and casseroles are served, and all are good.
Ratatouille, meat lasagne, vegetarian lasagne, and a broccoli and cheddar cheese
quiche are among your choices. Sandwiches include tuna salad, ham, and turkey, or
you might want to try the delightful date-nut bread and cream-cheese finger sandwiches served with fresh fruit. The seafood salad, at $8.50, is the most expensive
dish.

Go sparingly on the main course, however, for you will surely want to partake
of one of Bonnelle's 55 different desserts, such as banana cheesecake, fudgy chip pie,
raspberry mousse cake, mocha torte, apple pie, strawberry-rhubarb pie, Kahlúa-
chocolate mousse pie, or a vanilla napoleon. We especially recommend any of the 18
chocolate-based desserts. Dessert crêpes are $5.50. Häagen-Dazs ice cream is served
($2.50 for a dish, $5 for one of several luscious sundae concoctions). The iced cappuccino, thick and creamy, is served in a huge goblet and is thick enough to eat with
a spoon—they include one, just in case! Hot beverages include several varieties of
regular and decaffeinated coffee and hot chocolate, as well as several varieties of tea.

Caffè Bonnelle is open Sunday through Thursday from 11 a.m. to 1 a.m., on
Friday and Saturday to 2 a.m.

The **23rd Street Bar and Grill,** 158 E. 23rd St., between Third and Lexington
avenues (tel. 533-8877), is a lively meeting place for a young professional crowd
after work and a great place to have an inexpensive meal. Turn-of-the-century
molded-tin ceilings and the curved wooden bar and high stools give this spot a flavor
reminiscent of the Roaring '20s. In fact, the bar was used in a scene in the movie
*Cotton Club.*

The dining room, complete with green tables and art deco lamps, is located in
the rear. The menu is the same for lunch and dinner. Entrees range between $5 and
$16. Burgers are large, and the smoked turkey with mozzarella, served with potato
salad, is a particularly tasty sandwich. There are several salads on the menu ranging
from $3.50 to $8. Try the pasta salad with dijon dressing. For entrees, served with
vegetable and potato, the batter-fried chicken and broiled filet of sole are good
choices.

Brunch is served from noon to 4 p.m. on the weekends and is $8, including
two cocktails. Choices include omelets, eggs Benedict, and french toast with ham,
sausage, or bacon, and maple syrup. The bar and restaurant are open from noon to
3 a.m. daily.

## AMERICAN/ITALIAN

**Ottomanelli's Café,** 337 Third Ave., at 25th Street (tel. 532-2929), is an unpretentious neighborhood spot specializing in pasta (made from scratch each morn-

ing with recipes that Angelica Ottomanelli, the owners' mother, learned from *her* mother in Bari, Italy), burgers, and pan pizza. The décor is simple and homey: red-and-white checkered tablecloths, James Dean posters, and hanging green plants are the trademarks.

The menu is limited, but the food is good and there are daily specials. Best of all, no entree is more than $9. Burgers range in price from $4.75 to $6, and are served with irresistible cross-hatch fries, lettuce, tomato, and a pickle. The chicken parmigiana ($8) is cooked to perfection, and comes with spaghetti and garlic bread. Pasta dishes, such as veal-sausage marinara and tortellini Alfredo, are $6 to $8. If you're feeling particularly sinful, finish your meal with fresh coffee and a slice of chocolate-mousse cake ($2.75).

There are 13 other branches of Ottomanelli's scattered throughout Manhattan, including one at 119 E. 18th St., between Park Avenue South and Irving Place.

Ottomanelli's is open Monday through Saturday from 11:30 a.m. to 10 p.m., and on Sunday from noon to 10 p.m. Reservations are not necessary.

## BARBECUE, BURGERS, AND RIBS

**R.J.'s Saloon,** 220 Madison Ave., at 37th Street (tel. 889-5553), brings a slice of the West to Murray Hill. You bring your biggest appetite, because R.J.'s serves a lot of food. R.J.'s has a huge barrel of unshelled peanuts to snack from, and fresh popcorn on the tables. It has some winning civilities more common in costly restaurants. Like the hot towels that come after you've finished feasting, or the free hot appetizers at happy hour (5 to 8 p.m. every weekday) that alone will fill you up. During the happy hour Tuesday through Friday there is live music.

Just about anything you order here is sure to be giant-size—even a half order of crispy onion loaf is still more than two people can eat. A half order of vegetable tempura is a meal in itself. The barbecued beef is succulent—your meal includes ribs with choice of potato, cornbread, and extra sauce. We like the tangy barbecue sauce best, even more than the Oriental sauce. The half chicken, charcoal roasted and served with potato, corn muffin, and sauce, is also good. The menu has lots of other choices, including chicken salad or two types of spinach salad. Entrees range between $8 and $16. Wines are $3 a glass; draft beers, $2.75 (there's a long list). And the desserts, should you be able to manage one, are knockouts. There are treats like chocolate mud cake and Arkansas pecan pie. And the chocolate climax is a boggling concoction of chocolate cake, chocolate chips, vanilla ice cream, fudge, nuts, and whipped cream, served in a huge goblet.

R.J.'s is open for lunch Monday through Friday from 11:30 a.m. to 4 p.m., and for dinner daily from 4 to 10 p.m. (on Friday until 11 p.m.). The bar stays open until midnight. During the summer, R.J.'s is closed on weekends. Reservations are not needed except for large parties.

**Checkers,** 201 E. 34th St., just off Third Avenue (tel. 684-7803), is a fast-food barbecue place with eat-in room and lots of Manhattan pizzazz. Checkers promises healthy food at reasonable prices. The focus of the shop is the huge grill, with its lines of chicken and ribs in various stages of cooking. The aroma is wonderful. But Checkers is also decorated with imagination, so you won't feel that you're just chowing down in a take-out kitchen (even though you are!). The floor is black-and-white tile, very clean in spite of the traffic. There are black tables set with red ashtrays, modern art on the walls, and salsa and rock music overhead.

You can order à la carte—a quarter of a three-pound chicken is also available in half- or whole-bird sizes. There are three sauces: the traditional red barbecue sauce with a kick (some may find it too salty), a sweet-and-sour, and a mustard. A small portion of salad is enough to feed two—choose from potato salad with natural mayonnaise, potato salad, pasta salad, and our favorite, red cabbage cole slaw with white raisins and a sweet-sour dressing. You can also order meat-salad combinations, like a quarter of a three-pound chicken with a choice of salad, extra barbecue sauce, and fresh whole-wheat, rye, or pita bread. Platters cost $4.75 to $10. A chicken-and-ribs combination with the same accompaniments is $9. Checkers has canned sodas, and apple-walnut pie, carrot cake, and brownies for dessert ($1.50 to $2.50 each).

Open Monday through Friday from noon to 11 p.m. and on Saturday and Sunday from 1 to 11 p.m.

**Jackson Hole** came east (to the Upper East Side of New York, that is), and now it's come south, to Murray Hill. The hamburger cookery chain has a restaurant at Third Avenue and 35th Street (tel. 679-3264). It's a good local place to satisfy a craving for a big, round, seven-ounce hamburger at low prices in a restaurant setting. This one is quite attractive (check out the pair of antique skis in the downstairs doorway), with an original mosaic floor, wood tables, and ski posters of the real West. A hamburger here is $3.75. There are all sorts of toppings and platters, plus omelets priced from $3.25 to a loaded combo for $7.25. A full meal averages about $7, and most items are a lot less. From salads to sandwiches to burgers and beer, there's something for everyone. The older Jackson Holes (except the resort!) are all uptown, but the menus are the same.

Open Monday through Saturday from 10:30 a.m. to 1 a.m., and on Sunday from noon to midnight.

Also, see "Steakhouses," toward the end of this section.

## COFFEESHOPS AND SPECIALTY SHOPS

**East Bay,** 491 First Ave., at 29th Street (tel. 683-7770), is our idea of a good coffeeshop. It's clean and spiffy with no worn corners. The spacious interior is Early American, with Delft-look tiles behind the counter, comfortable booths with blue seats, a brick floor, paneling, and a beamed ceiling with chandeliers.

East Bay's menu is almost as big as the dining room—over 200 budget-priced items. There are 49 sandwiches alone, as varied as salami and egg. Jumbo daily specials include a chopped sirloin steak with onion rings, potato, vegetable, and salad; meatloaf with potato, vegetable, and salad; baked shrimp with mushrooms, rice, and salad; and quiche with soup or salad. The owners are Greek, and charming. Cakes and pies are baked on the premises—try the strawberry cheesecake, chocolate-chip cake, or the dreamy lemon meringue pie. The rice pudding is not to be overlooked. Egg creams (at $1.25) are made just right. There is a full bar. The staff is polite, and the dining room is often full of doctors and nurses from Bellevue Hospital across the street.

East Bay is open 24 hours a day every day.

The **Tivoli,** 515 Third Ave., between 34th and 35th streets (tel. 532-3300), is another first-rate coffeeshop. In the heart of Murray Hill, it's worth a short walk from 34th Street stores (Macy's, Herald Square Center, B. Altman and Co., etc.) or anywhere. The Tivoli has what we call class—it's spotless and modern, with a long wooden counter up front and tile floors. The dining room in back seems almost private and is quite attractive—blond-wood tables, fresh flowers, brass, a mirrored back wall, and Ultrasuede-like seats. The food is excellent, and the Tivoli has nice touches, like leaving baskets of pickles at each table.

Sandwiches are priced from $3.50 for tuna salad or chicken salad to $6.25 for a turkey club. A hamburger with fries is $4.25. Entrees—seafood, steaks, Italian pastas, chicken, and chops—are priced $7 to $14, with most around $9. Daily specials include the likes of moussaka with a vegetable and salad ($8), or roast chicken ($9). Our favorite seafood dish is stuffed filet of sole with crabmeat ($14). Fresh fish is available every day.

The Tivoli is also open 24 hours daily.

**Sarge's,** at 548 Third Ave. between 36th and 37th streets (tel. 679-0442), is a true New York deli, with a counter full of roast meats and pies up front and the dining room with wood walls and wood captain's chairs beyond. The food is delicious, the portions large, and the prices reasonable. Sandwiches are priced from $3 for cream cheese and jelly to $8 for a combination of turkey, pastrami, and swiss cheese. A burger with lettuce, tomato, and fries is $4. Entrees include corned-beef hash with poached egg and potato at $8, and go as high as $16 for a prime shell steak with salad and baked potato. Desserts are $1.25 to $3.25. Sarge's serves a $9 weekend brunch between 11 a.m. and 3 p.m. that includes a drink or fresh-squeezed orange juice, and coffee. Entrees include eggs Benedict, french toast stuffed with meat and cheese, and a lox, eggs, and onion omelet with a bagel and cream cheese.

Sarge's is open 24 hours daily, of course.

## CHINESE

Our selections in this section of town are listed in order of expense and elegance.

The delights of a dim sum lunch or brunch at **Hee Seung Fung,** or **HSF,** 578 Second Ave., near 32nd Street (tel. 689-6969), will teach you that it's not rude to point. Dim sum is the venerable Hong Kong tradition of dining on many tidbits, and it literally means to point to what your heart wants most. At HSF, the companion of a famed Chinatown restaurant, it is civilized indeed. You pick from a cart, or order from the special menu (ask). HSF is very elegant, very hi-tech, with subdued browns and whites, thick linens, and columned walls. Set way back from the hurly-burly street (HSF is in one of the few suburban-looking shopping arcades in Manhattan), lunching here is a real respite. Dim sum morsels are not inexpensive—at $2 and $2.75, they can add up quickly—but keep in mind that three or four will satisfy most people. Among the delectables: beef shiu mai, stuffed crab claws, shredded chicken roll, crispy spring roll, and pork dumplings.

On the regular lunch menu, chicken dishes are $7; pork, $6.50; beef, $7.50; and seafood, $9. The dinner menu is past our budget, alas, but is certainly worth it if you want to splurge.

HSF is open from 11:30 a.m. to 11:30 p.m. Sunday through Thursday, to 12:30 a.m. on Friday and Saturday. Reservations suggested.

**Dragon Szechuan,** 338 Lexington Ave., between 39th and 40th streets (tel. 370-9647), is done in bright Oriental reds and greens, with flowers on the tables and traditional tasseled lamps hanging from the ceiling of the narrow room. Its décor is that of the old-fashioned Chinese restaurant—very dragon-y, with dressed-up glitz. On the back wall, a lit-from-within cartoon salutes your good dining. The food is good, and priced comparably to other restaurants. We recommend going at lunchtime, when entrees are 50¢ to $1 less. For an appetizer, try sharing a dish of cold noodles with nutty-tasting sesame sauce ($4). The menu also has two "king-size" entrees that are easily shared: the Buddhist delight, a medley of sautéed vegetables ($7.25 at lunch), or the sweet-and-sour combination of pork, shrimp, and chicken ($9.50 at lunch). Other entrees are $6.75 to $10.50 at lunch, and about $7 to $11 at dinner.

Open daily for lunch from 11:30 a.m. to 3 p.m., and for dinner from 5 to 10 p.m. Reservations suggested.

**Hunan K's,** 455 Second Ave., between 25th and 26th streets (tel. 689-3857), is a good place for lunch, when the weekday special is only $4. You get a choice of 21 entrees, including pork and broccoli with garlic sauce, spicy beef and Buddhist delight, a choice of white or fried rice, a choice of soup or an eggroll, and a pot of tea. Shrimp and lamb dishes are $4.25. A fortune cookie and a dish of delicious caramelized walnuts follow your meal, a treat not on the menu. Another charming gesture also not on the menu—with new customers, owner Kent Huang sometimes brings over a complimentary cordial of plum wine, one for you and one for him, and he toasts you!

At dinner many entrees under $8 are available. But you can't beat the luncheon special. The service here is fast, attentive, and friendly. The restaurant itself is pleasantly dressed up, with cane chairs, brown tablecloths, and fabric roses in bud vases on each table. There are two rooms and a full bar.

Hunan K's is open daily Monday through Thursday from 11:30 a.m. to 11 p.m., on Friday and Saturday to midnight, and on Sunday from 1 to 11 p.m. The luncheon special is served Monday through Friday only, from 11:30 a.m. to 3 p.m. Reservations are not necessary, except for large parties.

## CHINESE/JAPANESE

Extraordinary is the only word for **Genroku Sushi,** 366 Fifth Ave., between 34th and 35th streets (tel. 947-7940), a completely automated Chinese/Japanese restaurant. There are over 125 in Japan alone, and you'll find that the restaurant here is almost always crowded. The chain is the brainstorm of Taiwanese fast-food magnate Kin Syo Chin, who brings a *Modern Times* efficiency to the old Hong Kong dim sum. We'd love to see Charlie Chaplin have a go at the morsels here. How? You sit on backless stools at a Formica counter, as food travels by, believe it or not, on an oval conveyor belt from the kitchen. What you like, you take, and at the end the waitress counts up your plates and gives you the tab. All dishes are a standard $2 each, except sashimi ($5) and a beef or curry bowl ($4.50). Combination platters range from $5.75 to $8.25.

Among the many choices are Japanese miso soup (clear broth) and tempura, Chinese chop suey, fried rice, fried chicken, and lots of sushi—tuna, shrimp, salmon, octopus, egg, mackerel, squid, etc. It's clanky and clattery, but great fun.

Open Monday through Friday from 11 a.m. to 8 p.m. (to 8:30 p.m. on Thursday), on Saturday to 7:30 p.m., and on Sunday from noon to 6 p.m.

## ENGLISH

We love **Billy Budd,** 303 Lexington Ave., at 37th Street, in the Shelburne Hotel (tel. 686-0110), a neighborly place in the middle of expensive Murray Hill. The restaurant is as dark as a Dickensian garret, but cozy. Wood tables are set with small white candles and heavy pewter service plates. Brass bed-warmers, scuttles, and hunting horns hang everywhere on the dark paneling.

Lunch and dinner are similar except for a slight increase in price. Good and hearty fish and chips is $10 at lunch, $12 at dinner. Chicken francese is light and lemony for $11.75 at dinner. Entrees come with salad and potato. There are also British staples like steak-and-kidney pie ($11.25 at dinner). On Saturday, Sunday, and Monday nights there's a special dinner of thick prime rib, baked potato, Yorkshire pudding, and salad for $9.50, but supplies run out before the evening does because of the demand, so come early. For dessert, trifle (whipped cream, fruit, and pound cake, with a nip of sherry) for $4.50 hits the spot.

Sunday brunch includes a Bloody Mary, entree or eggs, and coffee ($9).

Billy Budd's serves lunch from 11:30 a.m. to about 4 p.m., then dinner until about midnight daily. On Saturday evenings there is live music. Sunday brunch is from 11 a.m. to 4 p.m. Reservations are not necessary, but recommended for weekend evenings.

## GREEK

**Z,** 117 E. 15th St., between Irving Place and Park Avenue South, a block from the newly renovated Union Square (tel. 254-0960), is one of the nicest restaurants anywhere. Its red awning, spotless white paint, and tiled entry brighten an otherwise drab street; three steps down is the beautiful taverna. Owner Jerry Vontas is usually at the door—for more than 15 years he's been getting rave reviews for excellent food, service, and atmosphere. You walk past the spotless open kitchen, where waiters heap generous portions of delicious-looking food. The narrow front room positively glows: gleaming wood tables set with red napkins and red candles, a wine bar with red-and-white checkered cloths and more candles, a fireplace. Beyond are two more rooms and a fenced summer garden with benches and ten tables. Throughout, there are white stucco walls, cozy low ceilings, and wall hangings of colorful woven fabrics.

Lunch and dinner menus are similar, except that at lunch there are sandwiches, like souvlaki for $4. The antipasto is big enough to share. Or you might try a taramosalata appetizer of caviar and raw onion. Entrees come with a Greek salad, rice, vegetable, and bread and butter. Moussaka is $8.25 at lunch, $9.50 at dinner; and there is lamb and seafood. Customer favorites include yavetsi—shank of baby lamb baked with seasoned Greek pasta—and the broiled scampi. There are Greek wines and rich desserts—try the baklava ($1.75).

Z is open Monday through Friday from 11:30 a.m. to 3 p.m. for lunch, 4:30 to 11 p.m. for dinner (to 11:30 p.m. on Friday). On Saturday dinner is from 1 to 11:30 p.m., and on Sunday to 11 p.m. (no lunch). Reservations suggested for parties of five or more.

**Deno's Place,** 155 E. 26th St., at the corner of Third Avenue (tel. 725-9386), with its brick and ironwork, is very Victorian and lovely. The glass-enclosed Corner Café is white and summery inside, with green cushions on white bentwood chairs, lots of flowers, a few small antique carousel horses in the corner window, white wrought iron, a terracotta tile floor, and white latticework and a stained-glass effect at the ceiling. The café is as expensive as it looks, however. Dinner is past our budget. For lunch, you might want to share an appetizer of mussels marinara ($5.50). Fettuccine is $7.25 with meat sauce, $7 with red or white clam sauce. A classic Greek moussaka with eggplant, ground beef, and béchamel sauce is $6.75. One dinner entree is past our budget but worth a splurge. Frutta di mare ($13.50) translates as "fruits of the sea" and includes shrimp, clams, mussels, calamari, scallops, and octopus, served over a bed of lettuce. Other choices are tortellini and veal parmigiana. For dessert there's chocolate-mousse cake ($4); cappuccino ($2.50) and espresso ($1.50) are also served.

Lunch at the Corner Café is Monday through Friday from noon to 4 p.m. Dinner is served from 5 p.m. to midnight every night.

## INDIAN/PAKISTANI/BANGLADESHI

**Curry in a Hurry,** 130 E. 29th St., between Lexington and Third avenues (tel. 889-1159), is a no-frills fast-food place for Indian, Pakistani, and Bangladeshi meals. Décor consists of mirrored walls, brown dinette chairs and brown Formica tables. The linoleum floor is well worn, but everything is clean. You'll often see Indian families eating here. There's a small steam table, which fills the room with the smell of cumin. You order from the overhead menu. A la carte items are priced at $1.50 to $4.25. A platter of beef or chicken curry, with one vegetable curry, pilaf rice with vegetables, bread, and salad, is $5.25, or $4.75 with just vegetable curries. The special of beef or chicken curry, pakora (a savory fritter) or a kebab, a vegetable curry, pilaf rice, bread, and salad is $6.50. Sweets are $1.50 each.

Open Monday through Saturday from 11:30 a.m. to 9 p.m., on Sunday and holidays until 7 p.m.

**Shaheen,** 99 Lexington Ave., at the corner of 27th Street (tel. 683-2139), is a little Pakistani cafeteria—clean, bright, and new. There's piped-in Indian music overhead, but no decoration. The menu is on the wall. A half plate of lamb or chicken curry, rice, a piece of bread, and raita (yogurt) or dhal (lentil sauce) is $5. Niharee, a beef curry, with two pieces of nan (or naan) bread and dhal is $4.50. Snacks and sweets are the real treats here, priced at $6 per pound. There are Pakistani doughnuts, jalabi (a sweet pretzel of sugar and flour), kheer mohan (deep-fried cottage cheese with cream on top), coconut and cheese balls, and several kinds of halvah including pistachio, milk fudge, pink and almond fudge, and many more.

Shaheen is open daily from 11 a.m. to 10:30 p.m.

**Shalimar,** 39 E. 29th St., between Park Avenue South and Madison Avenue (tel. 889-1977), has offered good northern Indian food in a charming setting since 1977. From a nondescript commercial street, you step into an attractive, white grotto-like bar/lounge area and then into the dining room. All is kept very simple —white walls with Indian-motif mosaics imbedded in the stucco, plants and fresh flowers, white tablecloths draped over red, and a tin ceiling.

The lunch special is a good deal. For $4.50 you choose from fish, lamb, chicken, a minced-beef dish, and vegetable curries. Lunch comes with rice, dhal (lentil sauce), onion chutney, and coffee or tea. The shrimp do piaj is spicy with onions and tomatoes ($6). Definitely do not miss those marvelous breads—the huge, unleavened naan, or deep-fried poori, puffed and light.

Dinner à la carte is not out of reach. You might try an appetizer of bhujia, fried vegetable and chickpea balls ($1.50), or a samosa turnover (85¢). Entrees are served with rice, dhal, and onion relish. Chicken curry or spicy vindaloo is $7.75; a keema muttar (minced beef with peas) is $7.25. Lamb entrees are $7.50 to $7.75. Fish masala (curry) is $7.50, and other seafood is more expensive. For dessert, gulab jaman, a deep-fried pastry in syrup, is good ($1.50). Or for more money ($12 to $17), you can feast on a complete dinner with appetizer, soup, entree, dessert, and beverage.

Open daily from noon to midnight. The luncheon special is also served daily, from noon to 3 p.m. Reservations for large parties only.

## IRISH

The first thing you'll notice when walking into **Molly Malone's Pub,** 287 Third Ave., at 23rd Street (tel. 725-8375), is the sawdust on the floor, and the second, the friendly banter of the bartender who greets the regulars and nonregulars alike with the same Irish charm. Molly's is the place to go in the winter, when the fireplace is kept crackling throughout those long nights. The bar runs almost the entire length of one wall, and is backed by wood beams crisscrossed on an off-white stucco wall giving the room a down-to-earth, relaxed feeling. Against the other wall, and flanking the fireplace, are sets of wood booths just perfect for quaffing a stein of Irish beer or sipping a cup of good Irish coffee.

For traditional Irish fare, try the Cork Dublin Irish lamb stew, a combination of fresh vegetables and lamb in a thick sauce for $11. The roast leg of lamb with mint jelly is $11. For $10 you can try fish-and-chips Dublin style—filets of gray sole dipped in ale batter. All dinners come with salad and french fries. For the hearty appetite, try Molly Malone's shepherd's pie ($10), which consists of ground beef sirloin with sautéed fresh vegetables, topped with mashed potatoes and baked. Of course dinner wouldn't be complete without Irish coffee, which Molly's serves for $1.50. And for dessert, try cheesecake ($2.75) or apple pie, with or without melted cheese ($2.75).

Lunch is served from 11:30 a.m. to 5 p.m. weekdays, and dinner from 5 p.m. to 2 a.m. On Saturday and Sunday, brunch, including Irish sausage, bacon, black pudding, eggs, soda bread, and a cocktail ($8), is from noon to 5 p.m.

## ITALIAN

**Pasta Presto,** 513 Second Ave., between 33rd and 34th streets (tel. 889-4131), is popular with the natives. The prices are reasonable, and the décor is cheerful and inviting. You step down into a room of white-brick walls, trimmed in red, with a snowy white stucco ceiling and, in summer, old-fashioned ceiling fans.

Appetizers, which range in price from $2.50 to $5, include fresh mozzarella and sun-dried tomatoes ($4) and fusilli and curried chicken breast ($5). The pasta dishes are $6 to $12. Try the whole-wheat linguine with spinach, mushrooms, and sun-dried tomato pesto, or the spaghetti bolognese. Another popular item is the fettuccine and Italian sausage in Dijon mustard. The dessert selection features a creamy cheesecake ($3) and key lime pie ($3).

Pasta Presto is open every day from noon to 11:30 p.m. No reservations are taken.

## JAPANESE

**East,** 366 Third Ave., between 26th and 27th streets (tel. 889-2326), is an attractive restaurant that seats about 50. Lattice and bamboo partitions, and colorful ornaments festooned about, help create an exotic yet intimate setting. The service here is friendly and attentive.

Lunch entrees are $7 to $10, and come with soup, a small salad with soy dressing, and rice. Try the chicken katsu, a platter of deep-fried boneless chicken cutlet ($7), or something more exotic, like negima ($8.50), scallions rolled with sliced beef and broiled in teriyaki sauce. Sushi and sashimi dishes range from $6.25 to $12 for a deluxe platter. Noodle dishes are $6.50.

The menu at dinner is slightly larger than at lunch, and the prices higher. Entrees range from $8.50 to $16 for a lobster-crabmeat combination platter. Sushi and sashimi can be ordered individually ($1 to $2.50).

For dessert, don't miss the pudding à la mode ($2.75). It's not listed on the lunch menu, so simply ask for it. It features red-bean ice cream (a rare treat), pudding, and slices of fresh pineapple and kiwi, all topped with whipped cream. Two can easily share one serving.

East is open for lunch every day except Sunday from noon to 2:30 p.m., and every evening for dinner from 5 p.m. to midnight. Reservations for dinner are recommended.

There's a branch of **Larmen Dosanko,** a chain of Japanese noodle shops, at 329 Fifth Ave., between 32nd and 33rd streets (tel. 686-9259). It's all bright and cheery, from the tiled floor to the Formica tables, but also spacious and modern. The noodles—fried, in soup, in soy sauce, or chilled—are tasty and different. And cheap! A bowl of larmen (noodles) in soup is $4.50; stir-fried with beef and vegetables, and with a salad, it's $5. Six pork dumplings with sauce (gyoza) are $3.25, or $5.25 with a salad. Or you can really stuff yourself: Japanese-style fried chicken, with salad, vegetable, and rice or noodles for $5.75. To drink, there are Japanese and American beers and wines for $1.75 to $2.50. Find out why there are over 12,000 Larmen Dosankos in Japan. They're fun, fast food!

The Fifth Avenue Larmen Dosanko is open from 11 a.m. to 10 p.m. Monday through Friday, and from noon to 8 p.m. on Saturday and Sunday.

## MEXICAN

Fresh flowers, pink table linen, red brick, and a beamed ceiling make **Mexico Lindo,** 459 Second Ave., at 26th Street (tel. 679-3665), a convivial place. Amber lamps, a terracotta tiled floor, and attractive oil paintings add to the south-of-the-border atmosphere. And strolling guitarists, Wednesday through Sunday nights (6:30 to 11 p.m.), will win your heart.

Menus are similar at lunch and dinner, except for price. There are 19 combination platters with favorites like tacos, chicken enchiladas with green sauce and sour cream, and tamales, priced from $4.75 to $5.25 at lunch and $8.25 to $9.75 at dinner. There's seafood too, including four spicy shrimp entrees. Try the flan for dessert.

Mexico Lindo is open Monday through Thursday from noon to 11 p.m., and on Friday to midnight (lunch prices are in effect until 3 p.m.). On Saturday dinner is 4 p.m. to midnight, and on Sunday to 11 p.m. Reservations not required.

Grab your topsiders, khaki slacks, and a striped shirt and join the rest of New York's yuppies at the **Lorango** Mexican restaurant and bar, 321 Third Ave., at 24th Street (tel. 679-1122). The long, rectangular room offers plenty of opportunity for those up and coming to size up the competition. Large windows flank the street and provide ample lighting for those milling around the bar. Lorango serves up authentic Mexican food. Portions can be on the small size—so heartier appetites may want an appetizer plus main course.

For starters try the quesadillas at $3.75 and you get three soft flour tortillas filled with cheese. Single-entree dinners range from about $7.50 and up. The typical double-entree combination dinner—from a choice of tacos, enchiladas, tostadas, or burritos, with rice and beans on the side—is $9. Wash it down with Dos Equis beer.

Lunch is served from 11:30 a.m. to 5 p.m., and dinner, from 5 p.m. to midnight, seven days a week. A $7 brunch is served on Sunday from 11:30 a.m. to 4 p.m.

## MIDDLE EASTERN

**Cedars of Lebanon,** 39 E. 30th St., between Park and Madison avenues (tel. 725-9251), takes its name from the national symbol of Lebanon. Under the green awning, you enter the first of its two rooms, the bar/lounge. The bar is black and padded, and the walls are covered with textured wallpaper. The dining room has a simple, spacious elegance. Chairs are cushioned in red, tables are covered in white linens, and the wallpaper has a gold-toned tree motif. Oil paintings hang on the walls.

A weekday lunch special includes soup, a choice of entree (the likes of shish kebab, lamb chops, and keftah kebab), baklava for dessert, and American coffee, for $8. There is also a dinner special for $17, with soup, four appetizers, a choice of most of the entrees on the menu, any dessert, and American or Turkish coffee. Or you might try the mezza, or appetizers, instead of an entree. With pita bread, the mezza can be a full meal. Among them are hummus (mashed chickpeas with sesame), falafel (deep-fried vegetable burgers), and tabouli (chopped parsley, mint, and scallions), priced from $2 to $3 each. Prices for dinner à la carte range from $6 for grape leaves stuffed with minted lamb to $11 for a seafood kebab.

Cedars of Lebanon is open daily from 11:45 a.m. to 11 p.m., until 3 a.m. on Friday and Saturday. The luncheon special is served Monday through Friday from 11:50 a.m. to 3 p.m. Reservations are suggested, especially for Friday and Saturday, when entertainment (dancers and musicians) starts at 10 p.m.

## SPANISH

It may not be sunny Spain, but the authentic atmosphere at the **Olé** restaurant at 434 Second Ave., between 24th and 25th streets (tel. 725-1953), will take you there for the space of one meal. Run and owned by the Lugares brothers, the restaurant features live entertainment every night except Monday. Patrons sometimes sing along to familiar tunes, and Pepe Lugares sometimes gets up on a table to display his talent for downing an entire decanter of wine in one long gulp.

The food here is simple, peasant-style cooking, served in generous portions. For lunch, try the Spanish red sausages with rice or the veal in wine sauce. Shrimp in garlic sauce and a beautiful paella with chicken, sausages, clams, mussels, shrimp, and rice cost $8.50. For dinner, we suggest splitting one order of paella, served in a huge pot for $13.25, which is more than enough for two people. Dinner prices ($9.75 to $17) are slightly higher than lunch prices ($7.25 to $9.25) in general. Try the gazpacho soup (a cold vegetable soup) or the caldo gallego (a traditional peasant soup made with beans or other vegetables). Scallops in garlic sauce costs $14, and veal in wine sauce goes for the same price. For dessert, we recommend the pine nut cake, which is a moist, light delicacy for $2.75.

Open daily. Lunch is served from 11:30 a.m. to 3 p.m., dinner from 4 to 11 p.m., on Friday and Saturday until midnight.

## STEAKHOUSES

**Farnies Second Avenue Steak Parlor,** 311 Second Ave., at 18th Street (tel. 228-9280), is well on its way to becoming a New York institution. For a thick juicy steak or barbecued ribs at reasonable prices, it's hard to beat. In the window is a beef chart—a sure sign of serious eating. Inside it's decorated for fun: the walls are carpeted, mirrored, and cluttered with memorabilia, including huge likenesses of Laurel and Hardy, Charlie Chaplin, and W. C. Fields, oversize coins, and authentic advertisements from the turn of the century. The whole atmosphere is old New York —bustling and a little offbeat. Dinner entrees include chopped sirloin steak, barbecued spareribs, a junior sirloin, and char-broiled chicken. A lobster tail, or shrimp scampi entree, plus a choice of chicken, ribs, or sole (you figure out a combination) is

$11. Dinner entrees ($8 to $16) come with a large bowl of salad, garlic bread, and a choice of french fries, onion rings, baked potato, vegetable, or spaghetti. Lunch entrees ($3.50 to $5.50) come with a smaller salad and garlic bread, and are priced from $3.75 to $4.75 for omelets, ribs, steaks, sole, etc. Hamburgers are less ($3.50).

Farnies is open Monday through Thursday from 11:30 a.m. to midnight, on Friday to 1 a.m. On Saturday and Sunday it opens at 3 p.m. for dinner and closes at 1 a.m. on Saturday, at midnight on Sunday. There is free two-hour parking at dinner. Reservations suggested for parties of three or more only.

## TEX/MEX

One of the hottest spots in town, **America**, 9-13 E. 18th St., between Fifth Avenue and Broadway (tel. 505-2110), is one of those places where people from all walks of life will find their niche, and have fun and a good meal at low prices. You'll find no sign outside, so look instead for the raised star standard out front. The dining area is lit by track lights that accentuate the high ceilings and the art deco murals on the walls. Strips of red-and-white neon tubes stream along the ceiling above a center walkway that separates the dining room into two halves. Seating capacity is 400, and unlike many New York establishments, gives the diner ample elbow room. The atmosphere here is just plain fun. Dress is anywhere from New York sloppy to evening wear. Late-nighters lounge around the raised bar in the back that stretches nearly the width of the room. Gaze around. On one wall the Statue of Liberty gazes down on New York. On the other you get a bird's-eye view of a farm.

The menu conjures up a taste of Americana, with a variety of dishes from all four corners of the country, including burgers, pasta dishes, and many varieties of pizza. Entrees are $8 to $19, but salads, sandwiches, and omelets are cheaper. Try the Tex-Mex fajitas with a generous portion of marinated beef grilled on charcoal, served with sour cream, salsa sauce, and tortillas for wrapping it all up ($11). Or try the Cajun oyster po'boy sandwich, served with cole slaw and spuds ($7.50). Move over a few states and partake of New Mexican pulled-chicken casserole with corn chiles, tomatoes, and three cheeses served with warm tortillas and salsa. A meal from a little farther north might be the grilled Jersey pork chops with onions, gravy, and sautéed apples. The good old all-American hamburger is also available, and with a choice of toppings ($6.50).

Open daily from 11 a.m. to 3 a.m.

The hostess describes the clientele at **Albuquerque Eats,** 375 Third Ave., at 27th Street (tel. 683-6500), as "yuppie, hippie, and rock and roll." Evenings at the cocktail hour you'll find standing room only. Towering over the handsome wood bar is a stuffed American buffalo (actually, a bison), and at the top of a black metal staircase sits an authentic Sioux Indian water tank. While waiting for your meal, you can people-watch (large glass panels look out onto the street) or create a masterpiece with crayons on your paper table covering.

For starters, we recommend the montaña de nachos azules ($5), a "mountain" of blue-corn tortillas baked with three cheeses and served with salsa and guacamole. Also, try the guacamole cruda ($5). A Mexican fish stew (sopa de pescada) is offered for $5. Ensalada Albuquerque ($8) is a work of art: on a bed of spinach leaves, plentiful slices of avocado and fruit are arrayed. (In warm weather, enjoy luscious melon, kiwi, and orange.) Entrees are $7.50 to $9.50 at lunch and $10 to $15 at dinner. Try the obeja barbacoa—grilled lamb rubbed with garlic and herbs, and marinated with a Mexican barbecue sauce—or the ever-popular chimichangas. Dessert choices include flan almendrado ($3) and adobe mud cake ($4).

Open daily from 11:30 a.m. to 2 a.m. (dinner is served until 12:30 a.m.). Brunch is served on Saturday and Sunday from 11:30 a.m. to 4 p.m. For $10 you receive a drink, coffee, and an entree. Reservations taken only for large parties.

If you visit Albuquerque Eats at night, be sure to check out the Rodeo Bar, where bartenders serve up drinks from inside an old horse trailer. There is live music every night until the wee hours of the morning.

## TIBETAN

The **Tibetan Kitchen,** 444 Third Ave., at 31st Street (tel. 679-6286), offers a varied menu of Tibetan food. There are only a few seats, but servings are generous and prices reasonable. Beef, lamb, and chicken entrees run $5.75 to $7. Try the Himalayan khatsa—spicy hot cauliflower, fresh leeks, and bean curd, served cold on green leaf and hot bread—for $5.50. Or warm yourself up on a cold day with a cup of thang soup, a sort of spinach-and-egg drop concoction that's delicious ($1.75). Another traditional Tibetan beverage is bocha, a buttered and salted tea ($2 a pot), which is a perfect dessert complement to deysee—a steamed sweet rice with raisins, served with cold yogurt ($2.50).

Open Monday through Friday for lunch from noon to 3 p.m., and Monday through Saturday for dinner from 5:30 to 11 p.m. Closed Sunday.

---

# 14. Brighton Beach, Brooklyn

---

If you're heading to Coney Island for a day at the beach or to visit the New York Aquarium, or if you simply have the time: find your way to Brooklyn's Brighton Beach, where fantastic food, drink, and a full evening's worth of entertainment can be had for less than $10. The thousands of Russian Jews who have settled here in recent years call it "Little Odessa by the Sea." On the weekends they go all-out, partying and eating at dozens of local, authentic Russian restaurants. For the price of a subway token, and with the patience for the ride, you can join them. Take the IND D train all the way to the end of the line, Brighton Beach. Stop in at any one of the following restaurants for some of the best food in the area.

The **Kavkas Restaurant,** 405 Brighton Beach Ave. (tel. 718/891-5400), serves authentic Armenian food. The clientele is a mix of Russian immigrants and other New Yorkers, and it's the kind of place where friends and relatives wander in, pull up a chair, and reach without asking for one of the dishes of exotic food piled on the tables. Start with the red caviar served with pita bread, or with Ukrainian borscht, served hot and full of beef, cabbage, potatoes, and sour cream ($2.75), one of the 11 different soups. Specialties of the house range in price from $4 to $11 and include shaslik (grilled chunks of lamb that arrive on a skewer the size of a small sword), accompanied by a mountain of fried potatoes and raw onion; chicken Kiev; stuffed Ukrainian meat dumplings; and eggplant in walnut sauce. Things really heat up around 8 p.m., when a Russian band begins playing and the dance floor fills.

Kavkas serves food daily from 11 a.m. to midnight, but the music can go much later. Entertainment nightly; reservations a must on Saturday.

More of the same can be found at **Primorski,** 282B Brighton Beach Ave. (tel. 718/891-3111). This is a somewhat fancy place: dark-blue walls adorned with triangular mirrors, and tables covered in white linen. Try some of the cold appetizers, such as herring with onions, boiled potatoes, and vinaigrette ($1.85). House specialties include loolya kebab (ground meat with spices, grilled on skewers), roast lamb with potatoes, or chicken shaslik, all priced at $4.50; and sturgeon "moskau" style ($6.50).

Owner Buba Khotovli, who is from Georgia, has also instituted a "party" menu ($27 a head for groups of four or more on Saturday, somewhat less on other nights) that features a bottle of domestic vodka or Lambrusco, every hors d'oeuvre on the menu, three or four main courses, and a basket of fruit. A daily lunch special offers soup, salad, one of the 16 entrees, and coffee or tea for only $4.

Open daily from 11 a.m. to 2 a.m. Russian, Georgian, and Israeli music is played nightly from around 9 p.m.

Other spots to try in the neighborhood are the **Zodiac Restaurant,** 309 Brighton Beach Ave. (tel. 718/891-2000); **Sadko,** 129 Brighton Beach Ave. (tel. 718/

372-3088); and the **National Restaurant,** 273 Brighton Beach Ave. (tel. 718/646-1225). Each is a delight.

---

## 15. Especially for Brunch

---

Sunday, after an evening out on the town, treat yourself to a late morning in bed and then join native New Yorkers in their favorite weekend pastime: brunch. Even at expensive restaurants, brunch can be a real bargain. In the restaurant section we included many places that offer special deals for this in-between meal. Here's a slightly expanded list, by neighborhood, for easy reference.

### MIDTOWN WEST/TIMES SQUARE
**Landmark Tavern,** 626 Eleventh Ave., at 46th Street (tel. 757-8595).
**Caramba!,** 918 Eighth Ave., at 55th Street (tel. 245-7910).
**Cancún,** 937 Eighth Ave., near 55th Street (tel. 307-7307).
**K.C. Place,** 807 Ninth Ave., between 53rd and 54th streets (tel. 246-4258).
**Stage Deli,** 834 Seventh Ave., at 54th Street (tel. 245-7850).
**Arriba Arriba,** 762 Ninth Ave., between 51st and 52nd streets (tel. 489-0810).

### MIDTOWN EAST
**Hobeau's,** 882 First Ave., between 49th and 50th streets (tel. 421-2888).
**Extra Extra!,** in the Daily News Building, 767 Second Ave., at 41st Street (tel. 490-2900).
**Charley O's Bar and Grill,** Citicorp Center (tel. 752-2102).
**Au Natural,** 1043 Second Ave., at 55th Street (tel. 832-2922).

### UPPER EAST SIDE AND YORKVILLE
**Mumbles,** 1622 Third Ave., at 91st Street (tel. 427-4355).
**The Green Kitchen,** 1477 First Ave., at the corner of 77th Street (tel. 988-4163).
**T.G.I. Friday's,** 1152 First Ave., at 63rd Street (tel. 832-8512).
**Rupperts,** 1662 Second Ave., at 93rd Street (tel. 831-1900).
**Camelback and Central,** 1403 Second Ave., at the corner of 73rd Street (tel. 249-8380).
**Sarabeth's,** 1295 Madison Ave., near 92nd Street (tel. 410-7335).
**Drake's Drum,** 1629 Second Ave., between 84th and 85th streets (tel. 988-2826).
**The Summerhouse,** 50 E. 86th St., at Madison Avenue (tel. 249-6300).

### UPPER WEST SIDE
**West Side Storey,** 700A Columbus Ave., at 95th Street (tel. 749-1900).
**Marvin Gardens,** 2274 Broadway, between 81st and 82nd streets (tel. 799-0578).
**Popover Café,** 551 Amsterdam Ave., at 87th Street (tel. 595-8555).

### LINCOLN CENTER
**Opera Espresso,** 1928 Broadway, at 65th Street (tel. 799-3050).
**Los Panchos,** 71 W. 71st St., between Columbus Avenue and Central Park West (tel. 864-7336).
**Captain Nemo's,** 137 W. 72nd St., between Columbus and Amsterdam avenues (tel. 595-5600).
**Eclair,** 141 W. 72nd St., between Columbus and Amsterdam avenues (tel. 873-7700).

**Lincoln Square Coffee Shop,** 2 Lincoln Square, between 65th and 66th streets (tel. 799-4000).

## PENNSYLVANIA STATION/CHELSEA

**Miss Ruby's Café,** 135 Eighth Ave., between 16th and 17th streets (tel. 620-4055).

**Empire Diner,** 210 Tenth Ave., between 21st and 22nd streets (tel. 243-2736).

**Gefen's Kosher Dairy,** 297 Seventh Ave., between 26th and 27th streets (tel. 929-6476) (Sunday only).

**La Cascada Café,** 132 Ninth Ave., at 18th Street (tel. 255-6529).

## GREENWICH VILLAGE

**Ye Waverly Inn,** 16 Bank St., at Waverly Place (tel. 929-4377).

**The Lion's Head,** 59 Christopher St., just off Seventh Avenue South (tel. 929-0670).

**Cottonwood Café,** 415 Bleecker St., between West 11th and Bank streets (tel. 924-6271).

**Woody's,** 140 Seventh Ave. South, between West 10th and Charles streets (tel. 242-1200).

**14 Christopher Street,** at the corner of Gay Street (tel. 620-9594).

**The Corner Bistro,** 331 W. 4th St., at the corner of Jane Street and Eighth Avenue (tel. 242-9502).

**David's Pot Belly,** 98 Christopher St., between Bleecker and Bedford streets (tel. 243-9614).

**Cedar Tavern,** 82 University Pl., between 11th and 12th streets (tel. 929-9089).

**Covent Garden,** 133 W. 13th St., between Sixth and Seventh avenues (tel. 675-0020).

**Acme Bar & Grill,** 9 Great Jones St., at the corner of Lafayette Street (tel. 420-1934).

**Pizza Piazza,** 785 Broadway, at East 10th Street (tel. 505-0977).

**The NoHo Star,** 330 Lafayette St., at the corner of Bleecker Street (tel. 925-0070).

**Elephant and Castle,** 68 Greenwich Ave., between West 10th Street and Seventh Avenue (tel. 243-1400).

**Sazerac House,** 533 Hudson St., at the corner of Charles Street (tel. 989-0313).

**Caramba!,** 684 Broadway, at Great Jones Street (tel. 420-9817).

**The Pink Teacup,** 42 Grove St., near Bleecker Street (tel. 807-6755).

## SOHO

**Food,** 127 Prince St., at the corner of Wooster Street (tel. 473-8790).

**Moondance,** 80 Ave. of the Americas, at Grand Street (tel. 226-1191).

**Cupping Room Café,** 359 West Broadway, between Broome and Grand streets (tel. 925-2898).

**Spring Street Natural Restaurant and Bar,** 149 Spring St., between West Broadway and Wooster Street (tel. 966-0290).

**La Dolce Vita,** 195 Spring St., between Sullivan and Thompson streets (tel. 431-1315).

**Ear Inn,** 326 Spring St., between Washington and Greenwich streets (tel. 226-9060).

**Elephant and Castle,** 183 Prince St., between Sullivan and Thompson streets (tel. 260-3600).

**Dean and DeLuca** (pastries are their specialty), 560 Broadway, at Prince Street (tel. 431-1691).

## LOWER MANHATTAN/TRIBECA

**Bridge Café,** 279 Water St., at Dover Street (tel. 227-3344).

**Smoke Stacks Lightnin',** 380 Canal St., at West Broadway (tel. 226-0485).

**Walker's Restaurant,** 16 North Moore St., at Varick Street (tel. 941-0142).

**211 West Broadway,** at Franklin Street (tel. 925-7202).

**riverrun,** 176 Franklin St., between Greenwich and Hudson streets (tel. 966-3894).

**how's bayou,** 355 Greenwich St., at Harrison Street (tel. 925-5405).

**Ham Heaven,** 49 Warren St., between West Broadway and Greenwich Street (tel. 513-7224).

**Hors d'Oeuvrerie,** One World Trade Center (tel. 938-1111).

**Front Street Restaurant,** 228 Front St., between Beekman Street and Peck Slip (tel. 406-1560).

**Exterminator Chili,** 305 Church St., two blocks south of Canal Street (tel. 219-3070).

**Café Café,** 89 South St., Pier 17 (tel. 406-2870).

**The Square Diner,** 33 Leonard St., at West Broadway (tel. 925-7188).

## CHINATOWN

**Hee Seung Fung,** 46 Bowery, between Canal Street and Chatham Square (tel. 374-1319).

**The Nice Restaurant,** 35 East Broadway (tel. 406-9510).

**Silver Palace,** 50 Bowery, near Canal Street (tel. 964-1204).

## LITTLE ITALY

**Ferrara's,** 195 Grand St., between Mott and Mulberry streets (tel. 226-6150).

**Caffè Roma,** 385 Broome St., at Mulberry Street (tel. 226-8413).

## LOWER EAST SIDE/EAST VILLAGE

**Ratner's,** 138 Delancey St., between Norfolk and Suffolk streets (tel. 677-5588).

**Yonah Schimmel,** 137 E. Houston St., between Eldridge and Forsyth streets (tel. 477-2858).

**Around the Clock Café,** 8 Stuyvesant Pl., off Third Avenue (tel. 598-0402).

**103 Second Restaurant,** 103 Second Ave., at East 6th Street (tel. 533-0769).

**Cloister Café,** 238 E. 9th St., between Second and Third avenues (tel. 777-9128).

## MURRAY HILL/GRAMERCY PARK

**Mumbles,** 603 Second Ave., at 33rd Street (tel. 889-0750).

**Sarge's,** 548 Third Ave., between 36th and 37th streets (tel. 679-0442).

**Tuesday's,** 190 Third Ave., at 17th Street (tel. 533-7900).

**Hee Seung Fung (HSF),** 578 Second Ave., near 32nd Street (tel. 689-6969).

**Pete's Tavern,** 129 E. 18th St., at 18th Street and Irving Place (tel. 473-7676).

**Albuquerque Eats,** 375 Third Ave., at 27th Street (tel. 683-6500).

**Molly Malone's Pub,** 287 Third Ave., at 23rd Street (tel. 725-8375).

**Lorango,** 321 Third Ave., at 24th Street (tel. 679-1122).

# 16. Around the Clock

New York City is the place that never stops. When a craving for pastrami on rye, bagels and lox, a hamburger, or an honest-to-goodness breakfast strikes at 5 a.m., chances are that a place is right around the corner to satiate your munchies. And for the ultimate in convenience, many of them deliver for free, so ask. Listed here are

24-hour (or close) eateries; almost all have full writeups in the restaurant sections, above.

## MIDTOWN WEST/TIMES SQUARE
**Market Diner,** 572 Eleventh Ave., at 43rd Street (tel. 244-6033). Open 24 hours daily.

## MIDTOWN EAST
**Jumbo Bagels & Bialys,** 1070 Second Ave., between 56th and 57th streets (tel. 355-6185). Open 24 hours daily.

## UPPER EAST SIDE/YORKVILLE
The **Green Kitchen,** 1477 First Ave., at 77th Street (tel. 988-4163). Open 24 hours daily.

## UPPER WEST SIDE
**The Burger Joint,** 2175 Broadway, between 76th and 77th streets (tel. 362-9238), and **The Pizza Joint,** same address (tel. 724-2010). Open from 6 a.m. to 5 a.m. daily.

## PENNSYLVANIA STATION/CHELSEA
**Lox Around the Clock,** 676 Sixth Ave., at 21st Street (tel. 691-3535). Open 24 hours daily.
**Empire Diner,** 210 Tenth Ave., between 21st and 22nd streets (tel. 243-2736). Open 24 hours daily (but closed Monday from midnight to 4 a.m.)

## GREENWICH VILLAGE
**David's Pot Belly,** 98 Christopher St., between Bleecker and Bedford streets (tel. 243-9614). Open daily from 11 a.m. to 6 a.m.
**The Pink Teacup,** 42 Grove St., near Bleecker Street (tel. 807-6755). On Friday and Saturday only, open 24 hours (until midnight on Sunday).
**Restaurant Florent,** 69 Gansevoort St., between Washington and Greenwich streets (tel. 989-5779). Open 24 hours daily.

## SOHO
**Moondance,** 80 Sixth Ave., at Grand Street (tel. 226-1191). Open 24 hours on Friday and Saturday only.

## CHINATOWN
**Wo Hop,** 15 and 17 Mott St., near Chatham Square (tel. 766-9160 and 406-3973). At 15 Mott St., open 24 hours daily; at 17 Mott St., until 5 a.m. daily.
**Lin's Garden,** 53 Bayard St., at the corner of Elizabeth Street (tel. 962-9085). Open until 6 a.m. daily.
**Hong Fat,** 63 Mott St., between Bayard and Canal streets (tel. 962-9588). Open until 5 a.m. daily.
**Kam Bo Rice Shoppe,** 51 Bayard St. (tel. 233-5440). Open until 3 a.m. daily.

## LOWER EAST SIDE/EAST VILLAGE
**Kiev International Restaurant,** 117 Second Ave., at East 7th Street (tel. 674-4040). Open 24 hours daily.

**Around the Clock Café,** 8 Stuyvesant Pl., east of Third Avenue (tel. 598-0402). Open 24 hours daily.

**103 Second Restaurant,** 103 Second Ave., at East 6th Street (tel. 533-0769). Open 24 hours daily.

## MURRAY HILL/GRAMERCY PARK

**East Bay,** 491 First Ave., at 29th Street (tel. 683-7770). Open 24 hours daily.

**Tivoli,** 515 Third Ave., between 34th and 35th streets (tel. 532-3300). Open 24 hours daily.

**Sarge's,** 548 Third Ave., between 36th and 37th streets (tel. 679-0442). Open 24 hours daily.

---

# 17. Early-Bird Dinner Specials

Some restaurants offer dinner at lower prices during certain hours—hard-to-find specials dear to the hearts of budget-wise travelers. Listed here are a few good bets.

## UPPER EAST SIDE

**The Green Kitchen,** 1477 First Ave., at 77th Street (tel. 988-4163).

## UPPER WEST SIDE

**Broadway Bay,** 2180 Broadway, at 77th Street (tel. 362-4360).

## GREENWICH VILLAGE

**14 Christopher Street,** off Gay Street (tel. 620-9594).

---

# 18. Big-Splurge Restaurants

Here are some special choices to consider for a big night on the town.

## MIDTOWN WEST/TIMES SQUARE

**Café Un, Deux, Trois,** 123 W. 44th St., between Sixth and Seventh avenues (tel. 354-4148).

**Rasputin,** 371 W. 46th St., between Eighth and Ninth avenues (tel. 581-1860).

**The Russian Tea Room,** 150 W. 57th St., between Sixth and Seventh avenues (tel. 265-0947).

**Patsy's,** 236 W. 56th St., between Eighth Avenue and Broadway (tel. 247-3491).

## MIDTOWN EAST

**Mimi's,** 984 Second Ave., at 52nd Street (tel. 688-4692).

**Oyster Bar,** in Grand Central Terminal (lower concourse level), East 42nd Street, between Vanderbilt and Lexington avenues (tel. 490-6650).

**Hatsuhana,** 17 E. 48th St., between Fifth and Madison avenues (tel. 355-3345).

**Kenny's Steak Pub,** 565 Lexington Ave., between 50th and 51st streets (tel. 355-0666).

**Les Sans-Culottes,** 1085 Second Ave., at 57th Street (tel. 838-6660).

**Auberge Suisse,** Citicorp Center (tel. 421-1420).

**Les Tournebroches,** Citicorp Center (tel. 935-6029).

**Oscar's Salt of the Sea II,** Citicorp Center (tel. 371-2201).
**Beijing Duck House,** 144 E. 52nd St., between Lexington and Third avenues (tel. 759-8260).

## UPPER EAST SIDE/YORKVILLE
**Camelback & Central,** 1403 Second Ave., at 73rd Street (tel. 249-8380).
**Vasata,** 339 E. 75th St., between First and Second avenues (tel. 988-7166).
**Kleine Konditorei,** 234 E. 86th St., between Second and Third avenues (tel. 737-7130).
**Jim McMullen's,** 1341 Third Ave., near 76th Street (tel. 861-4700).

## UPPER WEST SIDE
**Marvin Gardens,** 2274 Broadway, between 81st and 82nd streets (tel. 799-0578).
**Genoa,** 271 Amsterdam Ave., between 72nd and 73rd Streets (tel. 787-1094).

## LINCOLN CENTER
**Captain Nemo's,** 137 W. 72nd St., between Columbus and Amsterdam avenues (tel. 595-5600).

## PENNSYLVANIA STATION/CHELSEA
**Centro Vasco,** 208 W. 23rd St., between Eighth and Ninth avenues (tel. 741-1408).

## GREENWICH VILLAGE
**Covent Garden,** 133 W. 13th St., between Sixth and Seventh avenues (tel. 675-0020).
**Café Loup,** 18 E. 13th St., between University Place and Fifth Avenue (tel. 255-4746).

## LOWER MANHATTAN/TRIBECA
**Capsouto Frères,** 451 Washington St., at Watts Street (tel. 966-4900).
**The Grille,** Fulton Market, Beekman and Front streets (tel. 227-9328).
**Liberty Café,** Pier 17, 89 South St., Third Floor (tel. 406-1111).

## MURRAY HILL/GRAMERCY PARK
**HSF,** 578 Second Ave., near 32nd Street (tel. 689-6969).

# III

# THE TOP SIGHTS AND CULTURAL ATTRACTIONS

1. SIGHTS NOT TO BE MISSED
2. MUSEUMS
3. GALLERIES, THEATER, CONCERTS, OPERA, AND DANCE
4. ENTERTAINMENT
5. ZOOS AND BOTANICAL GARDENS
6. SPORTS AND RECREATIONAL FACILITIES
7. MORE SIGHTS
8. CHURCHES AND SYNAGOGUES
9. HISTORIC HOUSES

New York almost became the permanent capital of the United States after the American Revolution, although that honor went farther south for political reasons. Today New York is viewed by many as the artistic and cultural capital of the country, if not the world. We think New York's art and entertainment are simply the best anywhere! You could take years and not exhaust the city's diverse treasures, but since you're here for only a short time, we've planned this chapter as your key to unlocking as much as you can. Don't be surprised if you're tired—but happy—at the end of a sightseeing day, because just walking around this on-the-go city is a wonderful adventure. If we sound biased, we are, and avidly so. Do as much exploring as you can, and you'll see why!

Don't let stories about how expensive New York is intimidate you. Yes, it can be costly here, but the city is a never-ending show packed with loads of freebies from street musicians (the good and the outlandish) to the U.N. General Assembly. In fact, your biggest expense might be for a sturdy pair of walking shoes, for this chapter will take you on those freebies, from a tour of the venerable New York Stock Exchange on Wall Street, to swank midtown art galleries, to blossoming Central Park.

We've put more than 300 places on your list to visit. To help you choose among them, here's a quick outline of how we've arranged everything.

**Sights Not To Be Missed:** These are what we consider New York's best: things not to be missed in a visit to the city.

**Museums/Galleries, Theater, Concerts, Opera, and Dance:** New York City is recognized throughout the world as a leader in cultural happenings. Not only are some of the most prestigious museums in the nation and the world located here, but Manhattan art galleries are known for setting trends in the art world.

**Entertainment:** We have tips for beating the skyrocketing costs of movies, as well as for seeing a taping of a favorite TV show.

**Zoos and Botanical Gardens:** The Bronx Zoo is superb; the Central Park Children's Zoo endearing. The New York Botanical Garden is astonishingly beautiful.

**Sports and Recreational Facilities:** If you haven't joined the national fitness craze, we'll show you how it's done in New York. Look at all the business suits with sneakers—walking (like you'll be doing) is a popular exercise here. And we'll tell you how to see your favorite sports star or team.

**More Sights:** For those with more time, or a penchant for the different.

**Churches and Synagogues:** New York's melting pot has filled the city with buildings sacred to countless sects and faiths. Many of these buildings are noteworthy for their history and architecture, others for their innovative dance and musical offerings.

**Historic Houses:** Beneath that famed Manhattan skyline you can still find Old New York, in buildings and homes preserved by concerned citizens and the city government.

Have fun!

# 1. Sights Not To Be Missed

## WORLD TRADE CENTER

They have none of the romance inherent in the Empire State Building, but the twin towers of the World Trade Center—each 110 stories and 1,350 feet tall—are imposing and impressive. On any given day nearly 130,000 people pass through the center's revolving doors—50,000 to work, another 80,000 as tourists. Many of the latter come to marvel at the breathtaking panorama from the observation deck on the 107th floor in the No. 2 World Trade Center building—a quarter of a mile in the air—and from the rooftop platform just above it (open only when the weather permits; tel. 466-7377). The vista can't be beat: on a crystal-clear day you can see 60 miles in every direction. Diagrams on the floor-to-ceiling windows identify buildings and other points of interest. The ride up is swift (at 20 miles per hour, it takes just under a minute) and silent. In addition to the view there's a display on the history of trade, a souvenir shop, and a classy fast-food snackbar with a stupendous view.

The observation deck is open daily from 9:30 a.m. to 9:30 p.m., except on Thanksgiving and Christmas Eve (9:30 a.m. to 5 p.m.) and Christmas and New Year's Days (11 a.m. to 7 p.m.). Admission is $3.50 for adults, $1.75 for children ages 6 to 12 and individuals over 62, and free to children under 6.

Down below the concourse, underneath the buildings, there's a complete city in itself, with restaurants and shops. There's also a pleasant, if windy, outdoor plaza with benches and plants centered around a large fountain and a huge bronze sculpted globe. It's a pleasant place to picnic.

To get to the World Trade Center, take the IRT–Seventh Avenue local subway (no. 1 or 9) or the BMT subway (N or R) to Cortlandt Street; or the IND–Eighth Avenue subway (A, C, or E) to the Chambers Street–World Trade Center station. Located at Liberty, Church, Chambers, and Vesey streets.

## BATTERY PARK CITY

Across the street from the twin monoliths that are the World Trade Center lies Battery Park City, a masterwork of urban planning completed in 1988 that is destined to become another treasured New York cityscape. This brand-new neighborhood was constructed literally from the ground up. Built on a 92-acre landfill, the development is a meticulous orchestration of office towers, residential buildings, and public spaces.

At the heart of Battery Park City is the **World Financial Center,** a complex of office towers, restaurants, shops, a yacht harbor, outdoor plazas, and indoor gardens. Designed by architect Cesar Pelli, the project displays an eloquent respect for the city's architectural history with breathtaking anticipation of things to come.

Perhaps the center's most stunning feature is its sparkling centerpiece, the **Winter Garden.** The glass-and-steel structure arches 80 feet into the air, enclosing an 18,500-square-foot marble plaza where, no matter what the temperature outside, strollers can enjoy the sun inside. Palm trees stretch 45 feet into the air in this public space that has become one of the city's most popular and pleasing informal settings for music, dance, and other live performances. The free evening and afternoon programs during the Winter Garden's first season displayed an amazing array of diverse artistic talents, from the Herbie Hancock Trio and Buster Poindexter and His Banshees of Blue to the Vienna Boys Choir, the Basel Ballet, and Siberian folk dancers. There are usually several performances each week either at 12:15 p.m. or sometime between 6 and 8 p.m. During the summer, there are also performances on the outdoor plaza just west of the Winter Garden. (For more information, call 945-0505.)

Even if there are no performances scheduled, a stroll through Battery Park City can be an interesting and relaxing diversion any day of the week. The shaded walkways south of the Winter Garden through the residential developments offer a retreat into radiant gardens, some designed to give the impression of untouched nature. On the west side of Battery Park City, the landscaped *esplanade* along the Hudson River is a romantic waterfront park that recalls the Hudson's shoreline as it was during the 18th and 19th centuries.

You can get to Battery Park City by taking the IRT–Seventh Avenue local subway (no. 1 or 9) or the BMT subway (N or R) to Cortlandt Street; or the IND–Eighth Avenue subway (A, C, or E) to Chambers Street–World Trade Center, and then walking west. In front of the World Trade Center, a pedestrian bridge at Vesey Street and another at Liberty Street can take you over the traffic on West Street and into Battery Park City.

## EMPIRE STATE BUILDING

When it opened its doors in 1931, the 102-story Empire State Building, on Fifth Avenue between 33rd and 34th streets, was the tallest building in the world and was often called "The Eighth Wonder of the World," "The Everest on Fifth Avenue," or "The Miracle on 34th Street." Depression-struck New Yorkers scrimped for weeks to save the then-$1 admission fee.

It no longer is the tallest building in the world, of course (it was eclipsed by two Chicago skyscrapers and the twin-towered World Trade Center downtown), but it remains one of the most beloved of the city's buildings, and a symbol of romantic skylines everywhere.

It's difficult to imagine a picture of New York's skyline without the profile of the 1,250-foot tower and familiar silver spire. Each year more than two million tourists flock to the building's observation decks on the 86th and 102nd floors, where on a clear day the view is a spectacular one of 60 miles or more. The building provides an entirely different vista of the city from the view at the World Trade Center tower; from here, you're right in the middle of a concrete forest of skyscrapers, looking down on them. The viewing area on the 86th floor has been opened up with a raised walkway platform backed by mirrors, and you can venture outside to the promenade if you wish. On the 102nd floor, viewing is from the inside only, through round porthole windows.

Take one of the building's elevators to the observation deck any day of the year, from 9:30 a.m. to midnight (last admissions before 11:25 p.m.), except on Christmas and New Year's Eve, when the deck closes at 7 p.m. Cost is $3.50 for adults, $2.75 for students with identification, $1.75 for children under 12 and senior citizens. Summer days and weekends all year long are especially crowded, so you might want to try a weekday, or better still, a star-studded evening.

If you've got children along, you might also want to stop in at the **Guinness World Record Exhibit Hall,** on the concourse level (open from 9 a.m. to 9 p.m. Monday through Thursday, to 10 p.m. Friday through Sunday; $4 for adults, $2.75 for children 11 and under). See Chapter VIII for details.

## STATUE OF LIBERTY

The statue, a gift from France, welcomes to America the world's "homeless, tempest-tossed . . . huddled masses yearning to breathe free." She's 152 feet tall, weighs 18,000 pounds, and has a 35-foot waist and a 4½-foot nose. Since she was shipped to the United States in 214 crates and erected in 1886, she has stood in New York's lower harbor as a symbol of freedom and a lady of hope for the country's immigrants.

Closed for renovation in 1984, the statue was reopened to the public in a gala Centennial celebration on July 4, 1986. Now cleaned and strengthened, with corroded iron ribs replaced by stainless steel, Miss Liberty holds a new, handcrafted torch with a gold-plated flame.

For a spectacular view of New York Harbor, take the new, glass-walled elevator to the top of the pedestal. From there, you can climb the spiral staircase to the statue's crown, if the prospect of climbing 168 steps doesn't dampen your enthusiasm.

In the pedestal, be sure to visit the museum exhibits on the second- and third-floor levels. The Statue of Liberty exhibit, featuring displays on the history, restoration, and symbolism of the statue, includes the original torch and flame plus a full-scale copper replica of the statue's face. Another exhibit offers a portrait of America's immigrants through artifacts, slides, and evocative black-and-white photographs of famous and obscure immigrants.

The Statue of Liberty is open daily (except Christmas) from 9:15 a.m. to 5 p.m., and the entrance fee is $1 for visitors aged 12 to 62. To avoid long lines, plan to arrive before noon. For information about special events at the statue, and possible extended hours during summer, call 363-3200.

To get to Liberty Island, take the Circle Line Statue of Liberty ferry leaving from Battery Park, at the bottom tip of Manhattan; take the IRT–Seventh Avenue local subway (no. 1 or 9) to South Ferry station, the IRT–Lexington Avenue express subway (no. 4 or 5) to Bowling Green, or the BMT local (N or R) to the Whitehall Street–South Ferry station). Boats leave at 9:15 a.m., and then every half hour from 10 a.m. to 4 p.m. The round-trip fare is $3.25 for adults, $1.50 for children under 12. The trip takes 45 minutes if you stay on the boat; or if you wander around the small park, allow at least one hour and 45 minutes. For more information call 269-5755.

## UNITED NATIONS

Like a sea-green monolith, the Secretariat building at the United Nations, on First Avenue between 42nd and 49th streets (tel. 963-7713), towers over a white marble plaza with the grandeur befitting its international status. Built on land that is internationally owned, it's the meeting place for delegates from over 150 nations, who discuss everything from disarmament to fishing rights.

General Assembly meetings are sometimes open to the public, and admission is free. Check the *New York Times* or call 963-7558 for information about meetings. Tickets are issued on a first-come, first-served basis, and meetings are sometimes cancelled on short notice.

The U.N. also offers a guided tour of its huge assembly halls, decorated with donations from Scandinavian countries. Your tour guide will probably speak more than one language, and will describe the U.N.'s history from its inception. Some tours even include a briefing with one of the delegates. Tours are given every half hour from 9:15 a.m. to 4:45 p.m. daily, and last for approximately an hour. Admission is $4.50 for adults, $2.50 for students. Children under 5 are not admitted.

The U.N. also shows free films about its history and about different U.N. projects, for ninth-graders and above. Call the day before you plan to visit and tell them which subjects you would like to see on film.

## LINCOLN CENTER FOR THE PERFORMING ARTS

New York City has nothing more impressive than Lincoln Center. It's home to the city's premier performing artists—the Metropolitan Opera, the New York City Opera, the New York Philharmonic, the New York City Ballet, and the Juilliard School of Music. It's a complex of eight tremendous theaters separated artfully by fountains, cafés, and tree-filled parks which stretches in length from 62nd to 66th streets and in width from Amsterdam to Columbus avenues. When you walk up the steps to the central plaza, the noise of the traffic fades and there is a sense that this is an island untouched by the city's commotion. It's worth a visit just to sit on the fountain's edge and watch the sleek and glittery theater-goers gather outside during the intermission, or to see the two immense and colorful Chagalls behind the glass façade of the Metropolitan Opera House.

The construction of Lincoln Center in the 1960s—at a cost of about $165 million—was surrounded by controversy. It transformed what was once a sprawling ghetto into a prime real estate area, but also increased traffic. Architects and architectural critics alike debated endlessly and angrily over whether to build it in the classical or modern style. What finally emerged was a blend of both.

The 2,800-seat **New York State Theater** (at the left side of the plaza), designed for ballet and musical theater, is the most clearly classical building. It has a lobby decorated lavishly in the baroque style, and above that there's a grand foyer with decorative metal balcony railings, colored chain drapery, and a gold velvet ceiling.

The **Metropolitan Opera House,** also built in classical style, has a grand auditorium of red and gold, but most noteworthy here are the Chagalls in the front lobby facing the central plaza.

**Avery Fisher Hall** (on the right side of the plaza), built for musical performances, was the most architecturally controversial because of its widely publicized acoustical problems. Rebuilt several times, the building finally emerged as a mix of modern and classical styles. Its auditorium is a classic European rectangle, but its simple flat planes derive from modern architectural notions. These three buildings, separated by an open plaza with a fountain, are banked by five other theaters, including **Alice Tully Hall** and the **Vivian Beaumont Theater.**

This cultural playground should not be missed by anyone visiting the city. Performances are expensive, but anyone can wander in and out of the buildings, or for the price of a drink, sit in one of the outdoor cafés or indoor restaurants. There are also one-hour tours every day for $6.25 for adults, $5.25 for students and seniors, and $3.50 for children 14 and under. The schedule changes daily, so call 877-1800, ext. 512, before 10 a.m. the day you plan to visit. A special program, Meet the Artists, offers visitors a chance to talk with some of the performers. For information, call 877-1800, ext. 547.

Nestled behind the Metropolitan Opera House is the **New York Public Library at Lincoln Center** (the Library and Museum of the Performing Arts), 111 Amsterdam Ave., near 65th Street (tel. 870-1630). On the "A" floor are four exhibition galleries and an auditorium which often offers free performances. The first floor shelves hundreds of books and scores for drama, dance, and music. The second floor has a projection room for films and an extensive children's library, and the third, a gallery collection of old clippings, photos, playbills, and costumes. There are research libraries with large and varied collections of material on dance, music, and

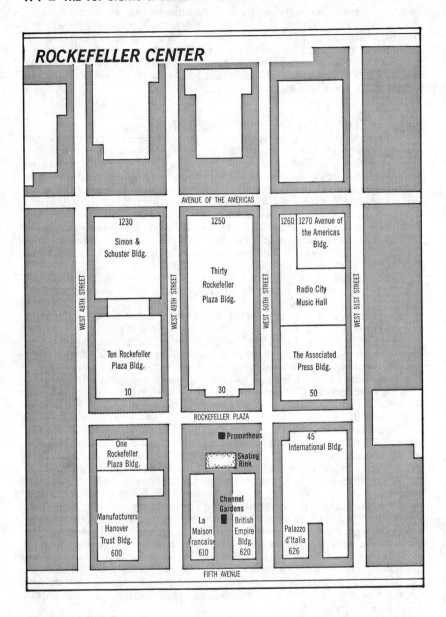

ROCKEFELLER CENTER

AVENUE OF THE AMERICAS

WEST 48TH STREET

WEST 49TH STREET

WEST 50TH STREET

WEST 51ST STREET

1230
Simon &
Schuster Bldg.

1250
Thirty
Rockefeller
Plaza Bldg.

1260 | 1270 Avenue of
the Americas
Bldg.

Radio City
Music Hall

Ten Rockefeller
Plaza Bldg.

10

30

The Associated
Press Bldg.

50

ROCKEFELLER PLAZA

One
Rockefeller
Plaza Bldg.

Manufacturers
Hanover
Trust Bldg.

600

Prometheus

Skating
Rink

Channel
Gardens

La
Maison
Francaise

610

British
Empire
Bldg.

620

45
International Bldg.

Palazzo
d'Italia

626

FIFTH AVENUE

theater. It also has records, earphones, and turntables available for public use. Open Monday through Saturday; hours vary, so call for the daily schedule.

## ROCKEFELLER CENTER

To see Rockefeller Center is to see a microcosm of New York. Skyscrapers, plazas, stores, and theaters all come together between 47th and 50th streets from Fifth to Sixth avenues in this magnificent complex—America's first and foremost urban mall. A promenade lined with stores and offices leads to Rockefeller Center's famous sunken ice-skating rink, marked by an immense gold-colored statue of *Prometheus,* and during the Christmas season, by an enormous, brightly lit tree. (This winter playground becomes a festive outdoor café in the summer.) At the center of the mall is a cluster of skyscrapers capped with rooftop cafés and gardens that offer spectacular views of Manhattan. One of the most noteworthy structures is the **RCA Building,** which has a magnificent black granite lobby lined with murals by José Maria Sert. But most impressive is the celebrated **Radio City Music Hall.** It has a 6,000-seat theater and 60-foot-high lobby. On one wall is Ezra Winter's richly gold-and-bronze painting *Fountain of Youth,* and on the staircase is a perfectly patterned art deco rug. Taken as a whole, the building is empowered with all the grandeur of the decade in which it was built—the 1930s.

The theater's productions are as grandiose as its architecture. There are concerts, ice extravaganzas, circuses, and special 90-minute Christmas and Easter spectaculars.

No view of New York is complete without seeing this mall. And unlike many of the city's attractions, Rockefeller Center can be enjoyed inexpensively. Tickets for performances at Radio City start around $18, but for only $6 there's a guided tour of the theater that might prove just as entertaining. For information, call 632-4000.

## TRUMP TOWER

One of the newer buildings in the city, and certainly one of the most spectacular, glamorous, and exciting to visit, is the Trump Tower on Fifth Avenue between 56th and 57th streets. The tall glass-sided building is primarily a residence for tenants capable of shelling out upward of $1 million for an apartment. But the best part is a gorgeous pink-marble lobby and atrium where browsers can stop in at expensive shops and just look around. There is something so New York about the Trump Tower that we definitely recommend a visit.

## NEW YORK STOCK EXCHANGE

At the heart of Wall Street—so named because in 1653 the Dutch governor, Peter Stuyvesant, ordered that a wall of thick planks be constructed to protect the city from marauding Indians from the north—lies the New York Stock Exchange. The forerunner of the present-day Exchange was founded in 1792 by 24 brokers who sealed the bargains with a mere handshake. Times have indeed changed, as any visitor to the Exchange will see firsthand. From the gallery overlooking the floor of the Exchange you can watch the frenetic and seemingly chaotic trading from 9:15 a.m. (when the floor opens) to 4 p.m. Monday through Friday. Tickets are free, but a limited number are handed out beginning at 9 a.m., so arrive early to guarantee yourself a spot. There is a taped explanation of the floor activities, and audio-visual exhibits and a short film presentation of the Exchange's history and present-day operations.

The Exchange is located at 20 Broad St., off Wall Street, on the third floor. For groups of more than ten, reservations are recommended: phone 656-5168. You can get there on either the IRT–Seventh Avenue (no. 2 or 3) or the IRT–Lexington Avenue (no. 4 or 5) trains; get off at the Wall Street station.

## COOPER UNION FOUNDATION BUILDING

The brownstone building at 41 Cooper Square, at Third Avenue and East 7th Street (tel. 254-6374), is today a tuition-free school of art, architecture, and engineering. It was founded by Peter Cooper, an industrialist and philanthropist whose early poverty prevented him from gaining an education, and spurred him in later years to begin the first privately endowed, tuition-free college in the country.

The building, which opened in 1859, is technologically interesting—it was among the first anywhere to use rolled-iron beams in construction, which earned it the designation as a forerunner to the modern skyscraper. It is also of political and historical interest. It provided New York City with its first free reading room, and the building's "Great Hall" (which seats about 950), was once the largest public auditorium in the city. That hall was the site of the first free public lecture series in the nation, and it has been a mecca for debate. It drew Abraham Lincoln arguing against the extension of slavery, Susan B. Anthony calling for women's suffrage, Mark Twain, Ulysses S. Grant, Theodore Roosevelt, and Margaret Mead, among many others. It was here that the campaign to overthrow the New York Tweed Ring was launched and here that a meeting leading to the establishment of the National Association for the Advancement of Colored People was held.

The three-nights-a-week music, poetry, and lecture series—and the roster of notable speakers—continues today from October through April. Call for scheduled events.

The building is open to visitors from 9 a.m. to 5 p.m. Monday through Friday year round (closed holidays).

## SOUTH STREET SEAPORT

In these days of telecommunication and air travel, it's easy to forget that New York rose to its present greatness from its original role as the nation's greatest seaport. At the restored South Street Seaport, located on 11 square blocks of downtown Manhattan, along Fulton and Water streets and on piers 15, 16, and 17 on the East River, that heritage is preserved in a revitalized area that contains one of the city's most exciting educational and recreational attractions. As you explore the Seaport's all-pedestrian cobblestone streets, restaurants, specialty stores, public terraces with waterfront views, and restored 19th-century rowhouses, you'll be caught up in the whole new spirit of enterprise and imagination that has magically brought the old port back to life, recalling the days when China clippers, transatlantic packets, Caribbean schooners, grain barges, and Long Island Sound steamboats crowded its teeming wharves.

Your tour should begin at the **Pilot House** on Pier 16, where you can purchase an admission ticket to the South Street Seaport Museum that includes a guided walking tour of the historic district and antique ships, and admission to the Seaport Gallery ($4 for adults, $3 for senior citizens, and $2 for children 12 and under). You might also want to take in *The Seaport Experience,* a multiscreen, multimedia entertainment at 210 Front St. in the Trans-Lux Seaport Theater. Complete with seaspray, fog, and 150 other special effects, the presentation ($4.75 for adults, $4 for senior citizens, and $3.25 for children 12 and under) provides a fine introduction to the Seaport's past and present and the ships that have docked at its piers. Shows run hourly from 10:30 a.m. Call 608-7888 for more information.

On the same museum block of new and renovated buildings as the theater, visit the **Seaport Gallery,** 215 Water St., for a schematic indoor tour of the area's historic buildings. See Chapter VII for a full description of the shops in the Museum Block, along **Cannon's Walk,** a charming interior courtyard tucked away in the center of the block, and along **Fulton Street,** named for Robert Fulton, inventor of the steamboat who inaugurated the Fulton Ferry to Brooklyn at the foot of the street. Also on Fulton Street is **Schermerhorn Row,** an architectural treasure of a red-brick blockfront dating back to 1811.

The festive-looking three-story brick-and-granite building occupying the block bordered by Fulton, Front, Beekman, and South Streets is the fourth **Fulton Market Building** on this site since 1822. Colored with the vitality and rich confusion of traditional market activity, the new Fulton Market incorporates the stalls of honest-to-goodness fresh fish and seafood merchants (along South Street) as well as an extraordinary variety of restaurants, outdoor cafés, and food shops. Just like the good old days, only better.

The tang of salty air will lead you across South Street to the **piers** where the old ships are moored: the four-masted steel bark *Peking* and the U.S. Coast Guard lightship *Ambrose*. You can also take a 90-minute excursion on the *Andrew Fletcher,* a sidewheel paddle ship modeled after 19th-century paddlewheel streamers. (Andrew Fletcher was the name of a father and son who were leading builders of sidewheel engines in the latter half of the 19th century.) From the deck of the boat, you'll get a closeup view of the Statue of Liberty as well as the spectacular sights of the lower Manhattan skyline. The boat departs from Pier 16 three times daily, and the price is $10 for adults, $6 for children 12 and under. Call 385-0791 for information.

Finally, you might cap off your trip to the Seaport with a visit to the **Pier 17 Pavilion,** a three-story glass-and-steel structure on the water's edge. Inside are more than 100 shops and restaurants; each floor has an outdoor promenade, and the top floor offers spectacular views of the Statue of Liberty, Brooklyn Bridge, and waterborne traffic on the East River.

Most Seaport attractions are open from 10 a.m. to 5 p.m. daily, except Thanksgiving, Christmas, and New Year's Days, with ship hours shorter during the winter. On Memorial Day weekend, July 4th weekend, Labor Day weekend, and New Year's Eve, the Seaport comes alive with spectacular fireworks presentations, live indoor and outdoor concerts, and other entertainment. Call 406-3434 for more information. To get there, take the IRT–Lexington Avenue express (no. 4 or 5) train, or the IRT–Seventh Avenue express (no. 2 or 3) train, to Fulton Street and walk east toward the waterfront.

---

## MANHATTAN NEIGHBORHOOD TROLLEY

One of the newest and most innovative tours starts at Pier 17 at South Street Seaport and goes to Battery Park, the World Trade Center, the World Financial District, City Hall, Chinatown, Little Italy, and to various spots on the Lower East Side. The trolley seats 35 and is designed to look like the trolleys used in Manhattan in the 1940s and 1950s. Because you're allowed to get out wherever you want, wander around, and get back on later, you can turn this into a full-day excursion.

You can buy a full-day pass ($3.50 for adults, $2.50 for children) in front of Pier 17, at the corner of South Street and Fulton St. Trolleys leave every hour on the hour from 11 a.m. to 4 p.m., Wednesday through Sunday, and the last one returns to the Seaport at 5 p.m. When you purchase your pass, pick up a map and guide of the neighborhoods you'll be visiting, for $2. For more information, call 226-3569.

---

## STATEN ISLAND FERRY

The ferry is probably the best deal in town, and certainly one of the most restful things any tour-weary visitor can do. For a mere 25¢ you can take a five-mile, 25-minute voyage and watch tugs nosing tankers and sun sparkling off the water, gaze on the shadowy silhouette of the Verrazano-Narrows Bridge, glide past the Statue of Liberty and Governor's Island, and listen to the cry of gulls. Day or night, the view of the Manhattan skyline from the ferry is superb.

The ferry runs every half hour from 6:30 a.m. to 11:30 p.m. weekdays, then every hour until the next morning; weekend rides are on a similar schedule. With a car, the trip costs $2 plus 25¢ per person from the Manhattan side and $2 from the Staten Island side.

To get to the ferry, take the IRT–Seventh Avenue local subway (no. 1 or 9) to South Ferry, the IRT–Lexington Avenue express (no. 4 or 5) to Bowling Green, or the BMT local (N or R) to the Whitehall Street–South Ferry station.

## CHINATOWN

Tucked below Greenwich Village and expanding into Little Italy is Chinatown, now the largest Chinese community in the United States. Many of its residents are recent immigrants, and there's a sense in this area that English is a second language. Bordered roughly by Canal Street to the north and Worth Street to the south, stretching west from the Bowery, its narrow, winding streets are packed with shops selling Oriental clothing, jewelry, and art, and with food stores selling herbs, teas, and fresh fish—even live chickens and ducks. There are just as many restaurants, and while some are lavishly decorated, others are no more than storefronts with a few wooden tables. During the Chinese New Year (held in February) the streets explode with fireworks, and are animated with masked dancers, paper lions and dragons.

IRT–Seventh Avenue local (no. 1 or 9); IRT–Lexington Avenue Express (no. 5); IND (A); BMT (R or N) all stop at Canal Street.

## GRAND CENTRAL TERMINAL

This is no mere train station: it has been New York City's great hall for more than 75 years, a place consummately public yet able to provide a private nook. It is a distillate of the city itself, a collision of the rich with the destitute, an intermingling of a glamorous past with a less romantic and more commercial present.

The Beaux Arts building at Park Avenue and 42nd Street, completed in 1913, has often been called "a city within the city," and aptly so. It was once the largest enclosed space in the world, and today houses more than 60 stores and banks. Within its corridors you can buy French pastries or potted plants, books, bric-a-brac, booze, or a basketball. You can place a bet, fill a prescription, have a pair of shoes or a watch repaired, dine on a fine meal or a variety of fast food.

It throbs at rush hour. On a normal weekday one million people stride through its corridors, concourse, and waiting room, plunging into or out of the tubes and tunnels. In their wake they leave six or seven tons of litter daily—enough to require a 55-man cleanup crew. Yet for all its swirling hubbub, there are quiet eddies too. The lower level is nearly always tranquil, and one can sit peacefully on the long wooden benches of the waiting room, underneath the ornate brass chandeliers and carved ceiling beams. Upstairs, take time to behold the wonderful ceiling mural of the Mediterranean winter sky, with 2,500 stars painted in gold, vaulting over the concourse. The subdued marble and stone elegance of both that room and the waiting room evoke an earlier era, when your train might be the *Twentieth Century* to Chicago, instead of a commuter to Connecticut. Or stop off at the "kissing room" on the main concourse level near Track 41. This waiting room for incoming trains has been renovated to the smallest detail of how it looked in 1913.

A sign of modern times is provided, however, by the presence of the world's largest color slide, courtesy of Kodak, and the world's largest clock and running news-strip, courtesy of *Newsweek* magazine, both in the main concourse.

## THE BROOKLYN BRIDGE

"All modern New York, heroic New York, started with the Brooklyn Bridge," said the British art historian Kenneth Clark. The bridge, which celebrated its centennial on May 24, 1983, was the first link over the East River between what were then the separate cities of New York and Brooklyn. But it was—and is—much more than that. It was the first great bridge, the longest suspension bridge in the world at the time, a brilliant feat of engineering. It took 16 years to build, piece by piece, by hand. In its time it was as daring an event as a space shot. And it is an architectural triumph: its roadway and great stone gateways on either end make the cables look more like delicate cobwebs than the heavy steel strands they are. And the bridge provided New

York City, which then had buildings of only five and six stories, with its first sky-scrapers: the two huge granite towers, each 276 feet above high water, were the tall-est and grandest man-made thing in the city. The roadway itself provided a spectacular panorama of Manhattan.

Today the panorama is far different, but no less stunning. Daily, some 5,000 pedestrians and bicyclists walk, jog, or wheel across the bridge's mile-long wooden promenade; and if you have time, you should consider becoming one of them. A walk across the bridge, in either direction, is an experience unlike anything else New York offers: the view of the Manhattan skyline is spectacular, and strolling under-neath the crisscross of cables, with the tumult of the traffic below, all makes the cross-ing a kind of ceremony.

You can reach the bridge by taking the IRT–Lexington Avenue subway (no. 4, 5, or 6) to the Brooklyn Bridge–City Hall station. (If you feel like continuing your jaunt after crossing the bridge, you can journey a short distance to the East River promenade in Brooklyn Heights, where benches provide a perfect place to rest.) Or take the IND–Eighth Avenue subway (A or C) to High Street–Brooklyn Bridge in Brooklyn and return on foot to Manhattan over the bridge.

## ELLIS ISLAND

The drafty old brick buildings on Ellis Island are empty now, and restoration work is well under way, but the island is expected to reopen in 1990. At that time, be sure to visit the Ellis Island Museum, which will feature exhibits and displays on immigration and the island's illustrious history.

Between 1892, when the federal government opened the buildings as an immi-gration center, and 1924, when the massive influx of immigrants tapered off, the island was the first point of entry for more than 17 million hopeful, weary, anxious people seeking a new beginning. The island closed in 1954 and was proclaimed a national monument in 1965. Now there are plans afoot to remake the entire island, which may take until 1998. The Great Hall and other long-neglected key buildings are currently being restored.

To get to the island when it reopens, take a Circle Line boat, leaving from Bat-tery Park (at the lower tip of Manhattan). At this writing, sailing times and prices were unavailable. For more information on the boats and the proposed opening of the island, call the Circle Line ticket office at 269-5755.

To get to Battery Park, take either the IRT–Seventh Avenue local (no. 1 or 9) train to South Ferry station, the IRT–Lexington Avenue express train (no. 4 or 5) to Bowling Green, or the BMT subway (N or R) to the Whitehall Street–South Ferry station.

## CENTRAL PARK

More than just a park, this 2½-mile expanse of greenery, extending from 59th to 110th streets and from Fifth Avenue to Eighth Avenue, offers something for everyone—from culture to sports, nature to architecture. The park was planned and laid out between 1859 and 1870 by Frederick Law Olmstead and Calvert Vaux, whose "Greensward" plan had won a park-design competition sponsored by the city of New York. Designed to give the illusion of being far removed from the crowded city streets, the park became a haven for urban dwellers: a place to relax and rejuve-nate with nature in a scenic, even rural setting.

Designated a national landmark in 1965, Central Park reflects the diversity of New York City. It's a family park, a place where singles congregate, couples stroll hand in hand, and city workers get a breath of fresh air at lunchtime. It's a place where you can rent bikes and boats, ice skate in winter, swim in summer, and jog all year round. You might even spot a celebrity or two doing laps around the **Reservoir,** one of the most popular jogging tracks in New York.

During the spring and summer, the park hosts free performances of all kinds: Shakespeare at the **Delacorte Theater,** concerts by the New York Philharmonic and the Metropolitan Opera, as well as jazz and rock music by top recording artists, on the **Great Lawn** and at the **Goldman Band Shell** in the **Mall.** For children, there are two **zoos,** playgrounds, model-boat sailing at **Conservatory Pond,** story-telling at the **Hans Christian Andersen statue,** an **Alice in Wonderland statue** to climb, and of course, the **Carousel,** with its hand-painted horses.

In recent years, an influx of city funds and private donations have helped to revitalize the park. Statues, fountains, and bridges have been cleaned and renovated, walkways lined with new trees and shrubs, and gardens newly planted with wild-flowers and bulbs. For one of the best views of the park, visit **Belvedere Castle,** in-side the park at approximately 79th Street, a replica of a medieval castle which is now a weather station and learning lab. For a prime example of Victorian architecture, don't miss the **Dairy,** inside the park at approximately 64th Street, one of Olmstead and Vaux's original park buildings. Recently renovated, the Dairy offers frequent exhibits, concerts, and a walk/talk series. For information about events at the Dairy, as well as park events in general, call 397-3156. A map and guide of all the paths and features of Central Park is available at the Castle and the Dairy for 50¢.

A final word: Like any other place, safety in Central Park is a matter of good judgment. Although the park is patrolled frequently by Parks Department staff and city police you should stick to well-populated areas (in general, south of 96th Street), don't frequent the park at night unless attending a special event, and don't wear expensive jewelry. To keep track of your whereabouts in the park, check the numbers on any lamppost. The first two digits represent the nearest cross street; the second two digits represent east or west (west if odd, east if even).

We suggest that you plan several visits to Central Park if time permits, for it's not only a top sight, it's also a great place to relax when you're ready for a break from sightseeing. (For more detailed information on specific places and events in Central Park, check appropriate chapters throughout this book.)

---

# 2. Museums

---

Contrary to popular belief, you don't have to travel to Europe to see great works of art—you can find examples of most everything you want to see right here in New York City. For years the city has been considered a "melting pot" for various nation-alities and cultural backgrounds, and a mecca for artists, art dealers, and collectors. The result? An *island* with more than 100 museums featuring exhibits ranging from fine arts to natural history, crafts, and ethnic cultures. Chances are good that if you have a specialized interest, New York City has a museum that caters to it. In this section, we give a taste of what the city has to offer.

*Points to Remember:* Some museums have fixed fees; others ask for contribu-tions. Senior citizens and students should carry some form of identification to qualify for special rates. Few museums open before 10 a.m., and most are closed one day during the week, so a call beforehand is often wise.

## METROPOLITAN MUSEUM OF ART

The grande dame of American museums, the Metropolitan Museum of Art, located at Fifth Avenue and 82nd Street (tel. 535-7710), has something to interest almost everyone. Its collection, the largest in the Western Hemisphere, comprises everything from ancient Greek vases and Renaissance paintings to Native American masks and a room designed by Frank Lloyd Wright. In addition to its permanent collection, the Met offers several special exhibitions of works on loan from around the world each year. The museum's Costume Institute, which preserves clothing from as far back as the 1600s, organizes some gorgeous exhibitions of period or regional clothing, and rooms exquisitely furnished in period styles offer a glimpse of life in ages past. The American Wing gives a comprehensive picture of three centuries of American life and art, and its glassed-in sculpture garden is a lovely place to pause and relax a bit. At one side of the garden you'll find some breathtaking stained-glass windows created in the much-acclaimed Tiffany Studios.

In June 1983 the final 13 galleries of the Met's Egyptian collection opened, marking the end of a 25-year project and the first time that the entire collection has been on public view. With an estimated 40,000 objects spanning over 500,000 years of Egyptian history, the collection is, in fact, so large that it requires 32 galleries to accommodate it! In the 25th gallery, visitors will find the Temple of Dendur, circa 15 B.C. from Lower Nubia. As part of a project to preserve Egypt's treasures from destruction during the building of the Aswan High Dam, this temple was excavated, sent piece by piece to the Met, and painstakingly rebuilt for public viewing. Visitors are invited to walk around the temple to experience its beauty firsthand.

Also of note is the Michael C. Rockefeller Wing, which exhibits a fascinating array of native art from Africa, the Americas, and the Pacific Islands. In addition, visitors can relax in the Iris and B. Gerald Cantor Roof Garden, a 10,000-square-foot open-air garden with an installation of 20th-century sculpture. The garden affords a spectacular view of the New York City skyline and Central Park, and is open May through October. Or if you'd rather rest indoors, you can visit the Lila Acheson Wing for 20th-century art and the Japanese Galleries. The mood in these galleries—which display ceramics, kimonos, armor, and woodblock prints—is enhanced by traditional Japanese architecture and by an indoor garden that replicates a contemporary Japanese garden.

As most visitors to the Met like to break for lunch, you may want to join them for a cup of coffee or a bite to eat at the museum restaurant. Weather permitting, you can also sit on the steps outside the front entrance and join other museum-goers munching hot dogs and watching the antics of street performers. A bit more tranquil are the tree-shaded park benches off to the side, where the splashing of the fountains drowns out the noise of the traffic.

Gorgeous as it is, the Met's size can be taxing for even the hardiest of museum-goers, so even if you've budgeted a whole day to see it, you should take a few minutes with a copy of the floor plan (available free at any of the information booths at the entrances) to plot out which exhibits you want to see. You also might want to take a free guided tour. There are daily tours given in English and weekly tours given in Spanish. (French tours can be arranged by appointment, and German-speaking visitors can rent an audio tour for a nominal fee.)

In addition, audio tours of the permanent collection are available for rental in the main lobby, and these, too, are available in a variety of languages: German, French, Japanese, Italian, Spanish, English, to name a few. (Inquire at the Visitors' Center for details.)

The Met's Uris Center for Education offers a variety of student- and family-oriented programs (see Chapter VIII for more details on activities for children). For information on museum facilities for the physically disabled, call 879-0421 or 570-3828.

The Met is open Tuesday through Thursday from 9:30 a.m. to 5:15 p.m. and Friday and Saturday from 9:30 a.m. to 8:45 p.m.; Sunday from 9:30 a.m. to 5:15 p.m.; closed Monday. A contribution of $5 is suggested for nonmembers; $2.50 for students and senior citizens. Children under 12 go in for free when accompanied by an adult.

## MUSEUM OF MODERN ART

The Museum of Modern Art (MOMA), 11 W. 53rd St., between Fifth Avenue and Avenue of the Americas (tel. 708-9500), is one of the world's great museums. Founded in 1929, the museum offers an unrivaled survey of the modern arts from 1880 to the present. Its collection includes over 100,000 paintings, sculptures, drawings, prints, photographs, architectural models and plans, and superbly designed objects, as well as 8,000 films, four million film stills, and a library containing some 80,000 books and periodicals. The museum's changing exhibitions focus on specific artists' works, styles, and modern art movements. You can explore the development of modern art—from the masterpieces of post-impressionists like van Gogh and Cézanne to works by modern masters Rauschenberg and Stella—in more than 20 galleries. And—against a soothing backdrop of weeping birch and beech trees, reflecting pools, and fountains—you can enjoy the sculpture of Picasso, Rodin, and many others in MOMA's Abby Aldrich Rockefeller Sculpture Garden.

Films—mainly by international and American independent filmmakers—are shown daily in the museum's two theaters, and video exhibitions are screened in the Video Gallery. Both are free with admission. For information on film showings, call 708-9490.

MOMA is open on Thursday from 11 a.m. to 9 p.m. and Friday through Tuesday to 6 p.m.; closed Wednesday and Christmas Day. For information on current exhibitions, call 708-9480. Admission is $6 for adults, $3.50 for students, $3 for senior citizens, and free for children under 16 accompanied by an adult; on Thursday, from 5 to 9 p.m., pay as you wish.

## GUGGENHEIM MUSEUM

Called a "giant snail" by some and "the most beautiful building in New York" by architect Philip Johnson, the Solomon R. Guggenheim Museum, 1071 Fifth Ave., at 89th Street (tel. 360-3500), is justly famous for its striking design by Frank Lloyd Wright and for its collection of more than 3,000 works from every major period in 20th-century painting and sculpture. The museum is shaped like a chambered nautilus, and in order to view most of the paintings, you must walk along the gently curving ramp that coils for seven stories down to the large circular ground floor.

Displayed on the ramp are works by new artists, as well as rotating exhibits of art by modern masters. On permanent display are such modern masterpieces as Picasso's *Mandolin and Guitar,* Bracque's *The Buffet,* and Chagall's *The Green Violinist.* The museum also has 20 other Picassos and one of the largest collections of works by Vasily Kandinsky in the world. In the permanently installed Justin K. Thannhauser Collection, off the main building, hang paintings by such luminaries as Manet, Renoir, Cézanne, Gauguin, and van Gogh.

The Guggenheim is open Wednesday through Sunday from 11 a.m. to 4:45 p.m., and on Tuesday until 7:45 p.m.; closed Monday. To get to the museum, take the no. 2, 3, or 4 Madison Avenue bus to 88th Street and walk a block to Fifth Avenue; or take the IRT–Lexington Avenue subway (no. 4, 5, or 6) to 86th Street and walk over to Fifth Avenue. Admission is $4.50 for adults, $2.50 for students and senior citizens; children under 7 are free. On Tuesday evening from 5 to 7:45 p.m. no admission is charged.

*Note:* The museum will be closed sometime during 1990–1991 in order to expand and restore its facilities. Visitors should call for current information.

## WHITNEY MUSEUM OF AMERICAN ART

In the heart of the gallery district, the Whitney Museum, 945 Madison Ave., at 75th Street (tel. 570-3611), is devoted to American art, concentrating on 20th-century works. Even the building is a piece of modern art. Designed by Marcel Breuer (the creator of the tubular-steel chair that bears his name), the Whitney is made out of rich gray granite and looks like an inverted pyramid.

Here you'll see paintings that reflect all the historical trends in American art from John Sloan to Julian Schnabel: naturalism, impressionism, pop art, throwaways, abstractionism, up to the stylistic pluralism of the present. Don't miss the whimsical *Circus* stabile by Alexander Calder on the first floor. Made out of steel, metal, felt, and fiber, this circus is a delightful creation of cavorting animals and swinging acrobats. On the upper floors, the Whitney displays pieces from its renowned permanent collection and highlights changing exhibits. Every two years the Whitney presents a show that features the work of both new and accomplished artists, and provides a revealing look at new trends in American art. There is also a pleasant, plant-filled restaurant where you can have a light meal and a cup of coffee.

The Whitney operates the **New American Filmmakers' Series,** which provides a showcase for the work of independent film producers. Call 570-0537 for a schedule. (Admission to the films is included in the general admission fee.)

Open on Tuesday from 1 to 8 p.m., Wednesday through Saturday from 11 a.m. to 5 p.m., and on Sunday from noon to 6 p.m.; closed Monday. Admission is $4.50 for adults, $2.50 for senior citizens (62 and older), and free for students and children under 12 accompanied by an adult. On Tuesday nights from 6 to 8 p.m. no admission is charged.

## FRICK MUSEUM

The Frick, 1 E. 70th St., at Fifth Avenue (tel. 288-0700), is a jewel. Its collection belonged to Pittsburgh coal-and-steel magnate Henry Clay Frick, and the museum was once his home. Although the Frick is not as large or as well known as some of her New York sisters, it is priceless in presentation. It's much like visiting the home of a very rich—and hospitable—friend who just happens to have Gainsboroughs in the dining room, a drawing room full of Fragonards, Titians in the living room, and an El Greco over the fireplace. The Fricks collected art for 40 years, lived with it, and arranged to turn it over to the public upon their deaths. The museum trustees have abided by their wishes; and even though the magnificent house has been expanded to almost double its original size, it still looks like a home complete with books and easy chairs among the grander antiques. Two of the more notable additions made since the Frick opened in 1935 are the serene garden court with splashing fountain and a lovely garden designed by British landscape artist Russell Paige.

The Frick Museum and its gift shop are open Tuesday through Saturday from 10 a.m. to 6 p.m., on Sunday and holidays from 1 to 6 p.m.; closed Monday. Admission is $3 for adults, $1.50 for students and senior citizens. No children under 10 are allowed in, and those under 16 must be with an adult. Call or write for information on lectures and weekly concerts (tickets must be arranged in advance).

## THE CLOISTERS

Isolated on a Manhattan hilltop in Fort Tryon Park at the upper tip of the island (tel. 923-3700), this uptown branch of the Metropolitan Museum of Art resembles a medieval monastery in location and appearance. Built in the 1930s by Charles Collens, the architect of Riverside Church, this stone complex combines parts of five medieval monasteries, a 12th-century chapter house, a Romanesque chapel, and a 12th-century Spanish apse into one. The Cloisters contains the Met's vast collection of medieval art, including the famous *Unicorn Tapestries* (seven 16th-century tapestries that depict the hunt of the mythical one-horned creature). Among other spectacular pieces on view is the famous *Altarpiece of the Annunciation,* as well as important illuminated manuscripts and striking stained-glass windows. You may want to take a free guided tour, which is given at 3 p.m. Tuesday through Saturday. After looking at the collection, sit in the herb garden and soak in the tranquility of this serene oasis far removed from the noise and bustle of midtown.

This unusual museum is well worth the half-hour trip from downtown. To get there by subway, take the IND–Eighth Avenue A train to 190th Street–Overlook Terrace. Then take the no. 4 bus or walk through Fort Tryon Park to the museum. By bus, take the Madison Avenue no. 4 to the Fort Tryon Park–The Cloisters stop.

Open Tuesday through Sunday from 9:30 a.m. to 5:15 p.m. Suggested admission is $5 for adults, $2.50 for students and senior citizens, and free for children under 12 accompanied by an adult.

## THE BROOKLYN MUSEUM

At Eastern Parkway and Washington Avenue (tel. 718/638-5000), the Brooklyn Museum contains perhaps the finest collection of Egyptian art in the country. The museum also owns a large selection of Oriental art, as well as an excellent group of American paintings from colonial times to the present. There are 28 American period rooms, the best assortment of Russian costumes and textiles outside the Soviet Union, and an outdoor sculpture garden consisting of architectural sections from demolished New York buildings. In the gift shop you can purchase original folk art from around the world. The museum has an art reference library with more than 100,000 volumes and the Wilbur Library of Egyptology that has more than 25,000 books on the subject.

To get to the museum, take the IRT–Seventh Avenue express subway (no. 2 or 3) or the IRT–Lexington Avenue no. 4 express train to the Eastern Parkway–Brooklyn Museum stop. Open Wednesday through Monday from 10 a.m. to 5 p.m.; closed Tuesday. Suggested contribution is $3 for adults, $1.50 for students, and $1 for senior citizens; free to children under 12.

## AMERICAN MUSEUM OF NATURAL HISTORY

Animal and human life in all its forms is the theme of this vast museum located at Central Park West and 79th Street (tel. 769-5100). With more than 34 million artifacts and specimens, the museum offers the visitor an incredible range of objects to view, from a miniscule chromosome to a 94-foot replica of the blue whale, the largest mammal that ever lived. But don't try to see all the exhibits or else you'll quickly become overwhelmed.

Among the many excellent exhibits are the Gardner D. Stout Hall of Asian Peoples, which features over 3,000 artifacts and artworks; the Hall of Mexico and Central America, which has an impressive collection of pre-Columbian jade and carved stone pieces; the Hall of Man in Africa; and the recently opened Hall of South American Peoples. Also on display are dioramas of many preserved animals shown in every type of habitat from the savannah to the tundra.

The museum's Naturemax Film Theater offers features sure to delight anyone with a sense of adventure. The Naturemax motion picture format uses a film frame ten times the size of a standard 35-mm frame, resulting in a display of breathtaking images unsurpassed in resolution and detail. Tickets—$4 for adults, $2 for children—can be purchased at the box office in the main lobby. Call 769-5650 for shows and times.

The museum also has a pleasant gift shop, a reference library, a cafeteria, and a restaurant.

Open every day from 10 a.m. to 5:45 p.m. (until 9 p.m. on Wednesday, Friday, and Saturday). Suggested admission is $4.50 for adults, $2 for students and children. On Friday and Saturday evenings admission is free after 5 p.m. For subway directions, see the Hayden Planetarium, below.

## THE HAYDEN PLANETARIUM

The closest thing to stargazing you're likely to get in Manhattan is a Sky Show at the Hayden Planetarium, at Central Park West and 81st Street (tel. 769-5920). When the lights go out and the quarter-million-dollar Zeiss VI projector splashes a star-studded sky on the 75-foot dome ceiling, you'd almost believe you were sitting on a mountaintop. That is, until the prerecorded show begins. The shows, which vary from season to season, trace man's fascination with the stars and the planets, the mythical and scientific explanations for cosmic phenomena, and the possibilities for future exploration. Shows take place weekdays at 1:30 and 3:30 p.m., on Saturday and Sunday at 1, 2, 3, 4, and 5 p.m. (an 11 a.m. Saturday show is added October through June).

The planetarium also contains exhibits explaining such things as orbital patterns, gamma rays, rainbows, and why the sky is blue. Its Hall of the Sun is the largest exhibit in the world devoted entirely to our nearest star. And if you're curious to know what you'd weigh on Mars, Jupiter, Venus, the sun, or the moon, jump onto a scale in "Your Weight on Other Worlds."

Most popular with the young crowd is the **Laser Show,** a dazzling show that combines laser images with rock music to create a vibrant kaleidoscopic effect. Shows are Friday and Saturday at 7, 8:30, and 10 p.m. Tickets cost $6 and at times sell out, so you should plan to arrive early (the box office opens at 6 p.m.) or to buy tickets in advance at Ticketron. For Laser Show information, call 769-5921.

The planetarium opens one hour before the first show and closes an hour after the last. Admission is $3.75 for adults, $2.75 for students with ID and senior citizens, and $2 for children 12 and under.

To get to the planetarium, take the IND–Eighth Avenue local subway (C) or the IND–Sixth Avenue local subway (B) to 81st Street, or the IRT–Seventh Avenue local train (no. 1 or 9) to 79th Street and walk east from Broadway.

## NEW-YORK HISTORICAL SOCIETY

This museum's old punctuation of "New-York" shows how determined it is to preserve the past. At 170 Central Park West, at 77th Street (tel. 873-3400), this library and museum of American history (with a special emphasis on New York) was founded in 1804 and is still one of the city's most important cultural institutions. The society houses New York's oldest museum and a renowned research library. The museum rotates exhibits from its excellent collection of Hudson River landscape paintings, early American portraits, furniture, New York silver, and early American toys. The museum has period rooms from the 17th and early 18th centuries, and a wonderful Tiffany glass gallery. Although they are not always on view, the museum boasts 422 *Birds of America* watercolors by John Jay Audubon. There is also a print and photographic department, and an excellent research library (for which a small user's fee is charged).

Open Tuesday through Sunday from 10 a.m. to 5 p.m.; closed Monday. Suggested donation is $2 for adults, $1.50 for senior citizens, and $1 for children under 12. Tuesday, pay as you wish.

## FRAUNCES TAVERN MUSEUM

This fascinating museum of early American history and culture is housed in the site of Fraunces Tavern, a landmark 18th-century building at the corner of Broad and Pearl streets in lower Manhattan (tel. 425-1778). The museum's permanent collections include Early Americana, Revolutionary War memorabilia, and portraits of President George Washington, the tavern's most famous guest. The museum also boasts two fully furnished period rooms: the Long Room, site of Washington's emotional farewell to his officers in 1783, and the 19th-century Clinton Dining Room. The museum hosts lectures, workshops, concerts, and theatrical performances, as well as special exhibitions on such topics as "Education in the Early Republic."

Open Monday through Friday from 10 a.m. to 4 p.m. Suggested contributions are $2.50 for adults and $1 for students, senior citizens, and children under 12 (admission is free on Thursday). Group tours are available by appointment.

## MUSEUM OF THE CITY OF NEW YORK

In a beautiful old Georgian building at Fifth Avenue and 103rd Street (tel. 534-1672), this museum contains a collection of New York City memorabilia presented in an entertaining and informative way. Even if you yawn at the thought of history, this museum will spark your interest. Through slide shows, colorful dioramas, and detailed exhibits, the museum glides you through the "Big Apple's" history from the time when the city was the Dutch colony of New Amsterdam to the present. Permanent exhibits capture the mood of Wall Street and the activity of New York Harbor with slide shows, taped sounds, and enlarged photographs. The museum has an excellent collection of American silver and some fine portraits of early American patriots and statesmen. Rooms filled with models, photographs, old fire engines, maps, toys—plus period recreations of furniture and dress—provide a sense of the city's rich social and cultural past.

Open Tuesday through Saturday from 10 a.m. to 5 p.m. and on Sunday from 1 to 5 p.m.; closed Monday. Suggested donation is $3 for adults, $1.50 for students and seniors, and $1 for children.

## THE COOPER-HEWITT MUSEUM

The Smithsonian Institution established its National Museum of Design in the elegant former Andrew Carnegie mansion at 2 E. 91st St., at Fifth Avenue (tel. 860-6868). The museum's name honors its founders: Peter Cooper, a 19th-century philanthropist and his three granddaughters; and the Hewitts, who envisioned a museum for the designer, the artisan, and the student. Since the Hewitt sisters started the museum in 1897, the collection has grown into one of the foremost collections of decorative arts and design in the world, including objects from every historical period over a span of 3,000 years: drawings, prints, wallpapers, textiles, porcelain, glass, furniture, woodwork, metalwork, jewelry, and woven and printed fabrics. The museum's collection of original architecture and design drawings is the largest in the United States.

The permanent collections are not on view, but the regularly changing exhibitions always relate to some aspect of design—from the dash and style of engraved and sculpted cane handles to the skyscrapers built in Manhattan in the 1920s and 1930s. Watch for coming exhibitions on a variety of design themes. Don't miss the peaceful garden on the southern side of the museum, which is lined with shaded benches; it's a very pleasant place for a moment's rest.

Open Wednesday through Saturday from 10 a.m. to 5 p.m., on Sunday from noon to 5 p.m., and on Tuesday from 10 a.m. to 9 p.m. (free after 5 p.m.); closed Monday and major holidays. Admission other times is $3 for adults, $1.50 for students and senior citizens, and free for children under 12.

## THE JEWISH MUSEUM

This museum, housed in the former Warburg mansion at 1109 Fifth Ave., at 92nd Street (tel. 860-1888), contains the most comprehensive collection of Judaica in the United States, and one of the largest in the world. The museum addresses the entire Jewish experience, from biblical times to the present. The permanent collection includes ceremonial objects, antiquities, paintings, prints, drawings, sculpture, photographs, textiles, decorative arts, broadcast material, and coins and medals from around the world. Though once known as a forum for any type of avant-garde art, the museum now displays only modern art with a Jewish content. Concerts, lectures, films, and children's programs are scheduled regularly, along with art courses and music programs.

Open on Monday, Wednesday, and Thursday from noon to 5 p.m., on Tuesday to 8 p.m., and on Sunday from 11 a.m. to 6 p.m.; closed Friday, Saturday, and major Jewish holidays. Admission is $4 for adults, and $2 for children, students, and senior citizens. On Tuesday from 5 to 8 p.m. admission is free.

## MUSEUM OF THE AMERICAN INDIAN—HEYE FOUNDATION

Located on the Upper West Side at Broadway and 155th Street (tel. 283-2420), this museum contains the world's largest and finest collection of artifacts made by the Indians of the Western Hemisphere. Attractively arranged in three floors of exhibits, these artifacts vividly catalog the ceremonies and daily activities of Indian cul-

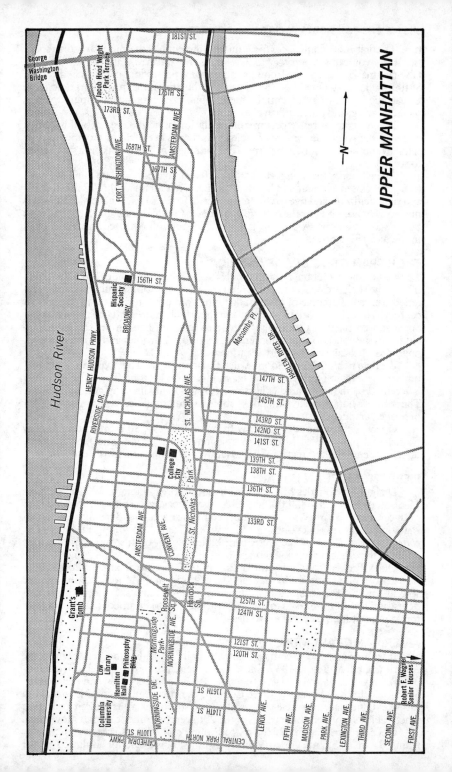

UPPER MANHATTAN

ture. The first and second floors focus on the different North American Indian societies. Here you can see everyday tools, such as the tomahawk, along with dramatic
false-face masks worn by the Iroquois and personal possessions of chiefs Red Cloud,
Sitting Bull, Crazy Horse, and Arapoosh. On the third floor are exhibits describing
Indian life in South and Central America, plus collections of wampum, games,
pipes, weaving, and other Indian crafts.

The museum currently occupies one of the imposing and elegant buildings that
make up the Audubon Terrace complex, but there's been talk of moving the museum to another location; so be sure to call the museum before making a special visit
to see it.

Open Tuesday through Saturday from 10 a.m. to 5 p.m. and on Sunday from 1
to 5 p.m.; closed Monday and holidays. Admission is $3 for adults, $2 for students
and senior citizens, and free to children under 7. To get there, take the Madison Avenue no. 3 or no. 4 bus, or the Avenue of Americas (Sixth Avenue) no. 5 bus to 155th
Street and Broadway. By subway, take the IRT–Seventh Avenue local (no. 1 or 9)
uptown to 157th Street.

## THE HISPANIC SOCIETY OF AMERICA

Part of the Audubon Terrace complex at Broadway and 155th Street (tel. 690-
0743), the society owns an impressive collection of paintings, sculpture, and decorative arts representative of Hispanic culture from prehistoric days to the present
century. Though the society specializes in the art, literature, and cultural history of
Spain and Portugal, it also features a good selection of Latin American pieces. Included in the collection are paintings by El Greco, Velázquez, and Goya, plus such
objects as Mexican ceramics and Spanish earthenware.

With its rich terracotta floors, Valencia tapestries, and high ceiling, the museum's interior resembles a grand and majestic cathedral in tone. The air of solemnity
is accented by the sculptured effigies of Spanish nobility lined up against one wall.
The society's library, filled with books about Hispanic culture, conveys a similar air
of hushed grandeur.

Open Tuesday through Saturday from 10 a.m. to 4:30 p.m. and on Sunday
from 1 to 4 p.m.; closed Monday. Admission is free. See the listing for the (next-
door) Museum of the American Indian (above) for transportation directions.

## PIERPONT MORGAN LIBRARY

Designed by Charles McKim, the Pierpont Morgan Library, 29 E. 36th St., at
Madison Avenue (tel. 685-0008), is a Renaissance palazzo befitting its collection of
15th-century and earlier books, illuminated manuscripts, and drawings. Almost always on exhibit are selections from Morgan's collection, including Erasmus's *Defense of Folly* and one of the Gutenberg Bibles—both on display with other rare
books in the ornate East Room library.

Open Tuesday through Saturday from 10:30 a.m. to 5 p.m. and on Sunday
from 1 to 5 p.m.; closed Monday, holidays, Sunday and Monday in July, and the
second half of August. Suggested admission is $3 for adults. Senior citizens, students, and children are asked to donate as they can. Be forewarned: this is not a place
for young children; they will get restless.

## AMERICAN CRAFT MUSEUM

If your impression of crafts is limited to coil pots and potholders, then let the
American Craft Museum, 40 W. 53rd St., between Fifth and Sixth avenues (tel. 956-
3535), introduce you to the latest trends in clay, wood, fiber, glass, and metal crafts.
Sponsored by the American Craft Council, the museum mounts thematic and
group exhibitions and single-artist shows; it also houses a permanent collection
whose objects represent high points in the 20th-century American craft movement.

Open on Tuesday from 10 a.m. to 8 p.m., and Wednesday through Sunday
from 10 a.m. to 5 p.m.; closed Monday. Admission is $3.50 for adults, $1.50 for

students and senior citizens, and free to children under 12. On Tuesday evening from 5 to 8 p.m. no admission is charged.

## MUSEUM OF AMERICAN FOLK ART

Although still in the process of completing its new facilities on West 53rd Street, the museum is rotating exhibits at the Eva and Morris Feld Gallery, 2 Lincoln Square, on Columbus Avenue between 65th and 66th streets (tel. 595-9585). Visitors can see works drawn from all the American folk arts, such as painting, sculpture, needlepoint, quilts, woodcarvings, decoys, painted and decorative furniture, and decorative arts in the folk tradition. Since the museum is immediately adjacent to the Lincoln Center for the Performing Arts, and on the west side of Central Park, theater-goers and Sunday strollers can take advantage of the gallery's flexible hours — it's open seven days a week, including most holidays, from 9 a.m. to 9 p.m. Admission is free.

If you're more in the mood to browse, take a stroll through the museum's crafts shop. It's open on Monday, Tuesday, and Saturday from 11 a.m. to 6 p.m., Wednesday through Friday from 11 a.m. to 7:30 p.m., and on Sunday from noon to 6 p.m. Enthusiasts might also want to visit the museum's other gift shop, at 62 W. 50th St., between Fifth and Sixth avenues, open Monday through Saturday from 10:30 a.m. to 5:30 p.m.

## INTERNATIONAL CENTER OF PHOTOGRAPHY

One of the museums on Fifth Avenue's "Museum Mile," the ICP is in an elegant landmark building at 1130 Fifth Ave., at 94th Street (tel. 860-1777). Its exhibitions, under the stewardship of Cornell Capa, show the sophistication and diversity of contemporary photography and the techniques and styles of the past. Changing exhibits sometimes focus on one photographer or on one genre, such as still-lifes, photo essays, or portraits. In the permanent collection are works by such famous photographers as Henri Cartier-Bresson, W. Eugene Smith, and Andreas Feininger. For those striving to become famous, the museum offers photography classes throughout the year for every level of experience. A large selection of photography books, postcards, and posters are sold in the first-floor shop.

Open on Tuesday from noon to 8 p.m. (free after 5 p.m.), Wednesday through Friday from noon to 5 p.m., and on Sunday from 11 a.m. to 6 p.m.; closed Monday. Admission is $3 for adults, $1 for students and seniors, and free for children under 12.

## THE NEW YORK PUBLIC LIBRARY

On the steps of the enormous New York Public Library, on Fifth Avenue between 40th and 42nd streets (tel. 340-0849), street musicians, vendors, and undiscovered comedians vie for the attention of the bustling crowds. Inside the library, the horns and noise of the street are forgotten. At table after table, in room after room, people pore intently over books. But there is more to do here than read. The library, one of the centers of New York's artistic and cultural life, also has exhibition rooms, art galleries, and permanent displays of 19th-century American paintings. To find out about special events, check the library's publication titled *Events,* available at all branches. All exhibits and programs are free.

The Main Reading Room is open Monday through Wednesday from 10 a.m. to 9 p.m. and Thursday through Saturday from 10 a.m. to 6 p.m.; closed Sunday. Call for information about the library's other branches.

## IBM GALLERY OF SCIENCE AND ART

Located in the IBM Building at Madison Avenue and 56th Street (tel. 745-3500), the city's largest "lobby" gallery offers a wide variety of exhibits. In the past, these have included "Sorolla: The Painter of Light," "The Flag Paintings of Childe Hassam," and "Frontier America: Works from the Buffalo Bill Historical Center."

The gallery, which has 13,000 square feet of exhibition space, usually offers two shows at a time. Be sure to visit the adjacent botanical garden tended by the New York Botanical Garden. In the midst of Manhattan's concrete hustle and bustle, it's a soothing oasis of horticultural beauty.

Open Tuesday through Saturday 11 a.m. to 6 p.m. and admission is free.

## FORBES GALLERIES

Located at 62 Fifth Ave., at 12th Street, in Greenwich Village (tel. 620-2389), these galleries offer a permanent exhibit of the world's largest collection of Fabergé Imperial Easter Eggs and special exhibits, such as "The Constitution: Two Centuries of America."

The galleries are open to the public on Tuesday, Wednesday, Friday, and Saturday from 10 a.m. to 4 p.m. Admission is free.

## ASIA SOCIETY GALLERIES

Located in the society's earth-toned headquarters at 725 Park Ave., at 70th Street (tel. 288-6400), the galleries provide a permanent home for the Mr. and Mrs. John D. Rockefeller III Collection of Asian Art. Included in this prodigious collection of art from China, Japan, India, and Southeast Asia are dancing Krishna statues, Ming porcelain, and delicate Japanese folding screens. The first-floor exhibit space is devoted to changing exhibits on specific themes in Asian art.

Open Tuesday through Saturday from 11 a.m. to 6 p.m. and on Sunday from noon to 5 p.m.; closed Monday. Admission is $2 for adults, $1 for students and senior citizens, and free for children under 12.

## YESHIVA UNIVERSITY MUSEUM

Featured in this university collection at 2520 Amsterdam Ave., at 185th Street (tel. 960-5390), are paintings, photographs, and ceremonial objects that record the Jewish historical experience. Of special interest is the museum's exhibit of detailed architectural models of ten famous synagogues.

Open Tuesday through Thursday from 10:30 a.m. to 5 p.m. and on Sunday from noon to 6 p.m.; closed Monday, Friday, and Saturday. Admission is $3 for adults, $1.50 for children under 16 and senior citizens.

## CHINA HOUSE GALLERY

Fascinating exhibits of classical Chinese art are presented semiannually at the China House Gallery at 125 E. 65th St., between Lexington and Park avenues (tel. 744-8181). A recent show featured Chinese women artists from 1300 to 1910.

Open Monday through Saturday from 10 a.m. to 5 p.m.; closed Sunday. Admission is free, though contributions are welcome.

## MUSEUM OF BROADCASTING

With more than 10,000 videotaped television shows and 7,000 radio shows, this comfortable place at 1 E. 53rd St., just off Fifth Avenue (tel. 752-7684), is a mecca for fans of popular culture, entertainment, and American history. Founded in 1975, this museum collects, preserves, and interprets radio and TV programs. All tapes can be screened by the public. At 23 broadcasting consoles, you can listen to Edward R. Murrow's London broadcasts or FDR's fireside chats. You can also view TV programs of all kinds, from Sid Caesar's comic routines to shots of the moon or serious documentaries.

Open on Tuesday from noon to 8 p.m. and Wednesday through Saturday from noon to 5 p.m.; closed Sunday and Monday. Suggested admission is $4 for adults, $3 for students, $2 for senior citizens and children under 13.

## MUSEUM OF HOLOGRAPHY

At 11 Mercer St., in SoHo, half a block north of Canal Street and one block west of Broadway (tel. 925-0581), this museum is devoted to the display of holograms, three-dimensional images made by exposing photographic film to laser beams. The result is images that never stop moving and often trick the eye. For example, in one display, miniature holographic images of celebrities, such as the artist Andy Warhol and the opera singer Beverly Sills, seem to move and vibrate as though alive. This is a fascinating museum for anyone curious about light, science, or new directions in art made possible by technology. The museum store has books, jewelry, pendants, and fine art by holographic artists for sale. For example, you can buy a holographic recording of a human eye, or the inside of a clock. And the museum offers workshops. Those interested should call for information.

Open Tuesday through Sunday from 11 a.m. to 6 p.m. (on Wednesday from 10:30 a.m.); closed Monday. Admission is $3.50 for adults, $2.50 for students and seniors, and $2 for children under 12. To get there, take the bus or subway to any Canal Street stop.

## THE NEW MUSEUM

At 583 Broadway in SoHo, between Houston and Prince streets, the New Museum (tel. 219-1222) is devoted to contemporary art. What makes it different from more traditional institutions is its support for new and unrecognized art. The museum has no permanent collection, but shows all kinds of artworks, from painting and sculpture to conceptual art, in temporary exhibits. The works, never more than ten years old, are often experimental, innovative, and radically different.

Open from noon to 6 p.m. Wednesday through Sunday (until 8 p.m. on Friday and Saturday); closed Monday and Tuesday. Suggested admission is $2.50 for adults, $1.50 for students, artists, and senior citizens.

## UKRAINIAN MUSEUM

Tucked away in a small building at 203 Second Ave., between 12th and 13th streets (tel. 228-0110), this museum features Ukrainian folk art from the 19th and 20th centuries: textiles, ceramics, metalwork, and woodwork. Because of the museum's limited space, only a few of its 2,000 craft items can be displayed at any one time. Highlights of the collection include festive folk costumes on permanent display and the museum's annual Easter exhibition of pysanky (colored Easter eggs). Pieces from the permanent collection are shown throughout the year in rotating exhibits.

Open Wednesday through Sunday from 1 to 5 p.m.; closed Monday and Tuesday. Admission is $1 for adults, 50¢ for students and senior citizens. Children under 6 are admitted for free.

## STUDIO MUSEUM IN HARLEM

This museum, at 144 W. 125th St., near Lenox Avenue (tel. 864-4500), features the work of prominent and emerging Afro-American, African, and Caribbean artists. Changing exhibits present the work of such artists as Romare Bearden, James Van Der Zee, and Beauford Delaney. The museum's permanent collection includes paintings, prints, sculpture, and photographs. Its gift shop has arts and crafts from all over the world.

Open Wednesday through Friday from 10 a.m. to 5 p.m., on Saturday and Sunday from 1 to 6 p.m.; closed Monday and Tuesday. Admission is $2 for adults, $1.50 for students and children under 12, and $1 for seniors. To get there, take the IRT–Seventh Avenue subway (no. 2 or 3) to 125th Street and Lenox Avenue, then walk across 125th Street toward Adam Clayton Powell Boulevard.

## EL MUSEO DEL BARRIO

Located at 1230 Fifth Ave., at 104th Street (tel. 831-7272), this museum records the vivid culture of Puerto Rico and Latin America through sculpture, paintings, graphics, and photography. Recently, the museum has featured major exhibitions of pre-Columbian artifacts and Puerto Rican *santos* (wood-carved figures of saints). All extended shows are supplemented with changing exhibits that focus on Puerto Rican culture on the island, in New York City, and in the Americas.

Open Wednesday through Sunday from 11 a.m. to 5 p.m.; closed Monday and Tuesday. Suggested contribution is $2 for adults and $1 for students and senior citizens. Children under 12 are admitted free.

## THE NATIONAL ACADEMY OF DESIGN

Founded in 1825 as an art school and exhibition space, the National Academy of Design, 1083 Fifth Ave., at 89th Street (tel. 369-4880), has a permanent collection of 19th- and 20th-century fine arts, and organizes exhibitions whose eclectic range aims to introduce new subjects to an American audience. Recent exhibits have focused on the work of little-known European masters and neglected American 19th-century talents.

The museum is open from noon to 8 p.m. on Tuesday, and from noon to 5 p.m. Wednesday through Sunday; closed Monday. Admission is $2.50 for adults, $2 for students and seniors, and free for friends of the Academy and for all on Tuesday from 5 to 8 p.m.

## THE GROLIER CLUB

This private club for bibliophiles and book collectors, which recently celebrated its centennial, runs changing exhibits on anything to do with books, from the 19th-century British Gothic Revival, to the art of stencil, to Ezra Pound.

The museum, at 47 E. 60th St., between Park and Madison avenues (tel. 838-6690), is open to the public free of charge Monday through Saturday (Friday in the summer) from 10 a.m. to 5 p.m. The library at the club is open to scholars and members only.

# 3. Galleries, Theater, Concerts, Opera, and Dance

## ART GALLERIES

For artists, dealers, collectors, and art lovers around the world, New York is an irresistible magnet, drawing the newest, the finest, the most prestigious in the visual arts. Dozens of art galleries are continually setting new trends and making new reputations. Whatever you want to see, it's here—from the paintings of old masters to works on the cutting edge. Each gallery is an adventure, and after a quick tour of a few you'll feel like a knowledgeable insider to a chic and beautiful world. Remember, don't expect to cover all of New York's galleries in a day or two, so take your time and enjoy yourself.

Galleries don't charge admission—they're businesses with art to sell. The prices are posted, usually near the front desk. We've heard more than one gallery assistant complain that the prices are sometimes more interesting and usually more shocking to the public than the artworks, so if you're interested, go ahead and ask for them.

Below, we've listed many of the galleries that the art world takes seriously, as well as the type of work and artists each gallery features. For those who want the most current and up-to-date listings (galleries generally change shows monthly), the gallery-goer's bible is *Gallery Guide,* a glossy paperback published monthly that lists virtually every gallery's shows, plus maps. It's available free in most galleries. You can also pick up a copy of *Art in America* ($4.75) at a magazine stand, for gallery listings and maps, slick photos, and reviews with the latest, but not last, word on the ever-changing art scene.

Galleries are generally open Tuesday through Saturday from about 10 a.m. to 6 p.m., and may have special summer hours.

## Madison Avenue/Uptown

Prestigious Madison Avenue is lined with art galleries and expensive stores, and each block abounds with architectural and historic landmarks. Window-shop, browse, and join the well-heeled residents of the brownstones, townhouses, mansions, and apartment houses that line the side streets off Madison Avenue.

At the **Forum Gallery,** 1018 Madison Ave., between 78th and 79th streets (tel. 772-7666), you can enjoy your art al fresco, because the gallery exhibits its contemporary sculpture in a charming penthouse roof garden. Inside, admire the works of American figurative painters and sculptors.

In the same building, the **Rachel Adler Gallery** (tel. 517-4005) specializes in early–20th-century Russian art and European works of the 1920s and 1930s. It also shows works by the Dadaists and Italian futurists.

The **Graham Gallery,** 1014 Madison Ave., at 78th Street (tel. 535-5767), features three floors of eye-pleasing art. The first two floors show 19th- and 20th-century American paintings and sculpture, plus British pottery. The third floor, Graham Modern, shows contemporary paintings and sculpture.

The focus at the **David Findlay Gallery,** 984 Madison Ave., at 77th Street (tel. 249-2909), is 19th- and 20th-century French art. The ambience is appropriately intimate and chic, and you can view old French favorites like Dufy and Vuillard.

On the second floor of 851 Madison Ave., between 70th and 71st streets, are three top-notch galleries. The **Barbara Mathes Gallery** (tel. 249-3600) shows Americans of the early 20th century such as Calder and Arthur Dove, works on paper by such Europeans as Matisse and Picasso, as well as contemporary artists. **Hirschl and Adler Modern** (tel. 744-6700) features contemporary paintings and sculptures, including works by Joseph Beuys, and paintings by Joan Snyder and Philip Pearlstein. And **Hirschl and Adler Folk** (tel. 988-FOLK) specializes in American folk art, mostly of the 18th and 19th centuries. You might see anything from calligraphy to Navaho weavings here.

Occupying a historic, landmark building at 21 E. 70th St., off Madison Avenue, is **Hirschl and Adler Galleries, Inc.** (tel. 535-8810). On the first two floors you will find museum-quality shows of art from the 18th to the 20th century. The range is dazzling: American paintings, watercolors, drawings, prints, and sculpture; 19th- and 20th-century American decorative arts; European impressionist painting; and modern art.

**M. Knoedler & Co.,** 19 E. 70th St., near the Frick Museum (tel. 794-0550), has an old-masters department, but much of its focus is on modern masters like Robert Motherwell, Frank Stella, Richard Diebenkorn, David Smith, and Adolph Gottlieb.

If you are interested in contemporary sculpture, the place to see it is **The Sculpture Center,** a nonprofit, alternative gallery specializing in emerging and mid-career sculptors. Located in an old carriage house at 167 E. 69th St., between Lexington and Third avenues (tel. 879-3500), the center also houses a school that teaches the traditional methods of sculpture—carving, clay modeling, and casting.

The **Richard York Gallery,** 21 E. 65th St., between Fifth and Madison avenues (tel. 772-9155), is the place to see important American art dating from 1800 to 1950. Featured are works by members of the Hudson River School, American impressionists like William Merritt Chase, early works by Georgia O'Keeffe, western art by Remington, and still-lifes and marine paintings.

At the **Wildenstein & Co. Gallery,** 19 E. 64th St., between Fifth and Madison avenues (tel. 879-0500), you can lose yourself in the dreamy colors of master French impressionists Monet, Manet, and Renoir.

## 57th Street/Midtown

Busy, bustling midtown is the geographical heart of the city. It moves to the beat of the well-dressed people moving in and out of its tall office buildings and upscale department stores. This area has long been home to many of the more established, blue-chip galleries that should be a part of any serious exploration of the city's art treasures. Most of the galleries aren't at street level; you'll find these hushed, pleasant spaces an elevator's ride above the noisy midtown crowds.

It's difficult to choose which galleries you should visit out of the many that are housed in the beautiful **Fuller Building,** 41 E. 57th St., at the corner of Madison Avenue. The structure itself is an architectural knockout that's considered one of the best examples of art deco design in the city. Look at the bronze doors, wall decorations, marble fixtures, and mosaic walls—and plan to spend some time investigating the many galleries within.

The **Robert Miller Gallery** (tel. 980-5454) features 20th-century and contemporary art by such artists as sculptor Louise Bourgeois, painter Joan Mitchell, and photographer Robert Mapplethorpe.

**André Emmerich** (tel. 752-0124) has two specialties. This gallery shows work by contemporary American and European artists like David Hockney, Helen Frankenthaler, Anthony Caro, and Hans Hofmann. But it also features ancient art. The lineup at the **James Goodman Gallery** (tel. 593-3737) includes Picasso, Matisse, Botero, Calder, and Klee, as well as contemporary masters like Rauschenberg and Rosenquist.

If you only have time to visit a few galleries while you're in New York, be sure to include the bustling **Pace Gallery,** 32 E. 57th St., between Fifth and Madison avenues (tel. 421-3292). This famous gallery shows an impressive array of modern and contemporary artists, from Picasso and Calder to photorealist Chuck Close and the maverick painter Julian Schnabel. Other modern greats on the gallery roster are Nevelson, Dubuffet, Rothko, Noguchi, and Dine. In the same building, **Pace Editions** (tel. 421-3237) shows contemporary and old-master prints and drawings, and **Pace Primitive** (tel. 421-3237) features turn-of-the-century African sculpture.

The **Pace/MacGill Gallery,** 11 E. 57th St., between Fifth and Madison avenues (tel. 759-7999), is a good place to see photography—from the classic works of Walker Evans to the avant-garde images of Joel-Peter Witkin.

The work at the **Holly Solomon Gallery,** 724 Fifth Ave., near 57th Street (tel. 757-7777), defies easy classification but should not be missed. Solomon is something of a legend in the art world for showing provocative work. You never know what you may see here—rows of television sets by Nam June Paik, videotapes of the artist William Wegman's dog, or the wild and colorful installations of Judy Pfaff.

In the same building are two other galleries you might want to visit. The **Merrin Gallery** (tel. 757-2884) shows only ancient art—classical Greek and Roman, Etruscan, pre-Columbian, and Egyptian—from finely woven textiles to polished stone sculptures. The **Grace Borgenicht Gallery** (tel. 247-2111) hosts an unpredictable and eclectic mix of work by old masters, established modern artists, and emerging younger artists.

A few doors down at **Blum Helman,** 20 W. 57th St., between Fifth and Sixth avenues (tel. 245-2888), the focus is on American and European postwar and contemporary painting and sculpture, with works by heavyweights like Ellsworth Kelly, the contemporary landscape painter David Deutsch, and sculptor Bryan Hunt.

At the **New York Gallery Building,** 24 W. 57th St., between Fifth and Sixth avenues, several galleries are worth a visit. Among them are the **Marian Goodman Gallery** (tel. 977-7160), which shows contemporary art in all media, with an emphasis on well-known Europeans like German artist Anselm Kiefer, and French artist Christian Boltanski. Two floors up, at **Arnold Herstand & Co.** (tel. 664-1379), you'll find African art and modern and contemporary art by such masters as Jean Dubuffet and Roberto Matta.

If you are a modern art aficionado, the **Marlborough Gallery** is not to be missed. Located in a skyscraper office building at 40 W. 57th St., between Fifth and Sixth avenues (tel. 541-4900), this prestigious gallery exhibits the gurus and greats of modern art, masters like Moore, Calder, Sutherland, Botero, Feininger, and Arp.

In the same building, stop in at the **Kennedy Gallery** (tel. 541-9600), where the walls are lined with collector-quality 18th-, 19th-, and 20th-century American paintings, drawings, and prints. Savor especially the works of John Marin, John Copley, Georgia O'Keeffe, and Charles Prendergast.

There are ten galleries at 50 W. 57th St., between Fifth and Sixth avenues. One of the best is the **Frumkin/Adams Gallery** (tel. 757-6655), which specializes in work by such well-known contemporary artists as James Surls, Jack Beal, and Roy De Forest, many of whom hail from Texas and California.

The **Sidney Janis Gallery,** 110 W. 57th St., between Sixth and Seventh avenues (tel. 586-0110), shows a wide range of modern and contemporary art—from legends like Mondrian, Brancusi, Léger, and Segal to aspiring legends like Crash (John Matos) and Maya Lin, the sculptor who designed the controversial Vietnam War Memorial in Washington, D.C.

## SoHo

When rents in nearby Chelsea and Greenwich Village soared in the early 1960s, artists moved to SoHo (which stands for south of Houston Street), attracted to airy lofts in the commercial buildings. Today SoHo is a chic neighborhood of restaurants, bookstores, antique shops, and boutiques. And rents in the area have risen so high that most artists can no longer afford to work here. Still, SoHo remains one of the commercial centers of the art world. You'll find more than 200 art galleries in just five square blocks of SoHo, and many of these galleries are housed in 19th-century cast-iron buildings. Visually, SoHo is one of the most stimulating neighborhoods in the city. So as you wander from gallery to gallery, be sure to check out the trendy shops and shoppers.

You might begin your tour at the **Leo Castelli Gallery,** 420 West Broadway, between Prince and Spring streets (tel. 431-5160). Castelli's unerring knack of spotting ground-breaking modern artists is legendary. At this, one of his three galleries in the city, you'll see work by "old" greats (Warhol, Johns, Stella, Lichtenstein, and Oldenburg), by newer greats (Dan Flavin, Donald Judd, and Ed Ruscha), and by rising stars like Charles Simonds, whose miniature clay sculptures are reminiscent of lost cities.

At the same address you'll find the highly regarded **Sonnabend Gallery** (tel. 966-6160), which features the works of such contemporary artists as sculptor Jannis Kounellis, photographer John Baldessari, and artist Jeff Koons; and **Germans Van Eck** (tel. 219-0717), which shows an eclectic mix of contemporary American and European art.

The **Mary Boone Gallery,** across the street at 417 West Broadway (tel. 431-1818), has become one of SoHo's institutions, with an impressive roster of contemporary artists like Eric Fischl, Sigmar Polke, Sherrie Levine, Barbara Kruger, Ross Bleckner, and A. R. Penke.

At the **Barbara Gladstone Gallery,** 99 Greene St., between Prince and Spring streets (tel. 431-3334), the work is hard to classify. But many artists who show here are the talk of the town. They include Jenny Holzer, whose work incorporates moving electric message signs, and Leon Golub, who is known for his sociopolitical paintings.

The **John Weber Gallery,** 142 Greene St., between Houston and Prince streets (tel. 966-6115), is associated with conceptual, minimal, and architecturally oriented art. You might see the famous grid-works of sculptor Sol Lewitt, the feminist photopanels of Victor Burgin, or the politically oriented sculptures of Hans Haacke.

In the same building, visit the **Sperone Westwater Gallery** (tel. 431-3685), which shows important contemporary artists such as the Italian neo-expressionists Chia and Clement; Cy Twombly, who is known for his elegant scribble-like drawings; and painter Susan Rothenberg.

Down the street, at **Barbara Toll,** 146 Greene St. (tel. 431-1788), you might find anything from a Garden of Eden, complete with flora, fauna, and a working fountain, to photographs of famous figures in the art world. And at **Metro Pictures,** 150 Greene St. (tel. 925-8335), you might see Cindy Sherman's provocative photographic portraits (in which she herself stars); Robert Longo's hefty, large-scale sculptures; or Louise Lawler's controversial photographs of other artists' artwork.

The **Paula Cooper Gallery,** 155 Wooster St., just south of Houston Street (tel. 674-0766), shows a mixed bag of well-known contemporary artists. They include painters Jennifer Bartlett and Elizabeth Murray, and sculptors Donald Judd, Jonathan Borofsky, and Joel Shapiro.

On Broadway, in the first two blocks below Houston, several recently renovated buildings now house a variety of galleries specializing in contemporary art. While some of these galleries are brand new, others have moved here from elsewhere in SoHo and from the fast-fading art scene of the East Village.

You might begin this leg of your art tour in the two adjoining buildings at 578 and 568 Broadway. On the first floor, the **Marcus Pfeifer Gallery Ltd.** (tel. 226-2251) is a great place to see photography. As the sign on the front desk says, there are "works on hand from Atgee to Weegee."

On the third floor, two more Castelli galleries—**Leo Castelli** and **Castelli Graphics** (tel. 941-9885)—exhibit more works from the impressario's stable of illustrious artists. The **Phoenix Gallery,** on the fifth floor (tel. 226-8711), is the oldest cooperative gallery in the city, with over 200 artists from around the country as members. The art may not be well known, but it may be the most affordable art in SoHo (we saw a few small paintings going for as little as $200). The gallery also hosts musical events, but is closed in the summer.

A trip all the way up to the **Lorence Monk Gallery,** on the 11th floor (tel. 431-3555), is worth it. The gallery features work in all media—for example, prints by Johns and Rauschenberg and photographs of life-size tableaux with titles like *Germs Are Everywhere* and *Radioactive Cats* by Sandy Skoglund.

The building at 560 Broadway, near the corner of Prince Street, houses another newly renovated cluster of art galleries. We've picked out just a few; but if you have time, we'd urge you to ride the elevator and explore other galleries in the building as well.

The **Dianne Brown Gallery,** on the second floor (tel. 219-1060), is known for its theme shows of contemporary sculpture. A recent exhibit consisted of pieces that artists considered their failures—and discussions of how such failures spurred their development into new directions. On the same floor, the **Max Protetch Gallery** (tel. 966-5454) specializes in American and European art and architecture. And the **Wolff Gallery** (tel. 431-7833) shows works by younger artists and has some interesting theme shows. For example, a recent exhibit of performance art featured Chris Burden's photographs of himself crawling through broken glass and getting shot in the arm.

**Gracie Mansion,** 532 Broadway, between Prince and Spring streets (tel. 477-7331), is a newcomer to SoHo, but not to the art scene. The owner, Gracie Mansion, named herself and her gallery after the New York City mayor's official residence. But the gallery is a far cry from its namesake. The gallery recently moved here from the funky East Village, where it grabbed the spotlight with its unconventional shows. How new is the work shown? "They call it post-contemporary," said one young gallery worker, "because they hang it before it dries."

## TriBeCa/Downtown

Just a few blocks south of SoHo is another old loft district turned trendy—TriBeCa. (Here again, the name describes the area's geography: triangle below Canal Street.) TriBeCa was once the center of the city's produce industry. But in the late 1960s developers relocated much of that industry to make way for the construction of the World Trade Center. In the 1970s artists fleeing the rents and trendiness of SoHo moved into TriBeCa and revitalized the area. In many ways today's TriBeCa resembles the SoHo of 15 years ago, but this relatively quiet neighborhood—where five-story buildings predominate and iron canopies, like sidewalk rooftops, still run along whole blocks—has its own personality. Among the key art attractions:

**Artists Space,** 223 West Broadway, between White and Franklin streets (tel. 226-3970), is one of New York City's most active alternative spaces. It focuses on emerging artists; for instance, a recent show featured paintings and sculptures by young artists from Eastern Europe who had never before shown in the West.

The **Alternative Museum,** 17 White St. (tel. 966-4444), also exhibits works in a variety of media by unknown or underrecognized artists. Much of the work has a sociopolitical content.

The **Clocktower,** 108 Leonard St., on the 13th floor (tel. 233-1096), is one of two exhibition spaces run by the Institute for Art and Urban Resources. Housed inside one of Manhattan's few existing clocktowers, it features provocative contemporary art—for example, the entries in an architectural competition to unite the two islands in the Bering Strait. The Clocktower also features concert programs and performances, and offers low-rent studios to artists from the U.S. and abroad.

**Hal Bromm,** 90 West Broadway, at Chambers Street (tel. 732-6196), is a well-lit second-floor gallery that features interesting and thought-provoking art in a variety of media. A recent exhibit consisted of large-scale drawings by artist/critic Jude Schwendenwien.

## The East Village

A decade ago, this area between Third Avenue and Avenue C, and from East 1st to East 13th streets, wasn't even a blip on the cultural map. Then, overnight, the East Village became home to a funky genre of art that swept through the New York art world and drew packs of young collectors and yuppies to the area. Today the East Village gallery scene is in a state of near-oblivion. The successful galleries have either moved or plan to move to SoHo. And the less successful ones have succumbed to rising rents. But a few galleries remain, and if you're exploring the East Village, you may want to check them out. Both galleries listed below have rather laid-back hours. They're open Wednesday through Sunday from 1 to 6 p.m.

**Kenkeleba Gallery,** 214 E. 2nd St., between avenues B and C (tel. 674-3939), shows a wide range of known and unknown contemporary artists. **P.S. 122,** at 409 E. 9th St., (tel. 228-4249), is a nonprofit gallery housed in a 100-year-old public school. It shares this building with dance spaces, art studios, and a community day-care center, and is closed during July and August.

## Other Exhibition Spaces

The **Dia Art Foundation,** 548 W. 22nd St., between Tenth and Eleventh avenues (tel. 431-9232), is a nonprofit arts organization that has come up with an unusual way to give contemporary artists a chance to create and exhibit their work. Each of the four floors of its West 22nd Street exhibition space is devoted to the work of one artist, who works and shows in the space for a year. One such artist, Jenny

Holzer, created an installation of granite tombstones and her trademark electronic-message boards on her floor.

The Dia Art Foundation also has two exhibition spaces in SoHo, and each houses a single installation piece by Walter De Maria. At 393 West Broadway, between Spring and Broome streets (tel. 925-9397), you can see De Maria's *The Broken Kilometer,* a piece that consists of 500 solid brass rods, weighs 37,000 pounds, and spans a kilometer (six-tenths of a mile). At 141 Wooster St., between Houston and Prince streets, on the second floor (tel. 473-8072), you can see *The New York Earth Room,* an earth sculpture that consists of 250 cubic yards of earth covering 300 square feet of floor space.

Like the Clocktower in TriBeCa, **P.S. 1,** at 46-01 21st St., in Long Island City, *Queens* (tel. 718/784-2084), is run by the Institute for Art and Urban Resources and features high-caliber one-person and group shows, and also houses low-rent studios. As the name suggests, P.S. 1 is in the city's first public school, a Romanesque Revival building of the 1890s. The exhibition space is open Wednesday through Sunday from noon to 6 p.m. Admission is $2. To get there, take the IND–Eighth Avenue E train or IND–Sixth Avenue F train to 23rd Street–Ely Avenue, or the IRT no. 7 train to 45th Avenue–Courthouse Square.

So that more people can see art on a daily basis, several corporations have helped make it possible for the Whitney Museum of American Art to curate special shows of American art in three locations around the city. As reflected in the titles of some recent exhibits—"Straphangers" (the local term for the city's subway riders), "Urban Figures," and "Suburban Homelife: Tracking the American Dream"—these shows can be quite interesting, and they tend to be about topics close to the lives of the people viewing them. What's more, the museum-quality shows at the following three locations are free.

The **Whitney Museum of American Art at Equitable Center,** 181 Seventh Ave., at 52nd Street (tel. 554-1000), is open Monday through Friday from 11 a.m. to 6 p.m. (on Thursday to 7:30 p.m.), and on Saturday from noon to 5 p.m.

The **Whitney Museum of American Art at Philip Morris,** 120 Park Ave., at 42nd Street (tel. 878-2453), is actually two spaces. The first is a regular gallery open Monday through Saturday from 11 a.m. to 6 p.m. (on Thursday to 7:30 p.m.). The other, called the Sculpture Court, is a sun-drenched, indoor sculpture garden, open Monday through Saturday from 7:30 a.m. to 9:30 p.m. and on Sunday from 11 a.m. to 7 p.m.

In lower Manhattan, the **Whitney Museum of American Art,** downtown at Federal Reserve Plaza, 33 Maiden Lane, at Nassau Street (tel. 943-5655), is open Monday through Friday from 11 a.m. to 6 p.m.

If you are in downtown *Brooklyn,* visit the **Rotunda Gallery,** in the Brooklyn War Memorial, on Cadman Plaza West near Orange Street (tel. 718/875-4031). This nonprofit gallery has helped spark the careers of several Brooklyn artists who have earned national and international recognition.

## AUCTION HOUSES

The quality of a new piece of work can often be measured by the amount one is willing to bid for it. Artistic movements are made or forgotten at the city's great auction houses. Although you may have to pay a "bidding paddle" fee in order to buy something—one doesn't bid here by raising a hand—there are pre-auction exhibits open for public inspection at no charge.

Mention art auction and you must think of **Sotheby's,** the premier auction house, at 1334 York Ave., between 71st and 72nd streets (tel. 606-7000). The million-dollar art sales will have you holding your breath, but don't forget to check out the less pricey, more down-to-earth auctions of quilts, furniture, antique clothes, and autographs.

**Christie's Galleries,** 502 Park Ave., at the corner of 59th Street (tel. 546-

1000), auctions paintings and sculpture fit for a millionaire or a museum. At **Christie's East,** 219 E. 67th St., between Second and Third avenues (tel. 606-0400), you can pick up an entire collection of mounted hunting trophies, or if you have no room in your home for those, settle for perhaps a few prints, some antique clothing, dolls, or Victoriana.

**William Doyle,** 175 E. 87th St., between Third and Lexington avenues (tel. 427-2730), is another major-league gallery; sales are held every other Wednesday. You can view the items Saturday through Tuesday.

**Swann Galleries,** 104 E. 25th St., between Park Avenue South and Lexington Avenue (tel. 254-4710), is for you if you're interested in books, autographs, photographs, and the like. Fans of folk art, puppets, country furniture, and other upscale, down-home items may want to check out **Greenwich Auction Room Ltd.,** at 110 E. 13th St., between Third and Fourth avenues (tel. 533-5930).

## THEATER

Many visitors shun the New York theatrical scene because they consider it too expensive for all but the most avid and wealthy fans. But with a little imagination and persistence, almost anyone can see even the glossiest productions at reasonable prices.

For those with hearts set on the expensive, glittery **Broadway** shows, there are services that can help you beat the price. We have listed several of them below. For those willing to venture beyond mainstream theater, there's a vast array of small theaters and companies that produce highly competent work at lower cost. These are the **off- and off-off-Broadway theaters.** They produce more experimental and original shows, and because of that, have gained a luster of their own in recent years. Many theater-goers prefer off- and off-off-Broadway to their more conventional Broadway counterparts. With the increased patronage, off- and off-off-Broadway shows have also become more expensive, though they still undercut Broadway prices. Off-Broadway tickets cost between $15 and $35. Seats for off-off-Broadway performances, which are even more experimental and unusual, usually cost between $8 and $20.

### Obtaining Tickets

Without careful financial planning, the lights may be the only thing you'll see on Broadway. Tickets for most orchestra seats run between $35 and $55, and even the less expensive second-balcony tickets seldom start at less than $20. Inexpensive seats are more accessible during the slower, summer months. But even then, finding good, low-priced seats is difficult on short notice.

One solution is to attend previews—performances given before opening night, when the critics attend. You get to see the show at prices reduced by as much as a third. You also risk spending money on an unsuccessful performance. However, most New York theater-goers consider previews a good bet. They're listed in the *New York Times,* the *Village Voice,* and other local publications. Using **twofers** is another way to beat the system. These are coupons that buy two tickets for the price of one. When a production is nearing the end of its run or when the audience is sparse, producers distribute twofers to fill up empty seats. Less popular Broadway shows distribute the coupons prodigiously to hotels, drugstores, and barbershops. More successful productions keep circulation low to protect sales of full-price tickets at the box office. Producers send the coupons out through mailing lists and to clubs, organizations, colleges, labor unions, and doctors' offices, which makes obtaining them without an insider's knowledge difficult.

One reliable source of twofers is **Hit Shows.** Send a self-addressed, stamped envelope to their office at 630 Ninth Ave., New York, NY 10036, and ask to be placed on their mailing list. You can also call them at 212/581-4211, and after requesting their schedule, pick up the coupons at their office. The service is open Monday through Friday between 9:15 a.m. and 3:45 p.m. Another good source for two-fers is the **New York Convention and Visitors' Bureau** at 2 Columbus Circle and 158 W. 42nd St.

**TKTS, the Times Square Theater Center,** at Broadway and 47th Street (tel. 354-5800), is a third way to enjoy theater without blowing your budget. The non-profit service sells half-price tickets to Broadway and off-Broadway shows on the day of the performance (with a $1.50-per-ticket service charge). It's open Monday through Saturday from 3 to 8 p.m., and on Sunday from noon to closing. TKTS has a second office at 2 World Trade Center in the financial district, which is open Monday through Friday from 11 a.m. to 5:30 p.m., and on Saturday from 11:30 a.m. to 3:30 p.m. Tickets may be paid for with cash or traveler's checks only. The group that sponsors TKTS, the Theatre Development Fund, also offers a package of five off-off-Broadway vouchers to foreign students for only $15.

**"NYC/On Stage"** is a phone information service of the Theatre Development Fund. It provides information on what shows are playing, and dates and prices of available tickets. Call 212/587-1111 in New York State; or toll free 800/STAGE-NY in all other states. The service provides information on dance, music, and children's entertainment.

**Audience Extras,** 163 W. 23rd St., New York, NY 10011 (tel. 989-9550), of-fers its members free tickets to Broadway shows, off-Broadway shows, cabarets, comedy clubs, dance programs, and classical events. For a $79 yearly membership fee ($69 for people in the entertainment industry and students of the performing arts), you'll get an ID card and the 24-hour phone number of a taped message that lists all the programs that will let members in free when they present their card. There is a $1 to $3 charge per show for making member's reservations at the box office. Write, call, or stop by for an application.

## Some Special Theaters

The number and variety of theatrical productions in New York is unsurpassed in the world, and deciphering the scene to pick between Broadway, off- and off-off-Broadway can be a tricky business. One solution is to peruse the ads and reviews in the *New York Times,* the *New Yorker,* the *Village Voice, 7 DAYS,* and *New York* maga-zine. We have highlighted some of the most interesting, unusual, and inexpensive shows in town.

One of the best deals is the summertime **New York Shakespeare Festival.** Tuesday through Sunday from late June to early September, some 2,000 people fill the outdoor Delacorte Theater in Central Park (tel. 598-7100). Against a backdrop of thick, green summertime trees, the audience watches classic and modern plays such as *Twelfth Night* and the *Mystery of Edwin Drood.* The theater is one of the best in town, and it's free. No surprises, then, at the long lines in front of the Delacorte, which distributes tickets, one per person, at 4:30 p.m. (3:30 p.m. for popular shows) each night before the 8 p.m. show. The theater is accessible by the 79th Street en-trance on the East Side and 81st Street entrance on the West. Try to get there before 5:30 p.m. because the tickets run out fast.

When the summer months are over, the Shakespeare Festival returns to its per-manent home at the **Public Theater,** 425 Lafayette St., south of 8th Street and just east of Greenwich Village (tel. 598-7100). The theater's six playhouses, and one cinema, offer high-caliber shows year round by a variety of companies. Among the Shakespeare Festival's most notable productions here were *A Chorus Line* and *The Pirates of Penzance,* which became hits on Broadway. Public Theater tickets cost be-tween $25 and $30 apiece. But one-quarter of the seats are held to be sold at half price the day of the performance. These discount seats, known as Quiktix, are avail-able at 6 p.m. before evening shows and at 1 p.m. on matinee days.

The **Library and Museum of the Performing Arts,** 111 Amsterdam Ave., at 65th Street (tel. 870-1600), is another source of good, free theater. This Lincoln Center branch of the New York Public Library offers plays, solo and chamber concerts, dance programs, musicals, and films from September through June with no admission fees. Monday through Friday performances begin at 4 p.m. On Saturday the show is at 2:30 p.m. Information about current schedules is available at 870-1630 or at any public library branch.

The Performing Arts theater has a rival in the **Manhattan Theater Club,** 453 W. 16th St., between Ninth and Tenth avenues (tel. 645-5590). The club, which now produces its shows at The Space at the City Center, 131 W. 55th St., between Sixth and Seventh avenues (tel. 246-8989), is considered one of the best buys in town. As a member, you subscribe to plays, poetry readings, and musicals. During its Mainstage Season, it premiers plays by well-known contemporary writers performed by such actors as Glenn Close, Bernadette Peters, and Sam Waterston. The best way to see the club's plays is to become a subscriber, or member, by buying a five-play series membership for the September-to-June season. Memberships go for as little as $115 (call 645-5848 for details), and single tickets, which go on sale as each play opens, start at $32.50.

For musicals, comedy, and drama, the **West Side Theater,** at 407 W. 43rd St., between Ninth and Tenth avenues (tel. 541-8394), is a good place to go. Ticket prices average $15 to $27. Recent productions have included *Penn & Teller* and *The Kathy and Mo Show.*

The **Equity Library Theater,** a private theatrical company sponsored in part by the actor's union, gives performances from September to June at the Master's Institute, 103rd Street and Riverside Drive. Performances are Tuesday through Sunday at 8 p.m., with a matinee on Saturday and Sunday. Call 869-9266 for information and reservations. The suggested contribution for tickets is only $10.

The tiny, intimate **Mitzi Newhouse Theater,** on Broadway at 65th Street, in Lincoln Center (tel. 362-7600), should not be overlooked. Recently revived, this 299-seat theater presents contemporary works as well as classic plays rethought. Some of its most notable past productions include Spaulding Gray's *Swimming to Cambodia* and the all-star production of *Waiting for Godot* starring Robin Williams, Steve Martin, Bill Irwin, and F. Murray Abraham. All tickets are $30. Call Telecharge (tel. 239-6200) for tickets.

One inexpensive theater which gets kudos from savvy New Yorkers is the **American Place Theater,** 111 W. 46th St., near Radio City (tel. 840-2960). Since its inception in 1964, the theater has won almost 20 *Village Voice* Obies, awards for outstanding theater outside the mainstream. The theater produces plays by living American playwrights. Its talent list includes such recognized writers as Steve Tesich (who wrote the screenplay for *The World According to Garp*), Jules Feiffer, and Sam Shepard. Tickets cost $24.

For Spanish speakers and students, **Repertorio Español,** 138 E. 27th St., between Lexington and Third avenues (tel. 889-2850), performs classic Spanish works and contemporary Latin American drama, comedies, and musicals. Twice a year the company, which performs in the Gramercy Arts Theater at the same address, features a performance of flamenco dance. Tickets usually run $12 to $23, with a $5 discount available to students and seniors.

You don't have to endure the hustle-bustle of midtown to see some of the best theater the city has to offer. The **Circle Repertory Company,** at 99 Seventh Ave. South (tel. 924-7100), has been delighting audiences with new American plays performed by its highly acclaimed company for 20 years. William Hurt, Christopher Reeve, and John Malkovitch have all been members of this seasoned family of actors. The recipient of over 90 major awards, Circle Rep has dedicated itself to rediscovering the lyric realism of American theater. Landmark productions of plays by, among others, Tennessee Williams, Sam Shepard, and Lanford Wilson have gone on to enjoy extended runs on Broadway. Ticket prices range from $22.50 to $28. For more than 15 years from October through June, the **Ensemble Studio Theatre,** at 549 W. 52nd St., between Tenth and Eleventh avenues (tel. 247-3405), has been one of New York's greatest seedbeds for the development of new American playwrights.

E.S.T.'s yearly season is capped with the marathon of one-acts. Each night from mid-May through mid-June you can see 4 from a roster of 12 new one-act plays from such notables as Christopher Durang and Horton Foote. Ticket prices for the marathon range from $12 to $20, while tickets for the main season are $12 to $18. While you're watching the offerings at E.S.T., don't be surprised if you see some of its more illustrious members at work. Richard Dreyfus, Kevin Bacon, and Andrew McCarthy are all former marathoners.

## Off-Off-Broadway

Many of the off-off-Broadway theaters have gained reputations for producing excellent, innovative shows. Indeed, the theaters' departure from the slick Broadway tradition is considered a selling point by the most sophisticated theater fans. Under a special agreement with the actors' union, known as Actors' Equity, the off-off-Broadway, or "showcase," theaters use only Equity members. Though they work on very low budgets out of about 150 tiny theaters scattered about the city, the off-off-Broadway companies are considered a nurturing ground for up-and-coming actors, directors, and writers. Each year a few showcase productions move to Broadway, where they often achieve critical acclaim. If you're willing to experiment, you may be one of the first to see a Broadway hit or a new star at a relatively low cost.

The **Hudson Guild Theater,** at 441 W. 26th St., and **Playwright Horizons,** at 416 W. 42nd St., both between Ninth and Tenth avenues, also receive good reviews. The Hudson Guild has produced such award winners as *On Golden Pond* and *Da.* The theater's season runs from September to June. Tickets start at $18 and can be reserved by calling 760-9810. Playwright Horizons features new shows by American writers. Among its most notable is Wendy Wasserstein's *Heidi Chronicles,* which moved to Broadway and won a Tony for best play in 1989. Some plays in the process of being written are presented in workshops, free of charge. Tickets, starting at $22, can be reserved at 564-1235.

The **Asia Society,** 725 Park Ave., at 70th Street (tel. 288-6400), a nonprofit organization promoting a better understanding of Asian culture, sponsors both traditional and contemporary performing arts from Asia. Usually performed by visiting Asian artists or by Americans of Asian extraction, the society's performances combine drama, dance, music, and even puppetry. The high quality of its presentations is evidenced by the society's winning of a 1985 Obie for its contribution to off-Broadway theater. Admission to the society's 258-seat auditorium usually costs $6 to $25, although there are a limited number of the best tickets sold at a discount price to students, and some shows are free. Most performances are from September to June, but call for a current schedule.

For theater fans with a penchant for politics, there are two innovative companies sure to be intriguing. The **Veterans' Ensemble Theater Company** (tel. 860-6090) produces plays year round about everything from Agent Orange and the homeless to media involvement in Vietnam. Call for the current schedule and performance locations. The **New Federal Theater Group,** 466 Grand St. (tel. 598-0400), uses minority issues as themes for plays that run from September to June. Tickets for general-admission performances Thursday through Sunday cost $8 to $10. Since they don't have a continuous schedule, call first.

*Note:* For a backstage tour of Broadway, see our "More Sights/Unusual Tours" section in this chapter.

## POETRY/PROSE

As one of the world's publishing centers, New York always has something literary going on, whether it be a poetry reading, a book signing, or a symposium. Often churches, major bookstores, and universities sponsor such events, and generally at little or no charge. The *New York Times* entertainment section, the *Village Voice,* and *New York* magazine are good sources to check for current happenings.

A forum for some of the most highly regarded poets is the Poetry Center of the

**YM-YWHA** (called the 92nd Street Y by New Yorkers), at Lexington Avenue and 92nd Street (tel. 427-6000). Umberto Eco, Mark Strand, Harold Pinter, Gjertrud Schnackenberg, and Eugene Ionesco are among those who have recently read their work there. They follow Dylan Thomas, who made this theater the stage for his fabled readings in the 1950s. There is usually a large and interesting selection of poetry readings and lectures. Tickets, which sell on a first-come, first-served basis (unless you are a member, in which case they are reserved at the beginning of the season) cost $6 and up. Performances are usually on Monday nights from late September to early May.

A $95 membership fee includes admission to all 32 events of the season. On selected Sunday mornings, from October to May, the center also sponsors a lecture series, Biographers and Brunch. For $14 you can enjoy bagels, cream cheese, and fruit salad while listening to literary biographers such as James Atlas, Justin Kaplan, or Ian Hamilton. For a current schedule, check listings in the *New York Times* entertainment section or write to the Poetry Center at the above address.

**PEN,** a writers' organization based at 568 Broadway, near Prince Street (tel. 334-1660), periodically sponsors literary events such as readings and symposia, many of which are free, at its headquarters as well as at other locations around the city. Call for a current schedule.

Many branches of the **New York Public Library,** 455 Fifth Ave., at 42nd Street (tel. 221-7676), sponsor literary readings. Usually the most famous writers can be seen either at the **Donnell Library Center,** 20 W. 53rd St., off Fifth Avenue (tel. 621-0618), or at the **Jefferson Market branch** in the Village, 425 Ave. of the Americas, between 9th and 10th streets (tel. 243-4334). Call or stop by any branch for information.

The **Writer's Voice,** a literary program sponsored by the West Side YMCA, 5 W. 63rd St., between Broadway and Central Park West (tel. 787-6557), offers authors' readings every Friday from October to December and March to May at 8 p.m. All genres from mysteries to poetry are featured, and admission runs $5 to $10, depending on the individual event. The admission price also includes a reception and book party afterward. A $40 membership fee includes admission to all events in either the fall or spring season.

## CONCERTS

Free classical music performances are plentiful in New York. The **Juilliard School,** at Lincoln Center, Broadway at 66th Street (tel. 799-5000), is considered the best music school in the nation, and it offers a wide assortment of free concerts and recitals. Symphony, opera, dance, and chamber music are among the musical performances given most Friday nights at 8 p.m. between September and May. On occasion there is also a weekday performance. Phone 874-7515 for information and schedules.

The **Manhattan School of Music,** 120 Claremont Ave., at 122nd Street and Broadway (tel. 749-2802), is another highly rated music school. It offers free concerts and recitals throughout the week, usually at 5 p.m., from September to May. Call for current schedules. Performances of the faculty and students of **Mannes College of Music,** 150 W. 85th St., between Columbus and Amsterdam avenues (tel. 580-0210), are also open to the public. The free concerts are held September to June, usually at 8 p.m. Call for monthly performance information.

For decades, to play **Carnegie Hall,** West 57th Street at Seventh Avenue (tel. 247-7800), has meant "making it" for classical musicians. Fortunately for music lovers with more taste than money, the hall—which presents orchestras, instrumental and vocal recitals, plus jazz and pop music—offers student rush tickets (also available to seniors) for $5 starting at 6 p.m. the day of performance. Check that day with the box office to be sure tickets will be available. Carnegie Hall is closed mid-July through August. To the left of Carnegie Hall on 57th Street is the former Carnegie Recital Hall. Recently renamed the **Weill Recital Hall,** it presents lesser-known artists for smaller fees than its more famous sibling. Tickets cost $4 to $20, depending on the performance.

**Avery Fisher Hall,** Broadway at 65th Street, in Lincoln Center (tel. 874-2424), is home to the New York Philharmonic, which has its season from September to May. (It also houses many of the main events of the New York Jazz Festival, held every June for ten days.) Student rush tickets go on sale half an hour before performance time, generally on Tuesday and Thursday, and cost $5. The Philharmonic often has open rehearsals on Wednesday or Thursday at 10 a.m., for $4.

The **Alice Tully Hall,** also in Lincoln Center, at 1941 Broadway (tel. 362-1911), presents recitals and chamber music, as well as an end-of-summer jazz series. Because performances there are produced by various individuals and groups, check with the box office for specific shows.

The **Lincoln Center Library,** Amsterdam Avenue at West 65th Street (tel. 870-1630), frequently offers free concerts on Saturday at 2:30 p.m. and weekdays at 4 p.m.

**Merkin Concert Hall** at the Abraham Goodman House, 129 W. 67th St., between Broadway and Amsterdam avenues (tel. 362-8719), is a pleasant, intimate new hall on the concert circuit. Tickets cost $8 to $12, and reduced-price tickets are available to students and seniors. The hall is closed July and August.

**Symphony Space,** 2537 Broadway, at 95th Street (tel. 864-5400), offers a grab bag of concerts with everything from classical to contemporary music. The theater also presents dance, literary readings, and drama. While the price of tickets varies with the performance, it is rarely over $12. James Joyce devotees will want to catch the annual Bloomsday celebration in June, which marks the anniversary of the day chronicled in *Ulysses* with readings from Joyce's works by an all-star cast. In the works is "Wall-to-Wall Gershwin," a 12-hour marathon of free music honoring one of America's greatest composers.

Travelers with children might want to take the kids there to see the very popular Paper Bag Players, a theater troupe for children, during January and February.

Many of the city's major churches, such as **Riverside Church,** 490 Riverside Dr., at 121st Street (tel. 864-2929), the **Cathedral of St. John the Divine,** Amsterdam Avenue at 112th Street (tel. 316-7400), and **Christ and St. Steven's Church,** 120 W. 69th St., between Broadway and Columbus Avenue (tel. 787-2755), sponsor free or low-priced concerts, as do a number of universities and libraries. Our favorite is **St. Peter's Lutheran Church,** 619 Lexington Ave., at 54th Street (tel. 935-2200), where the Jazz Ministry conducts Sunday-night vespers. Call or stop by for information.

The Wall Street area features free lunchtime concerts in some of the city's oldest landmarks. Try **Trinity Church,** on Broadway and Wall Street, on Tuesday, or **St. Paul's Chapel,** at Broadway and Fulton Street, on Monday and Thursday. Call the **Noonday Concert Calendar Hotline** (tel. 606-0747) for details. On Wednesday, take your pastrami on rye over to the **Federal Hall National Memorial,** 26 Wall St. (tel. 264-8711), and enjoy the sunshine and sounds.

Many of the major midtown skyscrapers, such as the **IBM Building,** 590 Madison Ave., at 55th Street (tel. 407-6390), and the **Citicorp Center,** 153 E. 53rd St., at Lexington Avenue (tel. 559-2330), offer free concerts in their atria, especially during lunchtime.

In addition, the **New York Philharmonic** sounds off during the summer on Central Park's Great Lawn and also in other parks in all five boroughs. Some people who attend the concerts think the fireworks that accompany many of the performances are even better than the music! Call the Philharmonic parks hotline (tel. 877-2011) for details.

Watch the skyline of Manhattan as you listen to the music at **Bargemusic,** Fulton Ferry Landing in Brooklyn (tel. 718/624-4061). The enclosed concert space aboard a boat provides a delightful change of musical scenery. The boat doesn't go anywhere, but it bobs up and down when the water gets rough. Concerts are on Thursday at 7:30 p.m. and on Sunday at 4 p.m. Tickets cost $15, $12 for students and seniors.

The **Brooklyn Museum,** Eastern Parkway and Washington Avenue, Brooklyn (tel. 718/638-5000, ext. 312), holds poetry readings as well as concerts. Performances are on Sunday from October to April. Call for specific schedules. To reach the museum, take the IRT–Seventh Avenue express subway (no. 2 or 3) or the IRT–Lexington Avenue no. 4 express train to Eastern Parkway, the Brooklyn Museum station.

The **Concert Theatre Club,** 2067 Broadway, Room 45 (tel. 718/855-9293), is one of the best ways to get inexpensive concert tickets. The $30, 12-month membership fee allows you two orchestra tickets to at least 100 concerts at Avery Fisher Hall, Alice Tully Hall, and Carnegie Hall. Members also get half-price tickets—known as twofers—to most Broadway and off-Broadway shows, and substantial discounts at a number of movie theaters and restaurants.

## OPERA

Some of the finest opera in New York is also inexpensive. The very popular **New York City Opera** at the New York State Theater, Lincoln Center, 64th Street and Broadway (tel. 870-5570), sells tickets for as little as $5. Check the *New York Times* or *New York* magazine for listings.

The **Amato Opera Theater** performs at 319 Bowery, near East 2nd Street (tel. 228-8200), featuring younger performers in the popular opera repertoire. Tickets for the 50 operas in its repertoire cost $15 per show.

The **Village Light Opera Group** puts on two shows a year at the Fashion Institute of Technology's main auditorium, 227 W. 27th St., at Seventh Avenue (tel. 563-1771). The fall show is typically a Gilbert and Sullivan operetta, while the spring show is either an operetta or a musical, such as *Brigadoon,* that comes close. The group does six performances of each show, with tickets costing $10 to $20.

The **Brooklyn Lyric Opera** (tel. 718/837-1176) produces four operas a year in the 400-seat Hirsch Hall at Temple Ansche Chesed, at 100th Street and West End Avenue. They also offer showcase productions, featuring rising opera talents. Tickets cost $10, with reduced rates for children, students, and seniors.

### The Metropolitan Opera

The Metropolitan Opera House, Lincoln Center, 64th Street and Broadway (tel. 362-6000), houses one of the finest opera companies in the world. In its modern and quite awesome theater, the company performs classics with an occasional foray into modern pieces. Performers include such internationally acclaimed operatic stars as Luciano Pavarotti, Placido Domingo, Mirella Freni, and Marilyn Horne. A trip to the opera is an expensive evening, but there are bargains to be found. The company offers free summertime concerts in Central Park, which are noted in local newspapers. The only regular bargains are the $8 to $11 standing-room tickets, which go on sale the Saturday before the performance. We recommend arriving two hours before the box office opens because lines are long and tickets sell fast. Other tickets range in price from $18 to $95 (for orchestra seats). Reservations can be made by phone for a $2 handling charge per ticket. The box office is open Monday through Saturday between 10 a.m. and 8 p.m., and on Sunday from noon to 8 p.m.

### BAM Opera

The Brooklyn Academy of Music (BAM) Opera, 30 Lafayette Ave., Brooklyn (tel. 718/636-4100), began its inaugural season in 1989 with a royal bang. With the Welsh National Opera on stage and Princess Di in the audience, BAM presented a remarkable production of *Falstaff*. During its first season, BAM also presented the Paris Opera in the first production in more than 200 years of Jean-Baptiste Lully's *Atys,* and Peter Sellars's *Das Kleine Mahagonny*. Upcoming BAM Opera productions will feature contemporary opera, unfamiliar and neglected works from the past, and new, fresh musical interpretations of more familiar operas.

Although BAM has not had a regular opera season since the 1920s, it staged its first opera in 1861, more than 20 years before the heralded Metropolitan Opera was founded. The innovation and excitement generated by the new BAM Opera has reverberated throughout New York's opera community. In the spring of 1991 the MET/BAM Project of opera co-productions will begin. This project will see the Metropolitan Opera visit Brooklyn for the first time in more than 50 years to mount experimental productions in the small, 900-seat Majestic Theater.

BAM Opera performs February to June. Tickets run $15 to $50. Call the BAM ticket office for details.

## DANCE

From the Rockettes to Nureyev, from Alvin Ailey to the Paul Taylor Dance Company, New York City is the apex of dance in the nation and the world. The city helped pioneer theatrical dance in the early 20th century, modern dance in the 1950s, and is still a beacon for the great names in dance. A typically glittering season includes visits by touring international troupes, from the Royal Danish Ballet to the Stuttgart Ballet. And we have our own New York City Ballet and the American Ballet Theater, as well as many smaller companies, covering everything from classical ballet to the experimental.

The **American Ballet Theater,** under the direction of the renowned Mikhail Baryshnikov, is the resident company at the Metropolitan Opera House (tel. 362-6000). The ABT presents classics like *Swan Lake* as well as new ballets by Mark Morris, Paul Taylor, and Twyla Tharp, among others. Generally, the ballet and opera companies keep the opera house busy year round, with the lights dimming only for August vacation.

Ticket prices for the ABT go as high as $52. You can ask for lower-priced balcony seats ($18 or $20), or top-of-the-house Family Circle tickets (bring opera glasses!) for $10 or $14. Standing-room tickets ($7 or $11) are sold the day of the performance, starting when the box office opens at 10 a.m. (at noon on Saturday); but be forewarned that many fans come at dawn with coffee and blankets in the hope of getting tickets.

The **New York City Ballet,** founded by the renowned George Balanchine, performs at the New York State Theater in Lincoln Center (tel. 870-5570). The spring season is all of May and June, and from November to February in winter. *The Nutcracker* is performed all December. Ticket prices at the New York City Ballet range from $6 to $45, with standing room going for $5 on the day of performance.

Justly famous as they are, the ABT and the New York City Ballet are far from the only dance performance options. We have listed a variety of other New York City troupes, from the new to the well known.

The **City Center,** 131 W. 55th St., between Sixth and Seventh avenues (tel. 581-7907), is in a landmark building that was once a Masonic temple. The City Center is the place to see performances by innovative American companies like the Paul Taylor Dance Company, Alvin Ailey, Merce Cunningham, the Dance Theater of Harlem, and companies from abroad. Tickets are generally priced between $15 and $40.

The bright new **Joyce Theater,** 175 Eighth Ave., at 19th Street (tel. 242-0800), has given a boost both to its Chelsea neighborhood and to the dance-going public. The theater stocks its fall and spring seasons with such performers as the Feld Ballet, the Laura Dean Dancers, and the American Ballroom Theater. Subscribers save 40% on ticket prices and also receive 2-for-1 discounts at Chelsea restaurants. Ticket prices vary with each performance, but are generally between $10 and $25.

The 125-year-old **Brooklyn Academy of Music,** 30 Lafayette Ave., in Brooklyn (tel. 718/636-4100), is well respected for its presentations of ballet and modern dance. Recently, BAM has garnered national attention for its Next Wave festival, an October-to-December celebration of new and avant garde in dance, music, and theater. The 1989 program included performances by Laurie Anderson and a tribute to Andy Warhol by Lou Reed and John Cale. BAM tickets cost $12 to $45.

The **Theater at Riverside Church,** 490 Riverside Dr., at 120th Street (tel. 864-2929), is one of the many cultural and other activities sponsored by this busy church. The theater highlights many types of dance and operates year round. General admission is around $10, with discounts for students and seniors. Come early enough to look around the church.

The **Martha Graham Center of Contemporary Dance,** 316 E. 63rd St., between First and Second avenues (tel. 832-9166), comprises the country's oldest dance company (founded in 1926 by the great lady herself, who still acts as its director) as well as a school where students are drawn from 30 different countries. The company generally performs a fall season at the City Center, 131 W. 55th St., between Sixth and Seventh avenues. Tickets to regular performances cost $10 to $40. Studio performances—which feature students and company members—are occasionally open to the public, and are either free or cost only $2 or $3. Call the center to see if there is a performance scheduled during your stay.

**Performance Space 122,** 150 First Ave., at East 9th Street (tel. 477-5288)—formerly P.S. (Public School) 122—features mostly experimental works in dance, theater, and music. Current offerings are always listed in the *Village Voice,* and tickets cost $4 for afternoon performances, $7 to $8 evenings.

**The Kitchen,** 512 W. 19th St., between Tenth and Eleventh avenues (tel. 255-5793), presents a similar array of dance, music, and performance art. Ticket prices range from $8 to $10, depending on the performance.

**Dance Theater Workshop,** at 219 W. 19th St., between Seventh and Eighth avenues (tel. 924-0077), is both a performance space for established artists and a forum for new choreographers and dancers. The workshop offers regular performances year round, including "Fresh Tracks," a program of five or six new works by up-and-coming choreographers. Tickets are $12 for 8 p.m. performances and $10 for 11 p.m. performances.

The world-famous **Dance Theater of Harlem,** 466 W. 152nd St., between Amsterdam and St. Nicholas avenues (tel. 967-3470), was founded in 1969 by Arthur Mitchell and Karel Shook as Mitchell's personal commitment to the people of Harlem following the assassination of Martin Luther King, Jr. It comprises both the renowned ballet company, which tours the world and performs at various New York theaters, and a school of allied arts. If you catch the company while it's in town, you're in for an impressive show, generally for prices that run $15 to $40. If you don't catch them, you might want to attend one of the school's open houses, which take place at 3 p.m. the second Sunday of every month from November to May. Depending on who's in town at the time, students and company and workshop ensemble members perform. Admission is only $3 for adults and $1.50 for children.

The **Danspace Project,** at St. Marks-in-the-Bowery, Second Avenue and East 10th Street (tel. 674-8112), sponsors a variety of dance performances in this historic corner church from October through June. Shows begin at 8:30 p.m., and cost $6.

The Great Hall program at the **Cooper Union,** 41 Cooper Square, at Third Avenue and East 7th Street (tel. 353-4155), includes free dance performances during fall and spring. Call to see what's scheduled.

Of course you'll find that dance activities change week by week. Check the newspapers and local magazines, especially the *Village Voice* and *New York* magazine, when you arrive. Chances are you'll find something interesting.

And before you call the box office, consider these money-saving tips: Some companies have "rush" tickets, sold at discount the day of performance to senior citizens and students with identification. Not all box offices have this, but if you qualify, ask! Both New York City Opera and Ballet give group discounts on tickets sold in blocks of 20 or more to some performances, but this must be established in advance.

Finally, try the **Bryant Park Music and Dance Tickets Booth,** at 42nd Street just east of the Avenue of the Americas, at the edge of Bryant Park, for low-priced ballet and concert tickets to events at such places as Lincoln Center, Carnegie Hall, and the 92nd Street Y. Tickets are sold on the day of performance at half price, with a small service charge. The booth is open on Tuesday, Thursday, and Friday from noon to 7 p.m., on Wednesday and Saturday from 11 a.m. to 7 p.m., and on Sunday from noon to 6 p.m. Call 382-2323 after 12:30 p.m. for information on ticket availability.

---

# 4. Entertainment

---

## TELEVISION

TV people are always looking for audiences to fill up their studios. Unfortunately for us, Hollywood has lured a lot of the entertainment industry away from New York, so there aren't nearly as many shows to visit now as there were in the early days of television. Participating in a studio audience is always a fun way to see how a show is produced, so it's worth a try to find a show that's open. Unless you're very lucky and see a network employee handing out tickets in Rockefeller Center on a weekday afternoon (which has happened to us), your best bet is to write to the studios well in advance. And there's another attraction to these studio broadcasts— they're absolutely free!

Below are the procedures the networks have set up for obtaining tickets.

### National Broadcasting Company (Channel 4)

NBC, located at 30 Rockefeller Plaza with an entrance on West 49th Street under the familiar peacock sign (tel. 664-3055), asks that you write ahead because some shows have long waiting lists. NBC has several popular shows based in Manhattan: "Late Night with David Letterman," "Saturday Night Live," "Donahue," and "The Cosby Show." To write for tickets, address your request to NBC Tickets (name of show requested), 30 Rockefeller Plaza, New York, NY 10112 (postcards only). There is a limit of two tickets per request, and you must be at least 16 years old to get into the studio. NBC doesn't air many pilots, and tickets for those pilots are usually given out the day before airing.

### American Broadcasting Company (Channel 7)

ABC, at 1330 Ave. of the Americas, also asks for a written request as much as ten months in advance. Requests, with a specific date, should be sent to ABC Guest Relations, 36A W. 66th St., New York, NY 10023 (not the Avenue of the Americas address). At press time, ABC ticketholders were invited to watch "The Morning Show," a talk show airing at 9 a.m. You, the audience, arrive at 8 a.m. ABC shoots its TV pilots in the summer. Call 887-3537 the day before you go to see if there's a show.

### Columbia Broadcasting System (Channel 2)

CBS, at 51 W. 52nd St., between Fifth and Sixth avenues, is housed in a black-glass tower sometimes called "Black Rock." CBS no longer tapes live shows in New

York, but they still film many of their pilots before live studio audiences. Look for CBS employees in blue blazers handing out tickets along Sixth Avenue or call 877-3537 for information about upcoming programs.

## MOVIES—FIRST RUN, CLASSIC, AND OTHERWISE

No city in the world has a selection of films comparable to New York's. As could be expected, there are a number of places where the cinema buff can see first-run films from the U.S. and abroad. Classic, avant-garde, and documentary films are screened at museums for the price of admission.

The **Museum of Modern Art,** 11 W. 53rd St., just west of Fifth Avenue (tel. 708-9490), screens film classics from their own fine collection as well as from other sources. The museum admission ($6 for adults, $3.50 for students, $3 for seniors) entitles you to admittance to the screening. The museum has two theaters, Titus 1 and Titus 2, and films are shown every day (except Wednesday when the museum is closed) in the early afternoon and early evening. Call for current schedules.

The New American Film and Video Series at the **Whitney Museum,** 945 Madison Ave., at 75th Street (tel. 570-0537), is one of the most important showcases for new, independent American film and video makers in the nation. The series features avant-garde, documentary, and feature films that are not apt to be shown in commercial theaters. Films are shown daily (except Monday when the museum is closed) each afternoon and on Tuesday evenings, but not in the summer. The Whitney also screens experimental videos and films in its second-floor film and video gallery. (Check the museum's daily calendar for titles and showing times.) The $4.50 admission charge gets you in to both the museum and the film series.

Also at the **Whitney Museum** is the Films and Video on Art Series, sponsored by the education department. This special summer series on artists and art movements is usually held every day in July or August (except Monday when the museum is closed).

The **American Museum of the Moving Image,** 35th Avenue at 36th Street, Astoria, Queens (tel. 718/784-0077), moved into the renovated former Paramount Pictures studio in the fall of 1988. The museum presents more than 700 film and video screenings annually in its two theaters, the 195-seat Riklis Theater, and the smaller 60-seat Warner Communications Screening Room. The programs range from silent films and Hollywood classics to experimental videos and animated works for children. Films are shown every day (except Monday when the museum is closed). The museum admission ($5 for adults, $2.50 for seniors and students) entitles you to admittance to the screenings. It is open from 11 a.m. to 5 p.m. Tuesday through Friday, and 11 a.m. to 6 p.m. on Saturday and Sunday. Call for a current schedule.

The **Donnell Library Media Center,** 20 W. 53rd St., a public library branch between Fifth and Sixth avenues, has a large collection of movies, and you can check out feature films as well as shorts with a permanent library card. You must, however, reserve most films in advance. Call 621-0609 to find out what's available. There are free screenings in the Donnell Auditorium, with frequent showings of documentaries, comedy classics, and children's movies. You can also request to screen film and video features in the study center. Call 621-0611 to make an appointment. A copy of the bimonthly publication *Events,* available free at the Donnell or any public library branch, lists current showings.

The **New York Public Library,** at 42nd Street and Fifth Avenue, and many of its 81 branches present free film programs, readings, and musical events throughout the year. Again, consult the publication *Events,* or call the library's public relations office at 221-7676.

The **American Museum of Natural History,** Central Park West between 77th and 81st streets (tel. 769-5100), presents anthropological and travel films in its auditorium at various times during the week. Your contribution upon entering the museum is the only cost. The museum also shows films in its Naturemax Theater.

The screen is 4 stories high and 66 feet wide, and is one of 12 of its kind in the Western Hemisphere. During the week, Naturemax screenings are every hour from 10:30 a.m. to 4:30 p.m.; on the weekends, to 7:30 p.m. Admission is $4 for adults, $2 for children.

Exceptional Japanese films, not readily available elsewhere, are regularly shown at the **Japan Society,** 333 E. 47th St., between First and Second avenues (tel. 752-0824). Screenings are usually on Friday at 6:30 p.m. from October to June. Admission is $6 for adults, $4.50 for students and seniors. All films are in Japanese with English subtitles.

The **French Institute,** 22 E. 60th St., just east of Fifth Avenue (tel. 355-6100), also presents films from abroad that are unlikely to gain commercial release in this country. Call for schedules and prices.

Free documentary films of topical interest are shown on Saturday and Sunday at 2 p.m. at the **Public Theater,** 425 Lafayette St., near Astor Place (tel. 598-7171). Ticket distribution begins at 1 p.m. Documentary and feature films are also shown every day except Monday. Tickets cost $5, $4 for students and seniors. Call for show times.

The **Millennium Media Center,** 66 E. 4th St., between Second Avenue and the Bowery (tel. 673-0090), includes an avant-garde film series, usually on weekend evenings but not in the summer. Filmmakers are often present to show and discuss their work. A contribution of $5 is asked for.

The **Collective for Living Cinema,** 41 White St., between Church Street and Broadway (tel. 925-2111), features new and old experimental films every night at 8 p.m. Admission is $5.

The **Film Forum,** 57 Watts St., two blocks north of Canal at Sixth Avenue (tel. 431-1590), offers foreign and art films and documentaries in one theater, and revivals and retrospectives in the second. Before, between, or after shows, you can enjoy fresh cake and cappuccino at the snackbar.

The **8th Street Playhouse,** 52 W. 8th St., between Fifth and Sixth avenues (tel. 674-6515), frequently runs festivals, such as an annual 3-D movie festival, and always has midnight showings of cult classics like the *Rocky Horror Picture Show* and *A Clockwork Orange,* as well as first-run features. Call for exact times of shows, prices, and current listings.

Other recommended theaters that regularly feature classic, foreign, and avant-garde films and retrospectives, are the **Thalia SoHo,** 15 Vandam St., between Sixth and Seventh avenues (tel. 675-0498); the **Bleecker St. Cinema,** 144 Bleecker St., between LaGuardia Place and Thompson Street (tel. 674-2560); **Cinema Village,** on 12th Street, east of Fifth Avenue (tel. 924-3363); and **Theater 80,** 80 St. Marks Pl., near First Avenue (tel. 254-7400).

Finally, not a week goes by without a special screening or film festival somewhere in the city. Check the weekly listings in the *Village Voice* or the Sunday *New York Times* for information.

## 5. Zoos and Botanical Gardens

The world-famous **Bronx Zoo** serves both as a fascinating educational and recreational center for animal lovers of all ages, and as one of the world's most successful repository/breeding centers for the earth's diminishing wildlife. With 265 acres, it's the largest urban zoo in the U.S. and is home to 4,500 wild animals. Among them are 75 species considered endangered and 4 species officially extinct in nature (look for them: Père David's deer, Mongolian wild horses, Formosan Sika deer, and the European bison). Each year there are more than 1,000 births among the zoo's animal population; other zoos throughout the country—and even the world—look to the Bronx Zoo for new acquisitions.

One of the zoo's most popular features is Wild Asia, an exciting 38 acres in which 19 species of Asian animals roam an open expanse of land cultivated to simulate their natural environment. The area, open May through October, is accessible only by monorail ($1.50 for adults, $1 for children), with a 22-minute tour narrated by a knowledgeable guide. Wild Asia hosts Siberian tigers, Asian elephants, gaur (the world's largest wild cattle), and axis deer, all of which pass before the windows of the monorail. One of the zoo's most ambitious projects is the award-winning Jungle World, a one-acre wood- and glass-enclosed habitat in which animals wander more or less freely through a re-created volcanic scrub forest, a mangrove swamp, a lowland evergreen rain forest, and a mountain rain forest. It uses an artful combination of real and artificial elements to simulate the natural habitats of the species it contains. Jungle World is open year round.

The zoo's newest feature is the Keith W. Johnson Zoo Center, home to Asian elephants and rhinoceroses. The Himalayan Highland Habitat is a 2½-acre haven for the endangered snow leopard, considered by many to be the most beautiful of the big cats. The habitat is built to resemble the mountainous terrain of northern India, Nepal, and Tibet, and is also home to red pandas, white-naped cranes, and pheasant.

One of the zoo's unique attractions is its participatory Children's Zoo, open from March through October. Here, youngsters can don giant fox ears and turtle shells, climb a giant rope spider web, and crawl through a prairie dog tunnel to see what it's like to be an animal. For an overview of the zoo, take the Safari train (closed in winter); to get from one end of the zoo to the other quickly, board the Skyfari tramway (also closed in winter). But for real excitement, climb atop a camel for the ride of your life.

You can easily spend an entire day at the zoo; and for those who do, there's a cafeteria with reasonably priced meals, snackbars throughout the park that stock traditional zoo fare—hot dogs, hamburgers, and sodas—or you can pack a lunch and eat at picnic tables.

Zoo hours are 10 a.m. to 5 p.m. Monday through Saturday, to 5:30 p.m. on Sunday and holidays (closes at 4:30 p.m. daily during the winter months). Admission is free Tuesday through Thursday; other days it's $3.75 for adults, $1.50 for children 2 to 12, and free for children under 2 and senior citizens. Rides and tours charge fees throughout the week. To get to the zoo by subway from Manhattan, take the IRT–Seventh Avenue no. 2 train or the IRT–Lexington Avenue no. 5 express to Pelham Parkway and proceed west to the Bronxdale entrance. Liberty Lines provides express bus service from stops in Manhattan on Madison Avenue (call 652-8400 for schedule and stops); the fare is $3.50 and you must have the exact change.

Near the zoo, but a healthy walk away, is the **New York Botanical Garden,** 200th Street and Southern Boulevard, Bronx Park. It is a lovely 250 acres of woods and waterways, lawns and carefully cultivated gardens, and a spectacular glass conservatory. Here, for a good part of a day, you can lose the sights of the city—if not its sounds—and you might even get lost yourself. Stroll through Rhododendron Valley or down Azalea Way, resplendent in middle to late May. Roam a 40-acre hemlock forest—the only uncut woodland in New York City. Follow the path along the Bronx River, past a waterfall to a restored 19th-century mill that now houses a riverside café. Above all, don't miss the famous Enid A. Haupt Conservatory, an acre of gardens in a gorgeous crystal palace, inspired by the 1844 Palm House of the Royal Botanic Gardens at Kew, England. Admission to the conservatory is $2.50 for adults, $1.25 for children; free on Saturday morning. Open Tuesday through Sunday from 10 a.m. to 4 p.m.

The museum building houses a gift shop for plant fanciers, and for the serious student of flora, one of the largest horticultural libraries in the world (open on Monday, Wednesday, and Friday from 9:30 a.m. to 4 p.m., and on Tuesday and Thursday from 9:30 a.m. to 8 p.m.). The garden grounds are open from 8 a.m. to 7 p.m. April through October and from 8 a.m. to 6 p.m. November through March. Call 220-8700 for information. By subway, take the IRT–Lexington Ave. no. 4 train to 200th Street and Jerome Avenue; on the IND–Sixth Avenue D train, ride to Bedford Park Boulevard. By railroad, take the Metro North Harlem local from Grand Central Terminal to the Botanical Garden Station.

The old **Central Park Zoo,** off Fifth Avenue at 64th Street, has been thoroughly renovated by the New York Zoological Society (creators of the wonderful Bronx Zoo). Visitors to the new, state-of-the-art zoo can wander through three "biomes" under the protection of a glass-covered colonnade. In the *polar zone,* a pool with windows gives visitors an underwater view of swimming polar bears. In the *tropic zone,* toucans and other birds fly freely in a giant aviary. In the *temperate zone,* Japanese snow monkeys live on an island habitat re-created expressly for them. The zoo has a cafeteria with indoor and outdoor seating, and a gift shop.

To get to the Central Park Zoo, take the IRT–Lexington Avenue local (no. 6) train to 68th Street and walk west to Fifth Avenue to enter the park. The zoo is open 365 days a year: from May to September, daily from 10 a.m. to 4 p.m. (until 7:30 p.m. on Tuesday); from October to April, daily from 10 a.m. to 4:30 p.m. (until 5 p.m. on weekends and holidays). Admission is $1 for adults, 50¢ for senior citizens, 25¢ for children 3 to 12, and free for children under 3.

While you're there, you might want to take your kids to **Lehman's Children's Zoo,** in Central Park just off 66th Street and Fifth Avenue. The zoo features playhouses in the style of a castle (home to the zoo's goats) and a barn (home to a donkey, cow, and barnyard birds that roam at will). There's also an awe-inspiring giant whale. Admission is an inflation-proof 10¢. Open daily from 10 a.m. to 4:30 p.m. For information call 408-0271.

Though outsized and outscoped by the Bronx gardens, the **Brooklyn Botanic Garden,** just east of Prospect Park, is nevertheless among the nation's leading botanical gardens. Reclaimed from a waste dump in 1910, the garden's 52 acres are densely planted with more than 12,000 types of vegetation. Most famous is the Japanese Hill-and-Pond Garden. In April and May the spectacle of masses of flowering cherry trees and fragrant magnolias is a sight to behold. The Rose Garden, at its peaks in June and September, is the third-largest public collection of roses on display in the U.S., boasting over 1,000 varieties. There is also a herb garden, a fragrance garden for the blind, a fresh fruit and vegetable garden grown by children, and a Shakespeare garden—carpeted with the violets, rosemary, chamomile, and other plants from the Bard's plays and sonnets.

The Garden's three-pavilion conservatory features desert, tropical, and temperate houses, as well as exotic bonsai, orchid, and aquatic houses. The complex also houses a restaurant and gift shop. From April to September the grounds are open Tuesday through Friday from 8 a.m. to 6 p.m. and on Saturday and Sunday from 10 a.m. to 6 p.m. (closed Monday); from March to October closing time is 4:30 p.m. Guided tours leave every Sunday from the administration building at 1 p.m. For information, call 718/622-4433. To get to the garden, take the IRT–Seventh Avenue express (no. 2 or 3) train or the IRT–Lexington Avenue no. 4 express to the Eastern Parkway station.

Popular as a pastoral respite for local residents, and worth a visit if you're in the borough, is the **Queens Botanical Gardens,** 43-50 Main St., in Flushing (tel. 718/886-3800). The gardens were built upon land recovered from use as a garbage dump, and the transformation has been complete. The 38 acres are planted with rose gardens (more than 8,000 bushes), a Victorian "wedding garden" (available by appointment for the big event), a crab apple grove, and an "all-American" display of native North American plants. Year round there are lectures and workshops open to the public. The garden boasts the largest display of European-style annuals in the U.S. Especially great for kids are the bird garden and the bee garden with an observatory hive. A plant shop on the grounds offers indoor and outdoor flora and gardening items.

The gardens are open from 9 a.m. to dusk. To get there from Manhattan by subway, take the IRT–Flushing line (no. 7 train) from Times Square or Grand Central, and get off at the last station, Main Street. Then take the Q44 bus south—or walk ten minutes—down Main Street to the Botanical Gardens on the right.

High on the banks of the Hudson River, in the hilly, tranquil Riverdale section of the Bronx, is the **Wave Hill** estate and public garden, at West 249th Street and Independence Avenue, the Bronx. Once home to the likes of Mark Twain, Theodore Roosevelt, and Arturo Toscanini, the 28-acre estate is now a public garden and cultural center with programs in education, garden history, and the visual and performing arts. For aspirants to the country-estate "good life" or just city-weary travelers, a visit to Wave Hill—with its manicured grounds, historic houses, and sweeping view of the Hudson River and the Palisades—is well worth the 45-minute bus and subway ride (30 minutes by car) it takes to get there. Built in 1843, the estate served for more than a century as home to various eminent Americans and foreign dignitaries. It was presented to the City of New York in 1960 by its last owners.

Today visitors can explore its four greenhouses, nature trails, formal and wild gardens, herb and aquatic gardens, and the only public alpine house east of the Rockies. In summer and fall Wave Hill hosts concerts and outdoor theater; year round there are lectures, and garden and bird walks; on Sunday at 2:15 p.m. there are guided greenhouse and garden tours. Wave Hill also boasts an archive of rare commercial recordings of Toscanini, as well as memorabilia from the maestro. Call 549-2055 for information on scheduling of events.

The estate is open daily from 10 a.m. to 4:30 p.m. (from Memorial Day to Labor Day, to 5:30 p.m.); on summer Wednesdays, to sunset; on summer Sundays, from 10 a.m. to 7 p.m. Admission is free Monday through Friday; on Saturday and Sunday, $1 for adults, 50¢ for seniors and students, and free for children under 14. Indoor and outdoor concerts and dance performances, scheduled intermittently, are frequently on Saturday and Sunday afternoons, with admissions running from $4 to $9. Express bus service is provided by Liberty Lines from mid-Manhattan via both the East and West Sides. Have the exact fare ready: $3.50. Call 652-8400 for Liberty's Manhattan Riverdale Express bus schedule.

*Note:* Both the **Queens Zoo,** in Flushing Meadows (tel. 718/699-7239), and the **Brooklyn Zoo,** in Prospect Park (tel. 718/965-6560), are closed for renovations until the early 1990s.

# 6. Sports and Recreational Facilities

## APPLE PICKING

North of the city, within a two-hour drive, are a number of apple orchards where you can pick your own apples in September and October. Always call ahead for hours and prices. Among others, there is **Outhouse Orchards** in Croton Falls (tel. 914/277-3188), which is also our favorite for fresh-picked vegetables and homemade preserves, and **Wilkens Fruit Farm** in Yorktown (tel. 914/245-5111).

## BASEBALL

Baseball took over from horseracing as New York's most popular spectator sport in 1986 when the **New York Mets** won the World Series. You can see the Mets at Shea Stadium in Queens, where they play from April to October. Tickets start at $6, and the box office opens two hours before game time. Call 718/507-8499 for ticket information. You can reach Shea Stadium by taking the no. 7 IRT–Flushing train to the Shea Stadium stop.

American League fans can catch the **New York Yankees** at Yankee Stadium in the Bronx (tel. 293-6000). The Bronx Bombers and their controversial owner, George Steinbrenner, are guaranteed to entertain the fans both on the field and off. Tickets start at $4.50 for bleacher seats and go on sale two hours before the game. Box seats are on sale at the stadium ticket office. To reach Yankee Stadium, take the IND–Sixth Avenue D train or the IRT–Lexington Avenue no. 4 train (marked "Woodlawn") to the Yankee Stadium stop.

## BASKETBALL

For basketball fans, New York is a great town. Professionally, the **New York Knickerbockers** (the Knicks) play at Madison Square Garden from November through April (tel. 563-8300). After years of mediocrity, the Knicks won the Eastern Conference title in 1989 with their best record since the fabled 1971–1972 championship season. Patrick Ewing and company have established themselves as a force to be reckoned with in the 1990s. Tickets, which are hard to come by, start at $10. Reach the Garden by taking the IRT–Seventh Avenue no. 1, 2, or 3 train to the 34th Street–Pennsylvania Station stop.

The **New Jersey Nets** play at the Brendan Byrne Arena at the Meadowlands Sports Complex, East Rutherford, New Jersey (tel. 201/935-8888). Ticket prices start at $6. The arena is only a short bus trip from the Port Authority Bus Terminal (at Eighth Avenue and 42nd Street), and special buses run regularly on game nights.

On the college level, Madison Square Garden is also the home of the famous postseason **N.I.T.** collegiate tournaments. The tournaments are held in November and March and attract top college teams from around the nation. Call the Garden for ticket information.

## BICYCLING

During the warm-weather months, Central Park's many bike trails and wide park roads (which are closed to traffic on weekends) are jammed with cyclists. You can rent a bike at the **Loeb Boathouse,** Park Drive North at 72nd Street (tel. 861-4137), for $6 per hour or $24 for the whole day. If you go a few blocks away from the park, you can rent a bike for about $4 an hour ($6.50 an hour for a ten-speed) at **West Side Bicycle Store,** 231 W. 96th St., at Broadway (tel. 663-7531); **Metro Bicycles,** 1311 Lexington Ave., at 88th Street (tel. 427-4450); or **Gene's Bicycles,** 242 E. 79th St., at Second Avenue (tel. 249-9218), where after the first 3½ hours, the rest of the day is free. All the above businesses require identification and/or a substantial deposit. Call for details.

From early spring until well into the fall, **American Youth Hostels,** 75 Spring St., between Broadway and Lafayette Street (tel. 431-7100), organizes weekly bicycle tours (from $50 to $250) of the city and outlying areas. The tours are led by an experienced leader and are a great way to see the city. Call AYH for details and a schedule.

## BOATING

Rent a rowboat at Central Park's **Loeb Boathouse,** Park Drive North at 72nd Street (tel. 517-4723). From April until winter, you can drift along the lake and enjoy the beauty of Central Park from the water. It's only $6 an hour, but you must leave a $20 deposit.

If you prefer sailing on a 70-foot yawl, the **Petrel,** which is the fastest sailboat in New York Harbor, sails from the southeast corner of Battery Park, (tel. 825-1977), near the Statue of Liberty excursion lines. Prices range from $8 for 45 minutes to $20 for two hours. Open April through October.

## BOXING

Madison Square Garden stages pro boxing bouts twice a month on Thursday nights and occasionally a championship fight. The Felt Forum, a part of the Garden sports complex, also hosts the annual Golden Gloves amateur tournament, held in March or April. Phone 563-8164 for details on upcoming matches.

## FOOTBALL

The **New York Jets** are still nominally New York's home team even though they've left (some say deserted) Shea Stadium for the newer Giants Stadium in the Meadowlands Sports Complex across the river in New Jersey (tel. 201/935-8222). The Jets, who play from September to December, have plenty of company, as the **New York Giants** also play there. Tickets for the Jets start at $22.50, and those for the Giants at $23, but they're hard to come by in the former case and nearly impossible in the latter, because of all the season-ticket holders. Tickets for pre-season games in August are easier to get.

## HOCKEY

The competition between the **Islanders** and the **Rangers** makes New York a great place for rabid hockey fans. See the Rangers at Madison Square Garden (tel. 563-8136), with tickets starting at $11. The Islanders skate at the Nassau Coliseum, Hempstead Turnpike, Uniondale, N.Y. (tel. 516/587-9222), where tickets start at $10. To reach the Coliseum, take the Long Island Rail Road from Penn Station to Hempstead, and then take a bus from there (ask at the Hempstead station for directions to the bus), or take the train to Westbury and a taxi to the Coliseum.

## HORSERACING

New York's second most popular spectator sport is available year round. **Belmont Park,** Hempstead Turnpike and Plainfield Avenue, Elmont, N.Y. (tel. 718/641-4700), races thoroughbreds from May through July and September through mid-October. The Long Island Railroad goes to Belmont from Penn Station.

**Aqueduct Racetrack,** Rockaway Boulevard at 108th Street, Jamaica, Queens (tel. 718/641-4700), presents thoroughbred racing from mid-October through May.

The **Meadowlands Racetrack,** in East Rutherford, N.J. (tel. 201/935-8500), also races thoroughbreds September through mid-December and presents trotters late December through August, plus simulcasts other tracks year round.

**Yonkers Raceway,** in Yonkers, N.Y. (tel. 914/968-4200), races trotters year round, plus carries the simulcast from the various New York tracks during the day.

Most of the tracks have special bus service from the Port Authority Bus Terminal, 42nd Street and Eighth Avenue in Manhattan. For Aqueduct, take the IND–Eighth Avenue A train or the JFK special to the Aqueduct station.

## RIDING

The **Claremont Riding Academy,** 175 W. 89th St., between Columbus and Amsterdam avenues (tel. 724-5100), will provide you with a horse for cantering on the nearby Central Park bridle path. The cost is $27 an hour and you must be experienced riding in an English saddle. They also give riding lessons. It's open seven days a week: from 6:30 a.m. to 10 p.m. weekdays and 8 a.m. to 5 p.m. on weekends. Reservations are recommended for weekend rides.

## RUNNING

Contact the **New York Road Runners Club,** 9 E. 89th St., between Fifth and Madison avenues (tel. 860-4455), for information concerning evening group runs in Central Park and races ranging from short runs through Central Park to full-fledged marathons. (The Road Runners sponsor the annual New York City Marathon in November.)

## SKATING

Indoor ice skating is available year round at the **Sky Rink**—billed as the world's highest rink—located on the 16th floor at 450 W. 33rd St., between Ninth and Tenth avenues (tel. 695-6556). Admission is $6.50 during the day, $7 in the evening, plus $2.50 for skate rental.

A winter tradition is a whirl around the ice at the **Rockefeller Center Ice-Skating Rink** (tel. 757-5731). Few things are as enjoyable as skating around the giant Rockefeller Center Christmas tree on a brisk winter's evening. Sessions are $7 to $9, plus $4 for skate rental. The rink is open October through April.

The newly renovated **Wollman Rink** at 63rd Street and East Drive in Central Park is open from November to early April. Admission is $5 for adults and $2 for children, plus $2.50 for skate rental. The rink is open seven days a week. Call 517-4800 for hours.

Central Park also has the **Lasker Memorial Rink** at 107th Street near Lenox Avenue (tel. 397-3142). The rink is open Sunday through Thursday from 11 a.m. to 9:30 p.m. (on Monday to 5 p.m.) and on Friday and Saturday until 11 p.m.

## SKIING

If it's the middle of winter and you're longing to be outside cross-country skiing, there are a number of ski areas within a few hours of the city. The **Fairview Lake Touring Center** in Newton, N.J., has 12 miles of groomed trails. Trail fee is $5 for adults and $3 for children. Rental equipment is available. Call 201/383-9282 for information and directions.

The **White Memorial Foundation** in Litchfield, Connecticut, is a 4,000-acre wildlife sanctuary with 30 miles of old carriage roads and nature trails running through it. The skiing is free, but there are no rentals on site. But you can rent skis in the city at Eastern Mountain Sport, 611 Broadway at Houston Street (tel. 505-9860).

## SWIMMING

New York has a number of ocean beaches for swimming and recreation, none of them more than a subway or short train ride away. The crowds reflect the polyglot mix that is New York—stronger on earthiness than elegance.

## Beaches

World-famous **Coney Island** on Brooklyn's Atlantic coast has a sandy beach more than seven miles long and a welter of other attractions: roller coasters, carnival attractions, ferris wheels, and loop-the-loops. On a fine summer Sunday the air is overburdened with cries, laughter, and music while the smell of hot dogs and sticky cotton candy pervades the air, and rows of bodies are stretched out on the sand. Yet for all its continued popularity, Coney Island is in a rundown area, certainly safe by day because of the enormous crowds in season, but best avoided by night.

The beaches at Coney Island are free. To get there, take the IND–Sixth Avenue B, D, or F train, or the BMT N line, to the last stop in Brooklyn, Stillwell Avenue.

If you are taking a day at the beach, be sure to stop in at Astroland Amusement Park, which towers above the boardwalk and the beach. The **New York Aquarium** is nearby at West 8th Street and Surf Avenue (tel. 718/265-3474). Housing hundreds of examples of the world's fresh- and saltwater marine life, the Aquarium features three seal pools and a whale pool. It's open daily from 10 a.m. to 4:45 p.m., between Memorial Day and Labor Day, and on weekends until 5:45 p.m. Admission is $3.75 for adults, $1.50 for children 12 and under (seniors, free on weekdays after 2 p.m.).

Just east of Coney Island is **Brighton Beach.** The beach is the same but the atmosphere is a little less frenetic and the crowds a little smaller. Also, thanks to the recent wave of Soviet immigrants, you will hear more Russian and see more Russian eateries in a few blocks of Brighton than just about anywhere outside of Russia (see Chapter II). Take the IND–Sixth Avenue D or Q train to the Brighton Beach stop.

Beyond the city limits, but worth a visit, is **Jones Beach State Park.** In addition to a beautiful series of beaches, there are tennis courts, heated pools, outdoor roller-skating rinks, and fishing. You can get there on the Long Island Railroad, which leaves from Pennsylvania Station and connects with a shuttle bus at the Freeport, Long Island station. The railroad offers a special day-trip ticket for $8.50 for adults, $5 for children. The ticket covers round-trip rail and bus transportation. For details, call 718/454-5477.

## Pools

Within Manhattan there are a number of pools open to the public. Fees are minimal and some offer facilities for sports and picnicking as well. The city's pools are open generally from the first week in July until Labor Day; hours may vary seasonally.

**West 59th Street Pool,** 533 W. 59th St. (tel. 397-3159). Facilities include an indoor pool open during the winter, a gymnasium with weight room, handball court, and a small basketball court. Open from 11 a.m. to 7 p.m. Admission is free, but you must bring a padlock and towel. Take the IRT–Seventh Avenue no. 1, IND –Sixth Avenue B or D, or IND–Eighth Avenue A or C train to Columbus Circle.

**John Jay Pool,** East 77th Street and Cherokee Place, one block east of York Avenue (tel. 397-3177), is usually the busiest pool in Manhattan, with a view of the East River for sunbathers. Open from 11 a.m. to 7 p.m. seven days a week. Admission is free. Take the IRT–Lexington Avenue no. 6 train to 77th Street and Lexington Avenue. Transfer to the crosstown bus on 79th Street going east.

**East 54th Street Pool,** 54th Street between First and Second avenues (tel. 397-3148), is an indoor pool, open year round, Monday through Friday from 3 p.m. to 10 p.m. and on Saturday from 10 a.m. to 5 p.m. Bring a lock and a towel. There is a $2 yearly fee.

For more money ($14 on weekdays, $20 on weekends; children, half price), you can swim all day at the pool at the **Sheraton City Squire Motor Inn,** 790 Seventh Ave., at 51st Street (tel. 581-3300). See "Swimming" in Chapter VIII for more details.

## TENNIS

The annual **U.S. Open Championship** is played at the National Tennis Center at Flushing Meadow Park every fall during early September. The center can be reached by taking the IRT–Flushing line (no. 7 train) to the Shea Stadium stop. For ticket information, call 718/271-5100.

## URBAN HIKING

Every weekend the City's Urban Park Rangers lead free public walks and workshops in the city's parks. You can explore animal and plant life, history, and even astronomy in Central Park and Inwood Park in Manhattan, and other parks in the outer boroughs. Call 397-3080 for information on walks in Manhattan, 718/287-5252 in Brooklyn, 718/699-4204 in Queens, 718/816-5456 in Staten Island, or 548-7880 in the Bronx.

## WRESTLING

Nowhere has wrestlemania hit harder than New York. You can catch Hulk Hogan and "Rowdy" Roddy Piper in action at Madison Square Garden (tel. 563-8300). Ticket prices start at $9.

# CENTRAL PARK

1. Arsenal
2. Wollman Rink
3. Dairy
4. Chess and Checkers
5. Carousel
6. Delacorte Clock
7. Children's Zoo
8. Zoo
9. Tavern on the Green
10. The Mall
11. Naumburg Bandshell
12. Frick Museum
13. Bethesda Fountain
14. Cherry Hill Fountain
15. Loeb Boathouse
16. New-York Historical Society
17. American Museum of Natural History
18. Hayden Planetarium
19. Shakespeare Gardens
20. Delacorte Theater
21. Swedish Cottage
22. Metropolitan Museum of Art

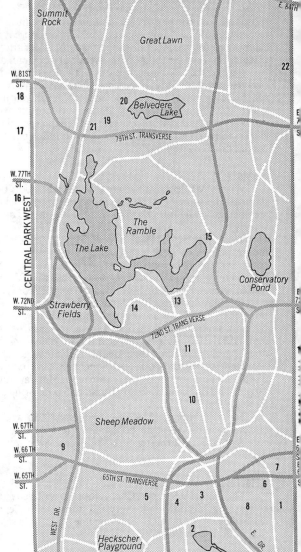

WEST     CENTER     EAST

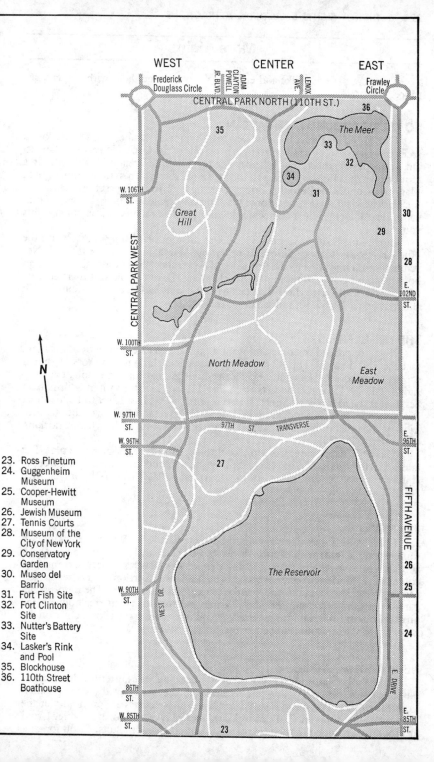

WEST  CENTER  EAST

Frederick
Douglass Circle

ADAM
CLAYTON
POWELL
JR. BLVD

LENOX
AVE.

Frawley
Circle

CENTRAL PARK NORTH (110TH ST.)

The Meer

36

35

33

32

34

31

W. 106TH
ST.

Great
Hill

30

29

28

E.
102ND
ST.

W. 100TH
ST.

CENTRAL PARK WEST

North Meadow

East
Meadow

N

W. 97TH
ST.

97TH  ST.  TRANSVERSE

E.
96TH
ST.

W. 96TH
ST.

23. Ross Pinetum
24. Guggenheim
    Museum
25. Cooper-Hewitt
    Museum
26. Jewish Museum
27. Tennis Courts
28. Museum of the
    City of New York
29. Conservatory
    Garden
30. Museo del
    Barrio
31. Fort Fish Site
32. Fort Clinton
    Site
33. Nutter's Battery
    Site
34. Lasker's Rink
    and Pool
35. Blockhouse
36. 110th Street
    Boathouse

27

The Reservoir

FIFTH AVENUE

26

25

24

W. 90TH
ST.

WEST DR.

86TH
ST.

E. DRIVE

E.
85TH
ST.

W. 85TH
ST.

23

# 7. More Sights

These are places we like and enjoy—places we urge those with longer visits to see.

## BOAT TRIP AROUND MANHATTAN

One of the best ways to view New York's famous skyline, bridges, and other architectural marvels is via a seagoing trip on one of the **Circle Line** boats (Manhattan, you will remember, is an island). The three-hour, 35-mile trip takes you on a cruise down the Hudson River, past the Statue of Liberty, across the lower harbor of Manhattan, under the Brooklyn Bridge, then up the East River past the U.N., across the Harlem River, under the George Washington Bridge, and back down the Hudson again. Along the way, a trained guide comments over a loudspeaker on the sights you pass.

Circle Line boats leave from Pier 83, at the foot of West 43rd Street (on the Hudson River). Boats begin operating in mid-March and continue through November. From mid-June to the first week of September boats depart about once an hour, beginning at 9:30 a.m. up until 4:15 p.m. The rest of the year there are two trips per day (call first to check the exact schedule: 563-3200). Fare for adults is $15; children under 12, $7.50; and seniors, $13.50.

## THE TNT EXPRESS

If you're pressed for time and want a quicker river's-eye view of Manhattan, take the TNT Express. This 82-foot Catamaran glides through New York Harbor at speeds of up to 29 knots and offers a one-hour guided tour of Manhattan's top sights. The TNT Express departs from Pier 11, two blocks south of South Street Seaport, at the foot of Wall Street. It travels north up the East River to 110th Street in Manhattan, turns around, heads back down the river, and glides past the Statue of Liberty, Ellis Island, World Financial Center, and Governor's Island before docking once again at Pier 11.

The TNT Express departs Monday through Saturday at noon and 2 p.m. The fare is $15 for adults, $13 for senior citizens, $8 for children under 12, and free for children under 5. For more information, call 201/CAT-RIDE or toll free 800/BOAT-RIDE.

## TRAMWAY

Glide along a steel tightrope high above the East River for a breathtaking five minutes on the **Roosevelt Island Tramway**. For $1.25 each way, you can rise high above it all and arrive almost instantly in Manhattan's newest and nearest commuter community (formerly Welfare Island, once a hospital and prison center), where garbage is collected by vacuum tubes and electric buses replace cars. The tramway departs from 60th Street and Second Avenue, and runs every quarter hour on the quarter hour until after midnight, every 7½ minutes during rush hour. Once on the island, have a stroll around and enjoy the green parks and clean streets.

## NEW YORK AQUARIUM

Sharks! Big ones, and plenty of them . . . dazzling little butterfly fish . . . a colony of comical penguins . . . white whales from the arctic and fearsome piranhas from the tropics. These and nearly 22,000 marine creatures are on display at the New York Aquarium (tel. 718/265-FISH), practically on the ocean at Coney Island in Brooklyn. Included in the price of admission ($3.75 for adults; $1.50 for children 12 and under; seniors, free after 2 p.m. on weekdays) is a whale- and dolphin-training show, an electric eel demonstration, and various special exhibits and demonstrations. For the kids there is a "Touch-It" exhibit, where you are invited to pick up sea stars and pet the fish. At the new Discovery Cove exhibit, visitors will encounter everything from the world's smallest invertebrates to its largest mammals through dioramas, graphic and photographic displays, push-button demonstrations, and participatory exhibits. For a view of continuous rocky coastal habitat, bringing together animals from the tips of both poles, visit the new Sea Cliffs exhibit, scheduled to open by 1990. Call for more information on exhibit activities.

Feeding times for the penguins, sharks, seals, and walruses vary, so call 718/266-8500 to catch the feedings. The Aquarium's hours are 10 a.m. to 4:45 p.m. weekdays, to 5:45 p.m. weekends and summer holidays.

To reach the aquarium, take the IND–Sixth Avenue D or F train to the West 8th Street Station in Brooklyn and walk down the ramp to Surf Avenue.

## LOOK INTO THE FUTURE

For those who suffer from technophobia, a visit to the fascinating **AT&T Infoquest Center** may be just the cure. The center, at 550 Madison Ave., at 56th Street (tel. 605-5555), is a permanent exhibit at AT&T World Headquarters. Infoquest features 40 interactive exhibits on lightwave communications, microelectronics, and computer software. There's a Telstar satellite, 32-screen multimedia presentation, and two robots on hand—one explains computer software, the other plays piano. Open on Tuesday from 10 a.m. to 9 p.m. and Wednesday through Sunday from 10 a.m. to 6 p.m.; closed Monday and holidays. Admission is free.

## ARCHITECTURAL AND NEIGHBORHOOD TOURING

For students of architecture, New York is a wonderland. From the very old to the very latest, it offers more variety of styles, forms, and types than probably any other New World city. From the fancifulness of the New York Yacht Club at 37 W. 44th St., off Fifth Avenue, and the Italian Renaissance Villard Houses on Madison Avenue between 50th and 51st streets, to the cast-iron warehouses of SoHo, you'll find treasures throughout the city just as you tour on your own. Check on what's happening in architecture in the city by reading Paul Goldberger's frequent columns in the *New York Times,* or consult his *The City Observed,* a guide to the architecture of New York. For the best walking tour of cast-iron buildings in SoHo and TriBeCa, consult the book by **Friends of Cast-Iron Architecture,** available at the Okay Harris Gallery on West Broadway near Grand Street.

Finally, the real story of the buildings and neighborhoods you'll see is the lives of the people who've lived there. For that, you might want to turn to Jeff Kisseloff's book *You Must Remember This: An Oral History of Manhattan from the 1890s to World War II,* a fascinating neighborhood-by-neighborhood portrait of the city by the people who lived in the first half of this century.

The **Municipal Art Society** (tel. 935-3960) offers a tour series which includes weekend walks through architectural areas of the city. Recent tours included "Tompkins Square Park," "Chinatown," and "Gardens of the Upper West Side." Guided walks are $12 for nonmembers and take place on Saturday and Sunday every week. Every Wednesday there's a free tour of Grand Central Terminal at 12:30 p.m.

Our favorite guided tours of New York are offered by the Graduate Department of Urban Affairs and Planning at Hunter College. **Planners' New York Tours** take you to the more unlikely areas for tourists—New York's neighborhoods and outer boroughs—and give you far more insight into the social reality of the city than you're likely to get from other tours. You will be taken by bus to such places as East Harlem, the South Bronx, Queens, and Brooklyn, as well as the more frequented neighborhoods of Manhattan. The guides—steeped in the nature and problems of urban life—will tell you the urban-planning histories of various neighborhoods and explain the challenges they are facing going into the 1990s. Tours are given to groups all year round and last two to six hours. Call 772-5605 for the most recent prices and scheduling assistance.

Take a "historywalk" with **Joyce Gold,** who teaches Manhattan history at the New School for Social Research and New York University, and gives tours of the financial district, Greenwich Village, Chelsea, and the East Village three Sundays each spring, summer, and fall for $10. She is also available anytime to give private tours to individuals or groups, and will mail you one of her books, which offer self-guided tours to select areas in lower Manhattan. Call or write to Joyce Gold, 141 W. 17th St., New York, NY 10011 (tel. 242-5762).

The **Museum of the City of New York** offers walking tours in all five boroughs with an emphasis on the architectural wonders of the city and the personal-interest stories of the people who made the Big Apple what it is today. Tours run in the spring and fall on Sunday and cost $10 for members and senior citizens, $15 for nonmembers. For details, call 534-1672.

Experts in their fields, the guides with the **92nd Street Y** tours come from all walks of life and can offer you everything from walking tours of gourmet eating places, artists' studios, or the political history of New York, to a Valentine's Day tour which takes you to the house where Marilyn Monroe lived and the residence where Valentino began his womanizing career. The Y specializes in "theme tours," and they do everything imaginable in this city that offers the most unimaginable things. Celebrate Independence Day by taking an all-night tour, including an escort by a fife-and-drum band and a visit to the mayor's office, or take a tour on roller skates or a bicycle. Tours are given most Sundays and often midweek, and are well worth the $10 to $15 fee. For around $50 the Y also offers tours outside the city to places like the Hudson River Valley and the U.S. Military Academy at West Point, the Boston Harbor, and the apple orchards and antique shops in upstate New York. For more information, write or call Batia Plotch, The 92nd Street Y, 1395 Lexington Ave., New York, NY 10128 (tel. 427-6000, ext. 599).

Russian, Middle Eastern, Italian, and Caribbean neighborhoods are viewed from above for those who take the **Discovery Tour of Brooklyn** bus tour. With stops at such famous sites as the Brooklyn Promenade, the Brooklyn Museum, and the Williamsburg Bank Tower, passengers also enjoy time for lunch at the Museum Café and browsing in the museum and garden gift shops. The tour lasts approximately six hours, and departs at 9:30 a.m. from the Gray Line Bus Terminal at 54th Street and Eighth Avenue in Manhattan. Buses run every Thursday and Saturday, May 4 through October 28. The tour costs $22. For more information, call the Gray Line Terminal at 397-2600.

## NATURE TOURS

You may not have come to the city to find nature, but the **Urban Park Rangers** offer interesting tours in all five boroughs of the many parks—over 500—in the area. For instance, in Manhattan's Central Park the rangers will take you on an early-morning wildlife walk with sightings of rabbits, raccoons, and all kinds of native birds. Very occasionally they also have a geology tour of glacial periods and rocks, history tours, and landscape design tours. In Brooklyn, the rangers have fashioned a nature trail at Marine Park, a chance to see the salt marshes and wetlands of an undeveloped area. They also give a "mounted tour" of Prospect Park—on horseback. Call two weeks in advance for this popular tour, which is the only one with a fee—$25. All the rangers' tours are offered all year round, usually on weekends, and best yet, they are *free.* Phone the ranger offices for more information: Bronx (tel. 548-7880), Brooklyn (tel. 718/287-3400), Manhattan (tel. 397-3091), Queens (tel. 718/699-4204), and Staten Island (tel. 718/442-1304).

Pick your own wild food with **"Wildman" Steve Brill,** who is an expert on the identification, collection, and use of the hundreds of vegetables, berries, fruits, nuts, herbs, seeds, and mushrooms that you can find—where you least expect them—in the city's parks. Mr. Brill offers leisurely four-hour walks, with a stop for lunch, on

Saturday and Sunday, March to December, and you can stuff yourself with such delights as black raspberries, cherries, and mulberries, or take home a load of gourmet mushrooms and wild spinach. These charming and educational walks will enchant anyone who has looked at a field of greenery and seen only grass. Call or write to "Wildman" Steve Brill, 143-25 84th Dr., no. 6C, Jamaica, NY 11435 (tel. 718/291-6825). All tours are free. Mr. Brill, a Parks Department naturalist, is also available for private groups.

## MORE TOURS

"Exploring the world within our reach . . . within our means" is the motto of **Adventure on a Shoestring,** a 26-year-old organization that arranges near-daily group visits to the unique places and people that make New York the exciting city it is. The group has some 2,000 members—including residents of 25 other states who visit the city regularly—all bound together by their common desire to explore the city's more offbeat and least-explored treasures. In recent years shoestringers have toured a factory that manufactures Rudolph ("the Red-nosed Reindeer") and Easter bunnies, backstage at the Metropolitan Opera House, and a subway training school for motormen and conductors, and have met with a vampire researcher, a Broadway playwright, a famous New York novelist, a lie-detection expert, an acclaimed watercolor artist, and a professional hypnotist who trained Mike Tyson.

For a free brochure describing the dozens of novel adventures, write Shoestring at 300 W. 53rd St., New York, NY 10019 (tel. 265-2663). Shoestring events cost members $3; an annual membership is $40. Events open to nonmembers cost them $5 per person. Shoestring also offers "Shoestring Safaris" for groups of five or more visiting the Big Apple. These walking tours are offered in different colorful areas of the city—from the Lower East Side and Chinatown, to the SoHo artists' area and even Brooklyn Heights. Often Shoestring will customize a tour to the interest of the group. Each tour features talks with members of the visited communities. For safaris, the fee varies according to the length of the tour, so call or write to arrange.

Theater lovers can take a unique, one-hour backstage tour of a Broadway theater through the graces of a group called **Backstage on Broadway.** The tours are led by Broadway stage managers, directors, lighting designers, and even leading actors and actresses. You'll see how a show is put together, from the hanging of the scenery to the blocking of the stage. Tours are usually scheduled for Monday through Saturday at 10:30 a.m., and advance reservations by phone only are essential—tours fill fast. For reservations, call 575-8065. Admission is $7 for adults, $6 for students and seniors. For information, write Backstage on Broadway, Suite 344, 228 W. 47th St., New York, NY 10036.

A great way to spend a Sunday afternoon is touring **Shapiro's Winery.** It's the only remaining winery in New York City, and the tour ends with a tasting of some of Shapiro's 40 varieties of wine. The tour takes you through the wine cellar and includes a chat with the winery's fourth-generation owner. Tours are every Sunday on the hour from 11 a.m. to 4 p.m., and cost $1 per person. Shapiro's is on the Lower East Side, at 126 Rivington St. (tel. 674-4404).

# 8. Churches and Synagogues

Many of New York's religious institutions are among the city's architectural gems. They are fascinating museums of religious art, and their tree-shaded churchyards are pleasant sanctuaries from the city's tumult. The budget-conscious traveler can also look to many of these houses of worship for inexpensive, high-quality entertainment. No longer are the melodic sounds emanating from altars and choirs limited to Gregorian chants, traditional organ tunes, and chorus recitals. New York's churches and synagogues have become increasingly alive with the sound of contemporary music, especially jazz, and they host first-rate concerts, dance recitals, and plays. Many of these events are free, and others can be attended at little cost. In this section, we've listed some of the city's best-known houses of worship.

## LOWER MANHATTAN

**Trinity Church:** This famous Episcopal church, consecrated in 1846, is the third Trinity to stand at the corner of Broadway and Wall Street (a corner valued at more than $25 million). The first, dating back to 1698, was destroyed in the Great Fire of 1839, and the second was torn down because of structural defects. Trinity may well be the city's premier Gothic Revival church; in the mid–19th century its spire was the highest structure on the New York skyline. Alexander Hamilton, Robert Fulton, Capt. James ("Don't give up the ship") Lawrence, and other historic figures are buried in a cemetery surrounding the church. The church is open from 7 a.m. to 6 p.m. on weekdays, from 8 a.m. to 4 p.m. on weekends. Its museum, with exhibits relating to Trinity's history, is open Monday through Friday from 9 to 11:45 a.m. and 1 to 3:45 p.m., on Saturday from 10 a.m. to 3:45 p.m., and on Sunday from 1 to 3:45 p.m. For details, phone 602-0800.

**St. Paul's Chapel:** This Episcopal church, at Broadway and Fulton Street, is the oldest public building in continuous use in Manhattan, dating from 1766. It is also one of the city's best examples of Georgian Revival–style architecture. Much of the chapel's interior, including a hand-carved altar and a handsome winding stair, was designed by Pierre L'Enfant, who also designed the city of Washington, D.C. George Washington prayed here from 1789 to 1791 (a replica of his original pew is intact), and the chapel was also the place of worship for the Marquis de Lafayette, Major André, Lord Cornwallis, Benjamin Harrison, and Grover Cleveland. St. Paul's now serves as a parish chapel for Trinity Church. There are daily services and free noonday concerts at both churches on Monday and Thursday. For details, phone 602-0874.

**St. Marks-in-the-Bowery:** St. Marks, at East 10th Street and Second Avenue, dates from 1799 and stands on the site of the Peter Stuyvesant family chapel. A blend of disparate styles, it has an Italianate cast-iron portico, a Georgian chapel, and a Greek Revival–style steeple. Stuyvesant is buried in a crypt beneath the church along with 70 of his descendants, and a bust of him (donated by Queen Wilhelmina of the Netherlands in 1915) stands in the tree-shaded courtyard. Heavily damaged by fire in 1978, the building is now almost fully restored. There are services at 6 p.m. on Wednesday and at 10:30 a.m. on Sunday. St. Marks is extremely active in the cultural and artistic life of the East Village. It hosts weekly dance concerts, weekly writing workshops, and poetry readings, though not during July or August. The readings, with a suggested contribution of $2, are particularly noteworthy; they've been going on for more than 20 years and often feature such well-known poets as Allen Ginsberg and Anne Waldman. Call 674-6377 for exact times and performer information.

**Friends Meeting House:** This typical Quaker meeting house is a good place to see in combination with a visit to St. Marks. It's located at 15 Rutherford Pl., off East 15th Street between Second and Third avenues. Built in 1860, the red-brick house is understated, especially for structures in the Gothic Revival style. In its southeast corner you can see a granite hitching post from William Penn's Philadelphia home. Meetings are on Sunday at 9:30 and 11 a.m. and on Tuesday at 7:30 p.m. For details, phone 777-8866.

**Marble Collegiate Church:** Marble Collegiate, at the corner of West 29th Street and Fifth Avenue, is the city's oldest Dutch Reformed church. Its elegant façade was constructed entirely of marble, hence the church's name. The church boasts a number of firsts: it was the first to be built with hanging balconies, the first to install an electronically operated pipe organ, the first to be air-conditioned, and the first to use closed-circuit television for overflow congregations. For years Marble Collegiate was the site where Dr. Norman Vincent Peale, the world-renowned author and theologian, gave his spirited sermons. The Sunday service is at 11:15 a.m. in the fall and winter months, and at 10:30 a.m. June through August. For information, call 686-2770.

**Church of the Transfiguration:** This picturesque Episcopal church, at 1 E. 29th St., near Fifth Avenue, is known throughout the world as "the little church around the corner." Built in 1849, it sits in a shrubbery-filled garden that's the closest thing New York has to an old English churchyard. The church is a traditional favorite with stage people—and with lovers too. In fact, legend has it that this church has seen more weddings than any other its size, and there's a "bride's altar" (in the Holy Family Chapel) built with funds donated by the thousands of couples who were married here. Among the church's many famous parishioners were writers Stephen Vincent Benet and William Sydney Porter (O. Henry). The chapel is open from 8 a.m. to 6 p.m. daily. A tour is given every Sunday after the 11 a.m. service. For details, phone 684-6770.

## MIDTOWN

**St. Patrick's Cathedral:** St. Patrick's, at 50th Street and Fifth Avenue, is the city's major Roman Catholic cathedral. Everything about the church (the second largest in Manhattan) is majestic. Its twin spires (modeled after the Cathedral of Cologne) rise to 330 feet above street level, and its great Rose Window measures 26 feet in diameter. Dedicated in 1879, the cathedral took 21 years to build. Inside, there's an impressive array of altars and shrines, including those of Elizabeth Ann Seton and John Neumann, the first American-born saints. The cathedral is open for worship or visiting from 7 a.m. to 8 p.m. daily. Sunday services are at 7, 8, 9, and 10:15 a.m., noon, and 1, 4, and 5:30 p.m. For information, phone 753-2261.

**St. Peter's Lutheran Church:** This modernistic church is nestled in a corner near the Citicorp skyscraper at 54th Street and Lexington Avenue. Built in 1977, the church impresses on visitors a sense of simplicity, dignity, and strength. In contrast to the bank's sleek, 900-foot aluminum-clad tower, the granite outer walls of the church reach humbly into the sky like two hands in prayer. The feeling is continued in the main sanctuary, an immense angular tent with butcher-block pews, and a beautiful, tiny white chapel designed by Louise Nevelson, the world-renowned artist. (The walls of the chapel are lined with three of Nevelson's enigmatic wood assemblages.) St. Peter's is particularly well known for its commitment to the performing arts. Many of the greatest names in jazz have performed at Jazz Vespers—a worship service held every Sunday at St. Peter's at 5 p.m. The service is conducted by the Rev. John Garcia Gensel, who serves as pastor to New York's jazz community and for whom Duke Ellington wrote "The Shepherd Who Watches Over The Night Flock." A more traditional Lutheran service takes place on Sunday at 8:45 and 11 a.m., and at various times during the week. For details, call 935-2200.

This is a good place to see in combination with a trip to the Citicorp complex, right next door, which features a fabulous collection of shops and restaurants.

**St. Bartholomew's Church:** This 155-year-old Episcopal church, on Park Avenue between 50th and 51st streets, was originally located downtown on Lafayette Street. In 1918 the church moved to its current home, which is distinguished by an Italian Romanesque portal and dome. Services are held at 9 and 11 a.m. on Sunday, and at various times during the week. Call 751-1616 for details.

**Central Synagogue:** This Reformed Jewish synagogue, at East 55th Street and Lexington Avenue, has been called the finest example of Moorish Revivial–style architecture in the city. It was erected in 1872 and has been designated a national landmark. Although the sanctuary is only open to the public during Friday-evening and Saturday-morning worship services, you can arrange for a tour by writing the synagogue office, 123 E. 55th St. For information, phone 838-5122.

**Temple Emanu-El:** Temple Emanu-El, at Fifth Avenue and East 65th Street, is the world's largest Reformed Jewish synagogue. It's also the third-largest house of worship in New York City, after the Cathedral of St. John the Divine and St. Patrick's. Built in 1929, this gray limestone structure is a lofty mix of Romanesque, Byzantine, and Gothic architecture, with occasional flourishes of art deco. Its stately and awe-inspiring main sanctuary is 77 feet wide, 147 feet long, and 103 feet high, with seating for 2,500. Daily services are at 5:30 p.m., on Friday at 5:15 p.m. There is also a service on Saturday at 10:30 a.m. A tour is available by appointment only. For information, phone 744-1400.

**Congregation Shearith Israel (The Spanish and Portuguese Synagogue):** Almost directly across the park from Temple Emanu-El, at Central Park West and 70th Street, is the Orthodox Spanish and Portuguese Synagogue. Founded in 1654, this Sephardic congregation is the oldest Jewish congregation in America. (Its first members were descendants of Jews who fled Spain and Portugal during the Inquisition and made their way to New York via Brazil.) In keeping with the Jewish tradition of not representing human images, the windows of this landmark, neoclassical structure were designed by Louis Comfort Tiffany in simple yet elegant patterns. Services are held daily—mornings and evenings. You can arrange for a tour by contacting the synagogue office, 8 W. 70th St. For information, phone 873-0300.

## UPPER WEST SIDE
**Cathedral Church of St. John the Divine:** St. John the Divine, at West 112th Street and Amsterdam Avenue, is the city's major Episcopal church and the largest Gothic cathedral on earth. (In fact, among all the world's churches, only St. Peter's Basilica in Rome is larger.) Its immense nave stretches more than 600 feet, the length of two football fields, and has a seating capacity of 5,000. Though its first ground-breaking ceremony took place in 1892, the building is still only two-thirds completed. Currently, in a building program evocative of the Middle Ages, a dozen young apprentices are putting chisel to stone to raise two 323-foot towers on the cathedral's west front. You'll want to spend lots of time at this church; its nave is bordered by an array of small, beautiful, and intimate chapels. And you can relax in the church's "Biblical Garden," which is planted with a variety of herbs and flowers mentioned in the Bible. Services are held on Sunday at 8, 9, 9:30, and 11 a.m., and at 7 p.m. There are tours Monday through Saturday at 11 a.m., and on Sunday at 12:30 p.m. For information, call 316-7400.

**The Riverside Church:** The best way to see this famous church is in conjunction with a trip to **Grant's Tomb.** Both are located on Riverside Drive between 120th and 122nd streets. As befits its status as one of the city's most active churches, Riverside's 392-foot tower looms high above the Upper West Side. Built in 1930, the Gothic-style church was funded by John D. Rockefeller, Jr., and modeled on the Cathedral of Chartres. Its main chapel features heroic statues of six Christian preachers, and one of the largest church organs (13,000 pipes) in the world.

Be sure to take an elevator to Riverside's 20th floor, where an antique practice clavier can be seen. From there, a narrow staircase winds through a 74-bell carillon (the largest in the world) to an observation platform, 355 feet above ground. For $1 you can purchase platform tickets in the lobby and get an unobstructed bird's-eye view of Manhattan and its environs. Platform hours are 11 a.m. to 3 p.m. Monday through Saturday and noon to 4 p.m. on Sunday. Riverside's congregation is inter-denominational, interracial, and international. The 10:45 a.m. Sunday services are led by Dr. James Alexander Forbes, Jr., whose sermons often focus on issues of great social import. Carillon recitals are given before and after the Sunday service as well as at many other times throughout the week. In addition, Riverside often sponsors special music, dance, and theater events. For further information, call 222-5900.

## HARLEM
**The Abyssinian Baptist Church:** New York's oldest and largest black church is at 132 W. 138th St., near Lenox Avenue. Built in 1808, the church is an intriguing mix of Gothic and Tudor architecture. In the 1950s and 1960s it was best known as

the parish of Harlem's renowned congressman and preacher, the Rev. Adam Clayton Powell, Jr. Now the church is famous for its 75-member choir, which has sung with the New York Philharmonic and Boston Pops orchestras. You can hear the choir any Sunday at 11 a.m. For information, phone 862-7474.

# 9. Historic Houses

Beneath that famed Manhattan skyline you can still find the old New York, in buildings and homes preserved by concerned citizens and the city government. Here are a few of our favorites, arranged by geographical location.

## LOWER MANHATTAN

**Fraunces Tavern:** Built in 1719, this landmark building at the corner of Broad and Pearl streets is a rare vestige of Colonial America—an America of old Dutch homes, cobblestone streets, and trading ships. The building takes its name from Samuel Fraunces, the West Indian innkeeper who converted it into a tavern in 1762. It was here, in a long banquet room on the second floor, that George Washington bade an emotional farewell to his officers in 1783. (Later, when Washington became president, Fraunces became his chief steward.) Restored in 1904 the tavern now houses a restaurant on the first floor (open weekdays from 7:30 a.m. to 9 p.m.) and a museum of early Americana (see "Museums," above). Its collection of Revolutionary War memorabilia—flags, musketry, colonial maps, and paintings—is particularly noteworthy. The tavern also holds a changing series of painting exhibitions throughout the year. In 1990, it will have an exhibit on the history of Wall Street.

Open weekdays and selected Sundays from 10 a.m. to 4 p.m.; closed weekends and holidays (except for Washington's Birthday and July 4th). To get there, take the BMT subway (N or R train) to the Whitehall Street station and walk to Pearl Street. For information, call 425-1778.

**Federal Hall National Memorial:** A few blocks north from Fraunces Tavern, at the corner of Wall and Nassau streets, is the Federal Hall National Memorial—the site of George Washington's inauguration as our country's first president. John Quincy Adams Ward's famous statue of Washington stands in front of the building. Completed in 1842, the building is considered one of the city's finest examples of Greek Revival architecture. A reconstruction of the original Federal Hall—the nation's first capitol building—it served as a U.S. Customs House and as a subtreasury before being converted into a national memorial. Inside, there's a museum with Washington's inaugural suit as well as several exhibitions commemorating the inauguration. There's also a colonial folksinger who re-creates, through song, the history of Colonial New York.

Open Monday through Friday from 9 a.m. to 5 p.m. Admission is free. For information, call 264-8711.

**Old Merchant's House:** Now a museum, the Old Merchant's House at 29 E. 4th St., between Lafayette Street and the Bowery, is a perfectly furnished period piece in an area that has been largely taken over by trucking companies. That the house survived is not surprising once you know its story. The five-story Georgian brick house was built in 1832 and bought three years later by Seabury Tredwell, a prosperous hardware merchant. Three of his six daughters lived there all their lives, keeping the house just as it had always been, and refusing to depart when the fashionable area of town moved north. When the youngest of those daughters died in 1933 at the age of 93, hardly anything had changed. The house still lacked plumbing and electricity; its original furnishings, linens, china, and family memorabilia were all intact. Closets and cabinets were filled with old clothes, much of it dating from the 1800s, remarkably preserved and apparently not touched for nearly a century: A playbill from an 1860s theatrical production was found in the pocket of one dress.

More than most such museums, the house has the haunting quality of time's having stopped, and the visitor cannot help but wonder at the lives of the reclusive spinster sisters who lived there. It has classic Greek Revival parlors with the original mahogany furniture, fine decorative plaster molding, and handsome hand-carved columns.

Three of the house's five stories are open to the public on Sunday from 1 to 4 p.m. (closed in August). Admission is $2 for adults and $1 for students and senior citizens. The museum can be reached by taking the IRT–Lexington Avenue local (no. 6) subway to the Astor Place–8th Street station and walking south on Lafayette to 4th Street. For special group tours or lectures, phone 777-1089.

**Theodore Roosevelt House:** This landmark house at 28 E. 20th St., between Broadway and Park Avenue South, is the birthplace of Teddy Roosevelt, the gutsy "Rough Rider" who first led the charge up San Juan Hill and later became the nation's 26th president. The house is actually a replica of the original, which was torn down in 1916, but it has much of the original's Victorian furnishings and 19th-century relics. Free chamber-music concerts are presented September through June on Saturday from 2 to 3:30 p.m. on the fourth floor.

The house is open Wednesday through Sunday from 9 a.m. to 5 p.m. Admission is $1 for adults, free for senior citizens and for children under 17. To get there, take the IRT–Lexington Avenue local (no. 6) subway to 23rd Street and Park Avenue South, or take the BMT subway (N or R train) to Park Avenue South and Broadway. For information, call 260-1616.

## EAST SIDE

**Abigail Adams Smith Museum:** Sitting on a raised grassy site at 421 E. 61st St., between York and First avenues (tel. 838-6878), is one of the few 18th-century buildings left in Manhattan. It was built in 1799 as the carriage house on the estate of Abigail Adams Smith, the daughter of President John Adams. Made of schist, a stone quarried in Colonial Manhattan, the house is furnished throughout with museum-quality antiques from the Federal period. Outside there's a path leading to a quiet garden and sitting area—a mainstay of homes of this era.

Open Monday through Friday from 10 a.m. to 4 p.m.; closed during the month of August. Admission is $2 for adults, $1 for senior citizens, free for children under 12. To get there, take the IRT–Lexington Avenue subway (no. 4, 5, or 6) to 59th Street, then walk four blocks east to First Avenue.

## UPPER EAST SIDE

**Gracie Mansion:** This elegant structure, at East 88th Street and East End Avenue (tel. 570-4751), has been home to New York mayors since 1942. Ironically, the leader of our most urban of urban areas lives in a pastoral sanctuary overlooking the East River. The mansion was in fact originally built as a country estate by Archibald Gracie, a New York merchant, in 1799. After years of disrepair, Gracie Mansion became the first home of the Museum of the City of New York, and was then restored as a home and reception site for civic events.

The peaceful grounds of Carl Shurz Park surrounding the house are open to the public on weekends. Tours of the house are available on Wednesday by phone appointment. There is a suggested donation of $3 for adults and children and $1 for senior citizens.

## HARLEM

**Morris-Jumel Mansion:** This white-columned Georgian-Federal mansion, at the corner of Edgecombe Avenue and 161st Street, is a remnant of a time when Upper Manhattan was predominantly rural: the summering place of New York's aristocracy. Built by Col. Roger Morris in 1765, it sits atop a grassy hill in the middle of a park filled with lilac and magnolia trees. Outside, there's a Colonial herb garden. This peaceful setting served first as Washington's headquarters and then as British headquarters during the Revolutionary War; later the widow of Stephen Jumel lived there with Aaron Burr, her second husband. The house recently became an accredited museum and there's a special exhibitions gallery on the third floor.

The mansion is open Tuesday through Sunday from 10 a.m. to 4 p.m.; closed Monday. Admission is $2 for adults, $1 for students and senior citizens. Children under 12 accompanied by an adult are admitted free. For information, call 923-8008. To get there, take the IND–Eighth Avenue A train or IND–Sixth Avenue B train to West 163rd Street. You can also take the Madison Avenue no. 2 or no. 3 bus.

## WASHINGTON HEIGHTS

The **Dyckman House:** This 18th-century Dutch Colonial farmhouse was built of brick, wood, and stone to replace one that was destroyed by the British. Occupied by both the Continental and British armies during the Revolutionary War, the house, at 204th Street and Broadway, is now a museum containing Dutch and English period furniture and possessions of the Dyckman family.

Open Tuesday through Sunday from 11 a.m. to 4 p.m. Admission is $1. For information, call 304-9422. To get there, take the IND–Eighth Avenue A train to the last stop, 207th Street, and walk three short blocks south on Broadway.

## THE BRONX

**Poe Cottage:** This wooden-frame cottage was the last home of author Edgar Allan Poe, the place where he wrote "Annabel Lee," "The Bells," and "Eureka." Built in 1812 and opened as a museum in 1917, it is a memorial to Poe, his life and times.

Poe Cottage is located on the Grand Concourse at East Kingsbridge Road. To get there, take the IRT–Lexington Avenue no. 4 train to the Kingsbridge station. Open Wednesday through Friday from 9 a.m. to 5 p.m., on Saturday from 10 a.m. to 4 p.m., and on Sunday from 1 to 5 p.m. Admission is $1 for adults; children under 12 are free. Group tours are available by appointment. For information, call 881-8900.

## STATEN ISLAND

**Richmondtown Restoration:** This recently completed restoration shows the development of a Staten Island village through the 17th, 18th, and 19th centuries. It includes a Dutch schoolhouse, general store, carriage house, and historical museum. The museum is open Monday through Friday from 10 a.m. to 5 p.m., and on Saturday and Sunday from 1 to 5 p.m. Admission is $4 for adults, $2.50 for seniors and children.

To get there, take the Staten Island Ferry; when you reach the other side, pick up a no. 113 bus to Court Place, then walk up Court Place to the visitor center. For information, phone 718/351-1617.

# IV

# A STROLL OR TWO

1. GREENWICH VILLAGE

2. THE LOWER EAST SIDE

3. THE GARMENT CENTER

4. YORKVILLE

5. SOHO

6. THE UPPER WEST SIDE: COLUMBUS AVENUE

7. CHINATOWN AND LITTLE ITALY

8. CHELSEA

9. TRIBECA

10. CENTRAL PARK

11. TIMES SQUARE

**T**o us, the most fascinating free activity in New York is a simple walk through several of Manhattan's fabled neighborhoods, including Greenwich Village, the Lower East Side, the Garment Center, Yorkville, SoHo, the refurbished Columbus Avenue area on the Upper West Side—and, of course, Chinatown and Little Italy downtown. Put on a pair of comfortable shoes and let's begin.

## 1. Greenwich Village

Take any IND subway (A, B, C, D, E, F, or Q train) to the West 4th Street station. Get out at the uptown exit, which will bring you to 8th Street and Avenue of the Americas, which New Yorkers simply call Sixth Avenue. Walk east on **8th Street** toward Fifth Avenue. This is one of the Village's main shopping streets, and as people have been saying for the past 40 years about the Village, it's not what it used to be. Fast-food restaurants, discount shoestores, and flashy clothing shops have invaded the street. There are still a few handcrafted jewelry and bookstores, but you're more likely to find inexpensive gift shops or record stores blaring music. Yet it's worth visiting. Just ignore the "joint" salesmen and occasional weirdos and concentrate on imagining Bob Dylan or Jack Kerouac walking this street.

When you reach Fifth Avenue, turn right and you'll see the magnificent Washington Square Arch, which was once treated with an antigraffiti chemical to prevent its being defaced by New York's indigenous art form. The Arch leads directly to **Washington Square Park,** the heart of the Village scene.

In its time, Washington Square has been many things—parade ground, cemetery, scene of riots and meetings—but it has always been the Village's major loafing place, and still is. On any day, the people in attendance will be partly made up of chess players (who fill the tables at the southwest corner), mothers and children, strollers and bench-warmers, skateboarders and disco roller-skaters, street performers and students, just sitting around the edge of the fountain in the center of the park. Summer Sunday afternoons are particularly lively, often filled with rock and jazz musicians. And over it all, the marble Washington Square Arch—gateway to Fifth Avenue—watches serenely. Unfortunately, that's not to say that the park doesn't have a seamier side. Winos and drug users, among others, use the park, as do pickpockets and other petty thieves. So use the park with the caution you would any other New York public place.

The north side of the square is lined with lovely, old buildings (dating back to the 1830s), one of which—no. 16—was the scene of Henry James's famous novel *Washington Square.* Some of the houses are still occupied by private individuals, but others have been taken over by various offshoots of New York University, whose headquarters are on the east side of the square.

To the south sprawls the old Italian section of town, a conglomeration of tenements, inexpensive restaurants, grocery stores whose windows are filled with hanging cheeses and cans of olive oil, funeral parlors, and finally, the famous nightclubs and coffeehouses of Greenwich Village.

Walk completely across the square to the south side, and then start exploring the streets to the south of the square: **MacDougal Street, Bleecker Street, Sullivan Street, Thompson Street**—all of which hold the largest cluster of nightspots and coffeehouses in the area, and all of which are as enjoyably seen in the daytime as at night.

MacDougal Street, once the heart of Bohemia, is now a blend of brassy boutiques and small eateries selling shish kebab or pizza. Bleecker Street has many faces, ranging from the artistic to the earthy to the flashy.

East of Sixth Avenue, you're reminded how sleazy commercialism can be. Still, the mood is lively and the street teeming with life. West of Sixth Avenue, Bleecker houses Italian food markets and private homes. Between Seventh and Eighth Avenues, Bleecker Street is an antique hunter's paradise with a greater variety of vintage wares than anywhere else in the city. Over 20 shops are clustered in the seven-block stretch, and the emphasis is on French country furniture.

When you have seen this area, walk back to Sixth Avenue and find West 4th Street—another important shopping street. Walk up West 4th Street to **Sheridan Square,** and then start exploring the streets and areas west of Sheridan Square—which are the most unchanged and most typical residential areas of the Village and currently the heart of New York's gay community. In particular, ask any passerby to point the way to: **Gay Street** (only one block long, but so crooked that you can't see one end from the other); **Christopher Street** (narrow, historic, and housing the famous Theatre de Lys, now the Lucille Lortel Theater, earliest and most successful of the off-Broadway theaters); **Bedford Street** (which contains the Edna St. Vincent Millay House, two stories high, but only eight feet wide).

You might want to spend extra time wandering around **Greenwich Avenue,** that famous angled street that runs into 8th Street; it is on these two streets that you'll see some of the Village's best boutiques and lots of uptowners coming to see what's happening in the Village. Start at upper Greenwich Avenue, working your way down toward 8th Street.

## An Architectural Tour

Greenwich Village abounds in interesting 19th-century architecture, but the area at the base of Fifth Avenue is perhaps the most interesting—it contains three streets filled with notable examples of early 19th-century architecture. A visit here is a must for history buffs who want to see some unusual relics of the past.

**MacDougal Alley,** a tiny street lined with buildings that used to be stables, is one of the most picturesque. The area was created in 1833 and through the years its buildings have been renovated into studios and private homes. The alley is situated on MacDougal Street, between 8th Street and Waverly Place.

Around the corner on the north side of **Washington Square** is a group of buildings regarded by the City Landmarks Commission as "the most important and imposing blockfront of early-19th-century townhouses in the city." Built in the early 1830s, these Greek Revival buildings were the homes of prosperous merchants and bankers.

As you walk east on Washington Square North, the next intersection you'll come to is Fifth Avenue. Turn left and a few steps in on your right you'll come to another delightful mews area. **Washington Mews,** a cobblestone street that is longer than MacDougal Alley, was also used in the 19th century to stable the horses of prominent families but is now used as private homes by lucky New Yorkers who can afford these unique vestiges of a bygone era.

## 2. The Lower East Side

For 50 years the Lower East Side was the home of tens of thousands of immigrant Jews from Eastern Europe, who soon proceeded to provide the city with important leaders in the labor movement, politics, education, industry, science, and the entertainment world. Today most of the old tenement buildings of this area still stand, but mixed among them on the narrow streets are modern housing projects. And side by side in what was once an exclusively Jewish neighborhood live Italians, Puerto Ricans, Ukrainians, blacks, and free-'n'-easy young types, as well as a few of the older Jewish residents who originally gave the area its flavor.

A trip to the Lower East Side will appeal not only to the sociologist, but to the bargain hunter as well. The streets abound in tiny stores of every variety, selling merchandise at prices a good 20% to 30% lower than in any other neighborhood in New York. Wear comfortable shoes, for after a subway ride down to Delancey Street, it's by foot all the way.

If you're planning to take your car, make sure you don't attempt to drive into the neighborhood, especially on a Sunday when it is crowded and impossible to park. Take the IND–Sixth Avenue F subway downtown to Delancey Street. When you leave the Delancey Street station, walk west to Essex Street, turn left down Essex Street, and on the east side of the street, between Broome and Delancey streets, you'll come to the first of the four city markets that stretch up to Stanton Street (three blocks across Delancey). It's fun to browse through the Essex Street Markets.

The cavernous indoor markets are crammed with stands and stalls (each rented from the city by private shopkeepers) displaying an enormous variety of food and delicacies, dry goods, hardware, clothing—even home furnishings. The markets cater almost equally to the Jewish and Spanish residents of the neighborhood, and you can buy *cabrito* (goat meat) or *queso blanco* (soft, white milk cheese), as well as the Jewish items more usually associated with the area—kosher pickles to munch on as you walk, or slabs of creamy halvah (ground sesame-seed candy).

As you leave the markets, look to your left toward East Broadway. East Broadway was once the Fleet Street of the Lower East Side, but now the last of the famous Yiddish newspapers, the *Forward,* has moved. At Rivington Street (north of Delancey Street), head west, passing shops housing barrels of smoked fish, bins of unusual candies, jars of dried fruits, bags of lentils, and similar exotica. The clothing and toy stores display their wares right on the sidewalk, each owner carrying on his business from the doorway. Many of these stores are owned by Orthodox Jews, and

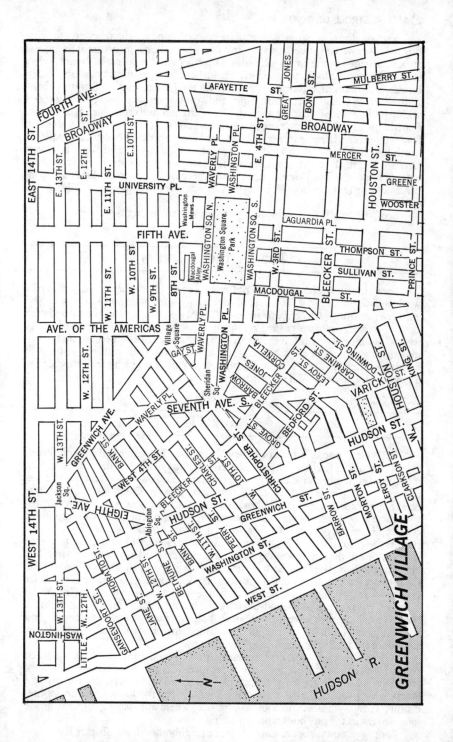

are therefore closed on Saturday, but all are open on Sunday, when they do a thriving
business. Cross Allen Street, turn left, and you'll be in the center of one of the busiest
antique sections in the city, specializing in copper and brass items. Narrow, dusty
stores sell copper candlesticks, crystal chandeliers, antique gift frames, brass headboards, and decorative antique accessories for the home—but no furniture. Now
walk down to Grand Street, turn right, and you'll soon pass rows of bridal shops
selling budget-priced wedding apparel. Then turn back and cross Allen Street again.
Remain on Grand Street as it becomes a linen and fabric section. You can stock up
here on sheets and towels at bargain prices, or have draperies or bedspreads made for
much less than you'd be charged anywhere else in the city. Grand Street intersects
Orchard Street, the heart of the shopping scene, with many stores for men's and
women's apparel. From Grand Street, return to Essex. Turn left at Essex and continue walking two blocks to Delancey Street, where you'll come to the IND subway
station.

See Chapter VII for specific shopping recommendations in this area.

## 3. The Garment Center

Save a lunchtime for the Garment Center, heart of New York's, and perhaps the
world's, fashion industry. The bulk of the activity takes place on Broadway or Seventh Avenue from 34th Street to around 42nd Street. The streets are crowded with
carts of women's clothes pushed recklessly by boys and men of every nationality
who look up only to admire the models, whose trademark—the makeup bags—
give them away. You'll see salesmen, executives, workers, all gathered in front of
buildings, often spilling over into the busy streets, gesturing with their hands, talk-
ing, wheeling, dealing—all in the name of fashion.

## 4. Yorkville

Yorkville is one of our favorite neighborhoods. Its center is East 86th Street,
one of New York's liveliest crosstown streets. Bustling during the day with shoppers,
it becomes even more alive at night with pleasure seekers who frequent its cafés and
restaurants, beer halls, and dance palaces. Places like the **Corso** (at no. 205) have
been popular for generations. Although some of the restaurants tend to get expensive, there are several German and Viennese restaurants where you can stop in for
coffee and delicate pastries. Our favorite is the **Kleine Konditorei** (no. 234).

At the eastern end of 86th Street, past the commercial section, lies East End
Avenue, one of the city's most expensive and quietest residential areas. There, also,
between the East River and East End Avenue is a broad expanse of greenery called
**Carl Schurz Park,** a place peopled with joggers, skateboarders, youngsters, and older
people who sit on the benches in good weather and watch the world go by. At the
north end of the park is **Gracie Mansion,** the beautiful 18th-century house that is
the home of New York's mayor. You can walk around the park near the mansion, and
if you're lucky you'll get a glimpse of the local and international notables who pop in
and out of the house for meetings and receptions.

Across East End Avenue between 86th and 87th Streets is a block of Queen
Anne 19th-century townhouses which has been designated a historic landmark
area. The back side of these red-brick buildings is on a tiny street called **Henderson
Place,** which you can enter from 86th Street. It has the flavor of a turn-of-the-
century village—unless you look to one side, where a massive apartment house
looms to dwarf the tiny houses underneath it.

For suggestions about restaurants in the neighborhood, see Chapter II.

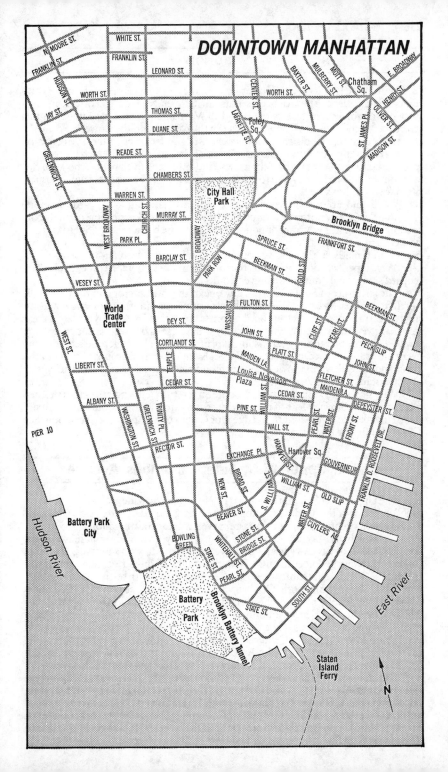

# 5. SoHo

Within the last decade SoHo has become the working center of the city's contemporary art scene. The area begins at its northern end at Houston Street, an east-west thoroughfare that bisects the island of Manhattan. SoHo is centered in the streets between Avenue of the Americas (Sixth Avenue) and the Bowery. Formerly this was a commercial district, with warehouses and factories in the 19th-century cast-iron buildings that line its streets. Now it's home to some 2,000 artists, photographers, craftspeople, dancers, filmmakers, and other creative talents who keep the area humming. SoHo is a place to see the latest in art and browse through unusual, often way-out shops.

You'll find an amazing variety of boutiques featuring avant-garde fashion, clothing that is art, pottery, antiques, records, books, and appealing natural-food restaurants as well as gourmet dining spots. Within the boundaries of SoHo you can find elegant creations that would be at home anywhere as well as the most experimental and trendy clothes you've ever seen. This is where the blue- and pink-haired New Wave types, walking their dyed-to-match punk-rock puppies, come to buy their leopard skin/vinyl/mini or whatever clothes.

The street life of SoHo is inarguably one of the most exciting in the city. Walk north from Canal Street on West Broadway on any weekend afternoon and you'll see impromptu flea markets set up on the corners or artists hawking their latest creations. We've seen a street performance by a Japanese artist who spent three days screwing common building screws into a platform while his colleague recorded his every move and the crowd's reaction. We've also heard myriad groups of street musicians, and once viewed a movie company filming in the dead of night on Thompson Street. SoHo, it seems, never sleeps.

Walk down West Broadway to Broome Street, turn left, and criss-cross the area west to Mercer Street. Most of the activity centers around these boundaries. To get to SoHo, take the IND–Eighth Avenue E or C train to the Spring Street station. See Chapter II for the best places to get a meal.

# 6. The Upper West Side: Columbus Avenue

The Upper West Side, aptly dubbed by *New York* magazine as the "Yupper West Side" in honor of the hordes of "yuppies" who have settled in here, has experienced a tremendous gentrification in the last few years. Heart of the action is Columbus Avenue, which has been transformed from a dirty, grimy thoroughfare into a smaller version of Greenwich Village, a lively strip for nonstop shopping, strolling, dining, drinking, people-watching. Centering around 72nd Street, extending north up into the 80s and south into the 60s, the avenue is lined with bistros and boutiques and crowds frequenting both. Old brownstones on the side streets have been transformed from grubby rooming houses into private homes and luxury apartments. The best time to experience Columbus Avenue is from late afternoon through early evening: some of the shops stay open until 8 p.m. Begin your stroll at 81st Street and walk south toward Lincoln Center. On your way down, you may want to meander off the avenue and stop in at the American Museum of Natural History at 77th Street, or the New-York Historical Society at 77th Street and Central Park West.

Two streets west of and parallel to Columbus, **Broadway** and **Amsterdam Avenue,** have retained some of the flavor of the "melting pot" West Side, but they, too, are changing fast. On Amsterdam you'll find botanicas and zapaterías next door to antique shops and boutiques forced off Columbus Avenue by skyrocketing rents. Stroll downtown on Broadway from about 85th Street to 79th Street and stop into **Zabar's** on 80th Street for gourmet treats par excellence. The **Apthorp** at Broadway and 78th Street and the **Ansonia** at 74th Street are quintessential Broadway apartment buildings and interesting examples of long-gone architectural styles.

---

## 7. Chinatown and Little Italy

---

One of the liveliest sections in the city, day or night, is **Chinatown,** a small area downtown bounded on the south by Worth Street, on the north by Canal Street. Its main commercial area stretches only a few blocks west from the Bowery. Best known for its abundance of low-priced Chinese restaurants, it is full of gift shops catering to the tourist trade and grocery and vegetable stores that are stocked with all kinds of Oriental foods. Its main streets are **Mott Street, Mulberry Street, Pell Street,** and **Doyers Street**—narrow, teeming roads that wind and intersect through the tiny neighborhood. You can enter the area from Canal Street at Mott or Mulberry, or from the Bowery at Pell Street. The Second Avenue bus is a good way to get here; ask the driver to let you off at Chatham Square. See Chapter II for our favorite eateries.

After you've seen Chinatown, walk up Mulberry to Canal Street, and as you keep going on Mulberry you will have entered the home of generations of Italian immigrants who have settled in this European-like community called **Little Italy.** Mulberry Street, above Canal, is the center of a booming activity from afternoon on, in restaurants and cafés that offer the best and lowest-priced Italian food in town. Besides the cafés and restaurants, there are lots of tiny shops that sell imported Italian groceries, cheeses, housewares, and a great array of sausage, and meat stores and tiny bakeries. The area, particularly Mulberry Street, has enjoyed a recent *risorgimento*—an effort to enhance and preserve the neighborhood's special character, its intimate scale, and bustling street life.

---

## 8. Chelsea

---

Like so many once-rundown areas of Manhattan, Chelsea is enjoying a renaissance. The area, which is loosely defined as bounded by Fifth Avenue on the east and the Hudson River on the west, runs from 14th Street to 34th Street. Chelsea was the center of the city from the mid–to late–19th century and is rich with historical interest. Before funding for the erection of the Statue of Liberty was completed, her hand (complete with torch) rested in **Madison Square Park** (Madison Avenue at 23rd Street). Madison Square Park, by the way, was the location of the original Madison Square Garden which encompassed the entire city block, Fourth Avenue (now Park Avenue South) to Madison Avenue and 26th to 27th streets.

Don't miss the **Flatiron Building,** a unique structure at the triangle formed by Broadway and Fifth Avenue at 23rd Street.

Walk west on **23rd Street,** once the heart of New York's theater district, dominated by the long-gone Grand Opera House on the corner of 23rd Street and Eighth Avenue. The **Chelsea Hotel** at 222 W. 23rd St., between Seventh and Eighth avenues, has been home to noted show business and literary figures, including Sherwood Anderson, O. Henry, Isadora Duncan, and Dylan Thomas. Today many rock stars enjoy the relative privacy of the Chelsea. Continue west on 23rd Street to Ninth Avenue, once the site of the home of Clement Clark Moore who wrote "The Night Before Christmas." Chelsea owes its name to Moore's father-in-law, a sea captain, who named his estate after a home for retired seamen—not the famous London district. When Moore died, he willed the land between 20th and 21st streets between Ninth and Tenth avenues to the **General Theological Seminary.** The seminary's beautiful gardens are open to the public during daylight hours.

The segment of Sixth Avenue in Chelsea from about 18th to 23rd streets was known as **Ladies Mile** during the mid-19th century and the street was lined with exclusive shops and stores. Ladies Mile continues to the east, on Broadway, from 20th Street south to 10th Street. The building on the southwest corner of Broadway and 20th Street, for example, was an early location of Lord & Taylor's department store.

Farther uptown, on Sixth Avenue, is the wholesale flower district between 26th and 29th streets. Buy yourself a bargain posy or stroll along West 28th Street between Fifth Avenue and Broadway and imagine it 100 years ago when it was the world's Tin Pan Alley.

## 9. TriBeCa

Another Manhattan artistic community is named for its location—the *Tri*-angle *Be*-low *Ca*-nal Street—and extends (loosely) south of Canal Street to the World Trade Center, and west of Broadway to the Hudson River. It can be reached by the IRT East Side subway, no. 4, 5, or 6 train to the Brooklyn Bridge stop. You'll emerge from the subway near **City Hall Park,** the scene of one of the first public readings of the Declaration of Independence, an event witnessed by George Washington and his troops. Several blocks south of the park, on Broadway at Vesey Street, is **St. Paul's Chapel.** Built in 1766, it's the oldest church building in Manhattan. Walk one block north from St. Paul's, along Broadway, and you'll encounter the **Woolworth Building.** This magnificent example of Gothic architecture was built in 1913 and for 18 years held the title of the world's tallest building. This "Cathedral of Commerce" possesses one of the most beautiful lobbies we have ever seen, with marble walls and floors, bronze wall decorations, and mosaic ceiling. If you enter the building from the Broadway entrance, look closely at the first archway to your left, and you'll see representations of Mr. Woolworth and his architect in each corner. In the rear of the lobby, a plaque details the history of the building.

Continue up Broadway to **Warren Street** and turn west toward the Hudson. This street is a bargain hunter's mecca, so do indulge if you'd like to buy a $30 man's shirt for $5 or a $27 book for $4.

North on Greenwich Street from Warren Street you'll see many factory buildings which have been born again as lofts. Despite fears of high-rent development, the loft-dwellers coexist peacefully with the olive oil/nut/coffee/produce businesses in the neighborhood. Continue up Greenwich Street to **Harrison Street** and you'll see a row of original Federal townhouses, saved from the wrecker and sold, by lottery, 25 years ago to lucky bidders.

**Hudson Street,** which runs parallel to and is one block east of Greenwich Street, is the main street of TriBeCa. The shops, galleries, and cafés in TriBeCa will give you a feeling of what SoHo was like before commercialization.

## 10. Central Park

A leafy oasis in the heart of Manhattan runs from Fifth Avenue to Eighth Avenue and from 59th to 110th streets—a total of 840 acres of boating, tennis, gardens, playgrounds, bridle paths, and statuary smack in the middle of some of the world's most expensive real estate. Plan to spend an afternoon in Central Park; it's perfectly safe during daylight hours as long as you proceed with caution—that is, don't let your wallet hang out of your back pocket or flash expensive jewelry.

You'll be able to experience a microcosm of city life in the park, from the English nannies and their charges, the East Side types sunning themselves behind the

Metropolitan Museum to the sounds of salsa, reggae, and rap drifting from the northernmost end of the park.

From the **horse-and-buggy rides** (hire a hack on the 59th Street side) to the **Wollman Ice-Skating Rink,** to the **zoo,** to the free Shakespeare in the **Delacorte Theater** in summer, Central Park is a nonstop attraction, much beloved by all New Yorkers.

Those who remember John Lennon will want to pay a visit to **Strawberry Fields,** a living memorial to the singer just across Central Park West from the Dakota Apartments at 72nd Street, where Lennon lived and where he was shot on December 9, 1980. Countries from around the world have contributed gifts to this "International Garden of Peace," whose initial $1 million funding came from Lennon's widow, Yoko Ono. A special spot.

---

# 11. Times Square

---

The Times Square area runs from 49th Street and Broadway to 42nd Street. It is, of course, home to New York's famed Broadway theater district. But it is also crammed with enough porno shows, pinball emporiums, pizza and souvlaki shops, and sleazy movie houses to supply the world. The area is nothing if not colorful. The section of 42nd Street between Seventh and Eighth avenues is best avoided, unless you're doing a sociological study on New York's lower depths. But the rest of the area is improving. The luxurious New York Marriott Marquis is here, between 45th and 46th streets, and other glamorous hotels and towering office buildings are under construction. Broadway and 42nd Street has been called the crossroads of the world, and rumor has it that if you stand on the corner long enough, you're sure to see at least half of all your friends. We can't guarantee that, surely, but you might see one of each type of person you've ever heard of. Clergy and streetwalkers, performers, cops, super-salesmen, pimps, office workers, out-of-towners, photographers, and just plain New Yorkers flock to the area for the movies, the girlie shows, and the theater. And there may be more gigantic billboards block for block here than anywhere else in the world.

---

**New York with Kids**

*The Candy Apple* by Bubbles Fisher, published by Prentice Hall Travel, $12.95, is a sure-fire hit of a book for people traveling to New York with children. Look for it in your local bookstore or write Prentice Hall Travel, 15 Columbus Circle, New York, NY 10023.

---

# V

# ONE-DAY EXCURSIONS
# FROM NEW YORK

## 1. UP THE HUDSON VALLEY
## 2. LONG ISLAND
## 3. NEW JERSEY

If you're planning to be in New York for a few weeks, you might very well want to spend some of your time traveling just outside of New York City—to the surrounding country areas which are noted for scenic beauty and a wide variety of gardens, beaches, old houses, and historical attractions. Most of these are within an hour or two's driving distance of mid-Manhattan. You can either rent a car and be on your own, or take a tour by bus or railroad.

The excursions described in this chapter will take you through the scenic Hudson River Valley to see the Historic Hudson Valley restorations, Museum Village in Orange County, the Mohonk Mountain House, Boscobel, Olana, Montgomery Place, Hyde Park (the home of Franklin D. Roosevelt), and some Hudson Valley wineries; then on to the unspoiled beauties of Long Island and to New York's favorite summer playground, Jones Beach; and a trip to Waterloo Village in nearby New Jersey.

## 1. Up the Hudson Valley

### THE HISTORIC HUDSON VALLEY
In addition to its natural beauty, the Hudson Valley has a rich colonial history; it is in this area that folk legends were created. The three Historic Hudson Valley restorations (tel. 914/631-8200) in the lower Hudson Valley were made possible by the generosity of John D. Rockefeller, Jr., who made his home in nearby Pocantico Hills. Located within a few miles of each other in the Tarrytown area, they span three centuries of Hudson Valley history. Admission to each property is $5 for adults, $4.50 for seniors, $3 for students; children under 6 are admitted free. Adults are given a comeback card after the first visit, which allows them to visit any other site for 20% off. A fourth property, Montgomery Place, is in Dutchess County (see below).

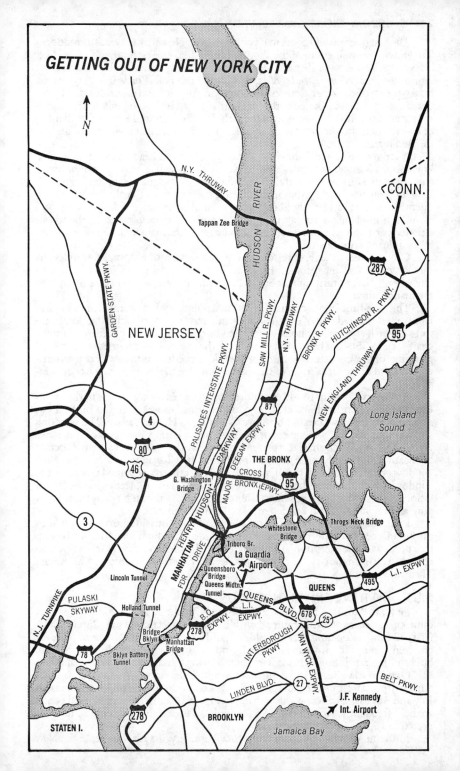

The first one you will come to if you drive from New York City is **Sunnyside,** in Tarrytown, one mile south of the Tappan Zee Bridge on West Sunnyside Lane (just off N.Y. 9). This was the 19th-century home of Washington Irving, the great literary figure who gave us *The Legend of Sleepy Hollow* and *Rip Van Winkle.* The gingerbread house is one of the most picturesque homes in America and is surrounded by orchards, gardens, and wooded paths that were planned by Irving himself. Inside, the rooms are furnished as they were in the early 19th century and are filled with many of Irving's personal momentos. Swans glide over the pond that Irving called his "little Mediterranean."

After you've visited Sunnyside, get in your car and head north on N.Y. 9 to **Philipsburg Manor,** two miles away in North Tarrytown. The stone manor house and gristmill date from the early 1700s and were the headquarters of the Philipses, a Dutch family who backed the British during the American Revolution and subsequently lost their vast land holdings. The gristmill is the scene of daily activity, and early farm implements and agricultural methods are demonstrated in the reconstructed barn nearby. A beautiful colonial kitchen in the main house is presided over by a guide in period costume.

Our favorite of the three restorations is **Van Cortlandt Manor,** a few miles farther up, off N.Y. 9 in Croton-on-Hudson. To get there, take the Croton Point Avenue exit off N.Y. 9, turn right at South Riverside Avenue, and go a quarter mile to the manor entrance.

This one-time home of an 18th-century politically important Dutch-English family is considered one of our most authentic restorations of early America. It features a Dutch-style manor house, a restored tavern, 18th-century gardens, fruit orchards, and a 750-foot brick walk connecting the manor house to the inn. There are plantings of flowers for every season and guides in period costumes who give horticultural and other focus tours of the estate, as well as early-American craft demonstrations.

Art lovers will want to add one more stop to this excursion: a visit to the **Union Church of Pocantico Hills,** close to Philipsburg Manor, to see the magnificent stained-glass windows created by Marc Chagall and Henri Matisse. The windows were commissioned by members of the Rockefeller family, members of this active church and congregation, and represent the final work completed by Matisse before his death and the only cycle of church windows by Chagall in this country. Nine windows were created by Chagall, who painted directly on the stained glass; the rose window, which shimmers high above the altar, is by Matisse. Sleepy Hollow Restorations conducts tours of the Union Church Wednesday through Friday from 1 to 4 p.m. and on Sunday from 2 to 5 p.m., April to December.

Philipsburg Manor, Van Cortlandt Manor, and Sunnyside are open daily April through December (only on weekends from January through March) from 10 a.m. to 5 p.m., with the exception of Thanksgiving, Christmas, and New Year's Days. To reach N.Y. 9 from the city, take the Major Deegan Expressway to the New York State Thruway.

## MUSEUM VILLAGE IN ORANGE COUNTY

Here, in Monroe, N.Y. (tel. 914/782-8247), is one of the country's largest outdoor museums of 19th century daily life. With a collection of over 250,000 artifacts, 32 exhibit/demonstration buildings, and a 17-acre site, this is a great place for children and the whole family. Demonstrations include broom-making, blacksmithing, printing, seasonal farm life, weavings, and a typical day in school.

Open in May, June, and September through December, Wednesday through Sunday from 10 a.m. to 2 p.m. on weekdays and noon to 5 p.m. on weekends; in July and August, Wednesday through Sunday from 10 a.m. to 5 p.m. Special events are held frequently. Admission is $5 for adults, $4 for senior citizens, $3 for children 6 to 15, and free for those under 6.

Museum Village is 50 miles from New York City. To get there, take the New

York State Thruway to Exit 16, Harriman. There, take N.Y. 17 west four miles to Exit 129 and follow the signs.

## MOHONK MOUNTAIN HOUSE

One of the most refreshing things a visitor can do to escape the frantic pace of New York is to spend a day at one of the last of the great mountain resorts of the 19th century: the famed Mohonk Mountain House in New Paltz, NY, 90 minutes away and a century apart. Both the sprawling Victorian castle that is the resort's center and the 7,500 acres of mountain splendor, including an alpine glacial lake, have been designated a National Historic Landmark. The Mohonk's public rooms are filled with an eclectic collection of 19th-century antiques, its walls hung with oil paintings and aging photographs of some famous Mohonk guests (among them four presidents, including Theodore Roosevelt), all drawn by the natural tranquility and beauty that the Mountain House still offers. Descendants of the Smileys, the Quaker family that founded the resort in 1869, are still in charge. Although overnight guests at the Mountain House pay top prices, day visitors can enjoy most of the indoor and outdoor facilities (except for use of the lake) simply by purchasing a meal, a rare bargain, indeed. Breakfast is $14.50; the midday buffet is $18 weekdays, $22 weekends; and dinner is $22. Advance reservations are a must, since capacity is limited (tel. 914/255-4500, or 233-2244 in New York).

Day visitors who wish to forgo the meal and bring a picnic lunch instead can be admitted to the grounds (but not to the Mountain House) by purchasing a day visitor's pass: $4 for adults midweek, $6 on weekends and holidays; $2 for children under 12 midweek, $3 on weekends and holidays. The pass entitles one to hike on the many miles of carriage roads, trails, and paths, to tour the extensive lawns and flower gardens, and to use the facilities of the Picnic Lodge, which is open daily from 11 a.m. to 6 p.m. in summer, and on weekends and holidays in spring and fall. Use of the lake is not included. For additional fees, day visitors may play golf or tennis or go horseback riding.

Mohonk Mountain House is open year round and it's a delight in all kinds of weather. In winter, it's very popular for cross-country skiing. To reach the resort, take the New York State Thruway to Exit 18. Turn left on N.Y. 299 and follow Main Street through New Paltz. Immediately after crossing the bridge over the Walkill River, turn right at the "Mohonk" sign, and after a quarter of a mile, bear left at the fork and follow the road up to the Mohonk gate.

## BOSCOBEL

Deeper into the Hudson Valley, but still less than a two-hour drive from midtown, is Boscobel (tel. 914/265-3638), the splendid Federal-style mansion that graces a bluff high above the Hudson River in the town of Garrison. It boasts one of the finest collections of Federal furnishings anywhere. The Dyckman family, descendants of Dutch colonists, who built the house in 1807, shopped for most of the furniture in New York and many of the pieces you will see came from the workshop of cabinetmaker Duncan Phyfe. Take time to stroll through the rose garden, the wildflower garden, and the herb garden, and visit the gift shop, with tasteful reproductions of Boscobel bowls, pottery, French linens, candles, and other items reminiscent of the 19th century.

Boscobel is eight miles north of the Bear Mountain Bridge on N.Y. 9D. It is open Wednesday through Monday throughout the year—except the months of January and February, and on Thanksgiving, Christmas, and New Year's Days—from 9:30 a.m. to 4:30 p.m. (to 3:30 p.m. in November, December, and March). Admission is $5 for adults, $4 for seniors, and $2.50 for children 6 to 14.

## HYDE PARK

In the same area, you shouldn't miss a visit to the **Home of Franklin D. Roosevelt National Historic Site,** more simply known as Hyde Park, birthplace of the late president. This is our favorite excursion. The house is maintained as it was during the Roosevelts' lifetimes, and both Franklin and Eleanor are buried in the Rose Garden, near the house. Don't miss seeing the library. It houses FDR's personal and presidential papers, as well as displays of priceless gifts he received while in the White House.

Open seven days a week from 9 a.m. to 5 p.m. April through October; closed on Tuesday and Wednesday from November through March. Admission is $3.50 for both house and library; seniors over 62 and children under 17, free.

From April through October, you have another special treat. A shuttle bus leaves from the Roosevelt home and takes guests two miles east to the **Eleanor Roosevelt National Historic Site** at Val-Kill. Val-Kill was Mrs. Roosevelt's home from 1945 to 1962, and it was here that she received such visitors as Nikita Khrushchev, Jawaharlal Nehru, Adlai Stevenson, and John F. Kennedy. A visit to Val-Kill includes a showing of a film biography of Mrs. Roosevelt, a tour of the cottage, the grounds, flower gardens, and wooded trails. There's a special charm about this place, the modest house that was Eleanor Roosevelt's special retreat and sanctuary.

Two miles farther north on N.Y. 9 is the **Vanderbilt Mansion** (tel. 914/229-9115). This is the millionaire's impressive home, built between 1896 and 1898. It's open seven days a week from 9 a.m. to 6 p.m. April through October, and Thursday through Monday from 9 a.m. to 5 p.m. November through March. Admission is $2.

Antique collectors and fans should be sure to visit the **Hyde Park Antiques Center** (tel. 914/229-8200), located between the Roosevelt and Vanderbilt Mansions right on N.Y. 9. Over 35 dealers feature furniture, glassware, china, jewelry, prints, toys, Orientalia, and collectibles. It's open daily from 10 a.m. to 5 p.m.

To drive to Hyde Park from Manhattan, take the West Side Highway to the Henry Hudson Parkway to the Saw Mill River Parkway to the Taconic Parkway. Then take Interstate 84 West to N.Y. 9 North at Fishkill, and follow N.Y. 9 to Hyde Park. Or take the Major Deegan Expressway to the New York State Thruway and get off at Exit 18 (New Paltz), following signs to the Mid-Hudson Bridge. After the bridge crossing, take the right ramp and follow signs to N.Y. 9 North.

## OLANA

About an hour's drive north of Hyde Park (and an hour's drive south of Albany) is what looks like an Islamic castle on the banks of the Hudson. This is the Olana State Historic Site, and all of it—house, studio, paintings, landscaping, furnishings—reflects the genius of the man who created it, the renowned landscape painter of the Hudson River School, Frederic Edwin Church. Inspired by a visit to Europe and the Near East in 1867, Church and his wife created a palace fit for an Oriental potentate, its lush Oriental trappings curiously mixed with Victorian furnishings. Outdoor views compete with those indoors: Olana is situated on a 500-foot hill overlooking the Hudson at a point where it abruptly becomes two miles wide, affording breathtaking vistas of the river and the Catskill Mountains.

The grounds of Olana are open every day from 8 a.m. to sunset. The castle can be viewed only on guided tours, which are held Wednesday through Sunday and also on Memorial Day, July 4th, and Labor Day. Tours begin at 10 a.m. from the first weekend in May to Labor Day, at noon from Labor Day to October 31. The last tour is at 4 p.m. There is a nominal fee for the tour, and because it is extremely popular, reservations are a must: contact Olana State Historic Site, R.D. 2, Hudson, NY 12534 (tel. 518/828-0135). For driving directions to Olana, which is on N.Y. 9G, five miles south of Hudson, phone the above number.

## MONTGOMERY PLACE

In this same northern reach of Dutchess County, about 50 miles south of Albany, visitors have a rare treat in store at Montgomery Place in Annandale-on-Hudson, a property of Historic Hudson Valley (see above). Montgomery Place, one of the great Hudson River Valley estates of the 19th century, was the ancestral

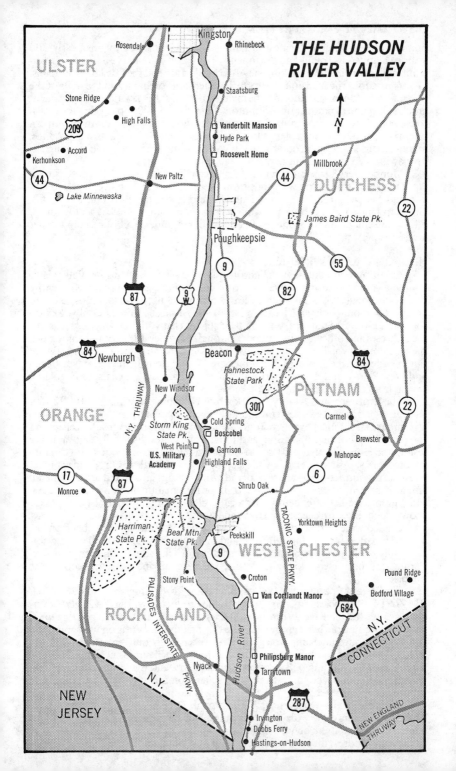

THE HUDSON RIVER VALLEY

ULSTER

Rosendale
Kingston
Rhinebeck
Stone Ridge
Staatsburg
209
High Falls
Vanderbilt Mansion
Accord
Hyde Park
Kerhonkson
Roosevelt Home
Millbrook
44
DUTCHESS
New Paltz
44
Lake Minnewaska
22
James Baird State Pk.
Poughkeepsie
9
87
9W
55
82
84
Newburgh
Beacon
84
Fahnestock
State Park
New Windsor
PUTNAM
301
ORANGE
Storm King
State Pk.
Cold Spring
Carmel
West Point
Boscobel
Brewster
U.S. Military
Garrison
Mahopac
Academy
Highland Falls
17
6
22
Monroe
87
Shrub Oak
Yorktown Heights
Harriman
State Pk.
Bear Mtn.
State Pk.
Peekskill
WESTCHESTER
9
Stony Point
Croton
Pound Ridge
Van Cortlandt Manor
Bedford Village
ROCKLAND
684
N.Y.
CONNECTICUT
Philipsburg Manor
NEW
Nyack
Tarrytown
JERSEY
287
NEW ENGLAND
Irvington
Dobbs Ferry
Hastings-on-Hudson

home of the prominent Livingston family, and its mansion contains nearly 200 years of family possessions and documents. The estate comprises 434 acres of river-front land, affording breathtaking views of the Hudson and the Catskill Mountains. Guests may tour the mansion, the formal gardens, the orchard, and the trails of the magnificent old woods. And they're invited to try out the lawn-game equipment, and have a game of croquet or badminton. More than 5,000 apple, pear, and peach trees are under cultivation in the farm portion of the estate, and in summer, you can purchase delicious Montgomery Place peaches, along with other seasonal produce, at the orchard's farm stand on N.Y. 9G. If you come during the fall, you're invited to "pick your own" in the apple orchards.

Montgomery Place is open every day except Tuesday from 10 a.m. to 5 p.m. April through October; on weekends from 10 a.m. to 4 p.m. in November, December, and March (grounds only on Thursday and Friday from 10 a.m. to 4 p.m.); closed in January and February. Admission to Montgomery Place is $5 for adults, $4.50 for seniors, $3 for students, free for children under 6. Grounds-only passes are $3 per person.

## HUDSON VALLEY WINERIES

Attention oenophiles! A delightful way to explore the Hudson Valley is to combine your sightseeing with a visit to a winery in the area—or plan your entire day around such a visit. There are at least 16 wineries in the region, most of them about a two-hour (or less) drive from New York. At most you're not only taken on tours and given free samples, but you'll be able to chat with the winemakers, savor local cheeses and other goodies, wander through the vineyards, stay and enjoy a pic-nic for as long as you like. There is a small admission charge to most wineries. Two of our favorites are the Brotherhood Winery in Washingtonville (close to Newburgh and West Point), and, farther north, the Regent Champagne Cellars, in Highland, not far from Poughkeepsie and Hyde Park.

The **Brotherhood Winery,** 35 North St., Washingtonville, NY 10992 (tel. 914/496-3661), is the oldest continuously operating winery in the United States. Visitors are taken on an extensive tour, invited to visit the underground cellars and the processing-bottling operation, and to taste the wines. Especially enjoyable is a visit to the Hors d'Oeuvrerie, a flower-bedecked outdoor patio, where you can nib-ble on cheeses, pastas, and pâtés while sipping wine by the glass. On Monday nights in August, gourmet meals are served and wine tastings are offered at the Vinehill Inn at Brotherhood for a cost of $45 (call for information and reservations). Sea-sonal events are held frequently: barbecues, grape-stomping festivals, antique car shows, "cooking with cheese" festivals, and holiday celebrations.

Guided wine-tasting tours are given every day May through October from 11 a.m. to 5 p.m. (January through April and in November and December, on week-ends only, from noon to 5 p.m.). Admission is $2 for adults; children visit free. Phone for group reservations and details. There's a gift and souvenir shop on the premises.

The **Regent Champagne Cellars,** Blue Point Road, Highland, NY 12528 (tel. 914/691-7296), boasts an entire "champagne production village," 425 acres over-looking the Hudson River. Visitors see everything, from vineyards to bottling lines. You can have a picnic here, enjoy a hayride through the vineyards on weekends, and take home a souvenir champagne glass. On weekends, six different champagnes are tasted with cheese and breadsticks. During the summer various evenings concerts are scheduled, including polka dances, jazz concerts, and the Hudson Valley Phil-harmonic. Various types of festivals are also held on the weekends, and the entire month of September sees the Grape Stomping Championships.

Tours are held on weekends, April through December from noon to 4 p.m. There are no tours on weekdays, only tastings. During the week, admission is $3 for adults, free for children; on weekends, $6 for adults, $2 for children. Phone or write to the above address for reservations, driving directions, and a schedule of events.

To get a free booklet on winery tours in the Hudson River region, plus information on historic sites and special events, phone 914/265-3066, or write to Hudson River Valley, 72 Main St., Cold Spring, NY 10516.

*Note to parents:* A visit to a winery makes for a delightful family outing—although the youngsters will not be given free samples!

## 2. Long Island

The **Long Island Rail Road** offers about 80 excellent, inexpensive escorted tours of Long Island, famed for its beaches and historic homes; they're scheduled during the summer and autumn months. The price of a ticket usually includes all admissions, transfers, and one meal. Write for the latest schedule to Customer Sales, Department 1723, Long Island Rail Road Co., Jamaica, NY 11435 (tel. 718/454-LIRR or 718/990-7498). Tickets for all tours may be purchased in advance or even 20 minutes before train time at the Long Island ticket office at Pennsylvania Station, 34th Street and Seventh Avenue.

There are two tours we think are most representative of what the area has to offer. First, the **Famous Homes and Garden Tour,** which will take you about 35 miles from the city, through Long Island's beautiful North Shore. You'll visit Sagamore Hill, home and summer White House of President Theodore Roosevelt; and then stop at the John S. Phipps Mansion and Old Westbury Gardens, one of the finest American examples of Georgian architecture, with the beautiful grounds surrounding it. Total cost (including dinner) is $27 for adults, $20 for children 5 to 11.

Some other Long Island Rail Road tours worthy of your attention include an all-day train-bus-boat tour on Wednesday to the **Cold Spring Harbor Fish Hatchery;** a Saturday or Sunday **ferryboat cruise** from Stony Brook Village to Bridgeport, Connecticut; and an all-day, 300-mile trip to the tip of Long Island, **Montauk Point,** with shopping time in Southampton Village.

### MANSIONS AND GARDENS
The legendary millionaires' estates of Long Island's "Gold Coast" have all but disappeared, but two grand ones still remain, and now welcome day visitors to enjoy their fabled interiors and splendid gardens. You'll need a car for this trip to Old Westbury Gardens in Old Westbury and/or Planting Fields Arboretum in Upper Brookville, Long Island. Driving time should be less than an hour from midtown Manhattan; the estates are about five miles from each other. Get an early start and you should be able to enjoy them both.

**Old Westbury Gardens** (tel. 516/333-0048 for information and driving directions), was the home of financier John S. Phipps: the mansion contains fabulous furnishings, curious artifacts, and a painting collection by late-19th- and early-20th-century giants. Behind the house are acres of superb gardens. There's plenty of room for a picnic, and a snackbar on the premises.

Old Westbury Gardens is open May through October, Wednesday through Sunday from 10 a.m. to 5 p.m. Admission to the gardens alone is $4.50 for adults, plus $3 for a tour of the house; for seniors, $3.50 for both house and gardens; for children 6 to 12, $1 for the gardens, $1.50 for the house. Picnic/pops concerts are held six times during the season (admission is $6 for adults, $3.50 for seniors, and $2 for children).

Much larger than Old Westbury Gardens, **Planting Fields Arboretum** (tel. 516/922-9206), is a joy for serious students of horticulture, photographers, and anyone who cherishes serenity and beauty. In the center of the 409-acre estate is Coe Hall, the former mansion of Englishman Robertson Coe. Planting Fields is open every day except Christmas, from 9:30 a.m. to 5 p.m. Concerts are often held. Admission is $3 per car.

## JONES BEACH

Beach lovers will want to visit Jones Beach, just a little over 30 miles from midtown. It offers everything from superb ocean swimming and white sandy beaches to paddle tennis and other sports, as well as a famous open-air theater for evening entertainment. Yes, it's crowded, especially on weekends. During the summer, a Long Island Rail Road package takes you there for a round-trip fare of $8.50 for adults, $5 for children. Another Long Island Rail Road package takes you to nearby Long Beach; the charge of $10 for adults includes admission to Ocean Beach Park. For information, phone 718/454-LIRR or 718/990-7498.

If you have your own wheels, you can drive to Jones Beach in about 1½ hours from midtown Manhattan. Jones Beach is at the end of the Meadowbrook and Wantagh State Parkways. You might also consider driving another 15 miles farther on to slightly less crowded Robert Moses State Park at the southern end of Sunken Meadow State Parkway. And if you prefer the mild waters of Long Island Sound to the sometimes rough surf of Jones Beach and Robert Moses State Park, try Sunken Meadow State Park, which is at the northern end of that same Southern Meadow State Parkway. For information, phone 516/669-1000.

---

# 3. New Jersey

---

## WATERLOO VILLAGE

New Jersey's restored Colonial-period hamlet in Stanhope is only 55 minutes by car from the George Washington Bridge. Set in the Allamuchy Mountain area, it offers a journey through American history. The little canal village contains historical homes and buildings dating from 1740 to 1860. Among them are the Canal House, a Revolutionary-period stone structure; a gristmill built in 1760; a blacksmith shop; and the Victorian Wellington House, dating from 1859. In all, 90 rooms have been refurbished in authentic period style. The village is also the scene of busy activity by craftspeople trained in early arts, whose work is sold in the general store that is part of the reconstruction.

On summer weekends, Waterloo is the site of a music festival with everything from orchestral and chamber concerts to jazz and bluegrass, featuring internationally known musicians—anyone from Arlo Guthrie to Alicia de Larrocha or Pete Seeger. Ticket prices start at $20, but the music festival is included with the village admission on most Sunday afternoons. For details, phone 201/347-4700.

Admission to the village Tuesday through Friday is $6 for adults, $4.50 for senior citizens, $3 for children 6 to 12; on Saturday and Sunday, $7.50 for adults, $5 for senior citizens, $3 for children. Prices are subject to change. Open Tuesday through Sunday from 10 a.m. to 6 p.m., from just after Easter through December (to 5 p.m. beginning in October). To get there, take the George Washington Bridge to Interstate 80 West to Exit 25. Then take N.J. 206 north and follow the signs to Waterloo Village. For further information, phone 201/347-0900.

# VI

# BARGAIN NIGHTSPOTS

## 1. BAR HOPPING
## 2. THE MUSIC SPOTS
## 3. DANCE, DANCE, DANCE
## 4. THEATRICAL AND NIGHTCLUB ENTERTAINMENT

**A**fter dusk falls, New York City's frantic daytime scurry reemerges in the nighttime spots—the cafés, clubs, bars, and cabarets. Quiet or closed during the day, they are transformed into glittery, swirling havens for people whose happiest times are at night. They become a night-person's paradise. You can do or find anything. There are piano bars, cabarets, and elegant watering holes for sophisticated fun. There are places for quiet conversation and a drink. And there are disco, jazz, and punk clubs for hot, sensual nights.

A night on the town can be expensive—as much as $100, sometimes more. But for the price of a moderate cover charge, or even just a drink, you can find lively and interesting entertainment. We've highlighted these places below.

Bars, which can be anything from chic celebrity hangouts to rowdy beer joints, make up the first section. They're described briefly with attention to atmosphere and crowd. Live music—from oldtime show tunes to jazz and New Wave—is a New York City trademark and the topic of the second section. The type of music, performers, and prices are noted. Our third major topic is the city's opportunities for you to "boogie," New York's dance spots. Cabarets and nightclubs comprise the final section. Again, prices and performers are noted.

## 1. Bar Hopping

### ROOMS WITH A VIEW

The view from the top of New York's skyscrapers is overwhelming. It spreads across Manhattan to the outer boroughs, showing off miles of crowded avenues, massive buildings, and elegant brownstones. Viewing all of this can be done relatively cheaply—provided you limit yourself to one cocktail.

At the top of the World Trade Center, with a 180° view, is the **Hors d'Oeuvrerie,** the bar at Windows on the World, One World Trade Center (107th floor; tel. 938-1111). Here you can have afternoon or evening drinks (house specialties start at about $5), along with tasty ethnic-style hors d'oeuvres ($4.75 to $15) while taking in the Statue of Liberty, Staten Island, or the Brooklyn Bridge and

Queens. Open to the public from 3 p.m. to 1 a.m. Monday through Saturday and on Sunday from 4 to 9 p.m., with hors d'oeuvres served after 4 p.m. Men must wear jackets, and no blue jeans are allowed.

The newly renovated 65th-floor **Rainbow Room,** at 30 Rockefeller Plaza (tel. 757-9090), rests about 850 feet above the city and the view from its three sides spreads at least 50 miles. You can see downtown Manhattan and Central Park directly below, and then as far afield as New Jersey. Meals at the restaurant are very formal and expensive; the **Rainbow and Stars** supper club charges a $35 cover for cabaret acts such as Tony Bennett and Rosemary Clooney. Better to go just for the view and a drink at the **Rainbow Promenade** bar, which is open weekdays from 3 p.m. to 1 a.m., on Saturday from noon to 1 a.m., and Sunday from noon to 11 p.m.

At **Top of the Tower,** atop the Beekman Tower Hotel, 49th Street and First Avenue (tel. 355-7300), the view spreads from the East River to the Empire State Building and the United Nations. There's also an outdoor terrace from which the scenery is even more pleasant. There's no cover or minimum, but drinks are expensive—between $4 and $7.50 apiece. Tuesday through Saturday a pianist entertains between 9 p.m. and 2 a.m.

Another skyscraper café is **Top of the Sixes,** on the 39th and top floor of 666 Fifth Ave. (tel. 757-6662). The scenery through its large windows includes Central Park, downtown Manhattan, and parts of New Jersey. Drinks are moderately priced at about $3.75 for cocktails and $2.50 for beer. There's entertainment Tuesday through Saturday. Open Tuesday through Saturday from 11:30 a.m. to midnight, with complimentary hors d'oeuvres served during happy hour, 5 to 7:30 p.m. Closed Sunday.

## HANGOUTS

On a weekend night in Manhattan, the bars and cafés are as seductive as anything in town. In the Village and on the East and West Sides they dot nearly every block; and when passing by you can't help but be enticed by what's inside—long bars lined with gleaming bottles and glasses, chatter and music that spills into the street, and the glitter of the famous and high-powered that frequent many of them. There is a bar for everyone—for artists, actors, students, musicians, politicos, and business types. They are the "in" places—though not always expensive—and as much a New York trademark as the Stock Exchange and Broadway.

We have listed the popular, famous, and more intriguing bars. Some have already been covered in the restaurant section, and in this case our description is cursory. Any drink prices not covered are moderate.

### Upper East Side

Oak wood bars, art nouveau, and Tiffany-style lamps are ubiquitous in Upper East Side bars. These are elegant and lavish watering holes, hoping also to become second homes for the chic or famous.

**Elaine's,** 1703 Second Ave., between 88th and 89th streets (tel. 534-8103), takes that image to its zenith. The bartender will tell you that Francis Ford Coppola and producer Robert Evans were in before you, and mention a few others familiar only to those with an insider's knowledge of the celebrity scene. For the price of a drink—about $4—you can sit at the bar and watch for celebrities, but don't expect gracious service unless you fit in with the glitterati. Open nightly until 4 a.m.

Housed in a 19th-century red-brick building, **P.J. Clarke's,** 915 Third Ave., at 55th Street (tel. 759-1650), is a remnant of a time when bars, tenements, and antique shops gave this area a real neighborhood feel. Next to the towering headquarters of Skidmore, Owings, and Merrill, Clarke's looks tiny and inconsequential. But inside it's the type of place that garners an avid following of celebrities and noncelebrities alike. It has one of the city's most ornate cut-glass and mahogany bars, and its two back dining rooms have black-and-white tiled floors covered with sawdust. What's more, Clarke's has one of the best jukeboxes in town, with oldies by

Sinatra, Peggy Lee, the Ink Spots, and the Mills Brothers. All this and you can get a beer for $2.25. Open nightly until 4 a.m.

A similar ambience, with a preppy twist, fills **Ruppert's,** 1662 Third Ave., at 93rd Street (tel. 831-1900). The split-level bar draws a young professional crowd which sports polo shirts, crew-neck sweaters, and tweed jackets. A pianist performs seven nights a week upstairs, and food is served downstairs until 12:30 a.m. Open nightly until 4 a.m.

**Drake's Drum,** 1629 Second Ave., between 84th and 85th streets (tel. 988-2826), has the feel of a British tavern. Rumor has it that the English tourists are almost always directed to the bar—which is owned by Englishmen—and that most regular customers have Cockney accents. British flags are stretched across the ceiling and the floor is covered with sawdust in this friendly and low-key bar. Open nightly until 4 a.m.

Whether your taste runs to flirting on the dance floor or to whispering "sweet nothings" over a quiet drink, you can find your niche in the Upper East Side singles bars.

The best spot in the neighborhood for singles on the prowl is **T.G.I. Friday's,** 1152 First Ave., at 63rd Street (tel. 832-8512), where you can try out your best one-liners until 1 a.m. weeknights and until about 3 a.m. on Friday and Saturday. The bartenders are chatty, friendly, and extremely well schooled in the art of moderating a boy-girl repartée.

## Upper West Side

**McGlade's New Pub,** 154 Columbus Ave., at 67th Street (tel. 595-9130), is reputed to be one of the best bars in New York. Its customers include many of the staff from ABC's network headquarters across the street. This is a relaxed bar for young professionals, and has a good mix of neighborhood people, writers, and artists. Open nightly until 2 a.m., later if it's happening.

Take a window seat at **Marvin Gardens,** 2274 Broadway, between 81st and 82nd streets (tel. 799-0578), and watch the crowds along Broadway. This clean, comfortable bar attracts a sophisticated set. Open Sunday through Wednesday until 2 a.m., Thursday through Saturday until 3 a.m.

**The All-State Café,** 250 W. 72nd St., between Broadway and West End Avenue (tel. 874-1883), is a friendly, no-fuss bar with a jukebox that won't quit and all the right brands of beer in bottles and on tap. The All-State is open daily from 11:30 a.m. to 2 or 3 a.m.

**Broadway Bay,** 2180 Broadway, at the corner of 77th Street (tel. 362-4360), is a pleasant watering hole with a Southwest flavor and good seats for the game or the videos or whatever else might be on the tube. The margaritas are large and salsa and chips are on the house. Open nightly until about 2 a.m.

Fun is the name of the game for young professionals who flock to **Amsterdam's,** 428 Amsterdam Ave., between 80th and 81st streets (tel. 874-1377), from all over Manhattan. This bar and rôtisserie has the flavor of a college football crowd ready to go wild and start cheering at any moment. Open from noon to 2 or 3 a.m. daily.

On the same block is **KCOU Radio,** 430 Amsterdam Ave., between 80th and 81st streets (tel. 580-0556). This bar rivals Amsterdam's in attracting local young professionals. Highlights of KCOU include a streamlined look with touches of blue neon lighting, and a jukebox that features rock and rhythm-and-blues. Open nightly until 4 a.m.

There's no sign marking the entrance to **Bamboo Bernie's,** 2268 Broadway, between 81st and 82nd streets (tel. 580-0200), just a primitive painting and a corrugated-tin overhang. Among other equatorial touches inside, there's a woven rattan ceiling and a tape of lively island music. Happy hour, from 5 to 8 p.m., features half-price frozen drinks and free popcorn. Open daily until about 4 a.m.

The ambience at **Lucy's,** 503 Columbus Ave., between 84th and 85th streets (tel. 787-3009), is strictly Southern California, a bit of Venice Beach in New York. Favored poisons are margaritas and Dos Equis beer—awesome, like totally. Open daily from 5 p.m. until the wee hours.

**Brat's Bar,** 2662 Broadway, between 101st and 102nd streets (tel. 678-9165), is a little-known secret, tucked in the middle of the block behind an unassuming façade. Inside, however, the atmosphere is pleasant, informal, and cozy. A fun group of regulars often gives the bartender grief and then buys rounds for the house. Open daily until about 2 a.m.

## Murray Hill/Gramercy Park

Be sure to check out the wood-paneled Rodeo Bar at **Albuquerque Eats,** 375 Third Ave., at 27th Street (tel. 683-6500), where bartenders serve up drinks from inside an old horse trailer. You genuinely feel as if you've been transported to the Wild West. There is live music every night until the wee hours of the morning. The hostess claims that the music goes until 4 or 5 a.m., but neighbors and members of the local constabulary may have a different story to tell. A beer is $3 to $3.75, depending on the label; mixed drinks are slightly higher. There is no cover charge, but a three-drink minimum at the tables.

## Midtown West/Times Square

Around Midtown West/Times Square, the bars and pubs attract audiences and performers from the nearby theater district, and if you're lucky you might very well stumble upon a Broadway star.

Try the fabled and very beautiful **Russian Tea Room,** 150 W. 57th St., between Sixth and Seventh avenues (tel. 265-0947). It has a second-floor bar that's a perfect roost for watching the passing parade of celebrity diners. A favorite with Carnegie Hall concert-goers, the restaurant was refurbished in the red-velvet opulence of a czar's palace. This is not a place to come in jeans and T-shirts, especially if you expect to get good service. While you're here, you might try one of the vodka specials that go by names like Ivan the Terrible, the Ballet Russe, the Moscow Mule, and the Nureyev. Open seven days a week until 11 p.m.

The line of tourists waiting to get into the **Hard Rock Café,** 221 W. 57th St., between Sixth and Seventh avenues (tel. 489-6565), is usually quite long, as befits this New York version of owner Isaac Tigrett's legendary London restaurant/bar. Like its London counterpart, this Hard Rock is a museum of rock-and-roll memorabilia, including 100 gold records, Prince's jacket from the movie *Purple Rain,* Chubby Checker's boots, and the guitars of Eric Clapton and Eddy Van Halen. Even the bar is shaped like a guitar. Open daily from 11:30 a.m. to 4 a.m.

The preferred watering hole of the Lincoln Center set is the **Ginger Man,** 51 W. 64th St., between Columbus Avenue and Central Park West (tel. 399-2358). Employees warn that this is not a casual bar, but a place for a quiet drink or light meal after the ballet or symphony. The crowd here is heavily sprinkled with celebrities, and the bar's interior is as elegant as its patrons. Brass railings ring the oak bar and old Lincoln Center posters (they've become collectors' items) line the walls. Open nightly until midnight.

Less expensive but also star-studded is **Joe Allen's,** 326 W. 46th St., between Eighth and Ninth avenues (tel. 581-6464), open daily until 2 a.m.; food served until 1:30 a.m. Another is the very similar **Charlie's,** 236 W. 45th St., between Broadway and Eighth Avenue (tel. 354-2911), open later, until 4 a.m.

For a more romantic, steeped-in-history atmosphere, head west to the **Landmark Tavern,** 626 Eleventh Ave., at 46th Street (tel. 757-8595). But don't wait too late; it closes at midnight during the week and at 1 a.m. on Saturday and Sunday.

Lodged in a historic oak dining room built by Andrew Carnegie, **Lavin's Restaurant and Wine Bar,** 23 W. 39th St., between Fifth and Sixth avenues (tel. 921-1288), is a relaxing place to educate your wine palate. The bar, with its cool white marble countertop and etched-glass lamps hanging overhead, is a genteel refuge on a hot summer day. The bar emphasizes California wines, though there are European wines available by the glass as well. Pleasant wines cost about $3.50 for each glass, but there is always a superior-quality wine to taste as well ($6 to $12). Weekdays only, from noon to 10 p.m.

## Greenwich Village

In Greenwich Village the bars tend to be more casual, less expensive, and livelier. In any one of a number of clubs and nightspots you can join an offbeat crowd of students, artists, musicians, and locals for music, a drink, and a good time.

The **Cottonwood Café**, 415 Bleecker St., between West 11th and Bank streets (tel. 924-6271), is a lone and rising star in the Village. Fairly new to the Village scene, it has broken the mold. It's Texas in Manhattan, serving up great Tex-Mex food, a can't-be-beat friendliness, and live folk and country-western music every night except Sunday. The bar closes at 2 a.m. nightly.

**Sazerac House**, 533 Hudson St., at the corner of Charles Street (tel. 989-0313), serves New Orleans–style food but its ambience is pure Old Village. It's a local crowd that frequents Sazerac's bar, but you can break in and provide some out-of-towner talk. Open nightly until 2 a.m.

For those with a literary bent, there's **The Lion's Head**, 59 Christopher St., just off Seventh Avenue South (tel. 929-0670). It's one of the most famous writers' bars in the city. Besides that, it's cozy and pubby. Open most nights until 4 a.m.

The legendary **White Horse Tavern**, 566 Hudson St., at the corner of West 11th Street (tel. 243-9260), is where Dylan Thomas once wolfed down 18 shots of whiskey in less than 20 minutes, and died several days later. The White Horse is still host to writers and artists. It serves good hamburgers and omelets, and is open until 1 or 2 a.m. every night.

For romance, there's **Ye Waverly Inn**, 16 Bank St., at Waverly Place (tel. 929-4377). This old and dimly lit tavern is perfect for a romantic date. It's not open very late though: Monday through Thursday until 10 p.m., on Friday and Saturday until 11 p.m., and on Sunday until 9 p.m.

One bar that's popular without drawing a specific type of crowd is **Woody's**, 140 Seventh Ave. South, between 10th and Charles streets (tel. 242-1200). It has a mix of regulars and occasionals, making for a friendly and even pleasantly rowdy atmosphere. Good food is served until 1 a.m. every day; the bar closes at 2 a.m.

If you want a late-night espresso instead of a drink, the **Peacock Caffé**, 24 Greenwich Ave., off 10th Street (tel. 242-9395), is a popular coffeehouse hangout. Its classical music and baroque columns provide a restful, pensive break from sightseeing or bar hopping. Open until 1 a.m. Tuesday through Thursday and on Sunday, until 2 a.m. on Friday and Saturday; closed Monday.

**Chumley's**, 86 Bedford St., at Barrow Street (tel. 675-4449), is the quintessence of Old Village atmosphere. The entrance is unmarked because it used to be a speakeasy, and this two-room basement establishment seems not to have changed a bit since the old days. The neighborhood regulars and local bohemians make Chumley's a relaxed and convivial place. Open seven nights a week until 2 or 3 a.m.

The bar at **The NoHo Star**, 330 Lafayette St., at the corner of Bleecker Street (tel. 925-0070), always seems crowded in the evenings with zippy folks on their way to someplace else—a gallery, a movie, a party, another bar. So latch on. The bar is open until midnight Sunday through Thursday, and until 1 a.m. on Friday and Saturday.

A quiet, old-fashioned neighborhood bar can be found at 331 W. 4th St., on the corner of Jane Street. **The Corner Bistro** (tel. 242-9502) will never be confused with a hot spot, but if relaxation, conversation, and a great hamburger are what you need, this is your place. Open until 4 a.m. every day.

For a traditional café society feeling, there's the bar at **One Fifth**, at One Fifth Ave., entrance around the corner on East 8th Street (tel. 260-3434). Wednesday through Saturday nights, a jazz pianist holds forth in this classy little room tricked up to look like a 1920s ocean liner. In addition to the standard drinks and wine list, clams, burgers, and shrimp are available until the bar closes—every night at midnight.

For late-night beer binges, try **Woody's** on Seventh Avenue South between West 10th and Charles streets (tel. 242-1200). You can sit at the glassed-in patio or take a seat at the 150-year-old Bavarian bar that features over 50 kinds of bottled beer. Woody's closes at 1 a.m. during the week; 2:30 a.m. on weekends.

For afternoon drink specials and a casual atmosphere, stroll down to the **Acme Bar & Grill,** 9 Great Jones St., near the corner of Lafayette Street (tel. 420-1934). The Acme is cheerful and rowdy, and closes at 1 a.m.

If you're craving Mexican food and want to choose one of 100 different kinds of fruit drinks, try **Panchito's,** 105 MacDougal Street, at Bleecker and West 3rd streets (tel. 487-8963). Panchito's closes at 4 a.m. Its drinks are pure and natural—no additives or premixes.

If you like theme bars, try the **Caliente Cab Company,** 21 Waverly Pl., at the corner of Greene Street (tel. 243-8517). Loud and festive, the Caliente features six TV screens and a video bar complete with a video DJ and ample room for sports fans. Open until 2 a.m. during the week and 3 a.m. on weekends.

The **Cedar Tavern,** 82 University Pl., at E. 11th Street (tel. 929-9089), is a popular nightspot with a full bar and affordable bar food. The tavern offers a dark and cozy atmosphere and its century-old bar caters to a student, business, and neighborhood crowd. Open daily until 3 a.m.

If you enjoy a funky Mexican atmosphere, you'll like the party at **Bayamo,** 704 Broadway, between Washington Place and East 4th Street (tel. 475-5151). Bayamo offers favorites like Ron Ponche de Piña and pineapple rum punch for $5. Open until 1:30 a.m. during the week, 2 a.m. on weekends.

## East Village

You'll feel welcome at **Dojo's,** 24 St. Marks Pl., between Second and Third avenues (tel. 674-9821), in the heart of the East Village. There are lots of friendly faces and good conversations here. Drink at the light-wood bar or, in the summer, under a canopied porch. Open Sunday through Thursday from 11 a.m. to midnight, on Friday and Saturday to 1 p.m.

No tour of the East Village bars would be complete without a visit to the **Grassroots Tavern,** on the same block at 20 St. Marks Pl. (tel. 475-9443), a fun, noisy bar with lots of life, and a solid crowd of regulars. Open daily from 4 p.m. to 3 a.m.

You'll find **Holiday,** 75 St. Marks Place (tel. 777-9637), usually crowded with locals, whether they are sitting on the jukebox or gathered around the bar. Lots of hard drinking is done in this smokey, boisterous establishment. Christmas lights, up all year round, add a bit of the holiday spirit. Open from 9 a.m. to 1 a.m. daily.

Lots of white-paint graffiti art decorate the black walls of **Downtown Beirut,** 156 First Ave., between 9th and 10th streets (tel. 777-9011). There are even drawings of rolls of barbed wire, suggesting off-limits areas of Beirut. Downtown Beirut has a clubhouse atmosphere for a younger set of punks and East Village types. Open daily from 1 p.m. to 4 a.m.

Officially **King Tut's Wa Wa Hut,** on the southeast corner of 7th Street and Avenue A (tel. 254-7772), has no name. Still, it is one of the more imaginative bars in the area. Every few months local artists redecorate the entire bar according to a particular theme. In the backroom furniture is arranged in little conversational settings. Open from 4 p.m. to 4 a.m. daily.

**Sugar Reef,** 93 Second Ave., between 5th and 6th streets (tel. 477-8427), features a huge selection of tropical drinks and a nonstop party atmosphere. A word of warning though: Don't be surprised if there's a line, especially on a weekend. The bar is open from 4 p.m. to 4 a.m. daily.

Walk into **Caramba !,** 684 Broadway, at Great Jones (East 3rd) Street (tel. 420-9817), and you walk into a fiesta. Students and young professionals gather at the large front bar to party and meet friends. They come especially for the margarita slushes, featured in three sizes: small (3½ ounces), medium (12 ounces), and ridiculous (26 ounces). Open from noon to midnight weekdays, until 1 a.m. weekends.

If you've got a margarita-only thirst, another good bet is **Bandito!,** 153 Second Ave., between 9th and 10th streets (tel. 777-4504). In warm weather, sit at one of their outdoor sidewalk tables and you'll have a ringside view of the East Village. Open from noon to midnight.

Although only men were allowed into the rustic rooms of **McSorley's Old Ale House,** 15 E. 7th St., near Third Avenue (tel. 473-9148), until 1970, the pub now hosts both men and women. There's a solid college crowd here, but old-timers sit around in front of the pot-bellied stove as well, downing steins of draft ale.

## SoHo

Over in SoHo, the **Broome Street Bar,** at the corner of Broome Street and West Broadway (tel. 925-2086), is popular among artists, writers, and musicians. There's an accent on tropical drinks, and jazz plays from the bar's sound system. Open weeknights to about 2 a.m., weekends until 3 a.m.

There's a similar clientele at the **Ear Inn,** 326 Spring St., between Washington and Greenwich streets (tel. 226-9060). Ear Inn offers a good jukebox, poetry readings, and for the creative customer, butcher-paper tablecloths, and crayons for scribbling. The bar is open until around 4 a.m.

For a warming hot toddy in winter or a cooling piña colada in summer, you might make a SoHo stop at the **Prince Street Bar and Restaurant,** 125 Prince St., at the corner of Wooster Street (tel. 228-8130). It's popular with SoHo locals. Open until 1 a.m. weekdays, to 2 a.m. on Friday and Saturday.

For wine connoisseurs, a SoHo must is the **SoHo Kitchen,** 103 Greene St., between Prince and Spring streets (tel. 925-1866). It serves 110 varieties of wine and champagne by the 2.5-ounce taste, the glass, or the bottle. Open until 2 a.m. weekdays, until 4 a.m. on weekends.

## Lower Manhattan/TriBeCa

In TriBeCa you can head for a late-night drink to **Smoke Stacks Lightnin',** 380 Canal St., at West Broadway (tel. 226-0485), open until 2:30 a.m. Sunday through Thursday, until 4 a.m. on Friday and Saturday.

Or there's the lovely, lofty **211 West Broadway,** at Franklin Street (tel. 925-7202), a place typical of TriBeCa's warehouse turned bar/restaurants, with a pressed-tin ceiling and cast-iron columns.

There's always a neighborhood crowd at **Puffy's Tavern,** 81 Hudson St., four blocks south of Canal Street (tel. 766-9159), open for late-night drinks and socializing.

And down the street, you can have a drink in one of the prettiest of the TriBeCa warehouse-restaurants: **Capsouto Frères,** 451 Washington St., at Watts Street (tel. 966-4900).

Sports fans will love **The Sporting Club,** 99 Hudson St., between Harrison and Franklin streets (tel. 219-0900), where the main draw is a ten-foot video screen and its companion, a computerized scoreboard, which tower above the oval bar.

One of the best places to hang out in the South Street Seaport area is **The North Star Pub,** 93 South St., at Fulton Street (tel. 509-6757), which serves several varieties of British ale in keeping with its British décor.

If you want to be close to the water, enjoy a drink at two of Pier 17's outdoor bar cafés: **Caroline's at the Seaport** (tel. 233-4900) or **Café Café** (tel. 406-2870), both at 89 South St.

## PIANO BARS

This is becoming one of New York's most popular scenes, and understandably so! Piano bars are more romantic, more fun, and more relaxed than singles bars.

And since few piano bars have either minimums or cover charges, they tend to be less expensive than jazz clubs.

One of the largest and most esteemed piano bars in Manhattan is **Joe's Pier 52,** 163 W. 52nd St., between Sixth and Seventh avenues (tel. 245-6652), a seafood restaurant and bar. Teddy Robson performs jazz in the "showboat lounge" from 8 p.m. to 1 a.m. on Friday and Saturday. On Sunday and Monday Teri Thornton plays. Drinks run $3 and $6; excellent cold appetizers (mostly seafood) run $7 to $10 and are available in the lounge, with many patrons cracking their lobsters as they sit at the bar.

**The Stage Door Canteen,** in Kippy's Pier 44, 700 Eighth Ave., between 44th and 45th streets (tel. 869-3600), a piano bar in the Milford Plaza Hotel, features Mike Cossi playing show tunes and popular music Monday through Saturday from 7 p.m. to 1 a.m. There is no minimum and no cover charge.

Piano bars are also popular on the East Side. One of the most frequented is **Mimi's,** 984 Second Ave., at 52nd Street (tel. 688-4692). A pianist is on duty Monday through Saturday between 9 p.m. and 4 a.m., and on Sunday from 6:30 p.m. to 12:30 a.m.

**The Toy Bar,** 401 E. 78th St., between First and York avenues (tel. 988-4530), is a tiny hole-in-the-wall offering jazz piano from 9 p.m. to 1 a.m. Monday through Thursday, and from 10 p.m. to 2 a.m. on Friday and Saturday. On Monday from 6 to 8 p.m. and Sunday from 7 to 9 p.m. a tarot-card reader holds forth.

Other piano bars on the East Side include **La Camelia,** 225 E. 58th St., between Second and Third avenues (tel. 751-5488), with live music by Clinton Hayes from 10 p.m. to 2 a.m. nightly, and **Nickels,** 227 E. 67th St., between Second and Third avenues (tel. 794-2331), where piano music can be heard from 10 p.m. to midnight.

Over in Murray Hill, pianist Lenny Metcalfe brings lots of warmth to **Billy Budd,** 303 Lexington Ave., at 37th Street (tel. 684-8227). There is music Tuesday through Thursday from 9 p.m. to 2 a.m., on Friday from 10 p.m. to 3 a.m., and on Saturday from 9 p.m. to 2 a.m.

Another highly recommended piano bar is at **The Village Green,** 531 Hudson St., between West 10th and Charles streets (tel. 255-1650). Open from 8:30 p.m. to 1 a.m. Tuesday through Saturday.

**The Village Corner,** Bleecker Street at LaGuardia Place (tel. 473-9762), is a good spot to escape from the hustle and bustle of Bleecker Street. Resident pianist Lance Hayward plays from 8 p.m. to 1 a.m. most nights. On the weekends there is a $6-per-person minimum.

## HOTEL BARS

You may not be able to afford a room in some of New York's posh hotels, but that shouldn't prevent you from enjoying their distinctive ambience or their cocktail hours.

The **Carlyle,** at Madison Avenue and 76th Street (tel. 744-1600), has its share of celebrity guests. You may glimpse a few in Bemelmans Bar (named after the illustrator whose delightful murals adorn the walls), a pleasing place with decorated columns, small dark tables, and a grand piano for the singers who perform nightly from 9:30 p.m. The cover charge is $5; during the entertainment, drinks start at $6. Adjoining the bar is the Gallery where you can sip your drinks while sitting on velvet couches and comfortable upholstered chairs. (In the afternoon—from 3 to 5:30 p.m. daily—it's a tea room.) The bar is open nightly until 1 a.m.

Also in the hotel, the elegant **Café Carlyle** is open for drinks and musical entertainment until 1 a.m. Performers do two shows nightly, at 10 p.m. and midnight. The cover charge varies, according to who's at the piano. (*Note:* The Café Carlyle is closed for the summer.)

At the **Regency,** Park Avenue at 61st Street (tel. 759-4100), the wood-paneled cocktail lounge with its subdued lighting and dramatic red floral murals attracts an international crowd. For the price of a glass of wine ($4.75) or a cocktail ($5.25 and up), you can enjoy the piano music every night from 6 to 9 p.m. and again from 10 p.m. to 1 a.m. Complimentary hors d'oeuvres are served from 5 to 7 p.m. Open nightly until 2 a.m.

An underrated institution is the **Monkey Bar** in the Hotel Élysée, 60 E. 54th St., between Park and Madison avenues (tel. 753-1066). The monkey wallpaper is reminiscent of Disney's *Jungle Book* and hasn't changed since the place opened 53 years ago. The leopard-spotted carpet, fake-lizard upholstery, and monkey lamps are a testament to kitsch. Mixed drinks are about $4 to $7; beer is $3.50. Monday through Saturday there are two sets of piano music, at 5:30 and 7:30 p.m. On Saturday they add a comedian and singer, and depending on who's on the bill, a $15 cover. Open daily to midnight.

For *New Yorker* magazine fans, or anyone interested in things literary, what could be more exciting than a drink at the **Algonquin Hotel,** 59 W. 44th St., between Fifth and Sixth avenues (tel. 840-6800). The Algonquin was home to the magazine's celebrated "Round Table"—Franklin Pierce Adams, James Thurber, Dorothy Parker, Alexander Woollcott, and Heywood Broun. You can still see *New Yorker* writers and editors sipping drinks in either the lobby bar or the adjoining Blue Bar. Both bars serve drinks until 2 a.m. The bartenders make a point of being gracious to everyone. Top cabaret headliners, such as Christopher Mason and Harry Connick, Jr., appear in the dark and romantic Oak Room, just off the lobby. There are shows Tuesday through Saturday at 9:15 p.m., with an additional show on Friday and Saturday at 11:15 p.m., with a $15 food and drink minimum. Reservations are suggested.

Across the street from the Algonquin is **The Royalton,** 44 W. 44th St., between Fifth and Sixth avenues (tel. 869-4400). This is an ideal spot to take tea over a game of checkers or chess, or grab an after-theater bite to eat. The Nehru-jacketed staff is cordial and the futuristic furniture in the minimalist lobby is oddly relaxing. Two can snack on a sandwich plate, such as the goat cheese with black olive and sun-dried tomato purée ($9.50) or the crabmeat salad with orange ($11.50). No alcohol is served, but a pot of fruit ambrosia tea ($3.50) takes the edge off the day, as does a cup of orange cappuccino ($4). The toasted pound cake with berries and sweet cream is also a hit ($7.50). Open weekdays for tea from 2:30 p.m. to midnight.

Comfortable leather chairs and banquettes in the classic Oak Bar at the **Westin Plaza,** Fifth Avenue at 59th Street (tel. 546-5321), offer a lovely view of Central Park South. The dark Edwardian interior of this handsome room, with oak-paneled walls, an ornate ceiling, and original Everett Shinn murals, evoke the spirit of old New York. An informal pub-style menu is offered and house wines and beer start at $4, cocktails from $6.50. Open daily from 11:30 a.m. to 2 a.m.

At the **Waldorf-Astoria,** Park Avenue and 50th Street (tel. 355-3000), an international clientele gathers nightly at three distinctive and extravagantly decorated bars. Sir Harry's Bar has an African-safari motif with trophy heads and zebra skins on the walls. The Cocktail Terrace overlooks the exquisite art deco Park Avenue lobby and is open for tea from 2:30 to 10 p.m. Peacock Alley is next to a two-ton, nine-foot-tall, bronze clock that's capped with a miniature of the Statue of Liberty. The main attraction at this famous bar is songwriter Cole Porter's personal piano. Porter lived at the Waldorf for several years, and his tunes are played on the piano nightly. Open nightly until midnight. There are no cover charges at any of the bars. Drinks start at $5.50 for cocktails and $4 for beer.

Harry's is an inexplicably popular name for New York hotel bars. Harry's at the **New York Helmsley,** 212 E. 42nd St., between Lexington and Third avenues (tel. 490-8900), has one feature not to be missed—a lavish complimentary buffet served between 5 and 7 p.m. which includes shrimp cocktails, fresh vegetables, and quiches. A pianist entertains while you dine. Drinks start at $5.25 for cocktails and $4.50 for wine, but anyone with a large appetite will make out fine. The bar closes at 1 a.m

The **Helmsley Palace,** at 455 Madison Ave., between 50th and 51st streets (tel. 888-7000), has yet another Harry's Bar, named for Mr. Helmsley himself! For $8 you can buy a glass of champagne and pretend you're staying at one of the world's most expensive hotels. The bar has a pianist between 6 p.m. and 1 a.m. Located in the adjoining Villard House, a landmark and the hotel's trademark, is the elegant Hunt Bar. Soft couches and corner tables offer privacy and piano music plays nightly until 2 a.m.

But if it's a summery evening, you might want to sit at the outdoor Café de la Paix, at the **St. Moritz,** 50 Central Park South, at 59th Street and Sixth Avenue (tel. 755-5800). For the price of a glass of wine ($3.75), this Parisian-style café offers the perfect setting for a romantic interlude or a tête-à-tête. Open daily from noon to midnight, weather permitting. The indoor bar is open from 4 p.m. to 1 a.m.

## PLACES TO SEE AND BE SEEN

The watering holes of the glitterati flame and die as unpredictably as the stars they attract. Still popular, though, is the **Odeon,** 145 West Broadway, in TriBeCa (tel. 233-0507). Formerly a working-class cafeteria, it was refurbished and redecorated to become a sleek-looking place with lots of chrome and art deco set against a color scheme of black and white. It attracts painters, sculptors, and entertainers. Keith Haring, Robert DeNiro, and Jack Nicholson are said to be among the regulars. Open weekdays until 2 or 3 a.m. depending on the crowd, on weekends until 3:30 a.m.

**Café des Artistes,** 1 W. 67th St., off Central Park West (tel. 877-3500), attracts soap opera stars filming at the nearby ABC studios. The bar is decorated with turn-of-the-century Howard Chandler Christy murals, with some of the artist's original sketches. For some, these wood nymphs may prove as intriguing as the stars. Open Monday through Saturday from noon to 3 p.m. and 5:30 p.m. to 12:30 a.m., on Sunday from 10 a.m. to 4 p.m. and 5 to 11 p.m.

The **Gotham Bar and Grill,** 12 E. 12th St., between Fifth Avenue and University Place (tel. 620-4020), is one of Greenwich Village's chicest restaurants. Its postmodern design, done in a pink-and-green color scheme, with cloud-like parachute lights, creates the ambience of an outdoor café. The spacious bar area provides views of the fashion-, music-, and art-world movers and shakers who come for the superb American fare. Open Monday through Thursday from 6 to 10:30 p.m., 6 to 11:30 p.m. on Friday and Saturday, and 5:30 to 9:45 p.m. on Sunday.

The **Empire Diner,** 210 Tenth Ave., at 22nd Street (tel. 243-2736), is the pride of Chelsea. Ensconced in an old roadside diner, it was refurbished in 1976 into a fashionable, art deco restaurant/bar with chrome chairs, stainless-steel walls, and black tabletops. Open 24 hours a day, this is the place to go after the nightclubs close. It has 16 types of imported beer and serves everything from standard diner fare to elaborate meals. The atmosphere is one of candlelight and romance, and a pianist performs from 7 to 11 p.m. Sunday through Thursday, and from 7 p.m. to 3 a.m. on Friday and Saturday.

The **River Café,** 1 Water St., Brooklyn (tel. 718/522-5200), is housed in a barge that floats beneath the Brooklyn Bridge. It has one of New York's best views of the river and lower Manhattan. This restaurant/bar is elegantly simple with wooden floors, fresh flowers, and one wall made entirely of glass. Though it's extremely expensive (dinner costs $55), you may want to drop by for a glimpse and a drink—also expensive at $5 to $6 a cocktail. Open nightly until 2 a.m.

---

# 2. The Music Spots

New York is a mecca for musicians; there are more places for them to perform than anywhere else, and the city is home to a plethora of clubs, bars, and music cafés where you can hear them play every night of the week. For the music lover, it's a feast. You can hear some of the best contemporary music in jazz clubs and lofts, as well as oldtime favorites at the many piano bars scattered through town. There are places that feature country music and others where rock is the fare. Some clubs charge no admission or minimum; others tack on a music charge that varies depending on who's playing that night. To be certain, phone ahead to ask what the cover or minimum is that evening.

## JAZZ

### Greenwich Village

For jazz lovers, New York is a paradise. Nowhere in the world will you find more jazz per square foot than in the Big Apple, and most of it is concentrated in Greenwich Village. We list both major clubs and those that are good bargains—happily, there's often a coincidence of good talent and good prices. For what's playing, check the weekly "Cafés and Clubs" listings in the *Village Voice* or call **Jazzline** (tel. 718/465-7500).

The most famous jazz club in New York—and perhaps in the world—is the **Village Vanguard,** 178 Seventh Ave. South, at 11th Street (tel. 255-4037). For more than 30 years, jazz aficionados have been walking down the long flight of steps into the Vanguard's smokey, dark basement room to hear the likes of John Coltrane, Miles Davis, Charles Mingus, Sonny Rollins, and Pharoah Sanders. Today the Vanguard is as popular as ever, and it still attracts the biggest names in town. Unlike many other jazz clubs, the Vanguard treats both its audience and its musicians with respect. There are no ringing cash registers in the background or hustling for drinks; customers are invited to sit back, relax, and concentrate on the music. Musicians love the place as much as does the audience; dozens of live albums have been recorded in the club over the years, and any night's performance can turn into a blistering set of jazz. Be sure to check out the Monday-night shows, with the Mel Lewis Jazz Orchestra—now in its 24th year, it has become a New York jazz tradition. Admission is $12, and there's a $6 drink minimum per set. Open daily with sets at 10 p.m., 11:30 p.m., and 1 a.m.

Around almost as long as the Village Vanguard is the famed **Village Gate,** 160 Bleecker St., at Thompson Street (tel. 475-5120). In the past few years the Gate has been presenting more off-Broadway musical revues, such as *Beehive,* and cabaret and rock singers such as Tania Maria and Dr. John. But jazz names still appear at the club. One of the best shows in town is the Monday-night "Salsa Meets Jazz" series. Each week two top Latin bands, such as Tito Puente's or Eddie Palmieri's appear with a top jazz soloist such as Dizzy Gillespie. The interaction is something to hear and the dance floor really heats up. Admission varies with the performer and the evening: for musical revues, tickets start at $25 on weeknights and $30 on weekends; the Monday-night salsa shows range from $12 to $20. On Monday and weekends there's a two-drink minimum. The Village Gate is open seven days a week, with jazz sets beginning at 10 p.m. on weeknights, 6 p.m. on Friday, Saturday, and Sunday. The Monday-night set begins at 9:30 p.m. and goes on until 3 a.m.

Another Village club is the **Blue Note,** 131 W. 3rd St., off Sixth Avenue (tel. 475-8592). According to a jazz-knowledgeable bartender, there have been dozens of clubs at this address, going all the way back to speakeasy days. This wood-paneled, blue-carpeted beauty of a club seems to be doing an admirable job of keeping up the tradition. The Blue Note books top jazz stars such as *Billboard's* number-one pianist, Michel Camilo, and Freddie Hubbard, Stanley Jordan, and Sarah Vaughan. Admission is a little high: there's a $15 to $40 cover and a $5 minimum at a table. If you arrive early and sit at the bar, however, there's a $7.50 cover and a one-drink minimum. Open nightly with sets at 9 and 11:30 p.m., with an occasional 1:30 a.m. show on Friday and Saturday nights. Food is also served.

**Sweet Basil,** 88 Seventh Ave. South, between Bleecker and Grove streets (tel. 242-1785), with its exposed-brick walls and glass façade, is one of the handsomer jazz clubs in the Village. It also books top jazz groups, and a wide range of them: from mainstream small combos to avant-garde big bands. If you sit at a table there's a $12 cover with a $6 minimum. At the bar the cover is $12, which includes one free drink. On weekends and holidays the cover is $15. Open nightly, with music beginning at 10 p.m. Reservations recommended.

One of the best places to hear jazz piano and bass in New York is the **Knickerbocker Saloon,** 33 University Pl., at 9th Street (tel. 228-8490). It's a pleasant corner restaurant and bar that's always crowded with attentive listeners—for good reason. Some of the most accomplished and most famous jazz pianists and bassists in the world play in the plush dining room at Knickerbocker's every night. Billy Taylor, Roland Hanna, Ron Carter, Walter Bishop, Jr., and Cecil McBee are just a few. The best seats are in the main dining room, where there's a $3.50 cover and a $7 minimum on music nights after 9 p.m. In the lounge there's also a $7 minimum, but you can sit at the bar and enjoy the music for the price of a drink. Music from 9:30 p.m. Tuesday through Saturday.

For both good jazz and fine food, **Zinno,** 126 W. 13th St., between Sixth and Seventh avenues (tel. 924-5182), may be the place to go. Dinners at this comfortable Italian restaurant start at $11 and come with very good small combos seven nights a week. During the summer, though, Zinno closes on Sunday. There is no cover charge, but the minimum is $15 per person at the tables. You may also sit at the bar, where the minimum is $10, but the combination of good food and music seems to be the thing here. The first set each evening starts at 8 p.m., the last one at 11:15 p.m.

Good conversationalists and all-star piano/bass duos are the hallmark of **Bradley's,** 70 University Pl., between 10th and 11th streets (tel. 228-6440). Musicians like Ron Carter, Tommy Flanagan, Red Mitchell, and Hank Jones play regularly in this clubby, wood-paneled room, with music nightly at around 9:45 p.m. There's usually a $5 to $10 cover, plus an $8 food-and-drink minimum at tables and a two-drink minimum at the bar.

**Carlos 1,** 432 Sixth Ave., between 9th and 10th streets (tel. 982-3260), is a swank supper club with a Caribbean-style menu that showcases traditional and modern jazz. Artists such as Benny Carter, Arthur Prysock, and the World Saxophone Quartet appear every night. Sets begin at 9:30 and 11:30 p.m. and at 1 a.m. on Friday and Saturday. Monday nights are devoted to blues singers, with sets at 9 and 11 p.m. Open seven days a week from 4:30 p.m. to 2 a.m., with a special jazz brunch on Sunday from noon to 5 p.m. The music charge is $10 to $15 with a $7 minimum for a table; at the bar the music charge is $10, with a drink included.

Adventurous jazz and good Spanish-style food are offered at **Visiones,** 125 MacDougal Street, at the corner of West 3rd Street (tel. 673-5576), where the atmosphere is funky; walls are decorated with record jackets and meals are served on hand-painted tiled tables. On Wednesday and Thursday nights at 9:30 and 11:30 p.m., when headliners such as Paul Motian, Dewey Redman, and Lee Konitz appear, there is a $5 cover and $7 beverage minimum. Up-and-coming artists are featured on Friday, Saturday, and Sunday at 9:30 and 11:30 p.m. and 1:15 a.m. with no cover charge, but the $7 beverage minimum still applies. Latin bands appear on Tuesday night.

## SoHo

**5 & 10 No Exaggeration,** 77 Greene St. (tel. 925-7414), is an irrepressibly creative "total environment" with live big-band-era music in a restaurant whose fine antique furnishings and art deco decorations are for sale. It also has a jewelry and antique shop and an art gallery, so you can dine, shop, and listen to bands playing Glenn Miller, Benny Goodman, and the Andrews Sisters. The cover charge changes depending on the act, but never exceeds $5. Dinner items on the varied menu start at $5.50 for a half-order of fettuccine. There is no minimum. The live music runs Wednesday through Saturday. Try their unique brunch on Sunday from 1 to 5 p.m., where live jazz accompanies silent movies. Reservations are recommended at all times; closed Monday.

At **Amazonas,** 492 Broome St., near West Broadway (tel. 966-3371), quality Brazilian jazz and an Amazon jungle-like décor create a unique ambience. There is no cover or minimum, but dinner will run at least $25 to $30 per person, including tips. If that's too pricey, try the bar, where there is no minimum. Or check out the restaurant's Sunday brunches, when you can take in the same music along with all you can eat of various Brazilian dishes at a more moderate price, from noon to 4 p.m. At night music runs from 5:30 p.m. to midnight Monday through Thursday, from 5:30 p.m. to 2:30 a.m. on Friday and Saturday, and from noon to 4 p.m. and 7:30 p.m. to midnight on Sunday.

## Chelsea

The **Angry Squire,** at 216 Seventh Ave., between 22nd and 23rd streets (tel. 242-9066), is a long, nautical-ambience pub and restaurant that has been a Chelsea fixture for many years. The Squire features contemporary vocalists, pianists, and mainstream jazz bands including one of our favorite trumpet players, Joe Magnarelli. There's a $3 to $6 cover and a two-drink minimum, but no cover at the bar. Good food is served, and the atmosphere is warm and lively. Music can be heard seven nights a week; sets start at 10 p.m.

**Lola's,** at 30 W. 22nd St., between Fifth and Sixth avenues (tel. 675-6700), is a fine, upscale restaurant, but don't let the pricey menu keep you from dropping into the lounge on Saturday night to hear some of the best jazz combos around. Our favorite is the Quartet Bargad, led by one of New York's hottest jazz pianists, Rob Bargad. There's no cover; drinks are $5.50, and beer is $4. A gracious and glamorous hostess, Lola greets you at the door and treats all her guests as if they're her good friends. The restaurant features a variety of musical entertainment on other nights of the week. Call for details.

## Murray Hill/Gramercy Park

For an evening with big-name jazz musicians in a cozy atmosphere, **Fat Tuesday's,** 190 Third Ave., at 17th Street (tel. 533-7902), is the place to go. This supper club features only headliners such as Dizzy Gillespie, Les McCann, and Stan Getz, and since it only seats 100, the view and sound from anywhere is good. There are two performances Sunday through Thursday, at 8 and 10 p.m. On Friday and Saturday show times are 8 p.m., 10 p.m., and midnight. The Les Paul Trio plays every Monday night at 8 and 10 p.m. The cover charge is $12.50 with a $7.50 minimum, applicable to food or drink, but there's no minimum at the bar. Reservations are suggested.

## Midtown East

One of the most unusual jazz rooms in New York, the **Fortune Garden Pavilion,** 209 E. 49th St., between Second and Third avenues (tel. 753-0101), serves fantastic gourmet Chinese food in an upstairs atrium room, while the best pianists in town play, in the round, under a skylight and sheltering trees. Sets begin at 8 and 9:45 p.m. every night, with an extra show on Friday and Saturday at 11:15 p.m.; on Sunday music starts at 7 p.m. There's a $20 food-and-drink minimum, with a modest $5 music charge added on Friday and Saturday.

## Upper West Side

Named for one of the great jazz nightclubs of the 1950s and '60s, the present-day **Birdland,** 2745 Broadway, at 105th Street (tel. 749-2228), presents excellent modern jazz by the likes of Dewey Redman, Barry Harris, and John Hicks. (Pianist Renée Rosnes and guitarist Freddy Bryant, who perform separately, are two of our favorites.) A wide-ranging menu, including a selection of Mexican specialties, is offered on an upper tier, overlooking the bar and bandstand. There is no cover or minimum upstairs. Sunday through Thursday a $5 cover and $5 minimum apply at the downstairs tables in front of the bandstand, with no cover at the bar. On weekends the cover goes up to $10, $5 at the bar. Sunday through Thursday, sets begin at 9 and 11 p.m.; on Friday and Saturday they start at 9 and 10:30 p.m. and midnight. There's also a Sunday jazz brunch from 11 a.m. to 4 p.m. The music has to compete with an often-boisterous bar crowd, so try to sit close to the bandstand.

**J's,** upstairs at 2581 Broadway, between 97th and 98th streets (tel. 666-3600), is a comfortable, friendly, high-ceilinged restaurant and bar overlooking upper Broadway. The jazz is nothing too boisterous, usually a piano trio or small group; the continental dinner menu is served every day except Sunday, beginning at 6:30 p.m. The music is served starting 8:30 p.m. Monday through Thursday, at 9 p.m. Friday and Saturday, and at 10 p.m. on Sunday. There's a $5 minimum at the bar, $10 at the tables, and never a cover charge.

**Mikell's,** 760 Columbus Ave., at 97th Street (tel. 864-8832), offers a potpourri of sounds from jazz fusion to ragtime to pop. Performers have included Milt Jackson, Ray Brown, Roy Ayers, and Art Blakey's Jazz Messengers. Cover charges range from $5 to $12 depending on the group, and there's a two-drink minimum. Open daily from 4 p.m. to 4 a.m., with music every night; Sunday features the best jam session in town, starting at 9 p.m., with no cover and a $7 minimum.

## DIXIELAND

**Red Blazer Too,** 349 W. 46th St., in the theater district between Eighth and Ninth avenues (tel. 262-3112), is home to big-band and Dixieland jazz enthusiasts. Live bands perform Tuesday through Sunday and usually attract a mostly middle-aged crowd to the dance floor. As a bartender noted, the theme of this very New York–looking bar, with Tiffany-style lamps and pictures of celebrities along the walls, is nostalgia. There's no cover and a two-drink minimum. Open nightly until 4 a.m.

**Michael's Pub,** 211 E. 55th St., between Second and Third avenues (tel. 758-2273), is also known as Woody Allen's pub, because the actor/director/writer plays clarinet with a Dixieland band here on Monday. Mr. Allen doesn't always show up on Monday, so don't be disappointed if you hear Dixieland without his clarinet. Michael's has other music on other nights; count on spending at least $30 per person at a table. Closed Sunday.

## NEW WAVE/ROCK

They Might Be Giants, the Feelies, and Big Fat Love are the names of some of New York's New Wave groups. The clubs—as bizarre as the groups' names—might typically have Renaissance-style paintings and old lace hanging next to black lights and strobes. The crowd's style will be as cacophonous as the music. For the past decade New Wave clubs have been thriving in New York. We've listed some of the most popular.

Granddaddy to the New Wave clubs, and still going strong, is **CBGB,** 315 Bowery, at Bleecker Street (tel. 982-4052). The club feels a bit like the inside of a rundown stable, with its exposed beams, splintery wood posts, and general decrepit state. Bookings include the likes of Richard Hell and Rude Buddha. On Sunday there are "hardcore matinees" ($5) featuring "severe punk" groups. Cover ranges from $4 to $8, and there's a two-drink minimum. CBGB, though historic in its own right, is located on the fringes of lower Manhattan, an area that should be approached with care.

If you want to hear some of New York's hottest new bands, the **Pyramid Club,**

101 Ave. A, near East 7th Street (tel. 420-1590), is the place to go. Although you might find transvestites dancing on the bar and patrons with shaved heads, the crowd is filled with "just folks" types too.

**The Cat Club,** 76 E. 13th St., near Fourth Avenue (tel. 505-0090), has ample dance room and bands that know how to make use of it. Inside businessmen in three-piece suits clink glasses with Village trendies in basic black. National underground and emerging acts like G. G. Allin and Fetchin' Bones appear during the week. On weekends, it's all about dancing at the Cat Club. Performances start late; admission for the big names is $10, and there's a two-drink minimum at the tables.

**Nirvana Club One,** One Times Square Plaza, 16th floor (tel. 486-6868), is a wild one. By day an Indian restaurant, by night a rock club spotlighting much of the best local talent—and spotlighting the elaborate Indian décor too. You'll find that the crowd is a little better-dressed than at most rock clubs, and Nirvana has, without a doubt, the best view of New York you'll ever see from a dance floor. The cover charge ranges from $10 to $20; call ahead for performers.

## BLUES

**Tramps,** 125 E. 15th St., between Third Avenue and Irving Place (tel. 777-5077), is New York's top blues club, featuring the best in Chicago and New Orleans blues acts. Luminaries in rock-and-roll, pop, and rhythm-and-blues appear here frequently. Music begins around 9:30 p.m. (there's a second show at 11:30 p.m. or midnight), and the club is open until 4 a.m. There's a $5 to $10 cover and a two-drink minimum at tables.

**Mondo Cane Blues Bar,** 205 Thompson St., at Bleecker Street (tel. 254-5166), is one of the newer venues for blues music in New York and is fast establishing itself as one of the most successful by booking such popular bands as the Spin Doctors, G.G.B., and Wild Bill Durkin and the Diplomats. The cover charge is between $5 and $10 with a two-drink minimum. Open from 9:30 p.m. to 3 a.m. seven days a week, with shows at 10 p.m. and midnight. On weekends this tiny bar fills up fast, so get there early.

For nothing but blues, head to **Dan Lynch,** 221 Second Ave., near 14th Street (tel. 473-8807). Though the tunes can be soulful, the atmosphere is lively and friendly. The club is small and intimate, getting you right up with some of the city's best-known blues musicians. Sets start at 9:30 p.m. and the music plays till 2:30 a.m. weeknights and 4 a.m. on weekends. Local musicians often jam here on weekends from 4 p.m. to about 8:30 p.m. There's no cover or minimum on weekdays, and a $5 cover on weekends.

## COUNTRY

**The Lone Star Café,** 240 W. 52nd St., between Broadway and Eighth Avenue (tel. 242-1664), brings the ambience of Austin, Texas, to New York, and presents country, blues, and rock artists from all around. Try to arrive early—the place opens at 7:30 p.m. on weekends—to grab a seat upstairs at one of the balcony tables. The cover is $10 to $15, and there's a two-drink minimum nightly. At the bar, however, you can nurse one drink for as long as you can and take in the music as you do. The Lone Star is open Monday through Friday from 11:30 a.m. to 3 a.m. and on Saturday and Sunday from 7:30 p.m. to 4 a.m. You can reserve a table by prepaying tickets during the week.

If it's pure country music and bluegrass you want, try **O'Lunney's,** 915 Second Ave., at 49th Street (tel. 751-5470). One of the oldest country-music spots in the city, O'Lunney's features local and big-name country bands and an occasional bluegrass group. Bands like King Vito and Tom Russell, Sheri Wagner and Southern Cooking, and Peach Fish Pie perform here regularly. Performances are Monday through Thursday from 9 p.m. to 2 a.m., on Friday and Saturday to 3 a.m. There's a $3 cover charge if you take a table. But if you sit at the bar you can hoot and holler with the bands for the price of a drink.

**Rodeo Bar,** 375 Third Ave., at 27th Street (tel. 683-6500), is fast establishing a reputation as the top spot for the younger and harder-rocking local country performers. The place has real honky-tonk spirit, and while you're listening to the Surreal McCoys or Richard Hayman, you'd do well to check out the barbecue. There's no cover, and there is music every night starting at 10 p.m.

## MIXED BAGS

**The Bitter End,** 147 Bleecker St., between Thompson Street and LaGuardia Place (tel. 673-7030), presents a variety of rock, reggae, folk, jazz, comedy, and country acts. It is one of the few Village clubs that presents three or four bands a night. This is a good place to catch some rising stars before they graduate to bigger (and more expensive) clubs. The cover is $5 and there is a two-drink minimum at the tables and a one-drink minimum at the bar. The club is open seven nights a week, with shows at 8, 9, 10 p.m., and midnight Sunday through Thursday. Friday and Saturday shows are at 8 and 10 p.m., midnight, and 1:30 a.m.

The Village's premier showcase for top rock and jazz groups is **The Bottom Line,** 15 W. 4th St., at the corner of Mercer Street (tel. 228-7880). It is the fancy supper club of the rock crowd; dinner is served from 6 p.m. to 1 a.m., but it is perfectly acceptable to stand at the bar. There is no minimum. The best thing about the Bottom Line is its large stage (good views from every corner of the room), excellent sound system, and first-rate bookings, such as The Roches, Doc Watson, and Buster Poindexter and his Banshees of Blue. Tickets are usually between $10 and $12.50. Shows Sunday through Thursday are at 8 and 11 p.m., and on Friday and Saturday at 8:30 and 11:30 p.m. Advance tickets are on sale at the box office or through the mail, and they are advised for the really popular acts.

**Kenny's Castaways,** 157 Bleecker St., near Thompson Street (tel. 473-9870), features young rock-and-roll bands on their way up. (Cyndi Lauper and the Smithereens both performed here). On Monday there's a midnight jam session; Tuesday through Sunday, sets start at 9:30 p.m. and midnight. There's a two-drink minimum per person per set. Closes at 4 a.m.

The nearby **Back Fence,** 155 Bleecker St. (tel. 475-9221), adds country to its repertoire of rock, blues, and folk. There's a two-drink minimum at the tables and one drink at the bar, plus a cover charge on weekends. Sets start at 8:30 p.m. and the club is open until 2 a.m. on weekdays, until 4 a.m. on weekends.

Folk lives and thrives at **Speakeasy,** 107 MacDougal St., near Bleecker Street, in the heart of the Village (tel. 598-9670). Walk right through the Greek restaurant in front to the darkened, intimate club in back. Operated by a local folk musicians' co-op in conjunction with the owner, this club features some of the strongest acts in folk music. The Washington Squares, Josh White, Jr., and Jesse Winchester are a few recent ones. Cover charge ranges from $4 to $10, depending on the act, and it all goes to the musicians. There is a two-drink minimum per set, or order a meal of Greek or Middle Eastern cuisine from the kitchen. Shows start at 8:30 and 10:30 p.m. Tuesday through Saturday, and at 8:30 p.m. on Sunday.

If you love traditional Irish music, run, don't walk, to **The Eagle Tavern,** 355 W. 14th St., between Eighth and Ninth avenues (tel. 924-0275). Stop at the bar in the front room for your drinks then walk straight back to the rear room where you'll find a friendly, welcoming crowd sipping Guinness. On Friday from 9:30 p.m. to 1 a.m. there is traditional Irish music, with musicians playing guitar, fiddle, and all manner of pipes. Admission is $5. Monday night at 9 p.m. is an open stage for Irish musicians, singers, and poets, and is free. On Tuesday at 7 p.m. there are tryouts for Thursday's 8 p.m. comedy show. On Saturday there is a continuing Irish concert series that brings in some of Ireland's most popular musicians. Admission to this is generally $5 with shows at 9 and 10:30 p.m.

If you're in the mood—and money—for a good splurge, go to **Upstairs at Greene Street,** 101 Greene St., between Prince and Spring streets (tel. 925-2415). Greene Street, a popular yuppie dinner spot in fashionable SoHo, is a complex of three separate restaurants; "Upstairs" is the least expensive, serving a snack menu. Its low lights, intimate acoustics, and immaculate white-tablecloth settings set the tone. The entertainment may be comedy, rhythm-and-blues, country-and-western, or a musical revue, so call ahead to make sure what's scheduled suits you. Reservations are advised. There is a $12.50 entertainment charge and a $10 food minimum. Shows on Friday are at 8 and 10 p.m. and midnight. On Saturday, at 8, 9:30, and 11 p.m. and 1 a.m. Admission to the late shows is $10.

**The Knitting Factory,** 47 E. Houston St., three blocks east of Broadway (tel. 219-3055), offers an eclectic variety of local and international talent ranging from poetry readings to folk music to modern jazz fusion. Upstairs, there's a $5 to $10 cover charge, depending on the act. Downstairs, the entertainment is free and the beer on tap is only $2. If you're in the mood for something a bit different, this place is definitely worth checking out. Open from 6 p.m. to 3 a.m. seven days a week.

---

## 3. Dance, Dance, Dance

---

The dance scene in New York is more popular than ever, and you'll find everything from old-style ballrooms offering swing music to the hop clubs where the young and the restless hang out. While New York's clubs generally open at 10 p.m., most people don't think about going out until at least 11 p.m. Clubs stay open until 4 a.m. In New York, tastes run the gamut and there is a club to fit any interest you might have.

Cover charges can range anywhere from $5 to $20 and drinks can cost more than $5 at the more expensive clubs. You might have to wait as long as an hour to get into the very popular ones. The more exclusive and expensive the club, the more "attitude" you can expect to get from an ever-present doorperson whose job it is to create the most interesting and stylish mix of people inside.

Any printed guide to the "in" scene is inevitably out of date. Clubs open and close with a bewildering frequency. And fame, as Andy Warhol, the late patron saint of New York nightlife, so aptly observed, is a fleeting thing. Today's trendy clubs often last longer than 15 minutes, but rarely make it past 15 months. By the time this book is in your hands, nocturnal New York may have a dramatically different landscape.

If you're hell-bent on tracking the glitterati to the very latest locales, pick up a copy of *Details, Interview,* or *Paper* magazine and scan the gossip columns and ads for clues. Listed below are the clubs that qualified as the very latest while we went to press.

### THE HOT SPOTS

Located in a tiny two-story building at 179 West Broadway near Leonard Street (tel. 941-8655), **Big Haus** caters to the cutting edge of Manhattan's downtown fashion scene. The décor is as spare as the Bauhaus style it emulates and the character of the crowd varies nightly. Generally, though, expect rap music and a young, aggressively cool crowd. Open Wednesday through Saturday. Admission is $5.

**Bolito,** at 3 W. 18th St., near Fifth Avenue (tel. 463-8899), may be New York's most exclusive spot. This small supper and dance club was opened by a woman who ran the door at Nell's while that club was the slickest spot in town. Bolito looks like a space-age Jetson's cartoon come to life. Don't try to get in without an invitation unless you're exceptionally beautiful, famous, or persuasive. Open Thursday through Sunday. Admission is $5 on Thursday and Sunday, $10 on Friday and Saturday.

**Carmelitas,** 150 E. 14th St., (tel. 673-9015), is a small hall rented out for weddings to a predominantly Hispanic clientele most of the week. But on Monday everyone can enjoy the kitschy ambience of disco balls and mirrored walls. The young, trendy crowd, with a heavy contingent of NYU students, sweats itself into a frenzy while dancing to vintage '70s disco. Admission is $5.

**Mars,** at 28 Tenth Ave., at 13th Street (tel. 691-6262), is Manhattan's latest large disco. Operated by Rudolph, the former owner of the legendary Danceteria, Mars offers a five-floor smörgåsbord of different styles ranging from '60s psychedelic to industrial postmodern. Music apes each floor's atmosphere. Unless the doorman decides you have an agreeable "look," expect a long wait outside. Open Thursday through Sunday. Admission is $15 on Friday and Saturday, $10 on Thursday and Sunday (Sunday is gay night, "Mars Needs Men").

**Nell's** is located at 246 W. 14th St., between Seventh and Eighth avenues (tel. 674-1567). The emphasis is on exclusive luxury and comfort, but the furniture is all tattered and the pictures hang crookedly on the walls. The door policy is completely up to the doorpeople, so be prepared to wait. Inside, the well-dressed and well-turned-out mix with the trendy. There is a light supper offered to the accompaniment of a jazz quartet. There are two rooms of overstuffed couches and chairs, and a dance floor where you can enjoy old favorites and sambas. Open daily. Sunday through Thursday the cover is $5, $10 on Friday and Saturday.

Like Mars, **Red Zone,** 438 W. 54th St. (tel. 582-2222), is another club that marks the return of megadiscos to Manhattan after a few years of small-scale clubs. Red Zone is a large open space packed with hi-tech lighting, video screens, and on most nights, celebrities with gossip columnists nipping at their heels. Expect a wait at the door, but persistence pays off and most people get in. Open Thursday through Sunday. Admission is $15 on Friday and Saturday, $10 on Thursday and Sunday.

Denied liquor licenses, many intrepid club impressarios have established "outlaw" clubs. This is a New York phenomena and we list a few for those of you who are truly "into" the club "scene." These nightspots are usually open the same day of the week at different locations, which are known to local club-goers by word of mouth. It's never very hard to track them down. Ask likely looking candidates you see on the street if they know where the following clubs are located this week. As of this writing, a club called **Milky Way** had just closed. But one called **Payday** was operating in different downtown locations every Friday night, and drawing huge crowds of young people eager to pay $5 to hear the city's cutting-edge dance DJs at work. **$100,000 Bar** was operating on a smaller scale every Saturday night at various spots throughout the Lower East Side. Expect other outlaw clubs named after candy bars to be in operation by the time you visit.

## DINOSAUR DISCOS

If you want to dance in a big glitzy environment and don't want to contend with doormen who may make you wait indefinitely for admission, there are several clubs that have lost their luster as celebrity nightspots, but remain entertaining nonetheless. These huge clubs need to draw large crowds, and coupons for discounted admission are available all over the city. Passes should be available at fashionable record and clothing stores. Tower Records, at 692 Broadway on the corner of East 4th Street, offers particularly good pass pickings.

**The Palladium,** 126 E. 14th St., between Third and Fourth avenues (tel. 473-7171), is housed in an incredibly well-designed and well-executed space. It has the latest in acoustic and lighting technology, and is decorated with murals by celebrity artists. All in all, very impressive. Open from 10 p.m. to 4 a.m. Thursday through Saturday. The cover is $15 on weeknights, $20 on weekends.

**The Tunnel,** 220 12th Ave., at 27th Street (tel. 244-6444), has replaced the Palladium as the place to have big public-relations events. Because the club is not conveniently located, you must take a cab to get there. The inside contrasts a length of exposed train tracks with elegant rooms and beautiful murals. The basement is for private parties and is reminiscent of an underground speakeasy. Open from 10 p.m. to 4 a.m. Wednesday through Saturday. Weekdays, the cover is $15; weekends, $20.

**Limelight,** 660 Sixth Ave., at 20th Street (tel. 807-7850), is in an old church. This upbeat disco is irreverent but fun. Open nightly. The cover charge is $15 Sunday through Thursday, $20 on Friday and Saturday.

**M.K.,** once arguably New York's most exclusive club, has now opened its doors to all comers. Housed in a large five-story brownstone at 204 Fifth Ave., at 24th Street (tel. 779-1340), M.K. was designed to please the new breed of young fogeys (young people with a taste for traditional style). M.K. features a formal dining room, a coat-check room in what was once a bank vault, and a bewildering array of antiques that includes a set of stuffed Dobermans. Open daily. Admission is $15 on Friday and Saturday, $5 the rest of the week.

**The World,** 254 E. 2nd St., at Avenue C (tel. 477-8677), is a blissful grab-bag of styles. This big besotted former ballroom books a variety of acts from big-name rock and rap performers to local heroes. Local cult-hero DJs spin a spare brand of disco known as "house music" between acts for the predominantly young and ethnic crowd. Nearly everyone gets in. Open daily. Admission is $10 on Friday and Saturday, $5 the rest of the week.

## LESS GLITTER BUT LOTS OF FUN

**Big Kahuna,** 622 Broadway, between Houston and Bleecker streets (tel. 460-9633), is very popular with the preppies. It also has the distinction of being not unlike the best-decorated frat party you've ever been to. The water coolers are stocked with rum punch and the blackboard above the bar lists the current surf conditions from Ala Moana to Pipeline. The kitchen serves up burgers and chili, and the music and videos are very fresh. In fact, Big Kahuna offers every element of surf culture except lifeguards. Open Wednesday through Saturday from 5 p.m. on. The cover is $5.

**The Surf Club,** 415 E. 91st St., between York and First avenues (tel. 410-1360), is also a preppie favorite. It, too, celebrates the surf theme. The crowd is young and dances all night. Admission is free on Tuesday, $5 on Wednesday and Thursday, and $10 on the weekends. Closed Sunday and Monday.

**Private Eyes,** 12 W. 21st St., between Fifth and Sixth avenues (tel. 206-7770), is clean and modern, and boasts the most television sets in New York, if not the world. Wednesday and Friday are gay nights; all other nights are mixed. The cover is $8 weekdays, $15 on weekends.

**Cave Canem,** 24 First Ave., between 1st and 2nd streets (tel. 529-9665) means "beware the dog" in Latin. But the only thing scary about this place is the price of the Roman-style dinners served in the dining room. An air of debauchery remains from the era when the building was a gay bathhouse. But these days the crowd is aggressively heterosexual. The bathhouse atmosphere has been left intact in the basement, where well-dressed people turn out on weekends to dance to disco music among the tiled tubs and tapestries. Open daily until 4 a.m. Admission is usually free, but occasionally $5.

## LIVE BANDS

**The Ritz** recently moved uptown to 254 W. 54th St., at Eighth Avenue (tel. 541-8900), the old haunts of the infamous Studio 54. For years the Ritz on East 11th Street booked national acts that had not yet graduated to the stadium circuit. At their new, larger location, you can still catch bands on the cusp of stardom. Buy your tickets ahead of time—most shows sell out. Open weekdays from 9 p.m., weekends from 11 p.m. Tickets cost $10 to $25.

**The Pyramid,** 101 Ave. A, near East 7th Street (tel. 420-1590), is the place to go for unrestricted fun. Hot new bands play here all the time, and the employees get into the act by dancing on the bar. Open nightly from 10 p.m. to 4 a.m. Cover charge is $5 to $10.

**CBGB,** 315 Bowery, at Bleecker Street (tel. 473-7743), has been the launching pad for many rock bands over the years, and it's still upholding the tradition. Everyone plays (or has played) here. Open nightly. Hardcore matinees on Sunday, four bands for $5.

**The Cat Club,** 76 E. 13th St., near Fourth Avenue (tel. 505-0090), leans toward heavy metal, but bands of all kinds showcase here. Open nightly; the cover is $8 on weekdays, $15 on weekends.

The **Lone Star Road House,** 240 W. 52nd St., between Broadway and Eighth Avenue (tel. 245-2950), is another hallowed New York tradition that recently migrated up out of the Village. This outpost of Texan esthetics is housed in a building that looks like a touring band's bus. The Lone Star books top country, blues, and rock-and-roll performers. Don't dare to order anything but a Lone Star beer, ya'all. Shows nightly at 9:30 and 11:30 p.m. Tickets are $7 to $20.

## MUSIC OF ANOTHER ERA

Disco is only one facet of New York's burgeoning dance scene. For example, if your tastes run to swing music, there's the 65-year-old **Roseland** ballroom, 239 W. 52nd St., between Broadway and Eighth Avenue (tel. 247-0200). Admission is $7 on Friday, $10 on Saturday, and $8 on Thursday and Sunday. A Latin band adds to the festivities on Thursday and Sunday till midnight and on Saturday until 11 p.m.

If you're willing to spend more, you can also "swing" at **Windows on the World,** top floor of One World Trade Center (tel. 938-1111), nightly from 7:30 p.m. to 12:30 a.m. when there's dancing and a cover charge of $3.50 per person; and at the **Café Carlyle** in the Carlyle Hotel, 35 E. 76th St., off Madison Avenue (tel. 744-1600), Tuesday through Saturday where the cover charge is $35 but there is no dancing.

For '50s and '60s music there's **Heartbreak,** a dance club at 179 Varick St., at Seventh Avenue (tel. 691-2388), where a live band plays on Monday and admission is $10 on weeknights and $15 on weekends.

**Café Society,** 915 Broadway at 21st Street (tel. 529-8282), looks more like the set of an MGM musical than a place where mere mortals are allowed to tread. But take heart—you can live out your Fred and Ginger fantasies. On weekends this enormous restaurant with dramatic illuminated pillars and 50-foot ceilings pulsates with modern music. But on Monday and Wednesday from 8 p.m. to midnight couples gather on the large dance floor while a big band plays Latin and swing music against the backdrop of an ornate mural. Admission is free, but if you eat dinner, be prepared for a $10-per-person music charge.

## REGGAE

At the **Reggae Lounge,** 285 West Broadway (tel. 226-4598), a crowd heavily sprinkled with Rastafarians, Africans, and Europeans dances to pop and Jamaican reggae in a setting of jungle greens and browns. Admission is $8 for women and $10 for men on Friday (women are admitted free on Wednesday and pay $3 on Thursday), $10 for everyone on Saturday, and $6 at all times for students.

## LATIN

One of the hottest places to dance in all of New York is **SOB's (Sounds of Brazil),** 204 Varick St., on Seventh Avenue (tel. 243-4940). The club is a time tunnel to the tropical club of some forgotten era. Calabash gourds and stuffed alligators adorn the walls. Onstage, the best international calypso, salsa, and reggae music is played to a very knowing—and well-dressed—audience. Dinner reservations are accepted.

During the week shows are at 9 and 11 p.m.; weekends, at 11 p.m. and 1 and 2:30 a.m. Tickets range from $10 to $25.

---

## 4. Theatrical and Nightclub Entertainment

The nightclub entertainment in New York varies from glossy cabarets to Middle Eastern belly dancing to improvisational comics, whose biggest act is drawing the audience into the show and sometimes up on stage.

**Don't Tell Mama,** 343 W. 46th St., between Eighth and Ninth avenues (tel. 757-0788), has a lively front room with a copper-topped bar where you can sit and listen to Dick Gallagher and Bob Bendorf play Broadway show tunes every night from 9:30 p.m. to 4 a.m. There is no cover charge and no minimum, and there's an "open-mike" policy that allows anyone to get up and sing. In the backroom there's a cabaret where performers give two shows a night, at 8 and 10 p.m. The cover charge is $6 to $10 and there's a two-drink minimum.

**Steve McGraw's,** 158 W. 72nd St., between Broadway and Columbus Avenue (tel. 595-7400), used to be called Palsson's. The new club features a main show Tuesday through Thursday at 8 p.m., and two shows on Friday and Saturday at 6:30 and 9:30 p.m. Tickets are $20 on weeknights and $22.50 on weekends. The club's weeknight cabaret (performances at 10:30 p.m.) is more affordable, with tickets priced between $8 and $15. Steve McGraw's is open until 2 a.m. during the week and 4 a.m. on weekends. Reservations are recommended.

**The Duplex,** 55 Grove St., between Seventh Avenue South and Bleecker Street (tel. 255-5438), presents a mixture of inexpensive entertainment. Downstairs there is a piano bar, and upstairs, Thursday through Sunday, there are original and Broadway cabaret shows. On weekends, the club fills up with a show called *It's Not Just Comedy* and such comedians as Teri Coyne and Danny McWilliams. Thursday-night shows are at 8 and 10 p.m., and on Friday and Saturday there's an additional midnight show. There's a two-drink minimum and a $7 cover charge.

If you like to sing along with Broadway show tunes from today and yesteryear, come down to **Eighty Eights,** 228 W. 10th St., between Bleecker and Hudson streets (tel. 924-0088). This casual, easygoing club highlights musical comedy shows like *Rebel: The James Dean Musical* and features singers like Broadway performers Sharon McNight and Hazelle Goodman. The club sometimes offers a lineup of comedy acts. Weeknight shows are at 8 and 10 p.m.; weekends, at 11 p.m. and 1 a.m., with an $8 to $12 cover and two-drink minimum. Reservations are recommended.

Dress casual New York style for an evening at **Danny's Skylight at the Grand Sea Palace,** 346 W. 46th St., between Eighth and Ninth avenues (tel. 265-8130). Special attractions include piano-bar entertainment and cabaret shows featuring such talent as Jill O'Hara (*Promises, Promises* and *Hair*). Weeknight shows begin at 9 p.m., on weekends at 9 and 11 p.m. Cover ranges between $8 and $12, with a $10 drink minimum. Reservations are recommended.

**The Ballroom,** 253 W. 28th St., between Seventh and Eighth avenues (tel. 244-3005), features cabaret acts, singers, comedians, and dancers. There are shows Tuesday through Saturday at 6:30, 9, and 11 p.m., with a $15 to $25 admission and a two-drink minimum.

## COMEDY

**The Improvisation,** (the original), 358 W. 44th St., off Ninth Avenue (tel. 765-8268), is the city's premier breeding ground for new talent. This highly regarded restaurant/nightclub features a constantly changing lineup of young singers and comics. The club's famous alums include Rodney Dangerfield, Liz Torres, Robert Klein, Robin Williams, and Joe Piscopo. The action begins nightly at 8 p.m., and there is an additional show at 11:30 p.m. Friday and 12:40 a.m. on Saturday. The cover charge is $8 Monday through Thursday and $9 Friday through Sunday, and there's a $5 to $8 drink minimum. Reservations are essential on weekends.

One of the best-known New York comedy clubs is **Dangerfield's,** 1118 First Ave., between 61st and 62nd streets (tel. 593-1650). The club is owned by Rodney ("I can't get no respect") Dangerfield, who performs whenever he's in town. Other performers have included Redd Foxx, Red Buttons, Jackie Mason, and Robin Williams, when he happens to be in the audience. There are shows Monday through Thursday at 9:15 p.m. with a $10 cover and a $7 minimum, on Friday at 9 p.m. with a $15 cover and a $7 minimum, and on Saturday at 8 and 10:30 p.m. and at 12:30 a.m. Reservations are recommended, especially on weekends.

Good comedy can also be found at **Catch a Rising Star,** 1487 First Ave., near 78th Street (tel. 794-1906). The club features some of the same headliners as at Dangerfield's, but it's best known as *the* place to see up-and-coming comics. Sunday through Thursday there's a show at 9 p.m., with an $8 cover; on Friday shows are at 8:30 and 11 p.m., with a $12 cover and a two-drink minimum; and Saturday shows are at 7:30 and 10 p.m. and 12:30 a.m. Reservations are suggested.

There are more laughs to be had at the following clubs:

At **The Comic Strip,** 1568 Second Ave., near 82nd Street (tel. 861-9386), aspiring comedians perform Sunday through Thursday at 9 p.m., with a $7 cover; on Friday and Saturday at 9 and 11 p.m., with a $12 cover on both nights. There's a two-drink minimum. Reservations are suggested.

If you're hungry for southern cooking and want to laugh off your meal, come down to **Caroline's at the Seaport,** 89 South St., at Pier 17 (tel. 233-4900). The well-known club spotlights comedians like Richard Lewis, Gilbert Godfried, and Kevin Meaney. Upstairs you can feast at Mobile, which features down-home southern Cajun cooking. Shows Sunday through Thursday are at 8 p.m., and the cover varies between $12.50 and $15. On Friday and Saturday shows are at 9 and 11:30 p.m., and the cover is $15 or $20. There is a two-drink minimum, and reservations are recommended.

**Mostly Magic,** 55 Carmine St. (tel. 924-1472), is a nightclub-theater featuring combination or solo comedy-magic routines. Showtimes are Wednesday and Thursday at 9 p.m., with a $10 cover and one-drink minimum; weekend shows are at 9 and 11 p.m., with a $15 cover and a one-drink minimum. Reservations are recommended.

At **The Comedy Cellar,** 117 MacDougal St. (tel. 254-3630), there are shows Sunday through Thursday at 9 p.m. ($5 cover), on Friday and Saturday at 9 and 11:30 p.m. ($10 cover), and on Saturday at 8 and 10 p.m. and midnight. There's also a two-drink minimum.

If you're interested in creative audience participation and improvisational comedy, check out **Chicago City Limits,** 351 E. 74th St., between First and Second avenues (tel. 722-8707). This non-alcohol club features improvisational comedians like the Touring Company, Rick Simpson, and Paul Zuckerman. The weeknight show starts at 8:30 p.m.; two weekend shows are at 8 and 10:30 p.m. Cover charge during the week is $10; weekends, $15. Reservations recommended.

The **First Amendment Comedy Troupe,** 31 W. 21st St., between Fifth and Sixth avenues (tel. 678-0076), is New York's longest-running comedy show. After 14 years, the troupe boasts such graduates as Bruce ("Moonlighting") Willis, Jane ("Dirty Dancing") Brucker, and HBO comedian Dom Irrera. Saturday night's show starts at 11 p.m. (sometimes there's a second show, so call to confirm) and costs $12.50. There's no food, but plenty of drinks and no minimum. Reservations are recommended.

New on the comedy frontier is **Stand Up New York,** 236 W. 78th St., at Broadway (tel. 595-0850). The club is modern and loft-like, and there is a light bar menu to choose from. Shows are Sunday through Thursday at 9 p.m. ($7 cover charge), and Friday and Saturday at 8 and 10 p.m. and 12:30 a.m. ($12 cover charge). There is a two-drink minimum.

## LAS VEGAS IN NEW YORK

**Club Ibis,** 151 E. 50th St., between Lexington and Third avenues (tel. 753-3429), is the Middle Eastern club on the floor above the posh Café Versailles. The entertainers' style is a little more Egyptian than Las Vegas, with belly dancing and other performances running from 11 p.m. to 3 a.m. The cover is $6, with a $15 minimum. Open weekdays until 3:30 a.m., weekends until 4 a.m.

**Chippendales,** 1110 First Ave., at 61st Street (tel. 935-6060), is a phenomenon of the '80s which gives new meaning to the phrase "girls' night out." Whatever happened to Mahjong and bridge? The club can draw up to 850 people, many of whom are women from out-of-town, who sit on bleacher-style seats in this arena/theater where an all-male burlesque revue ultimately gets down to the bare necessities—their G-strings. The show starts at 8 p.m. Wednesday through Saturday and is for women only. Admission on Wednesday and Thursday is $20; on Friday and Saturday, $25. The seats closest to the stage cost an additional $7 on Wednesday and Thursday, an additional $10 on Friday and Saturday, and can only be purchased at the time of admission. Drinks are priced at $3 to $5. Reservations required.

After the show, at about 10:30 p.m., the club becomes a disco and the stage a dance floor. Men are allowed. If you've just seen the show, the disco is free. If you're just coming in to dance there's a $20 cover charge. Open until 4 a.m.

## COLLEGE HANGOUTS

Among the nightspots we have described, there are a number of college hangouts—music clubs with lots of students, and bars where the drinks are reasonably priced and talk is of classes and beer blasts. We have listed some of these by area.

### Upper West Side

**Amsterdam's,** 428 Amsterdam Ave., between 80th and 81st streets (tel. 874-1377).

**Lucy's,** 503 Columbus Ave., between 84th and 85th streets (tel. 787-3009).

**Marvin Gardens,** 2274 Broadway, between 81st and 82nd streets (tel. 799-0578).

**Broadway Bay,** 2180 Broadway, at 77th Street (tel. 362-4360).

### Upper East Side

**Rupperts,** 1662 Third Ave., at 93rd Street (tel. 831-1900).

### East Village

**King Tut's WaWa Hut,** southeast corner of East 7th Street and Avenue A (tel. 254-7772).

**McSorley's Old Ale House,** 15 E. 7th St., near Third Avenue (tel. 473-8800).

**Grassroots Tavern,** 20 St. Marks Pl., between Second and Third avenues (tel. 475-9443).

## SINGLES BARS

Here are a few around town.

### Upper East Side

**Ruppert's,** 1662 Third Ave., at 93rd Street (tel. 831-1900).

**T.G.I. Friday's,** 1152 First Ave., at 63rd Street (tel. 832-8512).

### Upper West Side

**Marvin Gardens,** 2274 Broadway, between 81st and 82nd streets (tel. 799-0578).

**Broadway Bay,** 2180 Broadway, at 77th Street (tel. 362-4360).

## Midtown West

**Hard Rock Café,** 221 W. 57th St., between Sixth and Seventh avenues (tel. 489-6565).

## East Village

**Caramba!,** 684 Broadway, at Great Jones (East 3rd) Street (tel. 420-9817).
**Cave Canem,** 24 First Ave., between 1st and 2nd streets (tel. 529-9665).

## Greenwich Village

**Woody's,** 140 Seventh Ave. South, between West 10th and Charles streets (tel. 242-1200).

# VII

# THE BEST SHOPPING BUYS IN TOWN

**1. MEN'S AND WOMEN'S CLOTHING**
**2. AN ALPHABETICAL MISCELLANY**
**3. FOOD**

There is one point that all visitors—and all New Yorkers too—seem to agree on: New York is the shopping capital of the United States. Nowhere else in the world is there such a wealth of goods—made right here or imported from all over the world—to tempt the purchaser. Mexican wedding shirts, chic French jeans (even for pregnant women), African fabrics, Japanese kimonos, Berber capes, the latest imports from the Peoples Republic of China, Ukrainian Easter egg decorating kits, Indian saris—you'll find it all here, and much more, in great profusion. Indeed, shopping is one of the city's finest entertainments.

But the thrill of shopping in New York goes even beyond the seemingly infinite variety of merchandise. For whether you're looking for a new camera, a violin, a Parsons table, or a Dior original—you can get it for less in the Big Apple. The purpose of this chapter, then, is to steer both the visitor and the resident to the most exciting bargains in town. We'll begin with men's and women's clothing, then proceed alphabetically, listing everything from antiques to umbrellas. And we'll wind up with a gastronomical tour of the town—where to buy everything from eggroll wrappers to homemade mozzarella cheese.

*Note:* Many, many stores—especially on the Lower East Side—are open on Sunday, a viable shopping day in this city.

## 1. Men's and Women's Clothing

The fashion industry is at the very heart of New York life. New York's Garment Center—an area that runs along Seventh Avenue ("Fashion Avenue") from 20th to 40th streets—produces nearly half the dresses and suits worn in the United States. Accordingly, it's no wonder that there are many good buys in retail clothing. Of course, nothing is as cheap as it used to be, but inveterate New York bargain hunters have a system. They use the major department and specialty stores—Macy's, Bloomingdale's, Lord & Taylor, Saks Fifth Avenue, and the like—for browsing, learning, and for buying on sale; they make most of their purchases at designer discount stores and little shops off the beaten path where values are high and the strain on the pocketbook is manageable. Herewith, we share with you some of their secrets —and ours:

## WOMEN'S CLOTHING AND ACCESSORIES

The best of the department stores for across-the-board bargains is **Alexander's,** Lexington Avenue and 58th Street (tel. 593-0880), which manages to maintain both a high-fashion policy and a low-price profile. It's filled to the brim with merchandise from all parts of the world, selected by crack buying and merchandise teams who travel throughout the United States, Europe, South America, and the Far East in search of their wares. There are usually great buys in cashmere sweaters and knitwear. Alexander's is actually a diversified department store selling items that range from perfumes to video cassettes, toys, and appliances.

Open from 10 a.m. to 9 p.m. Monday through Saturday and on Sunday from noon to 5 p.m. If you're touring downtown New York, stop in at the Alexander's at the World Trade Center.

Now for an oddball among the city's inexpensive clothing shops. **Richards Army-Navy,** at 233 W. 42nd St., between Seventh and Eighth avenues (tel. 947-5018), was once a typical warehouse-type outlet for military surplus, and indeed the store's major stock in trade remains such items as regulation navy pea jackets, of which they sell several thousand a year. But Richards is also well known to designers of high-camp styles, the chicest dames in town, and even Yves St. Laurent, whose visits a few seasons back resulted in a line of military-looking clothes designed specifically for women, as well as sporting wear modeled after military fashions. Richard's has all these (at a much lower price than anywhere else), plus Levi denim jeans, Schott, and much more—everything from Adidas footwear to basketballs, leather flight jackets, and new camouflage fatigues. Newest rage for European tourists: their Dunham boots and shoes. And it also has one of the largest swim shops, with year-round selections of men's and women's professional and fashion swimsuits, goggles, and accessories. This is also one of the city's largest repositories of Jacques Cousteau skin- and scuba-diving equipment, in case you're interested.

Open Monday through Saturday from 9 a.m. to 7 p.m.

Another army-navy store catering to the uptown blue-jean set is **Ar-Bee,** 1598 Second Ave., at the corner of 83rd Street (tel. 737-4661), where shirts, jackets, and raincoats are available at rock-bottom prices. We bought a heavy-weather hooded navy raincoat for $35. Timberland shoes are a big seller here too. Another branch across the street at 1601 Second Ave. features camping equipment.

Open Monday through Friday from 9 a.m. to 6:45 p.m., on Saturday until 5:45 p.m.

### Designer and Other Discount Shops

We know how you feel—you love clothes by Norma Kamali and Givenchy; Oscar de la Renta and Calvin Klein do wonders for your spirits; and Perry Ellis, Harvé Benard, Cathy Hardwick, and the like design the outfits you really want to wear. If you can't afford the top designers at boutique prices, don't despair: New York has many off-price stores where the price is right.

A leader of the designer discount chains is **Loehmann's.** It has three branches in New York, the main one at 236th Street and Broadway in the Bronx (tel. 543-6420); the others are at 19 Duryea Pl., at Beverly Road, in Brooklyn, off Flatbush Avenue (tel. 718/469-9800), and in Rego Park, Queens, in Lefrak City (tel. 718/271-4000). Loehmann's offers an enormous selection of women's coats, suits, dresses, and sportswear, often in styles that are simultaneously being sold in Manhattan department stores for twice the price! You'll have to plow through seemingly dozens of racks, but the end result of your search can be a superb outfit at a wonderfully low price. *Caution:* All sales are final; there are no exchanges or refunds.

To reach Loehmann's in the Bronx, take the no. 1 train of the IRT–Seventh Avenue subway to 238th Street and walk two blocks back to 236th Street. To reach the Brooklyn location, take the BMT–Brighton line (D train) to Beverly Road; Loehmann's is located 3½ blocks west of the station. Phone each store for exact hours.

Right in Manhattan, in the downtown financial district (easily reached by taking the IRT–Seventh Avenue subway to Park Place), is another treasure trove of designer clothing at discount prices: **Syms,** 45 Park Pl., between Church Street and West Broadway, two blocks north of the World Trade Center (tel. 791-1199). The women's departments are on the first and basement levels. Everything has the nationally advertised price on it. Syms marks down ladies' dresses every ten days: for example, a $100 outfit goes on the racks at $59; after ten days it goes down to $48; ten more days, to $38; after 30 days, when the price becomes final, it's $29. The dates of markdowns are on the ticket, so you might want to trust your luck and wait for the lowest prices. We've also found excellent bargains here in fine leather bags, gloves and scarves, and lingerie. This is pipe-rack shopping and crowded community dressing rooms, but the bargains make it all worthwhile.

Syms is open on Tuesday and Wednesday from 8 a.m. to 6:30 p.m., on Thursday and Friday to 7:30 p.m., on Saturday from 10 a.m. to 6:30 p.m., and on Sunday from 11:30 a.m. to 5:30 p.m. *Note:* During early-morning shopping hours, the store is the least crowded.

Savvy New York shoppers have been celebrating—and buying—like crazy ever since **Daffy's** opened its first retail store in Manhattan a few years back, at 111 Fifth Ave., at 18th Street (tel. 529-4477). For years, New Yorkers either had to drive to Daffy's suburban New Jersey stores or just dream about those incredible, in-depth bargains their New Jersey friends always raved about. Daffy's New York store, 35,000 square feet of merchandising space in three floors, is nothing if not dramatic: vivid colors, glass staircases and twin glass elevators, a striking ambience that bespeaks fashion. And the values on the racks are even more dramatic. Daffy's buyers buy "opportunistically" from the best designers on Seventh Avenue and in Europe and offer their finds for anywhere from 40% to 80% off regular retail prices every day of the week. When there's a special sale going on, they practically give the goods away. Here's what you might find on a typical shopping day: 100% silk dresses, regularly $158, $70 here; hand-knit wool sweaters that would be $118 elsewhere, $20 here; silk crêpe-de-chine printed blouses, $48 in other stores, $17 to $20 here; flannel pants, $62 to $68 elsewhere, $30 here. There are also faux furs from France, leathers from Italy, cashmere sweaters from Scotland, lingerie, handbags, hats, and jewelry—all at amazingly good prices. Sizes range from 2 to 14, with some petites, and some fashions for larger women too. You won't find every item in every size and color here, but what you will find is extraordinary. Children's and men's clothing are also featured at great savings.

Daffy's is open Monday through Saturday from 10 a.m. to 10 p.m. and on Sunday from 11 a.m. to 6 p.m.

Juniors can have a field day shopping for name-brand sportswear at **What's New,** at 166 Madison Ave., between 32nd and 33rd streets (tel. 532-9226), where we spotted the likes of $64 cotton dresses for $35, a $24 sweat-pants-and-shirt set for $14. The store is tiny so it's best avoided during the lunch hour, when nearby office workers are out in full force.

Open from 10 a.m. to 6 p.m. weekdays, to 5 p.m. on Saturday. There's another What's New store at 122 E. 42nd St., on the subway level (tel. 867-0574), open from 8 a.m. to 6 p.m. Monday through Friday only.

If you're in the Lincoln Center area, you may want to walk a few blocks to check out the neighborhood branch of **Labels for Less,** 186 Amsterdam Ave., between 68th and 69th streets (tel. 787-0850), which sells designer fashions at good discounts. There are almost two dozen other locations throughout Manhattan.

There are hefty discounts on designer sportswear at **Fishkin's,** 314 Grand St., at Allen Street, and at 63 Orchard St., near Grand Street (tel. 226-6538)—sweaters, separates, bathing suits, cruisewear, shoes, handbags, etc. An additional unit at 318 Grand St. concentrates on fun weekend wear.

Open Monday through Thursday from 10 a.m. to 5 p.m., on Friday to 4 p.m., and on Sunday from 9 a.m. to 4:30 p.m.; closed Saturday.

And while you're perusing Lower East Side shops, don't miss **Sam's Knitwear,** 93 Orchard St., between Delancey and Broome streets (tel. 966-0390), where discounts of 50% and more are offered on name-brand and designer clothes. Sales are held year round. We bought a dress here for $30 that we had seen (but only coveted) at $80 elsewhere.

Open weekdays from 10 a.m. to 6 p.m., on Sunday from 9 a.m.; closed Saturday.

Wherever you go in Manhattan, it seems, you'll find a **Bolton's.** And no wonder: Bolton's is Manhattan's largest women's discount chain. It offers current contemporary merchandise at 20% to 50% off major department and specialty-store prices. Bolton's prides itself on buying key fashion merchandise made of top-quality fabrics and workmanship; there's no junk to weed through here, just lots of good buys in coats, dresses, suits, sportswear, loungewear, sleepwear, and accessories; we've had good luck here with handbags many times.

Most branches of Bolton's are open Monday through Saturday from 10 a.m. to 7 p.m. (on Thursday to 8:30 p.m.), and on Sunday from noon to 5 p.m. You'll find them on the East Side at 1180 Madison Ave., at 86th Street (tel. 722-4454); 1193 Third Ave., at 69th Street (tel. 628-7553); 685 Third Ave., at 43rd St. (tel. 682-5661); 4 E. 34th St., just off Fifth Avenue (tel. 684-3750); and 225 E. 57th St., near Second Ave. (tel. 755-2527). On the West Side, Bolton's is at 27 W. 57th St., between Fifth and Sixth avenues (tel. 935-4431); 53 W. 23rd St., between Fifth and Sixth avenues (tel. 924-6860); and 2251 Broadway, at 80th Street (tel. 873-8545). In the Village, the address is 19 E. 8th St. (tel. 475-9574); downtown, it's 59 Liberty St. (tel. 349-7464), closed Saturday.

You no longer have to go all the way to Boston to enjoy the legendary shopping buys of **Filene's Basement of Boston.** You just have to go to Queens, specifically to the Fresh Meadows Shopping Center in Flushing, to sample the wares of the world's original "bargain basement." While this new version of Filene's Basement lacks the frantic pace and frenzied atmosphere of the original, the bargains are still the same, if on a much smaller scale, and there is even an improvement: dressing rooms, which somehow they never thought of in Boston. Filene's buys up huge lots of perfect and "nearly perfect" merchandise from leading manufacturers, and also from famous stores that need to dispose of unsold goods or that are going out of business. Many of the original store labels—Neiman-Marcus, Saks Fifth Avenue, I. Magnin, Sakowitz—are right on the garments. And the prices are always fractions—small fractions—of the originals. We've seen Neiman-Marcus sports coats for $98, Maggie London dresses for $60, handbags from Stone Mountain at $20, Buxton all-leather clutches at $5. Designer names show up frequently among the name-brand merchandise. Buys in lingerie and loungewear are outstanding. There's also a shoe department and a downstairs store for the men. There's giftware too, and on occasion even Oriental rugs—whatever Filene's gets a great buy on. New merchandise arrives daily, so if you don't find anything you need one day, come back the next, and the next. Yes, they do give refunds.

Filene's is a bit of a trip by subway—IND–Eighth Avenue E train to 169th Street, then the Q17A bus—but it's easy driving: take the Long Island Expressway to Exit 25. There are other Filene's Basements on Long Island: in Manhasset at the

Miracle Mile, 1400 Northern Blvd.; in Huntington on N.Y. 110, adjacent to Walt Whitman Mall; in Copake at 1101 Sunrise Hwy., as well as in Scarsdale, NY, and Paramus, NJ. All stores are open seven days a week, Monday through Saturday from 10 a.m. to 9:30 p.m. and on Sunday from noon to 6 p.m.

**Aaron's,** 627 Fifth Ave., between 17th and 18th streets, in *Brooklyn* (tel. 718/768-5400), is a marvelous store that specializes in high-fashion women's wear at discount prices. Current merchandise is sold at 20% to 30% off regular price. Famous-brand, expensive knit dresses that go for $125 to $500 elsewhere cost $88 to $333 at the most here. Designer clothes of every type—coats, sportswear, furs, cashmere sweaters—are all sold here. There's a large community dressing room, but the sales staff is courteous and helpful.

Open Monday through Saturday from 9:30 a.m. to 6 p.m. Aaron's own parking field is across the street. To get there by subway, take the BMT R local train to Prospect Avenue. Walk one block to Fifth Avenue.

Across the street from New York's prestigious Fashion Institute of Technology, a small cluster of designer discount stores draw price-conscious shoppers. Weekends are a big shopping time here, and all stay open on Sunday. Very "in" with fashion-conscious New York women is **S & W,** which has four stores at the corner of 26th Street and Seventh Avenue (tel. 924-6656), all offering incredible buys in top-designer clothing. The shop at 165 W. 26th St. offers designer misses and junior suits, dresses, sportswear, matching separates, and evening wear; 283 Seventh Ave. carries designer handbags, shoes, and accessories; 287 Seventh Ave. has designer coats; and 171 W. 26th is the outlet store for the best buys of all. In Brooklyn S & W is at 4217 13th Ave. (tel. 718/483-9679). All stores are open Monday through Friday, 10 a.m. to 6 p.m., Thursdays till 8 p.m., closed Saturday.

The atmosphere is exciting and prices are inviting at **Unique Clothing Warehouse,** which has two stores, at 718 and 726 Broadway, below 8th Street in Greenwich Village (tel. 674-1767). Over 30,000 square feet is jammed with avant-garde clothing, which includes outerwear, lingerie, antique clothing, accessories. They also have toys, do-it-yourself T-shirt painting, and men's clothing too. Entertaining. Open Monday through Thursday from 10 a.m. to 9 p.m., on Friday and Saturday to midnight, and on Sunday from noon to 8 p.m.

**Bogie's Antique Clothing and Furs,** 201 E. 10th St., near Second Avenue (tel. 260-1199), is a mess, a jumble, a mixture of incredible designer, antique, and recycled clothing. If you know how to pick through the tables, you'll find bargains galore. We've seen models and other chic types sitting on the floor going through the piles. We've even seen patchwork quilts here in fairly good condition for low prices. Prices are so low they're unbelievable. Some items are in perfect condition, but many need a little fixing up. If you're clever with a needle, you could put together an entire wardrobe for $100. And if you need a cheap fur coat—something for under $100 —this is the place. They're all used, in good condition, and include lamb, mouton, the occasional raccoon or mink.

Open from 12:30 to 5:30 p.m. Monday through Thursday, until 6 p.m. on Friday and Saturday. They may be open on Sunday in winter, and sometimes close on hot summer Saturdays, so call first to check.

Rock-and-roll fun clothes for the young set—that's how **Trash and Vaudeville,** 4 St. Marks Pl. (which is East 8th Street), east of Third Avenue (tel. 982-3590), defines its style. One of the funkier stores in the funky East Village, TAV has women's and men's clothing and accessories both expensive and trendy and inexpensive and trendy. They're known for their huge collection of jeans (black, blue, stretch, regular, you-name-it), including their own brand, which sells for $48 to $72. They also have an enormous collection of shoes, everything from sporty to dressy to "outrageous." Motorcycle and bike wear, weird, way-out jewelry, and lots of London imports too.

Open Monday through Thursday from noon to 8 p.m., on Friday from 11:30

a.m. to 8 p.m., on Saturday from 11 a.m. to 8:30 p.m., and on Sunday from 1 to 7:30 p.m.

One of the best stores of this genre—and a tremendous favorite with young people—is **Canal Jean Co.,** a few blocks south of Houston Street at 504 Broadway (tel. 226-1130). A short walk from Chinatown, Little Italy, or the heart of SoHo, this store offers a wide selection of colorful merchandise, from antique clothing and military surplus to better sportswear for men and women to accessories and lingerie —and all at super-low discount prices. Start in front of the store, where bins always offer plenty of good values for inveterate bargain hunters. We once saw antique tweed coats and jackets for $1 and antique sweaters at three for $5. Inside, look for such popular basics as 100% cotton dyed T-shirts (five styles, ten colors at any given time at $5 each, or three for $12), or their own 100% cotton mock turtleneck for $17. Or expect the unexpected! Perhaps a Hawaiian aloha shirt at $9, brand-new American military trenchcoats at $30, a 100% cotton Canal Jean beach towel for under $5, or seasonal designer closeouts at 50% to 75% off regular retail prices.

Canal Jean Co. is open Sunday through Thursday from 10 a.m. to 8 p.m., until 9 p.m. on Friday and Saturday.

Most of the SoHo boutiques are of the pricey variety, so we were thrilled to find a genuine off-price store here. It's called **Three Wishes,** 355 West Broadway (tel. 226-7570), and it has at least three virtues we always wish for in a shop: good products, good prices, and that hard-to-find commodity known as good service. Three Wishes manufactures a good deal of sportswear and career clothing under its own label, and also carries many brand names that they can't disclose in print, all at discounts of at least 30% off regular prices. As examples of their price range, consider silk blouses for $34 to $46, dresses for $59 to $118, pants for about $30 to $40, and suits for $79 to $89. They also do a lot of knits, carry coats in winter, and are expanding their line of petites. Sizes run 4 to 14.

Three Wishes is open every day from noon to 7 p.m.

Every kind of silk you can imagine—crêpe de chine, silk charmeuse, silk chiffon, crushed silk, knitted silk, silk batiste (silk and cotton), and much more—can be found at **Royal Silk,** 79 Fifth Ave., between 15th and 16th streets (tel. 243-5507), the New York store for the national catalog company. Best of all, silk shirts, blouses, pants, skirts, sweaters, lingerie, and so on, can be found at much less than regular retail prices—we saw silk sweaters for $29, basic shirts for $31, and a dinner skirt for $52. Even better bargains are found in the downstairs clearance section. Incidentally, most of the garments are washable; after all, silkworms were doing their thing long before the invention of dry cleaners! Any woman who loves silk—does that exclude anybody?—should check this one out.

Royal Silk is open from 9:30 a.m. to 6 p.m. Monday through Saturday (to 8 p.m. on Thursday and Friday), and on Sunday from noon to 5 p.m.

**Century 21,** 12 Cortlandt St., between Church Street and Broadway (tel. 227-9092), is a smart shopper's paradise. First-quality, current-season, moderately priced to expensive designer clothes are offered at good and sometimes huge discounts. Also children's clothes, men's clothes, ladies' undergarments and sleepwear, beautiful shoes, linens, giftware, appliances, and much, much more.

Open Monday through Wednesday from 7:45 a.m. to 6:10 p.m., on Thursday and Friday until 6:25 p.m., and on Saturday from 10 a.m. to 5 p.m. They're also in *Brooklyn* at 472 86th St., open daily from 11 a.m. to 6 p.m. No try-ons allowed, but they do offer full refunds on all purchases.

**Deals,** 81 Worth St., in the downtown area (tel. 966-0214), specializes in career dressing for women. Their classic as well as contemporary styles show up in the best offices. Discounts of at least 40% to 60% can be found in all-wool tropical suits, for example, which might be $450 uptown, but $189 and $199 here. Rayon challis dresses, $160 in leading department stores, go for $80 here. Even accessories such as leather wallets, address books, and umbrellas by top designer names are discounted. There are men's and children's selections as well.

Deals is open Monday through Saturday from 9 a.m. to 6 p.m. (on Thursday until 8 p.m.); closed Sunday.

Big sellers in Europe and Japan, the clothing creations of **Reminiscence** are a favorite with the under-30 international set. The anchor store is at 74 Fifth Ave., near 13th Street at the top of Greenwich Village (tel. 342-2292). Green and pink walls, neon signs, and spotlights set the scene for Stewart Richer's award-winning designs that are a redefinition of the '50s with a New Wave accent. Richer designs clothes, mostly in natural fabrics, that are fun, comfortable, and exciting, a blend of antique and ultra-contemporary. Flight suits, army-surplus pants, coveralls, and jackets are all dyed unusual and brilliant colors. They also carry reproductions of antique and nostalgic clothing such as their own "Hawaiian" shirts, exact duplicates of the patterns and styles sold during the '50s. There are jewelry, housewares, and bath departments. In the front of the store is a selection of genuine antique clothes, all reasonably priced.

Open Monday through Saturday from 12:15 to 8 p.m. and on Sunday from 1 to 6 p.m. There are also Reminiscence boutiques on the second floor of Macy's and the fourth floor of Bloomingdale's.

**Fiorucci,** 125 E. 59th St., between Park and Lexington avenues (tel. 751-5638), is an assault on your eyes (they specialize in *bright*-colored clothing) and ears (and they play *loud* music), and is definitely a must-visit in New York if you are interested in what the rest of the nation will be wearing two or three years in the future. Fiorucci stocks the fad of the minute, from miniskirts to paper clothing to blinking electrified earrings. Elio Fiorucci's penchant for combining the classic with the absurd—for example, cowboy boots in gold leather, or a map of the world on a pleated accordion skirt, or industrial textiles used for earrings and belts—is evident everywhere. His far-out collection of T-shirts, along with designer jeans, form the basis of his collection. T-shirts run about $25; coats, about $250; tops, from $55 to $90; jeans, from $62 to $70. Although the upstairs, which shows women's and children's clothing, jewelry, hats, cards, and the like, is wild and fun, there's a conservative male bastion downstairs fashioned like a dressing room with armoire, roll-top desks, and Oriental rugs. Also downstairs is a Texas desert scene, complete with cactus, oil rigs, horse and saddle, and the like, featuring denim togs for both men and women. Well worth a visit for shopping as theater: live window displays, contemporary music tapes.

Open Monday through Saturday from 10 a.m. to 6:30 p.m., plus Sunday during the Christmas holiday season.

**The Gap** is a phenomenally successful chain of stores selling jeans, sweat clothes, shirts, blouses, and other casual sports clothes for men, women, and children at very reasonable prices. Their styles are sophisticated, their merchandise all top-quality. Nifty polo shirts run from about $25 up. You'll find The Gap, it seems, every few blocks, but some central locations are 22 W. 34th St., west of Fifth Avenue (tel. 695-2521); Pier 17 at the South Street Seaport (tel. 374-1051); and 734 Lexington Ave., at 59th Street (tel. 751-1543). Check almost two dozen other locations in the New York telephone directory. Hours of operation vary, so call ahead.

The **Forgotten Woman,** 888 Lexington Ave. (tel. 535-8848) and 60 W. 49th St. at Rockefeller Center (tel. 247-8888), caters to the larger-size woman who has difficulty finding stylish, upscale clothing. The store stocks both items that are currently in fashion and good basics that can be considered "investment dressing." While none of this is inexpensive (the price range goes from $49 separates to $16,000 fur coats), they are definitely good value, since one dress that fits well is worth five that pinch, stretch out of shape, rip at the seams, or are uncomfortable.

Store hours are Monday through Saturday from 10 a.m. to 6 p.m.

Downtown, the fashion-conscious larger woman has an ally in Carol Lefkowitz of **The Greater N.Y. Woman,** at 215 E. 23rd St., between Second and Third avenues (tel. 725-0505), who has a great eye for high style at decent prices. There's a large collection of sportswear, daytime dresses, and executive clothing, and knowledgeable salespeople to help the customer put it all together. A must for the big woman.

Open Monday through Saturday from 11 a.m. to 7 p.m. and on Sunday from noon to 5 p.m.

## Maternity

The immense selection of maternity clothing at **Reborn Maternity Discount,** with a location on the East Side at 1449 Third Ave., between 81st and 82nd streets (tel. 737-8817), and on the West Side at 564 Columbus Ave., between 87th and 88th streets (tel. 362-6965), is almost equal to all the other maternity shops in the city (including department stores) combined. First-quality merchandise costs 10% to 50% less than you'd pay at other stores. Expect to pay from $25 to $30 up for tops, $65 up for dresses. They're also featuring sophisticated designer fashions for pregnant women, including names like Belle France, J. G. Hook, and Sasson. Lingerie and exercise leotards are also discounted.

The East Side location is open Monday through Friday from 10 a.m. to 7 p.m. (on Thursday to 8:30 p.m.), on Saturday to 6 p.m., and on Sunday from 11 a.m. to 5 p.m. The West Side store is open Monday through Friday from 10:30 a.m. to 7 p.m. (on Wednesday to 8:30 p.m.), on Saturday from 10 a.m. to 6 p.m., and on Sunday from 11 a.m. to 5 p.m.

## Bridal Gowns, Wholesale and Retail

Bridal gowns are far from inexpensive these days, so every prospective bride should know about the buildings at 1385 Broadway and 499 Seventh Ave. in the Garment Center; they house some of the leading bridal manufacturers and designers in the country. On Saturday mornings, between 10 a.m. and noon, 1385 Broadway is wide open for brides, bridesmaids, mothers of the bride, and flower girls. To shop efficiently here, shop elsewhere first: know your merchandise and prices before you set foot in the door. Then you'll have a guide for comparison-shopping; and in some —but not every—case the savings can be enormous. For the best bargains, check the discontinued and sample racks.

Gaining access to the showrooms at 499 Seventh Ave. may sometimes be difficult, but worth a try; ask the elevator starters what floors will be open. Good bets are floors 15 and 21. Again, this one is for Saturday.

Want to keep within your budget and look as if you've spent a mint? We'll let you in on a special secret. For upward of $250 and $300 you can rent a fabulous creation by **Gene London,** a copy of a couture or antique wedding gown (or even a Victorian original for a higher price). These gowns sell for thousands, and some are made of Battenberg lace and have mile-long cinema satin or candlelit satin trains. Gene's customers are many of the stars from movies and television, and his loft is a great adventure. By appointment only (tel. 533-4105).

It will be well worth your while to take a trip to Brooklyn to shop for wedding clothes at **Kleinfeld and Son,** Fifth Avenue and 82nd Street, Bay Ridge (tel. 718/833-1100). Kleinfeld is known for one of the largest selections of designer bridal gowns, mother-of-the-bride clothes, designer evening wear, and special-occasion clothes in the country. Discounts range from 20% to 40%. There are many imports from England, France, and Italy in misses and junior sizes.

Open on Tuesday and Thursday from 11 a.m. to 9 p.m.; on Wednesday, Friday, and Saturday until 6 p.m.; closed Sunday and Monday, and Saturday during July and August. Phone for travel directions.

## Special-Occasion Dresses

If you're looking for party, prom, mother-of-the-bride, and other special-occasion dresses, make note of the wholesale building at 498 Seventh Ave. Call designer **Anne Marie Gardin** at 736-2895 to make an appointment: she has beautiful dresses, long and short, in lace, linen, and silk, and many mother-of-the-bride outfits. Prices are $200 to $500 wholesale.

## Resale Shops

Some of the best-dressed women in New York—glamorous types who look as if they've just stepped off the pages of *Vogue* or *Town and Country*—are actually wearing secondhand clothes that they purchased at chic Madison Avenue resale shops! These are the places where society women, actresses, models, and fashion editors on the best-dressed lists often take dresses, gowns, suits, and coats that they've worn only a few times. (The society columnists would notice, perish the thought, if they showed up in the same clothes too often!) The castoffs are then resold to customers like you, in excellent condition (they've received a thorough cleaning), and at a fraction of their original prices.

The resale shop with the highest fashion styles is **Michael's,** at 1041 Madison Ave., at 79th Street, second floor (tel. 737-7273), which resembles Bergdorf Goodman's more than a secondhand store. The clothing available here comes from some of the wealthiest and best-dressed women in the world; when they empty their closets, they fill Michael's with the very best collection of designer names you're apt to find under one roof anywhere: Valentino, Calvin Klein, Yves St. Laurent, Armani, Ungaro, Blass, etc. We've seen $500 coats priced at $125 (and you'd never know they weren't new). Believe it or not, there is even a $10 rack on which you might find a treasure.

Open Tuesday through Saturday from 9:30 a.m. to 6 p.m.; closed Saturday during July and August.

After exhausting the possibilities at Michael's, you'll do well to walk five blocks uptown to the **Encore Resale Dress Shop,** at 1132 Madison Ave., at 84th Street (tel. 879-2850), which also stocks an enormous supply of women's outer apparel at prices averaging a third what the original owners paid. In addition to terrific buys on designer clothing, you'll also find incredible values in fine furs. Many of the famous have unloaded wardrobes here. Note, too, a large supply of new clothing, and a great selection of accessories, including designer handbags, shoes, jewelry, scarves, belts, etc. There are two floors to browse through.

Open Monday through Saturday from 10:30 a.m. to 6 p.m. (on Thursday to 7 p.m.), and on Sunday from 12:30 to 6 p.m. Closed Sunday from July to mid-August.

## Buttons and Buckles

And now, after scouring the resale shops for bargains, you may decide all your new dress needs is some elegant buttons. A charming shop, **Tender Buttons,** at 143 E. 62nd St., between Lexington and Third avenues (tel. 758-7004), carries every kind of antique and modern button, plus exquisite antique buckles. Some buttons even have fascinating histories, which proprietresses Diana Epstein and Millicent Safro will be happy to tell you about. Note, too, that Tender Buttons has the largest collection of men's blazer buttons (antique and new) in the world, as well as antique men's cufflinks, dress sets, studs, and stickpins.

Open Monday through Friday from 11 a.m. to 6 p.m., until 5:30 p.m. on Saturday. Closed Saturday in July and August.

## Lingerie

**Fashions,** 331 Grand St. (tel. 966-1143), claims the city's largest bra and foundation department, and largest brand diversity—all at typical Orchard Street discount prices.

Open Sunday through Thursday from 10 a.m. to 5:30 p.m., on Friday until 3 p.m.; closed Saturday.

Another huge selection of the top names in ladies' lingerie can be found at

**Goldman & Cohen, Inc.,** 54 Orchard St., between Hester and Grand streets (tel. 966-0737). Discounts range from about 20% to 70%.

Open Sunday through Thursday from 9 a.m. to 5 p.m., on Friday until 3:30 p.m.

Ditto **A. W. Kaufman,** 73 Orchard St., between Grand and Broome streets (tel. 226-1629), which has vast selections of designer lingerie at greatly discounted prices: loungewear, sleepwear, camisole sets, ensemble sets, hostess gowns, cashmere and wool robes, bedjackets, slippers, etc., in silks, satins, and cottons.

Open Sunday through Thursday from 10 a.m. to 5 p.m., on Friday to 2:30 p.m.

**Ultra Smart,** 15 E. 30th St., between Fifth and Madison avenues (tel. 686-1564), buys up stockings from the big mills and puts them out under their own label. These are the exact stockings you'd pay up to five times as much for under a designer label.

Open weekdays only from 8 a.m. to 5 p.m.

## Handbags

For the best values in better handbags, head for the Lower East Side and **Fine and Klein Handbags,** 119 Orchard St., between Delancey and Rivington streets (tel. 674-6720). Their huge selection of name and designer bags spans three floors and offers such names as Jay Herbert, Varon, Sharif, and Susan Gail, at discounts of 35%.

Open daily except Saturday from 8:45 a.m. to 5:30 p.m.

You should also know about **Ber-Sel,** 79 Orchard St., between Broome and Grand streets (tel. 966-5517), where Anne Klein, Liz Claiborne, Dior, and many other top-brand and designer bags are sold at discounts of about 30%, along with beautiful wallets and umbrellas.

Open Sunday through Friday from 9:30 a.m. to 5:30 p.m.

## Shoes

In the downtown area, women should try **Anbar,** 93 Reade St., between Church Street and West Broadway (tel. 227-0253), for good prices on high-fashion shoes. These retailers of women's shoes do not have all sizes, but if you're lucky you'll get a bargain. Many designer names. Under the same ownership, **Shoe Steal,** around the corner from Anbar at 116 Duane St. (tel. 964-4017), has shoes at even lower prices ($15 to $40 a pair).

Both stores are open weekdays from 8 a.m. to 5:30 p.m. and on Saturday from 11 a.m. to 5 p.m. Closed Saturdays in July and August.

Several stores on the Lower East Side are well worth checking out, among them:

For over 25 years, **Lace Up Shoe Shop,** 110 Orchard St., at the corner of Delancey Street (tel. 475-8040), has been drawing women who love high-style European designer shoes (on Sunday, you may have to wait in line to gain entrance). Once inside, check the sales section on the top floor first; odd-sized shoes, leftovers, and the like are discounted from 50% to 80%; prices run $15 to $60. On the lower level, current shoes, sandals, and boots by European designers are discounted 20% to 40%; most go for $50 to $125. We once spotted a pair of $100 ankle-length leather boots for $55. All prices are inclusive of tax. If you're in town the third week in July or in February, check out their summer and winter clearance sales (call first).

Lace Up Shoe Shop is open Sunday through Friday from 9 a.m. to 5:30 p.m.; closed Saturday.

The **Orchard Bootery,** 75 Orchard St., between Broome and Grand streets (tel. 966-0688), has many designer shoes—Jacques Cohen, Bandolino, Evan Picone, Versani, Charles David, Peter Kaiser, Martinez Valero, Palizzio, d'Rossana, etc.— discounted 30% or more.

Open Monday through Friday from 9:30 a.m. to 5:30 p.m. and on Sunday to 6 p.m.; closed Saturday.

**Leslie Bootery,** 319 Grand St., off Orchard Street (tel. 431-9196). This Lower East Side standby has a new location, featuring mens', ladies', and designer shoes. You'll see such names as Bally, Cole, Perry Ellis, Esprit, Frye, Calvin Klein, Reebok, Rockport, Timberland, etc., all at a minimum of 20% off.

Open Sunday through Friday from 9:30 a.m. to 5:30 p.m.; closed Saturday.

**M.&M. Shoe Center,** 302 Grand St. (tel. 966-2702), and **Maximum,** 91 Orchard St. (tel. 966-4622), are two stores under the same management, both offering a wide range of top name-brand sandals, shoes, and boots at discounts of 20% to 25%. They stock everything from high-style designer shoes to comfortable everyday styles, and it's all first-quality, all-leather, current stock. Among the brands represented, we spotted Frank Cardone, Julienneli, Rangoni of Florence, Fefeo Meucci of Florence, Erica, Newton Elkin, Barefoot Originals, and Rockport (Rockports that sell for $70 to $80 uptown are $54 to $64 here). Check the big clearance sales in July and the end of December.

Open Sunday through Thursday from 9:30 a.m. to 5:45 p.m., on Friday until 4 p.m.

In Brooklyn, the same management runs **M.&M. Classics,** 45–26 13th Ave. (tel. 718/972-2737).

## Furs

Some of the best bargains in New York on gently used furs can be found at the **Ritz Thrift Shop,** 107 W. 57th St., between Sixth and Seventh avenues (tel. 265-4559). This is where New York's society women shed their furs, sometimes after only a few months' wear. All the coats, stoles, and jackets are in excellent condition. Mink coats currently sell for between $700 and $4,000. Other furs enjoying great popularity at the moment are raccoon, fox, beaver, and other long-haired furs, which start at about $600 and can go up to as much as $3,000. Not readily available, but very popular are sable, lynx, and fisher, which sell for between $2,000 and $20,000. All garments are altered at no charge. The Ritz encourages inquiries by those who have any fur to sell.

Open Monday through Saturday from 9 a.m. to 6 p.m. Closed Saturday in July.

A huge selection of used furs—as well as outstanding buys in new furs—can be found at the **New Yorker Fur Thrift Shop,** 822 Third Ave., between 50th and 51st streets (tel. 355-5090). Although the store specializes in "finer quality coats" (a good used mink would begin at $1,500), they also have lots of antique fun coats—remember sheared raccoons and sheared beavers, muskrats, and Persians?—in the $250 to $300 range. Since the New Yorker is a manufacturer, they can also offer brand-new fur coats at factory prices; we've seen fox jackets at around $400. All told, there are about 2,000 garments on hand. And the men's department is growing.

Open Monday through Saturday from 10 a.m. to 5 p.m. and on Sunday from noon to 5 p.m. (Closed Sunday from May to August; closed Saturday in July and August.)

## MEN'S CLOTHING AND ACCESSORIES

Before launching into our listings for menswear, we refer you back to **Richard's Army-Navy, Unique Clothing Warehouse,** and the downtown wholesale shoe district, which carry goods for men also and are described above in our "Women's Clothing and Accessories" section

## Suits, Pants, Jackets, Coats

A family business over 60 years old has taken on a new lease on life as **Rothman's,** 200 Park Ave. South (17th Street at Union Square; tel. 777-7400). Harry Rothman, the grandfather of the current owner, was the first discounter of men's quality clothing in New York. When the Fifth Avenue store lost its lease several years ago, his grandson, Ken Giddon, relocated to handsome new quarters and kept the same philosophy, discounting the high end of the menswear lines, the best-tailored clothes in the country, for 20% to 50% off regular retail prices. Everything is under the Rothman label—the top manufacturers who supply the store will not allow their labels to be used or advertised—but savvy shoppers who know their top designers can find them, sans labels, greatly discounted here: a suit we spotted uptown for $875 was going for $485 here; a $750 suit was $395. We also saw top designer suits for $299; $40 pinpoint (tightly woven) cotton shirts sell for $20; braces (suspenders) go for $15 to $50; ties, $15 to $30—all discounted 20% to 25%. With prices like this, it's no wonder that some of New York's best-dressed men do their scouting at prestigious emporiums like Saks Fifth Avenue or Barney's, then come to Rothman's for the bargains.

Rothman's is open from 10 a.m. to 7 p.m. Monday through Friday (on Thursday to 8 p.m.), on Saturday from 9 a.m. to 6 p.m., and on Sunday from noon to 5 p.m. Closed Sunday in summer.

A good midtown resource for traditional executive wear at discount prices is **L.S. Men's Clothing,** 18 W. 45th St., Suite 403, between Fifth and Sixth avenues (tel. 575-0933). Designer suits, natural shoulder suits, jackets, and coats are all American made and sold at 45% to 65% off their typical retail prices of $375 to $650. They also have a large selection of silk ties and slacks. There's a tailor on the premises.

Open on Sunday from 10 a.m. to 5 p.m., Monday through Thursday from 9 a.m. to 7 p.m., and on Friday to 3 p.m.

Traditional men's clothing at nontraditional prices is what you'll find at **Deals,** downtown at 81 Worth St. (tel. 966-0214). The store is huge, equally divided between men's and women's clothing (see above), with discounts from 30% to 50% the norm. You might see $45 pinpoint Oxford shirts for $20, $240 pure-wool tropical suits for $140, $60 all-wool natural-shoulder designer sweaters for $30. The store specializes in natural-fiber apparel—shirts are 100% cotton—and refuses to handle any blends or polyesters. They are especially proud of their handcrafted English shoes, made by the same company that has been making footwear for the English royal family since the mid-1700s: elsewhere, $235; here, $99.

Deals is open on Monday through Friday from 8:30 a.m. to 6 p.m. (on Thursday until 8 p.m.), and on Saturday from 9 a.m. to 6 p.m.

Although **Daffy's,** 111 Fifth Ave., at 18th Street (tel. 529-4477), is known primarily for women's fashions, husbands need not sit idly by while the wives get all the bargains. We spotted designer cotton sweaters that would sell for $80 to $150 elsewhere, $24 to $40 here; Italian wool gabardine trousers were $50 here, $100 in other stores; cotton sport shirts that were selling uptown for $40 to $62 were $14 to $20 here—just to give you an idea.

Daffy's is open from 10 a.m. to 10 p.m. Monday through Saturday and on Sunday from 11 a.m. to 6 p.m.

**Fenwick Clothes,** on the fifth floor of 22 W. 19th St., west of Fifth Avenue (tel. 243-1100), is a manufacturer of quality men's clothing which has opened its doors to the public. As a result you get to buy at wholesale prices and can purchase suits, overcoats, topcoats, jackets, slacks, etc., for about 40% to 50% off retail price. Suits that would retail for $475 to $775 are $269 to $389 here; sports jackets that cost $350 in the retail stores are $210; and slacks retailing for $135 are $79 to $99. Quality is excellent. Alterations extra.

Open weekdays from 9 a.m. to 5 p.m., on Saturday until 4 p.m. Closed Saturday in summer.

Values are also good at **Borislaw Custom Clothier,** at 2 E. 17th St., just off Fifth Avenue (tel. 242-8134), which sells ready-to-wear brand names, including suits, leather jackets, and pants, at varying discounts, and also does custom clothing. They also sell and rent wedding tuxedos. A recent sale advertised quality wool or wool-blend men's suits for $49 to $165.

Open weekdays only, from 8:30 a.m. to 6 p.m.

**Syms,** 45 Park Pl., between Church Street and West Broadway, two blocks north of the World Trade Center (tel. 791-1199), has three entire floors of men's apparel and accessories, including shoes. Many designer labels in every department, and the savings can be incredible. Men will find everything at Syms, from designer coats and suits, to jeans, shirts, warmup suits, and pajamas. Women's and children's clothing too (see above).

Syms is open on Tuesday and Wednesday from 8 a.m. to 6:30 p.m., on Thursday and Friday to 7:30 p.m., on Saturday from 10 a.m. to 6:30 p.m., and on Sunday from 11:30 a.m. to 5:30 p.m.

**Buyer's Factory Outlet (BFO),** 149 Fifth Ave., at 21st Street, on the second and sixth floors (tel. 254-0059), is another big outfit where prices can sometimes be discounted as much as 50% off regular retail. There's a large selection of Italian suits and sports coats, famous-brand shirts, ties, and sweaters. We've seen suits for $175 and up, sports coats for $105 and up, and many designer and big-name brands. Alterations available while you wait.

Open seven days, from 9:30 a.m. to 6 p.m.

On the Lower East Side, check out the following shops:

For designer jeans, **Arnie's Place,** 37 Orchard St., at Hester Street (tel. 925-0513), is a good bet. Good discounts on Calvin Klein, Lee, Sasson, Levis, and Landlubber jeans, among others.

Open weekdays from 9 a.m. to 5 p.m. and on Sunday from 8 a.m. to 5:30 p.m.

A tradition of quality and service keep the customers coming back to **Pan Am Men's Wear,** 50 Orchard St., between Grand and Hester streets (tel. 925-7032). They carry coats, jackets, suits, shirts, and sportswear by such top designers as Perry Ellis, Polo by Ralph Lauren, Alexander Julian, Charles Jourdan, Tallia, Lubiam, Marzotto of Italy, and a full line of Italian designers. Discounts are sizeable and expert tailoring is free. Garments may be returned within 14 days of purchase.

Open Sunday through Wednesday from 9:30 a.m. to 6 p.m., on Thursday until 8 p.m., on Friday to 3 p.m.

Similar wares and bargains are across the street at **G & G International,** 53 Orchard St. (tel. 431-4530)—Adolpho and Geoffrey Beene suits, clothing by San Remo, Lubiam, Bill Blass, Harvé Benard, and much more. Hathaway and Christian Dior shirts are discounted 20% to 30%. Free alterations.

Open Sunday through Wednesday from 9 a.m. to 6 p.m., on Thursday until 8 p.m., on Friday until an hour before sundown.

## Shirts

For excellent values in men's and women's shirts in the midtown area, stop in at **The Shirt Store,** 51 E. 44th St., at Vanderbilt Avenue (tel. 557-8040). All shirts are 100% cotton and are made by the owner in Pennsylvania, which assures affordable prices. Selections are wide and service is excellent: if for some strange reason you can't fit into their wide range of sizes (men's neck sizes 14 through 18½, sleeve lengths 32 through 37, or women's sizes 4 to 16), they will alter stock garments for a reasonable fee and have your shirt ready within the week. They also do made-to-measure garments. Prices for men's shirts are $25 to $75; for women's, $30 to $47.50. (Most women's shirts are tailored and 100% cotton; some are blends and there are also some fashion shirts). Varying sales promotions—when we were last there they were giving away free ties with every shirt purchased—add to the fun.

Open weekdays from 8 a.m. to 6:30 p.m. and on Saturday from 10 a.m. to 5 p.m.

On the Lower East Side's Orchard Street, you can pick and choose among many stores selling men's shirts at a discount. Our favorite is the **Victory Shirt Company,** 96 Orchard St., between Delancey and Broome streets (tel. 677-2020), which also has a store in the City Hall area at 10 Maiden Lane, between Broadway and Nassau Street (tel. 349-7111), and a new one in the midtown area at 485 Madison Ave., at 52nd Street (tel. 753-1679). They make all their own shirts, specializing in top-of-the-line 100% cotton fabrics—Oxford cloths, broadcloths, pinpoint, Egyptian, Sea

Island—and since you're buying from the manufacturer, savings are great. Shirts range from $35 to $90. Handmade silk ties go for $15 to $40, and women's shirts for $42.50 to $62.50.

The Orchard Street store is open weekdays and Sunday from 9 a.m. to 5 p.m. (until 4 p.m. on Friday); the Maiden Lane store is open weekdays only, from 9 a.m. to 6 p.m.; the Madison Avenue branch, Monday through Saturday from 9 a.m. to 6 p.m.

The **Penn Garden Grand Shirt Company,** 58 Orchard St., between Grand and Hester streets (tel. 431-8464), has designer and famous-name men's shirts at incredibly low prices—20% to 30% less than you'd pay elsewhere, from $15 to $90.

Open every day but Saturday, from 9 a.m. to 6 p.m. in summer, until 4 p.m. on Friday in winter, on Thursday to 8 p.m.

## Shoes

**Leslie Bootery,** 319 Grand St., off Orchard Street (tel. 431-9196), offers discounts of at least 20% on designer and name-brand men's shoes. Brand names include Rockport, Reebok, Bally, Cole-Haan, Keds, Timberland, and Unisa.

Open Sunday through Friday from 9:30 a.m. to 5:30 p.m.; closed Saturday.

For sneakers—Puma, Adidas, Nike, etc.—head to one of these four stores, all under the same ownership, and all open seven days a week from 9:30 a.m. to 5:30 p.m.: **Jules Harvey,** 132 Orchard St.; **H & J Shoes,** 131 Orchard St.; **All Star Shoes,** 135 Orchard St. (these three between Rivington and Delancey streets); and **Peck & Chase Shoes,** 163 Orchard St., between Rivington and Stanton streets (tel. 982-0840 for all four stores). They also carry many name-brand and designer shoes, boots, dress shoes, and work shoes, including Timberland.

**J. Sherman Shoes,** 121 Division St., at the south end of Orchard Street, one block south of Canal Street (tel. 233-7898), is a find for men looking for discounts of 20% to 70% on high-quality designer shoes. You'll find top brands from Switzerland, Italy, the U.S., and England, casual and dress shoes in contemporary styles.

Open from 9 a.m. to 5 p.m. Sunday through Thursday; they close at 3:30 p.m. on Friday, and all day Saturday.

## Ties

Ties are discounted at almost all the men's stores mentioned above. In addition, **Tie City,** at Grand Central Terminal, East 42nd Street (tel. 599-1121), offers a large assortment of patterns and materials for as little as $3 a tie; maximum price is $8 for a silk tie.

On the Lower East Side, **Allen Street** is tie street, with about ten stores located between Delancey and Houston streets. You can simply walk in and out of each shop until you find what you're looking for. All offer the low prices you'd expect in this area.

---

# 2. An Alphabetical Miscellany

---

## ANTIQUES

A personal favorite among the city's many antique shops is **Carol Alderman Antiques,** 353 Third Ave., at 26th Street (tel. 532-7242). Shopping here is always an adventure, since you never know what might turn up at this serendipitous spot: it could be anything from an art deco chandelier to an old perfume bottle. Great for gift giving: Carol's large collection of one-of-a-kind earrings, necklaces, bracelets, made of old artifacts, from $12.50 to $85. You'll probably also find mirrors, lamps, stained glass, and much more. Many people consider Carol to be "New York's best-kept secret."

Open most days, more or less from 1 to 8 p.m.

You'll need to make an appointment to see the collection of vintage clothing and props at **Early Halloween,** 130 W. 25th St., between Sixth and Seventh avenues (tel. 691-2933). You could find a slinky satin nightie, a poplin print housedress, or woolen jodhpurs. Shoes, ties and hats, jackets and coats, accessories in excellent condition—many never-worn items—at reasonable prices.

Open weekdays from noon to 6 p.m., by appointment only.

Connoisseurs of brass will want to peruse the merchandise at the **Brass Antique Shoppe,** 32 Allen St., between Canal and Hester streets (tel. 925-6660), which specializes in small items such as candlesticks and andirons at good prices. This Lower East Side shop also has vases, old Russian samovars, antique drawer pulls, kiddush cups, and much more.

Open Sunday through Thursday from 10 a.m. to 4:30 p.m.

These are but a fraction of the city's antique shops. For a weekend browsing session, you can explore Hudson Street in Greenwich Village, Amsterdam Avenue from 79th to 86th streets on the Upper West Side, or the cross streets from 72nd to 86th streets on the Upper East Side—all are areas with a concentration of antique shops.

## APPLIANCES

We'd never buy a stereo, radio, TV, camera, toaster, hairdryer, watch, sewing machine, blender, washing machine—or any other major or minor household appliance—without first comparison-shopping along Canal and Essex Streets on the Lower East Side. The stores listed below all stock a wide variety of brand-new, major-brand household appliances, in perfect condition, with the usual warranties —at prices up to 50% less than those in major department stores! Unless you know exactly what brand and model appliance you want, however, it's a good idea first to stop in at one of the city's better department stores and discuss pros and cons of every make and model with a knowledgeable salesperson. Then simply check out these Lower East Side shops (where gracious service is almost unheard of), and buy where the price is best: they won't give prices on the phone. Ask about refund and exchange policies when you buy, as some of these stores have neither. One last warning—you don't know the meaning of the word "mobbed" if you haven't seen one of these shops on a Sunday; best to go during the week, and preferably in the morning.

Along Essex Street, between Hester and Canal streets, try:

**Dembitzer Bros. Export Company,** 5 Essex St. (tel. 254-1310), open Sunday through Thursday from 10 a.m. to 6 p.m., on Friday until 2 p.m.

**Lewi Supply Company,** 15 Essex St. (tel. 777-6910), open Sunday through Thursday from 9 a.m. to 5:30 p.m., on Friday to 2 p.m.

**Essex Camera & Electronic Discount Center,** 17 Essex St. (tel. 677-6420), open Sunday through Thursday from 10 a.m. to 6 p.m., on Friday to 3 p.m.

**Foto Electric Supply Company,** 31 Essex St. (tel. 673-5222), open Sunday through Thursday from 9 a.m. to 7 p.m., on Friday until 2 p.m.

**Central Electronics,** 39 Essex St. (tel. 673-3220), open Sunday through Thursday from 9 a.m. to 6 p.m., on Friday until 3 p.m.

On Canal Street, between Essex and Orchard streets, try:

**ABC Trading Company,** 31 Canal St. (tel. 228-5080), open Sunday through Thursday from 10 a.m. to 6 p.m., on Friday to 2 p.m.

**Bondy Export Corporation,** 40 Canal St. (tel. 925-7785), open Sunday through Thursday from 10 a.m. to 6 p.m., on Friday until 2 p.m.

**Kunst Sales Corporation,** 45 Canal St. (tel. 966-1909), open Sunday through Thursday from 9:30 a.m. to 6 p.m.; closed Friday and Saturday.

## ARTIST'S SUPPLIES

Worth checking out for art supplies is **Eastern Artists,** 5 W. 22nd St., just west of Fifth Avenue (tel. 645-5555). Eastern offers a full line of artist's supplies at 20% to 50% off regular prices.

Open weekdays from 8:30 a.m. to 7 p.m., on Saturday from 11 a.m. to 6 p.m. except during June, July and August.

Also popular with New York artists for good prices on supplies is **Pearl Paint Company,** 308 Canal St., between Broadway and Church Street (tel. 431-7932).

Open Monday through Saturday from 9 a.m. to 5:30 p.m. (on Thursday until 7 p.m.), and on Sunday from 11 a.m. to 4:45 p.m. (Closed on Sunday in July and August.)

## AUCTIONS

The best place to find major antique pieces at sensible prices is at auction houses. Our favorite is **Sotheby's Arcade Auctions,** 1334 York Ave., at 72nd St. (tel. 606-7409), the "budget" gallery of the wildly expensive Sotheby's. You might be lucky enough to pick up a room-size Persian carpet for under $1,000 at their 10:15 a.m. Tuesday auctions. Items are on exhibit the preceding Thursday, Friday, Saturday, and Monday from 10 a.m. to 5 p.m. While you're there, don't hesitate to go up to Sotheby's main galleries on the second floor to ogle, perhaps, the likes of Egyptian carvings or Monet watercolors, or ice-cube-size diamond rings.

The **Lubin Galleries,** 30 W. 26th St., between Fifth and Sixth avenues (tel. 924-3777), is another place to pick up excellent values in antique and used furniture at auction every other Saturday all through the year, beginning at 10 a.m. Antique and traditional furniture, pianos, silver, bronzes, Oriental rugs and tapestries, porcelain, china, etc., are offered. You can see the items on display the Thursday (10 a.m. to 7 p.m.) and Friday (9 a.m. to 3 p.m.) before the sale. If you can't make the auction, you can leave your bid with a 25% deposit.

Other auctions of interest:

The **Police Department Auctions of Vehicles and General Property** (tel. 406-1369) for a complete recording of current police auction information—days, times, locations, etc.; for further information, phone 374-5905 and talk to a live person.

The **General Post Office Auction** holds sales every four to six weeks. Phone 967-8585 for information, or check the classified sections of the local papers.

Auctions on behalf of the **U.S. Customs Service** are now held by the Northrop Company in Jersey City, N.J., just across the river from Manhattan. They advertise for the three Sundays preceding the auction in the classified section of the *New York Times.* Their main office in Oklahoma (tel. 405/357-9194) also has information on forthcoming auctions.

At any of the above you might pick up anything and everything, from an unclaimed sofa to a box of hankies, all at extraordinary bargain prices.

## BABY CARRIAGES, TOYS, AND FURNITURE

A number of discount-type shops specialize in furniture and accessories for babies.

**Albee Baby Carriage,** 715 Amsterdam Ave., at the corner of 95th Street (tel. 662-5740), carries what may be the city's largest selection of carriages: everything from a lightweight aluminum umbrella stroller to custom-made English-style prams. In addition, they carry a full line of juvenile furniture and furnishings, plus a marvelous selection of cribs, beds, toys, and infant wear by leading manufacturers, yet all selling at considerable discounts, which vary with each item. They'll quote prices on the phone.

Open from 9 a.m. to 5:30 p.m. Monday through Saturday.

Maclaren strollers, made in England and the biggest-selling strollers in the world, are discounted at **Schneider's,** 20 Ave. A, at the corner of East 2nd Street (tel. 228-3540), in the East Village. Larger strollers and carriages include the Guess line from Germany; these are soft-bodied, have windows, and begin at $175. Schneider's also offers discount-priced baby furniture, as well as a full line of children's toys and nursery accessories.

Open Monday through Saturday from 10 a.m. to 6 p.m., on Sunday to 5 p.m.

In business since 1911, emphasizing customer service and very low prices, **Ben's Babyland,** 81 Ave. A, near East 6th Street (tel. 674-1353), is a large store with a wide selection of children's furniture, carriages, layettes, and all related items. A complete line of Silver Cross English prams is priced from $324.

Open Monday through Saturday from 9 a.m. to 5:30 p.m. and on Sunday from 10 a.m. to 5 p.m.

## BEAUTY PARLORS AND BARBERSHOPS

Hair care is very expensive in New York, but many women—and men too—have learned to beat the high costs by patronizing beauty schools or training sessions at some of the city's finest beauty salons. You'll be worked on by qualified students who need some live heads to practice on. No need to be alarmed—you can choose the style, the results are usually excellent, and the prices will certainly make you *feel* beautiful.

The biggest school, almost like a private beauty salon, is the **Robert Fiance Hair Design Institute,** 1628 Broadway, at 50th Street (tel. 757-2370), where a complete restyling by an advanced student supervised by an instructor—haircut, shampoo, and set—is under $5. Other services available include permanent waves, relaxing the hair, facials, manicures (but no pedicures), hair coloring, eyebrow trim, etc.—just about any service you would receive at a regular salon but at less than half the price.

Daytime hours are Monday through Saturday from 9:30 a.m. to 3 p.m. Evening hours are Monday through Thursday from 6 to 7 p.m. A senior citizen discount is offered on Monday, Tuesday, and Wednesday from 9:30 a.m. to 2 p.m. No appointment necessary.

**Atlas Haircutters,** 32 Third Ave., at the corner of 9th Street (tel. 475-1360), charges $5 for all haircuts, for men, women, and children. With shampoo and blow-dry, the price is $8.

Open Monday through Friday from 9 a.m. and on Saturday from 9 a.m. to 6 p.m. No appointment necessary.

The nicest thing about the training sessions at the fine beauty salons is that you can get your hair done absolutely free! Service is on a first-come, first-served basis (no appointments necessary), at **Daines,** 833 Madison Ave., between 69th and 70th streets (tel. 535-1563), which has training classes Tuesday evenings at 6 p.m. And you must arrive at 6 p.m. exactly to get your free shampoo, complete restyling (their choice of hairdo), and blow dry. Daines specializes in a natural look.

## BOOKS, NEW AND SECONDHAND

New York as the mecca for book retailing is legendary. Nationwide chains—**B. Dalton** and **Waldenbooks**—are well represented as well as the city's own **Doubleday stores**.

It is impossible to list *all* the interesting stores. We, therefore, give you only a small sampling of the diversity and list only some of the specialty stores.

The book store for bargain-hunters in town has to be the **Barnes & Noble Annex,** occupying half a city block on Fifth Avenue between 17th and 18th streets (tel. 633-3500). It's the only bookstore we've ever seen that provides supermarket baskets, but that's what you'll need to carry out your finds. Every book in the store (and there are hundreds of thousands) is discounted: *New York Times* hardcover bestsellers at 30% off, paperbacks from 10% to 25% off, children's books, remainders, reviewers' copies, and scholarly books. It also houses one of the largest classical record departments in New York City, as well as a video department with over 1,300 titles to choose from, many at discount prices. Just across the street is the main Barnes & Noble, which stocks nearly three million hardcovers, paperbacks, and new and used textbooks.

Both Barnes & Noble stores are open weekdays from 9:30 a.m. to 8 p.m., on Saturday to 6:30 p.m., and on Sunday from 11 a.m. to 6 p.m.

In the busy midtown area, budget-conscious bookworms head for the **Barnes & Noble** at 600 Fifth Ave., at 48th St. (tel. 765-0590), which offers generous discounts: 15% off on all hardcover books, 10% off on all paperback books, and 30% off on all *New York Times* hardcover bestsellers.

**Brentano's,** a division of Waldenbooks, occupies the landmark street-level floor at 597 Fifth Avenue, between 48th and 49th streets (tel. 826-2450), which had previously housed the famous Scribner Bookstore. The store opened in late 1989 and is worth a visit to see the 30-foot-high vaulted sales room and the central staircase and balcony with cast-iron railings. The Landmarks Preservation Commission describes it as "among the finest interiors in New York City." Open Monday through Saturday 10 a.m. to 7 p.m., Sunday from 11 a.m. to 5 p.m.

The once-famous secondhand book area of New York, between Fourth Avenue and Broadway, from 8th to 14th streets, is declining, but a few stores are still doing business in the old neighborhood. The biggest of these is the **Strand**, located for over 47 years at 828 Broadway, on the corner of 12th Street, which makes it something of a New York landmark (tel. 473-1452). Here, 32,000 feet of selling floor hold over 2,000,000 books on eight miles of shelves, making the Strand the largest used-book store in the country. It's a browser's paradise, with an extensive selection of books on history, art, law, journalism, and philosophy. Prices range from 50¢ to $35,000. There are plenty of remainders, and the newest reviewer's copies, including bestsellers and new paperbacks, are sold for half the publisher's list price. No trip to the Strand is complete without a visit to the Rare Book Rooms, where you will find a large selection of art books, modern first editions, and collector's copies in fine bindings.

The Strand is open Monday through Friday from 9:30 a.m. to 9:30 p.m., on Saturday to 6:30 p.m., and on Sunday from 11 a.m. to 6 p.m.

There is a second Strand located on John Street in the bustling South Street Seaport, where the best of the Strand specials are conveniently arranged on two miles of bookshelves.

The Seaport Strand is open from 10 a.m. to 7 p.m. In the summer, you can visit Strand kiosks at Central Park and Bryant Park, where Strand Specials are offered from 9:30 a.m. to dusk every fine day.

Some other interesting stores are:

**ART: Hacker Art Books,** 45 West 57th St. (between Fifth And Sixth avenues) (tel. 212/757-1450). Hacker's has been a gem for art-lovers for years, and it's now moved across the street from its old location. As of this writing the old store was still open, at 54 West 57th, as a special sale annex loaded with bargains. Open Monday through Saturday from 9:30 a.m. to 6 p.m.

**Wittenborn Art Books,** 1018 Madison Ave., between 78th and 79th streets, 2nd floor (tel. 288-1558). Open Monday through Saturday 10 a.m. to 5 p.m.

**Rizzoli Bookstore,** 31 West 57th St., between Fifth and Sixth avenues (tel. 759-2424). Give yourself lots of time to browse through Rizzoli, which boasts one of New York's most exhaustive and sophisticated collections of art books, classical and jazz recordings, and European magazines. Open Monday through Friday 9 a.m. to 10 p.m., Saturday from noon to 8 p.m.

**CHILDREN'S:** The granddaddy of New York's children's bookstores is **Eeyore's Books for Children,** with locations on both the East and West sides of town: at 25 E.

83rd St., between Fifth and Madison avenues (tel. 988-3404), and at 2212 Broadway, between 78th and 79th streets (tel. 362-0634). Eeyore's sells only children's books, and has a huge selection through which youngsters are invited to browse, and a friendly staff to advise parents. Look here for hard-to-find classics as well as current children's books, fiction and nonfiction; Eeyore's has them all. As if that weren't enough, they also schedule a number of special events and story hours during the year, all of them free; you might find Isaac Bashevis Singer here signing books, or a magic show, or a slide show on the wonderful world of sharks. If you'd like a schedule of these events, which are held January through May and September through December, write to either location.

The Broadway store is open Monday through Saturday from 10 a.m. to 6 p.m. and on Sunday from 10:30 a.m. to 5 p.m.; the Madison Avenue store is open Monday through Saturday from 10 a.m. to 6 p.m. and on Sunday from noon to 5 p.m. In July and August, the Broadway store's Sunday hours are shortened to noon to 5 p.m., and the Madison Avenue store is closed.

**Books of Wonder,** 132 Seventh Ave. at 18th Street (tel. 989-3270) and 464 Hudson St., at Barrow Street (tel. 645-8006), is New York's largest children's bookstore, and one of its most imaginative. Books are carefully selected to stimulate a love of reading in children, beginning with books for reading aloud to infants, all the way up to novels for those ages 10 to 17. Kids are encouraged to browse, sit on the floor, and handle the books; and you'll often find parents here reading aloud to their youngsters. Wide aisles and double doors accommodate strollers. In addition to a large selection of classic and modern books, the store also deals in collectible children's books, first editions and out-of-print books, including the world's largest collection of Oz books. Knowledgeable staff members can advise parents on selections. Write for free catalogs to the Seventh Avenue address.

Open Monday through Saturday from 11 a.m. to 7 p.m. and Sunday from noon to 6 p.m. The Hudson Street store is smaller, with fewer antiquarian and Oz books.

# DRAMA AND THEATER: **Applause Theatre Books,** 211 West 71st St., between
Broadway and West End Avenue (tel. 496-7511), offers plays, criticism, biographies, and books catering to actors and performers. Another branch of Applause, at 100 West 67th Street, specializes in books on film. Open daily from 10 a.m. to 8 p.m., Sunday from noon to 6 p.m.

**Drama Bookshop, Inc.,** 723 Seventh Ave. at 48th Street, 2nd floor (tel. 944-0595), is a performing arts specialty store and stocks plays, textbooks, criticism, and anthologies relating to theater, dance, and film. Hours are Monday through Friday 9:30 a.m. to 7 p.m., Thursday until 8 p.m., Saturday from 10:30 a.m. to 5:30 p.m., Sunday noon to 5 p.m.

**The Theater Arts Bookshop,** 405 West 42nd St., between Ninth and Tenth avenues (tel. 564-0402). Open Monday through Saturday 10 a.m. to 8 p.m., Sunday noon to 7 p.m.

# MYSTERY AND SCI-FI: **Forbidden Planet** has its original store downtown at
821 Broadway, between 11th and 12th streets (tel. 473-1576), and a newer store uptown at 227 E. 59th St., between Second and Third avenues (tel. 751-4386). Both locations feature science-fiction books, old and new comic books, original art from comic books, space and science-fiction-oriented toys and games, and sci-fi film memorabilia. They call themselves the largest of their kind, and we believe it.

The downtown store is open Monday through Saturday from 10 a.m. to 7 p.m., on Friday to 8 p.m., and on Sunday from noon to 6 p.m. The uptown store is open Monday through Friday from 11:30 a.m. to 8:30 p.m., on Saturday to 9 p.m., and on Sunday from noon to 7 p.m.

"Small but mighty" is the way the owners of the **Science Fiction Shop,** 56 Eighth Ave., at Horatio Street in Greenwich Village (tel. 741-0270), characterize their store, in business for 17 years and well known to readers worldwide, from Japan to Sweden to Sri Lanka. Science-fiction buffs come from all over the globe to visit the shop when they are in New York. The Science Fiction Shop deals exclusively in the literature of science fiction and fantasy, with a large backstock of titles in print in the United States, supplemented with books brought in from England, both hardcover and paperback. You may find yourself running into an autograph party or special event for such famous writers as Arthur C. Clarke, Isaac Asimov, Anne McCaffrey, and many others.

Open weekdays from 11:30 a.m. to 6:45 p.m., on Saturday to 6 p.m., and on Sunday from noon to 6 p.m.

**The Mysterious Bookshop,** 129 West 56th St., between Sixth and Seventh avenues (tel. 765-0900), stocks an extensive array of mystery, horror, detective, and true crime books. Open Monday through Saturday 11 a.m. to 7 p.m.

**Murder, Inc.,** 271 West 87th St., between West End Avenue and Broadway (tel. 362-8905). If it's a mystery or detective novel, you'll find it here. Remember, however, that Murder, Inc. doesn't accept credit cards—just cash and personal checks with proper identification. Open Wednesday through Saturday 1 p.m. to 7 p.m., Thursday 1 p.m. to 10 p.m.

**BUSINESS: McGraw-Hill Bookstore,** 1221 Avenue of the Americas (tel. 512-4100), tucked away in the basement of the McGraw-Hill building at Rockefeller Center, carries books from all publishers, with a special emphasis on business publications and compter books, software, and games. Hours are Monday through Saturday 10 a.m. to 5:45 p.m.

**Waldenbooks,** 57 Broadway at Exchange Place (tel. 269-1139) is another excellently stocked business bookstore. Hours are  Monday through Friday from 8 a.m. to 6 p.m.

**WOMEN AND GAYS: Judith's Room,** 681 Washington St. between 10th and Charles streets (tel. 727-7330), carries fiction by female authors, nonfiction titles about women's issues, and a variety of buttons, cards, and posters. Open Tuesday through Thursday noon to 8 p.m., Friday and Saturday noon to 10 p.m., Sunday noon to 7 p.m.

**A Different Light Bookstore,** 548 Hudson St., between Charles and Perry streets (tel. 989-4850), offers a huge selection of books that are of interest to the gay and lesbian community. Aside from novels and nonfiction titles concerning gay issues, you'll find a wide variety of magazines from around the country and around the world. Open Monday through Thursday 11 a.m. to 9 p.m., Saturday 11 a.m. to 11 p.m.

**Oscar Wilde Memorial Bookshop,** 15 Christopher St., across from Gay Street (tel. 255-8097), was one of the first bookstores catering to the gay and lesbian community and has been around for 23 years, offering a small but fascinating range of titles. Open daily noon to 7:30 p.m.

**MORE SPECIAL-INTEREST STORES: Kitchen Arts and Letters,** 1435 Lexington Ave., between 93rd and 94th streets (tel. 876-5550), offers a huge array of books on cooking, food, and wine, organized by both type of food and region. Open Monday 7 p.m. to 6 p.m., Tuesday through Friday 10 a.m. to 6:30 p.m., Saturday 11 a.m. to 6 p.m.

The bookstore of the **Asia Society,** 725 Park Avenue, at 70th Street (tel. 288-6400), is a superb resource for books on Asia, including Australia and the South Pacific islands, with titles in art, architecture, history, fiction, travel, philosophy, and religion. It's often a first stop for people about to move to or travel in Asian countries. Tapes of music are available, as are many imported titles and catalogs from exhibitions at the Asia Society. Adjoining it is a tasteful gift shop with posters, jewelry, pottery, cards, maps, wall decorations, and the like.

Open Monday through Friday from 10 a.m. to 6:30 p.m., Saturday from 11 a.m. to 6 p.m., Sunday from noon to 5 p.m.

For over 50 years, **Paragon Book Gallery,** 237 W. 72nd St., 2nd floor, between Broadway and West End Avenue (tel. 496-2378), has been a specialist in books on the Far East, South Asia, and the Middle East. They deal principally in art books, in and out of print, with some out-of-print titles in history and philosophy as well. Generalists, collectors, and dealers all seek them out for their large collection of everything from magnificent coffee-table books to worldwide imports, even including exhibition and auction catalogs from Europe and Asia, much prized by collectors.

Open weekdays from 10 a.m. to 6 p.m., Saturday from 11 a.m. to 5 p.m.

**Samuel Weiser,** 132 E. 24th St., between Lexington Avenue and Park Avenue South (tel. 777-6363), has been in business since 1927 and is perhaps the largest bookstore stocking books on metaphysics in the world. Its quarter-of-a-million volumes, including many rare and out-of-print works, cover a wide range of philosophical, occult, metaphysical, and New Age persuasions. They have many hard-to-find books published in India. After you've browsed the books (some people stay here for hours), check out the jewelry, crystals, crystal balls, and the very large selection of Tarot cards.

Open Monday, Tuesday, Wednesday, and Friday from 9 a.m. to 6 p.m.; Thursday from 10 a.m. to 7 p.m.; Saturday from 9:30 a.m. to 5 p.m.; Sunday from 11 a.m. to 5:30 p.m.

Another outstanding bookstore dealing in matters esoteric is **East West Books,** 78 Fifth Ave. at 14th Street (tel. 243-5994), an affiliate of the Himalayan Institute. There's a serene atmosphere here; an excellent collection of titles in religion, philosophy, New Age, health and nutrition, psychology, etc. Cassettes and CDs of New Age music are available, as are some jewelry and crystals. Open Monday through Thursday from 11 a.m. to 7:30 p.m., on Friday, Saturday, and Sunday from 11 a.m. to 6 p.m. Uptown, there's a smaller branch at 568 Columbus Ave., between 87th and 88th streets (tel. 787-7552), open Monday through Friday from noon to 7:30 p.m. and Saturday and Sunday from 11 a.m. to 6 p.m. Classes in hatha yoga, meditation, and cooking are available at both locations.

In the SoHo area, anyone interested in spiritual, holistic, and metaphysical studies should check the bookstore of **The Open Center,** a nonprofit holistic learning center at 83 Spring St., between Broadway and Lafayette Street (tel. 219-2527). The shop carries a selection of quality titles, music, calendars, crystals, cards, and jewelry; tapes from Open Center workshops are available as well. Open Monday through Friday from 11:30 a.m. to 10 p.m., on Saturday from 11 a.m. to 9 p.m., and on Sunday from 11 a.m. to 7 p.m.

In the midtown area, the **Quest Bookshop,** 240 E. 53rd St., between Second and Third avenues (tel. 758-5521), is the place to go for more esoteric books. A part of the New York Theosophical Society, it specializes in books on Theosophy, the mysticism of the great religions, mind science, health and healing, meditation and the like. Crystals, jewelry, tapes, some videos, round out a collection of some 4,000 carefully chosen titles. Open Monday through Friday from 10 a.m. to 6 p.m., and on Saturday from noon to 5 p.m.

**AND THEN THERE'S . . . :** New York's most famous literary bookstore is the **Gotham Book Mart,** 41 W. 47th St, between Fifth and Sixth avenues (tel. 719-4448), which has been in business since 1920. Its founder, Frances Stellof, who passed away recently at the age of 101, was an early champion of such modern writers as Henry Miller, Ernest Hemingway, and James Joyce; the James Joyce Society still meets here four times a year. The current owners carry on her dedication to modern literature—novels, poetry, film and theater books, with many first editions, hard-to-find and out-of-print literature, and a vast collection of literary magazines.

Their Christmas tree is famous, laden with antique ornaments, some of which are for sale. An authentic, old-fashioned piece of New York City, and a literary browser's idea of paradise.

Open Monday through Friday from 9:30 a.m. to 6:30 p.m., and Saturday to 6 p.m.

## CAMERAS AND COMPUTERS

See also "Appliances."

A dizzying display of photographic paraphernalia meets your eyes when you enter **Willoughby Camera Stores,** at 110 W. 32nd St., near Herald Square (tel. 564-1600), in business for 90 years and still growing! You can get just about anything in the photographic line here, from a Kodak pocket camera for around $20 to a Nikon that goes up into the hundreds. There are projectors, film photo albums, and a complete line of developing and darkroom gear. In addition to all that, Willoughby is also a leader in the computer, video equipment, audio, and electronic lines as well. They offer one of the largest selections of personal computers and advanced video equipment in the metropolitan area. Bargains are great!

They're open weekdays from 9 a.m. to 7 p.m. (on Thursday to 8 p.m.), on Saturday from 9 a.m. to 6:30 p.m., and on Sunday from 10:30 a.m. to 5:30 p.m. You can also come in from 7:30 a.m. on for early developing and printing services.

When New York's professional photographers need new equipment or film, chances are they'll head for a branch of **Camera Barn,** at 1272 Broadway, near 32nd Street (tel. 947-3510), or downtown at 198 Broadway, (tel. 233-3080). Whether you're interested in a simple Polaroid camera or a sophisticated 35-mm system, you'll find the right prices and a helpful staff.

Both branches are open from 8:30 a.m. to 6 p.m. on weekdays; 1272 Broadway is open on Saturday as well.

The buys are often spectacular in cameras, electronics, computers, typewriters, dictation equipment, watches, fine jewelry, and much more at **47th Street Photo,** 67 W. 47th St. between Fifth and Sixth avenues, 115 W. 45th St. between Sixth and Seventh avenues, 116 Nassau St., and 35 E. 18th St. between Fifth Avenue and Broadway (the latter called the "Professional Photography Store") (tel. 260-4410 or 608-6934, or toll free 800/221-7774 outside New York state). Huge ads in the *New York Times, Newsday,* and the *Wall Street Journal* list bargains almost daily. The store is often crowded, but the staff is knowledgeable and the bargains just great. We've seen portable cassette players with earphones selling for almost half the regular department store price, for example. Their prices on film can't be beat either!

Open Monday through Thursday from 9 a.m. to 6 p.m., on Friday to 2 p.m., and on Sunday from 10 a.m. to 5 p.m.; closed Saturday. Their catalog is available free for the asking.

**Brothers** is another big name in New York for good buys in cameras, electronics, and video, with a number of stores around town.

They have two locations on the East Side: at 466 Lexington Ave., at the corner of 45th Street (tel. 986-3323), open Monday through Saturday from 8:30 a.m. to 7 p.m. and on Sunday from 10 a.m. to 6 p.m.; and at 599 Lexington Ave., at 52nd Street (tel. 888-2090), open Monday through Friday from 9 a.m. to 8 p.m., Saturday to 7 p.m., and on Sunday from 10 a.m. to 6 p.m. The West Side location, 130 W. 34th St., opposite Macy's (tel. 695-4158), stays open on Monday, Thursday, and Friday from 9 a.m. to 8:30 p.m.; on Tuesday, Wednesday, and Saturday from 9 a.m. to 7:30 p.m.; and on Sunday from 10 a.m. to 6 p.m. The downtown store at 200 Broadway, between John and Fulton streets (tel. 619-8400) is open from 8:30 a.m. to 7 p.m. weekdays, noon to 6 p.m. on Sunday.

## CARPETS

**ABC Carpet Company,** two huge stores at 881 and 888 Broadway, at East 19th Street (tel. 677-6970), is perhaps New York's best-known name for rug and carpet values, with thousands of rolls of rugs at very good prices: a recent trip turned up all-wool imported Berber broadlooms, valued at $40 per square yard, selling for $10 here. Along with the carpet collection, the rug assortments are huge, encompassing everything from fine handmade Orientals selling for thousands, to handcrafted Indian and other rugs imported from around the world that might go for as little as $100 for a 9- by 12-foot. There's also an enormous selection of area rugs. New departments include a huge antique furniture department and a bed, bath, and linen shop.

Open from 10 a.m. to 8 p.m. on Monday and Thursday; to 7 p.m. on Tuesday, Wednesday, and Friday; to 6 p.m. on Saturday; and 11 a.m. to 6 p.m. on Sunday.

Uptown, on the busy Upper West Side, the **Rug Warehouse,** Broadway at 79th Street (tel. 787-6665), draws those with a keen eye for values. Owner Larry Feldman carries almost 3,000 new and used Oriental carpets of the finest quality and at some of the lowest prices you'll find anywhere in this country. Prices begin at less than $200 for a 9- by 12-foot Oriental-style carpet.

Open daily from 9 a.m. to 6 p.m. (until 8 p.m. on Thursday).

## CHILDREN'S CLOTHING

For fabulous discounts on children's clothing, we suggest you venture across the river and into **Brooklyn.** If you're willing to brave the largest shopping crowds you've ever encountered (leave the children at home when you visit this store), you'll discover superb discounts on better children's clothing (brand names every mother will recognize) at **Natan Borlam,** 157 Havemeyer St., near South 2nd Street, Brooklyn (tel. 718/387-2983). You'll find underwear, dresses, suits, snowsuits, coats, tights, polo shirts, etc.—many with top-name labels still in them and most at discounts ranging from 25% to 50%. They also carry teenage and ladies' clothing. Take the IRT–Lexington Avenue subway (no. 4) to Brooklyn Bridge, then change to the BMT (Jamaica line) Q train. Take the BMT to Marcy Avenue, get off, and walk four blocks to 157 Havemeyer St.

Borlam's is open Sunday through Thursday from 10 a.m. to 5 p.m. and on Friday from 10 a.m. to 2:30 p.m. If Borlam's doesn't have what you want (which is highly unlikely), then browse around Havemeyer Street; it's dotted with discount shops offering children's furniture and clothing.

Don't plan on getting the children's basic duds here, but do try **Daffy's,** 111 Fifth Ave., at 18th St. (tel. 529-4477), when you want to outfit your little darlings in the finest designer sportswear, including European imports. Designer and European samples go for 50% off regular prices, as do designer dresses for girls. Leather clothing for boys and girls is discounted 40% to 50%, as are cotton terry robes for both boys and girls. Especially nice is the 100% cotton layettewear at 50% off regular prices.

Daffy's is open Monday through Saturday from 10 a.m. to 10 p.m. and on Sunday from 11 a.m. to 6 p.m.

The discount houses offer the best value in new children's clothing; the **resale shops** offer the biggest bargains in hand-me-downs, some of them quite elegant and bearing name tags from high-fashion stores like Saks Fifth Avenue and Bergdorf Goodman. One of the oldest and best of these in town is **Second Act,** 1046 Madison Ave. (upstairs), between 79th and 80th streets (tel. 988-2440), where you can purchase outgrown clothing in excellent condition, often items that have been worn only a few times, at prices 50% less than the original. Many French and English imports, as well as American-made coats, toddlers' snowsuits, girls' skirts, boys' slacks, Levis, jackets, etc. We've even seen ski and riding gear. Every item is freshly cleaned and only the latest styles are sold. In addition, Second Act has a large selection of children's books (from 15¢ to $3), a smattering of handcrafted items at less than boutique prices, and used ice skates.

Open Tuesday through Saturday from 10 a.m. to 5 p.m. Closed Saturday in July and August.

As for New York department stores, nothing can beat the twice-yearly sales (usually around January and July) at **Saks Fifth Avenue,** 611 Fifth Ave., between 49th and 50th streets (tel. 753-4000), when crowds of hungry mothers from everywhere swoop down on the children's department to realize savings of anywhere from 30% to 50% on beautiful merchandise. (Savings are huge all over the store during these sales.)

Saks is open Monday through Saturday from 10 a.m. to 6 p.m. (on Thursday to 8 p.m.).

West Side mothers watch for the twice-yearly sales (July–August and January–February) at **Morris Brothers Department Store,** 2322 Broadway, at 84th Street (tel. 724-9000), when the pickings are good in name-brand children's clothing. The store has a large and varied selection and specializes in jeans—many of them for mothers and fathers as well as kids.

Open from 9:30 a.m. to 6:30 p.m. Monday through Saturday.

On New York's Lower East Side you should check out the following:

**A & G Infants & Children's Wear,** 261 Broome St., between Orchard and Allen streets (tel. 966-3775), sells name-brand (Healthtex, Ruth Scharf, Youngland, Carters, etc.) children's clothes at discounts of about 25%. You can get clothes here for infants to preteens.

Open Sunday through Thursday from 10 a.m. to 5 p.m., on Friday to sundown.

Similar wares and hours at **Rice & Breskin,** 323 Grand St., at the corner of Orchard Street (tel. 925-5515), and **M. Kreinen & Co., Inc.,** 301 Grand St., between Allen and Eldridge streets (tel. 925-0239).

## CHINA, POTTERY, CRYSTAL, AND GLASSWARE

We have no problem making our choice here: the most exciting, low-cost shop in the country for modern design in home accessories, tableware, and cookware is the **Pottery Barn,** which has eight New York City branches: the huge original store at 231 Tenth Ave., between 23rd and 24th streets (tel. 206-8118), consisting of three floors and a basement; a store at 117 E. 59th St., between Park and Lexington avenues (tel. 753-5424); at 250 W. 57th St., at Eighth Avenue (tel. 315-1855); one at 51 Greenwich Ave., between Sixth and Seventh avenues in the Village (tel. 807-6321); at 2109 Broadway, at 74th Street (tel. 595-5573); at 700 Broadway, at 4th Street (tel. 505-6377); at 1451 Second Ave., at 76th Street (tel. 988-4228); at 1297 Lexington Ave., at 87th Street (tel. 289-2477); and at Pier M at the South Street Seaport (tel. 233-2191). All are under the imaginative management of William Sonoma, who—through mass purchasing and low overhead—manages to sell stunning imported modernistic designs, most of which are manufactured according to his own specifications, at low, low prices. You'll find kitchenware, dishes, glassware, mugs, vases, baskets, picture frames, rugs, storage systems, and casual furniture. A recent visit turned up excellent buys in frames, white porcelain dinnerware, and 11-ounce wineglasses. The Pottery Barn will ship anywhere in the United States.

All stores are open on Sunday from noon to 5 p.m., and from 10:30 a.m. to 6:30 p.m. weekdays and Saturdays; most stores have some evening hours.

*Note:* A Pottery Barn catalog is available by writing to: Mail Order Department, Pottery Barn, P.O. Box 7044, San Francisco, CA 94120.

A high-rent, prime midtown location does not deter **Robin Importers,** 510 Madison Ave., between 52nd and 53rd streets (tel. 753-6475 or 752-5605), from offering generous discounts—30% to 60% on most items—on china, stainless flatware, stoneware, giftware, and table linens by major manufacturers. They show over 600 patterns in stainless and china.

Open Monday through Friday from 9:30 a.m. to 5:30 p.m. and on Saturday from 10 a.m. to 5 p.m. They ship anywhere in the United States via UPS.

On the Lower East Side are at least half a dozen shops offering excellent buys in china, crystal, and usually sterling silver. One of the best is **Greater New York Trading Company,** 81 Canal St. (tel. 226-2808), in business for 60 years, and regularly offering discounts of 25% to 60% on china, dinnerware, sterling silver, silver-plated and stainless flatware, as well as crystal. Frequent sales can bring the discounts up to as much as 70% off regular prices.

Open Monday through Thursday from 10 a.m. to 6 p.m., on Friday to 3 p.m., and on Sunday from 9:30 a.m. to 5:30 p.m.; closed Saturday.

**Eastside Gifts and Dinnerware,** 351 Grand St., near Essex Street, (tel. 928-7200 or 529-6328, or toll free 800/GIFTS-II outside New York state), offers discounts of from 35% to 60% on all major brands of china, crystal, and flatware, and ships anywhere.

Open Sunday through Thursday from 9 a.m. to 5:30 p.m. and on Friday to 3:30 p.m.; closed Saturday.

Similar wares and discounts are found at these other Lower East Side shops:

**Lanac Sales Company,** 73 Canal St., at the corner of Allen Street (tel. 925-6422), open Monday through Thursday from 10 a.m. to 6 p.m., on Friday to 2 p.m., and on Sunday from 10 a.m. to 5 p.m.; closed Saturday.

Over on Grand Street, between Ludlow and Essex streets, check out **Grand Sterling Company, Inc.,** 345 Grand St. (tel. 674-6450), open Sunday through Thursday from 10:30 a.m. to 5:30 p.m.; closed Friday and Saturday. They have another store at 4921 Thirteenth Ave. in Brooklyn (tel. 718/854-0623).

## CIGARS

Cigar lovers should run over to **J-R Tobacco,** 11 E. 45th St., just off Fifth Avenue (tel. 869-8777), where cigars are 30% to 40% off retail. A free newsletter (ask to be put on the mailing list) tells which cigars will be specially discounted; one brand is featured daily.

Open weekdays from 8 a.m. to 6 p.m. and on Saturday from 9 a.m. to 4 p.m. Other locations are: 1410 Broadway, at 39th Street; 505 Park Ave., at 59th Street; and 219 Broadway, between Vesey and Barclay streets, downtown. (The downtown stores are not open weekends.)

## COSMETICS

For fantastic buys in top-quality cosmetics, head for the **Make-Up Center,** 150 W. 55th St., between Sixth and Seventh avenues (tel. 977-9494), where models and actresses have been shopping for years. The center sells its own line of products for half of what regular name brands cost. Available treatments are eyebrow shaping and tweezing, makeup consultations, facials, manicures, and pedicures. Because so many models have their makeup applied here, you must make an appointment for the consultation. Best of all, there's no pressure to buy the products.

Open Monday through Friday from 10 a.m. to 6 p.m. (until 8 p.m. on Thursday), until 5 p.m. on Saturday.

**Clairol Consumer Research Forum,** 345 Park Ave., between 51st and 52nd streets (tel. 546-2707), is always seeking consumer responses to their new and existing hair- and skin-care products. Women and men are invited to make an appointment to come in to test products—using them as they would at home. You might be asked to test a hair-color, hair-care, or skin-care product. Each consumer who qualifies and participates is given a complimentary gift bag of products. Call the above number to arrange an appointment. To be absolutely sure of getting a convenient appointment, it might be wise to write or phone several weeks before your visit.

If you'd like to relax with a facial while you're in New York, call the **Christine Valmy International School,** 260 Fifth Ave., at 28th Street (tel. 581-1520). The beauty school from this famous Fifth Avenue salon will cream, massage, and pamper you for the bargain rate of $15. All the operators have completed the school course and are putting in hours of hands-on training. Your facial will be completely supervised by an instructor. Other services available are: makeup lesson and applications, waxing, nail art, and manicure.

Appointments, which should be scheduled two to three days in advance, are available Monday through Friday from 10 a.m. to 3 p.m. and Monday through Thursday from 6 to 7 p.m.

**Caswell-Massey Co., Ltd.,** 518 Lexington Ave., at 48th Street (tel. 755-2254), is still formulating and selling the same cologne that George Washington used. Try some if you're feeling presidential, or if you're in a lighter mood, buy a cake of any of their aromatic hard-milled soaps. Caswell-Massey is the oldest chemists and perfumers in America, founded in 1752, with a superb line of toiletries and personal-care items, many from Great Britain and Europe.

The main store on Lexington Avenue is open weekdays from 9 a.m. to 7 p.m. and on Saturday from 10 a.m. to 6 p.m. There are branches at 21 Fulton St., at the South Street Seaport (tel. 608-5401); at One Herald Square (tel. 244-0411); and in the World Financial Center (tel. 945-2630), all open Monday through Saturday.

**Boyd Chemist,** 655 Madison Ave., between 60th and 61st streets (tel. 838-6558), is the place to go for unusual and imported cosmetics and beauty supplies. The cosmeticians will gladly give you a demonstration of any product you buy, such as eye shadow, for a glamorous professional look. They also carry designer fashion jewelry.

Open Monday through Friday from 8:30 a.m. to 7 p.m. and on Saturday from 9:30 a.m. to 6 p.m. Closed Saturday in July and August.

## DISCOUNT HOUSES

**Dollar Bill's,** 90 E. 42nd St. (tel. 867-0212), a storefront in Grand Central Station, has a bargain-basement appearance, but there are treasures within. On a recent visit we saw scads of well-tailored gentlemen milling about a rack of Italian designer men's suits that were selling for $399. Since Dollar Bill's is not allowed to advertise or publicize designer's names, we won't spoil their secret, but the labels are there, and we will tell you that suits by this Italian designer normally sell for $800 to $1,000 elsewhere. A salesman let us in on the secret: the owner goes to Italy and buys directly from the designers, in huge quantities, and passes the extraordinary bargains on to the customer. Women's Italian knits are another specialty, none of them inexpensive, but of fine quality. The bargains go on and on, and there's simply no telling what you will turn up here.

Dollar Bill's is open on Monday, Tuesday, Wednesday, and Friday from 8 a.m. to 6:30 p.m., on Thursday to 8 p.m., and on Saturday from 10 a.m. to 6 p.m.; closed Sunday.

Depending on what they have in stock on the day you visit, a stop at **Job Lot Trading Company, Inc.** (also known as "The Puschcart"), downtown at 140 Church St., between Chambers and Warren streets, at 80 Nassau St., near Fulton Street (tel. 962-4142), and uptown at 412 Fifth Ave., at 37th Street (tel. 398-9210) and 1633 Broadway, at 50th Street (tel. 245-0275), could be one of the memorable shopping experiences of New York. You'll find everything and anything from famous-name children's toys to fishing rods, from toothpaste to knapsacks, to boxes of candy—all discounted at least 50%. The crowds are thick.

Most stores are open Monday through Saturday from 8 a.m. to 6 p.m., and on Sunday 11 a.m. to 5 p.m.; check for individual hours.

**Odd Job Trading,** 7 E. 40th St., just off Fifth Avenue (tel. 686-6825), 149 W. 32nd St., between Sixth and Seventh avenues, at the Penta Hotel (tel. 564-7370), and 66 W. 48th St., between Fifth and Sixth avenues (tel. 575-0477), sells brand-name close-out toiletries, linens, stationery, glassware and china, tools, toys, and just about anything else you could think of at low, low prices. Occasionally, you may luck into designer clothing and shoes; we once saw Joan and David shoes, which go from $120 to $220 uptown, here for only $25!

Open Monday through Friday from 8 a.m. to 6 p.m. All stores close early on Friday nights during the winter and are closed all day Saturday. Open on Sunday from 10 a.m. to 5 p.m.

Again, you never know what you're likely to find at **Weber's Closeout Cen-**

ters, another popular group of job-lot merchants. We've spotted $50 Italian designer summer sandals for $12, $20 straw hats for $4, and sweaters, jeans, housewares, tools, china, all for way-below-wholesale prices.

There are five branches of Weber's: downtown at 138 Church St. (tel. 406-2723), open Monday through Saturday from 7:45 a.m. to 6:15 p.m. and on Sunday from 11 a.m. to 5 p.m.; at 505 Eighth Ave., at 35th Street (tel. 564-7637), open from 9 a.m. to 6 p.m. Monday through Saturday (closed Sunday); at 132 Chambers St. (tel. 571-3283), open Monday through Saturday from 10 a.m. to 10 p.m. and on Sunday to 6 p.m.; at 45 W. 45th St., between Fifth and Sixth avenues (tel. 819-9780), open Monday through Wednesday from 8 a.m. to 7 p.m., on Thursday and Friday to 8 p.m., and on Saturday from 10 a.m. to 6 p.m.; and on the Upper West Side at 2064 Broadway, at 72nd Street (tel. 787-1644), open from 9 a.m. to 9 p.m. seven days.

If you've ever been to an oldtime bargain basement where everything is piled high on tables and you have to fight your way through mobs to get to the goodies, you'll have an idea of what shopping is like at **Conway,** with its main store at 1335 Broadway, at Herald Square (tel. 976-3460). Except that Conway stores are at street level and not in basements, and that there appears to be a Conway every few doors on West 34th Street, between Seventh and Eighth avenues. At last count New York had eight Conways, and there will probably be more by the time you read this. This is not designer shopping by a long shot, but standard items are deeply discounted. Most Conways sell men's, ladies' and children's clothing; a few sell health and beauty aids and towels and linens as well. On West 34th Street, there are now Conways at nos. 11, 225, 245, and 247, and at 450 Seventh Ave. at 34th Street. Downtown, there's a Conway for kids called **La Galeria,** at 37 Broad St., and a regular Conway at 45 Broad St.

Hours at all stores are the same: Monday, Wednesday, and Thursday from 8 a.m. to 7:30 p.m.; on Tuesday and Friday to 8 p.m.; on Saturday from 9:30 a.m. to 7:30 p.m.; and on Sunday from 11 a.m. to 6 p.m.

## DRUGS AND VITAMINS

Since they have 29 stores in Manhattan, it's not hard to find a branch of **Duane Reade,** in business for 30 years and the largest independently owned drugstore chain on the East Coast. Markups here are so low that prices can only be described as amazing—and the bargains extend all the way from prescriptions (averaging 50% off regular prices) to health and beauty aids, tobacco, cosmetics, fragrances, photo developing, hosiery, candies and cookies, convenience foods, and lots more. As for vitamins, they carry all the major national brands, many of the organic and natural brands, and their own generic vitamins, with savings again in the amazing range. Check the phone book for a complete list of Duane Reade stores, but for starters, in the most popular midtown areas, you'll find Duane Reade at 350 Fifth Ave., near 33rd Street (tel. 714-2417); at 215 W. 34th St., between Seventh and Eighth avenues, near Macy's (tel. 714-9410); and at 51 W. 51st St., near Radio City Music Hall (tel. 582-8525).

Midtown stores are open Monday through Saturday from 7:30 a.m. to 6 p.m.; closed Sunday.

For a complete line of drugstore items, as well as prescriptions, try the **Drug Loft** at 1103 Lexington Ave., at 77th Street (tel. 879-0910). Ordinary drugstore products are sold at a discount of at least 20%. Prescriptions are 20% to 50% lower than at regular drugstores. Vaporizers, hairdryers, surgical stockings, thermoses, electric heating pads, hot-water bottles, and everything else are all at low, low prices. Cosmetics, too, are discounted.

Open Monday through Friday from 8 a.m. to 7:30 p.m. and on Saturday from 9 a.m. to 5 p.m.

For the leading brands of natural and organic vitamins and supplements, it's hard to beat the values at **The Vitamin Shoppes**—discounts are at least 20%, and often go up to 40% or more on special sales. Popular brands here include Schiff, Solgar, and Twin Labs.

Among the seven Manhattan locations, a few of the most centrally located are the Vitamin Shoppes at 139 E. 57th St., at Lexington Avenue (tel. 371-3850), open from 9 a.m. to 7 p.m. Monday through Saturday (closed Sunday); 2086A Broadway, at 72nd Street (tel. 580-7620), open from 10 a.m. to 7 p.m. Monday through Saturday and on Sunday from 11 a.m. to 5 p.m.; 375 Ave. of the Americas, at Waverly Place, in Greenwich Village (tel. 929-6553), open from 10 a.m. to 7 p.m. Monday through Saturday and on Sunday from 11 a.m. to 5 p.m.; and 1375 Ave. of the Americas, at 56th Street (tel. 664-0048), open from 10 a.m. to 7 p.m. Monday through Saturday and 10 a.m. to 5 p.m. Sunday.

**Vitamin Factory Outlets,** located in Prescriptions Limited at 1151 Madison Ave., at 85th Street (tel. 628-3210), and at 1147 Third Ave., at 67th Street (tel. 879-5115), offers a huge selection and very low prices on all-natural and organic vitamins: they are hypo-allergens, with no sugar, starch, artificial colors, flavoring, salt, or preservatives. You can get a free vitamin consultation and a free catalog, which enables you to order from home via a toll-free number.

Both branches are open Monday through Friday from 9 a.m. to 6 p.m.; Saturday hours vary.

## DRY GOODS

For towels, linens, curtains, bedspreads, comforters with matching sheets, decorative pillows, and draperies, **Ezra Cohen,** 305 Grand St., at Allen Street, on the Lower East Side (tel. 925-7800), is a bargain shop that offers name brands at prices at least 25% lower than comparable uptown shops.

Open Sunday through Thursday from 9 a.m. to 5 p.m., on Friday to 4 p.m.

Continuing along Grand Street, between Allen and Forsyth streets, you'll find over ten more dry goods stores stocking similar wares. It's a good idea to comparison-shop for the best styles and prices.

**The Wholesale House,** 2960 Avenue U, off Nostrand Avenue, Brooklyn (tel. 718/891-5800), is worth a trip on the BMT to buy designer bedroom and bathroom linens and accessories at tremendous discounts. All the major brands are sold at below "White Sale" prices. They can custom-design your bedroom using sheet fabrics of your choice.

Open Monday through Saturday from 10 a.m. to 5:30 p.m. Take the IRT–Lexington Avenue subway to Brooklyn Bridge, and change there for the BMT (D train). Get off at Avenue U and take the Avenue U bus to Nostrand Avenue. They ship all over the country.

## ELECTROLYSIS

Electrolysis tends to be expensive in New York, but good prices and expert professional care are available from Margaret Railton-Jones at the **Radiant Skin Care Center,** 357 E. 57th St., between First and Second avenues (tel. 595-4633). Ms. Railton-Jones, who will use either sterilized or disposable needles, claims that she can get as much done in a quarter hour—for which she charges $20—as others can in a much longer period of time. She also offers very good rates on waxing, facials, nail care, and eyebrow styling, a particular specialty. Please mention this book for special rates.

## EYEGLASSES

The very best choice for huge discounts is **Cohen's Optical,** 117 Orchard St., at the corner of Delancey Street (tel. 674-1986), where the choice, including all top-designer frames—Givenchy, Dior, Pierre Cardin, Yves St. Laurent, etc.—numbers into the thousands! Prices begin at $15. They also have contact lenses. Another advantage of Cohen's is two hours of free parking (they reimburse you) at the Municipal Garage on Essex Street between Rivington and Delancey streets.

Open Monday through Saturday from 9 a.m. to 6 p.m., on Sunday to 5:45 p.m.

You can choose from hundreds of first-quality frames—many of them by top designers—at **Empire Optical,** 19 W. 34th St., between Fifth and Sixth avenues, Room 1107, 11th floor (tel. 244-8588). Discounts on frames and lenses are in the 30% to 50% range. Bring your prescription or a correct pair of glasses.

Open Monday through Thursday from 10 a.m. to 6 p.m., on Friday to 2 p.m.

## FABRICS, LOW COST

The Lower East Side of New York is the place to find fabrics at the cheapest prices in America. The streets here are jammed with little stores that are themselves jammed with bolts of cloth, scraps of cloth, bits of fur, and suit materials.

Also, be sure to shop West 40th Street between Seventh and Eighth Avenues for an exciting array of high-fashion fabrics at reasonable prices.

Your first stop could be at one of **Sam Beckenstein's** establishments. The shop at 125 Orchard St. (tel. 475-4525) features men's suiting fabrics, many from England and Italy, in pure worsteds and blends, for a fraction of the price charged in midtown textile marts. The ladies' shop, at 130 Orchard St. (tel. 475-4305), carries laces, embroideries, imported wools, and silk couturier fabrics, as well as patterns and notions. Another department here (tel. 529-9180) specializes in slipcovers, upholstery goods, and custom draperies made to order.

The stores are located between Rivington and Delancey streets, and are open Sunday through Friday from 9 a.m. to 5:30 p.m.

Pay a visit, too, to **Harry Snyder,** 70 Hester St., between Allen and Orchard streets (tel. 925-0855), which has lovely imports and designer fabrics—woolens, silks, cottons, novelty fabrics, etc., at about one-third the original cost.

Open Sunday through Thursday from 9 a.m. to 5:30 p.m.; closed Friday and Saturday.

Another good place to buy fabrics at near-wholesale prices is **Art Max,** 250 W. 40th St., between Seventh and Eighth avenues (tel. 398-0755). The store is jammed with bolts of imported and domestic fabrics of all types and patterns. Bridal fabrics —imported French laces, Swiss embroidered organza, and the like—are specialties here, as are "mother-of-the-bride fabrics"—imported beaded silk chiffons, chantilly and metallic laces. Salespeople are highly knowledgeable and are fluent in most languages. Be sure to go downstairs where lots of bargains are to be found.

Open from 8:30 a.m. to 6 p.m. Monday through Friday and on Saturday from 9 a.m. to 5 p.m.

If you're handy with a needle or know somebody who is, check out the terrific values at **Frontier Fabrics,** 144 Chambers St. right at the IRT subway stop (tel. 608-3283), a warehouse-outlet store for a huge line of fabrics for dresses, sportsware, and upholstery as well. Biggest sellers here are the printed materials (percale, poly-cotton blends, all cotton, etc.) for $1.75 a yard, which would sell for $4 to $6 elsewhere, and their solid-color materials at $1.50 and $2 a yard. Artists come here for their canvases, $1.50 and $2.50 a yard. And upholstery fabrics start at a low $3.50 a yard.

Open Monday through Saturday from 10 a.m. to 6 p.m. (on Wednesday to 7 p.m.).

The **Fabric Warehouse,** 406 Broadway, at Canal Street (tel. 431-9510), sells fabrics, trimmings, patterns, and anything else you might ever need for home sewing at amazing discount prices.

Open on Monday, Tuesday, Wednesday, and Friday from 9 a.m. to 6 p.m., on Thursday to 7:30 p.m., and on Saturday and Sunday from 10 a.m. to 5 p.m.

## FLEA MARKETS

Flea markets come and go with some rapidity in New York and the vendors who work the fleas can often be found in the streets—particularly around Sheridan Square in Greenwich Village and in the Lincoln Center area. Goods vary from junk to gems, from fine crafts to factory over-runs, seconds and just plain bargains, which may include hand-knit sweaters, copies of designer bags, jeans, cosmetics, jewelry, and more. A few of the more durable fleas include the following:

**I.S. 44 Flea Market, "Green Flea,"** 77th Street and Columbus Avenue (tel. 316-1088). Since Columbus Avenue in the 70s is one of the prime shopping and restaurant areas in town, it's only natural that a flea market here would be a great success—and it is. Going strong since 1984, it's the brainchild of the Parents Association of several local schools, and all proceeds go to fund after-school programs for children. Vendors crowd the schoolyard and the indoor cafeteria, selling collectibles, antiques, secondhand clothes, plus lots of new items like sweaters and knits from South America, hats, gloves, T-shirts, scads of jewelry, and books. Combined with the flea market is **Greenmarket,** a popular farmers' market that brings in fresh produce, freshly baked goods, ciders, jams, honeys, and other made-on-the-farm goodies from New York state and Pennsylvania farms. No wonder this one is such a delight!

It's open every Sunday year round from 10 a.m. to 6 p.m.

The **Antique Flea and Farmers Market,** held at P.S. 183, at East 67th Street and York Avenue, is the East Side equivalent of the I.S. 44 "Green Flea." Art, antiques, clothing, crafts, manufacturer's closeouts, etc., are sold inside the school building; outdoors is another popular farmers' market.

Open every Saturday year round from 6 a.m. to 6 p.m.

Many local artists and craftspeople can be found at the booths at the **Greenwich Village Flea Market,** held in the schoolyard at P.S. 41, Greenwich Avenue at Charles Street, on Saturday from noon to 7 p.m., year round.

**Annex Antiques and Flea Market,** Avenue of the Americas and 26th Street (tel. 243-5343), is open on Saturday and Sunday from 9 a.m. to 5 p.m. throughout the year. This is the town's biggest outdoor flea market, and it's prime hunting ground for antique lovers—everything from wicker furniture to old clocks and cameras to art deco pieces to stained glass to antique kitchenware turns up here. Admission is $1 for adults, free for children.

**Tower Market,** at Broadway between West 4th and Great Jones streets, in Greenwich Village, is great fun, showing work by many local craftspeople. It's open on Saturday and Sunday from 10 a.m. to 7 p.m., during warm weather.

Down on Canal Street, crowds throng the **Canal West Flea Market,** 370 Canal St., which is open on Saturday and Sunday from 7 a.m. to 6 p.m. Used tools, hardware, electronic items, plus clothing are more in evidence than antiques and crafts.

You don't need to wait for the weekend to visit **Walter's World-Famous Union Square Shoppes,** 873 Broadway, at 17th Street. Old magazines and periodicals, comic books, antique clothing and furniture, and costume jewelry are all popular sellers here.

Walter's is open Tuesday through Saturday from 10 a.m. to 6 p.m.

## FLOWERS AND PLANTS

The wholesale flower district of New York is located on Sixth Avenue around 28th Street—it's a tourist attraction in itself—and many of the wholesale distributors will sell to individuals at prices quite a bit lower than your corner florist would charge. If you're looking for something in particular—window-box plants, cacti, etc.—check out all the stores and comparison-shop.

One of the best stores in the area is **Bill's Flower Market,** 816 Sixth Ave., at 28th Street (tel. 889-8154), where top-quality fresh flowers can be had for very reasonable prices. Bill's also has dried flowers, seeds, and lovely silk flowers. They offer all florist services too—FTD, Interflora, etc.

Open Monday through Friday from 7:30 a.m. to 4:30 p.m.

## FOAM

**The Economy Foam and Futon Center,** 173 E. Houston St., at First Avenue (tel. 473-4462), cuts foam to size, custom covers cushions in vinyl or fabric, sells materials, quilts, pillows, mattresses, and highriser covers, all at discounted prices. Herculon upholstery fabric costs $7.50 here; it's normally $12.50 a yard or more elsewhere. They claim to have the lowest prices on futons, frames, and covers in the city, and the selection is large. You can also buy bedding, sheets, and pillow cases.

Open Sunday through Friday from 9:30 a.m. to 6 p.m. and on Saturday from 11 a.m. to 6 p.m.

## FURNITURE

The **Salvation Army Stores,** the larger of which is at 536 W. 46th St., between Tenth and Eleventh avenues (tel. 757-2311), are two large warehouses full of furniture, books, toys, clothing, and bedding. The furniture is old, some of it antique, some even stylish, but it costs peanuts, and can often be used for those staple furniture items (beds, for instance) whose appearance you may not care about. Speaking of beds, the Salvation Army Store has nearly an entire floor of them, assembled or disassembled into mattresses, frames, and bedsteads. A double bed with box spring, headboard, mattress, and frame recently went for $100.

Open from 9 a.m. to 4:45 p.m. Monday through Saturday. Delivery service is available. There are six other Salvation Army Stores in Manhattan; check your phonebook for listings.

Perhaps the most imaginative budget-priced furniture stores in town are the **Bon Marché** shops, in the Bon Marché building at 55 W. 13th St., between Fifth and Sixth avenues (furniture on the sixth and seventh floors, lamps and accessories on the sixth floor) (tel. 620-5550), and also at 1060 Third Ave., at 63rd Street (tel. 620-5592). They have literally cornered the market on young couples who want to decorate their apartments inexpensively in Scandinavian-modern style. They are best known for their price and range on all kinds of drawer units and bookcases (we've seen big teakwood bookcases selling for $90 to $100 each), Danish teak extension tables, and quality Italian chrome goods. Prices on their exclusive glove-soft leather sofas, made for them abroad are so special—under $1,000 for an 84-inch sofa, about $1,200 for a convertible double bed—that shipments regularly sell out. A recent trip turned up marble tops from Taiwan, Italy, and Portugal selling at one-third to one-quarter off the going price. Prices are considerably lower than comparable merchandise elsewhere. And, rare for New York, everything that's on the floor is in stock—which means instant delivery. Customers can pick up from the 13th Street store or pay for delivery. Just browsing here is a pleasure.

Both stores are open Monday through Saturday from 10:30 a.m. to 6:30 p.m.

The **Castro Convertible Showroom & Clearance Center,** 43 W. 23rd St., between Fifth and Sixth avenues (tel. 255-7000), has many floors (plus a mezzanine) jampacked with convertible sofas, modular groups, recliners, tables, bedroom furniture, wall units, box springs, mattresses, lamps, and much more. Convertibles can be custom-covered to your order; dozens of floor samples are ready for immediate delivery.

Open most days from 10 a.m. to 7 p.m. (to 9 p.m. on Monday and Thursday), and on Sunday from 11 a.m. to 6 p.m. They ship anywhere. There's free parking on the premises at all times.

**Plexi-Craft Quality Products Corporation,** 514 W. 24th St., between Tenth and Eleventh avenues (tel. 924-3244), is a factory that sells to the public at net prices —about 50% less than retail! They have Plexiglas and Lucite tables, chairs, magazine racks, telephone stands, cubes, shelving, television stands, you name it. Shipping is possible. A descriptive catalog is available for $2.

Open weekdays from 9:30 a.m. to 5 p.m. and on Saturday from 11 a.m. to 4 p.m.; closed Sunday.

Along the **Bowery,** between Hester and Delancey streets, are many restaurant supply stores that also sell to the public at far below list prices. The range of goods is wide—everything from bar stools, to tables, to commercial dishes and cooking equipment, cabinets, tables, chairs, etc.

## GIFTS AND MISCELLANEOUS ITEMS

See also "China, Pottery, Crystal, and Glassware."

New York's many Japanese shops are good places for inexpensive gifts. There's always an exciting selection of wares at **Azuma**—wicker furnishings, basketry, bedspreads, clothing, paper lampshades, toys, stationery, mugs, sake sets, tea services, posters, paper flowers, papier-mâché boxes, you name it! You'll feel as if you're at an exotic fair. One of the fine Azuma stores is at 666 Lexington Ave., near 56th Street (tel. 752-0599); see the phone book for other addresses.

**Hoffritz For Cutlery** has several locations around Manhattan, at Grand Central Terminal (tel. 682-7808); Penn Station (tel. 736-2443); 331 Madison Ave., at 43rd Street (tel. 697-7344); 203 W. 57th St., between Seventh and Eighth avenues (tel. 757-3431); 30 Rockefeller Plaza (tel. 757-3497); and 324 World Trade Center Concourse (tel. 938-1936). Try one of these shops for pocket knives, scissors, kitchen gadgets, unique shaving equipment, and imaginative gift items. They periodically hold 50% off sales on their high-quality cutlery, so you can really get an excellent buy at those times.

The stores are usually open from 9 a.m. to 6 p.m. Monday through Saturday; check with each individual store for exact hours.

## Gift Shopping at the South Street Seaport

The South Street Seaport and its Marketplace have a bevy of exciting shops, enough to make it a one-stop center for gift shopping. While many of the stores here are of the pricey variety (such as Laura Ashley, Abercrombie & Fitch, Pavo Real, Banana Republic), there are still dozens of shops where quality is high and prices competitive. The intriguing selection of goods and the crowds of people having a good time out shopping while enjoying the waterfront breezes and vistas add up to a delightful outing.

The main shopping action here is at the **Pier 17 Pavilion,** which offers some of the most scenic shopping in New York: public promenades of the steel-and-glass pavilion, set on a pier that extends out into the East River, open to vistas of the Brooklyn Bridge to the north and New York Harbor to the south. One of our favorite stores here is **The Sharper Image,** the ultimate catalog store, where people wait in line to try out state-of-the-art gadgetry like do-it-yourself acupressure massage tables or scales that speak. Then there's **A2Z, The Best of Everything,** with another array of marvelous gadgets, like "The World's First Waterproof Massager and Back Scrubber" ($15), a portable water sterilizer that weighs only two pounds and purifies drinking water anywhere in the world ($100), or a personal-size water cooler ($10). Don't postpone a visit to **The Last Wound-Up,** a store whose motto is "Don't Postpone Joy." It's available in bumper stickers for $1 or T-shirts for $7. A huge variety of windup toys priced from $2.50 to $5 can be played with in an area called "The Playpen." Adjoining it and under the same ownership is **Nathanial's Music Boxes,** with new and antique music boxes, plus some reproductions. Prices run $5 to $1,500. We also like the philosophy espoused by the people at **The Weather Store,** who say "you *can* do something about the weather—enjoy it." A good selection of raincoats, boots, umbrellas, water-repellant bags, and the like makes that possible.

If you can't get enough of penguins, you can get them on tote bags, on ties, emblazoned on T-shirts, and immortalized in "Penguin People," from eight-inch-tall hand puppets ($9) to giant stuffed penguins for $75, at **Next Stop, South Pole.** Another specialty store at Pier 17 is **New York, A View of the World,** where views of the city with whimsical geography appear on posters, cards, T-shirts, etc. You've probably seen local versions of this store in other cities around the country. Besides beautiful displays of mounted butterflies treated as works of art, **Mariposa, The Butterfly Gallery,** also has hand-worked paua-shell jewelry from New Zealand; small pieces begin around $20.

The most exciting clothing shopping at Pier 17 has to be at **Express,** a division of The Limited chain. You may have seen these shops elsewhere—there are over 400 around the country, and 4 in New York alone (at 34th Street just off Fifth Avenue, 75th Street and Columbus Avenue, 60th Street and Madison Avenue, and 62nd Street and Madison Avenue), but the Seaport location is one of the biggest and best. Both men and women can find fashionably, wonderfully priced, up-to-the-minute clothing here, for work into play, or just play. A recent look around turned up French racing tanks at two for $12, French beach shirts at $15, tie-dyes from India, handsome leather clothing, and silk shirts at $40, just to mention a few. And should you change your mind when you get back to your hotel, no problem; their motto is "No Sale Is Ever Final"—even up to a year after the time of purchase!

After you've shopped your heart out, you can pick up some food from the stalls at Pier 17, take it out to the decks, and usually watch some sort of free entertainment or the jaunty harbor craft chugging along the East River.

The **Fulton Market,** which was the Seaport's first shopping area, has considerably fewer stores, although it does boast, on the first floor, the marvelous **Zaro's Bread Basket,** which gives you a chance to sample traditional New York Jewish-style baking (everything here is kosher, by the way). Wonderful strawberry and blueberry cheesecakes, hearty breads like raisin pumpernickel, delicious pastries, and goodies galore are here. For $5 you can get a loaf of authentic Russian black bread. Trust that it's authentic: it's baked fresh in Moscow, then rushed to Zaro's by Aeroflot Soviet Airlines—"from Russia with love."

Also on the first floor of this building is **Merchant's Coffee, Tea and Spices,** whose huge sacks of fragrant coffee beans perfume the air. This store may well have the largest selection of coffees and pure-water-process decaffeinated coffees in the country. Consider, for example, decaffeinated amaretto, Irish cream, Swiss mocha almond, espresso roast, etc., for about $8 a pound. Luscious flavored coffees like Dutch mocha mint, cinnamon mocha royale, and chocolate cherry are about $7. Coffees from Africa, South and Central America, the Caribbean, and the Pacific are featured, and all are sold fresh and ground on the premises. They also offer coffee makers and mugs, cappuccino machines, loose and packaged teas, and more.

Scattered throughout both Pier 17 and the Fulton Market, and on the sidewalks as well, are seasonal kiosks that all bear the name **Beekman Market.** These come and go, but look for them: they often show among the most imaginative merchandise in the Seaport. For example, there's one called **Peace Frogs,** the creation of a young preppy entrepreneur who designs unisex shorts and T-shirts bearing flags and emblems of 105 nations. You could promote international peace by wearing a reversible pair of shorts with both U.S. and USSR emblems for all of $32. Another cute cart has soft sculpture of cats; it's called **Fraitie Kat and Friends; Rapunzel** shows hair accessories like barettes and combs; **The Bat Cart** is all about—you know—Batman. And so on.

Across from the Fulton Market is **Schermerhorn Row,** where there are a number of very entertaining shops to browse. Outstanding here is **The Nature Company,** a new branch of the national chain headquartered in Berkeley, California. Everything here is designed to provide products that will help people observe, understand, appreciate, and conserve the natural world. Nature lovers of all ages will find plenty here to keep them occupied, from "Moo Boxes" at $3, all the way to books, recordings, crystal clusters and crystal balls, fossil specimens, Native American jewelry, and magnificent animal sculptures that go up into the hundreds of dollars. Sierra Club posters and guides are sold here. The Nature Company also sponsors local events like a birding walk in Central Park; phone the store (tel. 422-8510) for information and reservations.

Also good fun to explore at Schermerhorn Row is **Williamson's Irish Imports,** which sports green ties, ties with shamrocks on them, handmade sweaters, Waterford crystal, lovely knitted caps and shawls, tweed hats and berets, and lots more. A poster of Irish names was just $9.

Gadget lovers should not miss **Brookstone,** which looks like a giant mail-order catalog of unusual hardware and gadgets come to life (it is). As soon as we win the lottery, we're going to get their Oriental Shiatsu massage chair for a mere $2,000. Kids have a good time here trying out the tabletop games. **Captain Hook's,** next door, is laden port to stern with marine antiques, brass fittings, seashells, and seashell jewelry. The **Seaport Museum Shop** in this block has nice T-shirts, tote bags, posters, cards, mugs, and the like.

There's another Seaport Museum Shop at nearby **Cannon's Walk,** which is larger, and shows lovely hand-painted pottery, books, prints, and home accessories in its Curiosity Shop. Cannon's Walk also has a branch of **Caswell-Massey,** America's oldest apothecary shop, whose goods arrived from Europe 200 years ago on these very docks. Try something traditional: perhaps the Williamsburg Potpourri, whose fragrance often fills the store.

In another part of the Seaport is **Browne & Co. Stationers,** a re-creation of a print shop typical of those found in mid–19th century New York, and named for a real firm established in 1775. It's located at 211 Water St., on the first floor of a Greek Revival building dating back to the 1830s. Here you will find demonstrations of letterpress printing, workshops, and classes, plus stationery items, antique and contemporary, for sale.

## HARDWARE

Come to Canal Street and rummage for bargains (job lot and closeout merchandise, for the most part) in the bins that line both street and stores in this area. **Canal Hardware,** 305 Canal St., at the corner of Mercer Street (tel. 226-0825), is typical of the genre. It's open Monday through Saturday from 8 a.m. to 6 p.m. and on Sunday from 10 a.m. to 5 p.m.

## JEWELRY

If you like crystals or geodes, amber, or semiprecious jewelry, check out **Astro Mineral Gallery,** 155 E. 34th St., between Lexington and Third avenues (tel. 889-9000). They have an extensive, well-priced collection of rocks, petrified wood, sculpture, and jewelry, all sold in a relaxed and beautiful gallery setting (with fountains and ponds). Their selection of crystals is outstanding. Admire precious rocks selling for thousands of dollars or purchase a string of beggar beads for under $10. There's a large selection of jewelry including tiger eye, garnet, carnelian, malachite, and rose quartz in the $10- to $20-per-strand price range. You may luck into a 50%-off sale.

Open Monday through Saturday from 10 a.m. to 6 p.m. (on Thursday to 8 p.m.), and on Sunday from 11 a.m. to 6 p.m.

For that special piece of jewelry you can't find anywhere else, take a little trip to the Upper West Side to **The Gold and Silver Man,** 2124 Broadway, between 74th and 75th streets (tel. 724-6393), where two talented craftsmen (one of them a seventh-generation jeweler to the King of Nepal), can create, copy, and repair any type of jewelry, from costume to museum pieces. Everything is made right in the store, so no need to worry that you'll see the same piece everywhere; and prices are reasonable for the quality and interest of the work. Earrings are a specialty (if you don't have pierced ears, they will pierce them for you or put the earring on a clip), starting at $4 and averaging about $50; and so are a wide variety of unusual pendants ranging from $25 to $35—we saw silver unicorns, OMs, Chais, stars, winged Pegasus horses, crosses, all of which can be matched to a large collection of silver chains or transformed into pins. There are wonderful beads made of lapis, black onyx, sterling silver, crystals and rose quartz; a collection of natural crystals; for men, cufflinks, tie pins, money clips, and rings. Nobody but an expert would know that the four-karat "diamond" ring set in sterling silver is really a cubic zircon, a most entertaining gift to yourself for $45.

Open weekdays from 11 a.m. to 6:30 p.m. and on Saturday from 11 a.m. to 5:30 p.m.; closed Sunday.

## KITCHENWARE

See also "China, Pottery, Crystal, and Glassware."

For pepping up your kitchen, the very French-looking but budget-priced **The Bridge,** at 212 E. 52nd St., between Second and Third avenues (tel. 688-4220), carries the most extensive and interesting housewares selection in town, and at substantially reduced prices—we've comparison-shopped. Prices start at 95¢ for wooden-handled spatulas (hard to find elsewhere), and go way up for gigantic copper pans which would cost much more anywhere else. This is where Julia Child buys the tiny French paring knife she used constantly on her television show "The French Chef." They also carry French white porcelainware, a full line of stainless-steel items, and the Zester, to make vegetable strips, twists, etc.

Open weekdays from 9 a.m. to 5:30 p.m. and on Saturday from 10 a.m. to 5 p.m.

Believe it or not, **Zabar's,** 2245 Broadway, at 80th Street (tel. 787-2000), world-famous home of appetizers, delicacies, fresh coffee, everything, has among the best prices in town on all kitchen equipment including the Robot-Coupe, the original Cuisinart. We once bought a model here for $80 on a special promotion and saw it selling elsewhere for $200! A marvelous shopping adventure.

Open Monday through Friday from 8 a.m. to 7:30 p.m., on Saturday to midnight, and on Sunday from 9 a.m. to 6 p.m. The mezzanine is open from 9 a.m. to 6 p.m. daily.

And **Conran's,** the American branch of the well-known London-based Habitat chain, has some fabulous buys in pottery, kitchenware, china, glass, and lots of other things (including furniture). Marvelous browsing here, even if you don't buy. One store is in the Citicorp Building, entrance at Third Avenue and 54th Street (tel. 371-2225); another is at 2-8 Astor Pl., near Broadway and 8th Street (tel. 505-1515); a third is at 2248 Broadway, at 81st Street (tel. 873-9250).

Open weekdays from 10 a.m. to 9 p.m., on Saturday to 7 p.m., and on Sunday from 11 a.m. to 6 p.m.

## LAMPS AND LIGHTING FIXTURES

On the Bowery, two stores offering vast selections of lamps, ceiling fans, and lighting fixtures at substantial discounts are: **New York Gas Lighting Co., Inc.,** 145-149 Bowery, between Broome and Grand streets (tel. 226-2840), open weekdays from 9 a.m. to 5 p.m. and on weekends from 10:30 a.m. to 5 p.m. (closed Saturday in July and August); and on the same block, **Bowery Lighting Corporation,** 132 Bowery (tel. 966-4034), open daily from 9 a.m. to 5:30 p.m.

## LUGGAGE

You simply can't beat the prices at **Bettinger's Luggage Shop,** 80 Rivington St., off Allen Street (tel. 674-9411). They offer discounts of 25% to 40% on first-quality brand-name luggage—Andiamo, American Tourister, Samsonite, etc.—plus exact replicas of the extremely popular nylon Sportsacs for 25% less, a full line of business and attaché cases, wallets, and much more. They also stock some seconds and irregulars.

Open Sunday through Friday from 9:15 a.m. to 6 p.m.

## MILLINERY AND NOTIONS

West 38th Street between Fifth Avenue and Avenue of the Americas is where New Yorkers go for ribbons, veils, buttons, feathers, hats, stones, and jewelry-making items. Wander in and out of the various shops, making sure to stop at **Manny's Millinery Supply Company,** 63 W. 38th St. (tel. 840-2235), where combs are only $2.50 a dozen and flowers to decorate them start at 40¢ a bunch.

Open weekdays from 9 a.m. to 5:30 p.m. and on Saturday from 9 a.m. to 3:15 p.m.

**Sheru Bead, Curtain, & Jewelry Designers,** 49 W. 38th St. (tel. 730-0766), is the spot for hobby supplies, buttons, flowers, millinery, ribbons, cloisonné, appliqués, beads, etc.

Open weekdays from 9 a.m. to 6 p.m. and on Saturday from 9:30 a.m. to 5 p.m.

**M and J Trimmings,** 1008 Ave. of the Americas, between 37th and 38th streets (tel. 391-6968), sells both retail and wholesale, with excellent prices for bridal headpieces, veils, and accessories, as well as trimmings of every kind.

Open weekdays from 9:30 a.m. to 6 p.m. and on Saturday from 10 a.m. to 5 p.m.

## MUSICAL INSTRUMENTS

For great buys (40% or more off) in new and secondhand musical instruments, particularly violins, call the **Ardsley Musical Instrument Service** in Westchester County (tel. 914/639-6639). They have an exclusive contract with a violin factory in Florence which manufactures handmade Italian violins in student sizes. They also carry a line of more advanced violins made in Bulgaria. And they have a Virtuoso Rental Plan for high-quality instruments. We also found new and used band instruments of every type, and tiny violins for tiny musicians.

Open Monday through Saturday, by appointment only.

## PAINTS

**Pearl Paint Company,** at 308 Canal St., between Broadway and Church Street (tel. 431-7932), is a bargain-hunter's store, and everyone from famous-name artists to household painters comes to Pearl's to stock up. Everything is sold at 20% to 50% off list price. Items are available by mail.

Open Monday through Saturday from 9 a.m. to 5:30 p.m. (on Thursday to 7 p.m.), and on Sunday from 11 a.m. to 4:45 p.m. Closed Sunday in July and August.

## PERFUME

Why spend a small fortune for expensive French perfumes when you can buy quality interpretations of the famous fragrances at a fraction of the price? Here's where to do it:

**Essential Products Company, Inc.,** 90 Water St. (between Wall Street and Hanover Square), New York, NY 10005 (tel. 344-4288), sells all its perfumes for a mere $19 an ounce, $10 for four ounces of men's colognes. They offer 45 perfumes, including highly popular new versions of Coco, Obsession, Poison, and Beautiful. Also available are 18 men's colognes; the newest versions of Antaeus, Giorgio, Obsession, Drakkar Noir, and Paul Sebastian. Mail orders are shipped promptly. Essential will send you free five fragrance cards, a fragrance list, and an order form if you call or write for information.

**Tuli-Latus Perfumes Ltd.** does a marvelous job of replicating such scents as Joy, L'Air du Temps, Lauren, Madame Rochas, Giorgio, Balà Versailles, Opium, Obsession, Coco, etc., as well as Cuir de Russie and other men's perfumes. Their version of Chanel No. 5 (Tuli-Latus No. 6) has long been a personal favorite. Prices range between $20 and $25 an ounce. They also have an excellent line of skin-care products. Phone 718/746-9337 for a catalog, or write them at 146–36 Thirteenth Ave. (P.O. Box 422), Whitestone, NY 11357.

## PETS AND PET SUPPLIES

Want to adopt a poor deserving little dog—an orphan, no less? Then go to the **ASPCA,** 441 E. 92nd St., at the corner of York Avenue (tel. 876-7711), and your only costs will be $8.50 for a license, which you can purchase right there, plus a $58.50 adoption fee. In addition to dogs, you can pick up cats, of course ($40 adoption fee), as well as more unusual animals (which occasionally include parakeets, hamsters, etc.); the ASPCA will examine the animal, inoculate it, and give it an optional free medical examination for up to two weeks after adoption, free vaccination, spaying or neutering, and free feline leukemia testing.

You can come in to adopt a pet from 11 a.m. to 7 p.m. daily. You must be at least 18 or have two forms of ID. The ASPCA also proudly presents the "Purina Pets for People" program for senior citizens aged 60 years and over who can adopt free of charge. For further information on this program, call the above number Monday through Friday from 11 a.m. to 7 p.m.

Another worthy animal-adoption agency is the smaller **Bide-A-Wee Home,** 410 E. 38th St., east of First Avenue (tel. 532-4455). They place dogs and cats, and ask a $30 to $55 donation depending on the animal's age. All animals here have been inoculated, already neutered if they are six months or older, and in perfect health. You must be at least 21 to adopt and have two forms of certificable ID.

Open Monday through Friday from 10 a.m. to 6 p.m. and on Saturday and Sunday from 10 a.m. to 4 p.m.

Everything you'll need to keep your new pet comfy and contented can be found—often at a discount—at **Pet Bowl,** 421 Amsterdam Ave., at 80th Street (tel. 595-4200). In addition to dog and cat food, they carry a large stock of accessories and furniture, including beds, toys, collars, leashes, etc. Stop in to put your name on their mailing list; you'll receive their catalog and be notified of special sales.

Open Monday through Friday from 10 a.m. to 7 p.m., on Saturday from 9:30 a.m. to 6 p.m., and on Sunday from noon to 5 p.m.

## PRINTS AND POSTERS

**Associated American Artists,** 20 W. 57th St., off Fifth Avenue (tel. 399-5510), has original graphics, etchings, lithographs, serigraphs, and woodcuts bearing the artists' signatures beginning at $40.

Open Tuesday through Saturday from 10 a.m. to 6 p.m. (June through August, Monday through Friday from 10 a.m. to 5 p.m.).

The **Argosy Book Store,** 116 E. 59th St., between Park and Lexington avenues (tel. 753-4455), places enormous bins of old maps, prints, and books out in front of the store (prints begin here at $2; inside, they begin at $1 and go way up). They also have catalogs of Americana, medicine, rare books, autographs, etc.

Open weekdays from 9 a.m. to 6 p.m. and on Saturday from 9:30 a.m. to 5:30 p.m. Closed Saturday from mid-May through Labor Day).

The **Gallery of Graphic Arts,** 1601 York Ave., between 84th and 85th streets (tel. 988-4731), has been presenting top-notch graphic art in an intimate, neighborhood setting for many years. Owner Ellie Seibold is an avid collector (and seller) of contemporary American, European, and Japanese lithographs, etchings, woodcuts, and authentic Mexican and New England tombstone rubbings. She's always on the lookout for works by young artists, and delights in selling quality work at prices people can afford. Small prints begin at around $50, and would sell for much more in a fancier gallery. She also does some very special framing work (some of the leading museums are her clients) and takes pride in framing the hard-to-frame—full-size quilts, tapestries, antique textiles, Indian beadwork, or whatever. If you need such work done, drop in to see Ellie or call and discuss it with her: send her the object, and she'll frame it superbly and mail it back to you. Her motto: "If there's any way to get it on the wall, we do it."

Gallery of Graphic Arts is open Monday through Saturday from 11 a.m. to 6:30 p.m.

**Poster Originals** has two locations, one at 924 Madison Ave., near 73rd Street (tel. 861-0422), in the uptown art district, and another downtown at 158 Spring St. (tel. 226-7720), in SoHo, New York's dynamic downtown art neighborhood. Both galleries carry an exciting array of posters by contemporary painters, both European and American. You might find Polish circus posters, as well as some from museums. Prices are reasonable, beginning at $15 for unframed posters.

The Madison Avenue gallery is open Monday through Saturday from 10 a.m. to 6 p.m.; the SoHo gallery, 10 a.m. to 6 p.m. daily.

**Untitled,** in SoHo at 159 Prince St. (tel. 982-2088), and 680 Broadway, at 3rd Street (tel. 254-1360), is a postcard store the likes of which you've never seen. Subjects run the gamut from cave paintings to the very latest in New Wave art cards. This is the place to finally start a postcard collection for yourself, or invest in a starter set for a friend as a remembrance of New York.

Hours are Monday through Saturday from 10 a.m. to 9 p.m. and on Sunday from noon to 8 p.m.

## RECORDS

Big record selections at great prices? You'll find them at **Sam Goody's** three Manhattan locations: on the West Side at 51 W. 51st St., at Sixth Avenue (tel. 246-8730), and on the East Side at 666 Third Ave., at 43rd Street (tel. 986-8480), and 1101 Third Ave., at 60th Street (tel. 751-5809). Goody's is one of the world's largest record and tape dealers in both classical and popular music; they also handle a full line of compact discs, portable radios, and all associated accessories. Each branch carries a complete line of these products, all selling at reasonable prices. Watch the newspapers for special sales.

Hours vary: call each store for specifics.

**Tower Records,** 692 Broadway, at East 4th Street (tel. 505-1500), and **Tower Video,** a block away at East 4th Street and Lafayette Street (tel. 505-1166), is as much a Village "happening" as a record store, with its three floors of records and tapes throbbing with excitement 365 days a year. The *New York Post* once called it "the hottest place to meet a member of the opposite sex," and that it is, as the crowds watch videos, attend special events, listen to music, and get to know one another. Well, even if you're just looking to buy records or tapes at good prices, Tower Records is good to know about. The largest eastern outpost of the well-known western chain, Tower has one of the world's largest collections, in all categories, from classical to rock to rhythm-and-blues. Records are often sold for as little as $7. There's another gigantic Tower Records uptown in the Lincoln Center area at 1967 Broadway, at 66th Street (tel. 799-2500), and a block north of that, at 1977 Broadway (tel. 496-2500), is Tower Video.

All stores are open every day of the year, from 9 a.m. to midnight.

## SPACE AGE GIFTS

Something like 2,000 products that show that "science and spirit are not incompatible" can be found at **Star Magic,** 743 Broadway, near 8th Street (tel. 228-7770), and 275 Amsterdam Ave., at the corner of 73rd Street (tel. 769-2020). Star Magic is a unique and magical store that should be experienced by anyone tuned in to either inner or outer space. Celestial music, flashing lights, and hi-tech design set the scene for a futuristic space in which you can find anything from telescopes, globes, robots, prisms, holograms, and space shuttle models to healing crystals, gemstone pendants, pyramids, books on higher consciousness, and statues of the Buddha. Tapes, albums, and CDs run the gamut from New Age and synthesized space music to Tibetan gongs. The price range is wide, from 25¢ for a sticker to $6,000 for a home planetarium. Among the Space Age jewelry, L.E.D. lapel pins go for $20. Rose quartz spheres can go from $100 to $500.

Both stores are open Monday through Saturday from 10 a.m. to 10 p.m. and on Sunday from 11 a.m. to 9 p.m. The original Star Magic is located in San Francisco, at 4026 24th St. in Noe Valley.

## SPORTING GOODS

The three outstanding sporting goods stores in New York are Herman's, Paragon, and Hudson's. Each of them has complete selections of name-brand equipment.

**Herman's World of Sporting Goods,** 135 W. 42nd St., between Broadway and Avenue of the Americas (tel. 730-7400); 845 Third Ave., at 51st Street (tel.

688-4603); 39 W. 34th St., off Fifth Avenue (tel. 279-8900); 110 Nassau St., between Ann and Beekman streets, downtown (tel. 233-0733), carries a full line of equipment and supplies for golf, racquet sports, hunting, fishing, camping, exercising, skiing, and team sports. Herman's also has a large selection of active sportswear and athletic apparel, athletic shoes, ski wear, and rugged outerwear for men, women, and children. Value is outstanding. And everything is geared to both the novice as well as the serious amateur athlete.

The uptown stores are open Monday through Friday from 9:30 a.m. to 7 p.m., on Saturday to 6 p.m., with the addition of Sunday from noon to 5 p.m. at 34th Street. The downtown store is open weekdays from 9 a.m. to 6 p.m., on Saturday to 5 p.m.; closed Sunday.

**Paragon,** 867 Broadway, between 17th and 18th streets (tel. 255-8036), has comparable items and specializes in camping equipment. Their prices are rock bottom for all kinds of backpacking and climbing gear, tents, and camping clothing, not to mention a wide variety of sporting goods and sports clothing.

Open Monday through Friday from 10 a.m. to 8 p.m., to 7 p.m. Saturday, and on Sunday from 11 a.m. to 6 p.m.

**Hudson's,** 97 Third Ave., from 12th to 13th streets (tel. 473-7320), is a whole city block of a store specializing in outdoor clothing and equipment. They have a big selection of leather jackets, jeanswear (501 jeans), footwear, and sports apparel at discount prices.

Open Monday through Thursday from 9:30 a.m. to 8 p.m., on Friday and Saturday to 7 p.m., and on Sunday from noon to 5 p.m.

## THRIFT SHOPS

Along Second and Third avenues in the 70s and 80s is a string of thrift shops which feature used merchandise—of every sort—sold in "as is" condition. The shops are staffed by public-spirited ladies in colorful smocks who donate their time and proceeds from sales to hospitals, nursing homes, and other charitable institutions. Some of the merchandise, admittedly, is hand-me-down, but very often you turn up excellent buys here. Many smart shoppers regularly canvas these shops for real finds.

Top choice of these shops is the **Girls' Club of New York Thrift Shop,** 202 E. 77th St., between Second and Third avenues (tel. 535-8570), which is almost elegant in appearance compared to many others of the genre. They feature men's, women's, and children's clothing in "mint condition," some of it new. Prices go from $5 up. They sell designer clothing and fine furs at reasonable prices. Also, furniture, bric-a-brac in excellent condition, many antiques in all categories, and books from 25¢ up.

Store hours are Monday through Saturday from 9:30 a.m. to 4:45 p.m. (on Thursday to 6 p.m.).

Among the others, you might try:

**Irvington Institute Thrift Shop,** 1534 Second Ave., at 80th Street (tel. 879-4555), which sells women's and men's clothing, from dollar items to designer numbers. They also have furs, linen, furniture, rugs, decorative accessories, paintings, porcelains, books, silver, and glassware. Proceeds go to Irvington Institute for Medical Research, affiliated with the Albert Einstein College of Medicine and Rockefeller University.

Open from 9:30 a.m. to 6 p.m. Monday through Saturday (on Wednesday until 8 p.m.); closed Sunday.

The **Trishop Quality Thrift Boutique,** 1689 First Ave., between 87th and 88th streets (tel. 369-2411), is a well-kept secret among many of the city's better-dressed women: this place handles mostly top-quality, brand-new merchandise contributed by manufacturers and famous Fifth Avenue department stores (proceeds from sales benefit the Mental Health Association of New York and Bronx Counties). You might find designer clothes for anywhere from $10 to $100. There is also a small section of gently used men's, women's, and children's clothing. While most of the

314 THE BEST SHOPPING BUYS IN TOWN

clothing is new, most of the furniture, lamps, bric-a-brac, etc., is used.

The shop is open Tuesday through Saturday from 9:30 a.m. to 4 p.m.

Downtown, the thrift-shop fans swear by **St. George's Thrift Shop,** 61 Gramercy Park North, near 21st Street and Park Avenue South (tel. 260-0350), which sells gently used clothing and accessories for men, women, and children, as well as bric-a-brac, books, records, linens, and lots more.

Open Monday through Friday from 10:30 a.m. to 5:30 p.m., and on Saturday from 10:30 a.m. to 4 p.m.

## TOYS

The new and collectible toys at **Mythology,** 370 Columbus Ave., at 78th Street (tel. 874-0744), seem as popular with grownups as with kids: there's always a flock of people ogling the antique windup toys, the posters, the unusual rubber stamps, earrings, architectural toys and kits, inflatable rafts and floats, Mexican masks, Burmese puppets, crazy salt and pepper shakers, just to give you an idea. If you can leave this little store without buying something, you have more sales resistance than we do! Unusual flip books, all kinds of tiny toys at tiny prices, and much, much more.

Open Monday through Saturday from 11 a.m. to 11 p.m., and on Sunday to 6 p.m.

**B. Shackman & Co.,** 85 Fifth Ave., near 16th Street (tel. 989-5162), sells wonderful reproductions of antique toys, picture books, and dolls. Here you'll find the kind of Victorian greeting cards and teddy bears that are sold in museum gift shops. Cat lovers will enjoy their Kitty Cucumber™ items.

Open Monday through Saturday from 10:30 a.m. to 4 p.m.

**Dollsandreams,** 1421 Lexington Ave., at 93rd Street (tel. 876-2434), is a dream of a toy store. They stock a lovely selection of dolls, toys, and art supplies, as well as a full line of Swiss Caran D'Ache art supplies (crayons, paints, markers, etc.). The dolls and toys here are of the highest quality, and prices are always fair.

Open Monday through Friday from 10:30 a.m. to 6 p.m. and on Saturday from 10 a.m. to 5 p.m. Closed on Saturday in summer.

For new and antique dollhouses, miniatures, and dolls, a good bet is **The Doll House,** 176 Ninth Ave., at 21st Street (tel. 989-5520). There is at least a 20% discount on everything and the selection is overwhelming for such a little place.

Open Wednesday through Friday from noon to 6 p.m. and on Saturday from 10 a.m. to 4:30 p.m.

## TYPEWRITERS

**Lexington Typewriter and Business Systems,** 300 Park Ave. South (tel. 674-8584), is one of the nicest places in New York to buy a typewriter. Not only do discounts range from 15% to 20% off manufacturer's suggested list price, but the typewriters are set up at tables with comfortable chairs, so you can really try them out. In marked contrast to the frenzied atmosphere at other typewriter discount marts, the staff here is really helpful with advice on which machine is best for your needs, and they will teach you how it works. Lexington, in business for over 47 years, is an authorized dealer for Smith Corona, IBM, Brothers, and Sharpe, with a wide range of electronic typewriters and word processors for home or office use. Owner Jeff Riggio advises that you can usually get a better price on a typewriter in Manhattan, where so many dealers must compete by offering good deals, than in a small town, where there may be only one dealer who will charge list prices. We priced the Smith Corona XL 1500 electronic typewriter here for $149, as against a list price of $229; the sophisticated Smith Corona PWP3000 was $499 here, $799 elsewhere. And for those of you who simply refuse to move ahead with progress, we even found a tiny manual typewriter—an Olivetti—for all of $69.

Lexington Typewriter is open week days only, from 8:30 a.m. to 5:30 p.m.

## UMBRELLAS

If you've never been able to find the perfect umbrella in your local stores, **Gloria Umbrellas,** 39 Essex St., on the Lower East Side (tel. 475-7388), should have one in stock to suit your fancy—and at a 30% discount! Whether you're looking for an oversize, folding, or windproof umbrella, we're sure you won't be disappointed here. They are also expert at repairing all types of umbrellas.

Open Sunday through Thursday from 9 a.m. to 5 p.m., on Friday until 2:30 p.m.

---

# 3. Food

Food, food, beautiful food. In New York, everyone's a gourmet. For the best prices on the essentials—plus the frills from Spanish saffron to Hungarian prune whip—consult the following:

## CHEESE

New York abounds with cheese stores, but it's hard to beat the prices at **Cheese of All Nations,** 153 Chambers St., between Hudson and Greenwich streets (tel. 732-0752). Almost a thousand varieties are in stock, all modestly priced. A trip down here is well worthwhile since the neighborhood abounds in bargain stores. And Chambers Street is right at the IRT–Seventh Avenue subway stop (take the no. 1, 2, 3, or 9 train).

Open Monday through Saturday from 8 a.m. to 5:30 p.m.

**Fairway,** 2127 Broadway, at 74th Street (tel. 595-1888), has a marvelous cheese section, at some of the best prices anywhere. Up front are acres of super-fresh fruits and vegetables, which, along with the cheeses and pastas and other goodies, bring the customers from far and wide. A few blocks farther uptown, at Broadway and 80th Street, **Zabar's** (tel. 787-2000), New York's great gourmet grocery, has another superb selection of cheeses (more highly priced, however, than at Fairway). Both stores are open every day.

**Ideal Cheese,** 1205 Second Ave., at 63rd Street (tel. 688-7579), just might be the best cheese store in New York—the best of everything, including the largest selection of goat and sheep cheese in the country; many are American made. They also claim to have the largest selection of low-fat, low-cholesterol cheeses in the country. You can usually find between 250 and 300 cheeses there at any given time. They also sell gift baskets, gourmet coffees, and pâtés. A free catalog goes with all cheese and gift items.

Open weekdays from 9 a.m. to 6:30 p.m., on Saturday to 6 p.m.

**Dean & De Luca,** 560 Broadway, at the corner of Prince Street, in SoHo (tel. 431-1691), has every type of cheese, great loaves of black bread, sweet ham, savory pies, pastries, pastas, condiments, coffees, and croissants to name a few categories. Everything is fabulous, but be warned: prices are high.

Open Monday through Saturday from 10 a.m. to 7 p.m., on Sunday to 6 p.m.

**Ben's,** 181 E. Houston St., between Allen and Orchard streets (tel. 254-8290), features homemade baked flavored farmer and cream cheese—strawberry, pepper, walnut, raisin—irresistible and relatively inexpensive. Not to mention fresh tub butter, and hundreds of varieties of domestic and imported cheeses.

Open Monday through Friday from 8:15 a.m. to 5:30 p.m. (closing at 3 p.m. on Friday in winter); on Sunday, it's 1:30 to 6 p.m.

**Murray's Cheese Store,** 42 Cornelia St., between Sixth Avenue and Bleecker Street (tel. 243-3289), has hundreds of varieties of imported cheeses at unbeatable prices. Frequent specials and excellent quality.

Open Monday through Saturday from 7:30 a.m. to 6 p.m.

## COFFEES AND TEAS

**McNulty's** has been serving coffee- and tea-loving New Yorkers since 1895 at 109 Christopher St., between Hudson and Bleecker streets (tel. 242-5351). They sell about 100 varieties of choice coffees and rare, hard-to-obtain teas.

Open Monday through Saturday from 11 a.m. to 11 p.m., and on Sunday from 1 to 7 p.m.

## GOURMET GROCERIES

**Paprikas Weiss Importers,** at 1546 Second Ave., between 80th and 81st streets in the Yorkville section of town (tel. 288-6117), specializes in Middle European foods, as well as unusual kitchen utensils from all over the world. Hard-to-find spices are available here in bulk (it's cheaper to buy it this way, rather than in the fancy bottles you get at the supermarket). Coffees and teas, ready-to-use strudel dough sheets, Hungarian salamis, nuts, cheeses, homemade jams and syrups, every kind of canned good imaginable, a huge selection of French pâtés, foie gras, and fresh goose livers, plus continental candies, make this place an international food bazaar par excellence. They also sell gift items from Hungary: hand-embroidered peasant blouses, kerchiefs, and shawls, for example. Send $1 to subscribe to their mail-order catalog.

Open Monday through Saturday from 9 a.m. to 6 p.m.

Still shopping Yorkville, **Bremen House,** 220 E. 86th St., between Second and Third avenues (tel. 288-5500), is a great place for cold cuts and sausages in every size, shape, and texture, cooked and raw. Cheeses, candies, German herrings, mustards, jams, herb teas, kitschy gift items like Black Forest cuckoo clocks, spices, European records, European cosmetics, and all sorts of imported canned and packaged goods, as well as German newspapers and magazines are also sold. A free catalog is available. Well worth a visit to the Yorkville area just to see this store.

Open Monday through Saturday from 9:30 a.m. to 7 p.m.

While you're in the neighborhood, stop in at **Schaller and Weber** for "gold medal award-winning" cold cuts and gourmet products. They're at 1654 Second Ave., at the corner of 86th Street (tel. 879-3047); and the **Elk Candy Co.,** at 240 E. 86th St., between Second and Third avenues (tel. 650-1177), for every kind of sweet imaginable.

**Basior-Schwartz,** 421 W. 14th St. (tel. 929-5368), is an enormous cooler which is also a large wholesale supplier to stores and restaurants. It services the retail customer as well, selling cheeses, pâtés, smoked fish, crackers, and biscuits at very big discounts, and much, much more. Olive oil, dried fruits and nuts, and tuna fish at great savings too.

Open from 5 to 10:30 a.m., weekdays only. It's in the bustling wholesale meat market district.

## GREENMARKETS

You wouldn't expect to find farmers' markets in the asphalt jungle, but New York does have them, and New Yorkers adore them. If you're in the neighborhood of the biggest and most popular of the Greenmarkets—the one held at **Union Square** (17th Street and Broadway) every Wednesday, Friday, and Saturday, year round, do take a stroll around. Whether or not you're cooking in, it's worth a visit to see and sample the wonderful produce, freshly baked breads and pastries, ciders, honeys, etc., that are grown by farmers in New York state and Pennsylvania, brought to the city and sold by the growers themselves. Prices are very reasonable and everything is the freshest and finest. On a recent summer visit, we spotted a variety of pies—shoofly, cherry, peach, and apple—baked by farm ladies from Pennsylvania's Amish country for around $5 each; they were also selling their own butter and cheese. Fishermen from Montauk on the tip of Long Island were selling freshly caught fish. New York state farms were selling wild mountain strawberries, fresh sweet corn, raspberry preserves, fresh apple cider, and hydroponically grown tomatoes, lettuce, and cucumbers. Pennsylvania Dutch farms were selling organically produced meats and handmade pretzels. There were goat cheeses and raspberry preserves and New York state wines, and scads of stands selling plants and fresh country flowers. In cold weather, you can often pick up a steaming bowl of potato chowder from one of the stands.

Other popular Greenmarkets that you may want to visit are the ones in **Greenwich Village,** at Gansevoort and Hudson Streets, in the heart of the meat market area, open on Saturday from June 3 to November 18; in the **East Village** at St. Marks Church, 10th Street and Second Avenue, on Tuesday from May 30 to November 21; **West 57th Street** and Ninth Avenue, on Wednesday and Saturday, year round; downtown at the **World Trade Center,** on Thursday year round and also on Tuesday from June 6 to December 19. The Greenmarket at **Columbus Avenue** and West 77th Street, in the schoolyard of I.S. 44, shares space with one of the city's most engaging flea markets, making it doubly delightful. It's known as "Greenflea."

Most Greenmarkets are open from 8 a.m. to 5 or 6 p.m., or until they sell out. The earlier you come, the fresher and better are the pickings.

For more information on Greenmarkets, phone or write the Council on the Environment of New York City, 51 Chambers St., New York, NY 10017 (tel. 566-0990).

## HEALTH AND NATURAL FOODS

It sometimes seems that half the people in New York are on a health and fitness kick. As a result, there are health-food stores every few blocks, plus huge natural-food emporiums here and there. Some of the best:

**Commodities,** 117 Hudson St., at the corner of North Moore Street, in TriBeCa (tel. 334-8330), is a macrobiotic superstore, with what they call perhaps the largest selection in the world of macrobiotic products. But there's also plenty for those who are not into macrobiotics in this huge store where almost 95% of the goods are organically grown—and that includes fresh fruits and vegetables, grains, beans, seaweeds, unusual flours (chestnut, chickpea, etc.), even the very pleasant Altura coffee from Mexico, which has half the usual amount of caffeine. Rows of bins house staple items; homeopathic and herbal remedies (including Dragon Eggs, a line of Chinese herbal medicines) comprise a natural pharmacy. Sections of cookwares and natural cosmetics too. And prices on these hard-to-find items are all discounted from 7% to 20%. Many people from out of the neighborhood come here on weekends to stack their cars with the good buys.

Commodities is open from 10 a.m. to 8 p.m. seven days a week, and closes only on Thanksgiving and Christmas Days.

**Earth Harvest Trading Company,** 700 Columbus Ave., at 94th Street (tel. 864-1376), is an uptown mecca for organic fruits and vegetables, meat, fish, and poultry, as well as a wide variety of natural-food products, vitamins, and herbal preparations. Their slogan is "Your Whole Week's Shopping Naturally," and they live up to their word.

Open weekdays from 9:30 a.m. to 7:30 p.m., and on Saturday and Sunday from 10 a.m. to 6 p.m.

Also popular in this area is **World Health Fitness Center,** 628 Columbus Ave., near 90th Street (tel. 874-0988), with excellent selections of all-natural foods, including vitamins, grains, beans, nuts, dried fruits, honeys, meat, fish, and dairy products.

Open Monday through Friday from 11 a.m. to 7:30 p.m., on Saturday to 7 p.m.

**The Health Nuts,** 2141 Broadway, at 75th Street (tel. 724-1972), is another outstanding source for natural foods (although they do not carry produce). They stock herbs, macrobiotic products, and natural foods from quality companies.

Open from 9 a.m. to 8 p.m. Monday through Saturday and on Sunday from 11 a.m. to 7 p.m. Other branches of The Health Nuts are at 2611 Broadway, at 99th Street (tel. 678-0054); and on the East Side at 852 Second Ave., between 44th and 45th streets (tel. 490-2979), and 1208 Second Ave., at 63rd Street (tel. 593-0016).

**The Good Earth,** 1334 First Ave., between 71st and 72nd streets (tel. 472-9055), carries a wide array of organic and natural foods—fruits, vegetables, meats, dairy products, breads, cakes—natural cosmetics, natural vitamins, etc. Their other store at 182 Amsterdam Ave., at 68th Street (tel. 496-1616), is just two minutes from Lincoln Center.

Open on Monday, Wednesday, and Thursday from 10 a.m. to 7 p.m., on Tuesday and Friday to 7:30 p.m., and on Saturday to 6 p.m.

Nutrition may be the "in" thing now, but at **Brownies,** 91 Fifth Ave., between 16th and 17th streets (tel. 242-2199), healthful eating has been the vogue for over 50 years. Brownies purveys vitamins, grains, beans, seeds, herbal teas, a full line of natural food items. Their home-baked cakes—carrot, maple walnut, carob, to give you an idea—are both healthful and scrumptious, using only whole-grain flours, honey, and other natural ingredients.

The retail store is open Monday through Friday from 9 a.m. to 7 p.m., until 6 p.m. on Saturday.

The best source for natural produce in the Village is **Down to Earth,** 337 Seventh Ave., between 12th and 13th streets (tel. 924-2711). This bustling, crowded emporium also has good supplies of macrobiotic staples, herbs, an excellent frozen-food section, and a counter for fresh juices and healthy snack items.

Open weekdays from 9:30 a.m. to 9:30 p.m., on Saturday from 10 a.m. to 8:30 p.m., and on Sunday from 12:30 to 8:30 p.m.

## HERBS AND SPICES

In Greenwich Village, **Aphrodisia,** 282 Bleecker St., between Sixth and Seventh avenues (tel. 989-6440), is the place to go for exotic herbs and spices. You can also purchase flower oils to make your own perfume or potpourri, *fo-ti* (an Oriental herb reputed to have healthful qualities), and dandelion root (a healthful coffee substitute); they even carry crystallized roses, a perfect cake decoration, which are hard to find. Lots of books for sale here on nature's own medicines, health foods, recipes, aphrodisiacs, and magical herbs.

Open Monday through Saturday from 11 a.m. to 7 p.m., and on Sunday (except in July and August) from noon to 5 p.m.

**Pete's Spice and Everything Nice,** 174 First Ave., between 10th and 11th streets (tel. 254-8773), is considered a prime source among the city's serious cooks and professional caterers. Almost everything here is sold in bulk (from an ounce to 100 pounds), and that includes herbs and spices, grains, flours, dried beans, dried fruit, shelled and unshelled nuts, plus various gourmet items—all at budget prices. Try the coffee beans—mocha java was going for a reasonable $5.25 a pound when last we looked in.

Open Monday through Saturday from 10 a.m. to 7:30 p.m. and on Sunday from 12:30 to 5 p.m.

## PRODUCE

The cheapest produce—as well as groceries, meat, and other items—in town is sold in the **City Markets,** which are warehouse-type buildings in which pushcart peddlers and other small food entrepreneurs place their carts, stalls, and bins. The food is more exotic than you'd find in the commercial groceries, very little of it is canned, and the prices are rock bottom. Several such markets exist, but our favorites are the ones located on **Essex Street,** between Stanton and Broome streets and on Essex between Delancey and Rivington streets on the Lower East Side (tel. 254-6655).

Open Monday through Saturday from 8 a.m. to 6 p.m.

## SWEETS AND DRIED FRUITS

Best buys here are on the Lower East Side. **Wolsk's Confections,** 81 Ludlow St., between Broome and Delancey streets (tel. 475-7946), has been here since 1939, both wholesaling and retailing dried fruits, nuts, candies, chocolates, halvah, and more. They have 50 varieties of nuts for eating or baking, 30 varieties of domestic and imported dried fruits. Nuts are roasted fresh daily on the premises. Hand-dipped chocolates, made of only the finest and purest ingredients, are made weekly. In lots of 100 or more, one can buy imported and domestic hard candies, licorice, gummies, boxed chocolates, etc., at 20% to 50% below regular retail prices.

Open Sunday through Thursday from 8 a.m. to 5 p.m., on Friday until 2 p.m. Mail order is available; they ship UPS.

Good buys are also available nearby at **Mutual Dried Fruit,** 127 Ludlow St., between Rivington and Delancey streets (tel. 673-3489), open Sunday through Thursday from 8:30 a.m. to 5:30 p.m., on Friday to about 4:45 p.m.

## WINES AND SPIRITS

Offering one of the city's most comprehensive and inexpensive selections of domestic and imported wines is **Astor Wines and Spirits,** 12 Astor Pl., between Broadway and Lafayette Street, just below 8th Street (tel. 674-7500). You can get a very nice imported French table wine for around $4, and prices on all their stock—especially their own Astor label—are most reasonable. In addition, a wide choice of liquors and liqueurs is sold at competitive prices.

Open Monday through Saturday from 9 a.m. to 9 p.m.

## THE BRONX'S ARTHUR AVENUE

One of the city's most unusual shopping areas is not in Manhattan but in the Bronx. The Arthur Avenue section is predominantly Italian, with lots of food shops and bakeries as well as a smattering of retail shops selling clothing and household items. But food is first on Arthur Avenue, and a walk along the avenue is a must for every gourmet who enjoys eating and cooking Italian food. Shoppers will be glad to learn that prices are considerably lower here than in most parts of Manhattan.

Our favorite stretch of the avenue is between 184th and 187th streets, where a number of the best shops are located. For fish, go to **Randazzo's** at 2340 Arthur Ave. (tel. 367-4139). On the sidewalk in front of the store a raised bench full of ice shavings holds an interesting array of mussels, clams, and unusual small fish. Inside you can buy anything from porgies to lobster, and the fish is always fresh and well priced. Occasionally the owners themselves have caught the fish they sell.

Open Monday through Saturday from 7 a.m. to 6 p.m.

The **Arthur Avenue Retail Market,** 2344 Arthur Ave., a big city public market chock full of privately operated stalls, each offering vegetables and fruit at competing prices. You can walk through and buy what you want after checking the price and quality of the various vendors. Meats and poultry, cheeses and sausages, espressos, coffees, pastries, all Italian specialties, housewares, and candies—spices, too—are all sold here under one roof and the atmosphere is very European. A good place to do your budget shopping.

Open Monday through Saturday from 8 a.m. to 6 p.m.

187th Street, which intersects Arthur Avenue, is a continuation of the Italian food shopping in this area. **De Lillo Pastry,** at 606 E. 187th St. (tel. 367-8198), offers all types of Italian goodies baked right on the premises.

Open every day from 8 a.m. to about 6 or 7 p.m.

**Danny's Pork Store,** 626 E. 187th St. (tel. 933-1690), sells every cut of pork imaginable, and specializes in homemade Italian pork sausage, made fresh every day. Dry-cured sweet and hot sausage (pepperoni), made daily from September through May, is another specialty.

Open Monday through Saturday from 9 a.m. to 5:30 p.m.

To reach the Arthur Avenue section by subway, take the IND–Sixth Avenue D train uptown to Fordham Road in the Bronx. Then take the no. 12 bus from Fordham Road to Hoffman Street, and walk one block to Arthur Avenue. The shopping area is three blocks away.

## CHINATOWN

A market shopping tour of Chinatown is educational as well as fun. Not to be missed is the fascinating **Kam Man Food Products, Inc.,** 200 Canal St., between

Mott and Mulberry streets (tel. 571-0330), a vast emporium offering everything from fish, meat, housewares, and vegetables, to furniture and exotic Chinese remedies for whatever ails you. Not only is the food and produce of excellent quality and relatively inexpensive, but the drug products come in intriguing little metal boxes and wonderful wrappings, all worth saving. The line in the front is generally for the barbecued duck hanging in the window. Wonderful for gift shopping or just browsing.

Open every day from 9 a.m. to 9 p.m.

**Kam Kuo,** 7 Mott St., near Park Row (tel. 349-3097), is a spanking-clean supermarket-like store selling everything from utensils to the actual ingredients—everything you need for Chinese cookery. Open the same hours as Kam Man.

The **United Super Market,** 84 Mulberry St., between Bayard and Canal streets (tel. 962-6440), specializes in Chinese meats—pork and liver sausages, dried duck, etc.

Open daily from 9 a.m. to 7:30 p.m.

## A LITTLE ITALY GASTRONOMIC ADVENTURE

The neighborhood people who live in Little Italy, a section that runs the length of Mulberry Street from East Houston Street to Canal Street, swear by the quality and low prices at the many food shops in the area. We have several favorites of our own (see also Chapter II).

A good bet for sausages—they've been making them at the same location since 1890—is **Fretta Brothers Italian Pork Products,** 116 Mott St., at Hester Street (tel. 226-0232). They call their products "the Rolls-Royce of sausages."

Open Tuesday through Saturday from 8 a.m. to 6 p.m., and on Sunday from 9 a.m. to 2 p.m.

For excellent homemade pasta, try either of the following:

**Piemonte Ravioli Company,** 190 Grand St., between Mott and Mulberry streets (tel. 226-0475), where owner Mario Bertorelli turns out ravioli, manicotti, cannelloni, gnocchi, cavatelle, spinach noodles, spinach lasagne, egg lasagne, and a host of other pastas.

Open Tuesday through Saturday from 8:30 a.m. to 6 p.m., and from 8:30 a.m. to 3 p.m. on Sunday.

**Raffetto's,** 144 W. Houston St., between MacDougal and Sullivan streets (tel. 777-1261), is another specialist in excellent homemade pasta.

It's open Tuesday through Saturday from 8 a.m. to 6 p.m.

For cheese, we like a store that has been doing business at the same address since 1925. **Di Palo's,** 206 Grand St., between Mott and Grand streets (tel. 226-1033), features cheese that is made on the premises—fresh mozzarella and ricotta made with whole milk—plus a good selection of imported cheeses. Provolone is available in weights from 2½ to 100 pounds.

Store hours are 8:30 a.m. to 6:30 p.m. Monday through Saturday, until 2 p.m. on Sunday.

In business even longer than Di Palo's, **Alleva Dairy,** 188 Grand St., at Mulberry Street (tel. 226-7990), has been offering fresh ricotta and mozzarella (try the smoked mozzarella) since 1892. They are the oldest makers of these products in America.

Open from 8:30 a.m. to 6 p.m. Monday through Saturday, until 2 p.m. on Sunday.

For specialty breads, Italian sausages, quality imported cheeses, fresh mozzarella, and salads, visit the **Italian Food Center,** just next door at 186 Grand St. (tel. 925-2954), open daily from 8 a.m. to 7 p.m.

The biggest supplier of bread in the area is the little **Parisi Bakery,** at 198 Mott St., between Kenmare and Spring streets (tel. 226-6378). Large and crusty loaves of bread sell for 95¢ to $1 each. You can also buy "lard and pepper" cookies and butter biscuits for $2.50 a pound.

Open Monday through Saturday from 7:30 a.m. to 6:30 p.m.

We get our Italian vegetables at **Caruso's Fruit Market,** 152 Mott St., between Broome and Grand streets (tel. 226-2978), which supplies some of the finest restaurants in Little Italy. All the hot and sweet peppers you may desire, as well as a good selection of the freshest fruits and a wide variety of other vegetables.

Open from 7:30 a.m. to 5:30 p.m. Monday through Saturday.

## A NINTH AVENUE GASTRONOMIC ADVENTURE

The city's most colorful market area, where prices are exceptionally low, is Ninth Avenue from 37th to 45th streets. Everywhere you look here, the eye is attracted by vivid color, the nose by tantalizing smells. Up and down the street, bins are overflowing with fresh seafood (crabs, shrimp, squid, mussels), fruits, and vegetables; bakery windows are crowded with still-warm French and Italian loaves and flaky pastries; huge cheeses, ripe enough to burst, beckon invitingly from inside dark groceries; butchers proudly advertise their rock-bottom prices, and announce via window posters fresh game, baby lamb, and other delicacies. Take an hour or more to see this one day.

Especially hospitable, and a personal favorite, is the family-owned **Poseidon Oriental Pastry Shop,** 629 Ninth Ave., between 44th and 45th streets (tel. 757-6173), a guaranteed hit if you're a fan of honey-rich delicacies made with the purest ingredients in a spotless environment. Look toward the back of the store and you'll see one of the good-looking sons of the owner in front of a large wooden table, busily spreading out the 16-square-foot sheets of paper-thin phyllo dough, used to make exotic pastries and strudels. Buy it and freeze it. Pistachio-filled honey rolls, rich baklava, and innumerable other exotic delights are for sale. Delicious cheese, spinach, meat, and vegetable pies are available in both cocktail and regular sizes. Everything, incidentally, can be frozen.

Open Tuesday through Saturday from 9 a.m. to 7 p.m. and on Sunday from 10 a.m. to 4 p.m.; closed Monday.

Stop in at the **Washington Beef Company,** 573 Ninth Ave., between 41st and 42nd streets (tel. 563-0200), whose very reasonably priced beef, pork, poultry, lamb, and other meats draw New York's most knowledgeable shoppers.

Open on Tuesday, Wednesday, and Saturday from 7 a.m. to 5:30 p.m., until 6:30 p.m. on Thursday and Friday.

The block between 39th and 40th Streets is where you'll find fresh fruit and spices. At **International Groceries and Meat Market,** 529 Ninth Ave. (tel. 279-5514), boxes of imported spices line the sidewalk, and inside are row upon row of burlap sacks filled with more spices (over 50 kinds in all), beans, and grains. You'll also find Middle Eastern and European delicacies here—everything from stuffed grape leaves to Spanish saffron. They also have a wide selection of olive oils and cheeses, a wide variety of dried fruits and nuts, plus freshly made pasta and Greek feta cheese, as well as fresh pita bread daily.

Open from 8 a.m. to 6 p.m. Monday through Saturday.

Hungry by now? Stop in at **Manganaro's,** 492 Ninth Ave., between 37th and 38th streets (tel. 947-7325), and order a "mile-high special," heaping big portions of meat and cheese: prosciutto, salami, mortadella (Italian baloney), capicola (cold shoulder loin of pork), cooked salami, provolone, fried peppers, tomato, lettuce, and spices. If you simply want to rest your feet and have some dessert, this is a good place to get delicious cappuccino, espresso, cheesecake, cannoli, and the like. Next door at 488 Ninth Ave. (tel. 563-5331) is its retail store, where you can buy the ingredients for the sandwich just described. Great cheeses and salamis are suspended from the ceiling, along with giant bags of Italian candy and pasta.

The restaurant is open Monday through Saturday from 6:30 a.m. to 7:30 p.m.; store hours are 8 a.m. to 7 p.m. on Monday and Saturday, to 8 p.m. Tuesday through Friday. More about Manganaro's in Chapter II.

# VIII

# NEW YORK WITH CHILDREN: BUDGET TIPS

**1. CULTURAL AND EDUCATIONAL ATTRACTIONS**

**2. RECREATION**

**3. ENTERTAINMENT**

**4. SHOPS FOR CHILDREN**

**5. SERVICES FOR CHILDREN**

**6. EATING OUT WITH CHILDREN**

**7. MAPPING OUT YOUR DAYS**

With its skyscrapers and busy streets, New York is a nonstop carnival for children. There's an endless list of activities for young people here, and chances are that small feet will grow tired long before you exhaust the full range of things to do.

We have listed activities that can be enjoyed with little or no expense. There are seven sections in this chapter: cultural and educational attractions, recreation, entertainment, shops, services, restaurants, and touring. Although the programs we've listed are for kids, adults may enjoy them too.

---

### Prentice Hall Travel and the Big Apple

Prentice Hall Travel has a guidebook on New York for virtually every kind of traveler—the business traveler, the casual tourist, travelers with children, budget travelers, students, the traveler with expensive tastes, travelers who are interested in cultural and architectural history.

Look for Prentice Hall Travel books in bookstores or write c/o 15 Columbus Circle, New York 10023. The different series names are: Access, American Express, Baedeker, the Economist, Frommer, Frommer Touring Guides, Gault Millau, Insight, Mobil Travel Guides, and the Real Guides.

---

# 1. Cultural and Educational Attractions

## MUSEUMS FOR CHILDREN

Although New York is home to some of the most sophisticated museums in the adult world (as described in Chapter III), the city has been generous in its efforts to provide museum activities that are of interest to young people. Exhibits and special programs for children cover a wide range of interests, and most are either free of charge or require a nominal contribution.

### From Tyrannosaurus Rex to Star Wars

Most native New Yorkers have fond childhood memories of the **American Museum of Natural History,** Central Park West at 79th Street (tel. 769-5100). This huge museum is a budding scientist's gold mine, featuring exhibits on animals, plants, humans, and the evolution of life as we know it. The dinosaur room, filled with huge skeletons of our prehistoric predecessors, is one of the museum's most popular exhibits. Visit the People Center, which offers lectures, poetry readings, and educational activities for children of all ages in the fall and spring. Other highlights are the Natural Science Center and the Discovery Room, which give kids a chance to learn about plants, animals, and geology of New York City. And don't miss the popular science films that are shown in the Naturemax Film Theater—the screen is four stories tall and projects images which have proven to be a delight for both children and adults alike. Naturemax tickets are $4 per adult; $2 for children ($6 and $3 for double features).

There's enough in this museum to fill several afternoons, so plan your hours carefully. It's worth a call to find out the schedule of activities. Open daily from 10 a.m. to 5:45 p.m., and until 9 p.m. on Wednesday, Friday, and Saturday evenings. Admission is pay-what-you-wish, with suggested fees of $4 for adults, $2 for children. On Friday and Saturday evenings admission is free.

For a dramatic journey in time and space, travel right next door to the **Hayden Planetarium,** Central Park West and 81st Street (tel. 769-5920). For more than 50 years the planetarium has been taking viewers of all ages out of this world with glittering sky shows on its huge domed ceiling. There's also a 14-ton meteorite, an exhibit exclusively devoted to the sun, and scales where you can find out what you would weigh on different planets (for show times, call 769-5920). Due to popular demand, the Planetarium has begun Saturday programs featuring shows especially for children under 10. Parents should call for show times and schedules.

Open daily except Thanksgiving and Christmas. Admission is $3.75 for adults, $2.75 for students and senior citizens with ID cards, and $2 for children. On Friday and Saturday nights the Planetarium presents Laser Rock Shows at 7, 8:30, and 10 p.m. (Cost: $6 per show.) Dazzling laser visuals dance to contemporary rock sounds. Call 769-5921 for current program.

One block to the south, children over 10 may find much that's interesting at the **New-York Historical Society,** 170 Central Park West, at 77th Street (tel. 873-3400). The fine collections here include Early American tin and cast-iron toys, Tiffany lamps, and although the entire collection is not always on view, the complete set of John James Audubon's *Birds of America* original watercolors.

Open Tuesday through Sunday from 10 a.m. to 5 p.m.; closed Monday. Admission is $2 for adults, $1.50 for senior citizens, and $1 for children under 12. Tuesday, pay as you wish.

### Museum Mile

Just across Central Park is the queen of Fifth Avenue's "Museum Mile" and one of the world's greatest museums—the **Metropolitan Museum of Art,** Fifth Avenue at 82nd Street (tel. 553-7710). To the eye-opening delight of children, there are displays of mummies, knights in armor, a real Egyptian temple, and some of the world's most famous paintings—all complemented by the beauty of the building itself and the Central Park backdrop. What's more, some of New York's finest street performers use the sidewalk in front of the museum as their stage.

Throughout the year the Met's Uris Center for Education offers family- and child-oriented workshops, gallery talks, discussions, and films. The events are usually an hour long and are presented on Tuesday evenings and weekends January through June, and weekdays only in July and August. Places are given on a first-come, first-served basis, and are free with museum admission. All materials are provided. Also, since family-program schedules vary, we suggest that you call ahead for details (tel. 535-7710; ask for Educational Services, ext. 3308).

The Met is open on Tuesday from 9:30 a.m. to 8:45 p.m. and Wednesday through Sunday from 9:30 a.m. to 5:15 p.m.; closed Monday. Suggested admission fees (which include workshops) are $5 for adults, $2.50 for students and senior citizens. Children under 12 are admitted free when accompanied by an adult.

To give your children a glimpse of New York City before the invasion of sky-scrapers and high-rise apartments, visit the **Museum of the City of New York,** Fifth Avenue at 103rd Street (tel. 534-1672), where slide shows, dioramas, and other exhibits trace the city's history from its founding as a Dutch colony in 1625. While older children may find the historical information here interesting, younger children can take a look at the museum's wonderful doll and dollhouse collection, which is the largest of its kind in the city. Displays of old fire engines, maps, and toys will also appeal to youngsters.

Open Tuesday through Saturday from 10 a.m. to 5 p.m., on Sunday and holidays from 1 to 5 p.m. Admission is $3 for adults, $1.50 for students and senior citizens, and $1 for children.

Although the **Guggenheim Museum,** Fifth Avenue at 89th Street (tel. 860-1300), doesn't have special children's programs, it is housed in a spectacular spiral building designed by the architect Frank Lloyd Wright. Visitors generally take the elevator to the top floor, then walk downhill in wide circles, viewing artworks along the curved walls. While parents view the museum's collection of avant-garde art dating back to the late 19th century, kids can get a kick out of the building's playful design.

Open on Tuesday from 11 a.m. to 8 p.m. and Wednesday through Sunday from 11 a.m. to 5 p.m.; closed Monday. Admission is free on Tuesday evening from 5 to 8 p.m.; other times, $4 for adults, $2.25 for students and seniors with ID cards, and free for children under 7. No strollers are allowed on the ramp, but there is a place to check them. *Note:* The museum will be closed sometime during 1990–1991 in order to expand and restore its facilities. Visitors should call for information.

The **Cooper-Hewitt Museum,** 2 E. 91st St., at Fifth Avenue (tel. 860-6868), is a must visit for aspiring designers and artists. As the Smithsonian Institution's National Museum of Design, it has an immense collection of historical and modern objects and designs from all over the world. While the permanent collection is not on view, the changing exhibits focus on various aspects of design, from hair styles to skyscrapers.

Open on Tuesday from 10 a.m. to 9 p.m., Wednesday through Saturday from 10 a.m. to 5 p.m., and on Sunday from noon to 5 p.m. Admission is free on Tuesday night from 5 to 9 p.m.; otherwise it's $3 for adults, $1.50 for senior citizens and students and free for children under 12.

The **Museum of Modern Art,** 11 W. 53rd St., between Fifth and Sixth avenues (tel. 708-9500), concentrates its educational efforts on classroom and school group activities, but this beautiful museum has plenty of powerfully communicative art children can appreciate. Monet's *Water Lilies,* Chagall's *I in the Village,* Calder's *Mobile,* Jackson Pollock's *No. 1,* and Picasso's *Goat* (in the sculpture garden) are just a few of the works popular with children.

Open Friday through Tuesday from 11 a.m. to 6 p.m., and until 9 p.m. on

Thursday; closed Wednesday. Admission is $6 for adults, $3.50 for students, $3 for senior citizens, free for children under 16 accompanied by an adult. Thursday from 5 to 9 p.m., pay as you wish.

**El Museo del Barrio,** 1230 Fifth Ave., at 104th Street (tel. 831-7272), records the vivid culture of Puerto Rico and Latin America through sculpture, paintings, graphics, and photography. For children interested in learning more about a vibrant but little-known culture shared by more than five million U.S. citizens, this museum is a must.

Open Wednesday through Sunday from 11 a.m. to 5 p.m.; closed Monday and Tuesday. Suggested contributions are $2 for adults, $1 for students and senior citizens; children under 12 are admitted free.

The **Jewish Museum,** 1109 Fifth Ave., at 92nd Street (tel. 860-1888), houses the world's largest collection of Jewish ceremonial art and historical objects and also presents exhibitions of 20th-century art. The museum offers some special family programs, usually for children 5 to 12, which focus on current exhibitions or upcoming Jewish holidays. Advance reservations are required, so call ahead to the education department (tel. 860-1863) for schedules and reservations.

Open on Monday, Wednesday, and Thursday from noon to 5 p.m., on Sunday from 11 a.m. to 6 p.m., and on Tuesday from noon to 8 p.m.; closed Friday, Saturday, and major Jewish holidays. Admission is $4 for adults, and $2 for senior citizens, students, and children. On Tuesday from 5 to 8 p.m. admission is free.

## Especially for Kids

The **Children's Museum of Manhattan,** at 314 W. 54th St., near Eighth Avenue (tel. 765-5904), is the borough's only participatory museum for children. This is a strictly hands-on place, where children have fun and learn by doing. The museum has permanent exhibitions in nature, science, and art as well as a changing major exhibition.

Open Tuesday through Friday from 1 to 5 p.m., and on Saturday and Sunday from 10 a.m. to 5 p.m. Admission on weekdays is $1 for adults, $2 for children; on weekends and holidays, $2 for adults, $3 for children.

The **Brooklyn Museum,** at Eastern Parkway and Washington Avenue, Brooklyn (tel. 718/638-5000), offers year-round weekend workshops and activities for children and families. "Arty Facts," for children 4 to 12 accompanied by an adult, takes place on Saturday. This workshop's main focus is to get kids involved with the creation of art. All materials are provided free of charge. If you would like your child to learn more about the museum's exhibits while you go off on your own, inquire about the new program called "What's Up?" for children ages 6 to 12. Each Saturday and Sunday the What's Up? group goes through certain galleries of the museum and discusses various aspects and bits of history about art. Both of these programs are free with museum admission. Call for information.

Open Wednesday through Monday from 10 a.m. to 5 p.m.; closed Tuesday. Suggested contribution is $3 for adults, $1.50 for students, and $1 for seniors; free to children under 12.

---

### How *Do* They Grow?

To teach urban youngsters how plants grow in the wild or on farms, the Brooklyn Botanic Garden has opened the **Chase Manhattan Discovery Center.** The center has exhibits, games, and self-guided demonstrations. Among the exhibits is a walk-through model of an oak tree with stuffed squirrels, chipmunks, owls, rabbits nestling in its trunk. The tiny doors in the bark reveal insects and acorns, and the leaves change with the seasons.

Other exhibits include letting children grind wheat into flour; a picture game which gives children a chance to move various vegetables around a supermarket—

into the produce section and then onto the shelves. Helping children learn the relationship between plants and food: tomatoes to ketchup; celery to cream of celery soup; corn to microwave popcorn is one of the main goals of this program.

The center is at 1000 Washington Ave., off Eastern Parkway in the Prospect Heights section of Brooklyn. Admission is free. Open Tuesday through Friday, 10 a.m. to 4 p.m.; Saturday and Sunday from 11 a.m. to 4 p.m. Call the Brooklyn Botanic Garden (tel. 718/622-4433) for more information.

Kids and parents alike will have a ball at the **Brooklyn Children's Museum,** 145 Brooklyn Ave., at St. Mark's Avenue, in the Crown Heights section of Brooklyn (tel. 718/735-4400). The museum—the first and oldest of its kind in the world—is housed in a remarkable $5-million multitiered structure and is a playground of participatory fun. Children enter by crossing a steel-mesh bridge and popping through the museum's entrance, an old-fashioned trolley-car kiosk. Inside they find themselves skittering down the People's Tube—a huge, simulated river with locks, dams, waterwheels, and a turbine that can be worked to make the water level rise or fall. The museum has a greenhouse, where children mix soil and gather seeds to grind into flour in a gristmill. On the more traditional side, the museum rotates exhibits from its collection of more than 20,000 artifacts from ancient China, Egypt, Europe, and Colonial America, along with a collection of more than 2,500 rare dolls. New to the museum is the Early Learners Arena, a section of activities for children under 5. In addition, the museum offers a number of daily workshops, classes, and films for children; call to find out daily and weekly schedules.

Open on Monday and Wednesday through Friday from 2 to 5 p.m., and on Saturday, Sunday, and all New York Public School holidays from 10 a.m. to 5 p.m.; closed Tuesday. Suggested admission is $2 per person.

To get there by subway, take the IRT–Seventh Avenue no. 3 ("New Lots" ) train or the IRT–Lexington Avenue no. 4 train to the Kingston Avenue station. Walk one block west to Brooklyn Avenue and then six short blocks up to Kingston Avenue and St. Mark's Avenue (you'll see Brower Park on the corner).

The **Staten Island Children's Museum** fits snugly in its new home in the Snug Harbor Cultural Center, 1000 Richmond Terrace (tel. 718/448-6557). The museum occupies a four-story building and offers exhibitions based on themes from the arts, sciences, and humanities; workshops for young children; theater performances; and an activity center, where children can be found learning anything from basket weaving with straws to printmaking on egg cartons. If you happen to be visiting in the spring, don't miss the famed Meadowfair, Snug Harbor's annual spring arts fair.

The museum is open Wednesday through Friday from 1 a.m. to 4 p.m., and on Saturday and Sunday from 11 a.m. to 5 p.m.; closed Monday and Tuesday. Admission is $2 per visitor. Reservations are required for all workshops and can be made by simply calling the museum. Take the ferry and a free ride on a motorized trolley to get there.

Kids will also love the **New York Hall of Science,** 48th Avenue and 111th Street, in the Flushing Meadows section of *Queens* (tel. 718/699-0675). The museum features hands-on science/technology exhibitions and demonstrations, a planetarium, and an amateur radio station.

The museum is open Wednesday through Sunday from 10 a.m. to 5 p.m. Admission is $2.50 for adults and $1.50 for children under 18 and senior citizens. On Wednesday and Thursday from 2 to 5 p.m. admission is free. To get there by subway, take the IRT–Flushing no. 7 train to the 111th Street–Roosevelt Avenue station. Then walk four blocks south to the museum.

## Ahoy Matey!

New York's still-thriving harbors are celebrated at the **South Street Seaport,** located along Fulton and Water streets at Piers 15 and 16 in lower Manhattan (tel.

732-7678). Recently restored and expanded, the Seaport is filled with exhibits, galleries, antique ships, seafood markets, food concessions, and 150 restaurants and shops. It's a great place to take a stroll, or get a cool drink, sit on the outdoor terrace, and view the majestic Brooklyn Bridge up close. The **South Street Seaport Museum,** 207 Front St. (tel. 669-9416), offers maritime exhibits and films, in addition to a number of family activities and children's workshops which deal mainly with the early social history of New York's maritime district. Some past exhibits displayed artifacts resulting from archeological digs under Wall Street, and an extensive exhibition of antique and reconstructed model ships. The museum's Children's Center, open year round, offers weekend activities, hands-on workshops, mock archeological digs, arts and crafts, and 19th-century games. Each activity is coordinated with subjects in the main gallery. All materials are provided. The museum's admission price is $5 for adults, $4 for senior citizens, $3 for students with valid ID, and $2 for children ages 4 to 12.

The museum also coordinates tours of the antique ships, docked at the Seaport (30 to 45 minutes), and walking tours of the Seaport's backstreet area (50 minutes). Both explain the history of the area's focus on commerce in the 1800s. Each tour is included in the price of the museum admission. For a combination charge, museum visitors can also experience life on the water in a replicated 1800s paddlewheeler. The boat ride runs from April through October and travels for 90 minutes around lower Manhattan and out to the Statue of Liberty (the boat does not dock at the statue). During April the boat usually runs only on weekends; from mid-May through October the boat runs on weekdays and weekends at noon, 2 p.m., and 4 p.m. Those who are interested in taking only the boat ride can do so. Prices are $12 for adults, and $8 for students, children, and senior citizens.

Separate from the museum, but around the corner, is the fabulous **Seaport Experience,** 210 Front St., on the corner of Beekman Street in the heart of the Seaport (tel. 608-7888). This multiscreen spectacular deals with the history of the 11-square-block area called the South Street Seaport. Viewers will be surrounded by fog, sea spray, sky rockets, cascades of fireworks, and ships ablaze. It is a must for anyone with a flair for the dramatic and children will love it (just don't forget to bring your raincoat!).

March 18 through January 1, shows run every hour, Monday through Thursday from 10:30 a.m. to 3:30 p.m., and on Friday, Saturday, and Sunday from 10:30 a.m. to 6:30 p.m. Admission is $4.75 for adults, $3.25 for children under 12, and $4 for senior citizens.

To get to the Seaport, take the IRT–Seventh Avenue express (no. 2 or 3) train or the IRT–Lexington Avenue express (no. 4 or 5) train to Fulton Street; walk east toward the water.

The *Intrepid* **Sea-Air-Space Museum,** on the Hudson River at the foot of West 46th Street and Twelfth Avenue, at Pier 86 (tel. 245-2533), is a fascinating museum of technology housed on an old aircraft carrier. There are four theme halls —each devoted to a particular aspect of our country's recent achievements on the seas, in the air, and beyond. Each hall offers a related film.

Admission is $4.75 for adults, $2.50 for children under 12, and $4 for senior citizens. Open Wednesday through Sunday from 10 a.m. to 5 p.m.

## Howdy Doody

The more than 25,000 videotapes and radio shows at the **Museum of Broadcasting,** 1 E. 53rd St., just off Fifth Avenue (tel. 752-7684), show younger generations that, yes, there was life before rock videos. Visitors can select tapes from the museum's holdings, and view them at individual consoles on a first-come, first-served basis. Why not pick out a few of your own favorite kids' shows—"Howdy Doody" and "Kukla, Fran, and Ollie" are all here—or let your kids choose reruns of their own favorites?

Open Wednesday through Saturday from noon to 5 p.m., on Tuesday to 8 p.m.; closed Sunday and Monday. Suggested donations are $4 for adults, $3 for students, and $2 for senior citizens and children under 13.

## A Special Easter Egg Hunt

Children don't have to hunt far for the world's largest collection of Fabergé Imperial Easter Eggs. The **Forbes Galleries,** located at 62 Fifth Ave., at 12th Street (tel. 620-2389), offer a permanent exhibit of these masterpieces. Also sure to delight children are the toy boats, toy soldiers, and trophies on display there.

The galleries are open to the public on Tuesday, Wednesday, Friday, and Saturday from 10 a.m. to 4 p.m. Admission is free.

## 3–D

Children and adults will enjoy being confounded at the **Museum of Holography,** 11 Mercer St., in SoHo, half a block north of Canal Street and one block west of Broadway (tel. 925-0581), where 3-D images seem to be alive and kicking in their own complete worlds. This museum features extensive educational displays, including a selection of the earliest and state-of-the-art holograms.

Admission is $3.50 for adults, $2.50 for students and senior citizens, and $2 for children under 12. Open Tuesday through Sunday from 11 a.m. to 6 p.m. (on Wednesday from 10:30 a.m.); closed Monday.

## First Aid for Dolls

The **New York Doll Hospital,** 787 Lexington Ave., between 61st and 62nd streets (tel. 838-7527), is the place to bring grandmother's wax doll for a facelift, or your injured Cabbage Patch kid for a specialist's care. The Doll Hospital began almost 90 years ago as a concession to a hairdressing salon—children could get their doll's hair done just like their mother's. Although there aren't any ambulances here, you're welcome to observe any of the "operations" and view the collections of bisque, foreign, and celebrity dolls. To get there, ring the bell at the sidewalk door and then go up one flight of crooked old stairs after you're buzzed in.

Open Monday through Saturday from 10 a.m. to 6 p.m.

## The Birth of America

A visit two centuries into the nation's past is the subject of the **Federal Hall National Memorial,** at the corner of Wall and Nassau streets in lower Manhattan (tel. 264-8711). The memorial, administered by the National Park Service, is housed in an 1842 building on the site where the Declaration of Independence was read in July of 1776, where the first Congress met to count the electoral votes of the first presidential election, and where George Washington was inaugurated in 1789 as the nation's first president. Anyone who is interested in this country's past will appreciate the museum's extended and temporary exhibits displaying art, architectural models, dioramas of the first inauguration, an eight-minute video on the history of the site, and a newly installed, hands-on computer exhibition called "A Celebration of the 200th Anniversary of the Constitution." The memorial itself is self-guiding; therefore children can explore as they wish. In addition, each Wednesday, year round, concerts are performed at 12:30 p.m. in the memorial's rotunda; admission is free.

Open Monday through Friday from 9 a.m. to 5 p.m. Admission is free. The memorial also has a bookstore which is open from 10 a.m. to 4:30 p.m.

## America's Greatest Tinkerer

Most children will enjoy an entire museum devoted to one of America's best-known homespun geniuses, inventor Thomas Edison. The **Con Edison Energy Museum,** 145 E. 14th St., just west of Third Avenue (tel. 460-6244), focuses on the development of electricity, from Edison's invention of the electric lightbulb to the present, and includes some hands-on exhibits.

Open Tuesday through Saturday from 10 a.m. to 4 p.m. Admission is free.

## Fire Engines

Nearly two centuries of fire-fighting history are stored away at the **Fire Department Museum,** 278 Spring St., between Hudson and Varick streets (tel. 691-1303). The oldest engine here dates back to 1820 and was hand-pulled by a team of volunteer firemen to the scene of a New York fire. Also on display are leather fire hoses, steam engines, Brooklyn's first fire bell, and pictures and drawings (including a Currier and Ives) of famous fires. There's even a stuffed dog named Chief, who earned his stripes by saving kittens from burning buildings.

Open Tuesday through Saturday from 10 a.m. to 4 p.m.; closed Sunday, Monday, and holidays. Donation suggested.

## New York's Finest

If anyone in your family is interested in the men and women in blue, try a visit to the **Police Academy Museum,** 235 E. 20th St., between Second and Third avenues (tel. 477-9753). This museum boasts one of the world's largest collections of police memorabilia—from weapons to handcuffs—plus exhibits on current police procedures and uniforms.

Open Monday through Friday from 9 a.m. to 3 p.m. (but call to make sure). Admission is free.

## The Hidden Wonders of Harlem and Washington Heights

Many guidebooks—and even natives—give the impression that sightseeing in northern Manhattan stops with the Upper West Side. This is an unfortunate misapprehension, and we would like to set the record straight! Manhattan continues to fascinate . . . even beyond 200th Street.

But before proceeding, it is wise to note that while this area is not dangerous if explored wisely, Harlem, more than anywhere else in Manhattan, demands street-smarts. Unless you are traveling with someone who lives in or is familiar with the neighborhood, visit during the day. You can map out the stops you want to make and take the most direct routes via several public transportation lines. MTA buses go uptown on Broadway and on Riverside Drive; the IRT and IND subway lines also serve the area. Consult subway and bus maps or call MTA route information (tel. 718/330-1234) for specifics. There are many organized tours that go through Harlem; for information, call the Uptown Chamber of Commerce (tel. 427-7200).

Visitors can view the country's largest collection of Black fashion design and memorabilia at the **Black Fashion Museum,** 126th Street between Lenox Avenue and Adam Clayton Powell, Jr., Boulevard (tel. 666-1320). The oldest pieces date from the late 1600s and the more recent from such Broadway plays as *The Wiz* and *Bubblin' Brown Sugar.*

Open by appointment only. Admission is free, but donations are accepted.

The **Studio Museum in Harlem,** 144 W. 125th St., between Lenox and Seventh avenues (tel. 864-4500), is an elegant museum dedicated to Black American culture and Harlem's vibrant local art. Programs for children—for example, weekend classes in batik, collage, silkscreening, and African masks—are offered throughout the year. Other frequently scheduled events include films and puppet shows about events in Black American history (for example, Rosa Parks and the bus boycott), and concerts, lectures, and readings by nationally known artists and scholars.

Museum hours are 10 a.m. to 5 p.m. on Wednesday, Thursday, and Friday, and 1 to 6 p.m. on Saturday and Sunday. Admission is $2 for adults; $1 for children under 12, students and seniors. Activities may cost extra; call for more information.

Once upon a time there lived a woman who saved so many toys and dolls in her lovely Harlem brownstone that she could hardly find room for them. Her name was —and is—Aunt Len, and you can meet her at **Aunt Len's Doll and Toy Museum,** located on one of Harlem's most historic blocks between 141st and 142nd streets

330 NEW YORK WITH CHILDREN: BUDGET TIPS

and Hamilton Terrace (look for the wooden sign near the corner) (tel. 281-4143). This is a very personal collection of more than 5,000 dolls and 100,000 assorted toys and trinkets; it includes antique Black dolls from all over the world, an American revival choir, Shirley Temple dolls, life-size English dolls sitting down to a tea party, and a Michael Jackson doll. Aunt Len (her real name is Mrs. Lenon H. Hoyte) gives classes in dollcraft to local children and is the inspiration behind a yearly doll pageant in Harlem.

Open by appointment only; donation suggested.

For a glimpse of America's indigenous past, visit the **Museum of the American Indian–Heye Foundation,** Broadway at 155th Street (tel. 283-2420). The museum is filled with artifacts from tribes as far north as the Arctic and as far south as Tierra del Fuego. There are masks, games, tomahawks, and the personal possessions of such famous chiefs as Red Cloud, Sitting Bull, Crazy Horse, and Arapoosh.

Admission is $3 for adults, $2 for students and senior citizens, and free to children under 7. Hours are Tuesday through Saturday from 10 a.m. to 5 p.m. and on Sunday from 1 to 5 p.m. This is the museum that's generated all the talk about moving elsewhere, so call first before making a special visit up to Harlem to see it.

Two other museums in the complex may be of special interest to older children: The **Hispanic Society of America** (tel. 690-0743), has a small yet lively collection of paintings by El Greco, Velázquez, Goya, and other Hispanic artists. With its terracotta floors and high ceilings, the building replicates a small Spanish villa. Walk through the Sorrolla Room, where there is a vivid series of murals painted by Joaquin Sorrolla y Bastida in 1911; the walls burst with scenes of fiesta life in regional Spain.

Admission is free but a donation is appreciated. Open Tuesday through Saturday from 10 a.m. to 4:30 p.m. and on Sunday from 1 to 4 p.m.

Coin collectors will appreciate the **American Numismatic Society,** at Broadway and 155th Street (tel. 234-3130). It features "The World of Coins," a comprehensive exhibit surveying the history of the world's coinage and paper money. Kids will delight in seeing coins made of salt, shells, and beads—and in learning how and why money has made "the world go round" for millennia. There's a computer on hand to provide detailed information on any coin or object in the show.

The exhibition room and library are open Tuesday through Saturday from 9 a.m. to 4:30 p.m., on Sunday the exhibition room only is open, from 1 to 4 p.m. Admission is free.

**The Cloisters** offer a welcome respite from the hustle and bustle of midtown Manhattan. Located in Fort Tryon Park in the Washington Heights section of Manhattan, this uptown branch of the Metropolitan Museum resembles a medieval monastery in location and appearance. The park itself is the perfect place for a family picnic.

Museum hours are Tuesday through Sunday from 9:30 a.m. to 5:15 p.m. Suggested admission is $5 for adults, $2.50 for students and senior citizens, and free to children under 12 accompanied by an adult. To get there by subway, take the IND–Eighth Avenue A train to 190th Street–Overlook Terrace. Then take the no. 4 bus or walk through Fort Tryon Park to the museum. By bus, take the Madison Avenue no. 4 to the Fort Tryon Park–The Cloisters stop.

## OTHER EDUCATIONAL ATTRACTIONS

In addition to the better-known museums, there are smaller, offbeat sights that will appeal to children as well.

### Banking

For a glimpse of the world of finance, young entrepreneurs should visit the **Federal Reserve Bank,** 33 Liberty St., between Nassau and William streets in lower Manhattan (tel. 720-6130). The tour here includes a visit to the gold vault, the currency-processing department, and an exhibit hall that explains the Federal Reserve's role in the economy.

Tours are given by reservation only—Monday through Friday at 10 a.m., 11 a.m., 1 p.m., and 2 p.m.—and must be made at least one week in advance by phone or by mail. To assure yourself a spot, we advise that you call two weeks ahead.

## The World's Largest Post Office

Kids 14 and older can see the U.S. mail at work in the huge **James A. Farley Post Office** at Eighth Avenue and 33rd Street (across from Penn Station), but you must make arrangements at least two weeks in advance. Write to the Communications Department, Room 3023, James A. Farley Building, New York, NY 10199–9461 (tel. 330-3604). Tours of nonmechanized facilities also are available for younger children. The post office will send you a letter confirming your reservation —be sure to bring it on the day of the tour. Tours take about 45 minutes. The Farley Building is one of the nicer buildings in the city—the two-block-long lobby has a magnificent ceiling and there aren't any loiterers. Admission is free.

## Around the World

From Australia to Zambia, governments from all over the world have consulates, U.N. missions, tourist bureaus, and information offices scattered around the city. You will come away from any of them with an armload of posters, brochures, and newspapers. Budding linguists can try using a few phrases of elementary French or Spanish, and others can try to decipher a newspaper written in Arabic. To get phone numbers or information, look up the country of your choice in the Manhattan telephone directory. Most offices are open during regular business hours.

## Great Graffiti

You don't have to go to Harlem to see graffiti in New York, but some of the best—and best intentioned—can be found at the **Graffiti Hall of Fame,** a neighborhood-improvement project on the playground walls behind Junior High School No. 13 at 106th Street and Park Avenue. Kids will appreciate the energy, vivid colors, and messages embedded in the designs. Other graffiti art can be seen on 125th Street between Fifth and Seventh avenues. The merchants here hire graffiti and spray-paint artists to decorate the roll-down shutters of their shopfronts. We recommend that you go on Sunday or before the shops open.

Nearby, on buildings at the corners of 104th Street and Lexington Avenue and Frawley Street and Fifth Avenue you will also find impressive murals depicting the life of the area.

## Videos, Computers, and Phones

If your kids like MTV, they'll enjoy directing their own music video at the **AT&T Infoquest Center,** on Madison Avenue at 56th Street (tel. 605-5555). The center has 4 levels and 40 interactive exhibits. Kids can learn about microchips and even help make one, meet Gor-Don the robot, and view phones of the past and future.

Infoquest is open on Tuesday from 10 a.m. to 9 p.m. and from 10 a.m. to 6 p.m. Wednesday through Sunday. Admission is free, but groups of ten or more must make reservations.

## Castle in the Park

See one of the best views of the city from the top of the **Belvedere Castle,** a majestic stone castle in Central Park, at 79th Street just south of the Great Lawn.

Inside is a National Weather Service station. Kids can make puppets and learn about the park through activities like leaf pressing in the participatory Discovery Chamber. Special Saturday workshops in science and art for children ages 5 to 11 run from 1 to 2:30 p.m. All workshops are free. You must make a reservation (tel. 772-0210).

The castle is open from 11 a.m. to 5 p.m. everyday except Monday and Friday, when it opens at 1 p.m.

## ZOOS FOR CHILDREN

If there's anyplace you can take your children and have just as much fun as they do, it's the zoo. New York's **Bronx Zoo,** at Fordham Road and Southern Boulevard, is among the world's finest. It is home and breeding ground for nearly 4,500 wild animals, many of which are endangered species, some even considered extinct in nature. The zoo is lovely as well as interesting, and the perfect place to take yourself and your children for a day away from the city proper.

Aside from the myriad animals in imaginative settings, the Bronx Zoo offers a special children's zoo. Conceived as a "participatory" zoo, it's a place where children can assume the behavior, live in the environments, and even don the body parts (fox's "ears," turtle shells) of wild animals, to find out just what it's like to be an animal. There's a prairie dog tunnel that is child-size and a giant rope spiderweb for climbing.

Also not to be missed is the camel ride ($1) (closed during winter), and a monorail ride ($1.50 for adults, $1 for children) through Wild Asia, where tigers, rhinos, and wild Asian deer roam relatively unconfined in a 38-acre area designed to simulate their natural environment. The zoo's most ambitious project is Jungle World, a one-acre wood- and glass-enclosed habitat in which animals wander more or less freely through a re-created volcanic scrub forest, a mangrove swamp, a low-land evergreen rain forest, and a mountain rain forest.

The zoo is open Monday through Saturday from 10 a.m. to 5 p.m. and until 5:30 p.m. on Sunday and holidays. Admission is free on Tuesday, Wednesday, and Thursday (rides and special exhibits have separate charges); other days, admission is $3.75 for adults and $1.50 for children above 2. To reach the zoo by subway, take the IRT–Seventh Avenue no. 2 express train to Pelham Parkway, or the IRT–Lexington Avenue no. 5 train to East 180th Street and transfer to the IRT–Seventh Avenue no. 2. From Pelham Parkway, walk west to the Bronxdale entrance to the zoo. Express bus service is available from mid-Manhattan; the fare is $3.50 (exact fare required). Call 652-8400 for schedule and stops.

At Central Park's **Lehman's Childrens Zoo,** off East 66th Street and Fifth Avenue (tel. 408-0271), a 10¢ admission brings children and adults into a fantasyland featuring a miniature bridge, a red barn, Noah's Ark, and a sculpted gray whale. The zoo's inhabitants are winsome ducks, rabbits, cows, and goats, plus more exotic critters like ferrets and African Pigmy goats.

Open daily from 10 a.m. to 4:30 p.m. Call the above number or park information (tel. 360-8111) for special events.

Also in Central Park, there's the **Carousel Ride,** a nice stroll in from either side of 65th Street. A ride on one of the gaily painted horses is 75¢. And if your children still want more, rustle them over to the **Alice in Wonderland statue** next to the model boat pond near the East 77th Street entrance to the park, and let them climb to their heart's content.

An internationally renowned collection of reptiles—including most species of U.S. rattlesnake—can be found at the **Staten Island Zoological Park and Children's Zoo,** 614 Broadway, Staten Island (tel. 718/442-3100). The zoo also features a pond, and feedable animals such as goats and sheep.

Open daily from 10 a.m. to 4:45 p.m. Admission is $1, free for senior citizens, disabled people, and kids under 3; on Wednesday, free to all. To get there by car, take the Verrazano Narrows Bridge to the Staten Island Expressway, to the Slosson Avenue exit. Follow Slosson to the zoo parking lot at Clove Road. By bus from the

Staten Island Ferry depot at St. George, take bus 107 to Forest Avenue at Broadway, then walk three blocks up Broadway.

*Note:* Both the **Queens Zoo and Children's Zoo** (tel. 718/699-7239) in Flushing Meadows and the **Brooklyn Zoo** (tel. 718/965-6560) in Prospect Park, including the Children's Farm, are closed for renovations until the early 1990s.

---

# 2. Recreation

---

Children who get cabin fever after a long hotel stay can run off steam in the city's wide range of recreational facilities. Below we've listed some inexpensive options, many of which can be found in Manhattan's Central Park—one of the best running, jumping, walking, ballplaying, ice-skating, roller-skating, theater-going, bicycling, kite-flying, picnicking, horsebackriding, concert-listening, napping, folk-dancing, sailboating, and people-watching spots anywhere.

## BICYCLING

Central Park's roadways are closed to cars on weekends throughout the year so that peddlers can make their way through the park unhindered. Biking hours are 8 p.m. Friday to 6 a.m. Monday. The park is also closed to cars on weekdays from early April to early November, from 10 a.m. to 3 p.m. and 7 to 10 p.m.

Among the shops where bicycles can be rented is **West Side Bicycle Store,** 231 W. 96th St., at Broadway (tel. 663-7531); **Metro Bicycles,** 1311 Lexington Ave., at 88th Street (tel. 427-4450); and **Gene's Bicycles,** 242 E. 79th St., at Second Avenue (tel. 249-9218). The cost for a bike is about $4 an hour for a three-speed and $6.50 for a ten-speed. There is a discount for a full-day rental. All the above businesses require identification and/or a substantial deposit.

## BOATING

There's nothing like a boat ride in Central Park on a sunny afternoon. You can rent rowboats at the **Loeb Boathouse,** on the east side of the 72nd Street lake (tel. 517-4723). Open seven days a week beginning in April (and until the weather becomes prohibitive) from 11:30 a.m. to 6 p.m. daily. A $20 deposit and $6 per hour gets you afloat.

## BOWLING

New York used to have more than 30 bowling lanes but now just a few remain. **Bowlmor Lanes,** 110 University Pl., between 12th and 13th streets (tel. 255-8188), has 44 lanes and is open Sunday through Thursday from 10 a.m. to 1 a.m. and on Friday and Saturday until 4 a.m. A game costs $2.40 and shoe rental is 75¢.

## CHESS

Have a grandmaster in your family? The **Manhattan Chess Club,** on the tenth floor of Carnegie Hall, 154 W. 57th St., at Seventh Avenue (tel. 333-5888), was established in 1870 and is one of the oldest chess clubs in the world. Bobby Fischer, among other chess stars, has played here. Your child can play chess all day for $5. Open daily from 11 a.m. to 10 p.m.

## HORSEBACK RIDING

Eager equestrians can rent horses at the **Claremont Riding Academy,** 175 W. 89th St., between Columbus and Amsterdam avenues, from 8 a.m. to 10 p.m. on weekends and until dark on weekdays for $27 an hour (no deposit required). Riding lessons and classes at different skill levels are also offered. Private lessons are $30 a half hour; group lessons, $30 an hour. For reservations and information, call 724-5101.

## ICE SKATING

The **Lasker Memorial Skating Rink,** at 107th Street in Central Park, at the 110th Street entrance opposite Lenox Avenue (tel. 397-3106), is an outdoor rink that doubles as a swimming pool in the summer. The winter season is from mid-November through early March. Admission is $1 for children, $2 for adults on weekdays; $2.50 for skate rental. Open Sunday and Tuesday through Thursday from 11 a.m. to 9:30 p.m., on Monday until 5 p.m., and on Friday and Saturday until 11 p.m.

The newly renovated **Wollman Rink,** at 63rd Street and East Drive in Central Park (tel. 517-4800), is open from November through early April, seven days a week. Admission is $5 for adults and $2 for children, plus $2.50 for skate rental. Call for hours.

For indoor skating year round, visit the **SkyRink,** on the 16th floor of 450 W. 33rd St., between Ninth and Tenth avenues (tel. 695-6556). The rink has afternoon and evening sessions for children and adults; call for the exact schedule. Admission is $7 for evening sessions, $6.50 for afternoon sessions. Skates can be rented for $2.50 a pair.

## KITE FLYING

The best place in Central Park to fly kites is in the **Sheep Meadow,** opposite the West 67th Street entrance to the park (also a good place to spread a blanket and relax).

For an unusual kite, try **Big City Kite Company,** at 1201 Lexington Ave., between 81st and 82nd streets (tel. 472-2623). It is open Monday through Saturday from 10 a.m. to 6 p.m. and on Sunday from noon to 5 p.m. Prices start at $3.50 and fly all the way up to $550.

## MODEL BOAT SAILING

**Conservatory Lake,** in Central Park at 72nd Street and Fifth Avenue, is the place to launch your model boat. You'll see some serious sailors and sailboats here, and as many adults as children. Races are held every Saturday beginning March 21 from 10 a.m. on.

## SWIMMING

The city also operates several swimming pools, open generally from early July to Labor Day. One favorite is the **John Jay Pool** on East 77th Street, one block east of York Avenue at Cherokee Place (tel. 397-3177). It's open daily from 11 a.m. to 7 p.m. Admission is free, but bring a lock and a towel.

Central Park has its own pool, the **Lasker Memorial Rink** at 107th Street (tel. 397-3106), which hangs up its skates for towels during the summer. Enter from East 110th Street opposite Lenox Avenue. Lasker has an Olympic-size pool (but only about three feet deep) and two wading pools. Admission is free. Open daily from 11 a.m. to 7:30 p.m.

If you're willing to pay to leave the crowds behind, swim at the **Sheraton City Squire Motel,** 790 Seventh Ave., between 51st and 52nd streets (tel. 581-3300). The pool, located on the fifth floor, is open to nonguests Monday through Friday from 6:30 a.m. to 7:45 p.m. and on weekends from 7:30 a.m. to 7:45 p.m. Fees are $14 on weekdays, $20 on weekends; children under 12 are half price. Towels and comfortable locker facilities are included, and you can stay all day if you wish. The pool is moderate-sized, with glass walls on three sides.

## PICNICS

On a warm, sunny day, a picnic is a special delight in the city, and it's as easy as picking up sandwiches and spreading a blanket. Central Park, of course, is just about the best place to go to stretch out, sunbathe, and let your kids run. In addition to the hot-dog vendors and orange-juice squeezers on most streetcorners, there are summertime kiosks at the **Bethesda Fountain** in Central Park at 72nd Street, where you can buy franks, sausages, drinks, and other snacks. More expensive are the special picnics-to-go that you can pick up at the **Tavern on the Green Restaurant,** 67th Street and Central Park West (tel. 873-3200), and other elegant eateries on the Upper East and West Sides.

On the West Side, you'll find a nice little park for lunch or a rest stop on **West 50th Street** between the Avenue of the Americas and Seventh Avenue, not far from Radio City Music Hall. The park has white patio chairs and tables, a fountain, and bronze life-like sculpture of a teenage boy reading a book on fishing. It's so realistic that you can read about angling over his right shoulder, but don't ask him to share the hamburger he also holds!

Another serene haven in the heart of the city is **Paley Park,** a few steps east of Fifth Avenue on 53rd Street, a tiny oasis about the size of a tennis court. High brick walls on three sides, vaulting honey locust trees, ivy, and pots of begonias shield you from the city's bustle. You can dine alfresco at patio tables, and there's a refreshment stand for light snacks. The park is open from 8 a.m. to 8 p.m. Monday through Saturday.

There are numerous **city-sponsored playgrounds,** but one of the roomiest and most pleasant is on First Avenue between 67th and 68th streets. It has safety swings, mini-theaters, and a log mountain with a giant slide. There's also a toddler area with a smaller slide and sand to play in. There are lots of tall trees and shaded benches. The park closes at dusk.

# 3. Entertainment

## THEATER AND PERFORMANCES

Stage lights and grease paint hold a special thrill for children, and New York theaters put on a wide variety of shows throughout the year that are appropriate for young people of all ages. Many productions are participatory, so your children may get a chance to step into the limelight.

For the most current and complete listings, check the *New York Times,* the *New Yorker, New York* magazine, the *Village Voice,* and *7 DAYS.* Below are a few playhouses and other entertainment establishments that regularly feature children's shows.

Audience participation is part of the charm at the **13th Street Repertory Company,** 50 W. 13th St., between Fifth and Sixth avenues (tel. 675-6677). The company performs two one- to two-hour-long plays with music, *Arlecchino* and *The Rose That Refused to Bloom.* Show times are Saturday and Sunday at 1 and 3 p.m. Admission is $4 for adults and children. Reservations are recommended. If you'd like to hold your child's birthday party here, call ahead and the company will set up a special table (cost: $10; you provide the food and decorations).

The **Little People's Theater,** at the Courtyard Playhouse at 39 Grove St., near Seventh Avenue South (tel. 765-9540), is one of the city's longest-running children's theater groups. From Labor Day till the end of June, it offers *Cinderella* and seven other participatory and comic adaptations of children's classics geared for kids between the ages of 3 and 8. Show times are 1:30 and 3 p.m. on Saturday and Sunday. Admission is $6 for adults and children; reservations are a must.

Other popular attractions include:

The **Market at Citicorp Center,** East 53rd Street at Lexington Avenue (tel. 559-2330), which presents a wide range of entertainment for children on Saturday from 11 a.m. to noon. Free admission. Call for schedule.

**Fourth Wall Theater,** 79 E. 4th St., between Second and Third avenues (tel

254-5060), presents rock-and-roll musicals for kids ages 3 to 13 at 3:30 p.m. on Saturday and Sunday. Admission is $6 for children, $10 for adults. Closed from mid-June through mid-September.

The **Big Apple Circus** is a delightful one-ring circus that performs at Lincoln Center, on Broadway between 62nd and 63rd streets, from October through January, then travels from borough to borough during the spring and summer. Call 391-0760 to check its schedule. Admission prices vary, from $8 to $30.

The **Paper Bag Players** (tel. 362-0431) are a much-praised, award-winning theater group that uses costumes made out of commonplace household items in an hour-long show of madcap musical skits and sketches. They perform on Saturday and Sunday at 2 p.m. from January through early March at Symphony Space, 2537 Broadway, at 95th Street. Admission is $11.

**On Stage Productions,** at the Hartley House, 413 W. 46th St., near Ninth Avenue (tel. 666-1716), offers six plays for family audiences from October to early May. Half the plays are for ages 3 to 12, the rest for ages 12 and up. Most are original musicals. Performances are at 1 and 3:30 p.m. on Saturday and 3:30 p.m. on Sunday. Ticket prices for the productions for ages 3 to 12 are $5. Those for age 12 and older are $8 for adults and $3 for students and seniors.

**Theater Works,** at the Promenade Theatre, at Broadway and 76th Street (tel. 677-5959), has been producing a variety of original, and often topical, plays for children. Offerings such as a musical celebration of the space program, *Footprints on the Moon,* and a musical introduction to Shakespeare, *The Play's the Thing,* have made this company one of the hottest tickets in New York children's theater. The company has performances on Saturday and Sunday at 12:30 p.m. from September through May. Tickets range from $9 to $15.

The **Jan Hus Playhouse,** 351 E. 74th St., between First and Second avenues (tel. 772-9180), presents musical comedies for children age 3 and up. *Jack and His Rock 'N' Roll Beanstalk, Pinocchio,* and *Peter Pan Meets the Wicked Wizard* are a few of the musicals offered from September through April. From April through June, the **Funzapoppin Magic Show** takes over. Performances are on Sunday at 1 and 2:30 p.m. and last about an hour. Tickets are $4.50.

If puppets are your child's passion, a visit to the **Cottage Marionette Theater,** near West 81st Street in Central Park (tel. 988-9093), is just the thing. Established in 1947, the playhouse presents puppet renditions of many children's classics including *Cinderella, The Magic Flute,* and *Rumpelstiltskin.* Admission is $2 and the season runs from October through May.

## OTHER ATTRACTIONS

Fun for children is not limited to the stage. Below are other events and entertainment that kids will enjoy.

### Record Breakers

Located in the concourse of the Empire State Building, which gets honorable mention here as the third-tallest building in the world, the **Guinness World Records Exhibit Hall** (tel. 947-2335) holds great appeal for children. Most of the displays are replicas of record holders, including a statue of the world's tallest man (8 feet 11 inches) and a model of the hand with the longest fingernails (uncut from 1952 to 1987). Admission is $4 for adults, $2.75 for children 11 and under. Open Monday through Thursday from 9 a.m. to 9 p.m., and Friday through Sunday to 10 p.m.

### Boat Excursions

The **Staten Island Ferry** is still the best deal in town, at 25¢ a ride. On a clear day you'll get a full view of the bay, including the Statue of Liberty, Brooklyn, Manhattan, New Jersey, Staten Island, Governor's Island, and the Verrazano-Narrows Bridge. To get to the ferry, take the IRT–Seventh Avenue no. 1 subway all the way to the South Ferry station. The Staten Island Ferry is used by commuters, so it's best to avoid rush hours when you go.

The **Statue of Liberty Ferry** to Liberty Island leaves from Battery Park (tel. 269-5755). It runs every half hour from 9 a.m. to 5 p.m. weekdays, from 8:30 a.m. on weekends. Adult fares are $3.25; children under 12 pay $1.50. The schedule often varies; please call ahead.

The **Circle Line** tour boats sail completely around Manhattan from Pier 83 at the foot of West 43rd Street (tel. 563-3200). The schedule changes, so call ahead for information on these three-hour tours. The pier is located in an area of town that should be approached with caution in the evening. Fares are $15 for adults, $7.50 for children under 12.

## Wild Animals and Amusement Park

If you feel like getting out of the city for a short day trip, you can go on a safari to the wilds of New Jersey at **Great Adventure,** Jackson, N.J. (tel. 201/928-3500). The 500-acre park has lions, bears, and giraffes which run freely in a natural setting. You can drive your own car through the safari route (windows and doors must be locked) or take a guided bus tour. There's also a big amusement park here, with all the expected rides and attractions.

The safari park is open from 9 a.m. to 5 p.m. schedule varies call ahead. A combined ticket for the safari and amusement park is $23 for adults, $15 for children 54 inches and under. Admission to the safari park alone is $9. Children under 3 are admitted free.

Great Adventure is about an hour's drive out of the city. By car, take the Jersey Turnpike to Exit 7A and follow signs to I-95 East. Exit at Mount Holly and turn south onto N.J. 537, which takes you to the park.

## THIS AND THAT ABOUT TOWN

Even traveling around New York can be an exciting visual adventure. Many buildings, especially in SoHo and Greenwich Village, have been decorated with huge murals and designs.

If you're on East 42nd Street, the art deco home of the city's largest-circulation newspaper, the **Daily News Building,** at 220 E. 42nd St., at Second Avenue, is worth a peek. The main lobby, open 24 hours a day, contains a huge globe that turns, and sometimes there's a show of newspaper photographs taken over the years.

One block east, the **Ford Foundation** building, at 320 E. 42nd St., looks like a huge terrarium. A small, fern-lined pool of water keeps the air moist for a jungle of plants. Sometimes, when enough moisture condenses on the glass roof above, there's a "rainstorm" inside the building. The garden is open to the public weekdays from 9 a.m. to 5 p.m.

The **Flatiron Building** is a fine example of how architects have used every available space in the city to create unusual structures. Wedge-shaped to fit into a triangular piece of property at the intersection of Broadway and Fifth Avenue, at 23rd Street, the building got its nickname for its obvious resemblance to the old-fashioned iron.

## Parades, Street Fairs, Festivals, Etc.

Each year New York hosts parades and festivals on a grand scale. The color and hoopla make them great events for kids, so we've sketched out a few time-tested favorites to watch for.

Topping the parade list is the **Macy's Thanksgiving Day Parade,** a must-see pageant of cartoon creatures, decked-out high school bands, mounted horsemen and women, wonderful flower-bedecked mechanical floats, gigantic helium balloons, and marching celebrities. The parade usually begins around 9 a.m. at Central Park West and 72nd Street, and travels down Broadway to Macy's at Herald Square (West 34th Street).

**St. Patrick's Day** (March 17) is the occasion for the granddaddy of all New York's parades. You'll be surprised by how many Irish accents you hear, but then, everyone's a little bit Irish on St. Paddy's Day. Be prepared for the revelry to get pretty wild. The parade travels up Fifth Avenue from 38th to 86th streets.

Chinatown and Little Italy both have raucous celebrations of their own. The **Chinese New Year,** on the first day of the full moon between January 21 and February 19, is ushered in with a dragon parade and fireworks throughout Chinatown (see Chapter II). And right next door to Chinatown is Little Italy, scene of the **Feast of San Gennaro,** in mid-September on Mulberry Street between Spring and Park streets. The feast is like a half-mile-long church fair, with game booths and stalls selling all kinds of Italian food.

Keep in mind that both Chinatown and Little Italy are among the oldest sections of New York, with narrow streets that are usually mobbed by nightfall of the respective celebration days. Those with small children in tow or claustrophobia should come early (in the afternoon, if possible) to beat the thickest crowds. Hang onto your wallets and have fun!

Come Easter, the Parks Department holds its annual **Easter Egg Rolling Contest** in Central Park. Check the newspaper for the time and location (other groups hold egg hunts as well, some free).

**You Gotta Have Park** is another natural classic that Central Park offers kids. For one weekend in mid-May, races, concerts, and games are arranged to support the theme of Central Park as an urban oasis. Throughout the year, call the Parks Department at 360-3444 or 360-1333 for a recording of weekly events.

Staten Island greets ferry riders and other visitors with its annual **Children's Day Fair,** held the first Sunday in June on the museum grounds at 75 Stuyvesant Pl., *Staten Island* (a five-minute walk from the ferry). A mini-zoo and other exhibits help celebrate such themes as "The World According to Puppets."

Readers of all ages shouldn't miss the biggest merchandizing day in the publishing industry, **New York Is Book Country,** featuring the largest concentration of bookstores in the nation. From bookbinding to book signing, authors, entertainers, and lovers of the printed word fill Fifth Avenue between 48th and 57th streets the third Sunday in September from 11 a.m. to 5 p.m.

A good number to call for information on just about anything happening in the city is the New York Visitors and Convention Bureau (tel. 397-8222).

**Christmas** is a special time in New York. The stores and streets are as pretty—and busy—as the songs say. The following stores usually have special windows for the holidays, with mechanized puppets and trains that tell a story or theme. Dress warmly, because chances are you'll have to stand in line. And call first to make sure the windows are up.

**Lord and Taylor,** 425 Fifth Ave., at 38th Street (tel. 391-3344).

**Saks,** 611 Fifth Ave., at 50th Street (tel. 753-4000).

**Macy's,** Broadway at 34th Street (tel. 736-5151).

---

# 4. Shops for Children

Toys are part of what being a kid is all about. A 28-foot animated Clock Tower welcomes you to the World of Toys as you enter **F.A.O. Schwarz,** 767 Fifth Ave., at the corner of 58th Street (tel. 644-9400). The two-story wonderland of toys features a Plush Animal Zoo, Little Madison Avenue, magnificent doll collection, and many other boutiques to delight the young and young-at-heart. The store is open Monday through Saturday from 10 a.m. to 6 p.m. (on Thursday until 8 p.m.), and on Sunday from noon to 5 p.m.

If you really want to do some buying, **Woolworth's** has discounts on Fisher-

Price toys and other brands. One of the chain's largest local branches is at 34th Street and Avenue of the Americas, across from Macy's (tel. 563-3523). It opens at 10 a.m. and stays open until various times throughout the week.

**Alexander's,** Lexington Avenue at 58th Street (tel. 593-0880), also has good buys in toys and other children's things. Open Monday through Saturday from 10 a.m. to 9 p.m., on Sunday from noon to 5 p.m.

**Macy's,** Broadway at 34th Street (tel. 695-4400), has a great, if higher-priced children's section on the fifth and sixth floors. Macy's is open on Monday, Thursday, and Friday from 9:45 a.m. to 8:30 p.m., on Tuesday and Wednesday to 6:45 p.m., on Saturday from 10 a.m. to 6:30 p.m., and on Sunday from 10 a.m. to 6 p.m.

**Polk's Model Craft Hobbies,** in the basement at 314 Fifth Ave., near 32nd Street (tel. 279-9034), has a good selection of kits and models—airplanes, boats, trains, rockets, scientific displays, etc. Don't miss the case of beautiful wooden ships, priced into the thousands. The handcrafted paddleboats, sidewheeler steamers, and clipper ships are lovely to behold. Open from 9:30 a.m. to 5:45 p.m. Monday through Saturday.

**Ace Hobbies, Inc.,** 35 W. 31st Street, between Fifth and Sixth avenues (tel. 268-4151), is the place to go for military and car models from around the world. In the back is a case of painstakingly completed models with magnificent detailing, and a jumbled work area where staffers work on models in their free time. It's a fascinating shop. Open Monday through Friday from 10 a.m. to 5:45 p.m. and on Saturday from 10 a.m. to 4:45 p.m.

**Mary Arnold Toys,** 962 Lexington Ave., between 70th and 71st streets (tel. 744-8510), has a nice selection of toys and classic family games that could be just what a desperate parent needs. Harried hotel-bound parents might also consider story tapes and cassettes, from $7.50 to $12. Open Monday through Friday from 9 a.m. to 6 p.m., on Saturday from 10 a.m. to 5 p.m.

Named after the woeful character in *Winnie the Pooh,* the two **Eeyore's,** 2212 Broadway at 79th Street (tel. 362-0634) and 25 E. 83rd Street, between Madison and Fifth avenues (tel. 988-3404), are bustling centers of activity. In addition to selling children's books for all ages, in at least three foreign languages, the stores sponsor story readings, art contests, and author appearances. The West Side branch is a cozy little place; the newer store on the East Side is attractively laid out, and has a huge stuffed Eeyore in the back for kids who want to cuddle between book browsing. Call or drop by to get a list of the store's activities.

**Pennywhistle Toys** has three locations: at 132 Spring St., between Wooster and Greene streets (tel. 925-2088); 448 Columbus Ave., between 81st and 82nd streets (tel. 873-9090); and at 1283 Madison Ave., at 91st Street (tel. 369-3868). At all three stores you'll be greeted at the door by a bubble-blowing, life-size stuffed bear, and the treats just begin there. There are age-appropriate and educational games, from soap bubbles to speak-aloud spelling games. Prices range from $2.50 into the thousands (for a jungle gym complete with swings, rope ladder, and a large tent for a backyard campout). The SoHo location is open every day from 11 a.m. to 7 p.m. The Upper West Side location is open on Monday from 11 a.m. to 7 p.m., Tuesday through Friday from 10:30 a.m. to 8 p.m., on Saturday from 10 a.m. to 6 p.m., and on Sunday from noon to 6 p.m. The Upper East Side location is open Monday through Friday from 9 a.m. to 8 p.m., on Saturday from 9 a.m. to 6 p.m., and on Sunday from noon to 5 p.m.

While the **Enchanted Forest,** 85 Mercer St., between Spring and Broome streets, in SoHo (tel. 925-6677), celebrates "the spirit of the animals, the old stories, and the child within," it is not exclusively a children's store. Many of the stuffed, carved, and painted animal figures are unique collector's items with price tags up to $1,500. See the *Coyote in Dapper Clothing* upstairs, for instance, and the exquisite *Puss n' Boots.* But the shop does stock plenty of less costly items for children, and it's worth a trip to see the shop's rainbow-colored rooms, waterfall, and tree-house-like second floor. Unusual, one-of-a-kind stuffed animals range in price from $5 to $25, and animal trinkets, notecards, coloring books, and wind-up toys are available from $2 to $10. Fine handmade kaleidoscopes run $10 to $150.

Open daily 11 a.m. to 7 p.m.

If you're after real bargains in kids' clothing, try **Rice & Breskin,** 323 Grand St., at Orchard Street, on the Lower East Side (tel. 925-5515). This store has three floors of just about everything for kids, with all the better-known American brands.

Open Monday through Friday and Sunday, 10 a.m. to 6 p.m.

For clothing that's fun, bordering on silly, visit **Mouse Dynasty,** at 503 Columbus Ave., at 84th Street (tel. 362-2806), which specializes in unique cartoon clothing and accessories.

**Kiddie City,** 35 W. 34th St., between Fifth and Sixth avenues (tel. 629-3070), carries 18,000 name-brand toys, all discounted. It's open Monday through Wednesday from 9:30 a.m. to 7 p.m., on Thursday to 9 p.m., on Friday and Saturday to 7 p.m., and on Sunday from 11 a.m. to 6 p.m.

There's no place like **Books of Wonder,** 132 Seventh Ave., near 18th Street (tel. 989-3270). This is one of the largest children's bookstores in New York, and it prides itself on carrying every book written about the Wizard of Oz. You can also visit the store's second location at 464 Hudson St., near Barrow Street (tel. 645-8006). They're open Monday through Saturday from 11 a.m. to 7 p.m. and on Sunday from noon to 6 p.m.

Kids (and adults too!) will love visiting the world's largest magic store, **Louis Tannen's,** on the fourth floor at 6 W. 32nd St., between Broadway and Fifth Avenue (tel. 239-8383). Inside you will find over 5,000 magic tricks for sale. The store also runs frequent magic shows. Open Monday through Friday from 9 a.m. to 5:30 p.m. (on Thursday to 7 p.m.) and on Saturday from 9 a.m. to 3 p.m.; closed Sunday.

Although it carries standard pet-store items, the main attraction at the **Crystal Aquarium,** 1659 Third Ave., at 93rd Street, (tel. 534-9003), is row after row of glass aquariums and their seemingly endless varieties of fish. In fact, local biology teachers often visit the store with their classes because it carries such a large stock of exotic sea creatures. Open daily from 9 a.m. to 5 p.m.

More than 300 fine feathered species fly free inside **Bird Jungle,** 401 Bleecker St., on the corner of West 11th Street (tel. 242-1757). The few cages Bird Jungle does employ usually have their doors open. Neighborhood residents have been known to befriend certain specimens, and careful visitors can start up a conversation of their own with the colorful birds or simply watch jungle inhabitants carry on with each other. Open Monday through Saturday from 12:30 to 6:30 p.m., and on Sunday from 12:30 to 5:30 p.m.

# 5. Services for Children

## BABYSITTERS

The sitters at **Gilbert Child Care Agency,** 119 W. 57th St. between 6th and 7th avenues (tel. 757-7900), come highly recommended. They charge $6.25 an hour for children nine months or older (infant care is more expensive) and $1 per hour for each additional sibling. The agency requires a minimum of four hours' work and asks you to pay $4 a day for the sitter's transportation before 8 p.m., and $8 after 8 p.m.

**Barnard College** women run a small babysitting service (tel. 854-2035 or 854-1754) and the charge is $4 an hour for up to two children and 50¢ per additional child. You must pay the sitter's cabfare home after 9 p.m.

Last-minute babysitters are available from **The Lynn Agency,** 2067 Broadway (tel. 874-6130). Babysitters can usually be arranged with only a few hours' notice. The agency charges $7 per hour for children 13 months or older (50¢ more for children 4 to 12 months old), and $1 extra per hour for each additional child. There is a four-hour work minimum, and you must pay $2 in carfare before 10 p.m., and $6.50 in carfare after 10 p.m.

## BARBERS

**Michael's** is a barbershop specializing in haircuts for children. Located at 91st Street and Madison Avenue (tel. 289-9612), they charge $17 per haircut. Hours are 9 a.m. to 5 p.m. daily and no appointment is necessary.

**Short Cuts,** 104 W. 83rd St., between Amsterdam and Columbus avenues (tel. 877-2277), is well worth a visit if you're on the Upper West Side. Here kids can get their hair cut and shop for toys or clothes. Haircuts cost $15, a few dollars more if the hair is very long. Toys and clothes are reasonably priced. Hours are Tuesday through Saturday from 10 a.m. to 6 p.m.

F.A.O. Schwarz, at 58th Street and Fifth Avenue, has **Shooting Star** (tel. 758-4344), a full-service child's salon. Open Tuesday through Saturday from noon to 5 p.m. Haircuts cost between $15 and $30. Appointments are not necessary.

Older children may prefer going to the hippest haircutters in the Village, **Astor Place Barbers,** at the corner of Astor Place and Broadway near 8th Street. The barbers here can cut your hair in any odd shape and color you can imagine—or stick to more conventional looks. Go early to avoid the crowds. Opens about 9:30 a.m., but by noon, particularly in summer, customers are lined up outside, creating a festive atmosphere as they wait their turns under the scissors. Haircuts are $7, $2 extra if you want your hair washed.

# 6. Eating Out With Children

Eating out is one of New York's great pleasures—and it's one that older kids may enjoy almost as much as their parents. But for diners with young children, a little bit of planning helps ensure a more pleasant meal. For one thing, most Manhattan restaurants just aren't accustomed to serving children—particularly the more fashionable or exotic spots. Often, waiters and waitresses haven't learned that serving families first helps them as well as you. For another thing, many restaurants don't have the kind of space a hungry, fidgety family needs—tables tend to be small and close together.

One easy way of settling on a restaurant that welcomes kids is to call ahead (even if it doesn't require reservations) and ask if it has highchairs. Many restaurants don't. The ones that do usually are used to serving families. Some New York parents recommend lugging along a "Sassy Seat" for your young child, if that's not too much trouble; this is an inexpensive, easily portable highchair that fits onto the end of just about any table.

Before you ever get to a restaurant, though, you and your kids will be tempted by savory smells on nearly every streetcorner. You'll find pushcarts and peddlars hawking a tremendous variety of foods—hot dogs, soft pretzels, roasted chestnuts, knishes, empanadas, little shish kebabs. For $1 or so apiece, you can literally eat your way down the street.

But save some room for pizza! Pizza joints abound everywhere, especially in areas like Greenwich Village, and nearly all sell pizza for $1 to $2 a slice.

And don't forget dessert! All over town, sweet tooths will find all kinds of ice-cream and cookie stands, Italian ices, and Tofutti.

Below we've listed a few, well-known, child-pleasing places.

The **Horn and Hardart Automat,** 200 E. 42nd St., at Third Avenue (tel. 599-1665), is a longtime children's favorite. The treat here is putting the tokens into the sandwich machines, and there's a David's Cookies stand in the restaurant for dessert.

**Nathan's Famous,** 1482 Broadway, at 43rd Street (tel. 382-0620), is one of the best places in town for a hot dog and fries. Originally a Coney Island institution, Nathan's has an amusement-park atmosphere, with murals of Coney Island, video games, brightly colored chairs and tables. The wide selection includes corn on the cob, knishes, even frogs' legs!

For reasonably priced barbecued chicken and ribs (always a kids' favorite), try the **Tony Roma's** chain restaurant at 450 Sixth Ave. between 10th and 11th streets (tel. 777-7417) or 400 E. 57th St. at 1st Ave. (tel. 308-2000). The décor is western-style diner, with booths and booster seats for those who prefer them. Small orders of ribs can be had for $5, and a giant brick of onion rings for around $4.

One of New York's best ice-cream parlors is **Peppermint Park,** 1225 First Ave., at 66th Street (tel. 288-5054). Everything is fresh, and there are more than enough flavors to satisfy the pickiest palates. Take-out ice-cream cones are $1.50 for a single scoop, plus an assortment of floats, sundaes, egg creams, frozen yogurts, and pastries. The café is cozy and bright, with white tables and green booths, and prices are moderate by New York standards.

**Rumpelmayer's,** in the St. Moritz Hotel, mid-block on glittering Central Park South, at 58th Street (tel. 755-5800), is a New York institution that's worth a peek if you're in the area. There are stuffed animals for sale, and an elegant marble soda fountain with pink padded stools. Beyond is the café, with mirrored arches, pink tables, and hanging ferns.

The two **Hamburger Harry's,** located at 145 W. 45th St., between Sixth Avenue and Broadway (tel. 840-2756), and 157 Chambers St., at West Broadway (tel. 267-4446), are terrific places to go with children. The burgers are mouthwatering, and children are heartily welcomed. Each table has paper tablecloths and a jar full of crayons. Kids will love the menu, which includes foot-long hot dogs, tacos, burgers, and grilled cheese sandwiches. Each item is reasonably priced at $2 to $3. Just make sure that you and your kids leave room for the generous ice-cream desserts! Booster seats are available at both locations.

The price is right ($7 per person), and the babysitting is provided at no additional charge, when you have Sunday brunch at **Extra! Extra!,** 767 Second Ave., at 41st Street (tel. 490-2900). Adults order from the regular brunch menu. Kids are taken care of in another section of the restaurant by young teachers and entertainers. The fun starts at noon and ends at 4 p.m.

# 7. Mapping Out Your Days

As any New Yorker will tell you, one of the keys to getting all you can of what the city offers is careful planning. That's particularly true when you're seeing the city with kids who want frequent pit-stops to eat, rest, or just be kids. Despite the city's simple street layout and its comprehensive transit system, getting around this crowded metropolis takes time. In other words, if you try to sightsee in more than a couple of areas of the city in one day, be prepared to spend a lot of time in subways, buses, or taxis.

Here we've listed suggestions for what to do with kids in different areas of Manhattan. For more information, check the detailed entries in other parts of this chapter and the rest of the guide. Keep in mind that streets are often crowded, even on Saturday, so a stroller for a small child is a good idea. And it's also a good idea to map out beforehand where you're going and how to get there.

## LOWER MANHATTAN

Lower Manhattan begins at the southern tip of the island, at the **Statue of Liberty, Battery Park** and the **Staten Island Ferry,** north to around **City Hall** and the **Brooklyn Bridge.** In between, the many sights and attractions include **Wall Street,** where you'll find the **stock exchanges, Federal Hall,** and **Trinity Church** and its cemetery, where such early American luminaries as Alexander Hamilton and Robert Fulton are buried. There's also the **South Street Seaport,** the ferry to "Lady Liberty," the **World Trade Center** (the observation deck on top is a must), the **Woolworth Building** at 233 Broadway, and **City Hall Park,** the site at which, on July 9, 1776, the Declaration of Independence was read to George Washington and his troops.

## SOHO

SoHo and TriBeCa are actually names that describe each area. SoHo stands for "South of Houston Street"; TriBeCa is the "Triangle Below Canal Street." Architecturally, SoHo is noted for its cast-iron loft buildings that house influential art galleries, and an ever-increasing number of fashionable restaurants and shops. Sights include the **Museum of Holography** (11 Mercer St.), but the real attractions are the galleries and shops, among them kids' clothing stores such as **Pennywhistle Toys** (132 Spring St.) and the **Enchanted Forest** (85 Mercer St.). The best sightseeing streets are West Broadway, Greene Street, Prince Street, and Spring Street.

It's an easy walk east of Broadway to **Little Italy** and **Chinatown.**

## GREENWICH VILLAGE

Greenwich Village generally covers the area north of Houston Street up to West 14th Street, between Broadway and the Hudson River. Here, the place to begin is **Washington Square Park,** at the foot of Fifth Avenue. Kids may like a stroll down Eighth Street, one block north, a bustling street crowded with stores, record shops, and a wide variety of eateries, including **BBQ** at the corner of University Place. Head west a few blocks, past Sixth Avenue, to find the narrow, winding streets that the Village is known for. Here also you'll find two children's theaters, the **13th St. Repertory Company** at 50 W. 13th St., and the **Little People's Theater,** at 39 Grove St., **Bird Jungle** (401 Bleecker St.) provides close encounters with exotic birds. For a great Sunday story hour, visit **Books of Wonder,** 464 Hudson St., at Barrow Street. For the best in records, try **Tower Records** at 692 Broadway, at East 4th Street.

## EAST VILLAGE/LOWER EAST SIDE

In just the last few years the East Village and the Lower East Side have become a magnet for artists, musicians, and punk style in general. It's also the center of the city's Ukrainian community. Here, attractions include the **Public Theater,** at Astor Place, and the rapidly increasing number of ultra-hip shops. Dine at the **Second Avenue Deli,** near East 10th Street, or at one of the many Indian restaurants on East 6th Street.

## MIDTOWN EAST

Midtown East takes in the area east of Fifth Avenue and north of 42nd Street to Central Park. A walk east on 42nd Street from **Grand Central Terminal** will take you past the **Chrysler Building,** the **Daily News Building,** the **Ford Foundation,** over to the **United Nations** at the East River's edge. A stroll up Fifth Avenue will bring you close to a host of world-famous places and stores: **Rockefeller Center, Radio City Music Hall, St. Patrick's Cathedral, Brooks Brothers, Tiffany's, Steuben Glass, F.A.O. Schwarz, Saks Fifth Avenue, Elizabeth Arden,** and more. A great place to stop for meals is the **Citicorp Center,** at Lexington Avenue and 53rd Street, which offers at least a half dozen different restaurant options, from a coffeeshop up to **Alfredo the Original of Rome,** which is a tad pricey but does offer great pasta, booster seats, and highchairs. After lunch, stop in at the **Museum of Broadcasting,** 1 E. 53rd St., to catch a classic episode of "Lassie" or another family favorite.

## MIDTOWN WEST

Midtown West includes the area west of Fifth Avenue, north of 42nd Street to Central Park. Attractions for kids are spread out, but one place to stop, rest, and get some fresh maps is the **Visitor Information Center** at 42nd Street and Broadway, at the base of **Times Square.** You'll probably want to avoid walking farther west on 42nd Street, which has become fairly seedy and for the unwary can be a dangerous place at night. Elsewhere in the area, special places for kids include: the **Intrepid Sea–Air–Space Museum** at the foot of 46th Street and the Hudson River; and the **Children's Museum of Manhattan,** at 314 W. 54th St.

## PENN STATION/CHELSEA

The focal point of another focal point of Manhattan activity is **Penn Station** (downstairs) and **Madison Square Garden** (upstairs), located at West 32nd Street between Seventh and Eighth avenues. A couple of blocks away is **Herald Square,** at the intersection of Sixth Avenue, Broadway, and 34th Street. There you'll find the mammoth main store of **Macy's.** And one block farther east at Fifth Avenue lies everyone's favorite tall building, the **Empire State Building** with the **Guinness World Records Exhibit Hall** down in the concourse.

## UPPER EAST SIDE

The Upper East Side, east of Central Park over to the East River, is generally considered the most elegant part of Manhattan. A sure kid-pleaser is the **Lehman's Children's Zoo** in Central Park, at 65th Street and Fifth Avenue. "Museum Mile" along Fifth Avenue includes the **Metropolitan Museum of Art** at 82nd Street, the **Guggenheim Museum** at 89th Street, the **Cooper-Hewitt Museum** and the **International Center of Photography** at 91st Street, the **Jewish Museum** at 92nd Street, and the **Museum of the City of New York** at 103rd Street, and **El Museo del Barrio** at 104th Street. For shopping, head one block east to Madison Avenue to **Eeyore's,** on 83rd Street; or for hamburgers, try **Jackson Hole Restaurant** at 91st Street.

## UPPER WEST SIDE

Most kids' attractions on the Upper West Side, the area west of Central Park, will be found around the **American Museum of Natural History** at Central Park West and 79th Street. Nearby are the **Hayden Planetarium,** behind the museum at 81st Street, and the **New-York Historical Society** at 77th Street. Pricey shops and restaurants line Columbus Avenue south to **Lincoln Center,** located between 65th and 62nd streets.

# IX

# FAST FACTS FOR NEW YORK

Here we give you a whole range of tips, tricks, and hints to help you make your way through New York as though you've lived here all your life. Few things are more frustrating than being in a strange city, having a tooth flare up and not knowing where to find a dentist, or getting front-row tickets to the show the critics are raving about and not having the faintest idea where to find a reliable babysitter. Check the alphabetical entries here and you can be well on your way to solving those problems. From the mundane to the serious, we offer the ABCs of life in New York, and hope they will help you feel right at home with the intricacies of the Big Apple.

**AIRPORT TRANSPORTATION: Carey Transportation** (tel. 718/632-0509) offers frequent bus service between New York City and both LaGuardia and John F. Kennedy International Airports. You can catch the buses at one of two locations: 125 Park Ave., near Grand Central Terminal between 41st and 42nd streets; or at the Air TransCenter at the Port Authority Bus Terminal, 42nd Street between Eighth and Ninth avenues. For John F. Kennedy, buses leave every 30 minutes from the Park Avenue terminal and about every 30 minutes from Port Authority ($8 one way, $13 round trip). For LaGuardia, buses leave every 20 minutes from the Park Avenue terminal, and every 30 minutes from Port Authority ($7.50). Plan on arriving at the airport about an hour and a half before your flight time.

There's also the **Train to the Plane,** the subway express to JFK Airport. Catch it at the IND–Sixth Avenue stations at 57th Street, 50th Street, 42nd Street, 34th Street, and West 4th Street, and the IND–Eighth Avenue stations at Chambers Street, Broadway-Nassau Street, and Borough Hall, Brooklyn. The train runs regularly every 20 minutes from 5 a.m. to midnight. From the last subway stop (Howard Beach, Queens) you will catch the connecting shuttle bus to the airport. It costs $6.50, plus subway fare. Allow at least one hour for the trip. Call 718/330-1234 for more information.

For bus service to Newark Airport, you can take **New Jersey Transit Bus no. 300** (tel. 201/460-8444) 24 hours a day from the Port Authority Bus Terminal's Air TransCenter, 42nd Street and Eighth Avenue. Or try **Olympia Trails** (tel. 964-6233) from Grand Central Terminal, 41st Street and Park Avenue, or from 1 World Trade Center from 5 a.m. to midnight. Both services cost $7 one way. Buses depart every 15 minutes and take approximately 40 minutes.

**Cab** fares are high, but you can cut costs by sharing. Fare from midtown to LaGuardia is approximately $20, about $30 to JFK, and $30 to Newark, plus tolls. Meter fares double when you cross state lines (such as going to Newark Airport). Group fares are about $8 per person, plus tolls, but are not always available. Ask the taxi dispatcher at the airport taxi stand. Cab drivers are supposed to give you an official airport fee schedule on request—beware of excessive fares. It's a good idea to get a fare receipt (you have to ask for one) so you can track down the taxi if you leave behind any of your belongings. Any problems or complaints about taxi service or fares should be reported: call 869-4237.

For reliable information on the best and least expensive way to get to any of New York City's airports (including Newark) from wherever you are, call toll free 800/AIR-RIDE, a service of the Port Authority. You'll find out where in the city you'll get your ride, how often it runs, and how much it costs.

**ALCOHOLISM:** To get help with problems of alcoholism, call **Alcoholics Anonymous** at 473-6200.

**Al-Anon** and **Alateen** offer help and support for family members of alcoholics; call 254-7230 for a recorded message providing the locations of meetings throughout the five boroughs.

**AMBULANCE:** If an emergency arises, call the police at 911, or simply dial the Operator, say there is an emergency, give him or her your telephone number, and location, and describe the problem.

**ANIMAL HOSPITAL:** If your pet gets injured or becomes sick, call the **Humane Society of New York**, 306 E. 59th St., near Second Avenue (tel. 752-4840). The clinic hours are weekdays from 9 a.m. to 4 p.m., on Saturday to 2 p.m., and on Sunday from 10 a.m. to 2 p.m.

For 24-hour emergency service, call the **Animal Medical Center**, 510 E. 62nd St. (tel. 838-8100), a private and expensive service.

**APARTMENTS:** The market is so tight in New York that finding an apartment can take weeks or months of tracking down leads and combing real estate ads. But if you want to stay for a while, try the Sunday real estate section of the *New York Times,* which comes out late Saturday night. Check the ads in the *Village Voice* (at the newsstands on Wednesday), and in the *Chelsea Clinton News* and other neighborhood papers. More important, though, ask all your friends and acquaintances—the best apartments are usually let before they even reach the real estate ads.

**BABYSITTERS:** The sitters at **Gilbert Child Care Agency,** 115 W. 57th St. (tel. 757-7900), come highly recommended. They charge $6.25 an hour for children nine months or older (infant care is more expensive) and $1 per hour for each additional sibling. The agency requires a minimum of four hours' work and asks you to pay $4 a day for the sitter's transportation before 8 p.m., and $8 after 8 p.m.

**Barnard College** women also run a small babysitting service (tel. 854-2035), and the charge is $4 an hour, plus the sitter's cabfare home after 9 p.m.

For more babysitting services, see Chapter VIII, "Services for Children."

**BATHROOMS:** If you don't want to spend money in a restaurant, there are many buildings with well-maintained public rest rooms. All the major retail stores: **Bloomingdale's** (1000 Third Ave., at 59th Street), **Bergdorf Goodman** (Fifth Avenue, at 58th Street), **Tiffany's** (727 Fifth Ave., near 57th Street), **Saks Fifth Ave.** (Fifth Avenue at 50th Street), **Lord & Taylor** (Fifth Avenue at 39th Street), and **Macy's** (Broadway at 34th Street). You can also use the facilities at most of the better hotels, many open 24 hours: the **Pierre** (Fifth Avenue at 61st Street; on the second floor and in the rotunda), the **Essex House** (160 Central Park South, near Seventh Avenue; in the lobby and on the second floor), the **Waldorf Astoria** (Park

Avenue at 50th Street; in the lobby), the **Grand Hyatt New York** (Park Avenue, at Grand Central Terminal; in the lobby); the **Parker Meridien** (118 W. 57th St., near Sixth Avenue; downstairs), the **Plaza** (Fifth Avenue at 59th Street; in the lobby), and the **Marriott Marquis Hotel** (1535 Broadway, near 45th Street; with a bathroom on every one of its eight floors).

Amid the steel and concrete are also a number of atriums that have lavatories and places to sit. (Some even have food stands): **Olympic Tower** (connects 51st and 52nd streets, east of Fifth Avenue), **Citicorp Center** (153 E. 53rd St.; lower level), the **Park Avenue Plaza** (55 E. 52nd St.), **875 Third Ave.** (at 52nd Street; ask the guard to unlock the rest rooms), the **Crystal Pavilion** (805 Third Ave., at 50th Street), the **IBM Garden Plaza** (590 Madison Ave., near 55th Street; lower level), **Trump Tower** (725 Fifth Ave., near 57th Street; downstairs), and the **RCA Building** (30 Rockefeller Plaza; concourse level).

## BUILDING AND HEAT COMPLAINTS: Call 334-9774.

## BUSES: The price of a bus ride in the city is currently $1.15, and they require exact change or a subway token. Bus drivers do not give change. If you need a transfer slip, ask for it as you board. The New York Convention and Visitors Bureau, at two locations—2 Columbus Circle and at Times Square on 42nd Street, between Broadway and Seventh Avenue—gives out excellent bus route maps, or call 718/330-1234 for bus information. Visitors 65 years old and older can ride city transportation at half fare (55¢) by showing a Medicare card or a half-fare card issued by the NYC Department for Aging. Call 577-0819 for details.

## CALENDAR OF SEASONAL EVENTS: These New York celebrations can be one of the highlights of a visit. The dates vary, so call or write ahead for details to the **New York Convention and Visitors Bureau,** 2 Columbus Circle at West 59th Street (tel. 397-8222); Madison Square Garden, 4 Pennsylvania Plaza (tel. 563-8000); or to the **Jacob K. Javits Convention Center,** 33rd Street and Seventh Avenue (tel. 216-2000). Be sure to call 360-1333 every few days to get a recorded message from the city's Parks and Recreation Department listing exciting things to do and see day by day.

**January:** Chinese New Year celebrations in Chinatown, on the first full moon after January 21; Ice Capades at Madison Square Garden; National Boat Show at the Javits Convention Center; Winter Antiques Show at the Seventh Regiment Armory, Park Avenue at 67th Street; Martin Luther King, Jr., Concert, on the third Sunday in January, at the Brooklyn Botanic Garden (tel. 718/622-4433).

**February:** USA Mobil Indoor Track and Field Championships at Madison Square Garden; Westminster Kennel Club Dog Show at Madison Square Garden; Black History Month, programs in all five boroughs; Greater New York Home and Apartment Show at the Javits Convention Center; early spring and Easter Flower Show, New York Botanical Garden.

**March:** St. Patrick's Day Parade on Fifth Avenue; Golden Gloves boxing finals at Madison Square Garden; Greek Independence Day Parade on Fifth Avenue; New York Flower Show of the Horticultural Society of New York (tel. 757-0915), at the Pier 90 Passenger Ship Terminal near 50th Street.

**April:** Baseball season opens at Yankee and Shea stadiums (call 397-8222 for exact dates); Ringling Brothers and Barnum & Bailey Circus at Madison Square Garden; Macy's Spring Flower Show (tel. 560-4495); Easter Parade in front of St. Patrick's Cathedral, Fifth Avenue at 50th Street, on Easter Sunday, late morning (wear your finest spring outfit and join in); American Ballet Theater at the Metropolitan Opera House; the Paul Taylor Dance Company at City Center.

**May:** Japanese Cherry Blossom Festival (with Japanese arts and entertainment) at the Brooklyn Botanic Garden (tel. 718/622-4433); Big Apple Circus at various locations (tel. 391-0760); Ninth Avenue International Festival (food and crafts), 37th to 57th streets on Ninth Avenue; Washington Square Outdoor Art Show on Memorial Day weekend; New York City beaches open on Memorial Day weekend; You Gotta Have Park, Central and Prospect parks.

**June:** Museum Mile Celebration on Fifth Avenue between 82nd and 105th streets; JVC Jazz Festival at various locations (tel. 787-2020); Puerto Rican Day Parade on Fifth Avenue; Popular Music Festival at Pier 84 begins (tel. 249-8870); Lower East Side Jewish Festival (tel. 475-6200); American Crafts Festival at Lincoln Center; Lesbian and Gay Pride Day Parade and street fair (tel. 777-1800).

**July:** Shakespeare in the Park begins at Delacorte Theatre in Central Park; Mostly Mozart Concerts at Lincoln Center (tel. 874-2424); Fireworks on the Fourth of July (call Macy's at 695-4400 for time and place); New York Philharmonic concerts in Central Park (tel. 397-3100); Festa Italiana Street Fair, Greenwich Village (tel. 989-6805).

**August:** U.S. Open Tennis Championships at the USTA National Tennis Center in Queens (tel. 718/592-8000); Avenue of the Americas Festival; Harlem Week (tel. 427-3315) in various locations around Harlem (check newspaper listings for specifics); Greenwich Village Jazz Festival; Lincoln Center Out-of-Doors Festival.

**September:** Labor Day Parade on Fifth Avenue; Feast of San Gennaro in Little Italy on Mulberry Street (tel. 226-9546); New York Is Book Country on Fifth Avenue; One World Festival on 35th Street and Second Avenue (tel. 686-0710); Mayor's Cup Schooner Race, South Street Seaport; West Indian American Day Parade in Brooklyn.

**October:** Columbus Day Parade on Fifth Avenue; Pulaski Day Parade on Fifth Avenue; Antiques Show at the Seventh Regiment Armory on 67th Street and Park Avenue; Halloween Parade in Greenwich Village; Hispanic Day Parade on Fifth Avenue; Rockefeller Center ice-skating pond opens (tel. 698-8500); New York Knicks basketball and New York Rangers hockey seasons open at Madison Square Garden.

**November:** New York City Marathon (to run in the race or volunteer, call 860-4455 well in advance); Big Apple Circus at Lincoln Center (tel. 391-0760); Macy's Thanksgiving Day Parade on Fifth Avenue; Veteran's Day Parade on Fifth Avenue; National Horse Show at Madison Square Garden.

**December:** Big Apple Circus at Lincoln Center (tel. 391-0760); Chanukah candle lighting at City Hall; Midnight Run and Fireworks in Central Park; Christmas windows in department stores; lighting of Rockefeller Center Christmas tree; New Year's Eve at Times Square; Christmas Star Show at the Hayden Planetarium.

**CAR STORAGE:** One of the cheapest in town on a weekly basis is the famous **Auto Baby Sitters** in Brooklyn. Call 718/493-9800 or write to them at 827 Sterling Pl., Brooklyn, NY 11216. They will pick up your car from the city for $15 and store it for $40 a week, $80 a month plus tax. They pick up and deliver to local airports as well. Their hours are 9 a.m. to 5 p.m. Monday through Friday, to 1 p.m. on Saturday. Closed Sunday and holidays.

**CHESS:** If you want to while away an afternoon over a chess game, you can play for $1.50 an hour at the **Chess Shop,** 230 Thompson St., at West 3rd Street (tel. 475-9580). They're open from noon to midnight every day of the year.

**CHILD ABUSE:** The **Childhelp National Child Abuse Hotline** (tel. toll free 800/422-4453) is staffed 24 hours a day by trained psychology professionals and social workers. The hotline is for parents having problems with children, as well as adolescents who are running away, pregnant, or worried about AIDS.

**CLEANERS:** New York City seems to have a dry cleaner on every block, and most of them can provide express service on the same day, if you bring in your things in the morning. Such speedy service, however, does cost more. If your clothes are just rumpled from a suitcase, try this old trick: hang the offending item in your hotel bathroom, shut the door, and run a hot shower (preferably with you in it to conserve water). In a few minutes the wrinkles should be steamed out and the garment ready to wear.

**CONSUMER-RELATED PROBLEMS:** To report any problems with merchants or ask consumer-related questions, call either the **Federal Trade Commission** (tel. 264-1207), the **Better Business Bureau** (tel. 533-6200), or the **Department of Consumer Affairs** (tel. 577-0111).

**CRISES:** If you need counseling and expert advice for any kind of real problem— loneliness, wife or child abuse, depression, extreme bewilderment—call **Help Line** (tel. 532-2400) or **Victim Services** (tel. 577-7777). Or call 673-3000 and ask for **The Samaritans,** who are there to lend an ear when you need a friend.

**DEAF CRISES:** Deaf people can call toll free 800/342-4357 and leave a message with a TTY machine if an emergency arises.

**DENTISTS:** If a tooth acts up in the middle of your visit, call the **New York University College of Dentistry,** 345 E. 24th St. near First Avenue (tel. 998-9976), open 24 hours a day, seven days a week. The **Dental Emergency Service** (tel. 679-3966, or 679-4172 after 8 p.m.) is a 24-hour answering service that will try to refer you to a dentist.

**DEPARTMENT OF HEALTH:** To report food poisoning or other health problems related to a restaurant or take-out eatery, call 566-3075. For problems with food bought in a grocery store or market, call 488-4820.

**DIAPER SERVICE:** A reliable, inexpensive diaper laundry is **Riteway Diaper Service,** 3329 Atlantic Ave., in Brooklyn (tel. 718/647-9000).

**DOCTORS:** Call the **Doctor's Home Referral/Home Call** service of the New York Medical Society (tel. 718/745-5900 or 718/238-2100) or the emergency services number, 911. Emergency wards are always open at **St. Vincent's Hospital,** Seventh Avenue and 11th Street (tel. 790-7000); **New York Hospital,** Cornell School of Medicine, East 70th Street at York Avenue (tel. 472-5454); and **Mt. Sinai Hospital,** at Madison Avenue and 100th Street (tel. 241-7171).

**DRUG ABUSE:** The **Drug Abuse Information Line** (tel. toll free 800/522-5353) is run by the State Division of Substance Abuse and is staffed around the clock to provide referrals for anyone with a drug problem.

**DRUGSTORES:** A good drugstore that is open 24 hours a day is **Kaufman's,** 50th Street and Lexington Avenue (tel. 755-2266). **Windsor Pharmacy,** at Sixth Avenue at 58th Street (tel. 247-1538), is open daily from 8 a.m. to midnight.

**ELECTRICAL APPLIANCES:** You can rent or buy anything and everything with a cord at **Electrical Appliances Rental and Sales Company,** 40 W. 29th St., near Broadway (tel. 686-8884). Open Monday through Friday from 8:30 a.m. to 5:30 p.m.

**EYE CARE:** An inexpensive place to get a general eye examination or referral is the Optometric Center, the clinic of the **State College of Optometry,** State University of New York. The offices are located at 100 E. 24th St., between Park Avenue South and Lexington Avenue. Call 420-4900 for information and appointments. Exams cost $35. Hours: Monday through Wednesday from 8:45 a.m. to 7 p.m., on Thursday from 8:45 a.m. to 5 p.m., and on Friday and Saturday from 8:45 a.m. to 4 p.m.

**FBI:** Its main number in Manhattan is 553-2700.

**FIRE:** Dial 911 to report a fire.

**FISHING:** If fishing is your passion, Long Island Sound offers some of the East Coast's best angling. Numerous charter companies and "party boats" line the sound on Long Island and in Connecticut. Similar services are located on Long Island and in New Jersey for fishing in the Atlantic Ocean.

**FOOD STAMPS:** For information about the food stamp program in New York, call 718/291-1900.

**FOREIGN CURRENCY:** If you're going abroad, you may want to take a small amount of the currency of the first country on your itinerary. Numerous New York agencies sell foreign currency. You can go to the excellent **Deak-Perera,** in Rockefeller Center at 630 Fifth Ave. (tel. 757-6915), or **Deak-Perera International, Inc.** at 41 E. 42nd St., off Madison Avenue (tel. 883-0400).

Exchanging foreign currency for dollars is also quite easy. **New York Foreign Exchange, Inc.,** at 26 Broadway, Room 767 (tel. 248-4700), will give dollar equivalents for any foreign currency. Their hours are 9 a.m. to 5 p.m. weekdays; closed weekends. And **Citibank** has two foreign-currency exchanges: at 54th Street and Lexington Avenue, and at JFK Airport. Many midtown hotels will exchange foreign currency if you are a registered guest.

**GAY AND LESBIAN CONCERNS:** Call **Gay Switchboard** (tel. 777-1800), with hours from noon to midnight, seven days a week. The volunteers staffing this telephone information and referral service have listings of more than 100 organizations and agencies ready to deal with the gay-related concerns of resident and visitor alike, regarding health, legal questions, religious issues, or whatever. When the volunteers aren't available, the same number will get you a recorded message listing gay social and entertainment possibilities.

The **National Gay/Lesbian Crisisline** (tel. 529-1604) is staffed Monday through Friday from 5 to 10 p.m., and on Saturday from 1 to 5 p.m. to council victims of anti-gay/anti-lesbian violence, people with AIDS, and people with other problems, questions, or concerns. The Crisisline can refer callers to more than 8,000 community services nationwide, including chapters of Parents and Friends of Lesbians and Gays.

**HANDBAG REPAIR: Modern Leather Goods,** 2 W. 32nd St. off Fifth Avenue (tel. 974-7770), will change the shape of last year's bag to keep up with the current fashions, mount needlepoint, or provide new handles when they get worn. Chain handles cost $25 and up; regalizing reptiles starts at $50. There is no charge for estimates.

**HELP FOR THE HANDICAPPED:** The city has many events and programs designed for those who are deaf, blind, or confined to a wheelchair. For information, call the **Mayor's Office of the Handicapped,** 52 Chambers St., Room 206 (tel. 566-0972); **New York Association for the Blind,** the Lighthouse, 111 E. 59th St. (tel. 355-2200); or the **New York Society for the Deaf,** 344 E. 14th St. (tel. 673-6500).

**INFORMATION:** Questions about New York will be answered by the **New York**

**Convention and Visitors Bureau** (tel. 397-8222—and be patient). The Visitors Bureau has two walk-in centers: 2 Columbus Circle at West 59th Street, open from 9 a.m. to 6 p.m. Monday through Friday; and at Times Square on West 42nd Street, between Broadway and Seventh Avenue, open from 9 a.m. to 6 p.m. Monday through Friday and 10 a.m. to 6 p.m. on weekends. The bureau is a gold mine of information about the city. It provides a guide and map to New York in six languages, lots of different brochures, guides to restaurants and stores in all boroughs, a list of free New York activities, bus maps, subway maps, tickets for TV shows, and twofers (two-for-the-price-of-one theater tickets), plus a complete listing of seasonal attractions. For a **recorded message** giving a rundown on all free events in New York, call 360-1333.

**NEWSPAPERS AND MAGAZINES (LOCAL):** New York City has four daily newspapers, including one, the *New York Times,* that is arguably the nation's finest. The city is also home to several weekly newspapers and two weekly magazines that you may find helpful. All are available on almost any newsstand in the city, or you might want to pick up an issue several weeks before you visit, since most events, cultural and otherwise, are announced in the press a few weeks ahead of time, and you'll be able to make reservations or buy tickets in advance.

**Daily Newspapers:** the *New York Times* (especially Friday and Sunday), *Daily News* (especially Friday), *New York Post, New York Newsday.*

**Weekly Publications:** *The New Yorker* (good for cultural events), *New York* magazine (now incorporates *Cue,* with excellent general listings), the *Village Voice* (particularly for music, cheap events, freebies, and off- and off-off-Broadway performances), *New York Observer* (a weekly paper with local listings), and *7 DAYS,* (an upscale *Village Voice*).

**NEWSPAPERS (OUT OF TOWN): Hotaling's,** 142 W. 42nd St., between Broadway and Sixth Avenue (tel. 840-1868), carries over 200 newspapers— everything from the *San Diego Union* to *Le Monde.*

**OPTICIAN:** You can get one-hour service at **Cohen's Optical Company,** 117 Orchard St., at the corner of Delancey Street (tel. 674-1986). With many branch locations, Cohen's has undoubtedly the lowest prices for eyeglass service in New York: about $17 to replace a broken lens, $42 for complete eye examinations and new glasses. Even better, Cohen's is open seven days a week from 9 a.m. to 6 p.m.

**PARKS DEPARTMENT EVENTS:** New York's many beautiful parks are great not only for general recreation but also as the sites for an extraordinary array of musical and operatic performances, plays, festivals, poetry readings, and much more. Of course, almost all of these outdoor events are in the summer. Call 360-1333 to get the Parks Department's recorded message giving all free events in the parks and in the rest of the city.

**PHOTOGRAPHY:** New York is a photographer's dream, not only because of its numerous visual treats but also because of its camera stores, which boast the lowest prices for camera equipment to be found in the United States. Dozens of cut-rate photo-supply stores dot the West Side. One of the best known is **47th Street Photo,** 67 W. 47th St., between Fifth and Sixth avenues (tel. 260-4410), plus its other branches—see the shopping chapter. Some tips on buying: Comparison-shop before you let a smooth-talking salesman con you into something you don't want, and try to bargain with the cut-rate places.

If you have your own equipment already, try to bring more than one lens—a 35-mm, 50-mm, and 135-mm lens should cover any photographic opportunity. Also, don't attract attention to your camera equipment by carrying it in a flashy, expensive camera bag. Bring a nondescript, surplus-type bag if you can. Don't bring your camera along to any area you don't feel comfortable in yourself, such as a lonesome, dark street late at night.

For a week's stay, you might want to bring 14 rolls of film, about two per day. Ten rolls (black-and-white or color) should be slow speed (ASA 64 or 100) and the remainder fast speed (ASA 400 or 1000) for taking either indoor photos without flash or night photos.

**POISON CONTROL CENTER:** For immediate 24-hour first-aid—or hospital referral if necessary—call 340-4494 or P-O-I-S-O-N-S (764-7667).

**POLICE:** Call **911** for life-threatening emergencies only; 374-5000 for normal matters.

**POLLUTION COMPLAINTS:** To report on air-, water-, sewer-, or noise-pollution violations, call the **New York Department of Environmental Protection** at 966-7500.

**POST OFFICE:** The **General Post Office,** 33rd Street and Eighth Avenue (tel. 967-8585), is open 24-hours daily.

**RADIO AND TELEVISION STATIONS:** It would take a chapter to list them all. Here are some major ones:

**AM Radio:** 660 (WFAN; sports), 710 (WOR; talk, news), 880 (WCBS; all news); 1010 (WINS; all news); 1560 (WQXR; classical music).

**FM Radio:** 88.3 (WBGO; jazz music); 93.1 (WPAT; easy-listening music); 93.9 (WNYC; Public Radio, classical music); 99.5 (WBAI; listener-sponsored radio), 101.1 (WCBS; "golden oldies" rock), 102.7 (WNEW; progressive rock); 104.3 (WNCN; classical music), 107.5 (WBLS; urban contemporary).

**Television Stations:** Channel 2 (WCBS, network), Channel 4 (WNBC, network), Channel 5 (WWNY, Fox network), Channel 7 (WABC, network), Channel 9 (WWOR, local), Channel 11 (WPIX, local), Channel 13 (WNET, public television), Channel 31 (WNYC, public television), Channel 47 (WNJU, mostly Spanish).

**RAILROAD INFORMATION:** New York has excellent rail connections to its suburbs and other major cities in the Northeast. For **Metro North** information (for Westchester County and other northern suburbs), phone 532-4900; phone 718/454-5477 for **Long Island Railroad** information (for all of Long Island); call toll free 800/USA-RAIL for **Amtrak** information.

**SAFETY:** Stay alert. Be aware of your immediate surroundings. Wear a money belt and don't sling your camera or purse over your shoulder; wear the strap diagonally across your body. This will minimize the possibility of your becoming a victim of crime. Every city has its criminals. It's your responsibility to be aware and be alert even in the most heavily touristed areas.

**SEXUALLY TRANSMITTED DISEASES AND AIDS:** The New York City Health Department's **AIDS Hotline** (tel. 718/485-8111) is staffed from 9 a.m. to 9 p.m. daily and can give information about HIV infection, set up appointments for counseling and testing, provide counseling, and refer callers to other sources of information about sexually transmitted diseases. (Testing can be anonymous.)

**SUBWAYS:** For information on how to get from one place to another on the subway, call 718/330-1234. Visitors 65 years old and older can ride on city transportation at half fare (55¢) by showing a Medicare card or a half-fare card issued by the NYC Department for Aging. Call 577-0819 for details. See Chapter 1 for details.

**SUICIDE:** Call the **Helpline** (tel. 532-2400) or the **The Samaritans** (tel. 673-3000) for help and counseling, anytime day or night. There are also walk-in mental-health clinics in most city hospitals—ask for an emergency appointment.

**TELEGRAMS:** Phone toll free 800/325-6000 for **Western Union,** which will also send a mailgram, singing telegram, cablegram, candygram, flowergram or opiniongram (to elected officials only).

**TELEPHONE CALLS IN THE NEW YORK CITY AREA:** The area code for Manhattan and the Bronx is 212. To call any other area code location (Brooklyn, Queens, and Staten Island, 718; Long Island, 516; Westchester and Rockland Counties, 914; Connecticut, 203; New Jersey, 201 and 609) dial 1, then the area code and number. The 718 area code is not a long-distance call.

**TELEPHONE DIRECTORIES (OUT OF TOWN):** The **New York Public Library,** 42nd Street and Fifth Avenue, maintains telephone directories of virtually every city in the world.

**TELEPHONE INFORMATION:** Dial 411 to get the number of any establishment or person in Manhattan and the Bronx; 718/555-1212 for the other boroughs. Long-distance information can be obtained by dialing 1, the area code of the city you want, then 555-1212.

**TELEPHONE RECORDINGS:** New York boasts a large collection of informational, interesting, and unique telephone services, all of which cost extra to reach. You can call the **Dow Jones Report,** 976-4141; **New York Lottery Results,** 976-2020; **Off-Track Betting,** 976-2121; **Sportsphone,** 976-1313.

For **Joyce Jolson Forecasts,** dial **Aries,** 976-5050; **Taurus,** 976-5151; **Gemini,** 976-5252; **Cancer,** 976-5353; **Leo,** 976-5454; **Virgo,** 976-5656; **Libra,** 976-5757; **Scorpio,** 976-5858; **Sagittarius,** 976-5959; **Capricorn,** 976-6060; **Aquarius,** 976-6161; **Pisces,** 976-6262.

**TIME:** Phone 976-1616.

**TIPPING:** The following should generally prove satisfactory: bellhops, 50¢ per bag; taxis, 15%, 50¢ minimum; waiters, 15%; chambermaid, $1 to $1.50 per night (for double or single room); barbers and hairdressers, 15%; manicurists, $1. Naturally, if any of the above provide extra services, your tip should be increased accordingly. Do not tip hotel desk clerks, theater ushers, employees of cafés where a "no tipping" sign is displayed, subway or bus operators.

**TRAVELERS AID:** If you're a stranger in the city, lost or destitute or in need of help of any kind, these folks can help. They have three offices: 2 Lafayette St., near City Hall (tel. 577-7700); 158-160 W. 42nd St., near Broadway (tel. 944-0013); and at the International Arrivals Building at JFK Airport (tel. 718/656-4870).

**WEATHER—WHAT TO WEAR:** The saying for New England's weather holds true for New York as well: if you don't like the weather, just wait a few minutes and it'll change. To be prepared for any contingency, always check the forecast in the morning. Phone 976-1212 for up-to-the-hour forecasts.

New York's temperature swings from the low average of 32° Fahrenheit in January to a high of 86° Fahrenheit in July. However, those are just averages; any New Yorker will tell you that it gets much warmer and colder than that. To help you decide what to pack for winter or summer in New York, here are some tips:

In **winter,** try to dress in layers. Not only will you be warmer, but you'll be able to take off layers when you go inside the frequently overheated restaurant or museum. A comfortable pair of warm, winter boots are essential if you want to take any winter walks, as are a hat, scarf, and gloves. An ideal coat for New York winter is a lightweight down-filled one. So if you own a parka, bring it along. It's considered perfectly acceptable in all but the poshest places.

**Summer** in New York can be downright blistering. Be sure to take along a light-weight hat to shade your head from the sun, thick-soled sandals or summer shoes to protect your feet from burning-hot pavement, and plenty of lightweight clothing. You might also want to tote a light sweater or jacket, since many restaurants and theaters keep a heavy hand on the air-conditioning switch.

If you dress for moderate weather in the **spring** and **fall,** you can't go wrong. And bring an umbrella in all seasons!

# INDEX

Abyssinian Baptist Church, 226–7
Accommodations, 26–54
  bed-and-breakfast, 52–3
  Chelsea, 45–6
  for families, 50–2
  Greenwich Village, 46–7
  Herald Square, 45
  hostels, 28–34; campus, 30–1; international, 33–4; for students, 32–4; women only, 31–2; YMCA, 31
  near Lincoln Center, 47–9
  Midtown: east, 49–50; west, 37–43; motor hotels, 42–3
  permanent residences, 34–6
  for service personnel, 36–7
  telephone traps, 27–8
  Upper East Side, 49–50
  Upper West Side, 47–9
  weekends and packages, 53–4
  West Fifties, 43–5
Address finder, 4, 6
AIDS information, 352
Airport transportation, 345–6
Alice Tully Hall, 173, 204
*Ambrose* (ship), 177
Ambulance service, 346
American Ballet Theater, 206
American Craft Museum, 188–9
American Folk Art, Museum of, 189
American Indian, Museum of the—Heye Foundation, 186, 188
American Museum of Natural History, 184, 209–10, 323
American Museum of the Moving Image, 209
*Andrew Fletcher* (ship), 177
Animal hospitals, 346
Antiques, shopping for, 288–9
Apartment hunting, 346
Appliances, shopping for, 289–90
Apple picking (outside New York City), 213
Aquarium, New York (Brooklyn), 216, 220–1
Architectural/neighborhood tours, 221–2
Arthur Avenue (The Bronx), 319
Art museums:
  American Craft Museum, 188–9
  American Folk Art, 189
  Brooklyn Museum, 184
  The Cloisters, 183–4
  Cooper-Hewitt Museum, 186
  El Museo del Barrio, 192
  Frick Museum, 183
  Guggenheim, 182
  Metropolitan, 180
  Museum of Modern Art, 181–2
  National Academy of Design, 192
  New Museum, 191
  Studio Museum in Harlem, 191–2
  Ukrainian Museum, 191
  Whitney Museum of American Art, 182–3
  *see also* Galleries
Asia Society Galleries, 190
AT&T Infoquest Center, 331
Auction houses, 198–9, 290
Avery Fisher Hall, 173, 204

Baby carriages, toys, and furniture, shopping for, 290–1
Babysitters, 340–1
Barbershops and beauty parlors, 291–2
Bars, 251–60
  hangouts, 252–7; East Village, 256–7; Greenwich Village, 255–6; Lower Manhattan and TriBeCa, 257; Midtown (west) and Times Square, 254–5; Murray Hill and Gramercy Park, 254; SoHo, 257; Upper East Side, 252–3; Upper West Side, 253–4
  hotel bars, 258–60
  "in" spots, 260
  piano bars, 257–8
  with a view, 251–2
Baseball, 213–14
Basketball, 214
Bathrooms, 346–7
Battery Park City, 170–1
Beaches, 216–17
Beaumont (Vivian) Theater, 173
Bed-and-breakfasts, 52–3
Belvedere Castle, 180, 331–2
Bicycling, 214
Blues music, 265
Boating, 214, 220
Books, shopping for, 291–5
Boroughs of New York, 3–4
  map of, 5
Botanical gardens, 170, 211–13
Boxing, 214–15
Brighton Beach (Brooklyn), 217
  restaurants, 162–3
Broadcasting, Museum of, 190–1, 327–8
Bronx Zoo, 210–11
Brooklyn Academy of Music (BAM), 205–7
Brooklyn restaurants, 162–3
Brooklyn Bridge, 18–19
Brooklyn Museum, 184, 325, 205
Brotherhood Winery (Washingtonville), 248
Bryant Park, 208
Building complaints, 347
Buses, 8–9, 347

Cameras and computers, shopping for, 296
Cannon's Walk, 176
Carnegie Hall, 203
Carpets, shopping for, 296
Cars and driving, 20, 348
Central Park, 179–80
  map of, 218–19
  walking around, 240–1
  zoo, 212
Central Synagogue, 225
Chase Manhattan Discovery Center, 325–6
Chelsea, 237, 240, 344
  accommodations, 45–6, 51
  jazz, 263
  restaurants, 101–6; American and continental, 101–2; brunch, 164; Chinese, 102–3; Cuban/Chinese, 103; Greek, 103–4; Italian, 104; Jewish, 104–5; Mexican, 105–6; Spanish, 105–6; splurge, 168; Thai, 106; 24-hour, 166

Chelsea Hotel, 237
Chess, 348
Child Abuse Hotline, 348
Children, traveling with, 223–44
  eating out, 341–2
  entertainment, 335–8
  recreation, 333–5
  services, 340–1
  shopping, 338–40
  sights and attractions, 342–4; banking,
    330–1; Belvedere Castle, 331–2; Graffiti
    Hall of Fame, 331; museums, 323–30; Post
    Office, 331; video, computers, and phones,
    331; zoos, 332–3
Children's Museum, Brooklyn, 326
Children's Museum, Staten Island, 326
Children's Museum of Manhattan, 325
China, shopping for, 298–9
China House Gallery, 190
Chinatown, 178, 237
  food shopping, 319–20
  restaurants, 132–8; brunch, 165; Cantonese,
    132–4; dim sum, 136–7; ice cream, 138;
    mixed bag, 135–6; noodle houses, 137–8;
    Shanghai, 134–5; Szechuan, 134; 24-hour,
    166
Christie's, 198–9
Churches and cathedrals, 170, 223–7
Cigars, shopping for, 299
City Center, 206
City Hall Park, 240
City of New York, Museum of the, 185–6, 324
Cleaners, 348–9
Cloisters, The, 183–4
Clothing, shopping for:
  children, 297–8
  men, 285–8
  women, 275–85; bridal gowns, 282; buttons
    and buckles, 283; designer and other dis-
    count shops, 276–82; furs, 285; handbags,
    284; lingerie, 283–4; maternity, 282; resale
    shops, 283; shoes, 284–5; special occasion,
    282–3
College hangouts, 273
Columbus Avenue, 236–7
Columbus Circle, accommodations near, 51
Computers and cameras, shopping for, 296
Comedy clubs, 271–3
Concerts, 203–5
Con Edison Energy Museum, 328
Coney Island (Brooklyn), 216
Cooper-Hewitt Museum, 186, 324
Cooper Union Foundation Building, 175–6
Cosmetics, shopping for, 299–300
Country music, 265–6
Crisis, 349
Crystal, shopping for, 298–9

Dance, 206–8
Dancing, 267–71
Delacorte Theater, 179–80
Dentists, 349
Design, National Academy of, 192
Dia Art Foundation, 197–8
Diaper service, 349
Discount houses, 300–1
Dixieland music, 264
Doctors, 349
Doll Hospital, New York, 28
Donnell Library, 209

Drug abuse, treatment for, 349
Drugstores, 301–2, 349
Dry cleaners, 348–9
Dry goods, shopping for, 302
Dyckman House (Washington Heights), 229

East Side: see East Village; Lower East Side; Midtown (east); Upper East Side; Yorkville
East Village, 343
  bar hopping, 256–7; college hangouts, 273;
    singles bars, 274
  galleries, 197
  restaurants, 141–50; American and continen-
    tal, 142–3; Brazilian, 143; brunch, 165;
    Caribbean, 143; Chinese, 143–4; Créole/
    Southern, 144; Indian/Bangladeshi,
    144–5; Italian, 144; Japanese, 145–6; Jew-
    ish, 146–7; luncheon, 149–50; Mexican,
    147–8; Middle Eastern, 148; Polish,
    148–9; 24-hour, 150, 166–7; Ukrainian,
    149
8th Street (Manhattan), 230–1
Electrolysis, 302
Electrical appliances, 349
Ellis Island, 179
El Museo del Barrio, 192, 325
Emanuel-El, Temple, 225–6
Emergencies, 349
Empire State Building, 171–2
Entertainment: see Nightlife and entertainment
Events, seasonal, 347–8
Excursions from Manhattan, 242–50
  Boscobel (Garrison), 245
  Hudson Valley, 242, 244–9
  Hyde Park (Hudson Valley), 245–6
  Long Island, 249–50
  map, 243
  Mohonk Mountain House (New Paltz), 245
  Museum Village in Orange County, 244–5
  New Jersey, 250
Eye care, 302, 349–50

Fabrics, shopping for, 303
Families, accommodations for, 50–2
Farley (James A.) Post Office, 331
FBI, 350
Federal Hall National Memorial, 227, 328
Ferry, Staten Island, 177–8
Films, 209–10
Fire Department Museum, 329
Fire emergencies, 350
Fisher (Avery) Hall, 173, 204
Flatiron Building, 237
Flea markets, 303–4
Flowers and plants, shopping for, 304
Foam mattresses, shopping for, 304–5
Food, shopping for, 315–21
  Arthur Avenue (The Bronx), 318–19
  cheese, 314
  Chinatown, 319–20
  coffees and teas, 315–16
  gourmet groceries, 316
  greenmarkets, 316–17
  health and natural foods, 317–18
  herbs and spices, 318
  Little Italy, 320–1
  Ninth Avenue, 321
  produce, 318
  sweets and dried fruits, 318–19
  wines and spirits, 319

Food stamps, 350
Football, 215
Forbes Gallery, 190, 328
Foreign currency, 350
Fraunces Tavern Museum, 185, 227
French Institute, 210
Frick Museum, 183
Friend's Meeting House, 224
Festivals, 338
Fulton Market Building, 176-7
Fulton Street, 176
Furniture, shopping for, 305

Galleries:
    Asia Society, 190
    China House, 190
    East Village, 197
    57th Street Midtown, 194-5
    Forbes, 190
    Madison Avenue/uptown, 193-4
    SoHo, 195-7
    TriBeCa, 197
    *see also* Art museums
Garment Center, 234
Gay and Lesbian concerns, 350
General Theology Seminary, 237
Gift shopping, 306-8
Glassware, shopping for, 298-9
Gracie Mansion, 228, 234
Graffiti Hall of Fame, 331
Gramercy Park:
    jazz, 263
    restaurants, 150-62; American and Continental, 150-2; American/Italian, 152-3; barbecue, burgers, and ribs, 153-4; brunch, 165; Chinese, 155-6; coffeeshops and specialty shops, 154-5; English, 156; Greek, 156-7; Indian, 157-8; Irish, 158; Italian, 158; Japanese, 156, 158-9; Mexican, 159-60; Middle Eastern, 160; Spanish, 160; splurge, 168; steakhouses, 160-1; Tex/Mex, 161; Tibetan, 162; 24-hour, 166
Grand Central Terminal, 178
Grant's Tomb, 226
Great Adventures (Jackson, NJ), 337
Greenwich Village, 230-2, 343
    accommodations, 46-7
    map of, 233
    bar hopping, 255, 274
    jazz, 261-2
    restaurants, 106-19; American and Continental, 107-11; brunch, 164; Cajun, 111-12; Caribbean, 112; Chinese, 112-13; Cuban, 113; early-bird dinner specials, 167; French, 113-14; Indian, 114; Italian, 114-15; Japanese, 115; Mexican, 115-17; Middle Eastern, 117; pizza, 117-18; Puerto Rican, 118; soul food, 118; Spanish, 118-19; splurge, 168; Thai, 119; 24-hour, 166
Grolier Club, 192
Guggenheim Museum, 182, 324
Guinness World Records Exhibit Hall, 336

Handbag repair, 350
Handicapped, help for the, 350
Hardware, shopping for, 308
Harlem, 226-9, 329-30
Harlem, Studio Museum in, 191-2

Hayden Planetarium, 184, 323
Health, Department of, 349
Heat complaints, 347
Henderson Place, 234
Herald Square accommodations, 45, 51
Heye Foundation—Museum of the American Indian, 186, 188
Hiking, urban, 217
Hispanic Society of America, 188
Historical museums:
    American Indian—Heye Foundation, 186, 188
    City of New York, 185-6
    Fraunces Tavern Museum, 185
    Hispanic Society of America, 188
    Jewish Museum, 186
    New-York Historical Society, 185, 323
    Yeshiva University Museum, 190
Historic houses, 170, 227-9
Hockey, 215
Holography, Museum of, 191, 328
Horseback riding, 215
Horseracing (outside of New York City), 215
Hostels, 28-34
    campus, 30-1
    international, 33-4
    student, 32-4
    women only, 31-2
    YMCA, 31
Hotels: *see* Accommodations
Hudson Valley, 242, 244-9
    map of, 247
    wineries, 248-9

IBM Gallery of Science and Art, 189-90
International Center of Photography, 189

Japan Society, 210
Jazz music, 261-4
Jewelry, shopping for, 308-9
Jewish Museum, 186, 325
Jones Beach (Long Island), 217, 250
Joyce Theater, 206-7
Juilliard School, 203

Kitchenware, shopping for, 298-9, 309

Lamps and lighting fixtures, shopping for, 309
Lehman's Children's Zoo, 212
Libraries:
    Donnell, 209
    Lincoln Center, 173-4, 204
    New York Public, 189, 209
    Pierpont Morgan, 188
Lincoln Center for the Performing Arts, 173
    accommodations near, 47-9
    library at, 204
    restaurants near, 98-101, 163-4, 168
Little Italy, 237
    food shopping, 320-1
    map of, 238-9
    restaurants, 138-41, 165
Long Island, 249-50
Long Island Railroad, 249
Lower East Side, 232, 234, 343
    restaurants, 141-50; American and Continental, 142-3; Brazilian, 143; brunch, 165; Carribean, 143; Chinese, 143-4; Créole/Southern, 144; Indian 144-5; Italian, 144;

Lower East Side (cont'd)
  Japanese, 145-6; Jewish, 146-7; luncheon, 149-50; Mexican, 147-8; Middle Eastern, 148; Polish, 148-9; 24-hour, 150, 166-7; Ukrainian, 149
Lower Manhattan, 224-5, 227-8, 342-3
  bar hopping, 257
  restaurants, 124-32; American and Continental, 124-7; brunch, 165; French, 127-8; Greek, 128; Irish, 128; Mediterranean, 128; Mexican, 128-9; mixed bag, 129; seafood, 130; South Street Seaport, 130-2; splurge, 168; Thai, 130

MacDougal Alley, 232
Macy's Thanksgiving Day Parade, 337
Madison Square Park, 237
Magazines and newspapers, 351
Manhattan: see specific neighborhoods and areas
Manhattan School of Music, 203
Mannes College of Music, 203
Maps, purchasing, 8
Marble Collegiate Church, 224-5
Merkin Concert Hall, 204
Metropolitan Museum of Art, 180-1, 323-4
Metropolitan Opera, 173, 205
Midtown:
  churches and cathedrals, 225-6
  galleries, 194-5
  map of, 57
  see also Midtown (east); Midtown (west)
Midtown (east), 343:
  jazz, 263
  restaurants, 67-75; American and Continental, 67-9; brunch, 163; Chinese, 69-70; French, 70; Irish, 70-1; Italian, 71; Japanese, 71-2; Mexican, 72; mixed bag, 72-4; Moroccan, 74; natural foods, 74; seafood, 74-5; splurge, 167-8; 24-hour, 166
Midtown (west), 234, 343-4
  accommodations, 37-43
  bar hopping, 254-5, 274
  restaurants, 55-6, 58-67; American and Continental, 55-6, 58-9; Argentinian, 59-60; Brazilian, 60; brunch, 163; Chinese, 60-1; Cuban/Chinese, 61; English/Irish, 61-2; French, 62-3; Greek, 63; international, 63; Italian, 63-4; Japanese, 64; Jewish, 64-5; Mexican, 65-6; Middle Eastern, 66; seafood, 66; splurge, 167; Thai, 66-7; 24-hour, 166
Military personnel, accommodations for, 36-7
Millennium Media Center, 210
Millinery and notions, shopping for, 309
Modern Art, Museum of (MOMA), 181-2, 209, 324-5
Montgomery Place (Hudson Valley), 246, 248
Morris-Jumel Mansion, 228-9
Motor hotels, 42-3
Murray Hill:
  bar hopping, 254
  jazz, 263
  restaurants, 150-62; American and Continental, 150-2; American/Italian, 152-3; barbecue, burgers, and ribs, 153-4; brunch, 165; Chinese, 155-6; Chinese/Japanese, 156; coffeeshops and specialty shops, 154-5; English, 156; Greek, 156-7; Indian, 157-8; Irish, 158; Italian, 158; Japanese, 158-9; Mexican, 159-60; Middle

Eastern, 160; Spanish, 160; splurge, 168; steakhouses, 160-1; Tex/Mex, 161; Tibetan, 162; 24-hour, 166
Museums: see specific museums and types of museums
Music spots and clubs, 260-7
  blues, 265
  country, 265-6
  Dixieland, 264
  jazz, 261-4
  mixed bag, 266-7
  new wave and rock, 264-5
Musical instruments, shopping for, 310

National Academy of Design, 192
Natural History, American Museum of, 184, 209-10
Nature tours, 222-3
New American Filmmakers Series, 183
New Jersey, 250
New Museum, 191
Newspapers and magazines, 351
New wave and rock music, 264-5
New York City:
  map of, 5, 7
  see also neighborhoods, areas, and specific places
New York City Ballet, 206
New York Hall of Science, 326
New-York Historical Society, 185, 323
New York State Theater, 173
New York Stock Exchange, 175
Nightlife and entertainment, 170, 251-74
  bar hopping, 251-60; college hangouts, 273; East Village, 256-7; Greenwich Village, 255; hotel bars, 258-60; Lower Manhattan, 257; Midtown (west) and Times Square, 254; Murray Hill and Gramercy Park, 254; piano bars, 257-8; "in" places, 258-60; singles bars, 273-4; SoHo, 257; Upper East Side, 252-3; Upper West Side, 253-4; views of Manhattan, 251-2
  children-oriented, 335-8
  college hangouts, 273-4
  comedy clubs, 271-3
  concerts, 203-5
  dance performances, 206-8
  dancing, 267-71; discos, 268-9; hot spots, 267-8; Latin, 270-1; to live bands, 269-70; nostalgic, 270; Reggae, 270
  music spots, 260-7; blues, 265; country, 265-6; Dixieland, 264; jazz, 261-4; mixed bag, 266-7; new wave and rock, 264-5
  opera, 205-6
  poetry/prose, 199-202
  television, 208-9
  theater, 199-202; for children, 335-6
  theatrical and nightclub, 271-3
Ninth Avenue, food shopping on, 321

Old Merchant's House, 227-8
Old Westbury Gardens, 249
Olana (Hudson Valley), 246
Opera, 205-6

Paint, shopping for, 310
Parades, 337-8
Parking, 20
Parks and gardens:
  botanical gardens, 170, 211-13
  Bryant, 208
  Carl Schurz Park, 234-5

Parks and Gardens (cont'd)
City Hall, 240
Madison Square Park, 237
Old Westbury Gardens (Long Island), 249
Washington Square Park, 231
Winter Garden, 171
see also Botanical gardens; Central Park
Parks Department, 351
Pennsylvania Station, restaurants near, 101–6;
American and Continental, 101–2;
brunch, 164; Chinese, 102–3; Cuban/
Chinese, 103; Greek, 103–4; Italian, 104;
Jewish, 104–5; Mexican, 105; Spanish,
105–6; splurge, 168; Thai, 106; 24-hour,
166
Perfume, shopping for, 310
Pets and pet supplies, 310–11
Photography, 351–2
Photography, International Center of, 189
Pierpont Morgan Library, 188
Pilot House, 176
Planetarium, Hayden, 184
Planting Fields Arboretum (Long Island), 249
Plants, shopping for, 304
Poe Cottage (The Bronx), 229
Poison Control Center, 352
Police, 352
Police Academy Museum, 329
Posters and prints, shopping for, 311–12
Pottery, shopping for, 298–9
Public Theater, 210

Queens Botanical Gardens, 212–13

Radio and television stations, 352
Records, shopping for, 312
Regent Champagne Cellars (Highland), 248–9
Reservoir, 179–80
Restaurants, 55–168
American and continental: Chelsea and Penn-
sylvania Station area, 101–2; East Village
and Lower East Side, 142–3; Greenwich
Village, 107–11; Lincoln Center area, 98;
Lower Manhattan and TriBeCa, 124–7;
Midtown (east), 67–9; Midtown (west)
and Times Square area, 55–6, 58–9; Mur-
ray Hill and Gramercy Park, 150–4, 160–1;
SoHo, 120–1; Upper East Side 75–6,
78–82; Upper West Side, 89–90, 92–3
Argentinian, 59–60
Brighton Beach, 162–3
Brazilian: East Village and Lower East Side,
143; Midtown (west) and Times Square
area, 60
brunch, 163–5
Cajun, 111–12
Caribbean: East Village and Lower East Side,
143; Greenwich Village, 112
Chinese: Chelsea and Pennsylvania Station
area, 102–3; East Village and Lower East
Side, 143–4; Greenwich Village, 112–13;
Lincoln Center area, 98–9; Midtown
(east), 69–70; Midtown (west) and Times
Square area, 60–1; Murray Hill and Gra-
mercy Park, 155–6; Upper East Side, 83;
Upper West Side, 93–4; see also Chinatown;
and Cuban/Chinese below
Créole, 144
Cuban: Greenwich Village, 113; Upper West
Side, 94

Cuban/Chinese: Chelsea and Pennsylvania
Station area, 103; Midtown (west) and
Times Square area, 61; Upper West Side, 94
Czechoslovakian, 83
dessert: Chinatown, 138; Lincoln Center area,
99; Little Italy, 141; SoHo, 123; Upper
East Side, 88–9
early-bird dinner specials, 167
English: Midtown (west) and Times Square
area, 61–2; Murray Hill and Gramercy
Park, 156; Upper East Side, 83–4
Ethiopian, 121–2
French: Greenwich Village, 113–14; Lower
Manhattan and TriBeCa, 127–8; Midtown
(east), 70; Midtown (west) and Times
Square area, 62–3; SoHo, 122
German, 84–5
Greek: Chelsea and Pennsylvania Station area,
103–4; Lower Manhattan and TriBeCa,
128; Midtown (west) and Times Square
area, 63; Murray Hill and Gramercy Park,
156–7; Upper East Side, 94–5
Hungarian: Upper East Side, 85; Upper West
Side, 95
Indian: East Village and Lower East Side,
144–5; Greenwich Village, 114; Murray
Hill and Gramercy Park, 157–8; Upper
East Side, 85–6; Upper West Side, 95
international: Midtown (west) and Times
Square area, 63; SoHo, 122–3
Irish: Lower Manhattan and TriBeCa, 128;
Midtown (east), 70–1; Midtown (west)
and Times Square area, 61–2; Murray Hill
and Gramercy Park, 158
Italian: Chelsea and Pennsylvania Station area,
104; East Village and Lower East Side, 144;
Greenwich Village, 114–5; Little Italy,
138–41; Midtown (east), 71; Midtown
(west) and Times Square area, 63–4; Mur-
ray Hill and Gramercy Park, 152–3, 158;
SoHo, 123; Upper East Side, 86–7; Upper
West Side, 95–6
Japanese: East Village and Lower East Side,
145–6; Greenwich Village, 115; Midtown
(east), 71–2; Midtown (west) and Times
Square area, 64; Murray Hill and Gramercy
Park, 156, 158–9; Upper West Side, 96
Jewish: Chelsea and Pennsylvania Station area,
104–5; East Village and Lower East Side,
146–7; Lincoln Center area, 99; Midtown
(west) and Times Square area, 64–5
macrobiotic, 96–7
Mediterranean, 128
Mexican: Chelsea and Pennsylvania Station
area, 105–6; East Village and Lower East
Side, 147–8; Greenwich Village, 115–17;
Lincoln Center area, 99–100; Lower Manhattan and TriBeCa, 128–9; Midtown
(east), 72; Midtown (west) and Times
Square area, 65–6; Murray Hill and Gramercy Park, 159–60; Upper East Side, 87
Middle Eastern: East Village and Lower East
Side, 148; Greenwich Village, 117; Midtown (west) and Times Square area, 66;
Murray Hill and Gramercy Park, 160; Upper East Side, 87–8; Upper West Side,
97
mixed bag: Chinatown, 135–6; Lower Manhattan and TriBeCa, 129; Midtown (east),
72–4

Restaurants (cont'd)
Moroccan, 74
natural foods: Midtown (east), 74; Upper West Side, 97
pizza, 117–18
Polish, 48–9
Puerto Rican, 118
seafood: Lincoln Center area, 100; Lower Manhattan and TriBeCa, 130; Midtown (east), 74–5; Midtown (west) and Times Square area, 66; Upper West Side, 97–8
soul food, 118
Spanish: Chelsea and Pennsylvania Station area, 105–6; Greenwich Village, 118–19; Murray Hill and Gramercy Park, 160
splurge, 167–8
Tex/Mex, 161
Thai: Chelsea and Pennsylvania Station area, 106; Greenwich Village, 119; Lower Manhattan and TriBeCa, 130; Midtown (west) and Times Square area, 66–7; Upper East Side, 88
Tibetan, 162
24-hour, 68–9, 150, 165–7
Ukrainian, 149
Viennese, 100–1
Richmondtown Restoration (Staten Island), 229
Riverside Church, 226
Rock and New Wave music, 264–5
Rockefeller Center, 174–5
accommodations near, 50–1
Roosevelt (Eleanor) National Historic Site (Hudson Valley), 246
Roosevelt (Franklin D.), Home of (Hudson Valley), 245–6
Roosevelt (Theodore) House, 228
Roosevelt Island Tramway, 220
Rotunda Gallery (Brooklyn), 198
Running, 215–16

Safety, 6, 8
St. Bartholomew's Church, 225
St. John the Divine, Cathedral Church of, 226
St. Marks-in-the-Bowery, 224
St. Patrick's Cathedral, 225
St. Paul's Chapel, 240
St. Paul's Church, 224
St. Peter's Lutheran Church, 225
Schermerhorn Row, 176
Schurz (Carl) Park, 234–5
Science and technology museums:
American Museum of Natural History, 184
Hayden Planetarium, 184
IBM Gallery of Science and Art, 189–90
New York Hall of Science, 326
Seaport Gallery, 176
Shearith Israel, Congregation (Spanish and Portuguese Synagogue), 226
Shopping, 276–321
antiques, 288–9
appliances, 289
auctions, 290
baby carriages, toys, and furniture, 290–1
beauty parlors and barbershops, 291
books, new and secondhand, 291–6
cameras and computers, 296
carpets, 296–9
for children, 297–8, 338–40
china, pottery, crystal, and glassware, 298–9
cigars, 299

cosmetics, 299–300
discount houses, 300–1
drugs and vitamins, 300–2
dry goods, 301–2
electrolysis, 302
eyeglasses, 302–3
fabrics, low cost, 303
flea markets, 303–4
flowers and plants, 304
foam, 304–5
food, 315–21; Arthur Avenue (The Bronx), 319; cheese, 315; Chinatown, 319–20; coffees and teas, 315; gourmet groceries, 316; greenmarkets, 316–17; health and natural foods, 317–18; herbs and spices, 318; Little Italy, 320–21; Ninth Avenue, 321; produce, 318; sweets and dried fruits, 318; wines and spirits, 319
furniture, 305
gifts, 306–8; space age, 312
hardware, 308
jewelry, 308–9
kitchenware, 309
lamps and lighting fixtures, 309
luggage, 309
men's clothing and accessories, 285–8
millinery and notions, 309–10
musical instruments, 310
paint, 310
perfume, 310
pets and pet supplies, 310–11
prints and posters, 311–12
records, 312
sporting goods, 312–13
thrift shops, 313–14
toys, 314
typewriters, 314
umbrellas, 314–15
women's clothing, 275–85; bridal gowns, 282; buttons and buckles, 283; designer and other discount shops, 276–82; furs, 285; handbags, 284; lingerie, 283–4; maternity, 282; resale shops, 283; shoes, 284–5; special occasion, 282–3
Sights and attractions, 169–213
art museums: American Craft Museum, 188–9; American Folk Art, 189; Brooklyn Museum, 184; The Cloisters, 183–4; Cooper-Hewitt Museum, 186; El Museo del Barrio, 192; Frick, 183; Guggenheim, 182; Metropolitan, 180; Museum of Modern Art, 181–2; National Academy of Design, 192; New Museum, 191; Studio Museum in Harlem, 191–2; Ukrainian, 191; Whitney, 182–3
for children: banking, 330–1; Belvedere Castle, 331–2; Graffiti Hall of Fame, 331; museums, 323–30; Post Office, 331; recreational, 335–6; video, computers, and phones, 331; zoos, 332–3
churches and synagogues, 223–7
galleries, 192–7; East Village, 197; 57th Street midtown, 194–5; Madison Avenue/uptown, 193–4; SoHo, 195–7; TriBeCa, 197
historic houses, 170, 227–9
historical museums: American Indian—Heye Foundation, 186, 188; City of New York, 185–6; Fraunces Tavern, 185; Hispanic Society of America, 188; Jewish Museum,

Sights and attractions (*cont'd*)
186; New-York Historical Society, 185; Yeshiva University, 190
miscellaneous, 220–3
science and technology museums: American
Museum of Natural History, 184; Hayden
Planetarium, 184; IBM Gallery of Science
and Art, 189–90; New York Hall of Science, 326
top sights: Battery Park City, 170–1; Brooklyn Bridge, 178–9; Central Park, 179–80;
Chinatown, 178; Cooper Union Foundation Building, 175–6; Ellis Island, 179;
Empire State Building, 171–2; Grand Central Terminal, 178; Lincoln Center for the
Performing Arts, 173–4; Rockefeller Center, 174–5; South Street Seaport, 176–7;
Staten Island Ferry, 177–8; Statue of Liberty, 172; Stock Exchange, 175; Trump Tower, 175; United Nations, 172–3; World
Trade Center, 170–80
zoos and botanical gardens, 210–13
*see also* Tours
Singles bars, 273–4
Skating, 216
Skiing (outside of New York City), 216
Smith (Abigail Adams) Museum, 228
SoHo, 236, 343
bar hopping, 257
galleries, 195–7
jazz, 262–3
map of, 238–9
restaurants, 119–23; American and Continen-
tal, 120–1; brunch, 164; dessert, 123;
Ethiopian, 121–2; French, 122; interna-
tional, 122–3; Italian, 123; 24-hour, 166
Sotheby's, 198
South Street Seaport, 176–7, 326–7
restaurants, 130–2
shopping, 305–7
Spanish and Portuguese Synagogue (Congrega-
tion Shearith Israel), 226
Sporting goods, shopping for, 312–13
Sports and recreation, 170, 213–17
Staten Island, 229
Staten Island Children's Museum, 326
Staten Island Ferry, 177–8
Statue of Liberty, 172
Stock Exchange, New York, 175
Strawberry Fields, 241
Street fairs, 338
Students, accommodations for, 32–6
Studio Museum in Harlem, 191–2
Subways, 9–19, 352
BMT, 18
IND 6th Avenue, 16–17
IND 8th Avenue, 14–15
IRT Broadway-7th Avenue, 10–11
IRT Lexington Avenue, 12–13
Suicide Helpline, 352
Swimming, 216–17, 334
Symphony Space, 204
Synagogues, 225–6

Taxis, 19
Telegrams, 252–3
Telephone traps, 27–8
Telephoning, 353
Television, 208–9
Temple Emanu-El, 225–6

Tennis, 217
Theater, 199–202
Theology Seminary, General, 237
Thrift shops, 313–14
Time, 353
Times Square, 6, 241
accommodations, 37–43, 50–1
bar hopping, 254–5
restaurants, 55–6, 58–67; American and
Continental, 55–6, 58–9; Argentinian, 59
–60; Brazilian, 60; brunch, 163; Chinese,
60–1; Cuban/Chinese, 61; English/Irish,
61–2; French, 62–3; Greek, 63; international, 63; Italian, 63–4; Japanese, 64; Jewish, 64–5; Mexican, 65–6; Middle Eastern,
66; seafood, 66; splurge, 167; Thai, 66–7;
24-hour, 166
Tipping, 353
TNT Express, 220
Tours:
architectural and neighborhood, 221–2
Broadway, 223
Long Island homes and gardens, 249
miscellaneous, 223
nature, 222–3
trolley, 177
Toys, shopping for, 314
Grand Central Terminal, 178
Long Island Railroad, 249
Transfiguration, Church of the, 225
Transportation, 8–20
airport, 345–6
buses, 8–9, 347
cars and driving, 20, 348
map: getting out of Manhattan, 243
Roosevelt Island Tramway, 220
Staten Island Ferry, 177–8
subways, 9–19, 352; BMT, 18; IND 6th Ave-
nue, 16–17; IND 8th Avenue, 14–15; IRT
Broadway-7th Avenue, 10–11; IRT Lexington Avenue, 12–13
taxis, 19
train travel, 352; Grand Central Terminal,
178; Long Island Railroad, 249
Travelers aid, 353
TriBeCa, 240
galleries, 197
restaurants, 124–32; American and Continental, 124–7; brunch, 165; French, 127–8;
Greek, 128; Irish, 128; Mediterranean,
128; Mexican, 128–9; mixed bag, 129;
seafood, 130; splurge, 168; Thai, 130
Trinity Church, 224
Trump Tower, 175
Tully (Alice) Hall, 173, 204
Typewriters, shopping for, 314–15

Ukrainian Museum, 191
Umbrellas, shopping for, 314–15
United Nations, 172–3
Upper East Side, 228, 344
accommodations, 49–50, 52
bar hopping, 252–3, 273
map of, 77
restaurants, 75–89; American and Continental, 75–6, 78–82; brunch, 163; Chinese,
83; Czechoslovakian, 83; dessert, 88–9;
early-bird dinner specials, 167; English,
83–4; German, 84–5; Hungarian, 85; Indian, 85–6; Italian, 86–7; light fare, 82–3;

Upper East Side (*cont'd*)
  Mexican, 87; Middle Eastern, 87–8; splurge, 168; Thai, 88; 24-hour, 166
Upper West Side, 226, 236–7, 344
  accommodations, 47–9, 51
  bar hopping, 253–4, 273–4
  jazz, 263–4
  map of, 91
  restaurants, 89–98; American and Continental, 89–90, 92–3; brunch, 163; Chinese, 93–4; Cuban, 94; Cuban/Chinese, 94; early-bird dinner specials, 167; Greek, 94–5; Hungarian, 95; Indian, 95; Italian, 95–6; Japanese, 96; macrobiotic, 96–7; Middle Eastern, 97; natural foods, 97; seafood, 97–8; splurge, 168; 24-hour, 166

Vanderbilt Mansion (Hudson Valley), 246
Vitamins, shopping for, 300–1
Vivian Beaumont Theater, 173

Washington Heights, 229, 329–30
Washington Mews, 232
Washington Square, 232
Washington Square Park, 231
Waterloo Village (New Jersey), 250
Wave Hill (Riverdale), 213
Weather, 353–4

West Side, Upper: *see* Upper West Side
Whitney Museum of American Art, 182–3, 198, 209
Wineries, Hudson Valley, 248–9
Winter Garden, 171
Women, accommodations for, 31–2, 35–6
Woolworth Building, 240
World Financial Center, 171
World Trade Center, 170–1
Wrestling, 217

Yeshiva University Museum, 190
Yorkville, 234–5
  accommodations in or near, 49–50, 52
  bar hopping, 252–3, 273
  restaurants, 75–89; American and Continental, 75–6, 78–82; brunch, 163; Chinese, 83; Czechoslovakian, 83; dessert, 88–9; early-bird dinner specials, 167; English, 83–4; German, 84–5; Hungarian, 85; Indian, 85–6; Italian, 86–7; light fare, 82–3; Mexican, 87; Middle Eastern, 87–8; splurge, 168; Thai, 88; 24-hour, 166
YMCAs, 31
YM-YWHA, 34–5

Zoos, 170, 210–13, 332–3

# NOW, SAVE MONEY ON ALL YOUR TRAVELS!
## Join Frommer's™ Dollarwise® Travel Club

Saving money while traveling is never a simple matter, which is why the **Dollarwise Travel Club** was formed 31 years ago. Developed in response to requests from Frommer Travel Guide readers, the Club provides cost-cutting travel strategies, up-to-date travel information, and a sense of community for value-conscious travelers from all over the world.

In keeping with the money-saving concept, the annual membership fee is low —$18 (U.S. residents) or $20 (residents of Canada, Mexico, and other countries)— and is immediately exceeded by the value of your benefits, which include:

1. Any TWO books listed on the following pages.
2. Plus any ONE Frommer City Guide.
3. A subscription to our quarterly newspaper, *The Dollarwise Traveler*.
4. A membership card that entitles you to purchase through the Club all Frommer publications for 33% to 50% off their retail price.

The eight-page *Dollarwise Traveler* tells you about the latest developments in good-value travel worldwide and includes the following columns: **Hospitality Exchange** (for those offering and seeking hospitality in cities all over the world); **Share-a-Trip** (for those looking for travel companions to share costs); and **Readers Ask . . . Readers Reply** (for those with travel questions that other members can answer).

Aside from the Frommer Guides, the Serious Shopper Guides, and the Gault Millau Guides, you can also choose from our Special Editions. These include such titles as **California with Kids** (a compendium of the best of California's accommodations, restaurants, and sightseeing attractions appropriate for those traveling with toddlers through teens); **Candy Apple: New York with Kids** (a spirited guide to the Big Apple by a savvy New York grandmother that's perfect for both visitors and residents); **Caribbean Hideaways** (the 100 most romantic places to stay in the Islands, all rated on ambience, food, sport opportunities, and price); **Honeymoon Destinations** (a guide to planning and choosing just the right destination from hundreds of possibilities in the U.S., Mexico, and the Caribbean); **Marilyn Wood's Wonderful Weekends** (a selection of the best mini-vacations within a 200-mile radius of New York City, including descriptions of country inns and other accommodations, restaurants, picnic spots, sights, and activities); and **Paris Rendez-Vous** (a delightful guide to the best places to meet in Paris whether for power breakfasts or dancing till dawn).

To join this Club, simply send the appropriate membership fee with your name and address to: Frommer's Dollarwise Travel Club, 15 Columbus Circle, New York, NY 10023. Remember to specify which single city guide and which two other guides you wish to receive in your initial package of member's benefits. Or tear out the next page, check off your choices, and send the page to us with your membership fee.

**FROMMER BOOKS**
**PRENTICE HALL TRAVEL**
**15 COLUMBUS CIRCLE**
**NEW YORK, NY 10023**
**212-373-8125**

**Date**_____

Friends:
Please send me the books checked below:

## FROMMER™ GUIDES

(Guides to sightseeing and tourist accommodations and facilities from budget to deluxe, with emphasis
on the medium-priced.)

| | | | |
|---|---|---|---|
| ☐ Alaska | $14.95 | ☐ Germany | $14.95 |
| ☐ Australia | $14.95 | ☐ Italy | $14.95 |
| ☐ Austria & Hungary | $14.95 | ☐ Japan & Hong Kong | $14.95 |
| ☐ Belgium, Holland & Luxembourg | $14.95 | ☐ Mid-Atlantic States | $14.95 |
| ☐ Bermuda & The Bahamas | $14.95 | ☐ New England | $14.95 |
| ☐ Brazil | $14.95 | ☐ New York State | $14.95 |
| ☐ Canada | $14.95 | ☐ Northwest | $14.95 |
| ☐ Caribbean | $14.95 | ☐ Portugal, Madeira & the Azores | $14.95 |
| ☐ Cruises (incl. Alaska, Carib, Mex, Hawaii, | | ☐ Skiing Europe | $14.95 |
| Panama, Canada & US) | $14.95 | ☐ South Pacific | $14.95 |
| ☐ California & Las Vegas | $14.95 | ☐ Southeast Asia | $14.95 |
| ☐ Egypt | $14.95 | ☐ Southern Atlantic States | $14.95 |
| ☐ England & Scotland | $14.95 | ☐ Southwest | $14.95 |
| ☐ Florida | $14.95 | ☐ Switzerland & Liechtenstein | $14.95 |
| ☐ France | $14.95 | ☐ USA | $15.95 |

## FROMMER $-A-DAY® GUIDES

(In-depth guides to sightseeing and low-cost tourist accommodations and facilities.)

| | | | |
|---|---|---|---|
| ☐ Europe on $40 a Day | $15.95 | ☐ New York on $60 a Day | $13.95 |
| ☐ Australia on $30 a Day | $12.95 | ☐ New Zealand on $45 a Day | $13.95 |
| ☐ Eastern Europe on $25 a Day | $13.95 | ☐ Scandinavia on $60 a Day | $13.95 |
| ☐ England on $50 a Day | $13.95 | ☐ Scotland & Wales on $40 a Day | $13.95 |
| ☐ Greece on $35 a Day | $13.95 | ☐ South America on $35 a Day | $13.95 |
| ☐ Hawaii on $60 a Day | $13.95 | ☐ Spain & Morocco on $40 a Day | $13.95 |
| ☐ India on $25 a Day | $12.95 | ☐ Turkey on $30 a Day | $13.95 |
| ☐ Ireland on $35 a Day | $13.95 | ☐ Washington, D.C. & Historic Va. on | |
| ☐ Israel on $40 a Day | $13.95 | $40 a Day | $13.95 |
| ☐ Mexico on $35 a Day | $13.95 | | |

## FROMMER TOURING GUIDES

(Color illustrated guides that include walking tours, cultural and historic sites, and other
vital travel information.)

| | | | |
|---|---|---|---|
| ☐ Australia | $9.95 | ☐ Paris | $8.95 |
| ☐ Egypt | $8.95 | ☐ Scotland | $9.95 |
| ☐ Florence | $8.95 | ☐ Thailand | $9.95 |
| ☐ London | $8.95 | ☐ Venice | $8.95 |

**TURN PAGE FOR ADDITONAL BOOKS AND ORDER FORM.**

0190

# FROMMER CITY GUIDES

(Pocket-size guides to sightseeing and tourist accommodations and facilities in all price ranges.)

| | |
|---|---|
| ☐ Amsterdam/Holland . . . . . . . . . . . . . . . .$7.95 | ☐ Minneapolis/St. Paul . . . . . . . . . . . . . . . .$7.95 |
| ☐ Athens. . . . . . . . . . . . . . . . . . . . . . . . . . .$7.95 | ☐ Montréal/Québec City . . . . . . . . . . . . . . .$7.95 |
| ☐ Atlantic City/Cape May . . . . . . . . . . . . . .$7.95 | ☐ New Orleans . . . . . . . . . . . . . . . . . . . . . . .$7.95 |
| ☐ Barcelona* . . . . . . . . . . . . . . . . . . . . . . . .$7.95 | ☐ New York . . . . . . . . . . . . . . . . . . . . . . . . . .$7.95 |
| ☐ Belgium . . . . . . . . . . . . . . . . . . . . . . . . . .$7.95 | ☐ Orlando/Disney World/EPCOT. . . . . . . . . .$7.95 |
| ☐ Boston . . . . . . . . . . . . . . . . . . . . . . . . . . .$7.95 | ☐ Paris. . . . . . . . . . . . . . . . . . . . . . . . . . . . . .$7.95 |
| ☐ Cancún/Cozumel/Yucatán . . . . . . . . . . . .$7.95 | ☐ Philadelphia . . . . . . . . . . . . . . . . . . . . . . .$7.95 |
| ☐ Chicago . . . . . . . . . . . . . . . . . . . . . . . . . .$7.95 | ☐ Rio. . . . . . . . . . . . . . . . . . . . . . . . . . . . . . . .$7.95 |
| ☐ Denver/Boulder* . . . . . . . . . . . . . . . . . . .$7.95 | ☐ Rome . . . . . . . . . . . . . . . . . . . . . . . . . . . . .$7.95 |
| ☐ Dublin/Ireland. . . . . . . . . . . . . . . . . . . . .$7.95 | ☐ San Francisco. . . . . . . . . . . . . . . . . . . . . . .$7.95 |
| ☐ Hawaii . . . . . . . . . . . . . . . . . . . . . . . . . . .$7.95 | ☐ Santa Fe/Taos/Albuquerque. . . . . . . . . . .$7.95 |
| ☐ Hong Kong* . . . . . . . . . . . . . . . . . . . . . . .$7.95 | ☐ Seattle/Portland* . . . . . . . . . . . . . . . . . . .$7.95 |
| ☐ Las Vegas . . . . . . . . . . . . . . . . . . . . . . . . .$7.95 | ☐ Sydney . . . . . . . . . . . . . . . . . . . . . . . . . . . .$7.95 |
| ☐ Lisbon/Madrid/Costa del Sol . . . . . . . . . .$7.95 | ☐ Tokyo* . . . . . . . . . . . . . . . . . . . . . . . . . . . .$7.95 |
| ☐ London. . . . . . . . . . . . . . . . . . . . . . . . . . .$7.95 | ☐ Vancouver/Victoria* . . . . . . . . . . . . . . . . .$7.95 |
| ☐ Los Angeles. . . . . . . . . . . . . . . . . . . . . . .$7.95 | ☐ Washington, D.C.. . . . . . . . . . . . . . . . . . . .$7.95 |
| ☐ Mexico City/Acapulco . . . . . . . . . . . . . . .$7.95 | *Available June 1990 |

# SPECIAL EDITIONS

| | |
|---|---|
| ☐ A Shopper's Guide to the Caribbean . . . . . .$12.95 | ☐ Manhattan's Outdoor Sculpture . . . . . . . . .$15.95 |
| ☐ Beat the High Cost of Travel. . . . . . . . . . . .$6.95 | ☐ Motorist's Phrase Book (Fr/Ger/Sp) . . . . . .$4.95 |
| ☐ Bed & Breakfast—N. America . . . . . . . . . .$11.95 | ☐ Paris Rendez-Vous. . . . . . . . . . . . . . . . . . .$10.95 |
| ☐ California with Kids . . . . . . . . . . . . . . . . .$14.95 | ☐ Swap and Go (Home Exchanging) . . . . . . . .$10.95 |
| ☐ Caribbean Hideaways . . . . . . . . . . . . . . . .$14.95 | ☐ The Candy Apple (NY with Kids) . . . . . . . . .$12.95 |
| ☐ Honeymoon Destinations (US, Mex & Carib). .$12.95 | ☐ Travel Diary and Record Book . . . . . . . . . . .$5.95 |
| ☐ Where to Stay USA (Lodging from $3 to $30 a night). . . . . . . . . . . . . . . . . . . . . . . . . . . . . . . . .$10.95 | |
| ☐ Marilyn Wood's Wonderful Weekends (Conn, Del, Mass, NH, NJ, NY, Pa, RI, VT). . . . . . . . . . . . . . . . .$11.95 | |
| ☐ The New World of Travel (Annual sourcebook by Arthur Frommer for savvy travelers) . . . . . . . . . . . . . . .$16.95 | |

# SERIOUS SHOPPER'S GUIDES

(Illustrated guides listing hundreds of stores, conveniently organized alphabetically by category.)

| | |
|---|---|
| ☐ Italy . . . . . . . . . . . . . . . . . . . . . . . . . . . .$15.95 | ☐ Los Angeles. . . . . . . . . . . . . . . . . . . . . . . .$14.95 |
| ☐ London. . . . . . . . . . . . . . . . . . . . . . . . . . .$15.95 | ☐ Paris. . . . . . . . . . . . . . . . . . . . . . . . . . . . . .$15.95 |

# GAULT MILLAU

(The only guides that distinguish the truly superlative from the merely overrated.)

| | |
|---|---|
| ☐ The Best of Chicago . . . . . . . . . . . . . . . . .$15.95 | ☐ The Best of Los Angeles. . . . . . . . . . . . . . .$14.95 |
| ☐ The Best of France . . . . . . . . . . . . . . . . . .$16.95 | ☐ The Best of New England. . . . . . . . . . . . . .$15.95 |
| ☐ The Best of Hong Kong . . . . . . . . . . . . . . .$16.95 | ☐ The Best of New York . . . . . . . . . . . . . . . .$14.95 |
| ☐ The Best of Italy . . . . . . . . . . . . . . . . . . . .$16.95 | ☐ The Best of Paris. . . . . . . . . . . . . . . . . . . .$16.95 |
| ☐ The Best of London. . . . . . . . . . . . . . . . . .$16.95 | ☐ The Best of San Francisco. . . . . . . . . . . . . .$14.95 |
| ☐ The Best of Washington, D.C. . . . . . . . . . . . .$14.95 | |

# ORDER NOW!

In U.S. include $2 shipping UPS for 1st book; $1 ea. add'l book. Outside U.S. $3 and $1, respectively.

Allow four to six weeks for delivery in U.S., longer outside U.S.

Enclosed is my check or money order for $_____

NAME _____

ADDRESS _____

CITY _____ STATE _____ ZIP _____

0190

# AMERICAN EXPRESS CAN DELIVER CASH AND A REPLACEMENT CARD TO YOU WITHIN 24 HOURS, AS LONG AS YOU'RE IN THIS GENERAL AREA.

No matter where you are in the world, if you lose your wallet, we can get a new American Express® Card and cash in your hands usually within 24 hours.*

If you're truly in the middle of nowhere, say the African Outback, it might take a little longer. Depending upon how many wandering hippos and fallen trees our local courier must contend with.

But more often than not, you'll have a new Card and cash the next day. Something you'd expect from American Express.

So carry the American Express Card. And no matter where on earth you go, you'll never leave civilization behind.

For assistance, call your nearest American Express office, or in the U.S. call our 24-hour number 1-800-252-3650; everywhere else call collect 602-954-1225. Don't leave home without it.®

## MEMBERSHIP HAS ITS PRIVILEGES℠

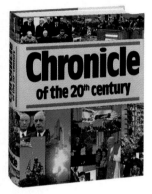
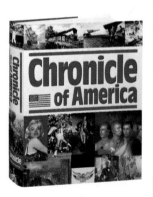